Communications
in Computer and Information Science 210

Mark Zhou (Ed.)

Education and Management

International Symposium, ISAEBD 2011
Dalian, China, August 6-7, 2011
Proceedings, Part III

Springer

Volume Editor

Mark Zhou
Hong Kong Education Society
The Sherwood No.8 Fuk Hang Tsuen Road
Tuen Mun, Hong Kong, China
E-mail: zhoumarkhk@sina.com

ISSN 1865-0929 e-ISSN 1865-0937
ISBN 978-3-642-23064-6 ISBN 978-3-642-23065-3 (eBook)
DOI 10.1007/978-3-642-23065-3
Springer Heidelberg Dordrecht London New York

Library of Congress Control Number: 2011933608

CR Subject Classification (1998): H.4, I.2, H.3, C.2, D.2, J.1

Typesetting: Camera-ready by author, data conversion by Scientific Publishing Services, Chennai, India

Printed on acid-free paper

Springer is part of Springer Science+Business Media (www.springer.com)

Preface

It is our pleasure to welcome you to the proceedings of the 2011 International Symposium on Applied Economics, Business and Development (ISAEBD 2011) which was held in Dalian, China. ISAEBD 2011 was the first conference dedicated to issues related to applied economics, business and development. This conference aims to provide a high-level international forum for researchers to present and discuss the recent advances in related issues, covering various research areas including economics, management, education and its applications.

The conference is sponsored by the Hong Kong Education Society, International Material Science Society and Information Engineering Research Institute. Their support is very important for our conference.

The conference was both stimulating and informative with an interesting array of keynote and invited speakers from all over the world. Delegates had a wide range of sessions to choose from.

The program consisted of invited sessions, technical workshops and discussions with eminent speakers covering a wide range of topics in applied economics, business and development. This rich program provided all attendees with the opportunity to meet and interact with one another.

We would like to thank the organization staff, the members of the Program Committees and the reviewers for their hard work.

We hope the attendees of ISAEBD 2011 had an enjoyable scientific gathering in Dalian, China. We look forward to seeing all of you at the next ISAEBD event.

Qingyuan Zhou

ISAEBD 2011 Organization

Honorary Conference Chairs

Chin-Chen Chang	Feng Chia University, Taiwan
Chris Price	Aberystwyth University, UK

General Chairs

Qinyuan Zhou	Jiangsu Teachers University of Technology, China
Junwu Zhu	Yangzhou University, China

Program Chairs

Honghua Tan	Wuhan Institute of Technology , China
Qihai Zhou	Southwestern University of Finance and Economics, China

Publication Chair

Mark Zhou	Hong Kong Education Society, Hong Kong

Local Chair

He Ping	Liaoning Police Academy, China

International Program Committee

Ming-Jyi Jang	Far-East University, Taiwan
Tzuu-Hseng S. Li	National Cheng Kung University, Taiwan
Yanwen Wu	Huazhong Normal University, China
Teh-Lu Liao	National Cheng Kung University, Taiwan
Yi-Pin Kuo	Far-East University, Taiwan
Qingtang Liu	Huazhong Normal University, China
Wei-Chang Du	I-Shou University, Taiwan
Jiuming Yang	Huazhong Normal University, China
Hui Jiang	Wuhan Golden Bridge-Network Security Technocogy Co. Ltd., China
Zhonghua Wang	Huazhong Normal University, China
Jun-Juh Yan	Shu-Te University, Taiwan
Dong Huang	Huazhong University of Science and Technology, China
JunQi Wu	Huazhong Normal University, China

Table of Contents – Part III

Earnings Management of Chinese Listed Firms: Discretionary Accruals and Earnings Benchmarks*

Ying Que[1] and Peter Secord[2]

[1] Management School, College of Foreign Studies, Jinan University, 601# Huangpu Dadao West, Guangzhou, P.R. China
tquey@jnu.edu.cn
[2] Sobey School of Business, Saint Mary's University, Halifax, Canada
Peter.Secord@smu.ca

Abstract. This paper examines how earnings benchmarks of firms listed in Mainland China may lead to earnings management through use of discretionary accruals. We compared discretionary accrual levels of small profit firms and small loss firms before and after controlling for the effect of two published benchmarks. We find that firms beating or missing both earnings level benchmark and earnings change benchmark tend to save discretionary accruals, while firms missing either of these benchmarks might employ extra discretionary accruals to meet the other earnings benchmark. Small loss firms reporting a bigger earnings increase might have driven accounting accruals up, and as a result small loss firms as a whole appear to have a high level of discretionary accruals not significantly different from small profit firms. Our findings provide direct evidence for earnings management of listed firms, and also give a reasonable explanation for the "kink" in earnings distribution.

Keywords: earnings management, earnings benchmark, discretionary accrual, small profit, small loss.

1 Introduction

Accounting earnings are viewed as the premier information item provided in financial statements. The importance attached to earnings, and the assumption that investors rely on simple heuristics suggest that reporting earnings that are positive (greater than last year) have positive valuation implications. Therefore, firms have strong incentives to exceed earnings benchmarks. Extensive research documents that firms manage earnings to beat benchmarks including earnings level, earnings changes, and analysts' consensus forecasts [1][2][3]. Burgstahler and Dichev build on Hayn by showing a kink in both the earnings change and the earnings level distributions and suggest the cause of the kink is earnings management [4]. Discretionary accruals are among the major earnings management methods where empirical evidence has been presented [5][6].

* The study is financially supported by China National Social Science Fund project No.07CJL022.

M. Zhou (Ed.): ISAEBD 2011, Part III, CCIS 210, pp. 1–7, 2011.

Observing a kink in the earnings distribution of firms listed in Mainland China, we wish to determine whether earnings management may have played a role. This question has rarely been addressed in China. Although studies have been conducted to examine the distribution of earnings around earnings level benchmark, the implicit assumption is that small loss firms do not manage earnings. However, small loss firms might have incentives to manage earnings so as to report positive earnings change. We examine discretionary accruals of firms around earnings benchmarks; we limit our discussion to earnings level and earnings change benchmarks because of limited analyst following of small firms. We focus on the properties of discretionary accruals for certain firms around earnings level benchmark, namely, small profit firms and small loss firms, taking into consideration the effect that an alternative benchmark may have. We hope our study will present a clearer picture of firm behavior with respect to earnings benchmarks.

Testing discretionary accrual properties with two different approaches, we obtain consistent results that both small profit firms and small loss firms manage earnings. Some small loss firms may drive up accruals to exceed the earnings change benchmark while some small profit firms may employ discretionary accruals to "save for the future". Our findings also offer an explanation for the kink in earnings distribution. Based on our findings, we suggest that researchers and users consider the effect of alternative goals of firms around an earnings benchmark.

Our paper proceeds in four sections. The remainder of the paper is organized as follows: Section 2 describes the data and sample selection; Section 3 presents research design and empirical results and Section 4 sets out our conclusions.

2 Data and Sample Selection

Our sample consists of firm-year observations gathered from the CSMAR and RESSET Databases from 2002 to 2009, which allows us to compute discretionary accruals using the statement of cash flows and to classify firms according to earnings level and earnings change. Banks and financial firms are excluded from our analysis because of related special requirements.

We classify each firm-year observation into an earnings level interval (ni_class) according to reported earnings (net income before special items) scaled by beginning-of-year market value of equity from year *t*. Scaled earnings are hereafter referred to as NI. Similarly, firms are classified into earnings change intervals (chgni-class) according to change in reported earnings from year *t-1* to year *t* scaled by beginning-of-year market value of equity from year *t-1*. Scaled earnings change is hereafter referred to as ChgNI. We classify firms into net income classes (ni_class), employing an earnings level interval width of 0.01 and defining each interval to include its lower boundary and exclude its upper boundary. We form our samples in a way consistent with Burgstahler and Dichev [4]. We refer to firms just missing earnings level benchmark (ni_class=-1, $-0.01 \leq NI<0$) as "small loss (SL) firms", firms just beating earnings level benchmark (ni_class=0, $0 \leq NI<0.01$) as "small profit (SP) firms". Firms just above earnings change benchmark (chgni_class=0, $0 \leq ChgNI<0.01$) are referred to as "small earnings increase (SEI) firms", firms just below earnings change level benchmark (chgni_class=-1, $-0.01 \leq ChgNI<0$) are referred to as "small earnings decrease (SED) firms". Similarly, firms with higher profits (ni_class>0) are referred to as "bigger profit (BP) firms", firms with bigger losses (ni_class<-1) as "bigger loss (BL) firms", firms with bigger earnings increases (chgni_class>0) as "bigger increase (BEI) firms", firms with bigger earnings decreases (chgni_class<-1) as "bigger decrease (BED) firms". Firm classification and sample selection are done in a similar way when analysis is based on pre-managed earnings.

Table 1 gives a brief description to discretionary accrual levels of firms as "beaters" or "missers" of either earnings benchmark. There is a kink in earnings distribution since three times as many firms report small profits as those report small losses. It appears that discretionary accruals might have been used to beat earnings benchmark(s).

Table 1. Data description to discretionary accruals of "beaters" and "missers"

		Pre-managed NI/ChgNI			Reported NI/ChgNI		
		No.	Mean	Median	No.	Mean	Median
Earnings Level Benchmark	BL	2917	0.05089	0.045200	1771	-0.03819	-0.03340
	SL	541	0.00531	0.012400	532	0.004222	0.006550
	SP	629	0.00321	0.008400	1621	0.011872	0.007300
	BP	4998	-0.02643	-0.01400	5161	0.013061	0.008000
Earnings Change Benchmark	BED	3437	0.049553	0.0363	2197	-0.03347	-0.0199
	SED	1125	0.009674	0.0089	1813	0.002523	0.0033
	SEI	1056	-0.00700	-0.0045	2245	0.008724	0.0073
	BEI	3467	-0.04400	-0.0296	2830	0.024959	0.01595

3 Research Design and Empirical Results

We use discretionary accrual levels as a proxy for earnings management. If firms manage earnings to avoid reporting losses, then we expect to observe higher discretionary accrual levels for firms reporting small profits than for firms reporting small losses. Under a simple loss avoidance story, it is not reasonable for a firm with a big loss to increase earnings to report a smaller loss; indeed, the opposite has been observed [7]. In fact, alternative benchmarks have complicated the story of "loss-avoidance". Contracts such as bonus plans that are conditional on earnings could create incentives for firms with small earnings (either positive or negative) to engage in income-increasing earnings management [8]. Hansen argues that firms below one benchmark might respond to other incentives or benchmarks [6].

We estimate discretionary accruals using the lagged model of Dechow et al. [9]:

$$\Delta REC_{it}=\alpha+k\Delta REV_{it}+\varepsilon_{it}\,. \tag{1}$$

$$TA_{it}=\alpha+\beta_1[(1+k)\Delta REV_{it}-\Delta REC_{it}]+\beta_2 PPE_{it}+\beta_3 LagTA_{it}+\varepsilon_{it}\,. \tag{2}$$

where:
TA_{it} =Total accruals for firm i for year t (difference between net income and cash flow from operations for firm i for year t);
ΔREV_{it} = Revenues change for firm i from year t-1 to year t;
ΔREC_{it} = Receivables change for firm i from year t-1 to year t;
PPE_{it} = Gross property plant and equipment for firm i for year t;
$LagTA_{it}$ =Total accruals for firm i for year t-1;
and all variables are scaled by lagged total assets.

We estimate the models separately for each two-digit SIC code and calendar year and eliminate from the sample any combination of two-digit SIC code and calendar year with less than ten observations. The estimated amount of discretionary accrual is the residual from equation (2).

Firms missing one benchmark may use discretionary accruals to meet an alternative benchmark, so we hypothesize that SL firms might use discretionary accruals to maintain positive earnings change, and SED firms might use discretionary accruals to maintain positive earnings. To investigate whether SP firms have higher discretionary accruals, we compare SP firms to all other firms and then to SL firms. To investigate whether discretionary accruals are higher for benchmark "beaters" after controlling for alternative benchmark, we make comparisons between SP firms and SL firms, between SEI firms and SED firms.

We find that SP firms and SEI firms have significantly higher ($p<0.0005$) discretionary accrual levels than other firms, 0.011872 vs. -0.000032 and 0.008724 vs. -0.000575 respectively (See Table 2). This finding is consistent with the earnings benchmark beating hypothesis: firms managing accruals up to shift from pre-managed loss group to reported small profit group, or from pre-managed earnings decrease group to reported small earnings increase group. We find discretionary accruals are not significantly different between firms just above and those just below earnings benchmarks, to be specific, between SP firms and SL firms, between SEI firms and SED firms.

If avoiding losses was the sole goal, it makes little sense for SL firms to manage accruals upward yet miss the benchmark by a small margin. Similarly, if positive earnings change is the target of firms, SED firms should have the least motivation to increase earnings with accruals. However, when firms are exposed to more than one benchmark, it is reasonable for missers of one benchmark to manage earnings in order to exceed another benchmark. In this case, it is not surprising to find that SL firms (earnings level benchmark missers) or SED firms (earnings change benchmark missers) have high discretionary accruals. Hence, it is necessary to control for the effect of alternative earnings benchmark(s) when comparing discretionary accrual levels between missers and beaters of a specific earnings benchmark. We delete from the samples firms that may be responding to alternative benchmarks and repeat the comparison between SL firms and SP firms as well as between SED firms and SEI firms respectively. We expect the mean discretionary accruals for SL firms to decline after deleting firms that have beat the earnings change benchmark, and that for SED firms to decline after deleting firms having beat the earnings level benchmark. Significant difference between each pair would imply that missers of one benchmark are nonetheless driven by the other benchmark to manage earnings upward.

Table 2. Comparison of discretionary accrual levels between benchmark missers and beaters

	Discretionary accruals				
Panel A: Comparison between small profit firms (SP) and all other firms, between small profit firms and small loss firm (SL) [earnings level benchmark]					
	Small profit (SP)	Other firms (OT)	t (p) value (SP) vs. (OT)	Small loss (SL)	t (p) value (SP) vs. (SL)
No.	532	*1621*		*6932*	
Mean	0.011872	-0.000032	5.501000	0.004222	-0.0922
Median	0.007300	0.002700	(<0.0005)	0.065500	(0.357)
Std. dev.	0.0708825	0.1047601		0.1870332	
Panel B: Comparison between firms with small earnings increases (SEI) and all other firms, between SEI and firms with small earnings decreases (SED) [earnings change benchmark]					
	SEI	OT	SEI vs. OT	SED	SEI vs. SED
No.	2245	5027		1813	
Mean	0.008724	0.001900	4.253	0.002523	2.255
Median	0.007300	-0.000575	(<0.0005)	0.003300	(0.074)
Std. dev.	0.0658218	0.1197420		0.1077778	

We exclude SEI firms from the SL sample, since they might have responded to incentives to beat earnings change benchmark. Further, SL firms that beat earnings change benchmark by large amounts may also signal that they are using discretion to try to meet earnings level benchmark, but they run out of discretionary room or are otherwise constrained. To avoid mixing up the effect of the benchmark we are studying (earnings level benchmark) and the benchmark firms are trying to beat (alternative benchmark), following Hansen, we exclude firms with higher level of earnings increases, namely firms with ChgNI bigger than 0.01[6].

We observe significantly higher (p=0.006) discretionary accruals for SP firms (mean=0.008571, median=0.004950) as compared to SL firms (mean=-0.013676, median=-0.001700) after deleting firms with earnings increases (both SEI and BEI). The mean discretionary accruals for SL firms drop from 0.004222 to -0.001238 by about 71% after deleting SEI firms. Meanwhile, difference between SP firms and SL firms becomes significant (p=0.027). After deleting firms with bigger earnings increases, we observe an incrementally significant decrease in both mean and median of discretionary accruals levels for the SL sample. This implies some SL firms have managed their accruals upward to beat earnings change benchmark even though they have failed to avoid loss.

Defond and Park find that firms smooth earnings by borrowing from future periods (saving for current period) when they know current earnings are poor (good) and expected future earnings are good (poor) [10]. Hansen reports consistent evidence of discretion-saving in SP firms meeting multiple benchmarks simultaneously [6]. We expect to observe discretionary accrual increase for the SP sample after deleting firms just beating earnings change benchmark. We find increase in both mean (from 0.011872 to 0.015608) and median (from 0.0073 to 0.0087) discretionary accruals for the SP sample with SEI firms deleted. Discretionary accruals are significantly higher for the SP sample after deleting the beaters of earnings change benchmark. This can be interpreted as evidence that firms meeting multiple benchmarks are discretion-saving from the good, current period to possibly benefit earnings in the future

The discretionary accrual levels for SP firms remain significantly higher than those for SL firms. We find a decline of about 30% in mean and median discretionary accruals after deleting firms with bigger earnings increases from the SP sample, and significant difference remains between SP firms and SL firms. These results are consistent with empirical evidence that SP firms are earnings managers: they might have driven up discretionary accruals to report positive earnings instead of negative earnings, and they might have managed their accruals down when they meet both earnings benchmarks to make accrual savings for future. Further, discretionary accruals may also be managed upward by SL firms just to meet earnings change benchmark, or to signal that they aim to and have potential to beat earnings level benchmark.

To examine the effect of earnings level benchmark as alternative benchmark on discretionary accruals, we follow the same steps as above, but SEI firms and SED firms are compared. When firms that may have responded to earnings level benchmark are excluded, the mean and median of discretionary accruals for the SED sample decrease by 174% and 42% respectively. The discretionary accrual levels for SEI sample turn significantly higher than those for the SED sample after controlling for effect of earnings level benchmark. The results imply that some SED firms might have responded to earnings level incentive and managed up discretionary accruals, and thereby inflate the discretionary accruals for the SED sample. After deleting SP firms from the SEI sample, we find a slight increase in both mean and median of discretionary accruals for the SEI sample, also implying that beaters of both earnings benchmarks are saving discretionary accruals for future use.

To get a straightforward picture of the effect of alternative benchmark, we examine discretionary accruals for firms shifting from missers to beaters of either earnings level benchmark or earnings change benchmark. We estimate pre-managed earnings (earnings change) by subtracting discretionary accruals from reported NI (ChgNI) and then assign firms to prmni_class (prmchgni_class). We employ 4 subsamples: 309 pre-managed bigger loss firms with reported small profit and earnings increase (BL to SP+EI), 318 pre-managed bigger loss firms with reported small profit and earnings decrease (BL to SP+ED), 130 pre-managed bigger loss firms with reported small loss and earnings increase (BL to SL+EI), 166 pre-managed bigger loss firms with reported small loss and earnings increase (BL to SL+ED). The results show that discretionary accruals are driven up to beat earnings benchmarks. Firms beating earnings change benchmark, BL to SP+EI firms and BL to SL+EI firms, have significantly higher (with p value of 0.031 and 0.004 respectively) discretionary accruals than missers. However, we find a smaller margin between earnings change benchmark beater (BL to SP) and misser (BL to SL). Discretion-saving by beaters of both earnings benchmarks might be an applicable reason for the smaller margin. There is a most significant difference (p value<0.0005) between firms beating both benchmarks (BL to SP+EI) and firms missing both benchmarks (BL to SL+ED), with mean discretionary accrual of 0.074395 vs. 0.038295. However, when beaters of earnings level benchmark but missers of earnings change benchmark (BL to SP+ED) are compared with beaters of earnings change benchmark but missers of earnings level benchmark (BL to SL+EI), the difference in discretionary accrual levels turns insignificant (P value = 0.335). These results imply that firms use discretionary accruals to beat either one or both earnings benchmarks.

4 Conclusions

We find evidence that firms record discretionary accruals in a manner consistent with earnings management to beat benchmarks, either earnings level benchmark, or earnings change benchmark, or both. We observe a significant difference in discretionary accrual levels for firms immediately around earnings level benchmark (earnings change benchmark) after controlling for effect of earnings change benchmark (earnings level benchmark). We provide a more complete story for discretionary accruals around earnings benchmarks: firms just below one earnings benchmark increase discretionary accruals to beat an alternative benchmark, and as a result, inflate the overall level of discretionary accruals for firms just below the one earnings benchmark. We also provide evidence that firms throughout the earnings level and earnings changes distributions (other than those immediately around the benchmarks) sometimes save discretionary accruals when certain alternative benchmarks have been met. Our findings highlight the need to consider alternative goals when conducting earnings management research.

Acknowledgements. We appreciate suggestions on data cleaning up from Eric Lee and Nguyen Quoc Duy. Ying Que appreciates academic guidance from Prof. Hua Wang, as well as help from her group of friends in data gathering and processing.

References

1. Hayn, C.: The Information Content of Losses. Journal of Accounting and Economics 20(2), 125–153 (1995)
2. Healy, M., Wahlen, J.: A review of the Earnings Management Literature and Its Implications for Standard Setting. Accounting Horizons 13(4), 365–383 (1999)
3. Ronen, J., Yaari, V.: Earnings Management: Emerging Insights in Theory, Practice, and Research. In: Demski, J. (ed.) Springer Series in Accounting Scholarship. Springer, New York (2008)
4. Burgstahler, D., Dichev, I.: Earnings Management to Avoid Earnings Decreases and Losses. Journal of Accounting and Economics 24(1), 99–126 (1997)
5. Burgstahler, D., Eames, I.: Management of Earnings and Analysts' Forecast to Achieve Zero and Small Positive Earnings Surprises. Journal of Business Finance and Accounting 33(5-6), 633–652 (2006)
6. Hansen, J.C.: The Effect of Alternative Goals on Earnings Management Studies: An Earnings Benchmark Examination. Account. Public Policy 29, 459–480 (2010)
7. Kirschenheiter, M., Melumad, N.D.: Can "Big Bath" and Earnings Smoothing Co-exist as Equilibrium Financial Reporting Strategies? Accounting Research 40(3), 761–796 (2002)
8. Watts, R.L., Zimmerman, J.L.: Positive Accounting Theory. Prentice Hall, New York (1986)
9. Dechow, P., Richardson, S., Tuna, I.: Why are Earnings Kinky? An Examination of the Earnings Management Explanation. Review of Accounting Studies 8(2-3), 355–384 (2003)
10. DeFond, M., Park, C.: Smoothing Income in Anticipation of Future Earnings. Journal of Accounting and Economics 23(2), 115–139 (1997)

Sports Consumption Behavior of Farmers in West China

Jiong Luo[1], Bing Zheng[2], and Lizheng Gong[1]

[1] School of Physical Education, Southwest University, Chongqing 400715
[2] Dep. of Physical Education, Tangshan Teachers College, Tangshan, Hebei 063000
Luojiong@swu.edu.cn, longbingchun@sohu.com,
gonglizheng@gmail.com

Abstract. To investigate 4000 rural inhabitants in sports consumption in West China, the aim of this study was to provide some suggestions for government. The results show that education background is the most key factor in sports consumption; gender, nationality and marital status also have significant effect on sports consumption; sports consumption level of women is higher than men(OR=1.429), the Han is higher than the minorities(OR=0.834), the married is higher than the unmarried(OR=1.446); when work hours reduce one unit, the sports consumption will significantly improve(OR=1.474); income exceeds certain limits, sports consumption will improve doubled. Family population, age, health status and village location have no significant effect on farmers' sports consumption. The study shows that sports consumption level is low in West China rural; the market potential is large and has large developing space. There are significant differences among income levels and education backgrounds, and its unbalance affects the development of rural sports consumption.

Keywords: West China, Farmer, Sports consumption, Correlation model.

1 Introduction

The 12 western provinces, autonomous regions and municipalities in China have a combined population of about 370 million. They include Chongqing, Sichuan, Guizhou, Yunnan, Tibet Autonomous Region, Shanxi, Gansu, Qinghai, the Ningxia Hui Autonomous Region, the Inner Mongolia Autonomous Region, the Xinjiang Uygur Autonomous Region, the Guangxi Zhuang Autonomous Region, where live the majority of the poor population in China . Due to historical reasons, its development is lag behind. Since 2000, the great strategy of Development of West China was launched, and it reached a great achievement by the end of the tenth five-year plan, and the eleventh five-year plan take "sports fitness project for farmers" as the key on the socialism new rural construction. Nowadays, Industry structures are progressively adjusted to balance in West China and make a pace to an advanced level. Along with shaking off poverty and setting out on a road to prosperity, the farmers have large leisure to control [1, 2, 3]. With the development of the economy in West China, the consumption structure of farmers are transforming from survival lifestyle to developmental lifestyle or enjoyable lifestyle. As a result, the sports consumption comes out. It meets the requirement of the sports consumption of farmers. This study

M. Zhou (Ed.): ISAEBD 2011, Part III, CCIS 210, pp. 8–13, 2011.

was subsidized by national social science fund, and investigated the farmers' living status, and then explored the key factors in limiting on sports consumption in West China, on the basis of the existing data and new questionnaire data, the authors build a model of farmers' living status and sports consumption, through the analysis of the effect and degree of the construction of this model, the authors reveals the key factors to improve the sports consumption in West China rural. Moreover, from the empirical research on the sports consumption of farmers, the study offers some important suggestions on sports consumption of farmers, and promotes the development of sports industry in China.

2 Method

2.1 Instrument

The instrument in which the data was obtained was a two-part self-report questionnaire. The questionnaire was divided into two parts: (a) actual sports consumption status which include 27 items; (b) limiting factors on sports consumption which contains 21 items.

2.2 Data Collection

The selection frame for this study was 66 villages with stratified sampling at random in 12 provinces, autonomous regions and municipality. Each village represented 60 samples. The sample had an even gender balance with approximately 50% female and male. Data were collected by village secretary. The study was conducted between Jan. 5, 2008 and April 26, 2008.

The stratified sampling by ages was used in the villagers over 18 years old and older. The rural inhabitants in this study refer to those who planting, working in the outside, businessman in local, worker in the town or village factory, craftsman etc.

The data collection procedure resulted in the distribution of 4000 questionnaires, with 3357 returned, and 3157 of them usable for this analysis, yielding a 78.9% valid rate.

2.3 Data Analysis

The crosstabs analysis and logistic regression analysis were used in this study. The significant level was set at $P< .05$ for all analyses. All statistical analyses were calculated using SPSS for Windows, version 16.0(SPSS Inc., USA).

3 Results

Table 1 shows some information as follows:

(1) By forward stepwise logistic regression, seven variables, including gender, nationality, marital status, education background, average family income, average personal income and work hours, were chosen. These variables are significant on the effect of farmers' sports consumption ($p<.05$).Family population, age, health status,

and distance to town are statistically insignificant to the effect of farmers' sports consumption, so they were excluded.

(2) Education background of farmers is the most key factor on sports consumption, odds ratio exp(β) is 1.696 times. from further multiple comparison , it shows: odds ratios of education level(a),education level (b)and education level(c) are 2.282,3.174 and 4.112 times, respectively, that is to say, from "illiteracy or little able to read" to "primary school" , "technical secondary school(high school included)"and "college or above", the frequency in participation in sports exercise will increase 2.282, 3.174 and 4.112 times, respectively. Therefore Cultural construction is as important as economy construction, or more important. The study shows that education poverty of farmer is the main origin of poverty, people who lived in poverty longtime, their cultural customs, thinking set and value orientation is adapted to poverty and self-maintenance [4,5,6].

(3) Sex factor has an important effect on sports consumption of farmers. Odds ratio exp(β) for female to male is 1.429, in other words, the probability of participating sports consumption of female farmers are 1.429 times as male. In other words, nowadays, the main sports consumption in West China is women, not men. The fact reveals equality between sexes in West China rural, sex discrimination doesn't exist and it also reflect the difference of social division of labor in West China rural. Most of the men go out to work, and women look after their houses which make women have more leisure for sports consumption than men.

(4) Odds ratio exp(β) for the minority to the Hans is 0.834 times, it means that when nationality type from the Han to the minority, the probability of sports consumption decreases. It showed that the Han's love to sports consumption is higher than the minority. Further study shows racial discrimination don't primarily exist in China. In this study, the minority population have the amount of 40% total population, The conscience of sports consumption is weak in the minority, its reason maybe base on the environment of their living condition. For example, Baiwan village, Aba prefecture, and Rili village, Lianshan prefecture, Sichuan province, Tangjia village Wuxi county in Chongqing city, Erlongtun village Youzhongqi county in the Inner Mongolia Autonomous Region, and these villages are remote, their economy, transportation and information are underdeveloped, especially sports consumption is weak, however, these regions are the hub of the minority ,therefore to enhance the constructing and propaganda of sports culture and sports consumption is necessary.

(5) Marital status of farmer has an important role on sports exercise. Its odds ratio exp(β) is 1.338 times. Based on the requirement of analysis, this study set marital status into 3 levels: unmarried, married, and other status. Here other status refers to unmarried after being divorced, married after being divorced, unmarried after being widowed, and married after being windowed. A multiple comparison has been performed when taking unmarried as control group (base), the result shows that the odds ratio of marital status "(a)" and "(b)"are 1.446 and 2.168 times respectively. It means when the marital status of farmer changes from unmarried to married or other status, the probability of sports consumption will increase to 1.446 and 2.168 times, respectively. The married have more stable and happy family than the unmarried; therefore, we can understand why the sports consumption of the married is better than unmarried. However, when the marital status of farmer changes from married to other status, the sports consumption

consciences is increased and even higher than the married, authors take this result as a puzzle. When they had an experience of marriage, why they are more active in sports consumption, this result is interesting; therefore, the reasons should be further explored.

(6) Work hours mainly refers to domestic chores, farm work etc. Table 1 shows that the odds ratio exp(β) for work hours to sports consumption hours is 1.474 times. It demonstrates that to emancipate farmers from hard work and increase leisure is another factor to improve farmers' sports consumption.

Table 1. Basic information of Sports consumption Status of Farmers in West China

Variable	Category	β	P	Exp(β)
Sex	Male (base)	0.357	.000	1.429
	Female			
Nationality	Han (base)	-0.181	.027	.834
	Minority			
Marital status		0.291	.000	1.338
	Unmarried (base)			
	Married(a)	0.369	.000	1.446
	Others(b)	0.774	.003	2.168
Education		0.528	.000	1.696
	College&above(c)	1.414	.000	4.112
	middle school(b)	1.155	.000	3.174
	Primary school (a)	0.825	.000	2.282
	Illiteracy (base)			
Family income		-0.465	.000	0.628
	~CNY1600 (base)			
	CNY 1601 – 6080(a)	-.581	.000	0.559
	CNY 6081 – CNY 10560(b)	-0.510	.008	0.600
	> CNY 10560 (c)	0.385	.582	1.470
Individual income		-0.166	.005	0.847
	~ CNY 500(base)			
	CNY 501 – 2800 (a)	-0.221	.003	0.802
	CNY 2801 – 5100 (b)	0.028	.941	1.028
	> CNY 5100 (c)	1.415	.092	4.116
Work hours		0.388	.001	1.474
Distance to town	P>0.05,excluded	Goodness of fit test:		
Family population	P>0.05,excluded	Chi-square X2=11.345,P=0.088>0.05;		
Age	P>0.05,excluded	Fit efficient of the model is better.		
Health status	P>0.05,excluded	Total test: ScoreX2=238.5; p=0.000<0.05;		
		Model has statistically significant.		

(7)The odds ratios for average family and personal income to sports consumption are 0.628 and 0.802 times, respectively. Obviously, both odds ratios show that the income of farmer is an adverse factor. It is an unusual result, however, by multiple comparisons; it shows that it is not the true result. When average family and personal income from below CNY 1600 and CNY 500 to CNY 10560 and CNY 5100 respectively, the odds ratio exp(β) of sports consumption on farmer are 1.470 and 4.116 times respectively. Therefore, the sports consumption depends on income. So far, income, consumer level, consumer structure and durable consumer items in rural are lag behind urban for more than 10 years [6, 7]. The economic base determines the superstructure. The economic base in rural is weak, and living level is low, it also limit the sports consumption in rural. When the increase of family and personal income keep in the range of middle and low income, the increase of income didn't promote their sports fitness consciences and motivation, but increase their desire to earn money, and then induce to ignore physical exercise. From interviewing, we find out that the family income of farmers remain at the level of basic living consumption and productivity consumption, there are a large gap to sports consumption [8, 9]. In the eye of these farmers, they believe that money is better than health. When they earned CNY 1000 last month, they try to earn CNY 2000 or more this month. This strongly desire to earning money makes them difficult to cost free time on physical exercise, so as the income increase, the sports consumption decrease. This phenomenon makes us upset, so the authority should be carefully.

4 Conclusions

As analyzed above, the authors draw some conclusions as follows: (1) Education level is the most key factor to limit sports consumption in farmers, when education level increases one level, physical exercise frequency will increase 1.696 times. Sex also has a significant effect on sports consumption. Female is significantly higher than male. There are significant difference in sports consumption behavior among nationalities, The Han is significantly higher than the minority. Marital status also affects the sports consumption of farmers. The married is significantly higher than the unmarried in sports consumption behavior.(2)Work hours and economic status are 2 key factors on sports consumption of farmer. The effect of economic status limits sports consumption to some extent, when family and personal income exceed certain value, the sports consumption will increase significantly, below certain value, income increment will makes the sports consumption decrease, and it become an adverse factor. The contribution of family population, age, health status, and village location to sports consumption is little, and it is insignificant, so they are excluded.

References

1. National People's Congress Standing Committee of the communiqué. National Economic and Social Development Five Year Plan (March 14, 2006)
2. Ma, X., Yang, L., Sha, L.: Sports in Rural Areas: A Bottleneck Restraining the Development of Mass Sports in China. Journal of Beijing University of Physical Education 27(10), 1310–1312 (2004)

3. Xi, Y., Liu, Y., Jin, T.: Analysis on Condition of Our Sports Goods Export. China Sport Science 25(12), 22–27 (2005)
4. Tian, Y.: Difference between Urban and Rural Areas of Our Social Sports in Well-off Society. China Sport Science 25(4), 3–6 (2005)
5. Qin, C., Meng, W., Miao, Z., et al.: The Imbalanced Development of Sport for All in China. Journal of Beijing University of Physical Education 27(7), 865–868 (2004)
6. Wang, J., Hu, Q.: Human Beings Oriented-New Ideal of Scientific Development of Rural Sports. Journal of Beijing University of Physical Education 28(12), 1602–1609 (2005)
7. Pei, L.: The Analysis on the Current Major Problems of Rural Sports For All. Sports & Science 24(3), 529 (2003)
8. Li, G., Zou, Y.: Family Changes in China Cities and Family Sports Service. Sports & Science (1), 11–14 (2004)
9. Lu, W., Liang, W., Sun, L., et al.: Research on Current Situation, Problems and Its Countermeasures about Public Sport Service Supply in Rural Areas of Western Region under the Circumstance of Constructing New Rural Areas. China Sport Science 30(2), 14–16 (2010)

IT Governance of Construction Information Based on COBIT Model

Xiao Chen[1,2] and Yanzhong Wang[2]

[1] School of Economics and Management, Tongji University, Siping Road.1239
200092 Shanghai, China
[2] Shanghai Jianke Project Management Co. Ltd, South Wanping Road.75
200032 Shanghai, China
{james919w,yzh_wang1015}@163.com

Abstract. The construction industry plays a decisive role in the development of national economy, which runs unique characteristics. IT Governance is built based on COBIT model in this paper to promote the progress of construction information smoothly.

Keywords: COBIT model, IT Governance, construction information.

1 Introduction

The construction industry is the pillar industry of national economy. In anytime, the construction industry plays a decisive role in the development of national economy. In order to effectively respond to the challenge of infomationization and networking, China has developed a series of related measures to promote the work of the information technology of the construction industry. After years of information construction, we had achieved certain results. However, compared with developed countries, the infomationization level of the construction industry is relatively low and exists a big gap. Compared with other constructions, information technology and process of information obviously is backward, which is bound to affect the industry as the pillar industry that should play a foundation supporting role. This paper will introduce the idea of IT governance to the construction of the process of information construction, which will make a useful exploration to raise the construction information efficiency, industry productivity and foundation supporting role.

2 Concept and Meaning of IT Governance

IT governance, introduced in 1990s, is also known as IT governance arrangements or IT governance structure. By reviewing of relevant literatures, IT governance is clearly brought up by many scholars and institutions. However, there seem to be no single, precise definition. Through careful analysis of relevant information, understanding of IT governance can be divided into two categories, the school of controlled IT governance and the school of guided IT governance.

M. Zhou (Ed.): ISAEBD 2011, Part III, CCIS 210, pp. 14–20, 2011.

The school of controlled IT governance emphasizes the controlling factors in the IT governance, whose main research idea is to balance IT risk and return, to control the use of company's IT resource and to realize effectiveness and efficiency of IT resource. Different with the school of controlled, the school of guided IT governance mainly emphasizes through guiding powers and responsibilities of institutional arrangements to promote the IT governance, whose research mainly includes the following aspects: IT governance mode (Allocation of IT decision-making power), IT governance mechanism (Organizational structure, processes and communication relations) and analysis of influencing factors in IT governance.

With comprehensive understanding of others to the IT governance, it is defined that IT governance refers to the activities and processes which the senior managers of enterprises ensure the implementation of IT strategy and promote strategic objectives by taking certain measures. The measures usually include construction of consistent relationship between IS strategy and business strategy, verifying powers and responsibilities of institutional arrangements during infomationization process, reasonably setting interrelated organizational structure, processes and communication relations, balancing IT resource and IT process's risk and return, increasing the added value of IT resource and process. IT governance is not only an organizational management tool, but a kind of management thought as well.

3 Operating Characteristics of the Construction Industry

Compared with other industry, it is a common phenomenon that the informatization level is low in construction industry, which exists not only in our country, but in some western developed countries. Investigating its reason, it is mainly decided by some characteristics of construction industry itself. Compared with other industry, a few characteristics of construction industry in the process of operation are as follows:

3.1 Taking Project as the Core

Project is taken as the core in the whole operation of construction. Project participants such as design, reconnaissance and construction, are working around the project all along. They are linked together through the project, which is also the carrier of the whole building products supply chain in construction industry. However, compared with ordinary commodities, project is characterized by large amount of investment, long production cycle, disposable etc. It also indicates that large quantities of repetitive production in construction industry are impossible. In the specific process, more often it needs case-by-case analysis. This brings out higher demand for the intelligent level of information system, and therefore puts forward greater challenges to the whole IS strategy.

3.2 Temporary Organization Structure

Compared with other industry, each node in the whole construction industry chain is not fixed. Construction production activities are under construction in different time, at different places, among different construction conditions and requirements of the project. Hence, for different construction project, the requirements for each node enterprise participating in building are different. In the specific process, this certainly will lead to project partnership between node enterprises instead of optimal resources strategic partnership, namely based on project objective, node enterprises establish cooperation relations which are not invariable. Therefore, usually there will be several temporary node enterprises in a fixed construction industry chain. This temporary will not only influence investment strength and passion of each node enterprise, but challenge the reasonable allocation of responsibilities in the process of informatization. Leading to mutual shuffle phenomenon, it will produce serious negative effect to the further development of informatization establishment.

3.3 Participants Diversity

The whole industry chain of construction is pull-type oriented by owners' demands. However, there are many participants in the process of project complete, except the owner, still including general contractor, subcontractors, material suppliers, supervising units, project management company, consultation unit, reconnaissance unit, government departments, etc. The roles of different participants played in each construction stage are distinct. The information they can provide and they are in need is also different. Compared with other industry, we need to spend more energy on coordinate and communicate, this will inevitably put forward higher request for abilities of reasonable allocation and communication of IS.

Anyhow, these characteristics of construction industry itself make higher demands for IS, so that the whole industry informatization establishment process need to overcome more difficulties.

4 IT Governance Used in Information Technology of the Construction Industry

In order to effectively overcome these difficulties and promote technology construction to proceed smoothly, we need to continuously introduce new ideas and tools to guide the information process. IT Governance is a suitable choice.

4.1 The Role of IT Governance

In the process of technology construction, we can effectively address the following aspects through the introduction of IT Governance:

Help to overcome the problem of information asymmetry between enterprises on supply chain. IT Governance objects to support various business activities including IT processes, IT resources involved in a variety of IT services. All of these are inextricably related to management information systems. Full use of the advantages of IT technology, building a good management information system can not only accurately and fully reflect all the business activities of enterprises, but also to meet the different needs of different types of information to provide various types of users with Information in time. Establishing an information system, information collection, processing, generation and transferring process is mainly done automatically by the system, reducing the number of manual intervention and setting in advance within the purview of the data made it very difficult tamper with, conceal. It is an addictive way to solve the problem of asymmetric information.

Through the reasonable set in relevant organizations, processes and communication mechanisms, IT Governance can effectively coordinate the process of the information for each participant of the project. The coordinating influence includes both the internal coordination of information in one participating party and the mutual coordination between participating parties, thus contributing to mutual trusts of the participants of the project, also enhancing the management efficiency and the quality of the whole industry chain in decision-making.

IT Governance is conducive to defer to the project management development mode. Led by the general contractor enterprise, it integrates resources and focuses on the distribution of powers, responsibilities and profits of related stakeholders, balancing the costs, benefits and risks. And IT governance can achieve business continuity management, meet the owners' needs and produce industrial chain revalue, thereby improving the productivity of the whole industry chain and competitiveness.

IT Governance is conducive to encouraging the application of IT. It can clear about the framework of the ownership and accountability of decision-making and keep the consistency of IT strategies and business ones, which realizes organization or supply chain's strategic target.

Generally, IT Governance will be introduced into the construction process of construction industry information, which can enhance the symmetry of information the parties involved in the project, improve the quality and efficiency of information, promote cooperation credit between the parties to increase, improve operational efficiency and reduce the industry Chain operating costs, the most scientific and rational distribution of benefits, link to the project objectives and business processes to improve productivity of the entire project. Figure 1 reflects the IT governance's role in the process of the informatization in the construction industry.

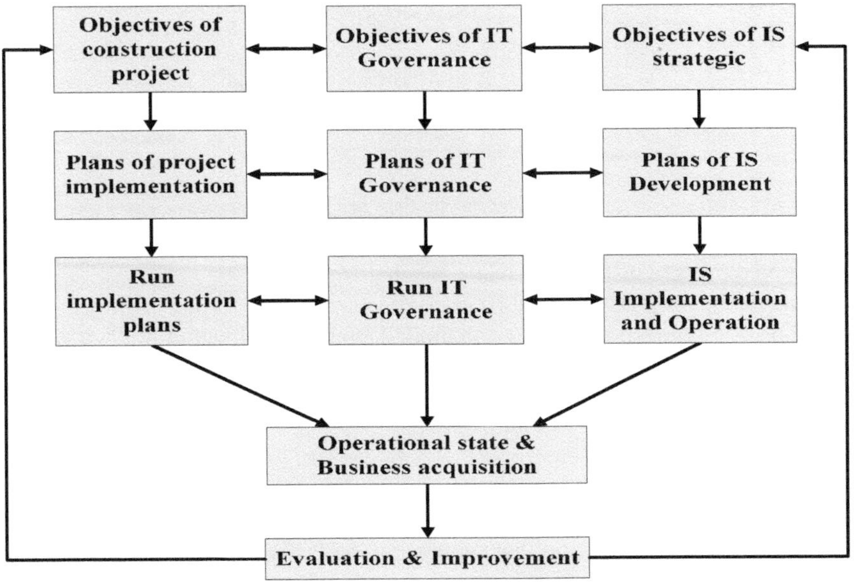

Fig. 1. The role of IT Governance in the process

4.2 IT Governance with COBIT Model

To apply the idea of IT management into informationization of building industry, adopting measurements to translate the idea into specific feasible methods is required, which is IT Governance mechanism. IT Governance mechanism is the interaction process of all the stakeholders who exploit and make use of IT resources. According to the latest edition of COBIT model, an effective IT Governance mechanism generally includes the following parts: executing manual, implementing tools, managing guide, auditing handbook, control objectives, etc.

Specifically, to build IT Governance mechanism on the basis of COBIT model in a concrete building project is to construct the operational process which uses managing guide as the tool, IT norm as the direction, IT process that controls objective model as the basic process, meanwhile introduces the auditing handbook.

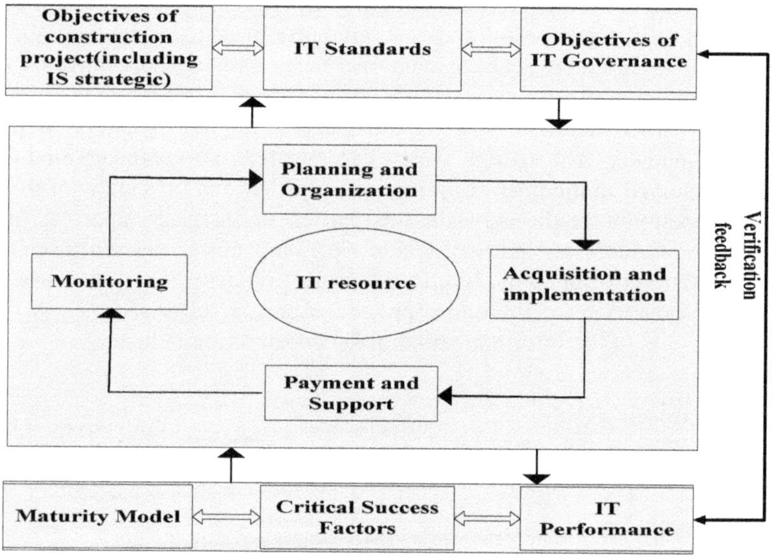

Fig. 2. The mechanism of IT Governance

Operational process of IT Governance mechanism:

In a specific project, based on head-contractor, administration of project participant should position the whole industry chain and every participant in line with situation of the construction and the business environment. And then obtain an information technology-based solution, IT criterion and the objective of IT management. COBIT framework describes the IT objective based on the quality standard of necessary information which helps enterprise to achieve the business objective, and COBIT treats IT objective as ensuring the information provided by the IT progress meet the requirements of specific quality standard. Generally, quality standard consist of availability of the information that supporting the business; lack of integrality and risk of security; efficiency (cost ratio of procedure and operation); reliability、effect and consistency.

Based on maturity model, ensuring the IT supervisory level of construction project and critical success factors. Critical success factors are the most important factors of IT process, which is strategic and technical process and activity, and can draw the outline of IT controlling.

Confirming the performance target of IT Governance. It contains key goal indicators and key performance indicators. The former measures "accomplish quality" of IT process, and the latter measures "how to accomplish" Governance targets. Monitoring and measuring IT performing indicators in the running process.

Under the direction of IT norms, utilize IT process to control and manage information resources, which separately through the processes of planning and organizing, gathering and implementing, delivering and supporting, and monitoring, etc. Meanwhile, to introduce auditing guide to ensure safety, reliability and order of resource management, thereby the panel point enterprises of industry chain of construction industry runs steadily and effectively. In achieving the project objectives but also to promote the development of their information technology, and then bring the advance of information technology of the whole industry, increase the industry productivity.

In addition, it is mentionable that changing in building process in traditional management methods usually lead to inefficiency of project operation. However, COBIT built change control process, and built control objectives which aimed at each activity in the process. Management set up parameters system to differentiate between emergency changes, establish procedures to give priority to control this change, to record and handle emergency changes, which could reduce the occurrence of adverse events in construction industry's chain.

5 Conclusion

Although China's infomationization level of the construction industry is relatively low and the use of IT technology by all participants in construction projects is also at a preliminary stage of exploration, if IT governance is introduced to the whole infomationization process in the early stage of information construction and IT operating mechanism is effectively integrated into current project management models, which will not only make the project participants practically find the advantages of IT technology, but also improve their initiative with implementation of information technology and enhance their desire and capacity of long-term planning. Moreover, in that way, the detours in the information process of other industries will be effectively avoided, the efficiency of infomationization construction of the building industry will be improved, and China's infomationization of construction industry will conduct smoothly. After all, the goal to enhance the productivity and competitiveness of the industry will be achieved.

Acknowledgement. The authors acknowledge the support of Science and technology project 'Research and integrated of knowledge-based multi-project information management platform' (2009-K9-35) of Ministry of Housing and Urban-rural Construction.

References

1. Zheng, X., Yang, J.: Interpretation of COBIT and its application in China. Productivity Research 17, 154–156 (2009)
2. Chen, W.: Analysis on governance processes of COBIT information system. Communication of Finance and Accounting 3, 120–121 (2010)
3. Li, H.: Application of IT governance in the construction supply chain management. Science & Technology Information 18, 790–792 (2010)
4. Shen, T.: Analysis of IT control based on COBIT. Science & Technology Information 5, 413 (2009)

The Study of New Energy Electric Automobile Project Feasibility Degree Evaluation Method

Kefei Wang

Department of Information Engineering
Jilin Business and Technology College
Changchun, China
wangkefei888@sina.com

Abstract. In this paper, we combine the status of electric vehicle with its development and future trends.We accord to the principle that combine subjective evaluation with objective evaluation,and give priority to objective evaluation, built electric vehicle project feasible degree evaluation index system.Used the Delphi method with AHP to subjectively evaluate electric automobile project feasibility degree. combined AHP withl cluster analysis objectively evaluate it, then determined the index weights each layer, on the base of prominent objective evaluation weight, using the subjective evaluation to score it,and thus make the analysis conclusions more objective and more scientific, Project investors can make investment decisions quantitative or numerical analysis of the adjustments.

Keywords: electric automobile, AHP, cluster analysis, feasibility degree.

1 Introduction[1]

Electric automobile is the world's only vehicle to achieve zero-emission. With the requirements of environmental protection, combined with new materials and new technology, electric automobile into the surge of development.From an environmental point of view or whether the energy point of view, the future of electric automobile needs to have a big development. In our nation, electric automobile has a unique market, the metropolis is the prevalence of serious traffic problems and car exhaust emission pollution[1], so electric vehicle in our country has unique conditions for the development and broad application prospects.

"Twelfth Five-Year Plan" is the new energy electric automobile project as a priority the development of industry and introduced the appropriate policy and industrial planning, I believe that electric automobile will rapid develop in the next five years in China. Electric automobile project must invest huge capital, many factors influence it, Market risk is high, As an emerging industry, and there is no historical experience to be followed. So the electric automobile project feasibility degree evaluation will help government and business to reference in the field for

[1] Education Department of Jilin Province, the "Eleventh Five-Year" science and technology research.(2010403).

M. Zhou (Ed.): ISAEBD 2011, Part III, CCIS 210, pp. 21–27, 2011.

investment, And be able to demonstrate scientific feasibility degree 、economic benefits and social benefits of the project.

Based on the development of domestic and international electric vehicle industry status and trends, We explored and studied the electric automobile project feasibility degree evaluation method.

2 The Electric Vehicle Project Feasibility Degree Evaluation Method Status in Domestic and International

Electric automobile industry is emerging industries.Still in the early stages of development, Greater uncertainty, many factors affect the feasibility. Therefore, the field of domestic industry in this feasibility degree study is relatively less, but most studies are based on subjective judgments and theoretical analysis, the main flaw is due to the following areas:

(1) Too much reliance on subjective analysis.

Evaluation index system is no reliable scientific data sources, appears entirely based on subjective indicators to judge.

(2) data analysis model is simple.

Most of the evaluation index system is not fully reflect the development of electric automobile in China. Meanwhile, data analysis is too one-sided.

(3)operational difference.

Standard Evaluation System for the fundamental purpose is to guide practice, but most studies there is scientific data from the selected indicators was untrue, so the conclusion can be operational difference.

In summary, scientific principles of the evaluation index system should be the following requirements:

(1) objectivity.

Evaluation index system, indicators are a scientific and reliable data sources, can not appear completely subjective indicators to judge.Evaluation index system of indicators to be strictly in accordance with the development of electric vehicle industry to determine the actual situation.

(2) comprehensive.

Evaluation index system to be able to more fully reflect the development of electric automobile in China, including hardware and software environment and the electric automobile project itself, so previous research to be comprehensive and thorough.Collective project of the evaluation index system can be modeled as a basis, as appropriate, increase or decrease based on the actual target.

(3) independence.

Evaluation System in response to each index to be able to separate their properties.

(4) operational.

Evaluation System of the fundamental purpose is to guide practice, so the index system is to be in line with, make sure that the selected indicators of scientific data sources, both in data processing should be comparable, consistent.

This paper combined with hierarchical cluster analysis method for electric automobile project objective evaluation of the extent practicable, determine the index weights each layer, in a prominent objective assessment of the weight of the principle, the use of subjective evaluation score, and thus make the conclusions more objective analysis more scientific, so the project can be based on quantitative numerical analysis of investors to make investment decisions or project adjustments.

In addition, the development of electric automobile in China is still at the exploratory stage, the paper also tries to establish the extent feasible electric automobile project evaluation system for the further development of electric automobile to provide a reference.

3 Electric Automobile Project Feasiblity Degree Evaluation

3.1 Build Feasible Degree Evaluation Index System

Electric automobile industry is emerging industries. Still in the early stages of development, the larger the uncertainty, Many factors affect the feasibility of it[3]. According to the current domestic and international research on electric automobile, focusing on the following five aspects to establish the simplified feasible degree evaluation index system: human resources, technical resources, regional location, the external environment, economic effects. Construction of the evaluation system shown in Figure 1.

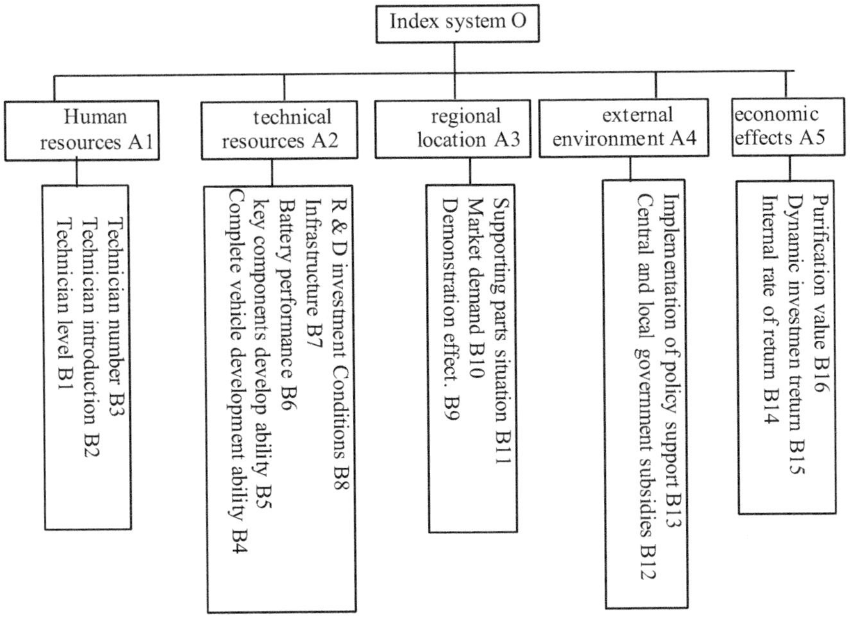

Fig. 1. New energy electric automobile project feasibility degree evaluation index system

3.2 The Study Process of Electric Automobile Project Feasibility Degree Evaluation System

3.2.1 Combined AHP with Cluster Analysis Construct Evaluation System

Based on the Index System of former, calculated the weight of the index system as follows.

In this step, 1 to 9 scale method are more applied which proposed by T.L.Saty, Importance of two factors comparison is showed by the scale[4-5]. Statistical data, you can get on the determine matrix of factors betwwen the under layer factors and uper layer factors.

Computed synthesis weight, then sorted it. determined the importance of bottom layer elements to the overall goal.

First, the single-level sort. Which factors determine the level of the adjacent levels of each factor on a priority.Sort of single-level include:

(1)Calculated to determine the largest eigenvalue matrix and the corresponding eigenvectors (or weight) W.

(2)test the consistency of comparison matrix. If the previous level A includes m factors A_1, A_2, ... A_m, the level of total ranking weights were a_1, a_2, ..., a_m, the next level of B_n factors, including B1, B2, ..., Bn, which for factor in the level of single-sort Ai weights were b1j, b2j, ..., bnj, the right sort at this time the total value of B-level Σaib1j ... Σaibnj.it shows as table 1:

Table 1. The total order weight of B layer

Layer b	Layer A A_1、A_2、...A_m a_1、a_2、...、a_m	The total order weight of B layer
b_1	b_{11}、b_{12}、...、b_{1m}	$\sum a_i b_{1j}$
...	...	...
b_n	b_{n1}、b_{n2}、...、b_{nm}	$\sum a_i b_{nj}$

3.2.2 Cluster Analysis Optimize the Results of AHP to Access to Each Layer Weights

Cluster analysis is an important application of fuzzy set theory, the main ambiguity is the real problem which by mathematical means to achieve certain classified and analyzed.

Classical clustering methods can be roughly divided into two categories: hierarchical clustering and non-hierarchical clustering method[6].In addition, this year to develop a series of intelligent clustering methods can be classified as a new category. First, the hierarchical analysis of multi group of experts on the index system to determine the weight and the corresponding weight matrix, and then by hierarchical clustering method shown in Table 2 (parts) data analysis:

Table 2. weights of determine layer(parts)

Experts number	human resources	technical resources	regional location	external environment	economic effects
1	.199500	.391000	.091000	.076000	.243000
2	.181800	.090900	.181800	.363600	.181800
3	.096300	.264300	.044100	.183400	.411700

First, a preliminary inspection of the data, using hierarchical clustering method to operate, the following conclusions, as shown in Table 3: column 1 lists the steps in the process of clustering number, column 2 and 3 out in a expert advice on what step in the merger.

Table 3. Layer cluster analysis table (parts)

Stage	Cluster Combined		Coefficients	Stage Cluster First Appears		Next Stage
	Cluster 1	Cluster 2		Cluster 1	Cluster 2	
1	13	22	.000	0	0	2
2	13	25	.000	1	0	3
3	13	24	.007	2	0	11

Cluster analysis yielded the most important result is the so-called pedigree chart, and some statistics books also call it a tree. The results generated by cluster analysis and found that the number is divided into categories is difficult to determine is reasonable, in order to determine the number into the appropriate categories, and named for each category, but also on the clustering results for further analysis.

K-means clustering is a non-hierarchical clustering method can be used for cluster analysis of large amounts of data, it is carried out according to the following steps

(1) First determine the number of cluster categories, in the actual analysis process, based upon the problem of repeated attempts to put data into several different categories, and compared to find the optimal solution.

(2) According to the analysis of cluster centers designated themselves, or by the data center itself, initially identified the structure of the original center of each category.

(3) each recorded one by one calculation of the distance from the center of each category, the individual records classified in accordance with the principle of the closest in all categories, and calculate the center of the newly formed category.

(4) According to the new center, to re-calculate the distance of each new class record of distance between the center and the center re-classified updated categories.

(5) Repeat step 4 until a certain convergence criteria, or to pre-specified number of iterations so far. Table 2 for the previous analysis, the experts tend to be divided into four categories, as shown in Table 4.

Table 4. K-means cluster analysis

	Cluster			
	1	2	3	4
Human resources.	.090036	.114150	.142260	.451897
Technical strength	.345004	.091900	.257020	.243939
regional location	.159560	.179250	.079655	.124927
Macro-environment	.093575	.319750	.082480	.101875
Economic benefits	.251794	.294900	.434770	.124417

Table 5. K-means Cluster analysis sorted

	Cluster		Error			
	Mean Square	df	Mean Square	df	F	Sig.
Human resources.	.216	3	.003	24	75.428	.000
Technical strength	.038	3	.002	24	16.971	.000
regional location	.012	3	.003	24	4.719	.010
Macro-environment	.033	3	.002	24	18.855	.000
Economic benefits	.147	3	.008	24	17.832	.000

From the Table 5 the size of the approximate F value of the variable by which the role of cluster analysis in a larger conclusion.

4 Evaluation Conclusion

According to F values, the F value of doing normalized index by five percentage weight in the evaluation, then the proportion by weight class from table 4 to extract the effective number of experts.

Effective means to take the weight of experts as the final evaluation of the index weight, and so, for the next layer of the evaluation index weights determined.

In accordance with the above method to obtain electric automobile project feasibility assessment model of the layers of the weight W_1 ... ... Wn.

Finally, most experts score the Delphi method, and data processing by experts score the indicators of the project data X_1 ... ... Xn.

$$A=WX=(W_1, W_2, \cdots W_n)(X_1, X_2, \cdots X_n)^T \tag{1}$$

A is the final score of the project's feasibility evaluation, investors can refer the project evaluation conclusion to the project investment decisions or adjustments.

5 Study Meaning and Value

This study is the decision-making electric automobile provides a scientific thesis on China's electric vehicle industry, the promotion and implementation of a scientific guarantee, in this research project decisions will be under the new energy to China's booming auto industry provide strong support.

It is estimated that in the coming decades, China's industrial restructuring in the electric vehicle project implementation and development will provide millions of jobs and trillions of economic benefits, the project's area of research for decision making can be scientific and rational basis, has far-reaching and immeasurable value.

References

1. Wang, J., Ma, L.: Electric cars are the future direction of chinese automobile. Corporation Research 12, 20–26 (2010)
2. Wang, G., Wang, J.: The future of electric cars to run the new industry model of the ideal chain. Energy Conservation 30, 4–10 (2010)
3. Wan, G.: Create a new era of electric vehicle industry. China Science & Technology Fortune 23, 11–14 (2010)
4. Gu, Z., Zhang, Z., Zhang, X.: AHP level of poverty in the poor students in the application of evaluation. Decision and Information 1, 96–97 (2010)
5. Wei, S., Zhang, Y.: Inland River Basin in Gansu assessment of sustainable utilization of water resources based on AHP method. Journal of Anhui Agricultural Sciences 1, 483–485 (2011)
6. Wei, J., Sun, Y., Su, N.: Interdisciplinary research based on Cluster analysis. Journal of the China Society for Scientific and Technical Information 6, 1066–1073 (2010)

Tentative Study on the Performance and Risks of Chinese Informal Finance

Xia Jiang

Central-China Development Research Institute, Wuhan University, Hubei Wuhan
jiangxia7633@yahoo.com.cn

Abstract. This paper elaborated on the performance and risks of Chinese rural informal finance.The author found that the Chinese informal finance has the economic efficiency,institutional efficiency and many market risks.The result shows that the economic efficiencies include optimizing resource allocation effect, capital accumulation effect, economic growth effect, employment promotion effect and promoting competition effect. The informal finance has the institutional superiorities in information, operation mode, speed, transaction costs and collaterals. In addition, the result shows that there exist moral risk, social risks, interest rate risk, operational risks and institutional risks in Chinese informal finance. In the end, the author concludes that we should take effective measures to regulate the development of Chinese rural informal finance.

Keywords: The informal finance, Effect, Risk, Superiority.

1 Introduction

Since reform and opening up to the world, the development of Chinese rural informal finance has become increasingly active.It has showed tenacious vitality and played a guiding role on the transition of financial system.Reports from IFAD (2001) have pointed out that Chinese farmers' loan from informal financial markets is about four times more than that of formal financial markets .Citigroup says that Chinese "underground financial" scale has reached 90 million yuan, which amounts to 6% of the Chinese GDP. According to estimates, only about 15% or so of Chinese 214 million farmers get loans from regular financial institutions, 85% of farmers getting loans basically through the folk lending to resolve (Chen xiwen,2004). Thus we can see the high incidence and wide coverage of informal finance is the widespread economic phenomenon in Chinese rural areas.

2 Performance Analysis of Chinese Informal Finance

2.1 Analysis of Economic Efficiency

2.1.1 Effect of Optimizing Resource Allocation

Firstly,the informal finance has overcome its congenital defects, linked to the final lenders and final borrowers, avoided the occurrence of moral hazard and improved the

M. Zhou (Ed.): ISAEBD 2011, Part III, CCIS 210, pp. 28–34, 2011.

situation of the information asymmetry between lenders and lenders.Thus,the informal finance has become beneficial supplement to failure of regular financial market. Under the condition of that rural regular finance can't meet the rural financial demand, the informal finance offers a solution to capital formation deficiency arisen from financial repression by collecting and investing the available funds outside the formal system.It has expanded the production-management funds in rural areas and especially played an important role on promoting the economic growth of rural areas.

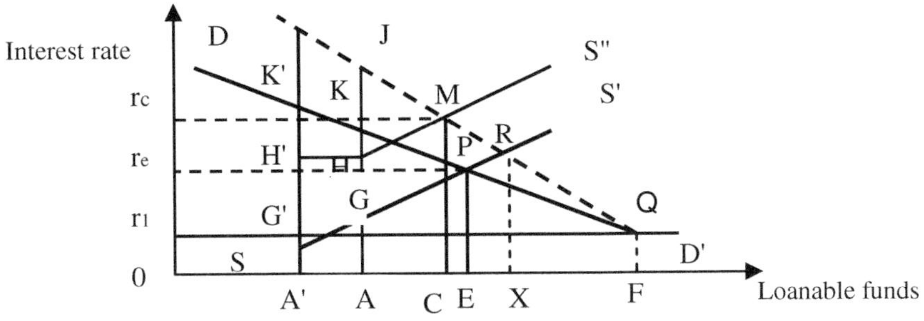

Fig. 1. Capital supply and demand of informal financial market and formal financial market

As shown in figure 1,the horizontal axis is loanable fund quantity and the vertical axis is interest rates. DD′ is loanable fund demand curve, it represents the investment demand function. SS' is loanable fund supply curve, it says that when residents' voluntary savings inflows formal department, it is positively related with interest rates. The intersection between loanable fund demand curve and loanable fund supply curve is P, the equilibrium interest rate is r_e,balanced quantity of loanable fund is OE. In figure 2-1, the slope of funds demand curve-JQ of informal financial market is steep than that of original funds demand curve -DD′. When the intrest rate of informal finance market equal to r_1, JQ will coincide with the initial capital demand curve-DD ' in Q. Under the condition of the interest rate liberalization, the financing quantity of regular financial institutions is OE, and in control of interest rate the financing quantity down to OA. Those capital demanders who can't get funds from formal market will turn to informal financial markets and strive to loanable fund with higher rates. Suppose the informal credit market is not in danger and the fund provider does not require risk compensation, then the capital supply line of informal sector will coincide with the regular capital supply line, namely the part of GS′ between G and S′. In this case, the financing quantity of informal market is AX, where the informal finance market plays an tintermediary role with financing effect.

Secondly, the rate of informal financial market is higher which is formed independently by market interest rates(r_c>r_1).It has promoted the transformation of savings into investment,reduced funding gap and the ratio of credit rationing and improved the efficiency of funds service.

2.1.2 Capital Accumulation Effect

Firstly, informal finance has the role to mobilize savings and promote rural investment.MaryKayGugerty (2005) think that rural informal finance group provided mandatory collective savings mechanism to mobilize farmers' savings. The rural of informal finance has mobilized rural idle capitals and will be beneficial to the formation of more large-scale investment funds and thus promote rural economic growth. At the same time, enterprises with good projects which are rejected by the formal finance can get credit support from informal finance,so the informal finance can reduce the cost of formal financial credit rationing and promoting the capital accumulation.Secondly, the informal finance plays an important role in solving capital accumulation of non-public economy. Nowadays, the formal financial support of non-public economy obviously lags behind and the difficulty in getting loans are still outstanding. In 2007, loans obtained by private enterprise and individual enterprise amount to 3507.66 billion yuan,only accounted for 1.34% of the total volume. Informal finance overcomes the defects of scale,amount and loan procedures of formal finance in a unique way, just make up for the inadequacy of formal finance and plays a role on providing capital supply for private economy.

2.1.3 Employment Promotion Effect

The rural informal finance promoting rural labor input,which is reflected by proportion improvement of rural employment. One is through the increase of capital's inputs to recruit more employees, another is that rural financial sector directly absorb the employment. In addition, the promotion employment effect of informal finance is also presented by private economy absorbing employment. Because the private economy get the funds support from informal financial markets, small and medium-sized enterprises,township enterprisethe, individually-owned business of non-state-owned economy get development and expansion ,and thus solve the employment of most of the non-agricultural population. According to the analysis of statistics yearbook data, by the end of 1998, the employed population of non-state-owned enterprises account for 87.53% of total urban and rural employed population.And by the end of 2005 the data has climbed to 91.78%. In recent years, both private enterprises and township enterprises have made great contributions in absorbing employment of laid-off workers from state-owned company and providing many job opportunities for rural areas.

2.1.4 Economic Growth Effect

The rural economy is dependent on strong capitals support.When other conditions remain unchanged, we can make use of private credit to increase conventional technologyto improve labor productivity and other resources utilization ratio, we can increase agriculture accumulation, increase the farmers' income and thus improve agricultural productivity. According to relevant data statistics, Chinese government provided fiscal capitals 574.93 billion yuan for farmers in 1995, the rural informal finance provided capital support 2147.6 billion yuan, which makes up of 17.87% of the rural GDP .In recent years, the contribution of informal finance has kept going down, but it still keeps above 10% on the whole. As shown in figure 2: the increase of rural economic gross domestic product (GDP) is positively correlated with the increase of the financing from informal finance. So,the development of rural informal finance has promoted the productivity of rural production factors, made great contribution to the development of Chinese rural economy and therefore, has the remarkable effect to promote economic growth.

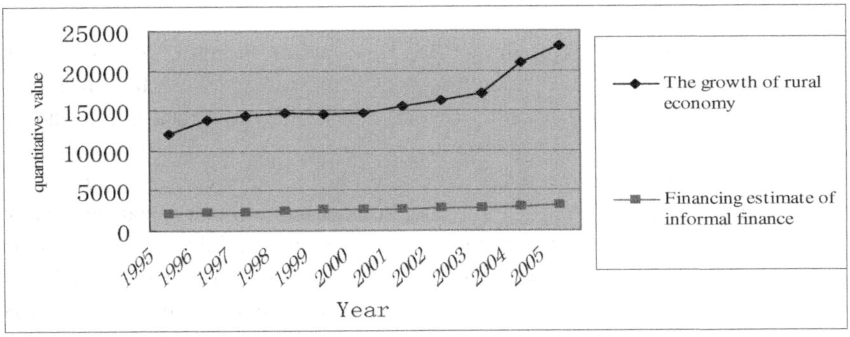

Fig. 2. Trend chart of rural economic growth and financing estimate of informal finance

Note: The economic data are from China Statistical Yearbook 2006 while the estimated data of informal finance come from Estimates of China's informal finance in rural areas by GuoPei, China Rural Survey, 2nd issue, 2004.

2.1.5 Competition-Inducing Effect

First, the informal finance has injected market factors and competitive factors to the whole financial system and further improved the financial institution system. The development of informal finance has changed the pattern of original financial institutions to certain extent, increased the diversification of China's financial system, promoted the competition of Chinese financial industries, improved the compition degree of rural financial market, promoted the marketization and development of whole rural financial market. Meanwhile, the diversification of China's financial institutions and development of informal finance are conducive to mobilize various saving resources to maximum,improve the speed and efficiency of transformation of savings into investment, avoid idle capitals and low-efficient allocation of fonds. Second, the development of informal finance will promote the innovation and development of existing financial institutions. The pressure from informal finance has became the driving force of formal financial reform. It stimulates entrepreneurial spirit of rural formal finance, prompts them to change their management concept, improves the service quality and efficiency, and thus promotes the whole financial service level.

2.2 Analysis of Institutional Efficiency

2.2.1 Information Superiority

William F.S, etal up (1997) thought that informal finance had comparative superiority in using local private information to solve the information asymmetry ,it is this superiority that cause the emergence of informal finance. The informal finance is established on the basis of relation with people, land,blood or other business relationship, the lenders can better understand the credit of borrowers, income status, reimbursement abilities and avoid or reduce the information asymmetry and other problems associated with it. It is this information superiority which informal finance institutions own that help the formal financial institutions solve information asymmetry problem to some extent and prevent the apperence of "moral hazard" and "adverse selection" (Braverman and Guash, 1986).

2.2.2 Operation Mode Superiority

The informal finance can be flexibly performed without lengthy procedures. It provides loans without approval procedures, it needs neither examination before credit nor after it. The loan contract can be simplified to a piece of paper, or even just oral commitment without any written materials, both parties of trade can make flexible innovation and reach consensus over the term of the loan, interest rates, repayment method with great flexibility.

2.2.3 Cost Superiority

Firstly, the informal finance is very concise and convenient. It excludes the spendings on fixed costs and pay rolls. It also has no many restrictions on trade time and thus can reduce the transaction cost of the informal financial institutions. Secondly, the implementation of informal financial contracts is often realized in accordance with community laws, and we can avoid lawsuit by a regular legal way at the high cost.

2.2.4 Speed Superiority

The operation of informal financial institutions is relatively simple, without complicated trading formalities, without examination involved. It's transaction process is quick, financing efficiency is high, the borrower can raise funds quickly and easily and make a deal as soon as possible.

2.2.5 Collateral Superiority

The flexible arrangement of informal financial organizations has eased the collateral constraint faced by the economical vulnerable groups and small and medium-sized enterprises. First, many things which cannot be as a guarantee in formal financial markets can be used as collateral in informal financial markets, such as property, land, etc. Secondly, the connection contract (interlinking contracts) is virtually a collateral. Thirdly, there is a social collateral mechanism ,or called recessive guarantee mechanism (implicit collateral) in informal financial markets.

3 Risk Analysis of Chinese Informal Finance

Due to the limitation of information and lack of the necessary norms and protection, there are also many market risks lurking behind high financial performance, which affect its operation efficiency to a certain extent.

3.1 Institutional Risks

The origin of informal finance make it only survive in narrow marginal space, make it more difficult to enjoy some advantages such as specialization and scale economy,therefore cannot enlarge the scale in the sunshine.Without the legal status granted by competent laws, the informal finance will lack a set of contract system which have legal effectiveness and protected by law. Financing body,actor's accountability for its duty and interests become blurred and difficult to discern due to lack of legal ownership. Meanwhile, the institutional framework which financial transactions requires is not sufficient, it is difficult for both capital providers and demanders to realize capital exchange and use, and so the financial resources cannot be allocated effectively.

3.2 Operational Risks

Most informal financial institutions in rural areas are not well organized and managed, Its internal management is more chaotic,there have neither standard internal control systems nor strict financial management and audit system in most informal financial institutions. They are less competent in fund-raising, credit investigation, assessment and approval, and thus vulnerable to market risks. In the meantime, most of the folk financial institutions do not extract the deposit reserves and bad debts reserves to resist the risk. They usually manage borrowers by experience rather than modern and scientific methods, and therefore have bigger operational risks.

3.3 Social Risks

The rural informal finance, not recognized by law, can only exist outside the formal financial system. It is hard to be standardized for lack of legal protection and necessary supervision and control. In this context, gray financial deals against direct legal items or stipulations of relevant departments are unavoidable, which are liable to cause social risks. When the Cooperation foundation close, collapse and fund-raising people flee with the money, extreme ways to solve the problem like retrieving the money with violence or even committing suicide or murder often ensue, sharpening the social contradictions and leading to the social instability.

3.4 Moral Risks

Generally, in the small range of rural folk finance, the moral risks are relatively smaller, but all forms of fund-raising conceals great moral risks. The fond-raisers often use information advantage to deceive, becloud investors, under the condition of high interests unfulfilled, they usually choose bankruptcy, surrender or fleeing with the money. There are two reasons leading to illegal fundraising events happened in succession, one is that fundraisers need capital desperately, the other is investors are lured by high returns. The high interests make use of people's unhealthy desire for profits, making them blind to their sources. Eventually more and more people involved in and it's scale becom lager and larger. Due to the unproductivity and repayment of this activity, the payment chain could finally break down, leading to the loss of participants' benefits and vicious impacts on the society.

3.5 Interest Rate Risk

Higher interest rate is one of the important features of rural informal financial market. With the sustained development of macro-economy and micro-economy becomes more and more actively, interest rate of rural informal finance raise to a new high level, and some places have come into "sudden huge profits" era. This high rate, more than 4 times larger than the rate given by the formal financial markets, would aggravated the economic burden and the cost of production, then make operation of the rural informal financial organization in danger. The operation model of the rural informal financial market's huge rate not only bring the borrowers high cost, but also make the capital chain become more and more fragile, and it even influence the survive of borrowers and cause interest risks. All of reasons will lead to collapse of financing chain and trigger financial risks.

4 Conclusions

The above analysis shows that as the product of private financial innovation,the Chinese rural informal finance has the economic efficiencies and incomparable institutional efficiencies. The Chinese informal finance is a kind of institutional arrangement,it comes into being as a result of the financial demands outside the extant system economy. To sum up, the informal finance is efficient and it has the character of efficiency improvement. However, due to the limitation of information and lack of the necessary norms and protection, there are also many market risks lurking behind high financial performance, which affect its operation efficiency in some degree. Therefore, some effective measures such as perfecting related laws and regulations, building effective supervisory system, improving market environment, setting up perfect service system and establishment of deposit insurance system for informal finance must be taken to regulate the development of Chinese informal finance.

References

1. IFAD: Rural Financial Services in China, Thematic Study. Volume I - Main Report. Report No. 1147-CN Rev. (2001)
2. Wang, L.: The theory of informal finance and economic growth and empirical research. Master Thesis of Chinese Northwestern University, pp.17–18 (2008)
3. Kong, D.: The internal defects of Chinese informal finance and regulating. Journal of Harbin Junior College (7), 15–16 (2010)
4. Gao, Y.: Rational thinking on the existence of rural informal finance. Journal of Anhui University (1), 115–116 (2007)
5. Guo, P.: Eestimate of Chinese rural informal finance. China's Rural Observation (2), 22–24 (2004)
6. Zhang, Q., Zhang, Q.: Study on market risk and supervision of informal finance. Hainan Finance (8), 51–52 (2010)
7. Conning, Udry: Rural financial markets in developing countries. The Handbook of Agricultural Economics (3), 35–37 (2005)
8. Liu, S., Cheng, K.: China's rural informal finance: performance, defect and governance. Journal of Xinjiang College of Finance and Economics 25(3), 35–37 (2005)
9. Cui, H.: Performance analysis on rural folk finance. Journal of the Central University of Finance and Economics (5), 40–41 (2005)

The Evolutionary Game Analysis on the Cooperative Relationship Stability of a Tea Company and a Tea Farmer

Guangyong Xu[1,2] and Xuemei Jin[2]

[1] School of Business, Renmin University of China, Beijing, Room 539, PINYUAN Building 3, No.59, Zhongguancun Street, Haidian District, Bejing 100872 P.R. China
xgypolo@163.com
[2] School of Business, Anhui University of Finance and Economics, Anhui Bengbu, China, 233041

Abstract. The paper established the dynamic evolution model of cooperative relationship of tea companies and tea farmers with the aid of the evolutionary stable strategy and replicator dynamics. Before forming stable evolution pattern, the model maybe both choose situation "low requirement-low requirement", forming equilibrium results of absolutely fair divide the net proceeds. However, these equilibrium results are only partial equilibrium points and the cooperative is not form evolution stable equilibrium results on the equilibrium points. Because the both participants constantly learn and adjust, the stable equilibrium results will eventually develop to both ends, that is, buyers and sellers will form cooperative strategy combinations with "high requirement-low requirement" or "low requirement-high requirements".

Keywords: a tea farmer, a tea company, the cooperative relationship, the stability, the evolutionary game.

1 Introduction

The cooperative of company and farmer is important cooperative problem in agriculture industry chain. "Company & famer" model completes effective connection between company and farmer through commodity contract form. The key of a stability of cooperative between company and farmer is reasonable and effective distribution economic interest. Tea industry chain optimization is necessary condition of tea industry upgrading, and the stability of cooperative and mutually benefit relationship is key link. The key is whether or not a tea farmer and a tea company can remain stable cooperative relations, and the key of stable cooperative relations is that economic benefit can be reasonable and effective distributed. The thesis puts the stability of the cooperative relationship as the core research problem, and builds an evolutionary game model in the condition of both limited rationality and learning and adjustment ability, then the thesis deeply analyses evolutionary game process and evolutionary balance style of cooperative behavior of tea farmer and tea company, the thesis's last part gives many advises about stabilizing cooperative relationship.

M. Zhou (Ed.): ISAEBD 2011, Part III, CCIS 210, pp. 35–40, 2011.

2 Theory Review

When game theory was widely used in economics, biologists got some revelation. They used strategic interaction idea to construct various biological competition evolution models, including the animal competition, gender distribution or plant growth and development, and so on (Lewontin, 1961). Then, biologists transformed traditional game theory according to the inherent laws of biological evolution, including transformed payment to fitness function, refined Nash equilibrium to evolutionary stable equilibrium through introducing mutation mechanism(Maynard Smith & Price, 1973) and constructed replicator dynamics model through introducing choice mechanism(Taylor & Jonker, 1978). The last stage was viewed as formatting the evolution game. (Foster&Young,1990;Weibull,2002; Schmidt , 2004; Young, 2007). Later on, economists referenced biologist thoughts in turn and applied evolutionary game to economics. That promoted the development of evolutionary game, including from evolutionarily stable equilibrium to stochastically stable equilibrium and from replicator dynamics model to the dynamic model of random individual learning (Foster & Young, 1990; Weibull, 2002; Schmidt, 2004; Young, 2007). Moreover, (Vincent &Brown, 2005) pointed out that meta-population dynamic model was transformed to evolutionary game model as long as establishing various evolution strategy and fitness and population growth rate relationship.

3 Construction of Model

The concept of evolutionary game is evolutionary stable strategy(ESS) and replicator dynamics (Weibull, 1998). ESS says a stable state of a population resistance mutation strategy. It is defined as: if strategy(S*) is a ESS, only if:

(1) S* Constitute a Nash equilibrium, that is, for any S, there will be U (S*,S*)≥ U (S*,S); (2) If S*≠S, U (S*,S*)=u (S*,S), there will be U (S*,S)> U (S,S)。 In fact, replicator dynamics describes dynamic differential equation that is the frequency a particular strategy being used. According to the principle of evolution, if the fitness of a strategy or payoff is beyond the average of population fitness, the strategy will develop in a population. Namely the survival of the fittest reflected in the growth rate of this strategy $1dx_k/x_kdt > 0$, and it can be said with the following differential equation:

$$\frac{1dx_k}{x_k\ d_t} = [U(K,S) - U(S,S)], K = 1,2,3\ldots,K \tag{1}$$

X_k means the ratio of strategy K being used in a population; U(K, S) means the fitness of strategy K being used; U(S,S) means the average fitness; K means the different strategies. ESS is a kind of strategy, not balanced. Strategy is in advance, Equilibrium in the later. Although evolutionary stable strategy is a biology concept, it provides robust criteria for all kinds of human behaviors. To make research objects do not break general, supposedly there are many tea farmers and many tea companies in the symbiosis of tea farmers and tea companies. They present two different groups who have intimate relationship. The game of two groups is randomly matched and dynamic evolutionary process.

3.1 Basic Hypothesis of Model

The hypothesis 1: There are two groups one of which is the buyer group composed with M tea companies, the other is the seller group composed with N tea farmers. Both parties of game get trade agreement after negotiations. The turnover is G as soon as PC=PF. The Pc is the bidding of a tea company, and the Pf is the bidding of a tea farmer.

The hypothesis 2: The initial cost of a tea company is CC, and the invested cost of a tea farmer is CF. For a tea company, G* PC-CC≥0, for tea farmer, G* PF-CF≥0. The total net income of both sides is NR= (G* PC-CC) + (G* PF-CF). The essence of this game fights for allocation proportion of the total net income. At the same time, if both don't reach a cooperation agreement, a tea company can get a only normal income R_{CO} through the other ways, and a tea farmer can get a only normal income R_{FO} through the way of produce and market all by oneself. Of course, R_{CO} or R_{FO} are all less than the income of cooperation, otherwise, the cooperation will lose its value.

The hypothesis 3: The proportion of high requirement in a tea companies is p, so the proportion of low requirement is 1-p; The proportion of high requirement in a tea farmer is q, so the proportion of low requirement is 1-q.

The hypothesis 4: The deviation degree of stable equilibrium in cooperate relationship is u_1 or u_2($0\le u_1\le 1/2$, $1/2\le u_2\le 1$).

3.2 Construct of Model

In the above hypothetical conditions, the both sides strategy set is {high requirement, low requirements}. The negotiation between the two game sides is conducted in the condition of an uncertain and limited rationality. The both must consider the other individual strategies and consider the relative fitness in itself group to select and adjustment their strategies. Table 1 is the pay matrix of cooperation game on both tea companies and tea farmers.

Table 1. Pay matrix of cooperation game on both a tea companies and a tea farmers

		Tea company	
Tea farmer		High requirement(p)	Low requirement (1-p)
	High requirement(q)	(R_{F0}, R_{CO})	(u_2NR, (1-u_2)NR)
	Low requirement(1-q)	(u_1NR, (1-u_1)NR)	(NR/2, NR/2)

The repeated game dynamic equation when a tea farmer selects high requirement is:

$$dq/dt=q(1-q)NR[u_2-1/2-(u_1+u_2-1/2)p] \tag{2}$$

Similarly, he repeated game dynamic equation when the tea company selects high requirement is:

$$dp/dt=p(1-p)NR[1/2-u_1-(3/2-u_1+u_2)q] \tag{3}$$

The system composed with (2) and (3) two differential equation describes the strategy evolutionary when a tea company and a tea farmer select high requirement. The stability of the evolutionary equilibrium points can be analysed by the local stability of

Jacobin matrix. The result includes 5 equilibrium points, two unstable points A(1,0) and C(0,1), two stable points O(0,0) and B(1,1) and the saddle point $D(\frac{1/2-u_1}{3/2-u_1-u_2}, \frac{u_2-1/2}{u_1+u_2-1/2})$. Because of the uncertainty of u1 and u_2, the saddle point is composed with many representative points. The detailed content will be presented in model analysis.

Figure 1 draws of each stable point and unstable and saddle points and shows the phase track of dynamic game evolutionary on cooperative relationship between a tea company and a tea farmer. In the figure 1, the broken line composed with two unstable points O, B and the saddle point D is the border line that shows system convergence in different state. The high requirement of a tea farmer converges in the upper left the broken line, meanwhile, a tea company selects low requirement strategy; the high requirement of the tea company converges in the upper lower left the broken line, meanwhile, the tea farmer selects low requirement strategy.

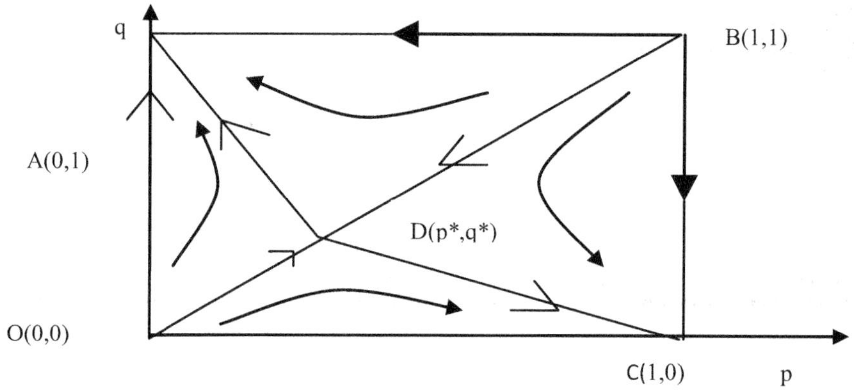

Fig. 1. The dynamic evolutionary of the cooperation between a tea company and a tea farmer

4 Analysis of Model

From the evolutionary model being constructed, we can conclude that the evolutionary equilibrium result between a tea company and a tea farmer can be {high requirement, low requirement} or {low requirement, high requirement}. Moreover, what path the evolutionary game is along with and which stable state will reach is closely related with the initial state and payoff matrix of game. So the fitness function and the initial value and change of two sides decide the game convergence of different equilibrium points. The saddle $D(\frac{1/2-u_1}{3/2-u_1-u_2}, \frac{u_2-1/2}{u_1+u_2-1/2})$ is the threshold value that shows the system characteristics change of evolutionary game. If initial state of the system is near the saddle point, the change of initial state or parameters minute changes will obviously affect system evolutionary results. Because the saddle is dynamic point, the below introduces several typical saddle points. The first, when the cooperate cost equals earning (G^* P_C=C_C and G^* P_F=C_F), the saddle is D(0.5, 0.5). In Figure 1, △AOC=△ABC that shows the evolutionary trend to O (0, 0) or B (1, 1) is same. That is, the stable probability of the cooperation between a tea company and a tea farmer is even. The second, when G^* $P_C \leq C_C$ and G^* $P_F \leq C_F$, the saddle D moves to left lower. In figure 1, the quadrilateral area ABCD is more than the quadrilateral area AOCD, in this case, the dynamic trend of evolutionary game is to be B (1, 1) and the probability of completely noncooperation is more than the probability of completely cooperation. The third, when G^* $P_C \geq C_C$ and G^* $P_F \geq C_F$, the saddle D moves to light upper. In figure 1, the quadrilateral area ABCD is less than the quadrilateral area AOCD, in this case, the dynamic trend of evolutionary game is to be B (1, 1) and the probability of completely noncooperation is less than the probability of completely cooperation. The fourth, when G^* $P_C \geq C_C$, and G^* $P_F \leq C_F$, this case is more complex, but overall, the saddle will fall near the right lower part of A. There are two kinds of cases, one is that the cooperation is not stable and moves to noncooperation because the power of noncooperation is stronger than the power of cooperation; The other is that the cooperation is stable and moves to cooperation because the power of cooperation is stronger than the power of noncooperation. The firth, when G* PC≤CC and G* PF≥CF, the saddle will fall near the left upper part of A. Of cause, also there are two kinds of cases, one is that the cooperation is not stable and moves to noncooperation because the power of noncooperation is stronger than the power of cooperation; The other is that the cooperation is stable and moves to cooperation because the power of cooperation is stronger than the power of noncooperation.

5 Conclusions

From the analysis of evolutionary game between the a tea company and a tea farmer in tea industry chain, Based on the game player's limited rationality, we can draw conclusions that the result of game can be noncooperation because of the choice "high requirement-high requirement (B in the figure 1)" and also can fairly divide the net income because of the choice "low requirement-low requirement (O in the figure 1)" before forming the stable evolutionary game. However, the two result of equilibrium only are temporary and partial equilibrium points, the cooperation cannot form stable evolutionary equilibrium result on above "equilibrium points".

Because the game player's Continuous learning and adjustment, the stable equilibrium result will trend to both ends (A or C in the figure 1), that is, contracting parties get the cooperation strategy of "high requirement-low requirement" or "low requirement-high requirement".

Acknowledgments. The study is supported by Research Fund of Anhui Province Philosophy and Social Science Planning, and we gratefully appreciate it. The fund program number is AHSKF09--10D05.

References

1. Foster, D., Young, P.H.: Stochastic Evolutionary Game Dynamics. Theoretical Population Biology 38, 219–232 (1990)
2. Lewontin, R.C.: Evolution and the Theory of Games. Journal of Theoretical Biology 1, 382–403 (1961)
3. Maynard Smith, J.: The Theory of Games and the Evolution of Animal Conflict. Journal of Theory Biology 47, 37–38 (1973)
4. Taylor, P., Jonker, L.: Evolutionary Stable Strategies and Game Dynamics. Mathematical Biosciences 40, 145–156 (1978)
5. Vincent, T.L., Brown, J.S.: Evolutionary Game Theory, Natural Selection, and Darwinian Dynamics. Cambridge University Press, London (2005)
6. Weibull, J.W.: Evolutionary Game Theory. MIT Press, Boston (1998)
7. Weibull, J.W.: What Have We Learned from Evolutionary Game Theory so Far? Working Papers From Industrial Institute for Economic and Social Research (2002)
8. Young, H.P.: In: Hendricks, V.F., Hansen, P.G. (eds.) Game Theory: Some Personal Reflections, From Game 5 Questions. Automatic Press (2007)

Study on Online Auction System of Group-Buying Based on Multi-agent

Yang Bai[1,2], Xiao Liu[1], Junping Li[3], and Yong Feng[3]

[1] School of Information technology, Eastern Liaoning University, Dandong, Liaoning 118000, P.R. China
[2] Institute of Systems Engineering, Dalian University of Technology, Dalian, Liaoning 116024, P.R. China
[3] School of Information, Liaoning University, Shenyang, Liaoning 110036, P.R. China
fengyong@lnu.edu.cn

Abstract. Group-buying online auction is a kind of dynamic pricing method. According to the weakness of the low-automation and advantages of the multi-agent, this paper introduces the multi-agent into the study on group-buying online auction. This paper discusses the automated negotiation protocols, negotiation strategies, system frame and provides the implementation algorithm of group-buying online auction by simulating the auction flow. The combination of multi-agent and the method of group-buying online auction not only supplements online auction theory but also has a good application prospect.

Keywords: multi-agent, group-buying, online auction, frame.

1 Introduction

With the wide use of e-commerce, online auction had been developed greatly due to its low cost, abundant species of items and the wide coverage of users. Among all kinds of online auction methods, group-buying has become the focus of current studies because it can bring the users all over the world together. Group-buying is also a kind of auction with the same quality of different items. And then all the bidders are considered as a group. More and more the bidders are, cheaper and cheaper the price is. So it is also called group pricing auction [1].

Because agent technology can simulate the whole steps of the online auction, it has become the main technology of auto-online-auction. Currently the application of agent technology in online auction has made some representative results. For example Lin et al. had invented an ODB system which can support dynamic online bargaining process and whose function was implemented by three agents [2]. Chan et al. had introduced a multi-access and multi-purpose auction system in which users can achieve a dynamic auction data access by Web, WAP devices and especially mobile agent [3]. When it is applied to the group-buying, there are also a lot of researchers who have been making studies on it. For example Kauffman and Wang had come to the conclusion that as the more the tenders were, the more the future tenders would be by analyzing the states

M. Zhou (Ed.): ISAEBD 2011, Part III, CCIS 210, pp. 41–47, 2011.

from Moboshop.com which was also called positive effect [4]. And also Chen et al. had made studies on the internal system of group-buying [5].

Though there are a lot of results related on the theory and practice of online-auction, there are still a lot of blanks, especially in the group-buying online auction system It is necessary to deepen the study on the protocols, strategies and the use of technology in the group-buying online auction system. Currently, the automatic of online auction is still very low. At the same time, it demands the auctioneer to check the whole auction process all the time. Therefore, the auctioneer has to spend a lot of energy and cost on the auction. As a result, to design a simple and effective group-buying online auction system has become the focus in this field. This paper introduces the multi-agent technology into the research of online auction. First it analyses the auction agreement of group-buying, the auction strategy and the auction process. And then it shows the design of online auction system based on the multi-agent technology including the system's frame and implementation algorithm. The last part is the summary of this research work. The group-buying online auction system based on the multi-agent technology can automate the auction process, and it can also bring auction participants a win-win result.

2 Group-Buying Online Auction Models

Whenever we make a model of auction, there will be a series of rules to restrain the system. During the process of group-buying auction, the auctioneer has to decide the auction strategy (increasing or decreasing) and the details of the auction (the quantity of item, the price curve and the time of auction). And the bidder will make the decision whether he wants to take part in the auction or not, if yes, how much he can give. The negotiation protocols and the negotiation strategies of the group-buying are the basic idea for the auction.

2.1 Group-Buying Auction Protocol

During the process of the auction, if there is just one auctioneer but there are N bidders, before the beginning of the auction, the auctioneer has to announce the following details about the auction. The first one is the price curve. If the price is marked step and step, the auctioneer has to give a detailed price to each corresponding step. If the price is decreasing, then it has to tell us how much the price will go down with the each increasing in the number of purchase. The second one is the deadline of the auction and the third one is the quantity of the items involved in the auction. Before the beginning of the auction, all the bidders will know the price curve, the time for the auction and the quantity of the items so that each bidder can have his own estimated price for the process of the auction. At the same time, each bidder can know the price curve of the other bidders but he cannot know the exact price. Each bidder can also know the detailed information about the former bidders. After they check all of price from the former bidders, he can give the best price and then he can also decide whether to give price or not. If the bidder's estimated price (q) is lower than the one given by theauctioneer, he will not make the bid. Otherwise, the expected utility will be less than 0. On the contrary, if the price is higher the one given by the auctioneer, then he can make the bid and then the expected utility will by greater than 0. The whole process of the auction has to be end within the time given by the auction otherwise it can be defined as invalid. All the items have been sold before the deadline of the auction. The auction will also be ended and all the bidders will be successful and will pay for the item with the same price.

2.2 Group-Buying Auction Strategies

Following the auction will end in any case: (1) the total number of bids reaches N, (2) the auction time reaches T. the auctioneer prior set a price range as a price vector Q, $Q = Q(q_1, q_2, ...q_N)$, in this, for any $i \in [1, N], q_1 \geq q_2 \geq ... \geq q_N$, i is the final number of goods sold, q_i is the price that each winning bidder must pay when the final number of goods sold. Auction only allowed discrete tender value, that bidders can only choose q_i, one of the elements in Q, as their tender value. ($i \in [1, N]$).

In group-buying, the successful bidder and their payment are according to the following strategies:

If the time is at t $t(t \leq T)$, and $n(n \leq N)$ bidders tender. If the bid vector is B= $(b_1, b_2...b_n)$, then the current price is current-price(B)= q_i, in which, i=max $(i|\sum_{j=1}^{n} H(b_j - q_i) \geq I$ and $i \in [0,N])$, when $x \geq 0$, then H(x)= 1; when $x < 0$ then H(x)= 0.

In order to describe the bidder's evaluation for the goods and tender value, as too as the price vector and their relationship, we define function as follow:

If $b \geq q_1$, then $\theta(b) = q_1$; if $b < q_N$ then $\theta(b) = q_{N+1}$; if $q_{j-1} > b \geq q_j$ and $j \in [2, N]$ then $\theta(b) = q_j$. Among them, the b is a real number, the q_j is the correspond element in price vector Q, and the j =1,2,..., N +1.

2.3 Group-Buying Auction Process

The group-buying auction is a very complicated process between the two parties in the auction. From the beginning of preparatory stage to reaching the negotiation protocols, the whole process includes so many different statuses. In order to make sure the process to be continued efficiently until to the consistent protocols reached, we should definite all the status of the auction and it is great importance to the process of the group-buying auction. In the following part we will give the picture of all the statuses of the auction which are displayed in figure 1 and figure 2 and in this picture there are two partied which are auctioneer agent and bidder agent [6].

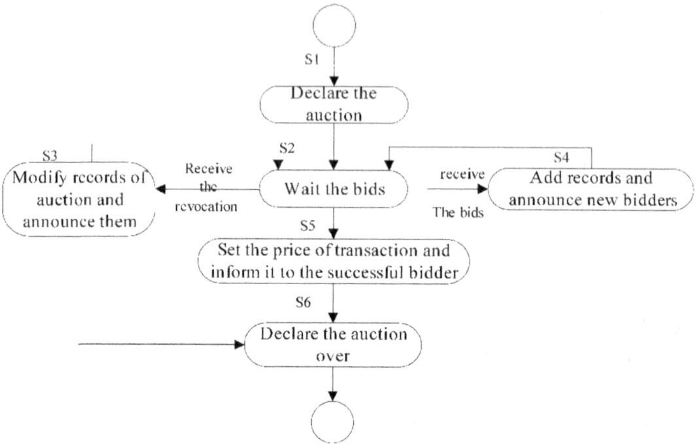

Fig. 1. Auctioneer agent negotiation finite state diagram

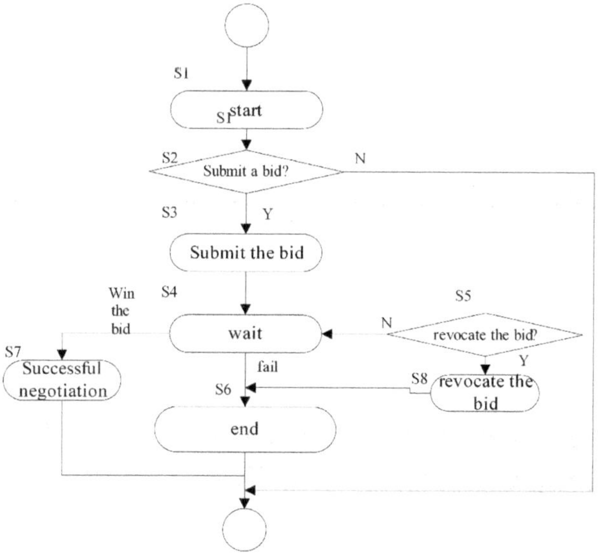

Fig. 2. Bidder agent negotiation finite state diagram

3 Designs on Online Auction System of Group-Buying Based on Multi-agent

3.1 System Frame

On the basis of group-buying auction model, connected with the online auctions, this paper comes out the frame of group-buying online auction system and the frame includes the following components as shown in figure 3.

(1) The Auction Management Agent

Auction management is the host of the auction process, who is responsible for announcing the auction mechanism, recording the information of the auction process, determining the time to stop the auction and interacting with all the user agents.

(2) The Search Agent

The main function of the search agent is to create a certain number of membership search based on the search task, to specify the practical information search and to screen the information of the commodity exchange and then it has to feedback the results to the auction management. The lower will exchange the data with the agent which works in the auction database.

(3) The Mechanism Agent

The main function of the mechanism agent is to provide the auction protocol and strategies of online management agent auction, and also to exchange data with the auction mechanism database.

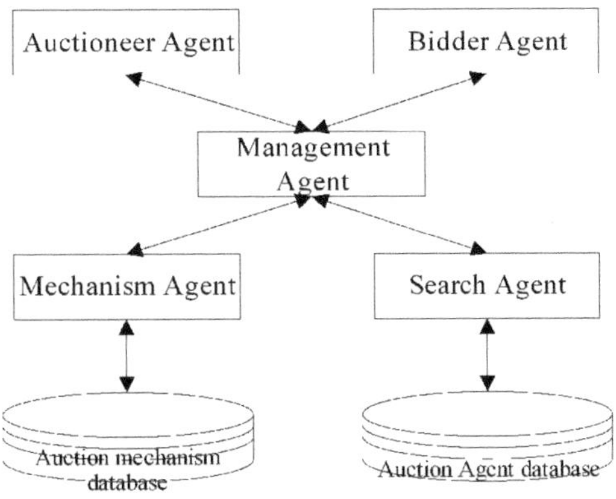

Fig. 3. Online auction system frame of group-buying based on multi-agent

3.2 Implementation Algorithm

In this paper, it uses IBM's Aglet as the prototype development platform. Aglet provides more comprehensive in agent programming model that allows effective and dynamic communication in agents. Aglet API builds the Aglet and its environment interface. It can provide a variety of creations in Aglet, messaging, dispatch, recovery, cloning, and termination methods. Aglet has many advantages in simple development, better scalability and better reusability. The online auction system is based on the agents in self-adjusting ability. The following statement gives the primary communication statements and implementation algorithm.

```
Void group-buying Auction () {
  t = 0; // auctioneer announces the price curve table, deadline time, delay interval (interval), the number of items and so on. Auctioneer announces the start of the auction;
    While (t <deadline) {
    for (i = 1 to m) { // bidding in order M;
    for (j = 1 to N) { // a number of N items;
    if (bidder i bid) // If the bidder i bids;
    {bid (bidder agent i); // bidder agent i bids;
    if (q> = qN) // bidder's valuation is lower than the auction price
    {selectedbid + = bid; //take the bid into current bid set
    If (Sum (selectedbid) = phase [j]) // If the goods number in bid collection equals with the item number in phase j number
    If (Max (selectedbid)> = q [j]) // If the auction price in bidding set not less than the price of the sequence in this very phase;
    current-price [j] = q [j]; // Change the current price into the price of the auction price series;
    else current-price [j] = null; // Otherwise, set the current price blank;
    if (t> deadline-interval)
    deadline = t-interval; // Delay;
    } else wait; // If no one bids, then waits;
    }
    }
    For (i = 0; i <N, i + +) Winnerbid [i] = selectedbid [i]; // Determine the successful bidder;
    buying-price = current-price [i]; // Determine the final transaction price;
  }
```

4 Conclusions

The online auction system of group-buying is the weak point in the e-commerce field. This paper introduces automated online auction of the multi-agent technology and also makes a detailed analysis of group-buying auction protocols, policies and processes. On this basis, the design, the system frame and algorithm of the online auction system based on the multi-agent technology are given to achieve the automation of group-buying online auction. The research on the group-buying auction system based on the multi-agent technology is important to improve the efficiency and automation of auction.

Acknowledgment. This work is supported by the Natural Science Foundation of Liaoning Province of China (Grant No. 20102083), China Postdoctoral Science Foundation (Grant No. 2010047147) and Social Science Youth Foundation of Ministry of Education of China (Grant No. 10YJC630063).

References

1. Chen, J., Chen, X., Song, X.P.: Comparison of The Group-buying Auction and The Fixed Pricing Mechanism. Decision Support System 43(2), 445–459 (2007)
2. Lin, F.R., Chang, K.Y.: A Multiagent Framework for Automated Online Bargaining. IEEE Intelligent Systems 16(4), 41–47 (2001)
3. Chan, H.C.B., Ho, I.S.K., Lee, R.S.T.: Design and Implementation of A Mobile Agent-based Auction System. In: IEEE Pacific Rim Conference on Communications, Computers and Signal Processing 2001, PACRIM 2001, Hawaii, vol. 2, pp. 740–743 (2001)
4. Kauffman, R.J., Wang, B.: New Buyers' Arrival Under Dynamic Pricing Market Microstructure: The Case of Group-Buying Discounts on the Internet. Management Information Systems 18(2), 157–188 (2001)
5. Liu, Y.H., Chen, J.: Retailer's Ordering Strategy under The Group-buying Online Auction. Systems Engineering-Theory & Practice 29(7), 35–42 (2009)
6. Yu, H.Y., Liu, Z.Y.: Study on Multi-attribute Auction System Based on Multi-agent. Computer Engineering and Applicationss 44(32), 194–196 (2008)

The Relationship between the Internal Governance and the Corporate Value of the Listed Companies

Helin Wang

Xinxiang University, Xinxiang China 453000
xxxywhl@163.com

Abstract. This paper provided evidence of significant positive correlation internal management and enterprise value of the listed companies. Ownership is highly concentrated in the listed company Henan province. And state-owned shares, state-owned shares form of subject, this means that the government is still in company management plays an important role. The establishment of a modern enterprise of the listed companies of Henan province, the governance mechanism for the situation changes, can get with creativity and necessary business, help companies to achieve business, improve the company's value.

Keywords: listed companies, internal governance, corporate value.

1 Introduction

In the mid 1980's and a century, China began to establish joint-stock enterprises. And Shanghai stock exchange and Shenzhen stock exchange, was established in December 1990 respectively in 1991 and April, marking the beginning of China's capital market. The first listed companies of Henan province in 1994, released on January 3, in Shanghai stock exchange, because when more and more companies from Henan province began to reform enterprise through the stock system to meet the development of the agriculture new market economy. December 31, 2009, by listed companies of Henan province there are 36 normal completely. Although the issuing time of the enterprises in Henan province is later than most other provinces, the rapid development of the listed companies, have very important influence economic development of Henan province. When beginning, we will provide a simple background in the former research. In the next section, statements, different cases studies involving possibility basic problems based on the knowledge that the panel data of Henan province from 2001 to 2009, the possibility of listed company: first, model and gives a complete relations; Then internal management and corporate value theory, proposes several Suggestions; Final consideration.

2 Theoretical Overview

Corporate governance is a system arrangement; solve the agency problems caused by the separation of proprietary rights, from management rights, which services to

M. Zhou (Ed.): ISAEBD 2011, Part III, CCIS 210, pp. 48–53, 2011.

investors. Exterior governance mainly by external market competition and external environment as a control means, including legal rights, such as market competition, control market. The main control internal governance institutional arrangements, including through the internal shareholders' supervision, plate, supervision, and top management personnel salary contact, institutional investors, etc. Good corporate governance has become the company's competitive advantage, this will help the company reduce the financing costs, improve the company's reputation and increase the value of the final victory. In China, corporate governance research started since 1990's, which is relatively late. Rapid development of the market economy reform smoothly, corporate governance has become a key realize the modern enterprise system. In China, the research and practice of company management development along with the development of social economy, the economic structure change and enterprise, the deepening of the reform of the evolution of company development strategy problem is very important.

Equity structure is important internal management, has serious influence for distribution enterprise control and agency. In the existing literature research on the relationship between ownership structure and corporate value is controversial. As early as in 1932, Berle and means proposed side and a negative correlation between ownership structure and corporate performance. The results confirmed that some scholars late, but some scholars provide the problem. - (1983) points out, the shareholding structure of company profit maximization service, and there is no correlation with the company value.

The board of directors has an important position in the company's business decision, also be very important internal governance structure. The board of directors features include many aspects, such as plate size, the board independence, leadership structure and the frequency of the board meeting, etc. Shleifer and suit, 2003 (1988) found that the correlation between the size of the board and tobin Q and is not a simple linear, but Yermack (1996) suggests they negatively correlated. Note here Millstein board independence is MacAvoy and positive correlation and enterprise value. In addition, significant problems are achieved by the board of directors meeting, so the board meeting frequency and efficiency of corporate governance and enterprise value influence directly. There is a positive correlation between internal management and enterprise value. But Jason (1993) hold different views, this is boarding conference is useless, didn't know what to do with company performance.

The company can be regarded as a kind of disease, facing disease formed between legal entity stakeholders of the contract. In these contract relations, the relationship between managers and owners is one of the core parts. An operator priority is responsible owner, it is necessary to safeguard the interests of the shareholders, but also achiever's biggest shareholder value, simultaneously. As market competition intensifies and ownership structure development, in 1960, big shareholders and senior management personnel and compromised competition. And pay design become the focus of attention. Most literatures on salary design is based on the principal-agent theory. Salary design, according to the interests of the principal and agent can converge and agency costs can be reduced, thus increasing the company's value. The positive correlation between the senior management personnel, salary and stock options, value the incentive effect significantly to senior management personnel (this, 1990).

3 Methodologies

3.1 Data

This paper mainly discusses using the unbalanced panel model to study the relationship between the internal management and enterprise value of the listed companies of Henan. In this paper, we sample company is listed companies from Henan province during 2001 to 2009. We exclude the company lack of available data. It leads to 37 companies, the final sample 270. Our data come from CSMAR database.

3.2 Empirical Model and Variable Measurement

The paper mainly studies from three aspects: the internal governance equity structure, the board of directors and senior management incentive mechanism construction. The shareholding ratio by SSR is the largest shareholder, measurement of ownership structure. Double is a virtual variable board leadership structure, when CEO is measured board chair, we define: 1, otherwise 0. INDE rate is independent directors of board seats, measuring level independence. BSIZE is a large number of board members, measuring plate size. The meeting of the board meeting is times during this fiscal year, measurement of the frequency of the board meeting. Income amount the top three executive's salary, measuring the salary incentive level of top managers. MSR and is executives shareholding equity incentive level measurement, the top managers. TobinQ (TobinQ) is a company's value; this is the relationship between computing indices, the company's market value and the value of replacement of assets.

Unbalanced take panel model method to measure the relationship and the internal management of the listed companies of Henan value. Find out the relationship between the internal management and enterprise value and performance, we ran back, using the following model:

$$\begin{aligned} TOBINQ_{a} &= \alpha_0 + \alpha_1 LNSIZE_{it} + \alpha_2 LEV_{it} + \alpha_3 SSR_{it} \\ &+ \alpha_4 DUAL_{it} + \alpha_5 LNDE_{it} + \alpha_6 BSIZE_{it} + \alpha_7 MEET_{it} \\ &+ \alpha_8 INCOME_{it} + \alpha_9 MSR_{it} + \varepsilon \end{aligned} \tag{1}$$

Where i= 1, 2 ,..., 37, means the sectional observation units; t=2001,2002 ,..., 2009, means the time-series observations.

The equation (1) expresses the panel model to test the relationship between internal governance and company value of Henan Province listed companies. The dependent variables are company value, which is measured by Tobin Q. The independent variables are SSR, DUAL, INDE, BSIZE, MEET, INCOME, MSR. And LNSIZE and LEV are control variables, which are the natural logarithm of total assets and leverage respectively.

Table 1. Construction of the variables of the research

Variables Name	Variables	Description
Company Value	TOBINQ	Tobin Q value.
Company Size	LNSIZE	The natural logarithm of total market capitalization of the companies.
Financial Leverage	LEV	Liability/asset ratio .
Ownership structure	SSR	Shareholding ratio of the first largest shareholder
Board leadership structure	DUAL	Dummy variable. If CEO also is the board chair, it is defined1, or else 0.
Independence level of the board	INDE	Ratio of independent director in the board.
the board size B	BSIZE	The number of board members.
Board meeting frequency	MEET	The times of board meetings during the fiscal year.
Salary incentive level of top managers	INCOME	The sum of the annual salary of top three executives
Equity incentive level of top managers	MSR	The sum of senior managers ' shareholding ratio

4 Empirical Results

4.1 Descriptive Statistics

It is a highly centralized. In the listed company, private enterprise and private enterprise is rare. In addition, the company's CEO 93% not board chair. 49 value board Numbers are even, 16.9% / 5 of total samples, the rest of the samples is odd, 83.1% board digital total samples. In order to avoid deadlock, this is popular when voting take odd number of plate size. This means that the independent directors quantitative 31%. 148 a sample, from 2001 to 2005, independent director's quantitative was 27%. 2006 there were 142 samples (including 2006), means that the independent directors to 35%. Quantitative the new company law takes effect, 1 January 2006; it increases the quota of independent directors. The average number of the board meeting was 7.8, the minimum value is 2, and the biggest is 31.

Table 2. Descriptive Statistics

Variables N	Number	Mean	Std. Dev	Minimum	Maximum
TOBINQ	290	1.386	0.769	0.401	8.405
SSR	290	47.567	15.628	15.26	79.73
DUAL	290	0.072	0.260	0	1
INDE	290	0.309	0.099	0	0.5
BSIZE	290	9.390	1.606	5	15
MEET	290	7.779	3.274	2	31
INCOME	290	482669.6	508378.5	38000	2711654
MSR	290	0.005	0.028	0	0.295
LNSIZE	290	21.492	1.132	18.676	25.355
LEV	290	0.578	0.381	0.065	4.465

4.2 Regression Analysis

Least-square method using the unbalanced panel data of the panel estimated balance correlation and internal management enterprise value, can overcome the sample selection bias. According to the test, hausman fixed effect model is more suitable for the model.

According to the regression results stata 10.0, by a significant positive correlation between the proportion in 0.05 level between the first big shareholders and corporate value. Henan concentration exists in most state holding listed companies. In a significant negative correlation between 0.1 and company level board meet the value of frequency. Have significantly positive correlation between the differences at 0. 05 level supreme manager and the shareholding ratio of value.

Table 3. Regression Results

Variables N	Coefficient	Std. Dev	t-Statistic	p-value
SSR	0.005**	0.002	2.00	0.047
DUAL	0.151	0.135	1.12	0.264
INDE	0.540	0.618	0.87	0.383
BSIZE	-0.024	0.023	-1.05	0.295
MEET	-0.020*	0.011	-1.82	0.070
INCOME	1.07E-07	8.39E-08	1.28	0.201
MSR	2.902**	1.269	2.29	0.023
LNSIZE	-0.180***	0.034	-5.26	0.000
LEV	0.208**	0.091	2.30	0.022
(Constant)	5.055***	0.814	6.21	0.000
Adj-R2		0.1100		
F		21.45***		
N		290		

Note: ***,**, * denote significance at 0.01, 0.05 and 0.1 level (2-tailed), respectively.

5 Conclusions

The result also shows that there is positively correlated with the frequency and the company value board meeting. In China, the larger the board of directors will greatly influence by the cost of an agreement, and a longer time. For decision-making, it can greatly reduce the company's value. Further, the evidence is that companies with poor performance have more meetings. According to Dongzhi gucci (transliteration) and (2001), in China, the board of directors of the company meet trends to increase quantity, the company performance decline. Obviously, the board meeting in China is not a positive act but a kind of passive actions, not may increase a company performance. And the meeting of the board may become a response performance Vafeas falling, 1999. According to this phenomenon, the board meeting shall be adjust gradually be from passive to active to really play their due function. The company's CEO, most companies not board chair, can avoid the excessive concentration of power and ensure the effective operation, the board of directors and management, improving both independence and autonomy. In China, the system of independent directors experienced a process from the start to standards. With the enforcement of new company law in 2006, independent director's power, the responsibility system and quantitative more clear. The independent directors for the quantitative are only 27% average before 2006. Beginning in 2006, this was up to 35%. Obviously, independent directors play a more and more important role in the internal governance structure. Therefore, it is necessary to establish an effective mechanism to ensure that the board of directors, not only scientific decision-making and timeliness and efficiency.

Average wages and equity incentive level of top managers are not high, but big difference. The results found that a significantly positive correlation, company executives of shareholding value. Through the equity incentives, the man's interests and shareholder unsmiling differences, this may be less reduce agency costs and achieve the goal of maximizing shareholder interest. It is necessary, the listed company establishes incentive mechanism according to the actual conditions and environment, and this will help reduce agency cost, the realization enterprise value eventually.

References

1. Barro, J., Barro, R.: Pay, Performance and Turnover of Bank CEOs. Journal of Labor Economics 8(4), 448–481 (1990)
2. Berle, A., Means, G.: The Modern Corporation and Private Property. Harcourt, Brace, & World, New York (1932)
3. Demsetz, H.: The structure of ownership and the theory of the firm. Journal of Law and Economics 26, 375–390 (1983)
4. Demsetz, H., Lehn, K.: The structure of corporate ownership: Causes and consequences. Journal of Political Economy 93, 1155–1177 (1985)
5. Gu, Q., Yu, D.: The Behaviors of Corporate Governance and Corporate Performance. Research On Financial and Economic Issues 1 (2001) (in Chinese)
6. Jensen, M.: The Modern Industrial Revolution, Exit, and the Failure of Internal Control Systems. Journal of Finance 48, 831–880 (1993)
7. Lipton, M., Lorsch, J.: A Modest Proposal for Improved Corporate Governance. Business Lawyer 48, 59–77 (1992)
8. MacAvoy, P.W., Millstein, I.M.: The Active Board of Directors and Its Effect on the Value of the Large Publicly Traded Corporation. Journal of Applied Corporate Finance 11(4), 8–20 (1999)
9. Morck, R., Shleifer, A., Vishny, R.W.: Management Ownership and Market Valuation: An Empricial Analysis. Journal of Financial Economics 20, 293–315 (1988)
10. Vafeas, N.: Board meeting frequency and firm performance. Journal of Financial Economics 53, 113–142 (1999)
11. Pearce, J.A., Zahra, S.A.: Board composition from a strategic contingency perspective. Journal of Management Studies 29, 411–438 (1992)
12. Hermalin, B., Weisbach, M.: The determinants of board composition. Journal of Economics 19, 589–606 (1988)
13. Yermack, D.: Higher Market Valuation of Companies with a Small Board of Directors. Journal of Financial Economics 40, 185–211 (1996)

The Relative Research on Rejection Sensitivity, Self-esteem, Social Support and Social Anxiety of Teenagers

Xia Li

The Vocational Education Institute, Jiangxi Science Technology & Normal University, Nanchang. 330013 Jiangxi, China
janebaby0523@yahoo.com.cn

Abstract. Purposes: to explore the effect of rejection sensitivity, self-esteem and social support on social anxiety. **Procedures:** to use stratified cluster sampling, 349 sample data were collected by means of group measuring. **Methods:** to adopt psychological evaluation method, the tools included Tendency to Expect Rejection Scale, Self-esteem Scale, and Perceived Social Support Scale, and Social Anxiety Scale. **Results**: the gender and area differences are found in the analysis of social anxiety, social anxiety is positively related to rejection sensitivity, higher social anxiety indicates lower self-esteem and perceived social support, they are significant. Rejection sensitivity and self-esteem are the effectively predictive factors in the regression analysis of social anxiety. **Conclusions**: In order to lower social anxiety, the efforts may be made to lower the rejection sensitivity, improve self-esteem, give them more social support to keep psychological health, the teenagers who are female or from village should be concerned very much.

Keywords: Social Anxiety, Rejection Sensitivity, Self-Esteem, Social Support.

1 Introduction

Social anxiety refers to the uncomfortable feeling in front of the others. The epidemiology studies show that the growing tendency appears obviously for social anxiety from children development stage to adolescence stage, the kind of problem exists extensively among teenagers, and has a profound effect. [1] Social anxiety becomes a common psychological disorder disease for teenagers.

The factors affecting social anxiety mainly include the internal and external aspects. Rejection sensitivity and self-esteem are proposed two important internal factors. Human beings have a pervasive drive to form and maintain at least a minimum quantity of lasting, positive, and significant interpersonal relationships, the deprivation of the need to belong is linked to a variety of ill effects on health, adjustment, and well-being. [2] Social rejection is one way of deprivation, which can result into bad consequences such as self-esteem, loneliness, depression, social anxiety, the decrease of pro-social behavior, and so on. [3]. In order to predict the sensitivity to social rejection, Rebacca developed a measuring tool. [4] The more one's Self-esteem refers to self-worth. According to sociometer theory, individual's

M. Zhou (Ed.): ISAEBD 2011, Part III, CCIS 210, pp. 54–60, 2011.

degree of inclusiveness in their social world paired with his or her level of the need to be included determines one's self-esteem, self-esteem serves as a mechanism for monitoring the likelihood of social exclusion at any given time. [5] So the level of self-esteem can affect social interaction behavior. Social support is proposed as one important external factor. it is considered as a mediating mechanism between stress and health, which means the mental and material help and support from others, and reflects the closeness degree of individual bonds with society. The social support includes two kinds, objective support and subjective support, the subjective social support is a kind of emotional experience and satisfaction of individual's being respected, supported, understood.

There are several assumptions, social anxiety is positively related to rejection sensitivity; the lower self-esteem level is, the higher social anxiety is; social anxiety is inversely related to subjective social support; the rejection sensitivity, self-esteem, and subjective social support can well predict the level of social anxiety.

2 Sample and Procedure

2.1 Sample

Participants were 360 undergraduates from colleges of JiangXi province, the efficient percentage of participants is 97%. Their age range is from 14 to 26 years old (*M*= 18.71 years, *SD*=1.873),there are 101 males, 248 females, 119 participants are from polytechnic school, 134 from junior college, 96 from university, 219 people are from village, 130 from town and city, 240 participants' major is the arts, the rest' major is the science, of these only 40 persons are the only child from the nuclear family.

2.2 Measures

The Tendency to Expect Rejection Scale. The scale in this study was translated to Chinese on the basis of Rebacca L.Jobe developed in 2003. [4] The opinions of English teacher, psychology postgraduates and experts were obtained during the translation. The scale is consisted of 18 items, this scale assesses individual sensitive tendency of being afraid of being rejected in the social context, participants are encouraged to mark out the degree of agreement with the sentence description on a five-point scale from very disagree (1) to very agree (5). The score range is from 18 to 90, The Cronbach'α reliability of this scale was 0.86, there were good congruent validity and convergent validity in it. Because this scale will be used in the cross-culture context, the reliability and validity need to be verified again.

The Symptom Checklist 90. There are 9 factors which are consisted of 90 items in this checklist, one of them is interpersonal sensitivity factor which refers to the uncomfortable, inferior complex, and negative expectation in the social context. [6] This dimension is the same as the trait of rejection sensitivity to some degree, it is specially selected as the proof of criterion validity of the tendency of expect rejection scale in the cross-culture context. This is a five-point scale ranging from never (1) to very serious (5), this scale had good reliability and validity.

The Self-Esteem Scale. The scale was developed by Rosenberg in 1965. Self-esteem refers to self-worth, This scale is consisted of 10 items, it had good reliability and validity after being used extensively, and became one of standard tools for testing teenagers' self-esteem in China, higher score means low self-esteem. [6]

The Perceived Social Support Scale. The scale was developed by Zimet. it emphasizes the subjective feeling of social support, which is consisted of 12 items with seven-point scale ranging from very diagree (1) to very agree (7), higher score indicates stronger feeling of social support. The Cronbach'α reliability was 0.88, the test-retest reliability was 0.85, and this scale was significantly inversely related to the depression of cancer patients in the clinic. [6]

The Social Anxiety Subscale of the Self-Consciousness Scale. The scale was developed by Scheier and Carver in 1985. it is consisted of 6 items, which doesn't only measure the subjective anxiety, but also measure the difficulty of language expression and behavior. The score range is from 0 to 18, higher scores indicate higher level of social anxiety, The Cronbach'α reliability was 0.79, the test-retest reliability was 0.77 after four weeks. [6]

2.3 Procedure

This study adopted the stratified cluster sampling with class as onc unit in JiangXi province, 360 undergraduates were tested through group measuring, and participants anonymously finished the questionnaires one time. Finally, the data was analyzed with SPSS11.5 statistical software package for statistical analysis.

3 Results

3.1 The Reliability and Validity of the Tendency of Expect Rejection Scale

Because the Chinese edition of the Tendency of Expect Rejection Scale was translated, it was necessary to verify the reliability and validity of this scale. 150 teenagers from college were randomly sampled to finish the scale and the interpersonal sensitivity factor of The Symptom Checklist 90 before other tests. The homogeneity reliability was adopted, the result showed the Cronbach'α reliability coefficient was 0.718, which was acceptable in psychometrics.

The interpersonal sensitivity factor of The Symptom Checklist 90 was selected as a criterion of validity, r=0.465(p<0.01), the correlation analysis result showed the criterion validity coefficient was good. In order to explore the relationship between rejection sensitivity and interpersonal sensitivity of SCL-90, the scores of in the Tendency of Expect Rejection Scale were sorted in descending order, 27% persons from the top were defined the high-score group, 27% persons from the end were defined the low-score group, then the difference of these two groups in the interpersonal sensitivity of SCL-90 was analyzed, $t = 5.064$ (p<0.001), so the scale had good discrimination in the interpersonal sensitivity of SCL-90.

Therefore, the Tendency of Expect Rejection Scale had good reliability and validity, which were acceptable in the psychometrics.

3.2 The Descriptive Statistical Analysis

The descriptive statistical results showed the score of social anxiety for this sample was 8.24±3.232. only 7% participants' scores are higher than 15, score 15 to 18 can be considered high social anxiety. To explore the effect of demographic variables on the social anxiety, the significant difference only in sex and family place was found, in the sex difference analysis, t = 2.089 (p<0.05), the score of social anxiety of females (M=8.57) was significantly higher than males (M=7.55). in the difference analysis of family place, t = 2.373 (p<0.05),the score of social anxiety from village (M=8.68) was significantly higher than people from town and city (M=7.60). There was no significantly difference in major, education, the number of children.

The significant difference in sex for the rejection sensitivity was found, t = 2.355 (p<0.05), the score of rejection sensitivity of females (M=61.96) was significantly higher than males (M=58.92). The significant difference in sex and education for the self-esteem was found, the sex difference was significant, t = 3.183 (p<0.01), the score of females' self-esteem (M=22.37) was significantly higher than males' (M=20.72); the difference in education was significant, F=7.255 (p<0.01),the score of participant from polytechnic school (M=22.95) was significantly higher than people from junior college (M=21.86) and university (M=20.70), the score of participants from junior college was significantly higher than from university, which indicated the self-esteem level became higher with the improvement of education degree, because low score indicates high self-esteem. No significant difference for social support was found in sex, education, family place, major, the number of children.

3.3 The Correlation Analysis

Table 1 showed the social anxiety was positively related to the rejection sensitivity, and self-esteem, negatively related to the social support, which indicated, the higher social anxiety was, the higher rejection sensitivity was, the lower the self-esteem and perceived social support were.

Table 1. Correlation Analysis of Social Anxiety, Rejection Sensitivity, Self-Esteem, Social Support

	rejection sensitivity	self-esteem	social support
Social anxiety	0.370**	0.358**	-0.227**

Note. ** P<0.01.

3.4 The Regression Analysis

In the stepwise regression analysis of social anxiety, the rejection sensitivity and self-esteem were entered the regression equation, they became the well predictive factors for social anxiety, and explains 16.7% of amount of variation. Which indicated rejection sensitivity was an important factor, and there were much more important variables affecting social anxiety.

Table 2. Stepwise Regression Analysis of Rejection Sensitivity, Self-Esteem, Social Support to Social Anxiety

Variables Entered	R	R square	F	β
1 rejection sensitivity	0.350	0.122	23.823***	0.350
2 self-esteem	0.409	0.167	17.088***	0.218

Note. *** *P*<0.01.

4 Discussion

Firstly, according to the distribution tendency of social anxiety, the score of this sample distributes 8.24±3.232, which indicates the social anxiety level in this study is not very high. All of them are students in school and university, college is one place where students learn new knowledge and skills, including social skills, how to be a nice person. The percentage of high social anxiety persons is 7%, but this kind of persons should be a focus group of the psychological health education in college. The results indicate the female social anxiety is significantly higher than the male's. the sex difference is found in the past study of social anxiety. [7] The following reasons are considered here, female character is different from male's, girls are more introverted, sensitive and shy, negatively assess themselves, it is also close to the parenting style, the boys are always encouraged to go out, to solve new problems, to shoulder the responsibility, after adolescence. The result also indicates the female rejection sensitivity is higher than male's. Meanwhile other study shows there is no significant difference in sex for social anxiety, [8] they think female and male are equal with the development of society. We think the reasons leading to different results are mainly related to measurement tool, the other reason is sampling, there should be no big difference in the number of male and female, these should be considered carefully in the future study. The social anxiety of students from village is higher than from town and city, the economical environment, parents' education degree, the information communication fall behind in village, and the inferiority is also an important cause.

Secondly, social anxiety is positively related to rejection sensitivity. Someone is sensitive to rejection, it would be shy for him or her to join others, he will experience more anxious interacting with others. In view of evolutionary psychology, because human can't survive and reproduce outside a group environment, anxiety evolved as a reaction to the experience of exclusion, it activates certain cognitions which prompt the person to terminate the undesirable behavior and engage in other behaviors which are more likely to result in acceptance and inclusion. Further, through experiencing anxiety, individuals learn what actions are associated with rejection and avoid them.

Self-esteem is an important psychological system for a person, the results indicate the higher social anxiety is, the lower self-esteem is, this is a proof of the sociometer theory which proposes self-esteem functions as sociometer, a cognitive-affective gauge that monitors the social environment for cues indicating disapproval, rejection, exclusion, the level of self-esteem is based on one's previous experiences of inclusion or exclusion. Low self-esteem is indicative of the history of being rejected, and the sensitivity to future rejection. So low-esteem theoretically means high rejection sensitivity and social anxiety, this assumption is verified here.

One study indicates people without enough social support experience more pressure than people with enough social support when facing social rejection. [9] Most think having a efficient social support does good for health, bad social support does harms to health. So if people perceive more social support, he will experience less social anxiety. The results show social support is negatively related to social anxiety on a significant level, which proves it very well.

Thirdly, the rejection sensitivity and self-esteem are tow powerful predictive factors, compared to the external factor, the internal factors play more important role in predicting social anxiety. Rejection sensitivity is especially important, it explains 12.2% of amount of variation. Meanwhile, there are more important factors affecting social anxiety. On the reasons resulting into the social anxiety, lots of factors are found, such as the biological factor, hereditary factor, temperament, personality, loss of social skills, negative self-assessment, life experience and so on. [10]

5 Conclusion

Several conclusions are summarized as follows: the Chinese edition of the Tendency of Expect Rejection Scale has good reliability and validity in China; Most teenagers' social anxiety level in this study is not very high, but people of high social anxiety are worthy of educator's attention in the psychological health education; Female's social anxiety, rejection sensitivity is significantly higher than male's, female's self-esteem is obviously lower than male's; The higher social anxiety is, the higher rejection sensitivity is, the lower self-esteem and perceived social support are; The rejection sensitivity and self-esteem are the well predictive factors for social anxiety, especially, rejection sensitivity, besides, there are more important factors affecting social anxiety.

On social anxiety, we should pay attention to the group of high rejection sensitivity, low self-esteem. In order to lower social anxiety, we can make efforts to lower the rejection sensitivity, improve self-esteem, give them more social support to keep psychological health, and the students who are female or from village should be concerned very much. In the future study of social anxiety, the rejection sensitivity could be thought as a important reason, sex and family place are important background variables for Chinese participants, the average ratio in these two variables should be considered seriously during sampling.

References

[1] Li, Z., Yang, X.: Social Anxiety of College Students: Survey and Analysis. Journal of Huhan University of Science and Technology (Social Science Edition) 2, 77–80 (2008)

[2] Baumeister, R.F., Leary, M.R.: The Need to Belong: Desire for Interpersonal Attachment as a Fundamental Human Motivation. Psychological Bulletin 3, 497–525 (1995)

[3] Kristine, M.K.: Measurement and Manifestation of the Need to belong (a dissertation for Doctor of Philosophy Degree). The University of Tennessee, Knoxville (1999)

[4] Rebecca, L.J.: Emotional and Physiological Reactions to Social Rejecton: The Development and Validation of the Tendency to Expect Rejection Scale and the Relationship between Rejection Expectancy and Responses to Exclusion (a dissertation for Doctor of Philosophy Degree). The University of Tennessee, Knoxville (2003)

[5] Leary, M.R., Downs, D.L.: Interpersonal Functions of Self-Esteem Motive: the Self-Esteem System as a Sociometer. In: Kernis, M.H. (ed.) Efficacy, Agency and Self-esteem, pp. 123–144. U.S. Plenum Press, New York (1995)
[6] Wang, X., Wang, X., Ma, H.: Rating Scales for Mental Health. Chinese Mental Health Press, Beijing (1999)
[7] Linyu, L.: Relationship among Social Anxiety, Attachment and Mental Health of College Students. China Journal of Health Psychology 2, 186–189 (2010)
[8] Juan, W.: Relationship between Social Anxiety and Type of Temperament in College Students. China Journal School Doctor 7, 500–501 (2010)
[9] Cohn, S., Wills, T.A.: Stress, Social Support, and the Buffering Hypothesis. Psychological Bulletin 98, 310–357 (1985)
[10] Xianyun, Z., Wei, F.: The Western Psychological Studies on Social Anxiety Disorder in Children and Youth. Chinese Journal of Special Education 4, 85–88 (2007)

The Research of Medical Expenditure in China

Ying Chen[1], Lin Chen[2], Qiangqing Wang[3], and Xiaosi Xu[3]

[1] Department of Student, Hebei United University, Tangshan, China
[2] School of Mechanical Engineering, Hebei United University, Tangshan, China
[3] School of Management, Hebei United University, Tangshan, China

Abstract. Medical expenditure has a rapid growth recently in China, and it is difficult to control the medical expenditure. Compared with the other countries, the paper discusses some factors which result the rapid increase of medical costs in China, including hygienic resource, the quantity and quality of practitioner, management system and inhabitant sanitary habit. Then, the paper gives some countermeasures and suggestions to control the medical expenditure in China, such as increasing government investment, improving the quantity and quality of hygienic technician, ameliorating social sanitary service system, reforming the medical management system and strengthening the education of resident sanitary habit.

Keywords: medical expenditure, hygienic resource, suggestions.

The medical expenditure of china has increased rapidly in recently ten years, and some very large and unreasonable fee-for-service has appeared, which makes some people can not be treated or have to give up treating. Now the government realizes that it has impacted the people's living standard and the social stability. How to control the medical expenditure is very important for medical system reform.

1 The Cause of Unreasonable Increase of Medical Expenditure

According to the data which disclosed by Information Center of Ministry of Health, the outpatients' medical expenditure and expense of medicine increase year by year, so do the inpatients'. In the past five years, the average income of townsman increased 8.9% per year, and the average income of countryman increased 2.4% per year, but the medical expenditure increased 13.5% and 11.8% respective. Apparently, the expenditure rises more rapid than the income, which brings the huge economic pressure and mental pressure for the family, and the main causes are below:

1.1 The Lack of State Expenditure of Health

From the Table 1, we can see the total health expenditure is 4.6% of GDP in 2009, the proportion is a little more than the India, but more low than the America, France and German. The proportion of individual expenditure in total health expenditure is 59.3%, lower than the 62.3% of South Africa and 75% of India, but much more than

M. Zhou (Ed.): ISAEBD 2011, Part III, CCIS 210, pp. 61–66, 2011.

the 12.7% of England and 18.7% of Japan. The proportion of state health expenditure in total health expenditure is 40.7%, lower than the proportion of the proportion of developing country. The proportion of state health expenditure in finance expenditure is 9.9%, is far lower than the proportion of developed countries. The health expenditure per capita is $216, is one thirtieth of America. The data above show the Chinese health expenditure is less than some other countries' heath expenditure.

Table 1. The health expenditure

Country	Total Health Expenditure as % of GDP 2006	Government Health Expenditure of Health Expenditure 2006	Private Health Expenditure of Health Expenditure 2006	Health Expenditure % of Government Expenditure 2006	Per Capita Health Expenditure(US$)2006
Australia	8.7	67.7	32.3	17.0	3119
Brazil	7.5	47.9	52.1	7.2	674
Canada	10.0	70.4	29.6	17.8	3673
China	4.6	40.7	59.3	9.9	216
Egypt	6.3	41.4	58.6	7.3	320
France	11.0	79.7	20.3	16.7	3420
Germany	10.3	76.9	23.1	17.9	3465
India	4.3	25.0	75.0	3.4	86
Italy	8.1	77.2	22.8	14.2	2631
Japan	7.7	81.3	18.7	17.9	2581
Mexico	6.6	44.2	55.8	11.8	778
Nigeria	3.8	29.7	70.3	3.5	59
Poland	6.2	70.0	30.0	9.9	919
Russian	5.3	63.2	36.8	10.8	698
SouthAfrica	8.0	37.7	62.3	9.1	715
Thailand	3.5	64.5	35.5	11.3	264
Turkey	4.8	72.5	27.5	10.6	584
UK	8.2	87.3	12.7	16.3	2815
USA	15.3	45.8	54.2	19.3	6719

Source: World Health Statistics 2009.

Table 2. The health resource per 1000 population 2000-2007

Country	Doctors	Nurses	Beds	Country	Doctors	Nurses	Beds
Australia	2.5	9.7	4	Japan	2.1	9.5	14
Brazil	1.2	3.8	2.4	Russian	4.3	8.5	9.7
Canada	1.9	10.1	3.4	South Africa	0.8	4.1	2.8
China	1.4	1	2.2	Thailand	0.4	2.8	2.2
France	3.4	8	7.3	UK	2.3	12.8	3.9
Germany	3.4	8	8.3	USA	2.6	9.4	3.1
India	0.6	1.3	0.7				

From the beds of hospital & health center per 1000 population we can know, it is 2.2 beds in China from 2000 to 2007, and more than in India, as many as in Thailand, and Chinese beds is one seventh of Japanese beds approximately, much less than that of the Russia, Franc and German. The number of beds reflects that it lack the medical resource in China.

1.2 Lack of Health Resource

From Table 3, we can know, the health institutions have increased from 1990 to 2009 in China, especially for the hospitals, some health institutions, such as health centers, outpatient department and clinics, village clinics, are decreased. By the end of 2009, it has 916571 health institutions in China, but a large mount of which are Outpatient Department & Clinic, Health Service Center for Community and village clinics, and the hospitals owned by state is 20291, among which the general hospitals is 13624, the outpatient hospitals is 174809, the village clinics is 632770, the TCM-hospitals and TCM-WM hospitals is 2973, the specialized hospitals is 3716, the MCH Centers is 3020. From the numbers of all kinds of health institutions, we can see that the distribution of medical institutes is not reasonable, a majority of them are village clinics, which have low medical technology and bad medical facilities, some doctors

Table 3. The number of health institutions

Institution	1990	2000	2005	2008	2009
Total	1012690	1034229	882206	891480	916571
Hospital	14377	16318	18703	19712	20291
Health Center	47749	49777	41694	39860	39627
Health Service Center for Community	-	-	17128	24260	27308
Outpatient Department & Clinic	129332	240934	207457	180752	182448
Village clinics	803956	709458	583209	613143	632770
Others	17276	17742	14015	13753	14127

and nurses can not deal with many difficult diseases, and lots of patients have to transfer to hospitals, which will bring the patients extra expenditure.

1.3 Limitations for Distribution System

Now the distribution system of Chinese health has some limitations, firstly, the medicine does not detach from the medical treatment. In China, there are about 80%-85% medicine sold by hospitals, so the hospitals monopolize the price of some medicine, which lead to the higher price of medicine in the markets. Some hospitals depend on the profits of medicine to keep the hospital run or get a higher benefit. At the same time, the patients have not the right to choose the medicine, and this may makes the doctors to abuse some medicine. Secondly, the industry of medicine is not centralized highly, and does not have a great competiveness. By now, there are more than 13000 medical wholesale companies, and there are more than 100000 retailing companies. They are small sizes, and have not stronger competitive. Thirdly, the management abilities of companies fall behind and have a higher distribution costs. The Chinese medicine companies are run by traditional management mode, and do not establish the modern information and logistics management system, this makes the companies have high costs.

1.4 The Way of Medical Service Is Not Reasonable

The medical institutions have the character of marketability and public welfare. The unreasonable running mechanisms of hospitals lead to over health check-up and over medicine-taking, and the hospitals pursue the high profits and do not take care of the public welfare, and use some new high-tech or new apparatus, and the patients pay more than before, so that the medical expenditures go up quickly. The year grow rates of outpatient and inpatient medical expenditure are shown by Figure 3, from which we can know the two rates are positive growth, and except 2006, the grow rates are more than 5% per year in near decades (except 2006), the over medical check-up and the over medicine-taking are mainly responsible for the growths.

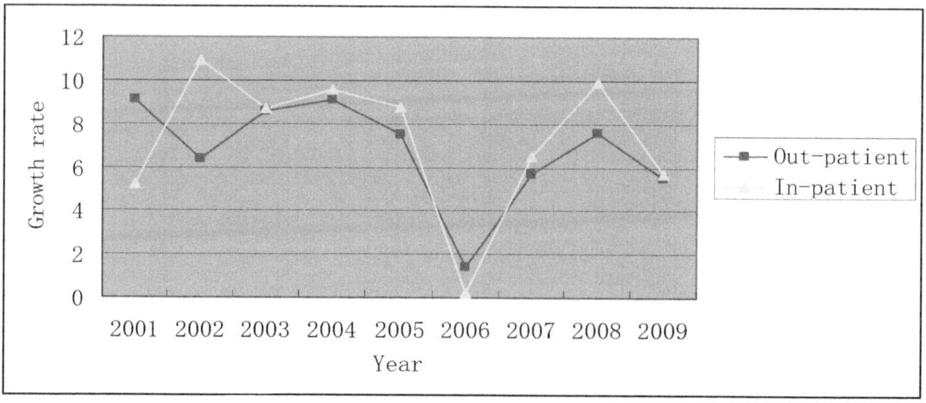

Fig. 1. The growth rate of out-patient and in-patient

2 Some Solutions to Controlling the Medical Expenditure

2.1 Increase the Government Investment and Enlarge the Coverage of Health Resource

The health resources have a character of public welfare, and government should play a fundamental role in allocating the health resources. The scheme of health system reformation points out the government must invest RMB 850 billion in improving the medical level in 2009-2011, and the state government must invest RMB 331.6 billion in building new hospitals, subsiding government hospitals and transferring payments, so that it can enlarge the coverage the health resource and promote equalization of health services. According to half of RMB850 billion to establish the new hospital, by 2011, the beds of hospital per 1000 population will be 3.97, and approximately equals to the Australia's beds and the British beds. The status of whole country can improve greatly.

2.2 Establish the Community of Health Service System and Improve General Practitioner Responsibility

The community of service system is the center of health of people and satisfies the basic health demands of family, including the prevention, medical treatment, health care, rehabilitation, health education, family planning, and so on. It is an effective, economic, convenient, comprehensive primary health service. Actively developing the community health services, it will improve urban health service system, improve efficiency and reduce costs.

It should establish the system of General Practitioners. The general practitioners must pass the examination, engaged by the government, and the salary paid by population who has served. Under the supervision of the patients and the government, the system can control the medical expenditure effectively.

2.3 Reform the Medical Management System and Optimize the Medical Resources

Controlling the medical expenditure, it should reform the medical management system, detach the medicine from the medical treatment, decrease and avoid the over medicine-taking. The hospitals emphasize on the medical treatment.

In order to reduce the costs of medicine management and retail, some medicine distribution center should be established, such as North East medicine distribution Center, North China medicine distribution Center, North West medicine distribution Center, South West medicine distribution Center, South East medicine distribution Center, and East China medicine distribution Center, which are based on the geographical location. It establishes the medicine distribution station and supply the medicine by point-to-point sell mode in cities. At the same time, some medicine supermarkets are set up so as to give convenient and efficient service.

2.4 Strengthen the Education of Health Awareness and Enhance the People's Physical Quality

Many people have no idea of healthy consciousness, and do not prevent the disease. The data show that the chronic diseases of the first ten incidences of disease are Gastrointestinal Disorders, Cardiovascular Disease, cardiopathy, Endocrine and metabolic disease, infectious disease and epidemic disease, which are related to the bad habit of sitology, the weakly healthy consciousness and self health care, which leaded to the continuous increase of incidence of disease and death rate.

The WHO puts forward the disease prevention and control as one way of healthy education and healthy promotion, Strengthening the national health education, establishing a scientific concept of health and promoting scientific way of life can effectively prevent some chronic diseases and reduce the medical expenditure. Firstly, spread propaganda and fully understand the importance of health education. We can use TV, broadcast and newspaper to propagandize some basic health knowledge, and bring up a good and healthy way of life. Secondly, strengthen and improve the health education system. We should improve and standardize the establishment of health education institutions, and establish the health education department in all kinds of medical institutions, and bring the health education into the teaching plan in schools, and improve basic health knowledge in primary school.

Acknowledgments. The paper is sponsored by National Nature Science Funds of China (70901003) and Social Science Funds of Hebei Province (HB09BYJ066).

References

1. Cunhai, T.: An economic analysis of the excessive increase of the medical in China. Journal of Jiangxi University of Finance and Economics 69, 11–15 (2010)
2. China Health Statistics Annual of 2009 (2009), `http://www.moh.gov.cn/publicfiles/business/htmlfiles/zwgkzt/ptjnj/200908/42635.htm`
3. Yuchun, T., Qian, W.: The empirical analysis of China's social medical insurance cost. Chinese Health Economics 29, 18–21 (2010)
4. Yulin, Z., Shizhu, L., Yilin, Z., et al.: Forecast research of health care expenditure in China. Chinese Health Economics 37, 16–18 (2008)
5. Jingwei, L.: From "separation of prescribing and dispensing" to Effective Control of Medical Cost. Chinese Health Economics 37, 61–62 (2008)
6. Youde, G.: An exploration on health expenditure and it controls. Chinese Health Resource 8, 114–115 (2005)

Empirical Analysis of Cotton Imports' Effect on Our Current and Long Term Production and Sales

Shurong Zhang[1] and Yongsheng Liu[2]

[1] Department of Economy and Management in Tianjin Agriculture University, 22 Jinjing Road, Xiqing District, Tianjin, China
zhangshurong@vip.sina.com

Abstract. Studies related to this paper mainly adopted model GTAP and ATPSM to explore the effect of importing on our cotton industry. To ensure the interest of weak group in the cotton industry--- the farmers, the paper used cointegration method to study the relationship between imports and sown area as well as sales, set up Error Correction Model to explore the current and long term effect of cotton importing on production and sales. The paper came to the conclusion: under open condition, the complementary between imported cotton and domestic one increases. Because of large subsidy to imported cotton, the paper puts forward the following countermeasures: we should improve our cotton subsidy policy and initiate the domestic minimum purchase price policy.

Keywords: Cotton Import, Effect, Empirical Analysis.

1 Introduction

Cotton is a kind of commodity related to the national economy and the people's livelihood. It is not only important for developing regional economy and guaranteeing farmers' income, but also influences the healthy development of downstream textile enterprises. China is not only a big cotton producer and consumer, but also a big importer in the world. According to statistics of the U.S. Department of Agriculture, during year 2009-2010, our output and consumption are respectively 30.66% and 40.70% of those of the world. In recent years, our cotton textile industry develops quickly, the cotton imports increase greatly. According the statistics of UN, our imports increased to 1758.9 thousand tons in 2009 from 245.1 thousand tons in 2002, degree of dependence on importing foreign cotton rose to 50% in 2006 from 4.04% in 2002, and has been keeping above 30% since 2007 despite a downward tendency that year. Large quantities of imports played an important role in regulating the supply and demand in domestic market, but also hampered the development of our own cotton industry to some extent, damaged the benefit of our cotton farmers, which led to the fact that our small scale production had to face more and more direct and keen competition overseas. This paper studied the effect of cotton importing on our domestic production and sales, with domestic production concerning sown area, output, yield per unit area, and domestic sales concerning volumes of sales, selling

M. Zhou (Ed.): ISAEBD 2011, Part III, CCIS 210, pp. 67–72, 2011.

price, merchandise rate, sales income. Since the sown area and volume of sale can better reflect the farmers' enthusiasm and market selling condition, the paper selected sown area reflecting production condition and volume of sales reflecting the sale condition to study the effect of cotton importing on our production and sales.

Studies related to this paper mainly adopted model GTAP and ATPSM to explore the effect of importing on our cotton industry. For example, Yang Jun etc used Global Trade Analysis Project Model (GTAP) in 2006 to discuss the effect of America's cancellation cotton subsidy on world and China's cotton textile industry, and reached a conclusion that the America's cancellation subsidy would increase the welfare of the world, promote our domestic production, push up our price and obstruct our exporting textile and cloth products. Song Juguo and Liu Zhuoyi also used GTAP to simulate the effect of importing on our cotton industry when they tried to establish an indicator system reflecting the safety condition of this industry and came to a conclusion that our cotton industry competitiveness dropped a lot, the degree of import dependence increased significantly, so there is development potential with increasing planting comparative income and increasing the customs tariff rate over imports beyond import quota will significantly reduce the cotton imports and promote our cotton industry development. GaoFeng used ATPSM model in 2006 to conduct a quantitative research on the effect of EU and America's subsidy on our cotton industry and drew a conclusion that high subsidy to cotton in EU and America greatly pushed down the international cotton price, damaged income and welfare of our cotton farmers, was harmful to our production and export. The above studies provided a good theoretical basis for our paper, but with a pity that all these studies did not notice the benefit of the vulnerable group in the industry--- the farmers, but in fact, the farmers play an important role in ensuring our cotton industry safety. This paper studied the effect of importing on our cotton production and sales from the point of farmers to make up for the negligence.

2 Study Method and Source of Data

Based on Cointegration analysis, this part tried to find out whether a long and stable relation exists between the cotton imports and the domestic output and sales. If it really exists, we would set up an Error Correction Model to study the current and long-term effect that cotton importing has our production and sales.

This paper selected our cotton imports during year 1986 to 2009 as explanatory variable and our cotton MJ and SALES during the corresponding years as explained variables. The imports and MJ data comes from China Statistical Yearbook, the SALE data is calculated according to our national cotton output and cotton commodity rate in Chinese Agricultural Products Cost and Profit Data Compilation, using the commodity rate during year 1990 to 2009 as that during year 1986 to 1989. At the same time, this paper uses the natural logarithm of the above three variables to get the corresponding logarithm variables LN(IMP), LN(MJ), LN(SALE), aiming to reduce the fluctuation.

3 Model Analysis

3.1 Unit Root Test

First, we did the unit root test on the three variables LN(IMP)􀀁 LN(MJ) and LN(SALE) to test their stability. The result shows that the three variables are all non-stationary time series. So, we did the Unit Root Test after getting the difference of the three variables and get the following results shown in table 1:

Table 1. The Unit Root Test of the variables

variables	Different order	(C,T,K)	D.W.	ADF	5% critical	1% critical	conclusion
LN(IMP)	1	(C,T,1)	2.12	-4.62	-3.63	-4.44	I (1) *
LN(MJ)	1	(C,0,1)	2.07	-5.32	-3.00	-3.77	I (1) *
LN(SALE)	1	(C,0,1)	1.74	-5.84	-3.01	-3.79	I (1) *

*(C, T, K)explains whether the unit root test include constant term, time trend term and lag time. * means that the variables passed the unit root test after being differentiated.*

The above test results shows that the three variables are all stationary time series after the first order differentials, LN(IMP)~I(1)、LN(MJ) ~I(1)、LN(SALE)~I(1). So, we set up the following equation:

$$LN(MJ)_t=C_0+ C_1LN(IMP)_t+\varepsilon_t. \tag{1}$$

$$LN(SALE)_t=C_0+ C_1LN(IMP)_t+\varepsilon_t \tag{2}$$

Then we estimated the above two equations and got the results:

$$\begin{gathered} LN(MJ)_t=15.084+ 0.029LN(IMP)_t+\varepsilon_t \\ (98.33) \quad (2.39) \end{gathered} \tag{3}$$

$$R^2=0.21 \quad D.W=0.75 \quad F=5.69.$$

$$\begin{gathered} LN(SALE)_t=14.475+0.071LN(IMP)_t+\varepsilon_t \\ (31.582) \quad (4.88) \end{gathered} \tag{4}$$

$$R^2=0.46 \quad D.W=0.82 \quad F=19.04$$

3.2 Residual Series Unit Root Test

We did the unit root test on the residual in equation 3 and 4 and got the test results shown in table 2.

Table 2. Residual Series Unit Root Test results

	D.W.	ADF	5% critical	1%critical	conclusion
Equation (3)	2.01	-2.22	-1.96	-2.669	I(0)
Equation (4)	1.92	-2.46	-1.96	-2.67	I(0)

Table 2 shows that under 5% significance level, the residuals in equation 3and 4 are all stable, cointegration relationship exists between our cotton imports and output, sales. So we set up ECM model between imports, output and sales respectively, and got the equation 5 and 6:

$$\Delta LN(MJ)_t=\alpha_0+\alpha_1\Delta LN(IMP)_t+\eta[LN(MJ)_{t-1}- k_0-k_1LN(IMP)_{t-1}]+\varepsilon_t. \tag{5}$$

$$\Delta LN(SALE)_t=\beta_0+\beta_1\Delta LN(IMP)_t+\lambda[LN(SALE)_{t-1}-\gamma_0-\gamma_1LN(IMP)_{t-1}]+\mu_t \tag{6}$$

$\Delta LN(MJ)$、 $\Delta LN(IMP)$ and $\Delta LN(SALE)$ stands for the first order differentials of IN(MJ), LN(IMP) and LN(SALE), η and λ are adjustment coefficients, $LN(MJ)_{t-1}-k_0-k_1LN(IMP)_{t-1}$ and $LN(SALE)_{t-1}-\gamma_0-\gamma_1LN(IMP)_{t-1}$ are residuals of equation 3 and 4. Then we put the results of equation 3 and 4 into equation 5 and 6, and got the following:

$$\Delta LN(MJ)_t=\alpha_0+\alpha_1\Delta LN(IMP)_t+\eta[LN(MJ)_{t-1}- 15.084- 0.029LN(IMP)_{t-1}]+\varepsilon_t. \tag{7}$$

$$\Delta LN(SALE)_t=\beta_0+\beta_1\Delta LN(IMP)_t+\lambda[LN(SALE)_{t-1}-14.475-0.071LN(IMP)_{t-1}]+\mu_t \tag{8}$$

Then we estimated the equation 7 and 8, and got the following results:

$$\begin{gathered}\Delta LN(MJ)_t=-0.01+0.043\Delta LN(IMP)_t-0.36[LN(MJ)_{t-1}- 15.084-\\ 0.029LN(IMP)_{t-1}]\\ (-0.41) \quad (2.94) \quad (-2.11)\\ R^2=0.41 \quad D.W=2.04 \quad F=6.88.\end{gathered} \tag{9}$$

$$\begin{gathered}\Delta LN(SALE)_t=0.008+0.043\Delta LN(IMP)_t-0.39[LN(SALE)_{t-1}-14.475-\\ 0.071LN(IMP)_{t-1}]\\ (0.25) \quad (2.14) \quad (-2.22)\\ R^2=0.29 \quad D.W=2.01 \quad F=4.12\end{gathered} \tag{10}$$

The above results show that the cotton imports long term elasticity on output and sales are respectively 0.029 and 0.071, short term elasticity are all 0.043, the adjustment coefficients are respectively -0.36 and -0.39.

3.3 Chow Test

Watching the regressional results in equation 3, we can find that despite the constant term and regressional coefficent passed the T test, the regressional results are not satisfactionary, goodness of fit and DW value are all too low. The reason of unperfect fitting may be the unstabiligy of regressional coefficents in the equations. So we did the stability test on equation 3 and found structural change appeared after year 1995. The test results are as follows:

So the longterm elasticiy of equation 3 changed too.

Chow Breakpoint Test: 1996

F-statistic	16.74096	Prob. F(2,20)	0.000053
Log likelihood ratio	23.60668	Prob. Chi-Square(2)	0.000007

4 Results Analysis

4.1 As a Whole, the Increasing Cotton Imports Will Lead to the Expansion of Production Scale

1% increase of cotton imports will lead to 0.043% increase in the production area in the short term and 0.029% increase in the long term. On one hand, imports increase means brisk demand for our cotton producers in the short term, which will help keep farmers enthusiasm and ensure an increase in sown area to some extent. On the other hand, a big supply gap has always existed in our cotton market, cotton importing is a supplement to our domestic supply to some extent, so imported cotton and domestic cotton are highly complementary.

4.2 Specifically, Reform of Exchange Regime and Circulating System Led to Change of Relationship between Cotton Imports and Domestic Production

During 1986 to 1994, cotton imports long and short term elasticity on output are respectively 0.04 and 0.028, while during 1995 to 2009, those elasticity are respectively 0.08 and 0.047. The reasons are as follows: the domestic cotton market was highly closed before 1994, the circulating system was not perfect, allocation was popular, the domestic cotton price elasticity was low, all of these led to low elasticity of cotton imports to domestic output during that period. Since 1994, Our domestic marketing system has been improved a lot, the price elasticity and devaluation of RMB played a role, domestic cotton industry developed quickly, the openness of domestic cotton market increased, the supply gap has always been expanding, the cotton imports and domestic cotton are more complementary, all of these help increase the long term and short term elasticity.

4.3 Cotton Importing Will Promote Domestic Sales to Some Extent

In the short term, the elasticity of cotton imports to domestic sales is 0.043, 1% increase of imports will lead to 0.043% increase in output and sales. This means our cotton import increase will lead to higher price in domestic and international market (which corresponds with the actual situation, higher price in international and domestic market happened during the years when china imported a large quantity of cotton.) , farmers would more likely sell the cotton instead of reserving it. In addition, the increase sales mean brisk demand currently, which will lead to import increase.

In the long term, the low price imported cotton will depress domestic sales. In the long term, the long term elasticity of cotton imports to sales is 0.071, 1% increase of cotton imports will bring 0.071% increase in domestic sales. As discussed above, cotton imports and domestic ones are complementary. Since there is a large supply gap in cotton market, the cotton imports will increase, which will complement the domestic supply, at the same time promote domestic sales through mechanism of price conduction. But imported cotton are highly subsidized at present, its low price will depress domestic cotton sales. So we should improve our cotton subsidy policy and initiate the mechanism of minimum purchase price.

5 Conclusion and Suggestions

5.1 Imported Cotton and Domestic Ones Are Increasingly Complementary Under Open Conditions

We can conclude through the above analysis that positive correlation exists between imported cotton and our domestic production and sales, which means that imported cotton and domestic ones are highly complementary. The imported cotton will regulate the supply. After the breakpoint analysis of year 1994, we know that the reform of exchange regime, the reform of circulating system and WTO entry all lead to increase of positive correlation coefficient between imported cotton and domestic production and sales. Under condition of complete market economy, imported cotton and domestic ones are more complementary.

5.2 We Should Improve Our Cotton Subsidy Policy and Initiate Mechanism of Minimum Purchase Price as Soon as Possible

Imported cotton with large quantity of subsidies leads to the failure of price conduction mechanism in domestic market, the price of imported cotton is lower than that of domestic one, the cotton users would like to purchase more imported cotton, which depress the sales of domestic one indirectly. To encourage the sale of domestic cotton and keep fair competition between imported cotton and domestic one, it is necessary to improve our cotton subsidy policy and initiate minimum purchase price mechanism as soon as possible. The minimum purchase price mechanism is a kind of yellow box subsidy, is admitted by the WTO. But at present our yellow box subsidy is far below the 8.5% top limit allowed by the WTO. Our annual output value is about 80 billon RMB, the yellow box subsidy should be 6.8 billon RMB on the basis of 8.5% level. But in recent years, our annual subsidy for purchasing superior crop varieties is at most 1.3 billion RMB, which is 1.5% of the total output value. So there is large space for us to increase our cotton subsidy.

References

1. Gao, F.: Study on the Effect of Cotton Subsidy in Europe and America on Our Cotton Industry. Chinese Academy of Agricultural Sciences, Beijing (2006)
2. Zhang, H., Yang, J., et al.: The effect of America's Cancellation of Cotton Subsidy on World and Our Cotton Industry. Problems of Agricultural Economy (1), 75–78 (2006)
3. Xiao, Y.: Study on Early-Warning of Dairy Food Trade to our Dairy Industry. Inner Mongolia Agricultural University, Hohehaote (2007)
4. Song, J., Liu, Y.Z.: Study on the Effect of Import on Our Cotton Industry. Journal of Agritechnical Economics (5) (2010)
5. Fan, H., Zhang, L.: EVIEWS Statistical Analysis and Application. China Machine Press, Beijing (2009)

The Economic Value of Forest Ecosystem Services Assessment Case Study of Hunan Province

Shaohua Yin and Wei Jiang

Business School, Central South University of Forestry and Technology,
Shaoshan Road 498, Changsha, Hunan, China
yinshaohua001@163.com

Abstract. This is a hot research issues related discipline about the economic value of forest ecosystem services assessment. This article synthesizes the domestic and foreign related research results, as use Hunan province for the study area, the use of valuation method, alternative engineering method, travel cost method and other methods, from economical, ecology and social three aspects to assess forest ecosystem 17 leadership service function value in 2007 in Hunan province. The evaluations show that the economic value of forest ecosystem comprehensive services is 558.554 billion yuan in Hunan province in 2007. It accounted ecological value for 89.96%; the economic value for 6.0%; social value accounting for 4.04%.

Keywords: Forest ecosystem, Services, Value, Hunan province.

1 Introduction

The forest ecosystem services, is the natural ecological processes of forests or the ecological balance of the contribution. The forest ecosystem services Function's value, are generally divided into economic value, ecological value and social value. And economic value includes forest production and forest sideline product value. The ecological value mainly includes the water conservation, soil conservation and fertility, the soil improvement, carbon sequestration and oxygen releasing, the environment purification, the forest protection, the biodiversity maintenance and so on. The social value mainly includes the forest amusement and rest, the sightseeing trip, the preliminary examination to explore and to increase the employment opportunity and so on. American scholar Douglas (Douglas J.Krieger) in 2001 considered that forest ecosystem service function summary had 8 aspects: climate control, the water treatment, food production, the traveling, raw material production, the soil maintain, biological control System and cultural services. And has provided its value monetization estimate result. Douglas's research, has provided a model for the forest ecosystem service function value estimate.

M. Zhou (Ed.): ISAEBD 2011, Part III, CCIS 210, pp. 73–77, 2011.

1.1 Study Area

Hunan province, located in central south of China, occupies 24°39'-30°08' north latitude, 08°47'-114°15' east longitude. The annual average of the temperature is 16℃~18℃ and the annual average sunshine is 1300~1800 hours while 278~300 days are frost-free days. The mean annual precipitation is 1200~1700 millimeters. So Hunan province enjoys a climate with distinctively-marked seasons with plenty of rainfall and sunshine. The natural condition is advantageous, which is known as "seven mountains, one river and two pieces of land". The statistical data indicated that, by the end of 2007, the province covers 21,183,500 hm2, which the forestry land area are 12,844,800 hm2, accounting for 60.64% of the provincial area. The forest coverage is 56.10%, with a 403 million stumpage saving and general output of 63 billion Yuan. It is one of most important forestry provinces in the south of China.

1.2 Evaluation Methods

Regarding the forest ecosystem service's value, the domestic and foreign scholars had already made many discussions. Based on the research results, forest ecosystem service economy value's can be divided into two categories. One is the alternative markets technology for the market that fit indirectly trading and market prices. But with alternative markets and prices of forest ecosystem services, it estimates substitute's expenditure economic value to replaces certain ecosystem service function. Evaluation methods include: cost expenditure approach, the market value method, opportunity cost, travel cost method and hedonic value method. The other is a simulated market technology, also known as the assumption market technology. The economic value is reflected by willingness-to-pay (WTP) and net-willingness-to-pay (NWTP) of forest ecosystem services which is a kind of ecosystem market services and resources value judged by men imaginary constructed market. The evaluation is only one, which is condition valuation method.

2 The Evaluation Index System

Hunan province forest ecosystem services evaluation system, consists of three evaluative features, ten function essential factors and seventeen evaluating indicators constitutes. Three evaluation features (economic value, ecological value and social value) are independent form of expression and clear lines. Ten functional elements of forest ecosystems are forest products, forest products, water conservation, solid soil fertilizer, carbon sequestration system oxygen, regulate climate, clean environment, biodiversity maintenance, recreation and health value and social and cultural values of the composition. It reflects and includes the forest ecosystem services, products and features the main effect of orientation. Seventeen evaluation of forest ecosystem services the formation of the object, directly used to assess the value of forest ecosystem services. Detailed in Table 1.

Table 1. Evaluation index system of Hunan province forest ecosystem service

<table>
<tr><th>Target layer</th><th>Element layer</th><th>Rule layer</th><th>Serial number</th><th>Index level</th></tr>
<tr><td rowspan="17">Evaluation of Hunan province forest ecosystem service</td><td rowspan="3">A_1 Economic value</td><td rowspan="2">B_1 Forest products value</td><td>C_{01}</td><td>Annual net growth of various trees value</td></tr>
<tr><td>C_{02}</td><td>Fire-wood value</td></tr>
<tr><td>B_2 Forest sideline product value</td><td>C_{03}</td><td>various Forest sideline product value</td></tr>
<tr><td rowspan="11">A_2 Ecological value</td><td>B_3Water conservation value</td><td>C_{04}</td><td>Water conservation value</td></tr>
<tr><td rowspan="2">B_4Fertilizer value of the solid earth</td><td>C_{05}</td><td>Solid earth value</td></tr>
<tr><td>C_{06}</td><td>Protects fertilizer value</td></tr>
<tr><td rowspan="2">B_5Oxygen value of carbon sequestration</td><td>C_{07}</td><td>Average annual value of the fixed CO2</td></tr>
<tr><td>C_{08}</td><td>annual release of O2 value</td></tr>
<tr><td rowspan="2">B_6Purification environment value</td><td>C_{09}</td><td>Absorption pollutant value</td></tr>
<tr><td>C_{10}</td><td>Hinders the dust the value</td></tr>
<tr><td rowspan="2">B_7Adjustment climate value</td><td>C_{11}</td><td>temperature regulation value</td></tr>
<tr><td>C_{12}</td><td>Adjustment humidity value</td></tr>
<tr><td rowspan="2">B_8 Biodiversity values</td><td>C_{13}</td><td>Biological habitat value</td></tr>
<tr><td>C_{14}</td><td>Genetic information (gene bank) value</td></tr>
<tr><td rowspan="3">A_3Social value</td><td>B_9 Recreational Health value</td><td>C_{15}</td><td>Recreational value</td></tr>
<tr><td rowspan="2">B_{10} Social culture value</td><td>C_{16}</td><td>Scientific research educational value</td></tr>
<tr><td>C_{17}</td><td>Social employment value</td></tr>
</table>

3 Evaluation System of Hunan Province Forest Ecosystem Service

All the data are quoted from the "Forest Resources of Hunan province Statistical Yearbook 2007" and "Development of Forestry in 2007 Report" etc.

3.1 Economic Value

The economic value of Hunan province forest ecosystems includes the value of a variety of trees, fuel wood value and the value of various forest products. According to statistics calculated in 2007, the economic value of Hunan province forest ecosystems was up to 33.551 billion yuan.

3.2 Evaluation of the Ecological Value

The ecological value of Hunan province forest ecosystems includes six major categories: water conservation, soil conservation, carbon sequestration and oxygen releasing, regulate climate, clean environment, biological diversity, maintenance of. According to relevant statistics and results at home and abroad in 2007, the ecological value of forest ecosystems in Hunan province, was 502.467 billion yuan.

3.3 Social Value

The social value of Hunan provincial forest ecosystems, mainly forms by three parts: the recreational value of forests, research and educational value and social value of employment. Under the Travel Cost Method (TCM) and related statistics, in Hunan province, the social value of forest ecosystems was 22.536 billion yuan in 2007.

3.4 Integrated Services Value

The forest ecosystem service value has comprehensive nature and synergy effects. There are overlapping between each evaluating indicator effects in an ecological function and that of another. But they promote and enhance each other sometimes. So the integrated forest ecosystem service value should be greater than the sum of value. But at the moment, the calculation of the integrated forest ecosystem service value is usually judged by the summation. Therefore, integrated forest ecosystem service value of Hunan province in 2007 was the combined value of ecosystem services in 2007, which was 558.554 billion yuan.

4 Evaluation Results and Discussions

From the Hunan provincial forest ecosystem service value quality synthetic evaluation result, we may draw the following conclusion:

4.1 Forest Ecosystem's Comprehension Service Value

In 2007 the Hunan provincial forest ecosystem's comprehension service value is 558,554,000,000 Yuan.Its value constitution is: The ecological value is 502,467,000,000 Yuan, accounts for 89.96%.The economic value is 33,551,000,000 Yuan, accounts for 6.0%. The social value is 22,536,000,000 Yuan, accounts for 4.04%. The ecological value is biggest, the economic value next best, the social value is smallest.

4.2 According to the Relevant Literature

The forest's ecological value of ecosystem services is about the direct economic value (timber value) of 8 to 20 times.From the evaluation results, Hunan province, the ecological value of forest ecosystems is 14.98 times of economic value, and 22.30 times of social value. Thus, the value of forest ecosystems in Hunan province, is not only in providing the raw materials of human, forest food, tea and beverages, wildlife resources, and direct economic value, but more important reflected in its regional economic and social development offered by the potential ecological value. And it provides the potential ecological value, much higher than the real value of the forest itself.

4.3 Looking from the Measure Results and the Entire Provincial GDP (GDP) Comparison

The Hunan provincial forest ecosystem's comprehension service value in 2007 occupies the entire provincial GDP as many as 61.1%, which was 8.86 times of the provincial forestry total output value in the same year. Every unit of forest land area service value is 5.32×104 Yuan $hm^{-2}a^{-1}$.

Just like Costanza said that "considered the huge uncertainty, we never can make the precise estimate of the ecosystem service". Therefore, this article on the value of forest ecosystem services in Hunan province carried out the evaluation, only a rough and conservative estimate, and the actual value far greater than the results of the assessment. In a sense, its value is infinite. Therefore, the evaluation results of this study are only given a general range of quantitative values and the potential to help people understand and recognize the value of forest ecosystem services, as well as to provide further analysis to provide information.

References

1. Brow, M.T., Ulgiati, S.: Emerge evaluation of the biosphere and natural capital. Ambio (1999)
2. Strange, E.M., Fausch, K.D., Covich, A.P.: Sustaining Ecosystem Services in Human-Dominated Watersheds: Biohydrology and Ecosystem Processes in the South Platte River Basin. Environmental Management 24(1) (1999)
3. Hargis, C.D., Bissonette, J.A., David, J.L.: The behavior of landscape metrics commonly used in the study of habitat fragmentation. Landscape Ecology (1998)
4. Odum, H.T., Odum, E.P.: The Energetic Basis for Valuation of Ecosystem Services. Ecosystems 3(1) (2000)
5. Pearce, D., Turner, D.: The environment of environment and natural resources, pp. 58–64. Earchscan, London (1990)
6. Costanza, R., d'Arge, R., de Groot, R., et al.: The Value of the World's Ecosystem Services and Natural Capital. Nature 387, 253–260 (1997)

Set Pairs Analysis Model for Synthetic Performance Appraisal

Wen-Liu Cai[1] and Jin-Song Li[2]

[1] School of Management, Hebei United University, 063009 Tang Shan, China
[2] School of Economics, Hebei United University, 063009 Tang Shan, China
caiwenliu2002@163.com

Abstract. Performance appraisal is the process of evaluating how well employees perform their jobs when compared to a set of standards and then communicating that information to employees. It is an important part in human resources management. The paper aims to introduce the authors' research on the set pair analysis (SPA) model and its application. Based on study of set pair analysis, the present paper had made a profound analysis of main features of the complex decision making process of effective management appraisal and identical-discrepancy-contrary (DC) system so as to establish the connection degree. At the same time, the authors have also calculated the connection degree of model and the quantitative analysis model. At last, the synthetic appraisal method of was explained how to use by an example. The appraisal results proved that it was an objective and scientific method.

Keywords: Set pair, Performance, Decision, Synthetic appraisal.

1 Introduction

Performance management is a bidirectional communicate process carrying by employee and their direct chief manager for achieving the organization object. Performance appraisal is different from performance management. It is the outcome of assessment program. Performance management includes prior plan, a matter of management and subsequent assessing. So performance appraisal is an important step in performance management program.

In the present performance appraisal methods both foreign and domestic, there are mainly four types of methods: (1) regression method, it based on a quantity of real data. But the simple regression analysis is difficult to express complex relation in the performance evaluates subjective and objective. Appraisal result is not correlated with actual measurement. And be subjected to restriction of the region condition while using. (2) Systematic analysis appraisal, represented by AHP and fuzzy mathematical method. It has a higher theoretical level and clear in analytical process. But in the two methods all want to use an expert to inspect grade point. So the appraisal result is suffered a great influence from human factor. (3) Gray comprehensive. It solved the problem which appraisal index is complex and fuzzy. But the values of whitening function, threshold of appraisal index and fuzzy cluster coefficient are confirmed by

M. Zhou (Ed.): ISAEBD 2011, Part III, CCIS 210, pp. 78–84, 2011.

experience range of each index. And when the appraisal result of clustering shows little difference, it is hard to select. (4) The others such as Attribute theory, Nerve network method similarly with gray theory.

Therefore, an synthetic assessment model of performance based on set pairs analysis was puts forward, which is easy to calculate and easy to understand and convenient to operate. What's the more important is that the evaluated result is closer to the actual situation and can be useful for the manager to make correct decisions.

2 Establishment of Performance Appraisal Index System

As an enterprise administrator, the most important four factors are specialized knowledge, performance, cooperation capability and exterior evaluation. So the main content of comprehensive appraisal system is listed in Figure 1.

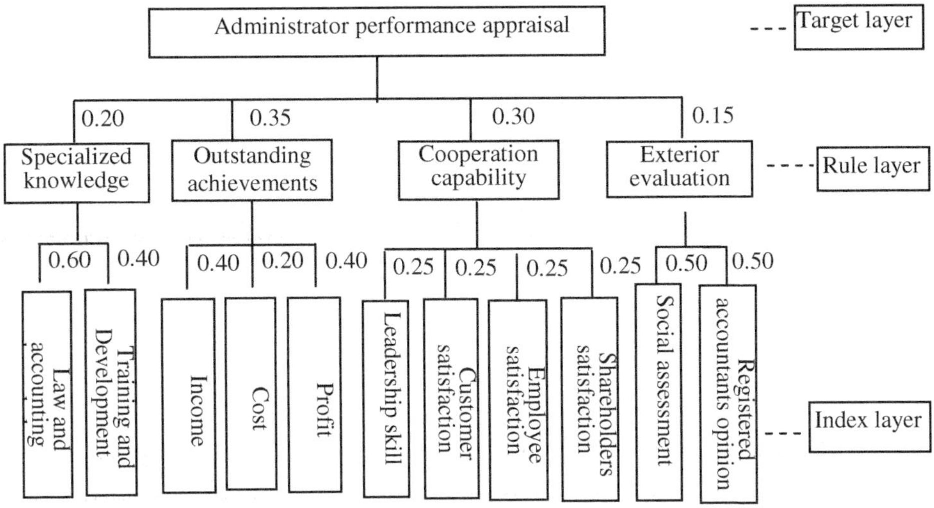

Fig. 1. Index system of administrator performance synthetic appraisal

3 Set Pairs Analysis Model of Performance Appraisal

3.1 Set Pairs Analysis Theory

Set pair is a pair of two related sets between which have three relations: identical, different and contrary, while set pair analysis is a method to process many kinds of uncertainty according to the connecting degree expression$\mu=a+b_i+c_j$. Furthermore, SPA can grasp the connection, change and transformation of two sets in set pairs to calculate the connecting degree.

In the connecting degree expression, $\mu$is the connecting degree, a, b, c is the identical degree, different degree and contrary degree respectively. i, j are the uncertain degree and the contrary degree respectively. Usually, a, b, c can be defined quantitatively, while *i*, *j* are only symbols that show the attribute of number terms. Particularly, *I*, *j* can be quantified, when j is denoted -1 to express that j term is opposite to a in number. *i* can be denoted a number from[-1, 1] which depends on the situation, while μcan turned to be connecting number.

In the connecting degree expression, *a,b,c* and *i,j* can describe the sets from two different levels, which *a*、*b*、c_is from the point of macroscopic level and *i*, *j* is microscopic level. And they can also describe the potential and possible tendency. For set pair analysis has gradation, $a+b_i+c_j$ can be extended as $(a_1+ a_2+\ldots,+a_n)+ (b_1+ b_2+\ldots,+b_n)i+(c_1+c_2+\ldots,+c_n)j$ in order to express and analyze the dynamic evolution and uncertain process of time extension and space expand.

It is thought by set pair theory that identity and contrary, certainty and uncertainty, are not only contrary, but also unit in a mathematic expression. When b is decomposed in the help of i and a and c can get benefit from this, the ratio of a and c can be changed to show the relationship between quantitative change and qualitative change. The certain conclusion can be drawn by use of the connecting degree but can be neglected by uncertainty, while in a certain condition the uncertainty can change into the certainty by neglecting itself, which can accomplish the unification of theory and practice.

3.2 Determination of Connection Number

Assumed *Z* which is the evaluate object space in the appraisal system as the administrator performance, if each condition of the administrator administration is to be evaluated in *Z*, main index used in appraisal are specialized knowledge, performance, cooperation capability and exterior evaluation, which can denote $I_1, I_2 \ldots I_m$. Next the set of *Z* is expressed as $(C_1, C_2, \ldots, C_k)$ and $C_k(1 \le k \le K)$ is the level of performance. The measured number should be come forth as figures. Then the standard of appraisal can be shown as table 1, which in fact is the quality level divided table of single factor in the appraisal index system. S_{ij} is classified limit of different classifications in table 1.

Table 1. Dividing grades of single index of performance

Index	C_1	C_2	C_3	…	C_k
I_1	$S_{10}-S_{11}$	$S_{11}-S_{12}$	$S_{12}-S_{13}$	…	$S_{1k-1}-S_{1k}$
I_2	$S_{20}-S_{21}$	$S_{21}-S_{22}$	$S_{22}-S_{23}$	…	$S_{2k-1}-S_{2k}$
			…….		
I_m	$S_{m0}-S_{m1}$	$S_{m1}-S_{m2}$	$S_{m2}-S_{m3}$	…	$S_{mk-1}-S_{mk}$

Set Pairs Analysis, which is different from the membership degree method, is a function structure of wide area and can improve the ratio of information utilization and ensure credibility of comprehensive result. It is the key to determine the accurate connecting degree to determine whether we can accept the classified result. The conformation method can be seen as follows: if the evaluated index is in the scope of the appraisal level, then it can be thought that they are identical and the connecting degree is 1; if the evaluated index is in the scope of separated level, then it can be considered that they are contrary and the connecting degree is -1; if the evaluated index is in the scope of the conterminous level, it will be determined as the equation (1) ~ (4).

(1) If j has the attribute the more, the better, and the performance appraisal index is at the condition of C_1={ excellent}:

$$\mu_{i1} = \begin{cases} 1 & x \in [S_{i(0)}, S_{i(1)}] \\ 1 + \dfrac{2(x - S_{i(1)})}{(S_{i(1)} - S_{i(2)})} & x \in [S_{i(1)}, S_{i(2)}] \\ -1 & x \in [S_{i(2)}, S_{i(5)}] \end{cases} \tag{1}$$

(2) If index of performance appraisal is at the condition of C_2={good}:

$$\mu_{i2} = \begin{cases} 1 + \dfrac{2(x - S_1)}{(S_{i(1)} - S_{i(0)})} & x \in [S_{i(0)}, S_{i(1)}] \\ 1 & x \in [S_{i(1)}, S_{i(2)}] \\ 1 + \dfrac{2(x - S_{i(2)})}{(S_{i(2)} - S_{i(3)})} & x \in [S_{i(2)}, S_{i(3)}] \\ -1 & x \in [S_{i(3)}, S_{i(5)}] \end{cases} \tag{2}$$

(3) If index of performance appraisal is at the condition of C_3={ medium}:

$$\mu_{i3} = \begin{cases} -1 & x \in [S_{i(0)}, S_{i(1)}] 或 x \in [S_{i(4)}, S_{i(5)}] \\ 1 + \dfrac{2(x - S_{i(2)})}{(S_{i(2)} - S_{i(1)})} & x \in [S_{i(1)}, S_{i(2)}] \\ 1 & x \in [S_{i(2)}, S_{i(3)}] \\ 1 + \dfrac{2(x - S_{i(3)})}{(S_{i(3)} - S_{i(4)})} & x \in [S_{i(3)}, S_{i(4)}] \end{cases} \tag{3}$$

(4) The μ_{i4} determining method is the same as that of μ_{i3}.

$$\mu_{i5} = \begin{cases} -1 & x \in [S_{i(0)}, S_{i(3)}] \\ 1 + \dfrac{2(x - S_{i(4)})}{(S_{i(4)} - S_{i(3)})} & x \in [S_{i(3)}, S_{i(4)}] \\ 1 & x \in [S_{i(4)}, S_{i(5)}] \end{cases} \tag{4}$$

3.3 Judgment of Appraisal Grades of Performance

After getting the connecting degree of every index by use of the method above, the total connecting degree can be determined according to equation (5):

$$\mu_j = \sum_{i=1}^{m} (\mu_{ij} \cdot w_i) \tag{5}$$

In the equation, w_i is the weight of the i index, μ_j is the total connecting degree which is every performance index for the j level. If

$$\mu_p = \max\{\mu_j\}, \quad 1 \le j \le k, p \in [1,2,\cdots,k] \tag{6}$$

Then it is thought that the performance belongs to the $C_{p.}$

3.4 Determined of Indices Weight

Indices weight can be determined using binary ratio reciprocal method of AHP, which is the indices are compared according to their importance to the assessment. Because the limitation of a specialist to the grade of information is 7±2, nine numbers division method is adopted.

The meanings of 1-9 are listed in table 2. The data has such characters as $a_{ij} > 0$, $a_{ij} = 1/a_{ji}$ and the meaning of $a_{ij} = 2$ is the index of number i is a little importance to number j.

Table 2. The meaning of nine number division method

Number	Meaning
1	same
3	important
5	More important
7	Very important
9	Extremely important
2 4 6 8	In the middle of the values it closed

According to judgment matrix, indices weights are required by mean square root. The computation result is followed and showed in Fig. 1.

4 Application of Appraisal Model

Administrator performance appraisal resorts to index system of fig 1. The index system is a treble system. Administrator performance is evaluated directly by every index of index layer. For simplification computing, the paper calculated every index through formula $S = \sum_i^n w_i \cdot s$ first. Its accuracy can also satisfy an appraisal request. The concrete process is as follows:

$I_1 = \{\text{Specialize d knowledge}\}$, $I_2 = \{\text{Cooperation capability}\}$, $I_3 = \{\text{Outstanding achievements}\}$, $I_4 = \{\text{Exterior evaluation}\}$ are supposed indices of rule layer. Performance grades are divided into five grades: excellent, good, medium, inferior and bad and which were denoted by C_1, C_2, C_3, C_4, C_5 respectively. Then to establish single index division table of administrator performance appraisal which was seen as table 3.

Table 3. Single index division table of administrator performance appraisal

Index	C_1	C_2	C_3	C_4	C_5
I_1	100~85	85~75	75~65	55~65	55~35
I_2	100~90	90~80	80~70	70~60	60~40
I_3	100~90	90~80	80~70	70~60	60~40
I_4	100~80	80~70	70~60	60~50	50~30

After the initial simplification, the fact score of each evaluate index of two Administrators performance from different corporation seen as table 4.

Table 4. Fact score of each appraisal index of two administrators performance from different corporation

Object	I_1	I_2	I_3	I_4
Admin A	94	81.5	91	49
Admin B	85	65	45	51

By using formula (1) ~ (4) and table 3, table 4, the fact score of two administrators, we can calculate the connection degree of single index. The result is shown in equation (7) and (8).

$$\text{(Admin A):} \quad \mu = (\mu_{ik})_{4\times 5} = \begin{array}{c} \begin{matrix} C_1 & C_2 & C_3 & C_4 & C_5 \end{matrix} \\ \left| \begin{matrix} 1.0 & -0.2 & -1.0 & -1.0 & -1.0 \\ -0.7 & 1.0 & 0.7 & -1.0 & -1.0 \\ 1.0 & 0.8 & -1 & -0.1 & -1.0 \\ -1.0 & -1.0 & -1.0 & 0.9 & 1.0 \end{matrix} \right| \begin{matrix} I_1 \\ I_2 \\ I_3 \\ I_4 \end{matrix} \end{array} \tag{7}$$

$$\text{(Admin B):} \quad \mu = (\mu_{ik})_{4\times 5} = \begin{array}{c} \begin{matrix} C_1 & C_2 & C_3 & C_4 & C_5 \end{matrix} \\ \left| \begin{matrix} 1.0 & 1.0 & -1.0 & -1.0 & -1.0 \\ -1.0 & -1.0 & 0 & 1.0 & -0.5 \\ -1.0 & -1.0 & -1.0 & -0.5 & 1.0 \\ -1.0 & -1.0 & -0.8 & -1.0 & -0.8 \end{matrix} \right| \begin{matrix} I_1 \\ I_2 \\ I_3 \\ I_4 \end{matrix} \end{array} \tag{8}$$

By using equation (7),(8) and formula (5), we can calculate the result.

$$\text{(Admin A):} \quad \begin{matrix} & C_1 & C_2 & C_3 & C_4 & C_5 \\ \mu_i = [& 0.11 & 0.40 & -0.41 & -0.40 & -0.7] \end{matrix} \tag{9}$$

$$\text{(Admin B):} \quad \begin{matrix} & C_1 & C_2 & C_3 & C_4 & C_5 \\ \mu_i = [& -0.60 & -0.60 & -0.62 & -0.15 & -0.20] \end{matrix} \tag{10}$$

Using the principle of the maximum degree of connection as equation (6) to evaluate, it is known that the result of Admin A is better. The results of this appraisal method are concordant with fuzzy comprehensive appraisal method and the calculation more simple. So it has even actual application worth.

5 Conclusions

Through quantitative analysis, we can get that the two administrator performance are excellent and good separately. Form the case we can see that using set pairs synthetic appraisal is viable and reliable. Here we may draw the following conclusions.

(1) Set Pairs Analysis is different from fuzzy subject degree. It is a function structure of wide area and pays much attention to the relativity and the fuzzy uncertainty during the process of dealing with the information. The principle of appraisal and its result are distinct and accurate, which can improve utilization of messages and ensure credibility of synthetic result.

(2) It is shown from the example that set pairs analysis appraisal model has explicit implication and easy operation, which can be spread and applied in the practice and is also a valid method to analyze uncertain problem with many targets.

(3) From the point of synthetic appraisal characteristics of performance, adopting set pairs synthetic appraisal can reflect the general state of the performance and get a new wholly effect which can't got through the normal synthetic appraisal methods.

References

1. Jiang, R.-h., Zhong, W.-l.: Performance Appraisal Summarize of Corporation Knowledge Management. Guangxi Social Science, 53–56 (2004)
2. Li, F.-x., Lu, X.-h., Mei, P.: SPA Model and Application of the Safety Prepare Appraisal in Coal Mine. Journal of Safety and Environment 5, 118–120 (2005)
3. Zhao, K.-q.: Set Pair Analysis for Describe and Handle of Uncertainty. Information and Control 24(3), 162–166 (1995)
4. Zheng, P.-e., Yue, C.-y.: The Credit Risk Analysis Based on Set Pair, vol. 37(1), pp. 84–88 (2004)

The Study on the Influence of the Motivation of the Domestic Enterprises' Mergers and Acquisitions on the Financing Instruments Choice

Chun Jiang[1] and Shuren Wang[2]

[1] Economics and Management School, Wuhan University, Wuhan 430072 China
[2] Economics and Management School, Wuhan University, Wuhan 430072 China
jiachun@whu.edu.cn, wangsrbj@sina.com

Abstract. The Financing Instruments Choice is a key to the success of Enterprises' Mergers and Acquisitions (M&A). Most of the previous studies on the M&A financing instruments choice only focus on the influence of the enterprises' financing structure rather than the motivation of M&A. This paper tries to use case study methodology to indicate the influence of the special motivations of domestic enterprises' M&A on the choice of financing tools. The results suggest that the non-market motivation of M&A in China has decisive impact on the choice of financing tools. Besides, the "internal people control under administrative intervention" determines that managers in the large and medium state-owned companies more focus on financing risk rather than financing cost and benefits. Meanwhile, the finance regulation policy and market environment, and the corporate M&A driven by local government aiming at "maintaining stability" are all motivation of the Domestic Enterprises' M&A on the Financing Instruments.

Keywords: Financing in M&A, Motivation of M&A, Choice of Financing instruments in M&A.

1 Introduction

M&A is a very important economic phenomenon in modern market economy. It not only makes the enterprises be bigger and stronger, but also enhance the enterprises to obtain the profitability quickly. As the famous American economist and Nobel laureate Stigler in his paper "The road leading to monopoly and oligopoly - Mergers" pointed out "a company through mergers of their way to become a giant business competitors is a prominent phenomenon in modern economic history "," No major U.S. companies need to grow up by a certain degree, some form of mergers and acquisitions, and almost no large companies mainly rely on internal expansion to grow up." Since the United States occurred the first wave of mergers and acquisitions nearly from the 19th century and early 20th century there has experienced five waves all over the world, and after each wave of M&A, some giants would appear. In recent years, with the constant improvement of China's capital markets, the corporate M&A are increasingly more and more universal as well.

M. Zhou (Ed.): ISAEBD 2011, Part III, CCIS 210, pp. 85–92, 2011.

M&A as a property transaction generally requires huge funds to complete the process. Meanwhile, the enterprises need to raise the adequate funds as quick as possible in a short time. Otherwise, the M & A activity may come to naught, they may even encounter anti-takeover. Therefore, choosing an appropriate financing instruments are an important guarantee to M&A success. According to the different financing channel, corporate finance M&A can be divided into internal financing and external financing. The internal financing mainly focus on the accumulation of its own funds. It cannot meet the huge number of M&A. Thus most companies rely on external financing to support its takeover. The M&A financing in this paper is mainly refers to external financing. In developed capital markets, the external M&A financing can be divided into three categories, the first is bank loans and leverage financing which are on behalf of the debt financing instruments. The second is preferred stock and common stock which are represented by equity financing. The third one is convertible bonds and warrants which are represented by the mixed financing tools. The firms choose the appropriate financing tools mainly based on the balancing of the costs of capital and the financing risks. Currently in China, although the three categories of external M&A financing exist, M & A financing tools are very limited in practice. In summary, the M&A financing tools which can be used in China are significantly different. This paper focuses on the impact of the motivation of the domestic enterprises' M&A on financing instruments choice.

2 The Literature Review

Different from the corporate financing strategies, M&A financing decision-making is an essential process in the whole M&A project. When the enterprises choose M&A financing instruments, they need to consider not only the company's capital structure and financial status, but also the case of Target Company and the purpose of M&A.

Generally the previous studies and researches in M&A field can be divided into four categories. One category begins from early Modigaliani and Miller (1958) called "MM" theory to modern financing structure theory which is on behalf of balance theory lately. This theory points out that the best capital structure for a company is balancing the tax shield effect and the results of the various costs which are caused by the increased financial problems' probability. The second category is Jensen and Meckling(1976) called "motivation theory" which developed after the introduction of the agency relationship. This theory indicates that the firm's capital structure depends on the marginal agency costs between debt and equity. After the research of Stulz (1990)、Harris and Raviv(1990), they appear that the value of the company, the probability of default and the growth opportunities of the firm have the positive or negative correlation with the optimal capital structures. The third category is Myers and Majluf(1984) introducing the dissymmetry information and establishing the Pecking Order Theory. The theory suggests that the enterprises need to select the internal financing, then choose the debt financing, and the issue of equity financing finally. That is using the least sensitive information tools firstly. Narayanan (1988)、Heinikel and Zechner (1990) explain the financing pecking order from the perspective of relationship between financing instruments choice and the stock price changing. The fourth category is the control of capital structure theory which is inferred by Grossman and Hart (1980). The theory indicates that companies choose different tools to obtain acquisition financing capital will produce different results when they consider the benefits of controlling. The administrators and shareholders will be different for the preferences of different financing instruments.

Recently, the studies and researches in domestic M&A financing instrument field are gradually increasing. Shen Qiang, Zheng Mingchuan et al (2003) indicated that the financing of mergers and acquisitions of listed companies showed the significant reverse selectivity, that is ignoring the internal financing, debt financing contempt, and preferring the equity financing.

There are three theories on the causes and motives of mergers of mergers among the western scholars. Firstly, On the basis of neo – classical assumption of profit maximization, mergers occur as the result of a profit maximizing behavior. They put forward the efficiency theory, the market power theory, undervalued theory and the signal & information theory. The efficiency theory summarizes that mergers and other forms of assets reorganization would make micro-economic entities improve the efficiency, and have the potential social benefits. The market power theory figures that an increase in the market share can increase profits because of reduced competition. The undervalued theory assumed that the M&A can save more costs than investing a new company, since the target company being undervalued. Accordingly it leads the M&A behavior to occur. The information and signal hypothesis suggest that the internal managers have more information than outliers. The company is able to perform and transfer the information by M&A. Secondly, on the basis of agency theory of management studies; the causes of mergers mainly include reducing the agency cost hypothesis, the free cash flow hypothesis and the over-conceited hypothesis. Fama、Jensen and Rubaek (1983) observed that the problem of agency cannot be controlled effectively by the market, however, the acquisition is good at solve this problem. Jesen(1986) further pointed out that M&A activity would help to resolve the conflict between shareholders and managers. Thirdly, from the new institutional economics point of view, merger is a way of reducing the transaction costs.

The domestic scholars have done lots of empirical research on domestic M&A. with a hypothesis of "value transformation and redistribution under the institutional factors", Xin Zhang (2003) proposed that some of the M&A should not have happened, or it cannot create value after M&A. However, the mergers occurred because of the institutional factors. Zengquan Li et al (2005) indicates that, based on the domestic specific institution, merger of listed companies to non-listed companies is a way of the local government and shareholders insisting or taking out the listed companies. Xing Huang and Weitao Chen twins (2006) showed that the large shareholders have a strong hollowed motivation in the performance of its excellent M&A of listed companies.

In summary, the current studies on causes and motives of mergers and choosing financial instruments mainly focus on analyzing the optimal financing arrangement, and comparing the pros and cons of financing instruments from the cost and risk point of view. The researchers less consider the causes and motives of mergers effect the selection of financing tools.

3 The Impact of the Motives of Domestic Mergers on the Choice of the Financing Instruments

Presently the financing facilities which can be chosen in China are debt financing such as bond loans, mergers loans, nongovernmental lend, corporation bond and trust credits, stock rights financing and mixed financing just as convertible bond. Their features and constraints are shown in Table 1.

Table 1. Major M&A Financing Facilities in China

Classification	Financing facilities	Features and constraints
Debt financing	Bank loans	Cannot make stock rights investment immediately if there is no certain approval.
	Mergers loans	Borrower needs to provide mortgage assurance. The equity leverage is no more than 2. The time limit is no more than 5 years.
	Nongovernmental lend	Higher financing costs, short time, and the exceeded accrual cannot receive statutory protection.
	Corporation bond	Connection block, long period issuing, high financial demanding, and lack of high level credit rating institutions.
	Trust credits	High level financing efficiency, low demand for information publishing, strict filtration of projects, requiring higher returns.
Stock rights financing	Ordinary shares	High costs, rigid restriction for issuing corporation, long period of issuing, low efficiency.
Mixed financing	Convertible bond	High conditional issuing, long period of financing, low efficiency.

Normally, there are three aspects for companies to choose the financing tools in their M&A. First, for those M&A on the purpose of increasing capital usage efficiency, they prefer to choose financing tools in long term with stable resource coming from. Secondly, for those M&A on the purpose of short term finance effect, they prefer to choose lever financing tool in short term with high risk. Thirdly, for those companies on the purpose of control benefits, they prefer debt financing tools as their first choice. Except all of these, some specific reason for M&A can also directly affect the choice of financing tools.

3.1 For the Opportunism M&A on the Purpose of Avoiding Control or Getting Specific Resource, They Prefer to Choose Debt Financing Tool Like Bank Debt

The "Opportunism M&A" is very normal at the beginning of M&A in China. The main purpose is to get national finance subsidiary or tax reduction, "buying shell" to get listed qualification, and making good results in order to keep Public company qualification. All these M&A shows short term Opportunism characteristics.

For those companies aiming to get national finance subsidiaries or tax reductions, most of them with limit resource and poor operational efficiency, so for the purpose of improving short term finance status, they may care more on the extent of easiness and cost in financing. Bank loans are their first choice.

For those companies who need "buy shell" to be listed, their ultimate purpose is to collect more funds through Capital Market. The pre-condition is that the company value is under-evaluated. Stakeholders would not sell their share before listing, so Bridge loans as a short term Bank Financing could be their best choice. These companies could also go for private lending once they are not able to get credits.

According to the provisions of the relevant securities laws and regulations, listed companies with continuous two years of losses will encounter special treatment, the risk of being delisted; listed companies with first three years of average net assets yield less than 10% are not allowed to share placements. To retain the "shell", some shareholders often use asset replacement or reorganization, through the inequality associated with specific transactions, to influence financial data of listed companies in order to improve the performance of enterprises, so as to avoid delisting or to reach the lower limit of placement requirements. "Shell" is treated rare by some local governments. Such kind of mergers and acquisitions often reflects the intention of the local government with direct or indirect government support. Therefore, the possible option for these companies is to obtain short term bank loans under intervention of government from executive perspective.

3.2 For the Purpose of Obtaining the Company's Domination, the Management-Buy-Out (MBO) of the State-Owned Enterprise (SOE) Tends to Choose Trust Credits etc. High Leverage Debt Financing Tools

The MBO is a behavior that the target company's management purchases all or most of the company's shares or assets to gain the domination of the company. The MBO is actually a particular kind of Leverage-Buy-out (LBO). This particularity embodies that the main body of the LBO is the management of the target company. The MBO in China mainly divided into two categories. One is the acquisition of the local SOE and the property rights of the collective enterprises; the other is mergers of non-circulated state-owned shares in the listed companies.

There are only two possible explanations existing. One is lots of personal loans, and another is that the management has accumulated a large number of illegal and unreasonable incomes. Thereby, when the management of SOE makes the MBO, for the protection of them avoiding suspicion, they will raise a part of funds by debt financing rather than using the self owned funds. At the same time, MBO is essentially a risky investment; management adapting debt financing can lock the financing costs in order to get higher returns by using financial leverage in the future. Finally, the high debt financing can let the outside investors know that the company has an optimistic future. Meanwhile, it is helpful to improve the company's future stock price. The self funds of the management cannot complete the acquisition of the target company abroad as well. Thereby, they normally adapt financial leverage to complete the acquisition especially for the listed companies.

According to the relative law in China, bank credit is not allowed to invest the equity. While on March 12th, 2003 the Ministry of Finance calls for suspension of direct MBO. Since the trust companies have the advantage of law to provide bridge loans, they are the important way after the suspension of direct MBO. The specific operation is as follows, the trust company make the target company shares as a collateral, and also make the dividend income as a future repayment to issue intrusting loans for the investors. Although the trust plan require the management to input part of their funds or assets in order to get rid of "moral hazard", the value of their assets or funds are still small in the whole acquisition.

3.3 Mergers Which Reflect State-Owned Enterprise Managers' Will Tend to Choose Stock Rights Financing Represented by Issuing Ordinary Shares to Expand the Firm's Scale

The "free cash flow hypothesis" from Jensen (1986) and the "over conceited hypothesis" from Roll(1986) both pointed out that managers carry out the acquisitions for the purpose of maximizing their own benefits, or making their ambition and self-motivation. The issue above is embodied particularly in China. Qingmu Cangyuan (1994) figured that the State-owned enterprises in the process of corporatization, the government lost the highly centralized corporate executive rights. We call it "internal control". This kind of "internal control" can make the original business managers and workers maximize their individual and small group benefits. Chunlin Zhang (1995) suggested that the domestic internal control can be referred as "internal control under the administrative intervention". The SOE managers will lose their place and controlling benefits, and if they adapt the debt-financing, it will lead to increase the probability of bankruptcy. Therefore, the stock rights financing becomes the first choice of the SEO managers. For instance, Wuhan iron and steel ltd. issued 1.2 billion state-owned corporate shares and 0.8 billion floating stocks in 2004. The company raised funds more than 9 billion in total. Wuhan Iron and Steel Group have raised funds to purchase the steel core business assets, and ultimately make the group's whole major assets be listed.

3.4 The M&A of Private Enterprises Tend to Choose Equity Financing for the Purpose of Emptying the Listed Companies

The strong shareholders and their family members of the private enterprises intervenes the operation of the firm with a strong motivation. They can wantonly make "emptying" the listed company and seriously infract the benefits of the minority shareholders. Classens and Djankov, Fan and Lang (1999) implies in their empirical studies that in East Asian countries including China, the main issues of corporate governance is the predatory behavior of the major shareholder to minor shareholders, and mergers and acquisitions of related companies is the very common form of "emptying".

Although the utility of funds through equity financing is under control by the Regulators, the intensity is still loose in the real operation. While the major shareholders who depend on the strength of "dominance" control the company's operation and business decisions. Low cost equity financing and long term occupation, even no dividends required in China, make it the best choice for private listed company to do M&A in form of "emptying". For example, in 1998, private enterprises called Tongliao famed-in 40 million stated owned shares and 6.5 million stated shares rights by total RMB 81.45 million(2.02 RMB per share) before the Sisha ltd. rationed shares. This made the Tongliao become the largest shareholder with 34.48% of the general capital. After that, the Tongliao takes the advantage of "Dominance", and successfully extracts 53 million RMB of Sisha Ltd.

3.5 Driven by Local Government, M&A Are Aiming for the Maintaining Stability

In recent years, impacted by international financial crisis and domestic industrial structure upgrade, a large number of export-oriented, labor-intensive large scale industries are encountering increasingly hard time, which also includes some public listed companies with serious business losses. Under this circumstance, a lot of government driven M&A appears aiming to maintain social stability and avoid company bankrupt liquidation.

4 Conclusion

Company M & A financing and the choice of specific financing tools are mainly affected by motivation of M&A, company capital structure, company risk preference and the capital market development status that the company facing.

We have strict control on financial environment, not fully developed capital market and specific corporate governance structure made companies have little choice on their financing tools. The motivation of M&A in our country has tremendous difference with developed market in western countries. Therefore, all these result in that traditional western financing tool on Choice cannot explain the choice of M&A financing tool in our country. In the same time, the choice of financing tool is also different with the financing sequence of those companies who ignore internal source financing, look down debt financing and prefer equity financing, which is mainly affected by some specific motivations of M&A in our country.

First, the non-market motivation of M&A in China has decisive impact on the choice of financing tool. This is highlighted in the Opportunism M&A aiming to avoid regulation or get specific resource, which less consider corporate capital structure optimization and information transferring characteristics.Under our current capital market environment, short term Bank Loan and private lending are the preference of these companies as their external financing tool.

Secondly, the "internal people control under administrative intervention" determines that managers in the large and medium state-owned companies, especially the listed state-owned companies, less consider financing cost and benefits in their choice of financing tool, but more focus on financing risk. "Conceited manager hypothesis " could explain their preference on equity financing, which is because the managers are concerned on that company bankruptcy could impact personal benefits.

Thirdly, subject to the M&A financing channels, finance regulation policy and market environment, some market-oriented company M&A prefer choosing specific external financing tool. It is first shown as the company management people choose using trusted curve MBO to reduce MBO risk and complications, since in any way they cannot get legitimate credit support; secondly due to the poor financing channels for private company, for those M&A aiming for "emptying", major shareholders prefer equity financing in their external financing.

Fourthly, corporate M&A driven by local government aiming at "maintaining stability" is the motivation with Chinese characteristics. In such acquisitions, The acquiring party need commit and guarantee the company employee employment status, which is the bargain chip in negotiation with local government and also the main cost in M&A. To the M&A aiming at "maintaining stability", it is not important the financing is equity financing or debt financing. The crucial part is that in the debt restructuring of Target Company, the previous creditors forced to cut debt usually bear the main cost of M&A ultimately.

References

1. Modigliani, F., Miller, M.: The Cost of Capital, Corporation Finance and the Theory of Investment. American Economic Review 48(3) (1958)
2. Stulz, R.M.: Managerial Discretion and Optimal Financing Policies. Journal of Financial Economics 26, 3–27 (1990)
3. Zhou, C.: Financing, M&A and Corporate Governance, 1st edn. Peking university Edition (2005)
4. Jensen, M.C., Meckling, W.H.: Theory of the Firm: Managerial Behavior Agency Cost and Ownership Structure. Journal of Financial Economics 3(4) (1976)
5. Chen, X., Zhang, T.: The market reflection of the M&A. The Economics Research (9) (1999)
6. Zhang, X.: Does the M&A create valuation — the Research of Theories and Practices on Securities Market in China. The Economics Research (2) (2003)

Analysis of Influence Factors of Real Estate Price Based on DEMATEL Approach

Yan-Xia Wu and Rong Guo

Xi'an University of Technology, School of Business Administration, Xi'an, China
xautguorong@163.com

Abstract. With the rapid development of real estate industry in China, more and more people from all walks of life have started to pay attention to real estate prices. According to scholars of research data on real estate prices, we screen out seven relevant factors which affect the real estate prices. We use DEMATEL method to analyze cause and effect relation among these influence factors and find out the main factors which affect real estate prices, including supply and demand situation, oneself condition and population factors. We expect to provide scientific basis for the government in the real estate industry to achieve effective of macro-control and management, and provide technical support for the investment decisions of the enterprise and the home buyers.

Keywords: Real estate prices, Influence factors, DEMATEL method.

1 Introduction

The real estate industry is an important pillar industry of the national economy. It plays an important role in improving people's living conditions and living standards, boosting economic growth, expanding employment and accelerating the urban construction. But the real estate market in China development is not balanced in fast development. It also appeared many worthy of our attention problems, such as, house prices have more than normal level, a real estate bubble phenomenon has become increasingly evident. The theory relating to real estate caused by the domestic and international scholars are highly valued. Actual bank loans, practical and real estate prices, they exist between long-term stable relations. House prices and the bank credit is the relationship between the real estate price changes affecting bank credit, rather than bank credit decided to real estate prices(Gerldch et al.,2005).The empirical analysis between the real estate price and real estate loans in the relationship, and the results show that, China's real estate price level and bank of real estate loans have strong positive correlation(ZHANG Tao et al.,2006).The risks of the real estate based on analytic hierarchy process and simulation(JIANG Gen-mou et al.,2007).The application of performance management in real estate enterprise to PLIZE real estate Co. LTD as an example(LIU Mei,2008). The influence factors of the real estate price analysis based on fuzzy evaluation (XU Jing et al.,2008). A set of the warning system design ideas in market of real estate (HANG Wei,2009).

M. Zhou (Ed.): ISAEBD 2011, Part III, CCIS 210, pp. 93–99, 2011.

Many factors influence the real estate price, from the national overall, national macroeconomic policies on real estate prices to adjust action appears very important. But must carry on the effective control, the recognition of the various factors, exactly what factors affect factors? What factors through other factors and its function? What factors can have an important impact on the real estate prices? This also is the key.

2 Determine Impact Factors of the Real Estate Price

Retrieving the papers in CNKI and WanFang database from 2000 to 1011, we all together find 2199 articles related to the real estate price, among which there are 139 articles which have great connection with the influencing factors of the real estate price. By using bibliometricsmethod, we screened out factors accounting for top 7 proportion as the main influencing factors of the real estate price, and they are: Supply and demand (S1), Oneself condition (S2), Environmental factors (S3), Demographic factors (S4), Economic factors (S5), Social factors (S6), Administrative factors (S7).

Judging from domestic and foreign research data, the main factors which influence the real estate prices in the following aspects:

(1) Supply and demand (S1)
Because real estate shall not mobility and alteration of the difficulty of the use function, decided to a real estate prices real level of this region, mainly is this kind of real estate supply and demand. Other types of estate supply and demand conditions of the property whether the impact of the price level and the extent. It depends on the spread of how supply and demand conditions may be.

(2) Oneself condition (S2)
Real estate oneself condition is good or bad, directly related to its price directly. The so-called oneself condition refers to the factors of natural objects state which reflect real estate itself, liking its own position, geology, topography, land area, land shape, sunshine, ventilated, wind direction, wind, temperature, humidity, annual rainfall, natural cyclical disasters and building appearance.

(3) Environmental factors (S3)
The environmental factors which influence the real estate price of real estate, it is to show those influential real estate prices around the physical factors. These factors include sound sleep environment, atmospheric environment, hydrological environment, visual environment, health environment.

(4) Demographic factors (S4)
Real estate requirements subject is people ,the number of people and quality of people has very big effect on real estate prices. Population factors on the influence of real estate prices, concrete can be divided into the population, population quality, the family size.

(5) Economic factors (S5)
The economic factors which influence the real estate price basically has economic development situation, savings, consumption level and the level of investment, revenues and expenditures level, financial status, prices (especially building materials price), building labour, the interest rate and the residents' income and real estate investment.

(6) Social factors (S6)
Social factors are: political stability condition, social security level, the real estate speculation, urbanization, etc.

(7)Administrative factors (S7)
The administrative factors which influence the real estate price, refers to the influence the real estate price system, policy and regulations and administrative measures and other factors. It mainly have land system, housing system, real estate prices, policy, administrative membership alteration, special policy, urban development strategy, urban planning, land use planning, tax policy, traffic control, etc.

3 The Specific Steps of DEMATEL Method

DEMATEL trial and evaluation decision making (laboratory), namely: "the decision test and evaluation test method ". Battelle Institute for research in Geneva which is to research complex and difficult problem of the world (such as race, hunger, environmental protection, energy issues, and so on) and put forward the method in 1973.

The specific steps of DEMATEL method:

Step1 First, examine the influence relationship of different factors, and set corresponding scale.

Through the expert scoring method is used to determine the direct impact between different factors level.

Assuming the direct influence matrix system for X:

$$X = \begin{bmatrix} 0 & x_{12} & \cdots & x_{1n} \\ x_{21} & 0 & \cdots & x_{2n} \\ \vdots & \cdots & \cdots & \cdots \\ x_{n1} & x_{n2} & \cdots & 0 \end{bmatrix} \tag{1}$$

Among, factor x_{ij}, (i=1,2, …,n, j=1,2, …,n, i≠j) shows the degree of direct influence of factor a_i to a_j .if i=j , x_{ij}=0.

Step 2 Standard directly influence matrix, and a conclusion that the standardized directly affect matrix-G,

$$G = \frac{1}{\max\limits_{1 \le i \le n} \sum_{j=1}^{n} X_{ij}} X \tag{2}$$

$$T = G + G^2 + \cdots + G^n \tag{3}$$

When n is large enough, you can use $G(1-G)^{-1}$ and approximatively calculate the aggregate impact matrix-T, where I is unit matrix.

Step 3 Calculate the impact degree and be affected degrees of each factor.

$$f_i = \sum_{j=1}^{n} t_{ij}, (i = 1,2,\cdots,n)$$
$$e_i = \sum_{j=1}^{n} t_{ji}, (i = 1,2,\cdots,n) \tag{4}$$

Step 4 Calculate the center degree of each factor which adding the impact degree and be affected degrees of system factors, and calculate the degree of causes of each factor which subtract the impact degree and be affected degrees of system factors.

$$m_i = f_i + e_i, (i = 1,2,\cdots,n)$$
$$n_i = f_i - e_i, (i = 1,2,\cdots,n) \tag{5}$$

Step 5 Through the center degree of each factor and the degree of causes of each factor to make the Cartesian coordinate system, mark the location of the coordinate system of each factor, analyze the importance of each factor, make recommendations for the actual system.

4 The Analysis of Influence Factors of the Real Estate Prices Based on DEMATEL Method

Through the use of DEMATEL methods, we analyze directly influencing relationship of all possible of a factor to other factors, establish directly impact matrix of seven factors which is shown in Table 1. According to the direct relationship among the various factors, we use fussy grade method. The "strong" marked 3, "middle" marked 2, "weak" marked 1. If the two factors have no effect, we use "0". We come to the relationship of these seven factors, the directional graph is shown in Table 1.

Table 1. Score sheet of factors

factors	S_1	S_2	S_3	S_4	S_5	S_6	S_7
S_1	0	0	0	0	0	0	0
S_2	3	0	0	2	0	0	0
S_3	2	2	0	1	6	3	0
S_4	3	0	0	0	0	5	6
S_5	2	3	2	2	0	0	1
S_6	1	2	1	2	1	3	0
S_7	1	2	0	1	1	0	0

The influence matrix X can be obtained through the above relationship.

$$X = \begin{bmatrix} 0 & 0 & 0 & 0 & 0 & 0 & 0 \\ 3 & 0 & 0 & 2 & 0 & 0 & 0 \\ 2 & 2 & 0 & 1 & 0 & 0 & 0 \\ 3 & 0 & 0 & 0 & 0 & 0 & 0 \\ 2 & 3 & 2 & 2 & 0 & 0 & 1 \\ 1 & 2 & 1 & 2 & 3 & 0 & 0 \\ 1 & 2 & 0 & 1 & 0 & 2 & 0 \end{bmatrix}$$

Standard directly influence matrix X, and get the matrix G:

$$G=\begin{bmatrix} 0 & 0 & 0 & 0 & 0 & 0 & 0 \\ 0.333 & 0 & 0 & 0.222 & 0 & 0 & 0 \\ 0.222 & 0.222 & 0 & 0.111 & 0 & 0 & 0 \\ 0.333 & 0 & 0 & 0 & 0 & 0 & 0 \\ 0.222 & 0.333 & 0.222 & 0.222 & 0 & 0 & 0.111 \\ 0.111 & 0.222 & 0.111 & 0.222 & 0.333 & 0 & 0 \\ 0.111 & 0.222 & 0 & 0.111 & 0 & 0..222 & 0 \end{bmatrix}$$

Calculate the matrix $T = G + G^2 + G^3 + G^4 + G^5 + G^6 + G^7$

$$T\begin{bmatrix} 0 & 0 & 0 & 0 & 0 & 0 & 0 \\ 0.406926 & 0 & 0 & 0 & 0 & 0 & 0 \\ 0.349301 & 0.222 & 0 & 0.160284 & 0 & 0 & 0 \\ 0.333 & 0 & 0 & 0 & 0 & 0 & 0 \\ 0.547633 & 0.416415 & 0.226594 & 0.359363 & 0.008273 & 0.0248440 & 0.111918 \\ 0.496366 & 0.385299 & 0.186451 & 0.408734 & 0.408734 & 0.008273 & 0.037266 \\ 0.348452 & 0.307533 & 0.04139 & 0.25101 & 0.74533 & 0.223837 & 0.008273 \end{bmatrix}$$

Calculate the influencing degree D, the influenced degree R, the centrality degree Di+Ri, and the causal degree Di-Ri, the result is shown in table 2 and table 3.

Table 2. The table of the influencing factors of real estate

Factors	S_1	S_2	S_3	S_4	S_5	S_6	S_7
S_1	0	0	0	0	0	0	0
S_2	0.406926	0	0	0.222	0	0	0
S_3	0.349301	0.222	0	0.160284	0	0	0
S_4	0.333	0	0	0	0	0	0
S_5	0.547633	0.416415	0.226594	0.359363	0.008273	0.024844	0.111918
S_6	0.496366	0.385299	0.186451	0.408734	0.335755	0.008273	0.037266
S_7	0.348452	0.307533	0.041390	0.251010	0.74533	0.223837	0.008273
SUM	2.133226	1.331247	0.454435	1.401391	1.089358	0.256954	0.157457

Table 3. The table of the influencing factors of real estate (follow table 2)

Factors	The sum of row	The centrality degree	The causal degree
S_1	0	2.133226	-2.133226
S_2	0.628926	1.960173	-0.702321
S_3	0.731585	0.787435	0.27715
S_4	0.333	1.734391	-1.068391
S_5	1.69504	2.784398	0.605682
S_6	1.858144	2.115098	1.60119
S_7	1.925825	2.083282	1.768368

According to the data in table 2 and table 3, through excel, the centrality degree as the abscissa and the causal degree as the longitudinal, we plot the cause and effect diagram of the influencing factors of real estate, which is as shown in fig 1.

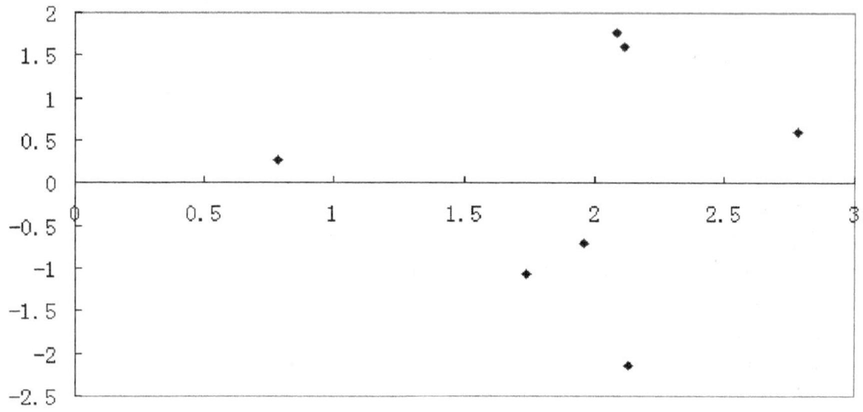

Fig. 1. The cause and effect diagram of the influencing factors of real estate

From the fig 1, we find the major be influenced factors of real estate: supply and demand situation, condition, population factors, the causal factors are environmental factors, economic factors and administrative factor.

The most fundamental factor which affects real estate prices is the supply and demand factor; supply and demand factor is the final factors of two in the formation of real estate price. Other factors affect the supply or the demand, then action on the real estate prices. The balance of supply and demand changes in the trends of real estate prices; socialist market economy under the conditions of real estate prices, both the amount of labor cost should be consistent with the price, but also social needs should be consistent with the price, which should be Supply price and demand a price consistent with the equilibrium price. The main part of real estate demand is person, the number of people and the quality of people have a big impact. The Government should strengthen the housing supply and demand projections, make macro-control for the unreasonable price and fluctuations of real estate.

S7 (administrative factors) and S5 (economic factors) direct role in S1 (supply and demand factors) to real estate price has changed. Since reform and opening up, China's real estate market has been tremendous development. However, until now, the Government is still the basic configuration of the main norms of the real estate market has not yet formed, administrative factors influence on the real estate prices. Both economic factors and personal factors are the sensitivity factors of the real estate price changes, in particular, the overall macroeconomic situation and the impact of land costs are very large. Through the above analysis, we should adopt strong measures which are administrative factors and economic factors to effectively control prices.

S6 (social factors) and S3 (environmental factors) direct role in S5 (own factor) and S1 (supply and demand factors) to real estate price has changed, while between economic factors and social factors have the interaction relationship. In political stability, social order in good condition, a high level of urbanization, regional environmental good circumstances, economic prosperity has support and protection, and boosting the confidence of investors to buy real estate, which is to maintain an active and stable factors of real estate prices. Also the building itself and environmental factors also significantly affect the development costs and thus affect the real estate prices. Therefore, we should be paid attention to social factors, environmental factors, the development and control of their own factors. Demographic factors Abstract in demographic economy and social impact to change in supply and demand. Real estate speculation is within the limits prescribed by law. It is the loopholes in the legal system for the formation of profit-driven behavior. If you want to be regulated by law, you may also inhibit lots of normal economic behavior. It is difficult to use the law to intervene. When speculation occurs, we can take necessary administrative means.

5 Conclusion

Firstly, under research data of domestic and international scholars on real estate prices, we summarize the impact factors of real estate prices. Through DEMATEL methods, we analyze and get the causal relationship between each factor structure. Finally, we conclude that supply and demand situation, its own conditions and demographic factors are most important to be influencing factors, administrative factors is the greatest factor that impact on other prices. We clearly get the importance of each factor and the interaction relation that can provide basis for determining real estate prices, and also provide important reference data for decision-makers.

References

1. Zhang, T., Gong, L.-t., Bo, Y.-x.: Return on assets, mortgage loans and equilibrium price of real estate. Financial Research 2, 1–11 (2006)
2. Wang, H.-g., YU, Z.-j.: The study of affect factors of juvenile crime analysis and empirical research based on DEMATEL. Youth Research of China 1, 153–157 (2006)
3. Jiang, G.-m., Hu, Z.-p., Jin, J.-y.: Quantitative Evaluation of Real Estate's Risk based on AHP and Simulation. Systems Engineering -Theory & Practice (2007)
4. Liu, M.: Application Research of Performance Management in the real estate enterprise. Chongqing University (2008)
5. Chen, Y.-j., Zeng, Y.-b.: Factors of the real estate price analysis by Fuzzy AHP. Anqing Teachers College 3, 25–29 (2008)
6. Jiang, C.-j.: Factors of the best real estate prices. Chinese Price 5, 35–38 (2009)
7. Hang, W.: Early Warning System and Research on Real Estate Market. Xi'an University of Architecture Technology (2009)
8. Xu, J., Wu, L.-j.: Structural model analysis of influence factors of Real estate prices. Finance and Economy 13, 22–23 (2009)
9. Liang, J.-h., Guo, D.: Factors of the Enterprise Human Resources Reputation based on DEMATEL. Human Resource Management 1, 153–157 (2009)
10. Xin, L., REN, A.-s.: Analyzing the influential factors of quality and safety of agricultural products based on DEMATEL method. Technology and Economic 4 (2009)
11. Rao, Q.-f., YANG, J.-h.: Influencing factors of SME financing based on DEMATEL. Modern-Commerce Industry 20, 135–138 (2009)

A Panel Regression Analysis on Relativity between China Regional Economic Development and Traffic Accidents Risks

Li Song[1,*], Gang He[1], and Cui Ding[2]

[1] Economy & Management School, Anhui University of Science & Technology, Huainan, Anhui 232001, P.R. China
lilysong@ustc.edu
[2] School of Resource and Safety Engineering, China University of Mining & Technology (Beijing), Beijing 100083, P.R. China

Abstract. Obvious regional traffic accident risks differences can be observed in China. This paper analyzed the contribution of regional economic development differences in regional traffic accidents risks by method of panel regression models. Results show that each economic development element has various effects on regional traffic accidents risks. Regional economic structure, (especially proportion of industry) and human resource are two obvious elements interpreting gaps in regional traffic accidents risks.

Keywords: Economic development, Traffic accidents, Panel regression model.

1 Introduction

Due to difference in many factors such as nature gift, history, location and social conditions, obvious gaps in production could be found among different regions in China. The East is the developed areas with higher economic speed, while the West is rather backward. Many researches found that economy development has relativity with traffic accidents. Eduard F van Beeck (2000) [1]used mortality and population data of the World Health Organization (WHO), and figures on motor vehicle ownership of the International Road Federation (IRF), examined cross-sectional and longitudinal associations of these traffic-related variables with the prosperity level per country, found a reversal from a positive relation between prosperity and traffic accident mortality in the 1960s to a negative association currently. In a long-term perspective, the relation between prosperity and traffic accident mortality appears to be non-linear: economic development first leads to a growing number of traffic-related deaths, but later becomes protective. Ulf-G. Gerdtham [2] used aggregate data for 23 Organization for Economic Cooperation and Development (OECD) countries over the 1960–1997 periods to examine the relationship between macroeconomic conditions and deaths, found that total mortality and deaths from several common causes rise when labor

[*] Corresponding author.

M. Zhou (Ed.): ISAEBD 2011, Part III, CCIS 210, pp. 100–105, 2011.

markets strengthen. For instance, controlling for year effects, a 1% point decrease in the national unemployment rate is associated with growth of 2.1% for motor vehicle deaths. Leonard J. Paulozzi [3] presented a cross-sectional regression analysis of recent national mortality in 44 countries using death certificate data provided by the World Health Organization. Results showed overall MVC mortality peaked among low-income countries at about US$ 2000 GNI per capita and at about 100 motor vehicles per 1000 people. Teik Hua Lawa[4] applied a fixed effects negative binomial regression analysis on a panel of 25 countries covering the period 1970–1999, proved the inverted U-shape relationship between economic development and traffic accidents. In early stages of development deaths would increase with increasing motorization. Eventually deaths decrease as technical, policy and political institutions respond to demands for increased safety. Thomas L. Traynor [5] used regression model to analyze relativity between gross domestic product and traffic accidents mortality, and found that traffic accident mortality had a non-liner relationship with gross domestic product. HE Xue-qiu, SONG Li [6] made an empirical study on Chinese regional work safety and socioeconomic development and found that there existed certain spatial safety distribution regularity which reflects regional economic wealth in China. But no research studied how regional economic development elements affect regional industrial accidents up till now.

There are 4 big economic regions in China: the East, the Midland, the West and the Northeast. Obvious difference in economic development among 4 economic regions could be found owing to influence of many factors such as resource gift, geographical and social condition. Figure 2 compared regional gross domestic product per capita during 2000-2007, which showed that the East is the richest area, and the West is rather backward. Figure 2 is a scatter diagram between regional traffic accidents occurrence rate per 10^5 people and regional gross domestic product during 2007. An obvious grads characteristic among 4 regions could be found. A region with high gross domestic product could be found high traffic accident risks.

This study aimed to explore whether regional economic development difference has effect on regional traffic accident risks.

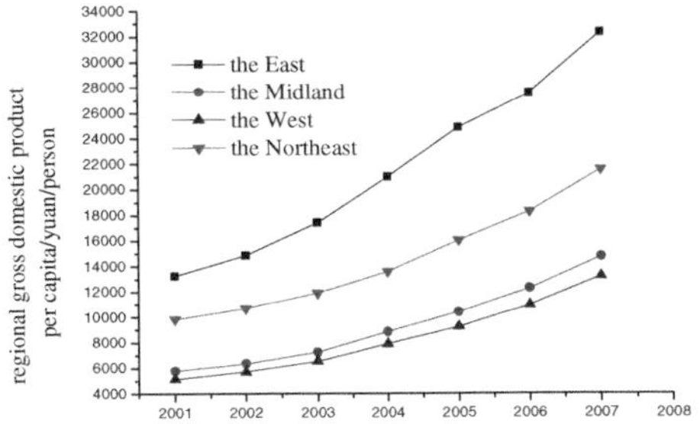

Fig. 1. regional gross domestic product per capita in 4 regions; 2001-2007

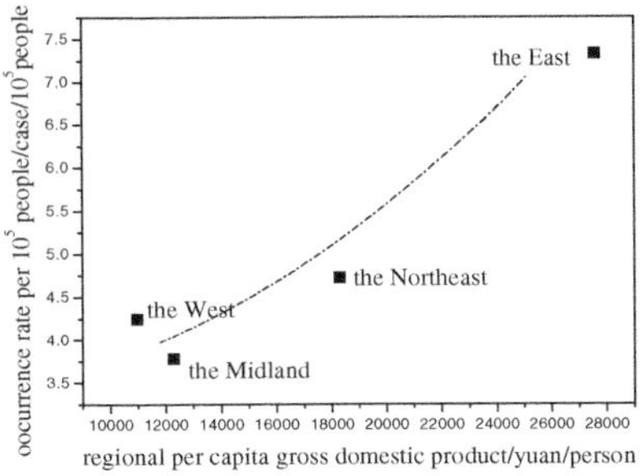

Fig. 2. traffic accidents risks and per capita gross domestic product; 2007

2 Method

2.1 Data

As regional economic development is a compound variant, we adopted compound variants including regional gross domestic product (LAG_i), regional industrial proportion (LIR_i), regional foreign trade value (LOP_i), regional technology value ($LTEP_i$), regional financial input on education (LHR_i) and production value of regional non-state enterprises (LMR_i). All of data on regional economic development come from China Statistics Yearbook each year. We adopted traffic accidents occurrence rate per 10^5 people (TOR_t) and injured rate per 10^5 people (THR_t) to describe traffic accident risks. Calculation formulas are shown as following:

$$TOR_t = \frac{N_t}{P_t} \quad (1) \qquad THR_t = \frac{H_t}{P_t} \quad (2)$$

where TOR_t is traffic accidents occurrence rate per 10^5 people, THR_t is injured rate per 10^5 people, H_t is number of injured people in traffic accidents, P_t is regional employed population, N_t is case number of regional traffic accidents, t is year. Data on regional employed population could be found in China Statistics Yearbook each year. Data on regional traffic accidents could be found in China Statistics Yearbook and China Work Safety Yearbook.

2.2 Method

We used regional traffic accidents and regional economic development data during 2000-2007 to build panel models. Three regression models are often used: mixed regression model, fixed effect model and random effect model [7]. To build a panel data model, we must test characteristics of panel data so as to find which kind of model is suitable to the data and improve validity of parameter estimate [8].

We used Eviews6.0 software to operate. Hausman test is usually used to test which kind of regression model should be made. Table 1 showed results of Hausman test. All of probabilities of Hausman statistics value were zero. This means that test results refused hypothesis "panel data could be made random effect models". Fix effect models should be built.

Table 1. Hausman test results of the panel data

Dependent variable	Statistics value	d.f.	Probability
LTNR	5.28	3	0.0520
LTHR	17.15	3	0.0007

note: If probability is zero, then reject random effect models.

We built fix effect regression model as following:

$$y_{it} = \delta_i + \lambda + \sum_{k=1}^{k} \beta_{ki} x_{kit} + u_{it} \tag{3}$$

Where y_{it} is LTNR and LTHR respectively. x_{kit} is regional economic development variances including LAG_i, LIR_i, $LTEP_i$, LHR_i, LOP_i and LMR_i.

$i = 1,2,3,4$. i referred 4 economic regions. $t = 1,2,...,8$, t referred time point. δ_i is intercept, λ is parameter of the model, β_{ki} is estimated parameter ; u_{it} is random error.

3 Results

We built individual fixed effect models, using industrial accidents variants including $LTNR_i$ and $LTHR_i$ as dependent variants, using regional economic development including LAG、LIR、LTEP、LHR、LOP、LMR as independent variants. Eviews6.0 is used to operate model. Results were shown in table 2. R^2 and adjusted R^2 were above 0.96, which means all of models had goodness of fit.

Fixed effect panel regression equation of regional traffic occurrence rate per 10^5 people and regional economic development is as following:

$$LTNR_i = \alpha_i + 9.67 - 2.16 \times LAG_i + 4.53 \times LIR_i - 0.09 \times LTEP_i - 1.37 \times LHR_i + 0.009 \times LOP_i + 0.004 \times LMR_i \tag{4}$$

where $i = 1,2,3,4$, $\alpha_1 = 1.59$, $\alpha_2 = -0.78$, $\alpha_3 = -0.61$, $\alpha_4 = -0.20$

Although traffic occurrence rate per 10^5 people in 4 regions had same trend during 2000-2007, difference among 4 regions is obvious, the East is much more than others. We compared absolute value of coefficients in above equation from big to small as following: LIR_i (4.53), LAG_i (2.16), LHR_i (1.37), $LTEP_i$ (0.09), LOP_i (0.009), LMR_i (0.004). All of economic development variants had different effect on regional death toll. Proportion of industry in regional economy, human resource and per capita gross domestic product were obvious influencing elements.

Equation 5 is fixed effect panel regression equation of regional fatality rate per 10^5 workers and regional economic development.

$$LTHR_i = \alpha_i - 13.63 + 0.25 \times LAG_i + 3.59 \times LIR_i + 0.11 \times LTEP_i - 0.58 \times LHR_i - 0.71 \times LOP_i + 0.05 \times LMR_i \tag{5}$$

Where, $i = 1,2,3,4$, $\alpha_1 = 1.63$, $\alpha_2 = -0.67$, $\alpha_3 = -0.27$, $\alpha_4 = -0.69$

Compared value of α_i, we can see obvious difference in injured rate per 10^5 people among 4 economic regions during 2000-2007, although they had same trend of variation.

According to absolute value of coefficient in above equation, we ranged variants as following: LIR_i (3.59), LOP_i (0.71), LHR_i (0.58), LAG_i (0.25), $LTEP_i$ (0.11), LMR_i (0.05). Regional industry proportion is the most obvious influencing elements.

Table 2. Panel regression results of regional traffic accidents & economic development

variables	$LTNR_i$ panel regression equation			$LTHR_i$ panel regression equation		
	β_{ki}	S.D	T-statistics	β_{ki}	S.D	T-statistics
C	9.67	14.12	0.68	-13.63	7.92	-1.72
LAG_i	-2.16	1.34	-1.61	0.25	0.73	0.34
LIR_i	4.53	2.55	1.78	3.59	1.33	2.69
$LTEP_i$	-0.09	0.27	-0.33	0.11	0.15	0.76
LHR_i	-1.37	2.15	-0.64	-0.58	1.12	-0.52
LOP_i	0.009	1.02	0.009	-0.71	0.56	-1.26
LMR_i	-0.004	0.08	-0.05	0.05	0.04	1.18
R^2	0.996		0.96		0.97	
adjusted R^2	0.994		0.93		0.95	
F-statistics	762.09		28.86		39.79	

4 Discussion of Results

Scatter diagram showed that regional traffic accidents risks had relativity with regional wealth. A region with high gross domestic product could be found high traffic accidents rate. Results of panel regression analysis on 4 regions during 2000-2007 showed that regional economic development could influence regional traffic accidents risks. Thereinto, gross domestic product per capita which could reflect wealth is one of economic elements effecting regional traffic accidents, but not the only one, nor obvious one. Regional economic structure (especially proportion of industry) and human resource were obvious elements effecting regional traffic accidents. Especially industrial proportion in regional economic structure is the most important element which increased regional traffic accidents during 2000-2007. Improvement of human resource would have benefit on decrease of regional traffic accidents.

5 Conclusions

In summary, the purpose of this study is to explore relativity between regional economic development and regional traffic accident risks. Findings were limited, possibly due to limited data, but still indicated that traffic accident risks could reflect regional economy, regional wealth increase is associated with decrease of traffic accidents rate. A higher income level is associated with higher traffic accidents levels. However, per capita gross domestic product reflecting regional wealth is not the only influencing element, different economic development element have various effects on traffic accident risks. Gaps in economic structure and human resource are the most obvious predictors of regional traffic accident risks. Industrial proportion in the East economy is above half. This could interpret the phenomena that the East has highest traffic accident risks in China. Along with adjustment of national economic structure encouraged by the Government since 2009, manufacturing and process industry in the

East have accelerated transfer speed from the East to the Midland and the West. The traffic accident risks would be forecast to rise, thus it is necessary to strengthen administration and control traffic accident risks in the Midland and the West.

Acknowledgment. This work is supported by the key project of Humanities and Social Science of Anhui education department (2011sk139zd), the university young teacher financial project of Anhui province (2007jqw062).

References

1. van Beeck, E.F., Borsboom, G.J.J., Mackenbach, J.P.: Economic development and traffic accident mortality in the industrialized world, 1962-1990. International Journal of Epidemiology 5, 42–46 (2000)
2. Gerdtham, U.-G., Ruhm, C.J.: Deaths rise in good economic times: Evidence from the OECD. Economics and Human Biology 4, 298–316 (2006)
3. Paulozzi, L.J., Ryan, G.W., Espitia-Hardeman, V.E., Xi, Y.: Economic development's effect on road transport-related mortality among different types of road users: A cross-sectional international study. Accident Analysis and Prevention 39, 606–617 (2007)
4. Lawa, T.H., Nolandb, R.B., Evansa, A.W.: Factors associated with the relationship between motorcycle deaths and economic growth. Accident Analysis and Prevention 41, 234–240 (2009)
5. Traynor, T.L.: Regional economic conditions and crash fatality rates – a cross-county analysis. Journal of Safety Research 39, 33–39 (2008)
6. He, X., Song, L., Nie, B.: Basic Features of Occupational Safety in China. China Safety Science Journal 1, 5–9 (2008)
7. Studenmund, A.H.: Using econometrics: a practical guide, 5th edn. China Machine Press, Beijing (2007)
8. Gao, T.: Methods and models of econometrics. Tinghua University Publishing House, Beijing (2008)

Research on the Exploration and Utilization of Contemporary Physical Information Resource

Peng Song[1], Jiong Luo[1], Yiding Gao[2], and Xiaozhu Yang[1]

[1] 2# Tiansheng Road, School of Physical Education, Southwest University, Beibei District, Chongqing, China 400715
[2] 2# Tiansheng Road, School of Psychology, Southwest University, Beibei District, Chongqing, China 400715

Abstract. As a sort of important resource, physical information is utilizing its great function in the field of physical. The more physical study depends on information updating, the more pressing physical information resource shows. Utilizing physical information resource fully is the fundament of physical information research. Therefore, this paper analyzed the basic characteristics of physical information resource and the way to unearth and utilize it. This paper aims at enhancing utilization of physical information resource and improving physical study.

Keywords: physical information resource, exploration utilization, search methods.

1 Introduction

With the rapid development and wide use of information technical, human stepped into information age. In information age, people produce and use information in large scale. Information has penetrated in every field and aspect of our daily life. Furthermore, it has become a key factor of developing economy, innovating technology, prospering culture. China is a developing country, a big power of physical education and research, with large number of scientific, academic information being produced per year. The information has great significance and value for workers of physical education and training, managers of government and corporation as well. At the same time, it is the bridge of international communication. However, the information grows in the form of explosion, and it will threaten existing and progress of human being. Thus, physical information resource study is very important, utilizing physical information resource in special.

2 The Connotation and Character of Physical Information Resource

2.1 The Connotation of Physical Information Resource

Information resource is a new concept derived from information and resource. It is a sort of information, even a section of information. Information quiet common, but not

M. Zhou (Ed.): ISAEBD 2011, Part III, CCIS 210, pp. 106–110, 2011.

all the information can be used. Only is the information managed, it is qualified to be resource. So that information resource can be defined as a gathering which was explored and managed by human. As for information resource, it is not only about information, but also relates with relevant factors of information activity. According to the definition of "contemporary Chinese dictionary", resource is the natural derivation of production and life. Therein, resource is necessary for normal operation of the whole society, the basic condition of each system. Combined with the concept of information and that of resource, we could define information resource as following: the first one is narrow definition. Physical information resource is physical document or physical data resource. Besides, it is the gather of different media and forms that relevant to physical, including words, audio, print, electronic information, data base and so forth. Another definition of physical information resource is the general designation of sorts of physical information resource, not only physical information itself, but also includes physical labors, equipment, skills and capital.

2.2 The Characteristics of Physical Information Resource

2.2.1 Physical Information Is Tremendous and Disorder

Physical information grows rapidly and disorder with a great number of useless information impeded users to utilize valuable information.

2.2.2 The Convenience and Share of Getting Physical Information

Internet information presents the form of dispersion, open and disorder. However, the typical hypertext linkage and powerful query strengthens the relation between information that enabled everyone could achieve information anywhere.

2.2.3 The Timeliness and Interactivity of Physical Information

The increasing speed and updating frequency fasts spreading speed and timeliness of information resource. As a result, high sensitivity of physical information resource requires us to collect, progress physical information resource in time.

2.2.4 Physical Information Resource Was Not Standard

Since physical information resource was not standard, the retrieval tools were not united; we may get different result by using different retrieval tool.

3 The Way to Obtain Physical Information Resource

Information resource, according to its carrier nature and application method, can be classified as follow: printing information resource, non-paper resource (electronic document, CD, full-text electronic database); virtual information resource. It is necessary for the development of physical industry to utilize physical information resource in every ways.

3.1 Utilizing Physical Information Resource by Periodical

Physical periodical is the main way of spreading latest physical technical information, benefits physical education, training, research and so forth. It is a pressing task to utilize and explore physical periodical information resource.

3.1.1 Concentrate and Process Physical Periodical Information Resource

Sifting from periodical information, dealing them into special topic index, bibliographic index, compilation of data. By analyzing physical information of physical periodical, we could work on it, present, sift and report it, even edit digest and organize title. We could extract essence; manage the document's comments, dynamic statement that relevant to physical study to reserve us, in order to provide us with data information and academic information accurately.

3.1.2 Workout the Keywords Catalog of Physical Periodical Thesis

Keywords, words or proper nouns, are chosen from a thesis to extend main meaning of this thesis. What they extend is the central content, basic scholar thoughts, extract of technical methods of this thesis. Keywords of physical thesis derive from physical workers' experience of long-term training and education. During the practice of technical innovation and knowledge innovation, several new theory, technology and new research findings will appear in their academic thesis, enlarging keywords constantly. Compared with other professional terms, this is a typical characteristic of academic keywords. According to name and scientific property of central physical periodical, we could register information, recording keywords of each thesis by sorts; with article title, journal title and issue number attached. Once keywords are inputted, articles that we need will be outputted immediately. It will satisfy physical worker's need for targeting information.

3.2 Unearth Physical Information Resource by Internet

With the rapid development of internet, it has become a main way of information communication and has been developed by leaps and bounds. The tendency gave birth to internet information resource. Internet information resource is the gather of all forms of information that contained in internet, including factors of information itself, carriers, ways of expressing, organization, ways of spreading and so forth. Internet database pioneered wild prospect for users to get information. It is not enough to search engine only for physical managers, trainers and teachers who expect accurate physical technical document that relevant to their research. There must be a specific, professional physical document database. At present, several document databases based on internet could be linked to the whole article. When users are searching this kind of database, they can find the clue of the document (including title, author, and publisher, abstract) by searching keywords, classification number. After making sure the suitable document, we could kick the linkage and scan the whole article. For example: "Chinese academic periodical website" (http;//www.cnki.net) sports features, master's and doctor's thesis; VIP Database of Chinese Journals, superstar full-text e-books library and so on. However, due to many factors of limitation, only a part of information could be found in these databases.

3.3 Unearth Physical Information by Grey Literature

Grey Literature is a sort of information that unpublicized, valuable and hard to get by usual way. What's more, Grey Literature is the document with complicated content, lager scale of information and high intelligence value.

Physical workers created a great deal of Grey Literature during their education, research and training. These documents are not only rich in number and specification, but also rich in its forms of production (printing, copying, hand-writing, describing, and photographing, duplicating). Getting understanding, supporting from leadership and having a close relationship, nice cooperation with Grey Literature holding work unit is the basic condition to utilize Grey Literature. We could unearth physical information from thesis that were written by physical workers; academic report and speech audio of specialist; material and thesis of academic conference; internal periodical of physical department; teaching reference of physical teacher; teaching outline, teaching plan, introduction of teaching experience, researching findings that published by physical college and research department. Besides, academic periodical, academic material and inside news are also Grey Literature. Many of them are unpublished with great potential.

3.4 Utilizing Potential Physical Information

The so called potential information resources refer to that information that didn't be discovered and publicized. Though in the past it in the obvious statement, yet it was ignored, abandoned, and deserted. The silent information and disappearing information formed the potential information. According to where the material exists the silent information can be made the information in book and in real material. The disappearing information includes often forgotten historic information and often losing information.

Taking advantage of the PE information can help us to find out language, character, data, audio, and video that comes from all kinds of document files, human and historical references and video cases. We can use many witnesses of historical information to find out the true information in order to make the potential information go further or recorded by documents. We also can receive special training for workmanship, skills, secret and other achievements which hide in brain. Teaching or using modern technology to store the information is a good way to protect the information.

The discovering of PE information is recreation. We could grasp its timeliness and the values of application according to the international and national situation. Beijing Olympic Game is the most fantastic party in history and it is also the milestone of China sports. The Beijing Olympic Game will push the development of China sports and make it into a new and prosperous era. The Sports information must be help a lot in Chinese sports career.

4 Conclusion and Suggestion

4.1 Conclusion

Sports journal aims at spreading and passing on the latest technological information of sports and acts as the main intelligence source of physical education, scientific research and practice. The utilization ratio of it should be further improved and the function is supposed to be brought into play to a larger extent. In addition, it is also necessary to update the professional knowledge of physical teachers, coaches and researchers on physics so as to enhance the teaching and researching qualities and apply to the developing needs of physics.

The physical information resources have been developing rapidly in our country; yet we should be aware that it still stays at the primary stage and the level is not advanced. The setting up of database lacks systematic organization and overall plan while the documentation of physics is for from being networked, unified and systematized. Consequently, the management of physical information resources need to be reinforced further.

The exploration of grey physical information resources requires not only encouragement and support from the leaders but also the cooperation of all parties concerned so that the collection of grey documentation could be standardized and systematized.

The exploration of the potential physical information consists of two parts: the silent information and the transient information. Compared with extrinsic information, the digging out of potential information is much more cumbersome and has the characteristic of being concealed, mixed and scattered.

4.2 Suggestion

The selection of the topic in physical information resources should be appropriate. As the scope of physics is increasingly extending, to gain an advantage in seeking a topic becomes more difficult. However, the selection of topic is the basis and must be attached importance to. The database establishment should be strengthened so that the current information resources may be digitalized and data based to support the promotion of physical information resources. Regarding the characteristics of being concealed, mixed and scattered, the researchers should select and sort out conscientiously. The exploration of physical information resources should be based on the changing situations both at home and abroad to keep its effectiveness and applied value.

References

1. Xiao, H.: Characteristics and use of network sports information resource. Journal of Hubei Normal University (Philosophy and Social Sciences) 5, 148–150 (2010)
2. Wu, X.: On the Basic Methods to Quickly Acquire and Use Information of Physical Education. Journal of Lishui Teachers College 3, 103–105 (2005)
3. Guo, J.: On utilization and integration of sports information resources. Journal of Wuhan Institute of Physical Education 9, 89–92 (2006)
4. Dong, H., Wu, X.: Research on the sports information resources and the methods of acquirement on internet. Neijiang Science 8, 20–21 (2008)

Dual Binary Labor Market Segmentation and the Wage Differentials in China

Guangrong Tong and Yanjun Yang

Economics and Management School, Wuhan University, Wuhan, Hubei, China
{tonggr2001,yangyanjun0221}@yahoo.com.cn

Abstract. The purpose of this article is to investigate the pattern of labor market segmentation and wage determination in China. Using the data from CHNS, we performed the analysis of variance to judge the significance of different variables which might lead to the wage differentials and found a multi-variation regression measurement model of labor market based on the Mincer model. The empirical results show that the pattern of labor market segmentation in China is dual binary labor market segmentation. In this labor market, though more educated workers have more advantage in wage distribution, significant wage differentials persist after controlling for individual attributes. Empirical analysis also provides evidence that the gender of the worker plays an important role in the wage determination mechanism in all the segmented labor markets.

Keywords: labor market, segmentation, wage differentials, CHNS.

1 Introduction

In recent year, just several years after lying off millions of factory workers, some areas in China are facing an increasingly acute labor shortage. Various domestic media reports put the labor supply gap at around a million people in Guangzhou and neighboring cities. For a country which still has significant surplus labor, the reportedly severe shortage of labor is rather baffling. Some researchers argue that China has now reached the Lewis turning point and China's economy is stepping out of the cheap labor era (Cai et al., 2007; Park et al., 2007; Wang, 2008)[1][2][3][4]. However, others argue that there is still evidence of widespread surplus labor in China (Kwan, 2009; Minami and Ma, 2009) [5] and the crucial reason leads to the coexistence of labor shortage and surplus labor is the segmentation of the labor market in China. In fact, the study of market segmentation is not a new theme in the literatures, several authors have done some research on this issue and proposed some useful conclusions. Cai et al (2007) argue that the hukou system is the institutional obstacles deterring labor mobility and population migration, which leads to the two coexisting crises [1]. Wu Zhongzhe (2007) believes that the urban labor market in China, in macro aspect, is manifested in binary form of in-system labor market and out-system labor market and there are also binary forms in both in-system labor market and out-system labor market respectively. So the labor market in China is in the state of dual binary form [6]. While Zhang Zhanxin (2004) argues that the

M. Zhou (Ed.): ISAEBD 2011, Part III, CCIS 210, pp. 111–117, 2011.

urban-rural segmentation and ownership segmentation are diminishing and the industry segmentation has become a new type of labor market segmentation since 1990s by using 2000 Census data, which implies a discrimination against certain group of worker to enter industries monopolized by the state [7].

Thus, it appears that different methodologies provide different pointers, and there is diverse data and evidence, resulting in conflicting conclusions. Our main concern in this paper is the pattern of labor market segmentation and the wage differentials between similar workers in different sectors in China. So the structure of our paper is as follows. Section 2 presents the methodology and several theoretical considerations. Section 3 discusses the data of CHNS, the main econometric results of the segmented labor market model and the alternative explanations for our findings. Section 4 is the conclusion.

2 Methodology

In the framework of SLM (segmented labor market) theory, the labor market consists of various sub-groups which have little crossover capability, which means: first, the labor market can be usefully thought of as being made up by several distinct segments with different rules for wage determination and employment policies; second, access to jobs in at least some sectors at some times is limited in the sense that more people want jobs than there are jobs offered [8]. Thus the market mechanisms in the labor market are seen as complemented or even replaced by a variety of other allocation mechanisms, the effects of which are to divide the labor market into separate, partial, segmented labor markets. A common example is dual labor market model.

There are several attributes common to many versions of labor market segmentation theory. The labor market can be usefully described as consisting of two major segments — primary and secondary. The primary sector consists of high-wage jobs with good working conditions, stable employment, and substantial returns to human capital variables such as education and experience; while the secondary sector consists of low-wage jobs with the opposite characteristics (Mincer, 1958, 1974) [9]. In order to identify the wage differentials between the workers in the segmented labor market, we propose a model as follow:

$$\log(w) = \alpha + \rho B + \mu \tag{1}$$

Where w is the average wage of the workers, B is the matrix of the important factors which affect the level of the wage. According to the labor market segmentation theory, the wage o f the workers depend on two aspects: the segment which workers in and the level of the human capital that the workers have. We assume that the function can be described as:

$$\log(w_i) = \alpha_0 + \theta_1 S_{i,1} + \theta_2 S_{i,2} +, \cdots, +\theta_k S_{i,k} + \beta_1 X_{i,1} +, \cdots, +\beta_j X_{i,j} + \mu_i \tag{2}$$

Where $S_{i,1}, S_{i,2} \cdots S_{i,k}$ are the dummy variables which identify the segment individual i works in, $X_{i,1}, \cdots, X_{i,j}$ typically include variables like the attributions of the workers themselves, which reflect the level of human capital of workers. The most widely used specification of empirical earnings equations and the point of departure for our analysis is the Mincer model:

$$\ln[Y(s,x)] = \alpha + \rho_s s + \beta_0 x + \beta_1 x^2 + \xi \quad (3)$$

Where $Y(s,x)$ is the wage or earnings at schooling level s and work experience x, ρ_s is the "rate of return to schooling" (assumed to be the same for all schooling levels) and ε is a mean zero residual. This regression model is motivated by two conceptually different frameworks used by Mincer (1958, 1974) [9][10][11]. Thus, we estimate the benchmark equation as follow:

$$\ln(w_i) = \alpha_0 + \theta_1 S_{i,1} + \theta_2 S_{i,2} +, \cdots, +\theta_k S_{i,k} + \beta_0 s_i + \beta_1 x_i + \beta_2 x_i^{\ 2} + \mu_i \quad (4)$$

Where β_0 is the "rate of return to schooling" and u_i is a random error term. The crucial identifying assumption is that w_i is uncorrelated with $S_{i,1}, S_{i,2} \cdots S_{i,k}$ .That is, any variable (observable or unobservable) which is correlated with earnings cannot be various with the change of the segments.

3 Empirical Analysis

3.1 The Data

The data used in this paper come from the China Health and Nutrition Survey (CHNS), an ongoing open cohort, was designed to examine the effects of the health, nutrition, and family planning policies and programs implemented by national and local governments and to see how the social and economic transformation of Chinese society is affecting the health and nutritional status of its population. The survey took place over a 3-day period using a multistage, random cluster process to draw a sample of about 4400 households with a total of 26,000 individuals in nine provinces that vary substantially in geography, economic development, public resources, and health indicators. In this paper, we focus on the pattern of the labor market segmentation, so we removed the samples of the unemployed, leaving 1954 samples of working-age employees with complete information.

3.2 Analysis of Variance

The primary and secondary segments are differentiated mainly by stability characteristics. The wages of primary jobs are relatively high and skills are often acquired on the job, while in secondary segmentation, wages are low and are mainly filled by migrant, unskilled workers and women. So we choose several variables to estimate different versions of model to analysis the pattern of labor market segmentation in China as follows:

Table 1. The variables of the model

Variables		Meaning
Dependent	wage	The individual wage earnings of the previous year
Independent	education	Education level
	experience	The work experience
	gender	The gender of the employees
	hukou	The household registration of the employees
	unit	The type of work unit
	area	The province in which the workers are
	occupation	The type of work occupation

The dependent variable (wage) only includes the average monthly individual wage earnings of the previous year. For the education indicator, we broadly classified it into 5 categories[1]. For the experience indicator, we evaluate it to 5 different categories[2]. For the hukou indicator, we classified it into urban and rural according to the household registration of the employees and in the survey, there are 12 types of occupations[3] and 8 types of units[4]. In order to judge the significance of the variables, we perform analysis of variance:

Table 2. The Results of Analysis of Variance

Varibles	F	Sig	Cross-term
gender	8.995	0.003	no
hukou	1.466	0.226	no
occupation	22.048	0.000	no
unit	0.013	0.908	no
area	7.004	0.008	no

[1] Education level includes 5 categories: graduated from primary school, lower middle school degree, upper middle school degree, technical or vocational degree ,university or college degree or higher.

[2] Experience indicator includes 5 categories: 0-9year, 10-19 year, 20-29 year, 30-39 year and 40-49year.

[3] Occupations included senior professional/technical worker (doctor, professor, lawyer, architect, engineer),junior professional/technical worker (midwife, nurse, teacher, editor, photographer), administrator/executive/manager (working proprietor, government official, section chief, department or bureau director, administrative cadre, village leader), office staff (secretary, office helper), farmer, fisherman, hunter, skilled worker (foreman, group leader, craftsman), non-skilled worker (ordinary laborer, logger), army officer, police officer, ordinary soldier, policeman, driver, service worker (housekeeper, cook, waiter, doorkeeper, hairdresser, counter salesperson, launderer, child care worker) , athlete, actor, musician.

[4] Units included government department, state service/ institution, state-owned enterprises, small collective enterprise (such as township-owned), large collective enterprise (such as owned by county, city, province), family contract farming, private, individual enterprise and three-capital enterprise (owned by foreigners, overseas Chinese and joint venture).

According to the results show in table 1, we can get the conclusion that, besides education and work experience, the area, occupation and gender are the most important factors which affect the level of the wage. That means the wage of different workers would differ not only in their different levels of schooling and work experience, but in their locations, occupation and gender as well. In this case, we will add the variables mentioned above into the Mincer model to estimate the model of pattern of the labor market segmentation in China.

3.3 Econometric Results and Discussion

To estimate the model of pattern of the labor market segmentation in China, we deal with the form of the variables at first and estimate the benchmark function as follow:

$$\log(wage_i) = \theta_0 + \theta_1 educ_i + \theta_2 \exp e_i + \theta_3 \exp e^2 + \theta_4 area_i + \theta_5 occup_i + \theta_6 gender_i + \mu_i \quad (5)$$

Where $educ_i$ denotes years of schooling, $expe_i$ stands for the work experience, which equals the years subtracting education plus 7 from age [12], area is the dummy variable of the work location (1 for eastern region and 0 for others), $occup_i$ is the dummy variable of the type of work occupation (1 for formal employment and 0 for informal employment) and gender is the dummy variable of the gender of the employees (1 for male and 0 for female). The coefficient of these variables can tell us whether the factors contribute to the wage differentials between workers.

The results show in table 3 suggest that, for the model of labor market segmentation in China, the significant wage differentials persist after controlling for individual

Table 3. The results of regression of lnwage

Variables	Model 1	Model 2	Model 3	Model 4	Model 5
constant	5.719***	5.665***	5.825***	5.625***	5.666***
	(72.349)	(71.142)	(72.719)	(71.652)	(70.504)
educ	0.075***	0.075***	0.058***	0.073***	0.059***
	(14.684)	(14.787)	(10.180)	(14.663)	(10.499)
expe	0.021***	0.020***	0.018***	0.021***	0.017***
	(4.743)	(4.472)	(4.140)	(4.893)	(4.042)
$expe^2$	-0.001**	0.000**	0.000**	0.000**	0.000**
	(-2.979)	(-2.724)	(-2.701)	(-3.615)	(-3.070)
area		0.116***			0.123***
		(4.387)			(4.785)
occup			0.191***		0.172***
			(6.262)		(5.740)
gender				0.227***	0.220***
				(8.361)	(8.183)
Adjusted R^2	0.327	0.510	0.453	0.471	0.603

Note: t-Statistic values are in parentheses.* means the coefficient is significant at the 10% level, ** means the coefficient is significant at the 5% level and *** means the coefficient is significant at the 1% level.

attributes and the pattern of segmentation of labor market in China is a dual binary labor market segmentation. Firstly, we examine the impact of the level of human capital on earnings. As shown in model 1 of table 3, applying the Mincer function in 2006 data, we obtain the positive coefficient of education and work experience, which implies that more educated workers have more advantage in wage distribution. When we control for other individual characteristics such as gender, occupation and area in model 2 to 5, the values of education and work experience return rates become lower, which means the significant wage differentials persist after controlling for individual attributes. Secondly, the variables, such as area, occupation and gender, in the model are all significant. This implies the pattern of segmentation of labor market in China is a dual binary labor market segmentation which has two meanings: on the one hand, there is region segmentation, the wage of the workers in eastern region is higher than the central region, and on another hand, there is occupation segmentation within different regions, the average income of the formal employees is higher than the informal. In addition, there is gender discrimination in the labor markets, under the same conditions of education and work experience, the average wage of the female is less than male workers.

4 Conclusion

In this paper we perform analysis of variance to judge the significance of the factors and found a multi-variation regression measurement model of labor market by using the data from CHNS to describe the pattern of the labor market segmentation in China. The empirical analysis results indicate:

First, though more educated workers have more advantage in wage distribution in China's labor market, the significant wage differentials persist after controlling for individual attributes. The values of education and work experience return rates become lower when we take individual characteristics, such as the area, occupation and gender, into account.

Second, the pattern of segmentation of labor market in China is a dual binary labor market segmentation, which has two meanings: on the one hand, there is region segmentation, the wage of the workers in eastern region is higher than the central region, and on another hand, there is occupation segmentation within different regions, the average income of the formal employees is higher than the informal.

In addition, there is gender discrimination in labor market, under the same condition of the education and work experience, the average wage of the female is less than male workers. The gender of the worker plays an important role in the wage determination mechanism in all the segmented labor markets.

References

1. Cai, F., Du, Y., Zhao, C.: Regional labour market integration since China's WTO entry: Evidence from household-level data, pp. 133–150. Asia Pacific Press (2007)
2. Park, Cai, F., Du, Y.: Can China meet her employment challenges. In: Conference Paper, vol. 11. Stanford University, Stanford (2007)

3. Cai, F., Wang, M.: A counterfactual of unlimited surplus labor in rural China. China and the World Economy 1, 51–65 (2008)
4. Wang, D.: Lewisian turning point: Chinese experience. Reports on Chinese Population and Growth No. 9: Linking up Lewis and Kuznets Turning Points (2008) (in Chinese)
5. Kwan, F.: Agricultural labor and the incidence of surplus labor: Experience from China during reform. Journal of Chinese Economic and Business Studies 7, 341–361 (2009)
6. Wu, Z.: Dual Binary Form:The Urban Labor Market in Unit System Transformation. Journal Of Social Sciences 4, 47–57 (2007) (in Chinese)
7. Zhang, Z.: Sectoral Segmentation of Labor Markets and the Labor Mobility. Population Science Of China 2, 45–52 (2004) (in Chinese)
8. Dickens, W.T., Lang, K.: The Reemergence of Segmented Labor Market Theory. The American Economic Review 78(2), 129–134 (1988)
9. Mincer, J.: Investment in human capital and personal income distribution. Journal of Political Economy 66, 281–302 (1958)
10. Mincer, J.: Schooling, Experience and Earnings. Columbia University Press for National Bureau of Economic Research, New York (1974)
11. Mincer, J., Polachek, S.: Family investment in human capital: Earnings of women. Journal of Political Economy 108, S76–S108 (1974)
12. Ning, G.: Can educational expansion improve income inequality? Economic Systems 34, 397–412 (2010)

Study on the Construction of Three-Dimensional Enterprise Education and Training System in Henan Province

Ying Chang

Henan Institute of Engineering, Zhengzhou Henan Province, P.R. China, 450007

Abstract. By adopting the questionnaire method and comparative analysis, we issued two kind of questionnaires to the entrepreneurial group and the college students and collected valilid questionnaires 228 and 210 respectively. After analyzing all the questionnaires statistically, we find some existing problems in the enterprise education and training environment in Henan province. According to the successful experience and lesson from both at home and abroad, this paper puts forward some suggestions on how to optimize the enterprise education and training environment in Henan province so as to optimize Henan entrepreneurial environment. The conclusion and innovation of this paper is that it puts forward the idea of constructing three-dimensional enterprise education and training system in Henan Province.

Keywords: Three-dimensional, Enterprise, Education and Training System.

1 Introduction

The conception of enterprise education was put forward and discussed first in an international proseminar called Faced 21st Century held by UNESCO in Beijing in Nov, 1989. And in 1991, the Office of the Asia-Pacific region of UNESCO made a Tokyo conference report and pointed out that enterprise education, in a broad sense, means to develop the initiative personality, which is very important for the salariat because the employers are paying increasingly attention to their employees' initiative, spirits of adventure, entrepreneurial abilities, abilities of working independently as well as their technological capabilities, social abilities and administrative abilities. Therefore, UNESCO requires that universities and colleges should make both entrepreneurial abilities and entrepreneurial spirits be the basic goals of higher education, which is as important as academic research and vocational education. In a narrow sense, the purpose of enterprise education is to develop the students' entrepreneurial consciousness, entrepreneurial qualities and entrepreneurial abilities so as to improve the comprehensive qualities of students and enhance the creative consciousness and entrepreneurial abilities of the students to meet the demand of *the knowledge economy age* for the innovative spirits and innovative abilities of the university and college Students.

M. Zhou (Ed.): ISAEBD 2011, Part III, CCIS 210, pp. 118–124, 2011.

2 Experience and Lesson from Home and Abroad

The enterprise activity is a symbol of regional economic activity, the success of which definitely dependeds on the enterprise environment of this region. And the most important environmental factor is the entrepreneurial education and training environment. At present, the countries and regions economically developed have plentiful experience in this aspect

2.1 International Experience

2.1.1 Enterprise Education System Starting from the Primary Period

Entrepreneurial consciousness should be developed from childhood. In the western developed countries, enterprise education is always conducted at the compulsory education stage. Some countries such as Japan and France have been trying to construct entrepreneurial education systems ranging from youth to manhood. By the end of the 20th century, many countries have made out the covering entrepreneurial education systems. For instance, the U.S. government set up a national fund for teaching entrepreneurs to promote the development of enterprise education. At present, the enterprise education in the U.S. has become a complete system including the normal education of primary school, secondary school, college or university and postgraduate. In January, 1998 the U.S. government carried out its Financial Anti-illiteracy Programme of 2001, by which the middle-school students learned the knowledges concerning finance, investment, marketing and business etc.

In 1999, Germany put forward a slogan requiring that the universities should become a melting pot for the entrepreneurs. Meanwhile, the Germany government aimed that within 10 years, there must be 20%-30% of the graduates who could start their own business each year. In British, courses in business administration were offered by middle schools and in order to promote the economic development, in 2005 the British government started the project to help the middle school students to do business, which required that all the students ranging from 12 to 18 take part in 2-week business training course. While in France, the entreprise education would be strengthened at the junior middle school.

Japan decided to carry out its enterprise education in elementary education in 1998 and in 1996 India put farward the conception of self-employment education to encourage the graduates to make a living by themselves making them not only be the applicants but also be the creators for the job opportunities. To some extent, the enterprise education in Japan has a high degree of universality, which has the characteristics of broad contents and various forms. By making full use of its characteristics, the schools are trying their best to create a positive entrepreneurial environment. With the motive of self-challenging and advanced technology transfer mechanism, the probability of success will be much higher in Japan.

2.1.2 Social Institution's Promotion in the Specialization and Universalness of Enterprise Education

Social institution should play an important and supplementary role in promoting enterprise education and set up classified courses according to different youth.

Junior Achievement, which holds the view that the entrepreneurial spirit should be developed from childhood, has set up 4 courses to teach the students some basic business concepts as well as covering knowledges. For the middle school students, JA set up the financing financial literacy to develop the students' company project which could provide the the students with internship opportunities. As for the college students, JA is always preparing the students to develop successful financial management habits, empowering them to explore the potential of becoming an entrepreneur, and providing them the skills necessary to succeed in a global economy. To some extent, JA is so influential in the U.S. that one fifth of CEOs hiring more than 50 employees are its members. Additionally, about one- quarter of entrepreneurs have taken part in the activities organized by JA. And among the senior high school students having attended courses of JA, there is about 85% students who are planning to found their own enterprises.

Making Cents International has been engaged in improving the professional abilities of enterprising supportive organizations from the world. According to different people and industries, it designed various levels of enterprise educational courses. Furthermore, according to some particular industries, it designed the courses such as Young Rural Entrepreneurs, Agricultural Enterprise and so on. The interdisciplinary courses include Business Simulation, Special Skill Training. It should be noticed that all the courses are designed according to the students of different ages, making it possible to teach students some relative knowledges about business and entrepreneurial spirits.

2.1.3 Duties Education

JA suggests that enterprise education should be carried out throughout the whole educational process. Therefore, apart from teaching business knowledges, the enterprise education should pay more attention to the education of students' character building so as to bring up more entrepreneurs with great sense of duties.

JA encourages successful entrepreneurs to participate in enterprise education and teach the students in the capacity as volunteers. At present, JA has 7,000 board members, who are all business leaders. And all of them are activitily calling for social duties by their own actions. There are 300,000 volunteers from enterprises and colleges every year who teach more than 9,000,000 students the courses of JA. And the students are respectively from primary schools, middle schools as well as colleges or universities.

2.2 State of Domestic Enterprise Education

With close cooperation between *International Labor Organization (ILO)* and t*he Ministry of Labor and Social Security (MOLSS)*, *Start Your Business (SYB)* has been introduced to China which can greatly support the entrepreneurs from minor enterprises. Although governments of all levels and the other relevant departments have done a lot of work, there are some existing problems.

2.2.1 Absence of Enterprise Education before Entering into Universities

The mainly existing problem of enterprise education in China is that we have laid more emphasis on the college students than that of the students of compulsory education stage. And exam-oriented education is still the main feature of the education in China.

2.2.2 Training Only for Special Groups

In recent years, China government and governments of all levels have issued a series of preferential policies on skill training for the returned migrant workers and laid-off workers. The people who attend the covering enterprise training organized by personnel departments and other training organizations can enjoy the preferential policies like tuition subsidies. But sometimes such kind of training can not result in desired result because of lack of teachers and incomplete teaching contents.

3 Current Situation of the Enterprise Education in Henan Province

The enterprise education in Henan province is mainly financed by the government and organized by the employment departments. By introducing the international courses like SYB and KAB, some universities have set up courses concerning entrepreneurial management. It is estimated that in Henan province there are 300,000 students attending entrepreneurial courses every year.

At present, the enterprise training is mainly for college students, overseas returnees, technicians, migrant worker, laid-off workers etc., who can enjoy some preferential policicies. Because the factor of different ages has not been taken into consideration, to some extent the enterprise training can not meet the requirements of all ages.

3.1 Collecting Questionnaires from the Entrepreneurs in Henan Province

According to 228 valilid questionnaires, the evaluation of service in the respects of enterprise training is shown below.

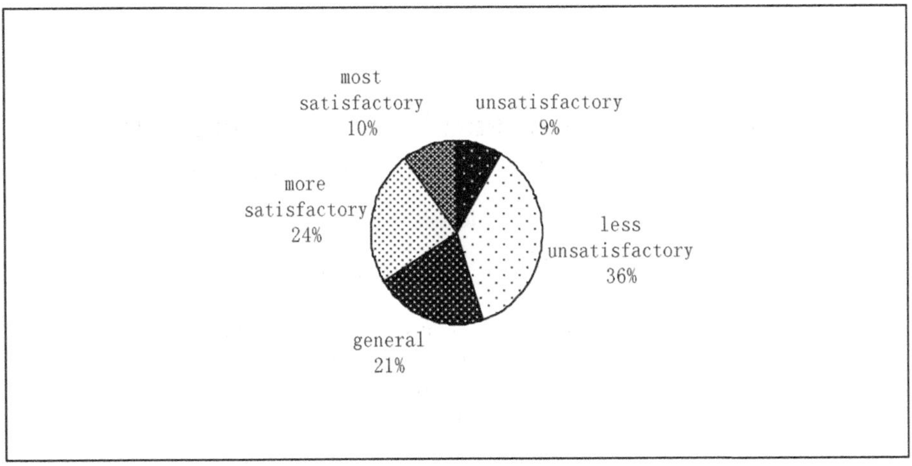

From the above diagram, we know that Henan province has made great efforts to provide the students with enterprise training services which have been recognized by 55% entrepreneurs. Since there are still 45% entrepreneurs who are not satisfied with the service, it is necessary for the government to provide more comprehensive, systematical and professional enterprise training.

3.2 Collecting Questionnaires about Entrepreneurial Environment in Henan Province

The questionnaires about entrepreneurial environment was issued by qq/email or through face-to-face talk with the result that 210 valid questionnaires were collected. The evaluation of enterprise training made by college students is shown below, and the full mark of each item is 5 points.

Contents	Marks
Enterprise Knowledges	3.052
Degree of Developing Enterprise Practical Activities	2.743
Entreprise Education Courses	2.581
Business and Administration Skills	2.443

From the above diagram, we can see that the marks graded by college students are not satisfactory. Therefore, the government, colleges and universities and enterprises should pay more attention to the improvement of entrepreneurial environment and it is essential for them to provide more entrepreneurial practising opportunities, set up enterprise training courses and provide more professional training on business and administration skills.

4 Constructing Three-Dimensional Enterprise Education Training System in Henan Province

4.1 Three-Dimensional Enterprise Education Training System

4.1.1 The Universal Enterprise Education

It should be noted that the enterprise education should not only be for the college students and laid-off workers etc. but also be for the entire people. Anyone suitable for business should be encouraged, supported and be well trained.

And the covering organizations should develop practical education and training system according to the characteristics of different people, which can include curriculum provision, writing training materials, option of training methods, training of teachers and training schedules etc.

4.1.2 The Whole-Process Enterprise Education

During the period of selecting projects, we should teach the trainees how to select suitable projects and help them analyze the possibilities of the covering projects scientifically. Meanwhile, it is advisable for us to put forward some advice to further perfect the projects so as to avoid unnessary failures resulting from wrongly selected projects.

In the early stage, the entrepreneurs should know how to effectively manage their own companies. Therefore, we should teach them some specific management skills according to specific situations in order to help them establish perfect management mode.

During the developing period, with the increase in profits, expansion of business scale, the entrepreneurs should carry out the standardized administration in its business. Therefore, we should pay more attention to the entrepreneurs' transformation of thinking mode. It is especially important to help them master scientific, standardized management method.

While in the mature period, the external environment will change greatly. Owing to the keen competition, the the entrepreneurs should take part in the training about second entrepreneurial spirits to ensure their sprits of continuous innovation.

4.1.3 The Enterprise Education for All Ages

Enterprise education should start from primary school and the guidance of entrepreneurial consciousness and sprits should be notices. For the middle school students, we should lay the emphasis on the education of social duties and help them to know the knowledges about society and business activities. And it will be useful for them to take one or two weeks to take part in some business activities. As for the college students, it is suggested that we should take effective measures to support them by accelerating enterprise training and providing practising opportunities. If it is possible, we should try our best to support the mature projects. In addition, we can help the graduates analyze and select the entrepreneurial projects and keep them informed all the latest information about entrepreneurial environment.

4.2 Mutual Cooperation

In order to make sure the establishment of the enterprise education and training system, the covering organizations should closely cooperate with each other.

4.2.1 The governments of all levels shuld work out more favourable policies and provide services of high quality.

4.2.2 The elementary and middle schools should build entrepreneurial consciousness and develop the students' enterprising spirits.

4.2.3 The colleges and universities should provide the students with systematical enterprising skills training and more practising opportunities.

4.2.4 The employment departments should provide the entrepreneurial service platform for the people who have entrepreneurial willingness and projects.

4.2.5 The function of Youth League Committees of all levels is to encourage more young people to enterprise and try their best to provide the communication and collaboration platform for the young entrepreneurs and young people.

4.2.6 The Women's Federation can help the female enterprising group accordingly.

4.2.7 The relative associations can provide some useful information and help the entrepreneurs to find and establish friendly relationship.

4.2.8 The training organizations should develop the covering enterprising training projects according to the specific situation and provide suitable training courses and professional guidence for the people who have different requirements.

5 Conclusion

Enterprise education is playing an important role in the development of our social economy and the government should implement strong supportive policy measures to ensure the success of the enterprising training projects.

References

1. Robertson, M., Collins, A., Medeira, N., et al.: Barriers to Start-up and Their Effect on Aspirant Entrepreneurs. Education and Training 45(6), 308–316 (2003)
2. Stevenson, H., Gumpert, D.: The Heart of Entrepreneurship. Harfard Business Review 63(2), 85–94 (1985)

Analysis on Legal Obstacles of Overseas M&A of Railway Enterprises against the High-Speed Railway Background

Xiang Zheng

Associate Professor of Department of Law, School of Humanities and Social Sciences of Beijing Jiaotong University Beijing, China, 100044
xzheng@bjtu.edu.cn

Abstract. The purpose of this article is to analyze legal obstacles of overseas M&A of Chinese railway enterprises and propose corresponding legal countermeasures. This article analyzes the motive to strengthen M&A of Chinese railway enterprises on the high-speed railway background, which have given rise to the increase of legal obstacles in overseas M&A. From the perspective of institutions, domestic legal obstacles with respect to national security review, anti-monopoly investigation, labor laws and IPR laws. The conclusion is that China should formulate overseas investment insurance laws to reduce risk in overseas M&A, improve government regulation efficiency, develop supporting policies for strategic industries considering the strategic position of railway output and strengthen international cooperation to protect IPR of railway enterprises.

Keywords: high-speed railway, Overseas M & A, legal obstacles, railway enterprises.

1 Introduction

Driven by industry globalization, while markets are integrating and foreign capitals are swarming into China, Chinese enterprises also actively investing abroad. The net outward investment has entered positive increase but remains a negative value. High-speed railway is a significant sign of the worldwide transport revolution. As the most effective approach to transport a large amount of passengers on a big channel quickly, high-speed railway has become a common development trend of railway throughout the world. On such a background, Chinese railway enterprises are gradually expanding overseas investment, but they also encounter some obstacles in this process. The purpose of this study is to analyze legal obstacles of overseas M&A of Chinese railway enterprises on the background of rapid development of high-speed railways and propose corresponding legal countermeasures on this basis.

2 The Development of High-Speed Railway Stimulates Overseas M&A by Railway Enterprises

High-speed railway is an international and epochal concept and a passenger transport vehicle adopted by a country according to its area, population distribution, industrial

M. Zhou (Ed.): ISAEBD 2011, Part III, CCIS 210, pp. 125–131, 2011.

and commercial layout, economic and technical strength as well as actual need. It is a complicated system engineering integrating most advanced railway technologies, advanced operation and management approaches, marketing and capital funding and has a highly efficient operation system. It involves technologies and management in many aspects such as infrastructure construction, locomotive configuration and railway operation rules. Characterized by advantages such as small land occupation, large transport capacity, little energy consumption and good comfort, high-speed railway has great significance for sustainable development of environment and creates excellent social and economic benefit. Meanwhile, economic globalization and the international situation that advocates low carbon economy also provide opportunity and room for development of high-speed railway[1].

China has become the country with most complete high-speed railway system technologies, strongest integration capacity, highest moving speed and largest scale under construction in the world[2]. The strong technical advantages of high-speed railway are mainly exhibited in following aspects: (1) large scale speed acceleration is possible on existing railway, which can accommodate motor train unit moving at 200-250 kmh. (2) China has the strongest capability to build extra-long high-speed railway network. The completed high-speed railways such as Wuhan-Guangzhou high-speed railway not only come top in the world in terms of one-time construction mileage but also operating speed for commercial use. The Beijing-Shanghai high-speed railway to be completed in 2011 is the longest high-speed railway built in one time throughout the world. On December 3rd 2010. (3) China's bridge construction level also comes top in the world. (4) China has more complicated geographic, geologic and climate conditions than Japan and Europe, and has world leading customization capacity for different environment. (5) China's high-speed railway also has advantage in price. The price of China-made EMU train is 1/2 to 1/3 that of its foreign counterpart and China also enjoys price advantage in labor and raw materials[3].

Considering the development trend of railway throughout the world, development of high-speed railway has become a consensus. Many countries and regions are perfecting their high-speed railway network at 300 km/h operating speed, including Japan's Shinkansen, France's TGV, Eurostar of UK, France and Belgium, Germany's ICE, Spain's AVE and South Korea's KTX. EU plans to build a high-speed railway network covering the whole Europe in 2020 consisting of 10,000km newly constructed high-speed rail lines and 15,000km reconstructed lines. the US government also announced its plan to build a nationwide high-speed railway network[4]. the popularization of high-speed railway technologies often relies on M&A of enterprises. For example, Red Nacional de Ferrocarriles Españoles (Renfe) signed a contract with Alstom to purchase high-speed train in 1998, and the latter bought shares of three Spanish companies to establish a new international group in which Alstom holds 55% share and three Spanish companies hold 15% share respectively. The three Spanish companies underwent modernized transformation and maintained their features of production and scope of products, becoming a locomotive production base of Alstom in Spain[5].

As a capital organization, any railway enterprise will seek maximum growth of capital, which is the major motive for M&A and complemented with the external pressure of market competition. The development of high-speed railway in China boosts the core competitiveness needed in internationalization of railway enterprises and promotes the growth of overseas investment of Chinese railway enterprises.

Through overseas M&A, railway enterprises could copy its core competitiveness and extend it in the international market. On December 7th 2010, GE signed a cooperation agreement with China South Locomotive and Rolling Stock Corporation to setup a joint venture in the US to promote China's high-speed railway technologies and rail transit technologies in the US market. The joint venture will manufacture high-speed trains locally in the US, which will run on US high-speed railway. China has reached an initial agreement with the California state government and GE to provide technologies, equipment, engineering and technical staff and part of capital for high-speed railway construction in California. Besides, the Ministry of Railways has initiated strategic cooperation with Industrial and Commercial Bank of China (ICBC) on implementation of high-speed railway technologies and financial capital. In January 2010, both sides signed Implementation of the railway "going out" strategic cooperation agreement. According to the agreement, the Ministry of Railways and ICBC will plan domestic resources with respect to technology, management, talent, capital and construction team in an all-round way under the direction of state policies, take part in international market competition, take strategic investment and financial service as an opportunity to carry out in-depth strategic cooperation mainly in supporting relevant industries of railway in China to go out and develop international market. Both sides will make joint efforts to popularize the mature "railway plus finance" cooperation model throughout the world and form a mutual benefit and win-win situation.

3 Legal Obstacles of Overseas M&A of Chinese Railway Enterprises

While adopting the "going out" strategy for the development of high-speed railway, we should recognize that overseas M&A of Chinese enterprises in recent years are no so optimistic. Obstacles in M&A are from many aspects, mainly including (1) political situation, (2) natural disaster, (3) religious belief, (4) cultural custom, (5) intellectual property right(IPR), (6) labor and employment, (7) other factors.[6] Chinese enterprises, especially state-owned enterprises, have had some failure cases in overseas M&A. Refer to Table 1 [7]for details.

Overseas M&A of Chinese enterprises are in the scope of regulation of international investment law, and its source of law includes source of international law and source of domestic law. The former is mainly manifested in international treaties and international practices, e.g. TRIMS agreement of WTO, Convention Establishing the Multilateral Investment Guarantee Agency, Convention on Settlement of Investment Disputes between States and Nationals of Other States, etc., while the latter includes laws of the investing country and the host country. The investing country provides protection for overseas M&A of its enterprises through diplomatic protection and overseas investment insurance system, strengthens macro control on capital and technology outflow by developing guidelines for overseas M&A of its enterprises and exerts impact on overseas M&A of its enterprises through tax laws and customs systems.

Table 1. Overseas M&A failure cases of Chinese enterprises in recent years

Year of acquisition	*Acquiring company*	*Target company*	*Country of the target company*	*Cause of failure*
2002-2003	TCL	Schneider / Thomson	Germany / France	Debt burden and law (conflict with labor unit)
2005	China National Offshore Oil Corporation	Unocal	US	Political interference
2006	China International Marine Containers	Burg Industries	Netherlands	EU antitrust investigation
2007	Huawei	3Com	US	National security investigation (political influences)
2009	Aluminum Corp. of China	Rio Tinto	Australia	Shareholders of Rio Tinto rejected capital injection of Aluminum Corp. (political influences)

Measures to regulate acquisition of local enterprises by foreign capital include limiting the scope of foreign investment, restricting the ratio of foreign capital shares, examination and approval of foreign investment projects, limiting foreign capital and its profit transfer method. From the perspective of law, legal obstacles in overseas M&A of railway enterprises mainly include following:

3.1 National Security Review System for Foreign Capital M&A

National security review system for foreign capital M&A means a legal system of a country to examine foreign capital M&A that may threatens its national security and take restrictive measures to eliminate national security threats. National defense security and technological security are the major factors to be considered in traditional national security review. The system has clear definition of review standard, market access and review procedures of foreign capital M&A and guarantee protection for domestic industries and key resources. Take the US for example, In 1992, the Congress passed Section 837(a) of the National Defense Authorization Act for Fiscal Year 1993 (P.L. 102-484), which amended Exon-Florio Amendment and added two situations that requiring review: the acquiring party is controlled by a foreign government or represents a foreign government, and the acquisition may cause the inter-state trader to be controlled and influence the national security of US. It is clear the new regulations are intended to prevent acquisition of primary enterprises or sensitive enterprises by any foreign enterprise with foreign background, and setup barriers for enterprises controlled or participated by the state, which is the situation in china, in acquisition of US enterprises[8]. Chinese railway enterprises are basically state-owned enterprises and often subject to special review by European and American developed countries in overseas M&A because of their public ownership and their ordinary commercial acts might be deemed as government act, which leads to unfair treatment.

3.2 Anti-trust Review System

In recent years, countries throughout the world have raised threshold of market access of overseas M&A through antitrust review system. Some barriers are substantive rules, while others are procedural rules. For example, the investigation process for antitrust in most countries includes initial investigation and detailed investigation. The former needs 30 days while the latter needs 36 months,which increases the unpredictability of acquisition risk. Since multi-party and multi-level regulation may exist in ant-trust review, so the acquiring enterprise may be investigated for anticompetitive effects by several authorities at the same time. China's advantage in high-speed railway is also likely to be judged as market monopoly position.

3.3 Labor Law

The success of overseas M&A depends on the integration process after the M&A. Legal disputes caused by employee affairs between the acquiring company and the acquisition target is a sensitive problem in overseas M&A[9]. Due to huge difference in cultural concept, market system and labor law between China and western countries, Chinese enterprise often cannot adapt to new rules of the international market. As a complicated system engineering, high-speed railway has higher requirement for staff and larger management pressure comparing with traditional railway transport. Proper coordination between local labor legal system and high-speed railway labor demand will directly determine the performance of M&A of railway enterprises.

3.4 Intellectual Property Right Legal System

Some other legal obstacles also exist in overseas M&A, e.g. intellectual property right(IPR) system. For example, the assertion that China's high-speed railway involves plagiarism and infringement is spread in the international high-speed railway market[10]. Actually, China borrowed some technologies from Japan, France and Germany when developing the high-speed railway and had an assimilation and digestion process, which should not be claimed infringement. Many innovation achievements are modified based on existing technologies and even have fundamental improvement.

3.5 Domestic Legal System

The Chinese government has formulated a series of policies for overseas investment management, such as Provisions on The Examination and Approval of Investment to Run Enterprises Abroad, Obstacle Report Rules on the Investment to Different Countries, and Catalogue of Countries and Industries for Guiding Investment Overseas, which has initially formed a legal system for overseas M&A. However, China still lacks a perfect overseas investment legal guarantee system for its enterprises, and cross-border M&A often involves various risks such as operation risk and transaction risk, which leads to considerable uncertainty. Moreover, due to low government regulation efficiency, Chinese enterprises have to pass through a series of complicated and inefficient approval procedures for cross-border investment, which influences the certainty of transaction.

4 Suggestions to Perfect Legal System of Overseas M&A of Railway Enterprises

4.1 Formulate Overseas Investment Insurance Laws to Reduce the Risk of Overseas M&A

It is suggested to fill the gap of overseas investment insurance laws through legislation, formulate dedicated Overseas Investment Law and Overseas Investment Insurance Law, establish overseas investment insurance institutions, expand the coverage of state bilateral investment protection agreement, strengthen the contact between overseas investment enterprises and venture capitals and insurance companies to setup a risk sharing mechanism and provide an all-round guarantee for political risks and commercial risks in overseas M&A for railway enterprises.

4.2 Improve Government Regulation Efficiency

The government regulation efficiency should be improved. One the one hand, the government should clearly define and standardize approval procedures, foreign exchange regulation policies, financial policies, national security policies, information service policies, insurance support policies and taxation policies in overseas M&A, gradually perfect the notification, management and statistic system of overseas M&A and provide guidance for overseas M&A; on the other hand, the government should also assist enterprises to understand overseas legal environment, know the role of foreign government and local regulations, conduct comprehensive and multi-level investigation to judge acquisition risks and reduce the barrier of market access for overseas M&A.

4.3 Develop Supporting Policies for Strategic Industries Considering the Strategic Position of Railway Output

The tenet of the supporting policies for strategic industries is to increase the input of production factors in strategic industries through strong government interference and boost the whole industry structure through extraordinary development of the strategic industry. The government can take some measures to support railway enterprises to "go out". It should be noted that Chinese enterprises in overseas M&A are mainly state-owned enterprises, Chinese enterprises may be subject to national security risk review. Therefore, state-owned railway enterprises are encouraged to adopt joint-stock system as the operation mode, introduce social capital and foreign capital to weaken the nature of state-owned enterprises.

4.4 Strengthen International Cooperation to Protect IPR of Railway Enterprises

Enterprise is the subject of creation, management, application and protection of intellectual properties. To protect intellectual property rights, we should take effective measures, make proper arrangement for ownership, sharing and protection of scientific achievements, actively take part in competition in international market, and strive for, maintain and develop advantage in fierce competition. In order to avoid legal obstacle in output of high-speed railway, we should timely register independent technologies at relevant countries and obtain valid certificate for intellectual property rights; properly evaluate the high-speed railway technologies and perfect technology transaction system; implement and perfect overseas IPR advocacy mechanism and protect the legitimate rights of railway enterprise as owners of intellectual properties.

Acknowledgments. This work is supported by HongGuoYuan Double-hundred Talented People Plan of Beijing Jiaotong University. (L10JB00040).

References

1. Zhang, Y., Zhang, H.: Constructivism Analysis of High-speed Railway Development in China. Transportation Enterprise Management (3) (2010)
2. China's High-speed Railway Enters US Market. Beijing Business News (December 8, 2010), http://finance.sina.com.cn/roll/20101208/01329070815.shtml
3. Gu, S.: Rapid Rise of China's High Speed Railway. Traffic and Transportation (4) (2010)
4. Zhang, X., Nie, Q.: High-Speed Rail Construction and the Regional Economic Integration in China. Modern City Study (6) (2010)
5. Xie, X.: Spain's High-Speed Railway Lines: Current Situation and Development. Railway Knowledge (3) (2006)
6. Wang, G.: Advantages, Unfavorable Factors and Countermeasures for "Going Out" Strategy of China's Railway. China Venture Capital (9) (2010)
7. Cheng, S.: Exploration of National Risk Problems in Overseas M&A of Chinese Enterprises. Jiangsu Commercial Forum (12) (2008)
8. Sun, X.: On the Changing System of US Security Review of M&A by Foreign Investors. World Economy (3)
9. Zhang, X.: Analysis of Legal Problems in Overseas M&A of Chinese Enterprises. Cards World (9) (2009)
10. Jiang, X.: Breaking the Diplomatic Barrier for China's High Speed Railway Going to the US and the World. Asia Weekly (51) (February 15, 2010), http://www.yzzk.com/cfm/Content_Archive.cfm?Channel=ae&Path=2184310972/51ae1a.cfm

Analysis of Heilongjiang Province Village Traveling Present Situation and Problem

Zhengjie Zhu

Tourism and Cuisine School
Harbin University of Commerce
Harbin, China
zzj966@yahoo.com.cn

Abstract. The characteristic of Heilongjiang province regional agricultural is distinct and agricultural tourist resources are rich. Besides, folk culture has different features and complete kinds. Rural tourism has the huge development space in Heilongjiang province. Since the construction of "New countryside", rural tourism in Heilongjiang province has got a vigorous development. But affected by history and geographical factors, its developing exist many problems that we must change from rural tourism products design, perfecting infrastructure, strengthening various marketing strategy application and so on to early maturity of the improvement of rural tourism in Heilongjiang province and realize benign circulation development.

Keywords: Rural tourism, Folk tourism, Heilongjiang.

Heilongjiang Province as our country's agricultural big province has the advantageous natural resources which lay the good foundation and growth potential for the village traveling development; Simultaneously Heilongjiang Province has the multitudinous mechanized farms and the agricultural village. The common social practice folk custom is unique which has provided the essential safeguard for the development of folk custom village traveling project. In the socialism new rural reconstruction, it is certain for Heilongjiang Province that the reasonable and order development of village traveling will become the new luminescent spot in processes of twice imbark the economy grows to our province.

1 The Heilongjiang Province Village Tourist Resources Superiority Highlights

Heilongjiang Province has 473,000 square kilometers area, ranging national sixth, where distributing the state-level, the provincial level forest park and each kind of state-level, provincial level nature protection area. The round-off work is 43.6%, the forest land area ranging national first. The rivers and streams in Heilongjiang Province are multitudinous, just like the world second big mountain imprisoned lake Chingpo lakes, the primitive ecology, water quality pure big boundary river Heilongjiang and

M. Zhou (Ed.): ISAEBD 2011, Part III, CCIS 210, pp. 132–138, 2011.

the Wusuli River and China and Russia lake Xingkai Lake. The Heilongjiang wetland area resides in the national first place and the relative centralism large expanse of has three river plain bog wetland, the Wryru River bog wetland and the Song'acha River bog wetland. The wetland landscape is a characteristic model and its type is rich, whose biodiversity is complete and has the primitive style. Heilongjiang Province is one of three big black earth regions around the world. Length and breadth Songnen Plain, three river plain are well-known in the nation. Since new China had been established, the country has constructed many large-scale modernized farm here, like the friendship farm, the Hong farm, the Xingkai Lake farm and so on. These farms have a very high well-knowness in domestic, which is the very good modern agriculture ecology sightseeing project. Taking the nature, plain, mysterious, rough as the characteristic, the big lake, the big wetland and the big forest all distribute in the general countryside and the forest region, which have laid the good foundation and the growth potential for the village traveling development.

Simultaneously, Heilongjiang Province has the multitudinous agricultural village and the common social practice folk custom is unique. Besides Han nationality, there also living together the Manchu nationality, the Korean National Minority, the Mongolian national minority, the Daur national minority, the Hezhe national minority, the Oroqen national minority, more than 20 national minorities and so on. The common social practice of the national minority is simple and honorable, where natural scenery is exquisite and the national culture breath is thick. Under all levels of government's attention, various national inhabitants have extended completely this nationality's unique habit and the custom. Among them, the national minority festival like the "the bonfire festival" of Oroqen national minority, the "Wu Rigong the congress" of Hezhe national minority, the "the fall evening festival" and "the full moon festival" of Korean National minority, the "discredits the festival" of Xibe national minority and so on are unique and colorful. From last century's end, the Heilongjiang Province national minority villages and towns as if by prior agreement use the local unique nationality history and culture resources to carry on the different traveling product development. More representative of the rural population with Jin Jiang Street Hezhe custom tour, iron force rural folk custom tour, the Korean Folk Customs Tour Mudanjiang, Qiqihar Mei Rees Daur District 2 tours, etc. It has played a great a lead role in the promotion of the region's economic development and cultural exchanges and has made great economic and social benefits.

2 The Present Situation of Heilongjiang Province Village Traveling Development

Heilongjiang Province presently governs 13 prefectures, 12 municipalities, 1 administrative office, 65 counties (city).In which county level city 19, 877 townships (town), in which town 462, 14488 villages. The rich village tourist resources have provided a good destination for the metropolis crowd, letting the people enjoy the nature, the experience of modern peasant family happiness in the exquisite environment, tasting the organic foods during weekend leisure.

Style type of rural tourism in Heilongjiang Province are also diverse, with different styles: ranch style with bold, fresh and simple style homes mountain people, ethnic minorities in northern styles, exotic style of the border, the forest Mountain style, there is a large recreational lodge wetland style, and widely distributed. These tourist spots are mainly located in rural outskirts of Harbin, Qiqihar, Mudanjiang, Jiamusi, Yichun, Hegang other places, transport facilities, rich flavor country. The main village tour lines in Heilongjiang province are as follows:

(1) Harbin, a city of gold to Beijing Cheng A History, A city Jintai Zu Ling, Jin Huining Prefecture sites, sub-ditch Cliff Jin, Asahi Hall, Song Fengshan tourist areas, Yuquan Hunting Ground, Harbin Northern Forest Zoo, Hirayama Resort, Xudong Science and Technology Park, Xiquanyan Reservoir tourist area, Yuquan Wei Hushan Forest Park, Yuquan Huaguoshan Zhuang, yew chong, Yuquan Hill Huambo, gold and Ling (Hu Kai Hill), the Korean style - Red New Village, where the singular ecological park.

(2) Harbin - Daqing - Dumont (Shoushan Resort, Mongolia, the village, when the Chennai eco-village) - Lindian (Shengli Village, Sanhe Town, Kwok ecological lake) - serial Lake (wetland tourism, waterfowl hunting, Mongolian style) - Qiqihar (Sahara Village Daur area, Gannan Xing fourth village, Zhalong Nature Reserve, the moon island, iron agricultural horticultural Resort).

(3) Harbin - Shuangyashan (shuangxing agricultural tourism demonstration area, Friendship Farm, Rao Xiang Zhe in four townships) - Jiamusi (Zhe Jiang village streets Tianjin port, good luck Tangyuan County township, huachuan Spark - the first collective farms, farms with Honghe River, Trinidad Ecological Park) - Hegang (East is Red, Dongshan District, Hua Chun Heung Korean Village, Gongqing farms, Luobei dawn village, five Gang).

(4) Harbin - Wudalianchi (eruptions, Lung Shizhaishan, ice cave, etc.) - Heihe (Yuan Hui museums, ancient ruins play warm).

(5) Harbin - Yichun (iron abundance of power on the Korean Autonomous Township, iron power farms, Jiayin Dinosaur National Geological Park, Poly Township, wulaga Oroqen Ethnic Village, Wing Tung Hu Village).

(6) Harbin - Mudanjiang (Ningan Lan Kong, ring the water village, the town of East Nanjing Divergence, bergamot Mountain National Forest Park, Seven Mile Ecological Park, and bar of the town river, national forest parks Hailin, Jingpohu source, North Korea Folk Village, Mudanjiang snow fort, large Hailin Xue Xiang) - Jixi (Xingkai farm, eight hundred fifty-six Farm, Unicorn Hill, birch forest, eight Lawrence Hill, tiger along the scenic, forest Heung Chicken Jidong County, Chengzihe area Yongfeng Township) - Qitaihe (Hongwei Town, the former village, English Village, Gold River triple, antlers ditch, Boli, senior station, Shuanghe, Longchuan spa).

(7) Harbin - Daxinganling (Jiagedaqi, Huma County, Hung Yen town, Arctic Village, Mohe, silver nano Township E family).

(8) Harbin Sun Island - Grape Kingdom - Harbin Botanical Garden - Provincial Academy of Agricultural Sciences Horticulture Branch (visit Sun Island Garden City

scenery, a variety of grape picking, wine tasting, tours of plant gardens and enjoy the autumn scenery, a variety of fruit and vegetable picking, Agricultural Science tour).

3 The Problems in the Development of Rural Tourism in Heilongjiang Province

3.1 The Understanding of Village Tourism Development Management Has Errors

At first, they think village tourist area can be built based on existing of farmland, Orchard, Ranch, and utilization of farm, insufficient awareness of other resources conditions to the development and construction of village tourism including agricultural resources foundation, village natural landscape and cultural landscape foundation, location conditions, social economic conditions, tourism foundation facilities conditions and investment conditions lacking marketing cooperation, scientific, standardization, and operating mode of scale.

Second, the application of the rural tourism market mechanisms and inadequate market configuration role is not enough. Most of the rural tourism operators and developers always put all the city residents into tourist market in rural areas by their wishful thinking. In fact, it is difficult for rural tourism to produce enough attractive on residents living in the small and medium-sized city with urban-rural integration features. That is mainly because the lower degree of industrialization and urbanization of small and medium-sized cities, public understanding of the village is near the city, rural scenery for their lack of strong attraction, tourism as strongly desire than residents of large cities. Besides, the product of rural tourism attraction is not very strong.

Operators will be happy to spend money on a device in the main building facilities rather than investing heavily in operating characteristics, quality of service and community environment.

3.2 The Planning and Design of Scenic Spots Lack of Rural Characteristic

At present, during the construction of many scenic generally only pursue scale and speed, lacking of summary of the local culture and extraction, building dull, towns featured being not highlight, construction-grade being not high, and glass curtain wall building high-rise buildings such as modernization of the rural tourism scenic spot planning standards, causing the smells increasingly weak. It has been difficult for city people to find their long interest in many villages of the rural landscape and natural tourism areas. Overall image of rural tourism in the minds of the public are not sharp and prominent, and on the tourism effect, city dweller more feeling is: there is no different between holidays in the countryside and tourism in urban areas. After all, it is because the planning of rural tourism scenic spot lacking of features and attractive smells of country. The accommodation reception facilities such as hat shanlv defensive wall or Stockade surrounding a village are too modern, rural countryside that the natural environment and the breath of life slightly weak.

3.3 Tourism Reception Facilities Are Not Complete and Management Is Disorder

Modern tourism activity is organic unity of "food, shelter, transportation, travel, shopping and entertainment". But many of the village scenic spots in Heilongjiang province only put emphasis on the development of scenic spots ignoring construction and management of tourist reception facilities leading to tourist reception low level, which is not only lost a lot of income-generating opportunities but also destroyed the destination image. Some new scenic spots rushing to open before service facilities having been built well, some old scenic spot development of service facilities lagging far behind the scenery itself, such as parking congestion, poor telephone booths are scarce, dining accommodation, scenic toilets shoddy, advisory centers lack and so on. Lagging in the development of service facilities can not meet the basic needs of tourists. For example, on September 2009, cross head mountains had attracted over 100,000 tourists mountaineering tours King, becoming year hottest of short tour line, but tourists generally reflected its road, and parking, and accommodation, and public toilets existing shortage problem and supporting facilities needs to be perfect.

The village tourism catering service also does not satisfactory in Heilongjiang province where most restaurants in tourism scenic are just pursuit economic interests, does not focus on catering quality, more is lack characteristics, regardless of real demand of tourists. Foods there also have many health problems just like raw materials of food are poor quality, food utensils disinfection measures are not in place, such as problems to be solved.

In addition, the economic costs of traffic and time costs affect the selection of leisure tourism scenic spots for urban residents. But many scenic spots are also exist road narrow and poor road conditions problems. Some tourist routes also access road dirt road, very muddy rain, could not pass through, traffic sense into which becoming critical of problems.

3.4 Weak Brand Awareness, Less Well Known

Tourism brand is not only the competition weapon of tourist enterprises even more bridges of communication with consumers, which is the bridge to convey information about the tourism products to consumers, culture, new way of life. At present, most of rural tourism in Heilongjiang province only from its own point of view to plan the brand unilaterally, ignoring from the relationship between consumer behavior and brand awareness to build brand. Rural tourism in Heilongjiang province is rich in resources, but not many strange, rare resources and most of ordinary. When compared with some excellent travel resources, it cannot form highlights, little attraction to tourists. Their Brand idea is confusion, slogan not loud, blindly following others and has no features. Innovation consciousness is weak, resulting in the slow development of the scenic spots. Target consumers are not clear, blind advertising, publicity, spending a lot of financial and material resources but not receiving good benefits. For example, the Sino-Russia boundary river-Xingkai Lake, the vast sea, sand and fine clear water, is a tourist attraction. Due to lack of scenic spot of the unique brand image support, coupled with the propaganda is not in place, its popularity is not high and very few tourists.

4 Rural Tourism Development Strategy of Heilongjiang Province

4.1 The Overall Planning and Rational Development

Rational development involving farmers, rural tourism and manpower planning problems of agricultural growth, the stability of rural areas, must be scientific and reasonable, hierarchy planning.

First, according to the guidance of nation and Heilongjiang province, in the county and township level, we can make appropriate plan, determining the thought of local development and focal point. In specific country we can guide and organize the villagers taking the path of joint development or decentralization, reasonable distribution of rural resources, taking into account the sustainable development of rural determines the specific development of the village. In the planning process, it should be suited to local conditions, avoiding copying and identical. The village and town which have conditions can hire professional planning organizations to provide intellectual support.

4.2 Keeping Local Characteristics, Highlighting the Experience of Tourism Products

In Heilongjiang province, regional differences are more obvious. The natural environment, location, level of economic development, cultural backgrounds, rural folk and other aspects of the differences around the village of tourism scenic area provide a broad source material. The characteristic design of rural tourism scenic should mine deeply connotation of smells in the country, cultural traditions and so on. We should take comprehensive inspection of location characteristic of scenic rural resources and pay attention to the historical context of inheritance, continuity and innovation. Characteristic design should also be based on creating life-rural area, which is a natural and simple life reflection on the original. When planning rural tourism scenic spot, the elements in the villages should be put to important positions, creating a natural pristine environment, making the rural small town into a beautiful, easy living and with a strong human touch of tourism space.

At the same time, rural tourism products are required to give visitor an easy feel and unforgettable experience. For the products of rural tourism in Heilongjiang province, it is a key to restraint the thinking that traditional tourist products design should based on simple resources. The design of tourism products should aim at promoting tourists to a passive position and enable the mind to be a great level of satisfaction from a passive and watching position, vigorously optimizing the structure of rural tourism in our province's products and improving the participation of tourism products. It is a wise idea to create a new stimulus, near misses, enabling visitors to participate in the experience of a special life fully and to get a meeting with the participation of and enjoy.

4.3 Improve Infrastructure Construction in Rural Areas

Under the influence of dual economy in Heilongjiang province, infrastructure construction is weak. In terms of infrastructure, we should in accordance with the requirements of the new rural construction, to build new premises, new facilities and new environment. Specifically, rural housing (especially of commercial housing) should be based on national and regional style, suiting measures to local conditions and construction, and focusing on energy saving and environmental protection. Roads, utilities, communications, medical and other facilities should be complete; Village streets and living environment should be maintained clear and the garbage disposal, sewage disposal and latrine construction should be improved. In the process of infrastructure construction, we should pay attention to economical use of land, maintain rural characteristics and smells in the country, avoiding the tendency of urbanization, avoiding excessive expansion of the village scale.

4.4 Establish a Distinctive Rural Tourism Brand

To establish brand image should first correctly understand the evaluation of the own resources and the environment, deeply mine characteristics of its own resources and determine the core competitiveness of precise positioning. At the same time we should also analysis the consumer psychology, mining depth psychological needs of consumers to resonate to tourism consumer's heart which will play a multiplier effect. Establish their brand of scenic spots also tend to rely on a large environmental impact. Heilongjiang province establishing a overall image of "COOL – China Tourism of Heilongjiang province" at home and abroad, special black culture, national culture and unique agricultural production culture are all the valuable wealth that can relied on to established brand of rural tourism.

At the same time to design distinctive rural tourism slogan is also necessary. To the natural environment of scenic spots, cultural and social environment as a background, based on the scenic landscape resources, summarizing the destinations most advantages of feature extraction into a slogan is a way to reach impress tourists and stimulate its tourism decision-making behavior. Echoes of tourism slogan and tourism image, with the most refined, the most relevant language just called out its own characteristics, while full of fascination and inflammatory, and conversational ease consumer memory. From the Batang Baram, Yilan 45 kilometres, successfully played "North first bleach" tourism slogan, occupies a leading position in the minds of the people. In addition, the theme of tourism image design also matters buckle of the pulse of the times, play a brand of overlay upgrade promotion, such as snow and ice ice-snow tourism activities + travel + mode of physical education lessons. For some of the low visibility and smaller, competitive and not first of all to the goals and focus of scenic spot based on the province, spreading and by growing and then layer break at home and abroad market.

References

1. Dou, b.: Study on the issue of rural tourist attractions planning for Heilongjiang province, pp. 36–46. Northeast Agriculture University, Harbin (2010)
2. Diao, z.: Rural tourism development and countermeasures in Heilongjiang province, vol. 9, pp. 13–15. HLJ Foreign Economic Relations & Trade, Heilongjiang (2010)
3. Li, q.: Rural tourism resource development of Heilongjiang, vol. 5, pp. 24–28. Northeast Agriculture University, Harbin (2010)
4. Heilongjiang encyclopedia, pp. 31–33. Encyclopedia of China Publishing House, Beijing (2009)

The Implementation of a Performance Management System in the Italian Army

Armando Suppa and Alessandro Zardini

University of Verona, Business Administration Department, via dell'Artigliere 19, 37129 Verona, Italy
{Armando.Suppa,Alessandro.Zardini}@univr.it

Abstract. The last reform program in the Italian public sector was realized by legislative decree 150/2009 that introduced the performance cycle, to improve the efficiency and effectiveness of the public organizations. The performance and its evaluation is one of new public management (NPM) pillars [1]. Control and accountability play an invaluable role in the institutional and organizational change [2]. The Italian Army is involved in this changing process, as well as the other public organizations, by implementing a performance management system (PMS), in order "to do more with less" [3]. By now, the army is in the middle of this process, several steps have been made, but furthers and more critics are going to be done to implement an effective Decision Support System (DSS). This article aims to respond to the following question: How is the Italian Army implementing PMS and what is its impact on the organization?

Keywords: New Public Management, Performance Management Systems, Change Management.

1 Introduction

The performance and its evaluation have been the main concern of the public reform of the most developed countries over the last twenty years. "Governments have demonstrated growing interest in the measurement of performance in the public sector" [4] to improve efficiency and effectiveness of public organizations. This focus on the performance had its genesis in the New Public Management Theory [1,5]. In fact the performance measurement and evaluation are both emphasized by NPM as management tools in government. Government initiatives worldwide have been carried out to promote the implementation and use of strategic performance measurement systems, for instance US Government Performance and Results Act of 1993, to improve the governmental three E's – economy, efficiency and effectiveness – by increasing the quality of public service and reinforcing the accountability of public managers [6-8]. The legislative decree 150/2009 introduces in the public administration the cycle of performance, characterized by the strategic planning and performance measurement, control and evaluation. It is a renew and strong attempt to move from a compliance of the rules to a management for results culture in Italian public administration. It is one of the major idea of the NPM "using performance information to increase performance by holding managers accountable for clearly and

M. Zhou (Ed.): ISAEBD 2011, Part III, CCIS 210, pp. 139–146, 2011.

specify goals" [9]. In order to manage for result, it is important to look "beyond the measurement of performance to the management of performance' [10]. Indeed, the performance measurement is the act of measure, whilst performance management is the reaction upon the performance information, it is "both measurement and management, about information and action" in the public sector management [11]. The adoption of a performance management system allows to integrate in a systemic board the function of planning, measurement, control and evaluation, that are usually considered in a separate way, to obtain a holistic performance management [12].

The Department of Defense, as well as the other public administrations, has been called to implement the performance cycle introducing a performance management system in order to obtain a positive impact on the output as well as on the outcome produced by the organization. The Italian Army (IA), being part of the Department of Defense, has begun the PMS adoption through the implementation of a strategic decision support system (DSS) that has been involving the whole organization, as every part of it has been called to contribute both in the translation of the strategic objectives into operative ones and action plans, and in the individuation of more appropriate indicators and metrics (Key Performance Indicators) to capture the effective impact of the administrative action. Such an information system, as soon as it becomes full operative, will allow to provide the public manager with an effective "tool" to support his decision and which can be the performance driver as you can't manage what you don't measure. The implementation of a strategic decision support system requires different steps [13]:

1. introduction of controller's office which is able to manage and use estimation models and what if analysis,
2. definition and mapping of organizational objectives, which are coherent and aligned to the politic priorities defined by the government,
3. identification and development of indicators, metrics and algorithms which allow to measure, monitor and value the achievement of planned objectives (Key performance indicator e Key performance area),
4. identification and adoption of advanced instruments for the control and strategic management under the methodological and technologic profile, through the development and adoption of informatics solutions.

By now, the Italian Army is in the third of the four phases over mentioned, as it has already instituted the controller's office which has been provided with a system of "what if analysis" and has already identified its own operative objectives, the action plans and the referring indicators for the evaluation through the involvement of the responsible units in the different sectors. That phase will be followed by the implementation of an advanced management performance system, which will be probably based on the balanced scorecard [14], following the example of other armies of the other western countries. The research question that will be proposed in that context is the following: How the Italian Army is implementing PMS and its impact on the organization?

In order to answer to the research question we will examine the current situation of that process, the "as is" and its probable future development, the "to be". This last one results to be one of the most delicate phases for the adoption of a PMS, as the whole organization will be called to contribute to the system in order to obtain an effective adoption of it, through the legitimating in all the units involved in the performance management process. Otherwise there will be the risk to obtain only a superficial implementation of that technique and its corruption which would bring to a formal and ceremonial use "ritual function" [15].

2 New Public Management in Italy

The NPM doctrines emerged during the late 80's, and it has been the principle element of stimulus for the change in the public sector on an international level over the last decades [16]. A first conceptualization of NPM could be the one of prescriptions' set, ideas and instruments taken from the private sector and used in order to reinvent the government of the public sector, so to obtain an "entrepreneurial government" more efficient and effective, focused on products and on results more than on input, less red-tape, decentralized, in which competition is promoted inside the organization as well as in the market, in order to "do more with less" [3]. Following that point of view, the citizen becomes the public administration client whose satisfaction is central [16]. This description sees the NPM as a tool box where to take the better instrument (best practices) from the business private sector in order to obtain a better organizational performance. Another definition, less functionalist, considers the NPM as constituted by a set of assumptions and principles declarations about how public organizations should be organized, managed and work [17]. The idea which is at the basis of the NPM is to make public structures and public servants, more similar to private organizations, that means more "business-like" and "market-oriented", where the efficiency, effectiveness and performance measurement and evaluation are crucial [18]. About the key elements and the based assumptions of the NPM, Diefenbach [17] identified the following:

- Market orientation, stakeholder orientation, customer orientation, cost reduction, downsizing, outsourcing and privatization, commodification of service under the slogan of "value for money";
- Decentralization and re-organization of organizational units, less hierarchy, standardizations and formalization of strategic and operational management,
- Systematic, regular and comprehensive capturing, measurement, monitoring and assessment of crucial aspects of organizational and individual performance through explicit targets, standards, performance indicators, measurement and control systems;
- Establishment of a management culture, emphasizing the primacy of management and "making the manages manage";
- Empowerment of the staff, that is expected to develop "business like attitudes".

The NPM theory is still one of the most debated matter in the academic field, the critics towards it are really strong, and some articles have even decreed its death "NPM is Dead…" [19]. Besides these critics, the NPM is still a paradigm of big influence on an international level, that has left its sign in the public sector [20]. The Italian government particularity has been that the ideas and the principles of NPM have been introduced both on a local and a central level through a multitude of legal prescriptions and formal rules that defined in a precise and punctual way the instruments and reform measures which should be adopted. Therefore, Italian NPM reforms have been almost exclusively "imposed" through the formal legislative instruments, "through law" [20]. The last of these presents itself in a logic of continuity with the previous ones and at the same time it is innovative, introducing the performance cycle and emphasizing planning, measurement, control and evaluation.

The performance cycle becomes the most important aspect of the reform which is taking place, constituting the point of strength for the change promotion in public administrations, for the improvement in efficiency, effectiveness and productivity, to increase the performance in quality and quantity terms. This initiative tries to "pursuits the performance" by introducing the performance management practices that have gradually became an integral part of modern governance arrangements.

Summarizing, planning, measurement, monitoring and evaluation of performances are the main functions that, if developed in a systematic and integrated way, should give birth to a new organizational model with a bigger "three Es of economy, efficiency and effectiveness" [21]. That reflects completely the NPM assumptions in which evaluation systems are considered "such an important player" in the public sector where the control plays an "extremely" crucial role in the area of institutional and organizational change.

3 Methodology and Data

In order to validate the research question and verify the theoretical referential framework, the analysis has been done inside the organizational structure of the Italian Army during the implementation of performance management system. The methodology used for that research is the Action-Research [22]. Inside the Action-Research we have later decided to use the technique of Multiview2 [23]. The theoretical model, following a dynamic and integrated process, must always be put in the context of the organizational environment. The theoretical preconfigured model should be put in the context and tested inside the socio-economic environment. According to the indication of the Action-Research, that gap should be reduced in order to make it possible that the theoretical model matches reasonably with the real model, for that reason, we should proceed with the modification of the theoretical framework in a recursive loop. In the study of the organizational environment, during the "as-is" step, we proceeded with a top-down approach. In this article we have analyzed the theoretical framework elaborated for the good functioning of the performance management system and we have observed the first results obtained through the implementation of the model. According to the Action-Research we are now only at the first step of the analysis as the model should be reiterated and validated in order to make the theoretical framework match with the "real" environment (matching of about 98%) so that it could be accepted. In order to analyze the theoretical model of PMS, we have proceeded through the assembling and rationalization of data and information deriving from the internal documents of the Department of Defense and of the IA which have been put at our disposal by the IA Controller's Office (UCIG), and from the analysis of the information which were already present in the Information Systems. Hence, we had boarded the framework and we proceeded with the improvement of it through a series of semi-structured interviews with some managers belonging to the over mentioned office of internal control. That process has allowed to understand the theoretical framework used to implement the company's performance management system. Finally, we have proceed with the testing of the model evaluating its function and the adherence to the final model, concluding that way the first cycle of Action-Research.

4 The Implementation of PMS in the Italian Army

4.1 Setting

During the last years the Italian Army has been interested on one side by a radical transformation that has reduced its strength from the previous 300.000 units to the actual 107.000 (all volunteer soldiers), on the other side to a bigger and bigger involvement in peace support operations, in fact an average of 7.000 personnel has been constantly developed all around the world on missions. By the way, the main issue which have to be faced by the army is the chronic lack of financial resources. In this respect at the present time the army has about 107.000, that is below the ceiling of 112.000 established by law, due to the strict limits of Defense budget. For the forgoing, it is possible to verify how important it is for the IA to manage the funds assigned in the more possible efficient and effective way, avoiding waste and cost duplications in order to obtain the higher possible performance, in consideration of budget constraints.

4.2 Organizational Environment

The IA has been engaged in the development and introduction of the performance management system for many years. Until 2009 the activity of management control was mainly of a financial nature, adopting some financial indicators that show the advance of expense, by comparing the allocated resources and the consequent use of them. That kind of indicators results to be less significant to explain the public outcome, as they do not underline profusions and inefficiency present inside the organizational environment. Hence, the model presented by Di Paolo [13] formalized a predictive model of "What if Analysis" which is an instrument able to evaluate the "productive capacity" of IA on the base of the assigned funds. It allows to operate some decisional simulations in real time, providing the rate of performance which are obtainable by the whole organization for each volume of allocated resources. The system permits also to do some drill-down operations, in order to obtain a specific What if Analysis for each sector or function. That allows to introduce an activity of benchmarking, identifying the objective target for each area of interest. The model is also able to determine the "threshold" behind which the allocated funds result to be insufficient to make the IA expresses a minimum level of operational capability. The overcoming of that level can produce serious repercussions in short and long term on the level of "national security". The borderline, which can be also defined as an "impairment limit", can even be declined for the single areas and functions allowing therefore to make some evaluations about the best allocation of the resources related to the army priorities. The What if Analysis appears to be a powerful instrument for the Decision Support Systems in order to identify ex-ante the systemic criticalities allowing to allocate the resources at disposal in an effective and efficient way.

The IA, thanks to the introduction of the integrated cycle of strategic-financial planning, has been elaborating since the 2010 its own objectives, indicators and metrics for evaluation and has provided to assign to them the relating financial resources. That integrated planning process involves the whole organization at its different hierarchy levels. That is made of one first phase during which the strategic planning is developed with the assignment of the objectives through a top-down process. In fact, starting from the politics priorities presented by the Department of Defense through the Minister act, the strategic objectives of the Defense are determined by a cascading process from them, as well as the operative objectives of the Army Chief of General Staff and the operative programs (PO) of the IA sector representatives and in this way along the whole commando chain. Therefore, the Department of Defense, through the Defense Chief of General Staff till the Army Chief of General Staff, on the basis of each own strategic priorities, assigns to the representatives the achievement of the underneath operative programs. These last ones are responsible for the planning of the activities which aim is the achievement of the PO (measurement, monitoring, control and adoption of the corrective actions). The representatives with an technical directive define and present the actions to do for the achievement of the objectives concerning the PO to the organism which have to execute them (main board executive organism, intermediate and final). The main board executive organism, once it has received that indications, identifies some more specific objectives that are communicated to the lower hierarchy level and ad so till the level of the final executive organism. During this phase, the different representatives must also provide to formulate and indicate the objective value (obtainable result if the activity was completely funded), the target value (the obtainable result whit the assigned resources) and the time frame, metrics and indicators for the objectives' achievement. From these considerations it appears evident that it is fundamental that objectives are correctly measured and quantified. Hence the individuation of suitable KPI in order to monitor their development on objective basis, also through the use of proxy variables, becomes one of the crucial moment in that process. In fact, the "little reliability and auto referentiality" of the indicators system related to the capabilities of the military instrument is one of the most critical factors for the "measurement of the complete performance of the defense organization". Therefore, it is possible to see how this process needs a further research in order to improve a model that provides an more objective representation of objectives. During the strategic planning, once the objectives have been identified and assigned to executive subordinate organisms, they are communicated to the superior command. Through this process it is realized: the definition of the parameters for the objectives (times, steps, metrics, indicators, etc.) from the subaltern organism in accordance with the superior one, the check of coherence and alignment of the all objectives which had been planned with the ones of the army. Once the strategic planning has been ended, the second step of the integrated strategic-financial planning begins. During this step, the strategic planning is integrated with the financial planning, this last one, on the contrary of the strategic planning is made through a bottom-up process. This way, the objectives determined during the strategic planning can receive the needed resources. Hence, only the activities that are relevant for the achievement of the strategic objective of the IA are funded, avoiding in this way the risk to allocate resources to activities that have not a "strategic" impact for the army. What has been described until now, is the present situation (as is) of the implementation process for the PMS of the Italian Army. The next step which has to be done by the IA (to be) will be the introduction and development of models and solutions in order to make easier the incorporation of information about performance into procedures, into the documents and in more in general way into the whole organization. The identified model has resulted to be the balance scorecard [14].

5 Conclusion

With the present study we have analyzed only the first step of the introduction of the performance management system inside the Italian Army. In detail, we have analyzed the theoretical framework introduced through the law 150/2009, which has taken birth from the principles assumed by the New Public Management. At the same time, it is correct to underline that the complete organizational effects will be seen only after the end of the implementation process of the PMS in the IA. As a matter of fact, the future and wished introduction of BSC alone will not be sufficient to guarantee that a performance management system has been effectively introduced. Summarizing, from our study on the introduction of the performance cycle in the IA it is possible to observe, after the fulfillment of the first steps of that process, the following aspects:

- introduction of a What if Analysis model's founded on objective basis for the decisions support systems;
- identification at the different levels of the organization of the actions to be done in order to achieve the organizational objectives, through the formalization of technical indications, identification of objectives which are aligned with the ones of the army, and related indicators and measurement metrics;
- adoption of an integrated strategic-financial planning, which assigns resources only to that activities which have resulted to be coherent with the achievement of the organizational objectives and which allows to avoid profusions and information redundancies.

References

1. Hood, C.: A public management for all seasons? Public Administration 69, 3–19 (1991)
2. Minelli, E., Rebora, G., Turri, M.: The risk of failure of controls and levers of change: an examination of two Italian public sectors. Journal of Accounting & Organizational Change 4(1), 5–25 (2008)
3. Osborne, D.: Reinventing Government. Public Productivity & Management Review 16(4), 349–356 (1993)
4. Micheli, P., Neely, A.: Performance measurement in the UK's public sector: searching for the golden thread. Public Administration Review 70(4), 591–600 (2010)
5. Hood, C.: The new public management in the 1980s: Variations on a theme. Accounting, Organizations and Society 20(2/3), 93–110 (1995)
6. Atkinson, A.A., McCrindell, J.Q.: Strategic performance measurement in government. CMA Magazine 71(3), 20–23 (1997)
7. Radnor, Z., Mcguire, M.: Performance management in the public sector: fact or finction? International Journal of Productivity And Performance Management 53(3), 245–260 (2004)

8. Cavalluzzo, K.S., Ittner, C.D.: Implementing Performance Measurement Innovations: Evidence From Government. Accounting, Organizations and Society 29(2), 243–267 (2004)
9. Moynihan, D.P.: Managing for results in state government: Evaluating a decade of reform. Public Administration Review 66, 77–89 (2006)
10. Otley, D.: Performance management: a framework for management control systems research. Management Accounting Research 10, 363–382 (1999)
11. Bouckaert, G., Van Dooren, W.: PerfromanceMeasurament and management in public sector organizations. In: Bovaiard, T., Loffler, E. (eds.) Public Management and Governance, 2nd edn., pp. 151–164. Routledge, New York (2009)
12. Bouckaert, G., Halligan, J.: Managing Performance, international comparison. Routledge, New York (2008)
13. Di Paolo, A.: l'introduzione del New Public Management e della Balanced Scorecard nel processo di riforma dell'Amministrazione pubblica italiana. Economia Pubblica 3-4, 156–179 (2007)
14. Kaplan, R.S., Norton, D.P.: Using the Balance Scorecard as a Strategic Management System. Harvard Business Review 74(1), 75–85 (1996)
15. Lozeau, D., Langley, A., Denis, J.L.: The corruption of managerial techniques by organizations. Human Relations 55(5), 537–564 (2002)
16. Osborne, D., Gaebler, T.: Reinventing Government: How the Entrepreneurial Spirit is Transforming the Public Sector. Addison-Wesley, Reading (1992)
17. Diefenbach, T.: New Public Management in Public Sector Organizations: The Dark Sides OfManagerialistic 'Enlightenment'. Public Administration 87(4), 892–909 (2009)
18. McAuley, J., Duberley, J., Cohen, L.: The Meaning Professionals give to Management and Strategy. Human Relations 53(1), 87–116 (2000)
19. Dunleavy, P., Margetts, H., Bastow, S., Tinkler, J.: New Public Management is DeadLong live Digital-Era Governance. Journal of Public Administration Research and Theory 16, 467–494 (2005)
20. Kulmann, S.: New Public Management for the "Classical Continental European Administration": modernization at the local level in Germany, France and Italy. Public Administration 88(4), 1116–1130 (2010)
21. Boland, T., Fowler, A.: A systems perspective of performance management in public sector organizations. The International Journal of Public Sector Management 13(5), 417–446 (2000)
22. Lewin, K.: Action Research and Minority Problems. Journal of Social Issues, 34–36 (1946)
23. Avison, D., Wood-Harper, A.T.: Bringing social and organisational issues into information systems development: the story of multiview. In: Socio-Technical and Human Cognition Elements of Information Systems, pp. 5–21. IGI Publishing, Hershey (2003)

An Empirical Study of One Western Province Public Department Budget in China

Yunjie Zhu and Shouguo Zhao

School of Economics and Management, Northwest University, 710127,
Xi'an, Shaanxi, P.R.C.
Yunjiezhu@Sohu.com

Abstract. Based on our survey on the public department budget of one western province in China, this paper summarizes the problems of budget management and implementation into five aspects, namely, lacking of standards for basic expenditure and project expenses, incomprehensive department budgetary plan, weakening constraint on department budget implementation, shirking legislature supervision and enormous gap between budget and final account. Then this paper discusses the corresponding reasons depending on the management theory. At last, this paper puts forward the suggestions on how to improve the public department budget management in China.

Keywords: Department Budget, Western Province, Management.

1 Introduction

In fiscal year of 2008, Chinese total fiscal revenue reached 6131.69 billion (2864.49 billion local government fiscal revenue contained) and its public expenditure was up to 6242.703 billion (including 4905.27 billion local government fiscal expenditure [1]. It is clear that sub-central government budget has been playing more and more important role in Chinese public budget. In 2009, sponsored by one western province NPC finance and economics committee in China, we studied systematically the ten government departments' budgetary statements of 2007 and communicated with them face-to-face. This paper, which is based on our survey, theoretically describes the reform of Chinese pubic department budget.

2 Problems of Province Government Department Budget

The government department budget plan, which is approved by legislature in accordance with statutory procedures, is characterized by time-limited, comprehensive, integrated, strict and mandatory. But our survey found five common and typical problems that are showed as below.

M. Zhou (Ed.): ISAEBD 2011, Part III, CCIS 210, pp. 147–153, 2011.

2.1 Lacks of Standards for Basic Expenditure and Project Expenses

Because there is no the quotas on government department staff, basic expenditure, and project expenses, our survey shows that there are two problems in both basic expenditure and project expenses budget.

(1) Enormous Margin of Per Capita Basic Expenditure Budget

The per capita basic appropriation of the office-bearers in 2007 is showed in table 1.In 2007, the average per capita basic budgetary appropriation of ten departments is 60.8 thousand Yuan, and the highest per capita expenditure is 135.3 thousand RMB, while the lowest is15.9 thousand RMB.

Table 1. Per Capita Basic Appropriation of the Office-Bearers in 2007 Units: Ten Thousand RMB

Department A	3.00	Department F	6.78
Department B	8.99	Department G	10.52
Department C	2.63	Department H	7.84
Department D	3.08	Department I	2.85
Department E	13.53	Department J	1.59

The budgetary appropriations of per capita salary and welfare, and per capita commodity and service for the office-bearers in 2007 are showed in table 2. As for the per capita salary and welfare of the ten departments, the highest is 39.1 thousand RMB, yet the lowest is 10.5 thousand RMB. The budget appropriation of per capita commodity and service expenses also exist the similar differences.

Table 2. Budgetary Appropriation of Per Capita Salary and Welfare, and Per Capita Commodity and Service in 2007 Units: Ten Thousand RMB

	per Capita Salary and Welfare,	per capita Commodity and Service
Department A	1.2578	0.8352
Department B	3.9111	4.2722
Department C	1.2119	1.2161
Department D	1.2860	0.9799
Department E	2.0703	2.6864
Department F	2.2229	4.4852
Department G	2.2210	2.1579
Department H	3.2701	2.7819
Department I	1.1329	0.4409
Department J	1.0529	0.3065

(2) Random Procedure and Bad Inefficiency for Project Expenditure Budget

Firstly, there is no a procedures of "argument, evaluation, declaration, setting up" for project budgetary. Most projects have no operating body and no basis to measure the expenditure. Few project's expenses budget introduce performance appraisal.

Secondly, it is common that most of project budgetary expenses only listed the total expenditures and are not classified into terms of economic type. For example, five departments' project budgetary expenses were packed into "other expenditures ", instead resolving into subjects of specific economic function.

Thirdly, the project budgetary surplus from last year-end occurs uninterruptedly. The survey reveals that 530.34 million of project budgetary surplus was carried forward from 2006 to 2007, which included 100.77 million of fiscal budgetary appropriations for ten departments. At the end of 2007, ten departments' project budgetary surplus was up to 614.33 million, which included 95.43 million of fiscal budgetary appropriations. This means that a large amount of public fund is idle.

2.2 Incomprehensive Department Budgetary Plan

Our investigation finds that ten departments' project budgetary plans do not contain infrastructure budgetary expenditure and it is impossible to discover the central transfer payment in their budget tables. At the same year, Department C, E, I and J didn't compile basic expenditure budget for their 11 subordinate units in 2007.

On the other hand, a few of non-tax revenue is brought into each department budget sheets. From 2004 to 2007, the total amount of this west province's non-tax revenue had increased fast and even exceeded its local tax revenue. However, such a large amount of money was never inside public financial budget management.

Table 3. Non-tax Revenue beyond Department Budget Units: Ten Thousand RMB

Department A	2446.46	Department F	2446.46
Department B	5423.34	Department G	123925.68
Department C	4624.85	Department H	3602.07
Department D	521.96	Department I	10064.88
Department E	98991.01	Department J	2065.83

We estimated the total amount of non-tax revenue of ten departments and it is showed in table 3. Table 3 shows that department G and department E respectively had 1.2 billion and 0.99 billion non-tax revenue exceeding supervision from the province public finance office and province NPC.

2.3 Weaken Constraint on Department Budget Implementing

Our survey finds that there are two typical problems along the department budget plan implementing.

The first is that the increase of a few department budgetary expenditures or transforming of the expenditures items had not been approved by legislature. The province public finance office allocated a supplementary budget of 14.4255 million to department A as its basic expenditures, 117.85 million to department J as its original administrative budget and 116.885 million to department J. However, the adjustment of the department budget did not be submitted to the province NPC.

The other is that the fund earmarked for administration funds and special funds is to be diverted to other purpose. For example, department G diverted the fund of 57.3304 million earmarked for administration funds and special funds to its retiree's added wages.

2.4 Shirking Budgetary Supervision and Control

Our survey even finds that department A, department I and department C didn't budget their government procurement in 2007. The government procurement budget of the other seven departments summed into 22.1993 million in 2007 (just 0.4 million more than it in 2006), and only equaled 0.54% of the sum of commodity and services spending in project budget and basic budget.

Meanwhile, each departments raise loans in a variety of indirect ways, which leads to a mass of implicit debt for government. Two departments' budgetary sheets of project expenses reflected their subordinate units' paybacking interest to the commercial banks. Department G should repaid interest as high as 0.537 billion for its subordinate units in 2007. The interest expense budget of department E was 3.9324 million. We estimated that its loan may be about 53 million according to one-year benchmark rate (7.29%) on Dec. 20, 2007.

2.5 Enormous Gaps between Budget and Final Account

The above problems lead to enormous gap between budget and final account. Ten departments' final revenue account is equivalent to 2.47 times of total budgetary revenue in 2007. For details, the final account of fiscal appropriation is 2.18 times as much as its original budget in 2007. Non-tax revenue is 1.84 times higher than control number in 2007. The other final revenue account is respectively equivalent to 7.89 times of budget number. Then, it is easy to understand that ten departments' total budget expenditure is in the proportion of the final accounts with 43.09% in 2007.

3 Why Province Department Budget Exists Problems

The developed countries budget system is characterized by the two aspects. The first is an efficient administrative supervising and controlling system, which mainly aim at administrative efficiency. And the other is legislature supervising and controlling system, which aims at performance. The well-work of these two supervising and controlling system depends on the centralizing powers and unifying accountability [2].

3.1 NPC's Limited Authority on the Department Budget

Chinese Budget Act does not authorize the power of government budget amendment to the province NPC. The Act just stipulates that the government budget should be re-submitted to the province NPC when the balance government budget is converted into imbalanced or government debts increased.

The other two reasons, which deteriorate the NPC's authority on the department budget, should be pointed out. The first is the confliction between the Budget Act and the Administrative Measures of the non-budgetary funds. The latter provides non-tax revenue, such as all kinds of fees, land rents and so on, with legal basis and most of them shirk the possible monitor from a province NPC. The second is that the vast transfer payment from Chinese central government has been "packed" integrally to the corresponding sub-department of province government. Actually, the revenue and expenditure of the non-budgetary funds and Chinese central government's transfer payment is not supervised or controlled by the province NPC at all.

3.2 The Separated Power of Initial Budget Distribution

The reform of the budget management system has not change the separated power of initial budget distribution among the government departments since 1994. For example, the initial distribution power of infrastructure investment is held by Province Development and Reform Commission, and the power of R&D funds is held by province R&D Department. It is means that the initial budget distribution power of one province is cut into piece [3]. For the more, each government department has certain power of allocating its non-budgetary funds. All of these lead to that each department does not have a complete and comprehensive budget submitted to the province public finance office and corresponding legislature.

3.3 Bad-Defined the Accountability of the Government Departments

It is easy to find that there are lacks of fundamental qualifications for the department budget. It is undoubtedly that it is one of the duties for a province public finance office to make up these fundamental qualifications. However, a province public finance office has no enough authority to eliminate the vested interest of other government departments. In fact it is impossible to work out the quotas on government department staff, basic expenditure, and project expenses for a province public finance office without reforming the government management system.

At the same time, the other government departments lack direct accountability to public and their directors control the power of using public funds. It is foreseeable that their expanding expenditure impulse could become true.

3.4 Inefficient Budgetary Control Links

Based on the management theory, "planning, measuring, checking and adjusting" consist of a whole control link. Complete information and participants' enough motivation are two fundamental factors to guarantee a well-running control link. For government budget, complete information only root in disclosing forcibly and participant's motivation resulting from public accountability.

At the beginning of department budget, there are no scientific the quotas on government department staff, basic expenditure, and project expenses, or they are not strictly enforced. As the budget executing and checking, the ineffective current control and the problems audit reported, a feed-back control mechanism also take a little effect because there are no mechanisms of forcibly disclosing and public accountability.

4 Suggestions

Under the Chinese current political power structure, the feasible choices to improve the budgetary system is to execute the government policy target and to improves expenditure organization's operation efficiency by total quantity control[4].

4.1 Reinforcing the NPC's Authority to Department Budget

A province NPC could draw up local budget act to stipulate its powers of rectifying a province draft budget and perfecting procedures of budget adjustment.,and to expand its authority to approve the central government transfer payments and non-tax revenue and so on. At the same time, NPC should extend the time for draft budget, found special budget committee and disclose the draft budget to the public to increase transparency in department budget.

4.2 Centralizing the Power of Initial Budget Distribution

It is necessary to increase government responsible through centralizing the budget distribution power into the government top leader.The first is to centralize the initial budget distribution power into a province public finance office depending on a special committee including the government R&D department and Development Revolution Committee. The second is that the actual distribution power of non-budgetary funds, fees, land rents and so on, which hold by each department, should be centralized into the province public finance office as quickly as possible.

4.3 Defining the Accountability of Government Departments

In order to achieve the government policy goal by public finance resources, a province public finance office should have distributing power on department draft budget. Its necessary responsibilities should include the following, such as balancing the government revenue and expenditure, distributing each department's expenditure according to the quotas, perfecting budget draft rules, procedures, and directing government departments to establish and perfect their internal control systems.

Other government departments' duties is to carry out its draft budget according to the relevant rules and procedures, to report its draft budget to a province public finance office, and to submit it to the province NPC with subsidiary ledger. It is no doubt that department director should take charge of the authenticity and legitimacy of its department budget.

4.4 Consummating the Budget Management Control Links

Based on the clearly definition of the power and accountability of department budget's participant, consummating the budget management control links require to bring the political "answerability" and "enforcement" accountability into effects [6].

"Answerability" requires the government department director to provide information about their actions and to testify their actions' legitimacy. "Enforcement" means that a province NPC (and a province public finance office) can award or publish the government department and its director depending on its actions.

It is clearly that perfecting the budget management control links needs a well-running information disclosing mechanism. To breaking the current face-to-face negotiations between province public finance office and each government department, a replaceable disclosure mechanism, which means that to open budgetary information among government departments, could be taken.

5 Conclusion

Obviously, the department budget reform has stronger political sense. Facing the Chinese current political states, we could choice the practical reforming steps to establish a fundamental budgetary support system and to perfect the budgetary control links. These practical reforming steps could help reaching higher public budget goals of accountability, transparency, participation and forecast.

References

1. Ministry of Finance People's Republic of China, `http://www.mof.gov.cn/mof/zhengwuxinxi`
2. Wang, S., Ma, J.: To "Budget Countries"—Financial Transition and National Construction. Public Administration Review, 1–37 (2008)
3. Ma, J., Niu, M.: Restructuring Chinese Public Budget System: Power and the Relationship–Based on the Investigation of Local Budgets. Observation of Chinese Development, 13–16 (2007)
4. Wang, Y.: China's Budget Reforms: Comment and Prospects. Economic and Social System Comparison, 38–46 (2008)
5. Schedler, A.: Conceptualizing Accountability. In: Schedler, A., Diamond, L., Platterner, M. (eds.) The Self-restraining State: Power and Accountability in New Democracies, p. 14. Boulder, Lynne Rienner (1999)

Study on Evaluation Tools of Harmonious Labor Relations in Enterprise

Qin He*

Beijing Union University, Beijing, P.R. China, 100101

Abstract. This paper is primarily focused on the study about the evaluation of harmonious degree in enterprise in terms of tool and technique for evaluation of labor relations, aiming at provision of reliable evaluation tool by which the government can carry out a sound critical estimate of status characteristics and trends of labor relations in the enterprise from macro views, and the enterprise can conduct micro-level investigation on its own labor relations status so as to effectively resolve and prevent the contradictory conflict as well as establish stable and harmonious labor relations. On the basis of theoretical analysis and document study, the paper has constituted the theoretical evaluation index system. Furthermore according to the experts in a two round survey, the evaluation indexes were screened by Subjective Delphi Technique and Objective Membership Analysis and the operational evaluation index system were established. Again using Delphi Technique in combination with Analytic Hierarchy Process (AHP), the weights of each evaluation index were determined. Test of discernment and independence for evaluation index system has been performed through correlation analysis and variation coefficient, and the results showed that the established evaluation index system in the paper was of comparatively better independence and representativeness as well as discrimination, and was capable of reflecting the labor relations status of evaluation objects comprehensively and systematically. The index system was consistent with the principles of design and selection, which was a reliable tool and technique for evaluation of labor relations with the enterprise.

Keywords: Harmonious labor relations, Evaluation, Index system, Tool.

1 Introduction

Since the 4th Plenary Session of the 16th Central Committee, the Party and National leaders have realized that keeping social development is as important as keeping economic development, and proposed the brand-new idea and great goal of building a socialist harmonious society timely. At 17th Party Congress, the goal to build a harmonious labor relation has been clearly put forward.

* HE Qin From Sichuan, was Associate Professor of School of Management, Beijing Union University. His main study fields include labor economics study and human resources.

M. Zhou (Ed.): ISAEBD 2011, Part III, CCIS 210, pp. 154–162, 2011.

In recent years, evaluation of harmonious labor relations in enterprise has gradually become a hotspot of study; however, the studies both abroad and domestic were carried out on evaluation of labor relations in the perspective of theory and practice, lack of the development of evaluation tools and techniques. This paper is primarily focused on the study about the evaluation of harmonious degree of enterprise in terms of tool and technique for evaluation of labor relations, aiming at provision of reliable evaluation tool and techniques by which the government could carry out a sound critical estimate of status characteristics and trends of labor relations of the enterprise from macro views, and the enterprise could conduct micro-level investigation on its own labor relations status so as to effectively resolve and prevent the contradictory conflict as well as establish stable and harmonious labor relations.

2 Establishing Evaluation Concept of Balance, Cooperation and Sharing

The evaluation of labor relations should have clear value assessment and concept. Concurrently the different values and assumptions for dominant position of labor relation evaluation by the researcher should play an important role on the evaluation process and results. The paper has proposed the evaluation value concept of "Balance, Cooperation and Sharing". To balance the interest between the employers and employees is the core of balanced labor. The key factors to achieve the balance of interests are the relatively equal rights and relatively balanced power of both parties, requiring the establishment of corresponding system and coordination mechanism as safeguard to facilitate the continual improvement of the balanced labor relations. The fundamental motive of labor-management cooperation is Pareto improvement of the interest between the labor and management. The employers or management should have due regard to the employee's preference and willingness with respect of the coordination and cooperation of labor relations, and build a reasonable interest balanced system to protect the employee's interest effectively. Such will contribute to culture cooperative style labor relations and promote the continual improvement of the interest between the employers and employees in the long run. The core of enterprise labor relations is the interest relations between human capital property right and physical capital property right. To improve the labor relations, it is essential to abandon the conventional practice in which the physical capital owner enjoys the surplus solely. With freedom of contract, the human capital of the employee should acquire the residual claim equivalent to the physical capital. Both capital share ownership of enterprise and achieve a communion of labor and management. Evaluation of labor relations is designed to transfix with measure of the present stage and that of its improvement, and to guide and promote the development and improvement of the enterprise labor relations using evaluation result of labor relations and its analysis. Therefore, the above-mentioned value concept is running through the study on enterprise labor relations and harmony evaluation, in order to provide a value assessment to evaluate the labor relations and guidance for the improvement.

3 Establishing Evaluation Index System of Harmonious Degree of Labor Relations in Enterprise

3.1 Design of Theoretical Index System

The study took Sandver theoretical model as framework for the harmonious degree evaluation, according to which the evaluation of enterprise labor relations should include two dimensions: work place factor and employee personal factor, and 7 aspects consisting of working environment, labor disputes, democratic participation, business management, business performance, achievement of employee rights and employee development.

Based on theoretical analysis, the study has established the evaluation theoretical index system of enterprise labor relations harmonious degree including 2 first-grade indexes, 7 second-grade indexes and 31 third-grade indexes.

3.2 Screening Evaluation Index

The study strived to overcome and compensate the defects and shortcomings in the previous study for establishment and screen of the index, and to carry out index screen in accordance with the principles of comprehensiveness and systematicness, representativeness, independence, authenticity, and availability.

Based on establishment of theoretical index system, the study initially modified the theoretical index system followed by subjective choice for the modified system with Delphi technique, then carried out an objective screen of the evaluation index through membership analysis, one of mathematical statistics.

3.2.1 Subjectivity Delphi Technique

(1) Composition of experts group

A total of 16 experts were selected in the group of the study. The experts were of wide coverage, consisting of 4 parts: senior management of human resources or labor relations; experts from trade unions; experts and scholars from the government department in charge of labor relations. The expert group structure had ensured that the expert's membership had professional knowledge, skills and experience. 1

(2) Analysis of the first round investigation results

The first round questionnaire was performed though non-structural interview followed by modification and supplement original theoretical index system.

3.2.2 Objective Method Membership Analysis Method

Modified theatrical index system was adopted in the structural question paper the second round investigation (table 2), with 2 first-grade index, 7 second-grade index and 33 third-grade index for the selection and judgment of the experts. They were required to select the most important one from 33 evaluation indexes in their own judgment according to their own professional knowledge and experience.

[1] Murry J W, Hammons J O. Delphi:a Versatile Methodology for Conducting Qualitive Research Review of Higher Education,1995,18(4):423-436.

Through statistical analysis on 16 valid questionnaires, membership of 34 evaluation indexes has been obtained.

Through the above membership analysis, the membership degree of the evaluation index less than 0.20 was deleted. Through subjective Delphi method and objective membership analysis, a feasible "operational index system" (table 4) was formed to reflect characteristics of enterprise labor relations. The modified operational index system included 2 first-grade indexes, 7 second-grade indexes and 28 third-grade indexes, of which 70% of original theoretical index system were kept constant, and 30 % was modified.

3.3 Determination of Weights of Evaluation Index System

Using Analytic Hierarchy Process (AHP) to determine the weight of each index, the procedure of calculation was accomplished by MATLAB 6.5 software. Based on the results of single hierarchical arrangement, the weights of each index were calculated

3.4 Verification of Evaluation Index System

The index was verified in the study statistically in order to ensure the established index system itself would not affect the evaluation results of index system.

3.4.1 Independence Test

The correlation analysis was adopted to carry out independence test for the evaluation system, and the original variables was analyzed by spss16.0 software, then correlative coefficient and two-tail test table original variables could be obtained.

The absolute value of correlative coefficient was closer to 1, indicating that there was a closer relation between the two variables, while the absolute value was close to 0, indicating the more closely related. With few exceptions, the correlation coefficient of each index variables was below 0.5, and was of significance at 0.01 levels, indicating each index had excellent independence, and the remaining indexes had better representativeness, which had remained the reflective content of index and avoided repetitive evaluation. The results showed that the established index system in the study had both independence and representativeness.

3.4.2 Discrimination Test

The discrimination test was performed for the index evaluation system in this study in the view of their variance coefficients. The discrimination ability of evaluation index is referred to the ability of index to discriminate the evaluation object. The discrimination ability of evaluation index of enterprise labor relations is to the ability to discriminate the different labor relations status. While the larger is the variable coefficient, the stronger is the discrimination ability of evaluation index; otherwise the discrimination ability is weaker. The calculation results were showed in Table 5. All variable coefficients of final selected variables in the study were larger than 0.2, indicating the index system had better discrimination ability and the screened index system met the requirements of variance and representativeness.

The verification results of the above methods showed that the established index system in the study had better independence, representativeness and discrimination ability, and also reflected the labor relations status of evaluated object comprehensively and systematically, as a reliable tool of evaluating enterprise labor relations in conformity with the principles of design and screen.

4 Empirical Study on Evaluation of Enterprise Labor Relations Harmony

The evaluation index system would served as the tool for the application of the evaluation the enterprise labor relations harmony after it was verified through theoretical analysis, screening index with subjective and objective methods, weight determination and statistical method. To verify the effectiveness of the established index system in the research, the empirical study was performed among 837 employees from 245 enterprises. A comprehensive evaluation of enterprise labor relations was carried out by fuzzy comprehensive evaluation.

4.1 Formulation of Scoring Standard

To evaluate something takes more than an evaluation tool, and formulation of scoring standard is needed, the present study has establish the quantitative scoring standard of enterprise labor relations harmony combining with the reality of small and medium-sized enterprises in Beijing based on theoretical study and document analysis.

4.2 Standardization of Index

Since each evaluation index with its own specific dimension was incomparable, not allowing the comparison of index value with different dimension, a direct comparison could be done between indexes in different units, also reduce the impact on the comprehensive evaluation due to fluctuation range of index value and dimension so as to minimize the loss of information. The standardization procedure of index data can usually be classified into Curve Undimensionalization, Polygonal Undimensionalization and Linear Undimensionalization. Extreme value method was adopted in the study to standardize the index data. The calculation formula is as follows:

$$L=(L-Lmin)/(Lmax-Lmin)x100$$

Lmin indicated the min value of each index, and Lmax indicated the Max value.

4.3 Evaluation of Enterprise Labor Relations Process with Fuzzy Comprehensive Assessment Method

The fuzzy comprehensive assessment method refers to introduce the idea and method of fuzzy mathematics into evaluation of something. Since many indexes are required comprehensive quantitative evaluation by enterprise labor relations, fuzzy comprehensive evaluation has become an effective method. The fuzzy comprehensive evaluation method in the study when applied in evaluation of enterprise labor relations includes the following steps:

(I) Determination of factor set

Establishment of evaluation index set

$$U=\{U_1,U_2,U_3,\ldots,U_m\} \quad (1),$$

It was the set of evaluation index L1-L28 in the study, and was classified two sub-factor sets, U1 indicating first-grade index set and U2 indicating second-grade index set, according to impact of labor relations.

$$U_i = U_{i1}, U_{i2}, \cdots, U_{in} \quad (2), \qquad \text{where } i = 1, 2, \cdots, s,$$

$U_1, U_2, \cdots, U_n$ and $U_{i1}, U_{i2}, \cdots, U_{in}$ were called as evaluation indexes, all of which can synthetically reflect the quality of evaluation object.

(II) Determination of evaluation set

$$V = \{v_1, v_2, \quad , v_m\} \quad (3)$$

Where Vm was comment which was previously determined available for selection, applicable for all evaluation factors in formula (1) and (2).The determined evaluation set in the study was stated as the part of full text scoring standard, with five grades including

$$V = \{\text{far greater, greater, equal, lower, far lower}\}$$

(III) Establishment of weight set

$$W=\{\mu_1,\mu_2, \mu_3,\ldots\mu_m\}$$

Weight reflects the importance of each evaluation index in a comprehensive evaluation, and $\sum\mu_m=1$

The set of weight of each index obtained by analytical hierarchy process was the weight set developed in the research.

$$W=\{0.043,0.048, 0.035,\ldots0.048\}$$

(IV) Determination of evaluation Matrix R

R_{ij} of evaluation Matrix R in the study was the score of each index for enterprise sample, which was obtained after standardization, scoring and calculation as defined by the proposed scoring standard, constituting the evaluation matrix of the research.

$$R=\begin{bmatrix} 74.3 & 54.3 & \ldots & 51.3 & 73.3 & 85.0 \\ 78.6 & 77.8 & \ldots & 61.3 & 33.3 & 56.3 \\ 65.7 & 50.0 & \ldots & 25.0 & 33.3 & 47.5 \\ \ldots & \ldots & \ldots & \ldots & \ldots & \ldots \\ 53.6 & 68.5 & \ldots & 58.8 & 66.7 & 47.5 \\ 92.9 & 84.0 & \ldots & 80.0 & 88.9 & 100.0 \\ 100 & 77.8 & \ldots & 87.5 & 66.7 & 70.0 \end{bmatrix}$$

(I) Fuzzy comprehensive evaluation

Through fuzzy transformation between weight matrix W and evaluation matrix R, fuzzy assessment set S was obtained.

$$S=W*R=\{\mu_1,\mu_2, \mu_3,\ldots\mu_m\}*\begin{bmatrix} r_{11} & r_{12}\ldots & r_{1m} \\ r_{21} & r_{212}\ldots & r_{2m} \\ \ldots & \ldots & \ldots \\ R_{n1} & r_{n2}\ldots & r_{nm} \end{bmatrix}$$

Through the values of established weight matrix set W and evaluation matrix R into fuzzy comprehensive assessment matrix formula, the results were as followed

$$\{0.043,0.048, 0.035,\ldots0.048\}*\begin{bmatrix} 74.3 & 54.3 & \ldots & 51.3 & 73.3 & 85.0 \\ 78.6 & 77.8 & \ldots & 61.3 & 33.3 & 56.3 \\ 65.7 & 50.0 & \ldots & 25.0 & 33.3 & 47.5 \\ \ldots & \ldots & \ldots & \ldots & \ldots & \ldots \\ 53.6 & 68.5 & \ldots & 58.8 & 66.7 & 47.5 \\ 92.9 & 84.0 & \ldots & 80.0 & 88.9 & 100.0 \\ 100 & 77.8 & \ldots & 87.5 & 66.7 & 70.0 \end{bmatrix}$$

4.4 Comprehensive Assessment Results and Analysis

The evaluation result in the enterprise labor relations evaluation index system, that was evaluation value, reflected the status of labor relations in enterprise. Using fuzzy comprehensive assessment, a comprehensive evaluation of labor relations was performed among 245 enterprises. The evaluation value was showed in Table 1.

Table 1. Statistics of evaluation of labor relations harmonious degree in enterprise

Enterprise No.	Evaluation value	Enterprise No.	Evaluation value	Enterprise No.	Evaluation value	Enterprise No.	Evaluation value	Enterprise No.	Evaluation value
1	60.48	50	54.42	99	58.97	148	46.21	197	59.63
2	52.85	51	57.66	100	48.97	149	52.86	198	44.13
3	50.49	52	50.55	101	50.27	150	54.78	199	50.97
4	52.13	53	51.65	102	52.00	151	56.34	200	45.64
5	58.27	54	37.87	103	52.47	152	46.66	201	52.15
6	49.49	55	58.53	104	50.39	153	50.55	202	53.34
7	50.78	56	48.35	105	57.80	154	50.39	203	46.26
8	55.84	57	47.90	106	42.78	155	63.73	204	52.44
9	57.05	58	52.58	107	47.92	156	55.03	205	47.64
10	41.35	59	49.12	108	50.21	157	48.20	206	53.79
11	54.88	60	41.73	109	47.03	158	58.22	207	52.10
12	42.54	61	57.16	110	44.91	159	43.98	208	60.11
13	59.02	62	53.20	111	60.19	160	48.45	209	54.27
14	64.42	63	59.13	112	40.10	161	58.42	210	51.25
15	67.80	64	64.75	113	55.16	162	49.10	211	43.99
16	62.32	65	55.66	114	48.97	163	52.55	212	42.24
17	51.49	66	51.98	115	37.21	164	47.82	213	42.05
18	50.87	67	60.82	116	54.84	165	61.98	214	44.51
19	62.26	68	50.83	117	45.16	166	56.59	215	54.04
20	57.42	69	58.52	118	54.58	167	54.28	216	57.46

Table 1 (*continued*)

21	52.46	70	56.61	119	46.87	168	43.41	217	58.78
22	52.12	71	51.99	120	55.79	169	45.90	218	56.09
23	49.19	72	47.49	121	47.16	170	50.30	219	57.04
24	55.96	73	48.67	122	59.62	171	53.21	220	44.81
25	53.06	74	42.90	123	45.36	172	48.76	221	49.19
26	53.86	75	59.85	124	49.98	173	54.00	222	63.88
27	47.74	76	55.46	125	51.32	174	47.57	223	54.66
28	56.89	77	58.31	126	49.71	175	40.12	224	63.62
29	58.77	78	48.19	127	51.17	176	45.89	225	49.36
30	56.13	79	60.12	128	38.71	177	41.37	226	53.93
31	61.30	80	56.96	129	59.40	178	61.92	227	61.69
32	49.70	81	58.15	130	48.40	179	60.98	228	50.88
33	54.73	82	57.09	131	53.07	180	47.32	229	51.92
34	57.84	83	51.87	132	50.14	181	46.18	230	52.97
35	49.90	84	49.08	133	58.86	182	55.26	231	48.57
36	59.32	85	52.22	134	49.33	183	57.29	232	49.78
37	52.14	86	54.39	135	49.54	184	48.42	233	53.18
38	55.46	87	44.47	136	43.49	185	59.38	234	56.39
39	59.06	88	53.49	137	55.38	186	58.13	235	51.77
40	41.56	89	36.07	138	54.29	187	60.45	236	58.57
41	51.23	90	49.03	139	58.75	188	56.49	237	40.02
42	38.33	91	52.89	140	42.19	189	58.78	238	46.08
43	57.25	92	50.03	141	50.04	190	50.22	239	61.05
44	67.56	93	46.80	142	46.58	191	57.46	240	46.51
45	58.53	94	52.26	143	36.01	192	57.97	241	44.33
46	50.93	95	63.47	144	65.83	193	52.26	242	52.59
47	44.05	96	57.86	145	59.10	194	51.40	243	50.54
48	40.31	97	61.74	146	49.82	195	60.21	244	66.69
49	55.54	98	42.27	147	52.29	196	49.17	245	61.67
Mean value:									

The study has classified the score according to different evaluation grade and adopted four grade comments that were score over 60 indicated excellent, 51-60 common, 41-50 poor and below 40 bad. See table 9 for scatter-gram of enterprise evaluation value.

Table 2. Scatter-gram of enterprise evaluation value

Evaluation grade	**Corresponding evaluation value**	**Number of enterprise**	**Proportion (%)**
Excellent labor relations	Over 60	21	8.57
Common labor relations	51-60	120	48.98
Poor labor relations	41-50	97	39.59
Bad labor relations	Below 40	7	2.86

In terms of overall evaluation value, the max score was 67.80, the min score was 38.33, and the mean value was 52.40. With regarding to distribution, 19 enterprises were in the status of "excellent labor relations", accounting for 7.76%; 126 were in the common status, accounting for 51.43%; 93 were in poor status, for 2.86%. The data showed that more than 50 percent of enterprises were in the state of "common labor relations", and enterprises in "poor and bad labor relations" were more numerous than those in "excellent labor relations". From the evaluation score distribution map of labor relations in investigated enterprise, the evaluation of labor relations was basically a normal distribution. Fewer enterprises were in the condition of excellent and bad labor relations, and dominated-enterprises were in the status of common and bad labor relations. The above results showed to some extent that labor relations of most enterprises must be dealt with as a matter of priority.

References

1. Katz, H.C., Kochan, T.A., Gobeille, K.R.: Industrial Relations Performance, Economic erformance and QWL Programs: An Interplant Analysis. Industrial and Labor Relations Review (2), 5–7 (1983)
2. Katz, H.C.: The Decentralization of collective bargaining: A Literature Review and comparative Analysis. Industrial and Labor Relations Review (13), 16–19 (1993)
3. Katz, H.,C., Kochan, T.A., Weber, M.R.: Assessing the Effects of Industrial, Relations Systems and Efforts to Improve the Quality of Working. The Academy of Management Journal (15), 15–20 (1985)
4. Kochan, T.A., et al.: The Transformation of American Industrial Relations. China Labor and Social Security Publishing House, Beijing (2008); Translated by Zhufei , Wang, K.
5. Hesheng: Studies on the evaluation of labor relations. Economic Review (2007)
6. Wang, H., Qiu, L.: Quantitative assessment model for labor relations in enterprises. Shanghai Enterprises (7), 10–13 (2001)

Analysis on Beijing's Low-Carbon City Evaluation Index System

Yanfang Yang, Xiling Li, and Haixia Zheng

School of Management, Beijing Union University
100101, P.R. China

Abstract. Beijing has large energy consumption and serious pollution. There is a research need to establish a suitable low-carbon city evaluation index system to measure the performance of low-carbon city planning and construction. In this paper, we established three-layer low-carbon city evaluation index system based on the PSR model and get the comprehensive evaluation score of Beijing's low-carbon city development in 2009.

Keywords: Low-Carbon City Evaluation Index System Beijing.

1 Introduction

The concept of low-carbon city was firstly proposed by the British, which refers to the cities with rapid economic development, low energy consumption and carbon dioxide emissions. City, as the center of human social and economic activities, brings together more than half of the world population. Greenhouse gas emissions in cities account for about 75% of the global emissions. With the rapid urbanization, urban population is increasing substantially. Urban energy consumption is a major source of global carbon emissions. As the capital of china, Beijing has large energy consumption and serious pollution. In 2010, population in Beijing exceeded 17.5 million and vehicles fleet exceeded 4.76 million. Beijing has a strong need to construct low-carbon city. During the "Eleventh Five-Year" Beijing has launched a series of low-carbon exploration and practice to meet the requirements of low-carbon development. Energy efficiency, industrial structure, energy structure, urban greening rate and low-carbon technology research have been optimized and improved, which laid a good foundation for low-carbon development of Beijing.

Currently, Beijing is at the initial stage of low-carbon city construction. Domestic low carbon-city research mainly focused on discussion of the necessity, design principles and methods. Studies that examined index system of the low-carbon city are limited and there is no standard evaluation and index system. There is a research need to establish a suitable low-carbon city evaluation index system to measure the performance of low-carbon city planning and construction. The low-carbon city evaluation index system has great significance to promote the Urban Construction management and sustainable development of Beijing.

M. Zhou (Ed.): ISAEBD 2011, Part III, CCIS 210, pp. 163–169, 2011.

2 Definition of Low-Carbon City

In order to build a low carbon city development index system, we need to make the definition of low-carbon city. Academia has different definition of low-carbon city. Low-carbon city development is to maintain energy consumption and carbon dioxide emissions at a lower level in the context of rapid economic development. Scholars believe that low-carbon cities not only include low-carbon energy and low-carbon production, but also include low-carbon consumption and low-carbon society. Xia Kunbao believe that low-carbon city is to implement low-carbon economy in the city, including low-carbon production , low-carbon consumption, the establishment of resource-saving and environment-friendly society and building a healthy sustainable energy ecosystem. On this basis, FuYun, Wang Yunlin and other scholars believe that the low-carbon city means to minimize the city's greenhouse gas emissions, shake off mass production, mass consumption and mass emission mode, develop clean, efficient low-carbon and sustainable development by developing low-carbon economy, innovating low-carbon technology and changing lifestyle. Zhuang Guiyang addressed that: the essence of low-carbon economy is energy efficiency and clean energy structure; the core is the innovation in energy technology and system; the goal is to alleviate climate change and promote sustainable human development. In Zhu Dajian's opinion: low-carbon city means the relative decoupling between energy consumption and CO2 emissions from the macro level; From the micro level it means comprehensive low-carbon in the process of importing, transforming and exporting.

This paper argues that the low-carbon city is essentially practical application of low carbon economy concept and low-carbon society concept in the urban development.The low-carbon city is defined as a comprehensive reflection of low-carbon production, low-carbon consumption, low-carbon environment and low-carbon urban planning.

3 Construction Ideas of Evaluation Index System for Low-Carbon City

In the late 1980s, Economic Cooperation and Development Organization and United Nations Environment Programme jointly proposed PSR (pressure-status-response) model to measure environmental indicators. In the PSR framework a particular environmental problem can be represented by three different types of indicators: pressure indicators reflect the impact of human activities on the environment; status indicators reflect environmental quality, natural resources and ecosystem conditions; response indicators reflect policies and measurement to deal with environmental problems. PSR model has a strong systematicness because it can classify environmental indicators from the interaction of human and environmental systems.

In this paper, we will establish three-layer low-carbon city evaluation index system based on the PSR model.

- ✓ Target Layer. In order to quantitatively reflect the status and development of low-carbon city development, the paper design target layer--- comprehensive evaluation of low-carbon city development index. This indicator is a comprehensive reflection in the process of developing low-carbon production, low-carbon consumption, low-carbon environment and low-carbon urban planning.

- ✓ Criterion layer. To better reflect the various influences that subsystems exert on the low-carbon city development, we design four criterion layers including low-carbon production, low-carbon consumption, low-carbon environment and low-carbon urban planning. The main pressure in the process of low-carbon city development comes from carbon emissions of production and consumption, so it is very important to emphasize low-carbon production and consumption in low-carbon city development. Low-carbon environment reflects the current state of the environment faced by the city. Low-carbon urban planning is a symbol of countermeasures people taken when they face environmental problems.
- ✓ Index layer. Index layer is described as the fundamental indexes in the process of low-carbon city development. This paper will add some related indicators based on the research of Chinese Academy of Sciences.

4 Evaluation Methods on Low-Carbon City Evaluation System

4.1 Determination of Weights

In previous discussion we can easily see that the evaluation of low-carbon city is a multi-level and multi-index comprehensive evaluation. In the comprehensive evaluation process, it is core issue how to define the weight of indicators scientifically and reasonably. In this paper the analytic hierarchy process (AHP) will be used to determine the index weight.

In this study, 10 experts are invited to join the analysis. We got comparison matrix of different layers. Extreme judgments in the matrix will be effectively eliminated, and then integrated into the community judgments. By way of scoring experts can determine the relative importance of each indicator. We can calculate the Max eigenvalue and corresponding standardized characteristic vector. If the consistency rates are available through consistency test, we can use YAAHP software to get comparison matrix of each index and index weight. The index weight is shown in table 1.

4.2 Determination of Index's Standard Value

Index's standard value will be determined according to the following principles.

✓ If there is national standard or international standard, try to use the standard value available.

✓ Determine the standard value according to the existing domestic or international good examples.

✓ Determine the standard value by making trend extrapolation of domestic status.

✓ As for the indicators, which is very important in the target system and statistical data are not very complete, can be temporarily replaced by a similar index.

4.3 Standardized Indicators

Individual index reflects different aspects of low-carbon city development. In order to reflect the complete picture we need to make comprehensive evaluation. Suppose the system evaluation index system come up with m objects. There is n factors for every object. The evaluation system can expressed by $n \times m$ matrix $X = (x_{ij})_{n \times m}$, where x_{ij} (i= 1, 2, , , n; j= 1, 2, , , m) represents the characteristic values . If the evaluation factors are qualitative indicators, x_{ij} is the expert score value.

Firstly, the indicators should be normalized. In general, all the indicators in low-carbon city evaluation can be divided into positive and negative index. For positive index, we can normalize as formula (1); and for negative index, we can normalize as formula (2);

$$r_{ij} = \begin{cases} x_{ij} / z_i & x_{ij} < z_i \\ 1 & x_{ij} \geq z_i \end{cases} \tag{1}$$

$$r_{ij} = \begin{cases} z_i / x_{ij} & x_{ij} > z_i \\ 1 & x_{ij} \leq z_i \end{cases} \tag{2}$$

x_{ij} is an actual value of a single index; z_i is the standard value of index i. Clearly, 0< r_{ij}< 1, the greater r_{ij}, the better for this index's evaluation. Because we need a percentile index evaluation, we need plus 100 on the basis of r_{ij}.

4.4 Synthetical Evaluation

The normalized matrix of evaluation factors in the index layer is R_{ij}. The weight of each index is w_{ij} , the value of index layer is $R_i = R_{ij} w_{ij}$, The weight of each index layer is u_i, The synthetical evaluation of this system will be $\sum_{i=1}^{n} u_i \times R_i$

We can use this model to calculate the level of low-carbon development.

5 Analysis of Beijing's Low-Carbon City Development in 2009

We can get the comprehensive evaluation score of Beijing's low-carbon city development in 2009 under the existing weights and the index score. It is shown in table 1.The value is 83, which indicates that the current low-carbon urban construction of Beijing has made some effectiveness in the low-carbon city development. There are high marks in low-carbon consumption and low-carbon envirment. It is a strong need to improve the low-carbon production and low-carbon urban planning.

Table 1. Analysis of Beijing's Low-Carbon City Development in 2009

Criterion Layer	Index Layer	Value of Index	Index's Standard Value	Score
Low-Carbon Production (0.2607)	Carbon Productivity(0.5179)	7400yuan/ton	12000 yuan/ton	62
	Energy Intensity per Unit GDP (0.3038)	0.54 tce /10^4 yuan	Average level in the world	80
	The Percentage of Tertiary Industry in GDP(0.1782)	75.8%	80%	94
Low-Carbon Consumption (0.2480)	CO2 Emission per Capita (0.4018)	9.3 tons per capita	5 tons per capital	77
	Energy Consumption Elasticity Index (0.2693)	0.38	<0.8	100
	Average Consumption CO2 Emission per Capita(0.3289)	1.7tons per capita	1.67	96.5
Low-Carbon Environment (0.2031)	Green Coverage (0.3017)	44.5%	45%.	99
	Disposal Rate of Sewage(0.2126)	80.3%	100%	80
	Harmless Treatment Rate of Garbage(0.2126)	98.2%	100%	98
	Percentage of Air Pollution Index at and better than Grade II (0.2730)	78.1%	85%	92
Low-Carbon Urban Planning (0.2882)	Proportion of Clean Energy(0.4092)	68%	Average value in the world.	76
	Proportion of Low Energy Building(0.2136)	75%	80%	94
	Popularization of Low-Carbon Concept(0.1839)	70	Score of questionnaire	70
	Proportion of Public Traffic(0.1933)	38.9%	50%	78

Over the past few years, Beijing has made a remarkable achievement in reducing carbon dioxide emissions. Average annual carbon emissions growth rate in Beijing is 1.87% which account for 1 / 3 of Shanghai' growth rate(4.43%). It is the lowest in cities of China; Per capita emission rate is -0.66%, which is also the lowest and the only negative growth in cities of China. The growth rate of carbon emissions per GDP is -12.81%. it is also the most significant decline.

Beijing has four major advantages in the Construction of low-carbon city:

(1)Beijing's industrial structure has been constantly adjusted and optimized. The proportion of the tertiary industry in the national economy has have risen rapidly;

(2) Efforts were intensified to reduce greenhouse gas emissions by conserving energy.

(3) Energetically strengthening ecological environment construction.

(4) The gradual establishment of government-led development mechanism.

There are still some bottlenecks in Beijing's low-carbon development city. Currently we are facing major challenges as followed:

(1) The energy structure is not reasonable. The proportion of clean energy, especially zero-carbon energy is low.

(2) Low-carbon city urban planning needs to be improved.

(3) With economic development, per capita carbon emissions and per capita carbon emissions may face a gradual increase pressure.

6 Summary

Based on the PSR model, this paper designed a preliminary evaluation system for low-carbon city. In the design process of this system we try to cover as much as possible indicators have a strong correlation with low-carbon city. We get quantitative evaluation results. However, due to the limitations of existing statistical data, the index system in the design process also need to make efforts in the following areas:

(1) The most important in the establishment of low-carbon city system is carbon emissions calculation. In this paper carbon emissions calculation is based on the estimate of energy use. The accuracy of the data needs to be improved.

(2) Due to data's limitations, the design had to give up some data which is very useful but difficult to obtain, such as urban planning-related indicators (availability of public facilities, the proportion of low-carbon buildings). This will have a negative impact on comprehensive evaluation of low-carbon cities. Low-carbon city evaluation index system needs strengthen the statistical work and provide data support by statistics, environmental protection, urban construction, and other government departments.

(3) We use the AHP method in determining the weight of subsystem. This method combines qualitative and quantitative. Subjectivity can not be completely eliminated because weights are based on expert judgment. In future studies, it is necessary to use other methods to determine the weights of subsystems in order to obtain more satisfactory results.

Acknowledgement. This paper is supported by National Natural Science Foundation (70703001), Beiing Union University Leading Academic Discipline Project of Regional Economics(11103541603) and Beijing Eduction Committee Social and Science program(SM201111417003).

References

1. Xia, H.: Developing Low-Carbon Economy and Making Sustainable Development of Cities. Environmental Protection 2, 33–35 (2008)
2. Fu, Y., Wang, Y., Li, D.: Research on the Path of Low-Carbon City Development. The Impact of Science on Society 2, 5–10 (2008)
3. Zhuang, G.: Low-Carbon Economy: China's Development Road in the Context of Climate Change. Meteorological Press, Beijing (2007)
4. Chen, F., Zhu, D.: The Content, Model and Target Strategies of Low-Carbon Cities. Urban Planning 4, 20–25 (2009)
5. Li, X.: Low-Carbon Economy Evaluation Method of Province based on Fuzzy AHP. East China Economic Management 24, 24–28 (2010)
6. Department of Trade and Industry(DTI). UK Energy White Paper: Our Energy Future—·Creating a Low-Carbon Economy. TSO, London (2003)
7. "2050 Japan Low-Carbon Society" Scenario team. Japan Scenarios and Actions towards Low-Carbon Societies (EB/OL), http://2050.nice.go.jp/material/2050_LCS_Scenarios_Actions_English080715.pdf
8. http://en.wikipedia.org/wiki/List_of_countries_by_carbon_dioxide_emissions_per_capita
9. http://www.docin.com/p-91378055.html
10. http://www.bjstats.gov.cn/

Risk Measurement and Early Warning in the Development of High-Tech Industry

Wei Liu, Hong Zhou, and Mujin Yuan

Institute of Techno-Economy and Management,
Economics and Management School,
Wuhan University
Wuhan, P.R. China, 430072

Abstract. High-tech industry development process associated with high risk. It promotes the transformation and upgrade of traditional industries structure, makes a growing contribution to economic growth and enhances national competitiveness. Risk measurement and early warning in the development of high-tech industry is a very complex and scientific issues. It is complicated because many factors affect their development. This paper analyzes the risk factors and features of high-tech industry, reviews existing risk measurement and early warning methods. Then we discuss the deficiency of existing methods and possible research directions.

Keywords: High-Tech industry, Risk measurement and early warning, Multivariate statistical analysis, Artificial neural network.

1 Introduction

High-tech industry is an enterprise cluster based on high and new technology, engaged in one or more technology and product research, development, production and technical services. The key technology often developed very difficult, but once developed, it has higher economic and social benefits. High-tech industry is knowledge-intensive and technology-intensive industries. The high and new technology often have higher contribution rate and strong industrial linkage, its marketization and industrialization can promote the rationalization and advancement of industrial structure, and play a tremendous role in promoting economic development. High-tech industry has formed a new industrial cluster and becomes a new growth point of national economy. It promotes the transformation and upgrade of traditional industries structure, makes a growing contribution to economic growth and enhances national competitiveness.

High-tech industry promotes the rapid development of world economy, meanwhile, in the course of its development is also associated with higher risk. This problem has attracted the attention of the world, many countries are struggling to find the methods to predict and prevent the risks. Conducting a reasonable risk measurement and early warning is an important task and an effective way to maintain sustainable development in the process of development of high-tech industries.

M. Zhou (Ed.): ISAEBD 2011, Part III, CCIS 210, pp. 170–176, 2011.

2 The Risk Factors and Features of High-Tech Industry

Compared with the traditional industries, high-tech industry has a greater risk in the development process. This risk is the result of many factors, such as the uncertainty of the external environment, the complexity of production and the limit of business activities and corporate capacity. Generally believed, there are many risk factors in the process of industrial development. For example, market demand, human resources, core technological innovation, capital, social environment, cultural differences and thinking, and natural disasters. Chen (2003) considered that the risk of high-tech industry mainly manifested as the development of risk, market risk, operational risk, personnel liquidity risk, policy risk. Zhang (2007) considered that the general mechanism of the formation of the high-tech industry risk are natural factors, social factors, economic factors, human factors and information factors, and other factors; Special causes are wrong decisions, science and technology (high cost and technical vulnerability), the unique market structure, government policy. Gao (2006) considered the risk of high-tech industry mainly comes from technology, capital, and market and so on.

Zhang (2007) considered that the risk of high-tech industry is characterized by the growth of objectivity, complexity, potential, relative, high losses and high-yield duality. On the other hand, high-tech industrialization has a relatively long period, while product has a short life cycle with updating faster and more effective(Gao 2006). In general, high-tech industrial development requires a large and long investment cycle external capital support, and needs for sound financial operation of the mechanism to counter the high risk.

3 Risk Measurement and Early Warning

Industry is a collection of several enterprises. Enterprise is the basic unit and microstructure of industry. Industrial development is the jointly of enterprises growth, reasonable risk measurement and early warning embodied within the industry for the high-tech enterprises measure and early warning. To measure business risk and early warning, risk should be identified first. Risks identification includes risk perception and risk analysis. The purpose of risks identification is to understand the nature of the risks and causes, and prepare for the budget and early warning. In practice, risk identification is generally based on the experience of decision makers, focusing on the qualitative analysis. In theory, identification methods are index analysis, financial statements act, flow chart, scenario analysis, decision analysis, dynamic analysis method and so on. In the current study on the risk identification, isolation, characterization, static methods are far more than integrated, quantitative, dynamic ones.

On the basis of the identification, the model of risk measurement and early warning can be established. Enterprise risk measurement and early warning related mainly to the following models: unary decision model, multivariate statistical analysis, artificial neural network (ANN) model, fuzzy evaluation method, entropy function method.

Enterprise risk measurement and early warning can be built on the financial early warning system, considering the financial and non financial indicators. Unary decision model predicts enterprise risk by a single indicator. By comparing 27 ST companies with the same size non-ST companies, Chen (1999) found that asset-liability ratio, current ratio, return on assets, return on net assets are four strong financial predictors and especially two or three years before bankruptcy the total return on assets is efficient. However, the generation of enterprise risk is the result of many factors, the unary decision model are often not precise enough. In 1968 Altman first used the multivariate statistical analysis to study the company's bankruptcy, proposed the famous Z-score model, and determine the threshold of bankruptcy. It is mainly through the statistical analysis of several financial indicators, calculate the weights, and then calculate the risk values by the weights and the indicators. Currently, the studies of multivariate statistical analysis mainly use of principal component analysis(PCA). PCA involves a mathematical procedure that transforms a number of (possibly) correlated variables into a smaller number of uncorrelated variables called principal components. The first principal component accounts for as much of the variability in the data as possible, and each succeeding component accounts for as much of the remaining variability as possible. The core of this method is through the principal component analysis to select a number of principal components, construct weights based on the variance contribution of principal components and then construct evaluation functions. It has the advantages of objective and scientific. When the first principal component of the variance contribution is large, we can directly use the first principal component to measure the risk of high-tech enterprises. Chung-Jen Chen, Chin-Chen Huang (2004) used principal component analysis to evaluate high-tech industries in Taiwan. It is concluded that the market potential is the biggest factor, followed by level of technology and government policy.

Artificial neural network (ANN), usually called neural network (NN), is a mathematical model or computational model that is inspired by the structure and/or functional aspects of biological neural networks. It can be used to solve identification and perception, evaluation and decision-making and other complex issues. It is a new rapidly developed subject. In some areas of scientific research and practical projects, it has shown a great power. An important feature of ANN is to improve the accuracy of prediction model by learning data. To some extent, it avoids the subjectivity of human identification. In the study of measuring and predicting the risk of high-tech enterprises, the use of more is back-propagation neural network (BP neural network) and its modification. BP neural network is a kind of three or more than three one-way transmission of a multilayer feedforward network. It consists of input layer, hidden layer and output layer. Hidden layer can have one or more. Each neuron receives a signal from the neurons in the previous layer, and each of those signals is multiplied by a separate weight value. The weighted inputs are summed, and passed through a limiting function which scales the output to a fixed range of values. The output of the limiter is then broadcast to all of the neurons in the next layer. In 1989, Hecht Nielson proved that a hidden layer of BP network can complete the n-dimensional to m-dimensional mapping. Wang, Gao and Guo (2003) used BP neural network to evaluate the international competitiveness of high-tech industry with satisfactory results.

There are no paper using BP neural network to analyze risk measurement and early warning in the development of High-tech industry yet, and more are using BP neural network to analyze it in high-tech enterprises level or in the micro level in the industry. For example, Li, Wang (2003) used the artificial neural network on the risk assessment,

Li, Qin and Wang (2008) evaluated the survival risk of high-tech enterprises in the High-tech Development Zone of Nanning. The current neural network topology shown in Fig.1. can be applied to the risk measurement and early warning in high-tech enterprise.

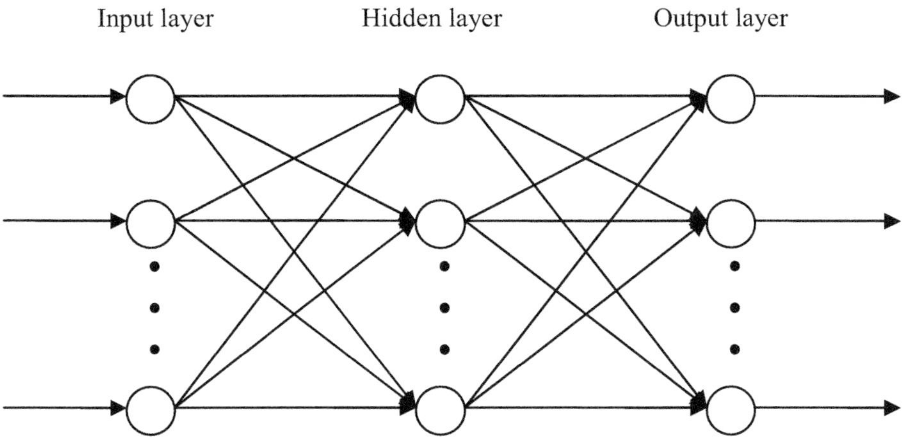

Fig. 1. The neural network topology

The risk measurement and early warning model of high-tech enterprises estimates the risk by calculating the output values. It uses error back propagation learning algorithm for modeling and determines the model by neural network learning. It can be seen as a nonlinear mapping which assesses the input of indicators to the output of the final evaluation of enterprise value. The calculation steps can be summarized as follows:

Step 1, select samples of high-tech enterprises, and determine the risk indicators a_i and the safety indicators c_i. Give the hidden layer connection weights ω_{ij}, bias values θ_j and the output layer connection weights γ_{jt}, bias values r_t any number at (-1,+1) , determine learning efficiency α and β, and set the allowable error range

Step 2, select the index data entry a_i, and find the output b_j of the hidden layer and output y_t of layer output. The formula is as follows:

$$b_j = f(\sum_{i=1}^{n} \omega_{ij} a_i - \theta_j)\text{, nis the number of input layer neurons} \tag{1}$$

$$y_t = f(\sum_{j=1}^{p} \gamma_{jt} b_j - r_t)\text{, p is the number of hidden layer neurons} \tag{2}$$

$f(\bullet)$ is the Sigmoid function:

$$f(x) = \frac{1}{1+e^{-x}} \tag{3}$$

The expected output from the learning data, find the error output layer unit t and hidden unit j of the error, calculated as follows:

Step 3, solve the error d_t^k of output layer unit t and the error e_j^k of output layer unit j from the learning data expected output c_t. The formula is as follows:

$$d_t^k = (c_t - y_t)y_t(1 - y_t) \tag{4}$$

$$e_j^k = (d_t^k \gamma_{jt})b_j(1 - b_j) \tag{5}$$

Step 4, amend hidden layer connection weight ω_{ij} and bias values θ_j, output layer connection weights γ_{jt} and bias values r_t.

$$\omega_{ij}(N+1) = \omega_{ij}(N) + \alpha e_j^k a_i \tag{6}$$

$$\theta_j(N+1) = \theta_j(N) + \beta e_j^k \tag{7}$$

$$\gamma_{jt}(N+1) = \gamma_{jt}(N) + \alpha d_t^k b_j \tag{8}$$

$$r_t(N+1) = r_t(N) + \beta d_t^k \tag{9}$$

Step 5, return to Step 2 until all the learning sample training is completed

Step 6, begin a new round of learning, until the error range meets the set requirements. Adjust the parameters to determine the neural network model.

Step 7, enter the test data to verify the correctness of the model.

When we need to forecast high-tech enterprises, just input indicator data, then get the output value calculated by the model to determine business risk and early warning. The main drawback of BP algorithm is: slow learning, local minimum, difficult to determine the hidden layers and the number of hidden layer nodes. In practice, there have been many improvements in algorithms. One is the heuristic learning algorithm, such as additional momentum method, adaptive learning rate adjustment method. Another is the use of more efficient optimization algorithm, such as the conjugate gradient method, quasi-Newton method, etc.

In addition, fuzzy evaluation, expert scoring method and other methods can be used to risk measurement and early warning, but they are not convincing in the process of applying weights to the subjective determination.

4 The Deficiency of Existing Methods and Possible Research Directions

High-tech product life cycle, business life cycle and industry growth cycle constitute the general rules of high-tech industry, and essentially determine the risk of the industry.

In the life cycle, the risks are not the same. For example, in the input stage the biggest risk are the commercialization of science and technology, government policies and other factors, and in the mature stage the biggest risk are market competition and enterprise behavior. Existing models do not consider the industrial life cycle, but put all enterprises together without distinction analysis. This may lead inaccurate models. A lot of enterprises which are competent may be misjudged as risky ones, so policy makers will make the wrong decisions. How to consider the life cycle when measure risk of high-tech enterprises or industries and add life cycle stages to early warning analysis is a direction can be studied.

Most of the current papers are to use the model to measure enterprises risk and early warning, very few do the risk measurement and early warning in the industry level. High-tech enterprise is the composed units of high-tech industry. When the high-tech enterprise risk increases, the high-tech industry risk also increases accordingly. However, on the other hand, high-tech industry as a cluster has a strong technology association effect, scale effect, scope economy effect, polarization effect, fusion effect and other economic characteristics which make the risk measurement and early warning of the high-tech industry more complex than the high-tech enterprise. How to measure enterprise risk reasonably and transform enterprise risk to industrial risk for early warning effectively may be a direction can be studied.

In practice, risk prevention relies mainly on the experience of managers and experts, and existing papers are mainly based on quantitative assessment of risk indicators. In fact, factors which the impact is difficult to quantify often have a greater risk. These factors must be considered in the model. We can combine artificial neural network, wavelet analysis and fuzzy evaluation method, establish risk measurement and early warning model in the development of high-tech industry based on fuzzy wavelet neural network. Specifically, we use fuzzy evaluation method to quantify the risk factors, and use the output of the fuzzy system as the input of neural network. Fuzzy wavelet neural network model achieves quantitative assessment of risk factors, and solves the existing subjective arbitrary, vague conclusions and other defects of the existing assessment methods. It also has higher fitting accuracy and faster convergence than the BP neural network.

The development of high-tech industry is a risky process, and the risk factors are many and complex. Risk measurement and early warning in the development of high-tech industry is a very complex and scientific issues. It is complicated because many factors affect their development. Many methods can be selected and it is difficult to explain which method is the most reliable and most accurate. On the other hand, with depth study and the development of science and technology, quantitative analysis will be more convincing and useful.

References

1. Chen, C.-J., Huang, C.-C.: A multiple criteria evaluation of high-tech industries for the science-based industrial park in Taiwan. Information & Management 41, 839–851 (2004)
2. Wang, W., Gao, C., Guo, C.: Application of Artificial Neural Networks in High-TechIndustry International Competitiveness Evaluation. Harbin University of Technology 8(5), 117–120 (2003)

3. Li, W., Qin, C., Wang, C.: Sustainable Development of High-Tech Enterprises, pp. 127–146. Economic Science Press (2008)
4. Zhang, G.: The Growth of High-Tech Industry the Framework of Qualitative Analysis of Uncertainty, pp. 17–44. China Economic Publishing House (2007)
5. Wu, M., Shao, Y.: High-Tech Industry's Definition based on Neural Network. Research and Development Management 12(2), 13–17 (2000)

The Study on the Impacts of Business-to-Business Relationship Commitment on Information Sharing

Xiao-Rong Jiang and Sui-Cheng Li

School of Business and Administration Management,
Xi'an University of Technology, P.R. China, 710054

Abstract. As the product life cycle become more shorter and the global market is increasingly competitive than before, great importance is attached to supplier management by manufacturing industry. Information sharing can promote high level of coordination between manufacture and supplier . It is necessary to research what factors impacts on information sharing. Based on the investigation among Chinese enterprises, The influencing factors on information sharing are examined in this paper on manufacturer's perspective. Firstly, the results show the relationship characteristics between manufacturer and supplier by influencing relationship commitment affects information sharing, The relationship characteristics between manufacturer and supplier include trust, power and product interdependence; Second, manufacturer internal factors through relationship commitment affects information sharing, manufacturer internal factors include executives support, technical support, innovative culture and employee capacity; Third, relationship commitment can be divided into three dimensions: normative relationship commitment, instrumental relationship commitment and emotional commitment. Manufacturing industry should pay attention to formation and maintenance of relationship with supplier, based on long-term orientation, it is beneficial to information sharing.

Keywords: information sharing, relationship commitment, trust, power
Supported by Human Social Science Research Program of the Ministry Education (10YJA630085), Shaanxi Provincial Soft Science Research Program (2010KRM70).

1 Introduction

As competition in the 1990s intensified and markets became global, so did the challenges associated with getting a product and service to the right place at the right time at the lowest cost.[1]The understanding and practicing of Supply Chain Management (SCM) has become an essential prerequisite for staying competitive in the global race and for enhancing profitably [2,3,4]. Information sharing is a key ingredient for any SCM system [5]. Information sharing leads to high levels of supply chain integration [6] by enabling organizations to make dependable delivery and introduce products to the market quickly. Quality information sharing contributes positively to customer satisfaction [7]. Although previous research discussed the importance of some factors affecting information sharing, But few studies have considered

M. Zhou (Ed.): ISAEBD 2011, Part III, CCIS 210, pp. 177–184, 2011.

simultaneously the impact of relationship characteristics between manufacturer and supplier , and manufacturer internal factors on information sharing in SCM. There is still much work to do in the field.

In this paper, we studied the influencing factors on information sharing based on the manufacturer perspective, specifically, our objectives are: First, to propose and empirically test a model. Secondly, to offer guidelines for practicing managers to enhance information sharing, information sharing could benefit both manufacturer and supplier, thus leading to a win–win situation for the whole supply chain.

2 Theoretical Background and Research Hypotheses

A. Information Sharing

Information sharing refers to the extent to which critical and proprietary information is communicated to one's supply chain partner [R.M.Monczka, K.J.Petersen, R.B.Handfield, G.L.Ragatz, 1998]. The empirical research by Child house will revealed that information flow which is simplified and made visible highly is coordinated and effective in the supply chain [P.Childhouse, D.R.Towill, 2003].

B. Relationship Commitment and Its Construction

In a supply chain, Relationship commitment is an attitude of supply chain partners about the development and maintenance of a stable, long-lasting mutual relationship (Anderson and Weitz, 1992; Moore, 1998).Relationship commitment can be classified as normative or instrumental (Brown et al., 1995). The relationship commitment in this paper can also be instrumental commitment, emotional commitment and normative commitment, of which emotional commitment is the recognition of the relationship and emotional dependence.

C. Information Sharing and Relationship Characteristics

As far as relationship characteristics between manufacturer and supplier are concerned, Trust among supply chain partners is believed as a key factor in elaborating the successful cooperation relationship. The more general concept of power has long been an important topic of study in organizational behavior(Drea et al.,1993).The partners have cooperated for each other in supply chain because of resources interdependence. This kind of relationship made them become a single entity which have joint productivity. Therefore, we hypothesize:

H1a: the higher level of trust the manufacturer for the suppliers, the higher the suppliers normative commitment.

H1b: the higher level of trust the manufacturer for the suppliers, the lower the suppliers instrumental commitment.

H1c: the higher level of trust the manufacturer for the suppliers, the higher the suppliers emotional commitment.

H1d: The greater power the manufacturer for the suppliers, the lower the suppliers normative commitment.

H1e: The greater power the manufacturer for the suppliers, the higher the suppliers instrumental commitment.

H1f: The greater power the manufacturer for the suppliers, the higher the suppliers emotional commitment.. .

H1g: The higher the manufacturer rely on suppliers, the higher the suppliers normative commitment.

H1h: The higher the manufacturer rely on suppliers, the lower the suppliers instrumental commitment.

H1i: The higher the manufacturer rely on suppliers, the lower the suppliers emotional commitment.

H2a:The greater power the manufacturer for the suppliers, the greater the information sharing.

H2b: the higher level of trust the manufacturer for the suppliers, the greater the information sharing.

H2c: The higher the manufacturer rely on suppliers, the greater the information sharing.

D. Information Sharing and Manufacturer Internal Factors

As far as manufacturer internal factors are concerned, executives support is needed in integrating information sharing strategy in SCM. Executives must understand the importance of information sharing and provide vision, guidance, and support for its implementation. Internet extends the scope of SCM practice by providing a cost effective communication backbone so that information can be shared efficiently and effectively. if the organization have strong innovation culture, the organization will try their best in the implementation of specific measures in information sharing. Employees capacity provides the probability for information sharing. Therefore, we hypothesize:

H3a: The more the executives support of the manufacturer, the higher the suppliers normative commitment.

H3b: The more the executives support of the manufacturer, the higher the suppliers instrumental commitment.

H3c: The more the executives support of the manufacturer, the higher the suppliers emotional commitment.

H3d: The more the technical support of the manufacturer, the higher the suppliers normative commitment.

H3e: The more the technical support of the manufacturer, the higher the suppliers instrumental commitment.

H3f: The more the technical support of the manufacturer, the higher the suppliers emotional commitment.

H3g: the higher level the innovation organization culture of the manufacturer, the higher the suppliers normative commitment.

H3h: The higher level the innovation organization culture of the manufacturer, the higher the suppliers instrumental commitment.

H3i: The higher level the innovation organization culture of the manufacturer, the higher the suppliers emotional commitment.

H3j: The stronger the ability of manufacturer personnel, the higher the suppliers normative commitment.

H3k: The stronger the ability of manufacturer personnel, the higher the suppliers instrumental commitment.

H3l: The stronger the ability of manufacturer personnel, the higher the suppliers emotional commitment.

H4a: The more the executives support of the manufacturer , the greater the information sharing.

H4b: the more the technical support of the manufacturer , the greater the information sharing.

H4c: the higher level the innovation organization culture of the manufacturer , the greater the information sharing.

H4d: The stronger the ability of manufacturer personnel, the greater the information sharing.

E. Information Sharing and Relationship Commitment

In the formation and maintenance of relationship, people think it is relationship commitment that is the key and basement between manufacturer and supplier. In short, a high level of relationship commitment will lead to increased cooperation and decreased opportunism. And information sharing is one of the cooperation elements. It reflects the willingness to share information and pass information to each other.

Therefore, we hypothesize:

H5a: the higher the suppliers normative commitment. the greater the information sharing.

H5b: the higher the suppliers instrumental commitment, the greater the information sharing.

H5c: the higher the suppliers emotional commitment, the greater the information sharing.

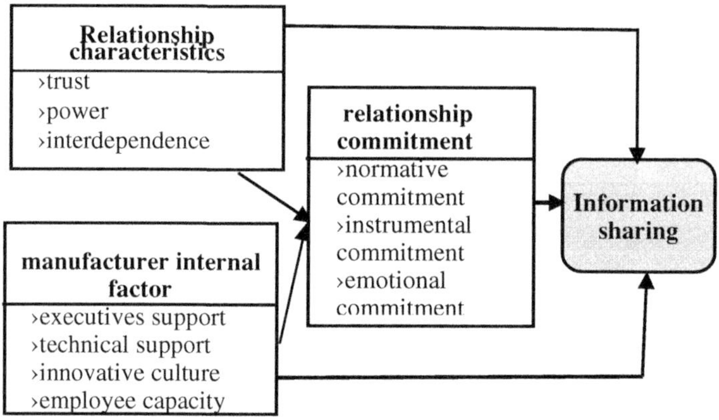

Fig. 1. Proposed model

3 Sample Survey and Descriptive Statistics

Owing to the survey involved all aspects of the situation of the enterprise, our subjects mainly focused on top-level managers, technical personnel, purchase personnel. the investigation release 500 questionnaires and withdraw 302 questionnaires in Xi'an, Beijing, Shanghai and Shenzhen ,from July to December in 2010, having analyzed the questionnaire, there are 281 valid questionnaires, of which effective questionnaire response rate of is 56.2 percent.

4 Analysis and Results

A. Scale reliability and construct validity

Exploratory factor analysis is ensure uni-dimensionality of the scale, then Cronbach's alpha for assessing reliability. EFA was used with principal components analysis for data reduction and determining the main constructs measured by the items. Varimax rotation with Kaiser normalization was used to clarify the factors (Loehlin, 1998). Cronbach's alpha of variables or factors is showed as below, they are all within an acceptable range (greater than 0.7), that indicated variables or factors have good reliability.

Table 1. Cronbach's α of variables or factors

Construct	Factors	No. of items	Alpha	Cronbach α
relationship characteristics	Trust	4	0.8477	0.8875
	Power	3	0.9125	
	Interdependence	2	0.7782	
Manufacturer internal factor	executives support	3	0.8512	0.9156
	technical support	3	0.9287	
	innovative culture	3	0.8863	
	employee capacity	2	0.9074	
relationship commitment	normative commitment	2	0.8621	0.9082
	instrumental commitment	3	0.7213	
	emotional commitment	3	0.8487	
information sharing	Sharing quantity	3	0.8245	0.9367
	Sharing quanlity	4	0.8832	

Table 2. The model fit measure indexes of confirmatory factor analysis of influencing factors on relationship performance

Fit Indices	χ^2	df	χ^2/df	RMSEA	GFI	AGFI	CFI	TLI
relationship characteristics	10.567	38	2.78	0.079	0.985	0.940	0.923	0.930
Manufacturer internal factor	67.63	24	2.80	0.081	0.951	0.908	0.942	0.913
relationship commitment	55.32	27	2.87	0.091	0.947	0.918	0.935	0.920
information sharing	10.631	30	3.54	0.061	0.929	0.868	0.922	0.866

B. Confirmatory Factor Analysis

Based on the above reliability and validity analysis, The reliability and validity has reached an acceptable level in this study. We use structural equation modeling to test the relationship between variables, here we use statistical software AMOS4.01.

When we observed numerical value of GFI, AGFI, NFI or TLI, CFI, IFI, these Five evaluation index above 0.90, it is said a better model, model can be received When

RMSEA less than 0.05, we believe it is a good model when numerical value of RMSEA is between 0.05-0.08, it said a better model; when numerical value of RMSEA is between 0.08-0.10,it is still accepted. However, if greater than 0.10, it indicates that the model don't fit well; generally x^2 / df require less than 5, More stringent requirements are less than 3.

Table 3. The overall analysis of the structural model fit measures

Fit measures	desired quantity	fitting results	Outcome
x^2/df（D/df）	<3	1.056	supported
GFI	>0.9	0.975	supported
AGFI	>0.9	0.937	supported
NFI	>0.9	0.948	supported
TLI	>0.9	0.996	supported
CFI	>0.9	0.998	supported
IFI	>0.9	0.988	supported
RMSEA	<0.08	0.014	supported

This study is based on the established literature at home and abroad, Combined with experience of practitioners and managers, Through effective test samples we determine a modified model. We use confirmatory factor analysis to verify validity. Results is shown as below:

According to statistics analysis of the results, we revised assumptions. the conclusions are as following table shows:

Table 4. The table of SEM results and Modified Hypothesis

path	path coefficients	t-values	P	Outcome
normative commitment <--- trust	.581	3.48	.000	supported
instrumental commitment <--- trust	.105	0.97	.150	supported
emotional commitment <--- trust	.381	3.27	.001	supported
normative commitment <--- power	.207	5.53	.043	supported
instrumental commitment <--- power	.389	2.78	.080	supported
emotional commitment <--- power	.372	2.53	.076	supported
normative commitment <--- interdependence	.545	3.75	.000	supported
instrumental commitment <--- interdependence	.489	2.37	.023	supported
emotional commitment <--- interdependence	.392	3.74	.022	supported
Information sharing<--- trust	.361	4.52	.048	supported

Table 4. (*continued*)

Information sharing<--- power	.060	0.86	.360	rejected
Information sharing<--- interdependence	.072	0.79	.289	rejected
normative commitment <--- executives support	.310	3.53	.009	supported
instrumental commitment <--- executives support	.357	4.12	.005	supported
emotional commitment <--- executives support	.340	5.26	.001	supported
normative commitment <--- technical support	.533	6.57	.042	supported
instrumental commitment <--- technical support	.376	3.37	.008	supported
emotional commitment <--- technical support	.380	7.95	.036	supported
normative commitment <--- innovative culture	.357	5.02	.015	supported
instrumental commitment <--- innovative culture	.484	5.67	.014	supported
emotional commitment <--- innovative culture	.513	6.74	.007	supported
normative commitment <--- employee capacity	.534	7.82	.005	supported
instrumental commitment<---employee capacity	.556	6.46	.009	supported
emotional commitment <--- employee capacity	.07	.79	.390	rejected
information sharing<--- executives support	.05	0.63	.280	rejected
information sharing<--- technical support	.421	3.32	.037	supported
information sharing<--- innovation culture	.372	4.51	.048	supported
information sharing<--- employee capacity	.03	0.58	.380	rejected
information sharing<--- normative commitment	.562	6.13	.007	supported
information sharing<---instrumental commitment	.513	7.14	.0045	supported
information sharing<--- emotional commitment	.548	6.68	.0063	supported

5 Discussion and Conclusion

The study explore the relationship among relationship characteristics between manufacturer and supplier, manufacturer internal factor, relationship commitment and information sharing through theoretical and empirical analysis.The result shows that relationship characteristics between manufacturer and supplier has a positive impact on relationship commitment, it shows that manufacturer internal factor has a positive impact on relationship commitment. It will lay the foundation of information sharing and interactive learning; therefore, managers should attach great importance to formation and maintenance of relationship commitment. It will increase information sharing and promote cooperation.

References

1. Li, S., Lin, B.: Accessing information sharing and information quality in supply chain management. Decision Support Systems 42(1), 1641–1656 (2006)
2. Childhouse, P., Towill, D.R.: Simplified material flow holds the key to supply chain integration. OMEGA 31(1), 17–27 (2003)
3. Rahman, Z.: Use of Internet in supply chain management: a study of Indian companies. Industrial Management and Data Systems 104(1), 31–41 (2004)
4. Tan, K.C., Lyman, S.B., Wisner, J.D.: Supply chain management: a strategic perspective. International Journal of Operations and Production Management 22(6), 614–631 (2002)
5. Moberg, C.R., Cutler, B.D., Gross, A., Speh, T.W.: Identifying antecedents of information exchange within supply chains. International Journal of Physical Distribution and Logistics Management 32(9), 755–770 (2002)
6. Jarrell, J.L.: Supply chain economics. World Trade 11(11), 58–61 (1998)
7. Spekman, R.E., Kamauff, J.W., Myhr, N.: An empirical investigation into supply chain management: a perspective on partnerships. Supply Chain Management 3(2), 53–67 (1998)

Modern Service Industry in Tianjin: Problem, System Construction and Measures

Shuhan Liu

Tianjin University of Commerce
Jinba Road, Beichen District, Tianjin, 300134, P.R. China
liushuhan@vip.163.com, liushuhan1666@126.com

Abstract. The growth rate of service industry in Tianjin has increased gradually since "The 11th Five-year Plan", however, compared with metropolis home and abroad, the gaps still exist. In accordance with the characteristics of modern service industry status quo in Tianjin and its urban function orientation, the approaches to and strategies for future development should be to transform traditional service industry, to accelerate high-end services, to focus on producer service industry, and continuously to improve health and security services. The paper also puts forward the system construction in public administration system, producer service industry system and consumer service industry system.

Keywords: modern service industry, development, system construction, producer service industry.

1 Introduction

With the globalization and development of information technology, modern service industry characterized by high technology, high added value, high human capital and low resource depletion and pollution has taken the place of manufacturing industry and has been the main impetus for world economy. With the adjustment and shifting of global industrial structure and the transition of developing mode in China, how to adjust economic structure has been the key issue in post crisis era. The development of service industry of metropolitan cities is imbalanced. The progress of service industry in Tianjin drops behind other cities in terms of service industry output and employment rate. The lagged development of service industry in Tianjin is becoming the bottleneck for future. However, the rapid growth of Tianjin economy paves the way for its further progress.

2 The Problems of Modern Service Industry in Tianjin

2.1 Small Scale of Total Volume and Slow Development of Emerging Service Industry

In spite of the rapid speed of Tianjin service industry, there are still obvious gaps compared with Beijing and Shanghai. The absolute added values of service industry

M. Zhou (Ed.): ISAEBD 2011, Part III, CCIS 210, pp. 185–191, 2011.

of Beijing and Shanghai are two and three times the amount of Tianjin respectively. The proportions of service industry in GDP in three cities are 75.9%, 59.3% and 43.5% respectively. The proportion of traditional services like transport, storage, hotels and restaurants is high, reaching 50%, while percentages of finance, information, design and education are comparatively low. These reflect that the tardiness and disperse of emerging service industry without scale and conglomeration effect. The knowledge intensive services like information consulting, manufacturing design and medical care are still to be improved. The connected effect, diffusion effect, interactive effect and united development among service sectors have not yet been integrated.

2.2 Low Level of Structure and Weak Strength of Producer Service

The process and tendency of global service industry demonstrate that knowledge and technology intensive services with high added value are the mainstream besides the fast speed and continuous upgrading of service industry. The statistics show the output of producer services in developed countries account for more than 50% of the total service industry. However, in spite of the fast industrialization in Tianjin, producer service industry is lagging behind. The scale advantage of producer service industry including finance, insurance, business, law, R&D, consulting and asset evaluation has not constructed.

2.3 Low Marketization in Service Industry

Service industry is quite competitive with high marketization degree and its globalization has been seen in the world. With service products transferring to developing countries from developed countries, innovation, knowledge based and internationalization have been the dominant tendency. Many emerging developing countries divert to “world office” from “world factory” in order to undertake a new round of international industrial transfer. Some core cities have owned “headquarter economy effect” in international industrial competition. Compared with 707 MNCs’ headquarters attracted by Shanghai, Tianjin possesses less 1/7 than Shanghai. Though Tianjin Binhai New Area Development Plan has been brought into the national overall development strategy, less publicity to international consortiums and MNCs, the monopoly of some service sectors and low level of private economy restrict the process in modern service industry.

3 The System Construction for Modern Service Industry Development in Tianjin

3.1 The Developing Design

Firstly, it is necessary to promote the industrial structure to shift from “manufacturing type” to “service type”. The focus of service should divert to Bohai Rim and international market from Tianjin and domestic market. Accelerating service industry will enhance the radiation and influence of Tianjin as an international metropolis.

Secondly, we should promote the integration of modern service industry and advanced manufacturing with reference to international experience. With the intensified competition, concentrating on intensive specification rather than scope economy has become corporations' universal demand. In order to be the advanced manufacturing R&D center, it is essential for Tianjin to separate some service functions as design, marketing and consulting from previous complete process of manufacturing and to accomplish the services by independent market. In this way, the internalization of producer service can be transformed to externalization. Combination integrating mode refers to the inputs and market research for new product R&D connect together. Computer and operation system is the example of binding integration. The derivatives consumption brings to manufacturing industry by movie, animation and sports are extended integration.

Thirdly, optimizing internal structure can help transit to high-end service industry. The added value of traditional service industry (transport, storage, postal service, wholesale and retail) occupied 40.03% of total service industry while finance sector, as the high-end service industry, 12.92%, and its contribution to GDP was only 5.6% in 2009. The proportions in Beijing and Shanghai were 14.5% and 12.2% respectively in same period. The added value of creative industry in Tianjin was RMB33.45 billion, while 325.07 billion and 272.54 billion in Beijing and Shanghai. It is obvious that high-end service industry in Tianjin is far behind. Therefore, the focus should be put on accelerating high-end service sectors like finance innovation, modern logistics, service outsourcing, creative industry, and headquarter economy.

3.2 Constructing Modern Service Industry Developing System

3.2.1 Public Administration Service Industry System

Urban public administration services include elementary education, public health, medical care, transport and communication, etc. Most fields are government agencies, public institutions, with large proportion of state-owned and high monopoly degree. They are still adopting planned economy instead of market economy and industrialization and their operation and management have common problems such as insufficient service supply, lack of humanization and low efficiency management level. Therefore, the key to upgrading soft strength is to optimize public service system. To accomplish the goal, it is necessary to break the system barriers and introduce competition mechanism to display the role of market allocation. Meanwhile, widening market access, breaking monopoly and constructing service evaluation system are other effective ways.

3.2.2 Producer Service Industry System

Producer service is the fastest growing service industry and is the focus and breakthrough of modern service development in Tianjin. Though having formed some scale, differences still exist compared with other cities. The main problems lie in unreasonable structure, insufficient emerging service industry and low degree of marketization and specialization. Therefore, the construction of Tianjin producer service industry should externalize manufacturer activity and professional service as well as strengthen the specialization and integration of services. Taking manufacturing as axis in production and market, the effective way is to form all round service system integrating R&D, consulting, logistics, finance and insurance, human resource training, marketing, law and intermediary service. At the same time, it is indispensable to expand new service fields and to establish cross-regional service system around Bohai Rim.

3.2.3 Consumer Service Industry System

The financial crisis not only impacted global entity economy, but also challenged China's economic growth mode led by exporting. The change of external environment will undoubtedly result in serious consequences on China's exports, especially on coastal cities like Tianjin. In 2009, the export trade volume declined to USD30 billion in 2009 from USD 42.23 billion. Transforming economic developing mode and driving domestic demand are the inevitable choices for keeping economic growth. The consumer service industry is the largest potential and innovative service field in Tianjin. In addition to overcoming insufficient effective supply, it is necessary to dig potential demand in emerging industries so as to meet the needs of different consumers in different living standard. The practical way at present is to foster advantageous products in education training, health service, culture, and tourism sectors.

4 The Key Fields of Modern Service Industry and Policy Suggestions on Development

4.1 The Key Fields of Public Administration Service Industry and Policy Suggestions

4.1.1 Executing System and Mechanism Innovation

In spite of the large scale reform on modern service industry, reform-legging is still a problem. The imperfect modern property right and corporation institution and low proportion of private enterprises have resulted in weak competitiveness. The private and foreign capitals are limited to enter market due to the low level of industrialization and marketization in some key fields. The reforms should be made on three aspects. First, introducing competition into monopoly industries, such as gas, water, electric power, and heating supply. The government should break the administrative barriers and widen the market access standard as well as push non state-owned capital to possess shares. Second, further improve the charging and monitoring of public and commonweal institutions, intermediary and other services. Third, push the reform on socialization of the rear-service of public organizations. Fourth, standardize the service industry criterion and establish strict charging and monitoring system in culture, education and medical care departments.

4.1.2 Improving the Implementation of Polices

Some imperfect policy effects can be seen in aspects as uneven policy support on service industries and tax preferential concentrating on infrastructure and hard environment. So we should adapt to the changing situations and social development and improve policy system. First is to review and old policies and abolish or liberalize the unreasonable ones. Second is to make policies clear and executive so as to carry out smoothly. Third is to develop E-government and improve the efficiency.

4.1.3 Introducing Competition and Evaluating System

The key to improving the service quality of public administration is to introduce competition system due to the high state-owned proportion and monopoly. First is to permit different economic entities to participate in the competition and operate in market economy. Second is to evaluate the service quality by third party. The last is to regulate market and industry standard to keep fair market order and environment.

4.2 The Key Fields and Policy Suggestions on Producer Service Industry

Generally speaking, it is necessary to execute financial and logistic innovation, to develop headquarter economy and service outsourcing as well as the exhibition economy.

4.2.1 Deepening Financial Reform

The global crisis triggered by American subprime mortgage crisis has exposed the excessive financial innovation and weak financial regulation which make virtue economy far beyond the capability of entity economy. Therefore, financial innovation and modern financial system must be established based on the scientific and cautious principle to control the risks. The primary measure is to widen financing channel and to perfect modern financial service system. In virtue of the experimental edge of financial innovation in Binhai New Area, various types of industrial investment fund can be developed. By trial operation of private equity, leasing, risk investment and venture investment fund, it is dispensable to regulate financial market transactions and perfect multi-level capital market and OTC market. The next is to deepen financial institutional reform and build sound financial organization system. The system innovation and preferential policy can attract MNCs' headquarters and transnational financial groups enter Tianjin and can encourage local legal person financial institutions to enhance core competitiveness. Meanwhile, by establishing and introducing trust corporations, factoring, assets management, insurance broker and assets evaluation, Tianjin can construct multi-level, compound, modern financial organization system. The third is to create financial services and products. Innovation can be executed in the fields like fund, factoring, leasing, private equity and offshore finance. The fourth is to perfect financial regulation and enhance risk management. Through the way to establishing united credit managing platform and regulating financial products and services, fair, reasonable and transparent market can be built.

4.2.2 Developing Modern Logistics

To correlate logistics with manufacturing, business and agriculture can shape complete industry and supply chain and can reduce costs. Extending the construction and service of "anhydrous port" and establishing electronic declaration system and one-stop service can make Tianjin be a modern logistic base. The next step is to build the logistic platform to cooperate with logistic enterprises home and abroad and to integrate with manufacturing industry and businesses. Further, based on TEDA, Tianjin Bonded Area and Dongxiang Bonded Port Area, logistic park can be built and will improve the intensive operation. By expanding logistic function, logistic services can be upgraded to supply chain finance from payment collection, settlement agency and pledge of warehouse receipts.

4.2.3 Developing Headquarter Economy

Headquarter economy is a service economy symbolizing with the characteristics of manufacture industry upgrading and advanced industrial level. It is suggested that we should take the transfer of high-end service industry in developed countries as an opportunity. The government should increase the strength on preferential policy, investment environment and talent pool reserve in order to attract headquarters, R&D centers, purchasing and marketing center.

4.2.4 Facilitating Exhibition Industry

Due to the lack of nationwide high quality exhibitions, it is essential to boost exhibition economy in Tianjin. By undertaking international well known exhibitions, business negotiation, tourism and trade can be expedited. The brand effect of universal acknowledged exhibitions can improve city image.

4.3 The Key Fields and Policy Suggestions on Consumer Service Industry

With the increase of income level, the demand to consumer service tends to be diversified and individualized. Besides satisfying popular demand, consumer service industry needs to seek breakthrough in innovation.

4.3.1 Education Training

With the scientific progress and faster speed of renewable knowledge, the demand for further education, enterprise training, re-employment training, vocational education and professional technology education has increased dramatically. Starting from vocational and technical training, the effective way is to foster skillful compound talents for Binhai Area. Aiming at various certificate examinations, perennial training institution or base with favorable brand should be established. In addition, it is helpful to introduce famous training organizations to cultivate high quality talents.

4.3.2 Tourism

With increasing living standard, consumption on tourism has occupied more and more proportion in individual consumption. Compared with Beijing and Shanghai, Tianjin is short of tourism resources. How to make attractive tourism highlight is the key to promoting tourism. Establishing large sized business mall integrating shopping, entertainment and hotels without influence of season and climate change will attract tourists and enhance city strength. Another approach is to upgrade the original brand tourism resources (city tour, Hai River tour, and Binhai New Area tour and mountain attractions tour). Perfecting the tourism incentive and punishment mechanism will improve the quality and supervision and management of tourism services.

4.3.3 Business Service

Based on urban characteristics, creating characteristic business areas is the effective way. Different from Gold Street Commercial Area, the construction of New Italian

Street and Ancient Culture Street should establish international business area, traditional brand business area and consumption flagship shops area to demonstrate particular features. In addition, to build community business service areas combined with the large business centers will construct "spider web" developing mode. Meanwhile, the government should reinforce infrastructure and regulation and introduce competition mechanism in order to achieve well-acknowledged image.

4 Conclusion

Expediting modern service industry is not only the main tendency of urban modernization but also can reflect the economic position of Tianjin. The exploitation and opening of Binhai New Area creates the opportunity for innovative development of modern service industry in Tianjin. Borrowing foreign and home experience and based on resource endowment and advantages, new measures and actions should be carried out by focusing on idea innovation, system innovation, management innovation and development mode innovation.

Acknowledgments. The author is indebted to Tianjin 10th Five-Year Social Science Research Key Project (TJ05-JL007): "The Research on Service Innovation Theory Based on New Schumpeter Economics" and Davos Forum 2010, Tianjin.

References

1. Li, J.: Interaction of Modern Service Industry and Urbanization. Theory & Moderniation (7) (2005)
2. Lin, M.: Study on Transition of China Economic Growth Mode. Journal of Henan Social Science (9) (2009)
3. Ma, X.: Rethinking on Developing Strategy on Service Industry in Tianjin. Tianjin Economy (8) (2009)
4. Ma, Y.: Trend and Characteristics of Modern Service Industry and Thought of Tianjin Service Industry Development. Northeast Asia Forum (7) (2008)
5. Campello, M., Graham, J.R., Harvey, C.R.: The Real Effects of Financial Constraints: Evidence from a Financial Crisis. Journal of Financial Economics (97) (2010)
6. Pomfret, R.: The Financial Sector and the Future of Capitalism. Economic Systems (34) (2010)
7. Wang, Y.: Adjustment and Transition: China's Economic Development in Post Financial Crisis Era. Marco-Economic Study (12) (2010)

The System Design on Performance of the Employees in Manufacture Enterprise

Ping Zang

Jilin Business and Technology College
Changchun, China
wangkefei888@sina.com

Abstract. With further development of the commodity economy, the competition of manufacture enterprise has become more and more intense in the market. One of the most important methods is to establish the performance measurement system in order to achieve those objectives.As one of the most useful technological tools in human resources management, performance measurement has become the key factor of the enterprise to compete successfully. This paper in written on the background of manufacture enterprise from the actual situation, has designed the key performance indicators (KPI) based on the performance measurement system and was in the guiding ideology of the Balanced Scorecard (BSC) from the system internal processes factors and etc. This paper has also established the performance measurement system for manufacture enterprise in order to enhance its human resources development and management and to improve its improve its market competitiveness.

Keywords: manufacture enterprise, human resources management, performance measurement.

1 Introduction

1.1 Performance Evaluation Objective

Constitute a Reasonable standards for performance measurement and detailed rules of Enterprise Staff. Feasibility of the enterprise data through the analysis, a detailed performance evaluation index system of standards and rules[1].

Determine Enterprise Staff's Numerical Weight of manufacture enterprise. Through the data analysis todeterminethe project performance evaluation indicators forthe development of new systems for data base.

Designed in detail manufacture enterprise Method of Enterprise Staff. Employee performance evaluation system through the establishment of employee performance evaluation data collection, development of manufacturing employees in the performance evaluation approach.

M. Zhou (Ed.): ISAEBD 2011, Part III, CCIS 210, pp. 192–197, 2011.

1.2 Meaning of Performance Measurement

1.2.1 Consideration about Sustaining Management Based on Manufacture Enterprise

In nowdays, with the restriction of inner culture and changing of external factors, enterprise raise new requirements on present talents[2]. Among them, the better way is making rational use of human resources and adjusting job positions rationally by knowing enterprise structure,so as to accelerate innovation speed of enterprise and increase enterprise competitiveness.

1.2.2 Design of Effective Performance Measurement Is the Key of Guaranteeing Enterprise Goal

Designing and Implementation of enterprise performance system will embody enterprise values, Encourage the Staff's Enthusiasm effectively. Meanwhile, enterprise culture also will be reflected during the course by operating Incentive Mechanism.

1.2.3 Employees Need Effective Performance Evaluation System to a Career

By considering the purpose of evaluation, decision making and other factors, to the more talented staff to provide personal career planning, so that they and the enterprises to establish a "trust contract " to maintain the common long-term growth and enterprise.

2 Definition of Performance Evaluation

Employee performance evaluation, is primarily used for an assessment of staff capability, is a measure of corporate productivity and competitiveness of the tools of organizational behavior and individual behavior is the result of measurement.

2.1 Performance Evaluation Method

Purpose of the evaluation according to different companies, requirements, use and corporate cultural differences, broadly divided into three:

Past-oriented assessment method: the evaluation by the form factors, employee behavior described in words, to differentiate the performance of staff selection, quantitative performance evaluation, employee data records[3].

Compared the method: The working conditions were all evaluators according to different evaluation criteria, listed in rank, in order to determine the level of performance in accordance with the merits.

Future-oriented assessment method: for different levels of staff, for different tests, making it the promotion of human planning and an important basis for decision-making to achieve maximum efficiency and effectiveness of organizations.

2.2 The Principles of Performance Evaluation System Design

The results of performance evaluation to ensure objectivity, impartiality and fairness, employee performance evaluation system manufacturers design should follow the following principles[4-5].

The principle of purpose: The purpose of performance evaluation is the overall objective of enterprise development organizations and individuals are divided into specific objectives, and translate into employee performance evaluation program, through the evaluation results with the salary, benefits and personal redeployment linked guide Staff personal development needs.

The principle of fairness: the development of performance evaluation at the same time, should be excluded from non-normal factors. Such as employee downtime due to maintenance of mechanical failure did not meet the standards set at this time if it is continue to assess indicators of performance evaluation criteria is clearly unfair. Performance evaluation system should be made more scientific and humane.

The principle of fairness: in determining the performance evaluation system or target, try to take the situation closer to the objective data available, to avoid the personal appraisal of both bias caused by misunderstanding. Therefore, the "sales employees "than " customer communication skills" is more easily evaluated, but also more likely to be accepted by the evaluation of the results obtained, to help clear their lack of staff, identify gaps.

Operational principles: objective, the data can not be notarized actual operation is invalid, and therefore the authenticity of the data obtained is important, the data should be simple and can be operational.

2.3 Employees Constitute a System of Performance Evaluation

Performance Evaluation System is a complete cycle management system, a management cycle can include four-part work: performance planning, performance guidance, performance appraisal and performance feedback.

Performance plan: based primarily on the objectives and work responsibilities, managers and employees participate in joint investment and reach a consensus on the performance expectations and make people make their own commitment to the objectives. Managers and employees for each position of the evaluation indicators designed to complete the project.

Performance guide: and staff through the joint efforts to help employees to achieve performance targets, and to give proper guidance and help. Timely resolution of problems found, and the performance plan to be adjusted. Focus on guidance from time to time, regular communication and evaluation, focusing on employee behavior and results and other key data collection.

Performance Assessment: Performance assessment at the end of a pre-planning, executive officer of the employee performance evaluation of implementation of the goals, the evaluation process based on guidance from the data collected, to distinguish between primary and secondary.

Performance Feedback: After the performance appraisal, supervisors should conduct feedback interviews with staff so that employees understand their expectations, while employees can complete the performance plan put forward in the process of the difficulties encountered.

3 Manufacturing Companies Design Employee Performance Evaluation System

3.1 Performance Design System Plan

(1) The work of the staff's overall goals and objectives of the company is closely related to the work of employees know their goals and the relationship between the overall objectives.

(2) staff responsibilities and describes the environment in accordance with existing organizations were modified to reflect the performance of the main content of the work during the period.

(3) administrators and managers in the task has reached a consensus process.

(4) managers and administrators are well aware of is the completion of the objectives of the obstacles encountered, and the managers offered clear support and help.

Table 1. Performance Design System

Rating scale	Reference points	Meaning
Excellent	90-100	Actual results than expected plans / goals, or the job requirements of the division of responsibilities in the planning / objectives or job responsibilities / requirements involved in the division have made very prominent in all aspects of the results.
Good	80-89	Actual results than expected plans / goals, or the job requirements of the division of responsibilities in the planning / objectives or job responsibilities / requirements involved in each division have made prominent achievements.
Qualified	70-79	Actual results to achieve the desired program / objectives or job requirements of the division of responsibilities, neither outstanding performance, there is no clear error.
Need to improve	60-69	Actual results did not achieve the desired program / objectives or requirements of the division of job responsibilities, or a key in many ways there is an obvious lack of or failure.
Unqualified	0-59	Actual performance fell far short of the expected plan / goals, the division of job responsibilities or requirements, in many respects there are significant or major deficiencies or omissions.

3.2 Performance Design System Guide

Select the appropriate content and methods of evaluation, the nature of the various departments and different standards and the development of performance indicators, evaluation focuses on content and relevance.

Clear evaluation criteria, norms job responsibilities and work, quantitative assessment, evaluation of records.

Evaluation results should be evaluated employee feedback, listen to staff reflect the description and claims.

Enhance democracy and transparency, so that an objective and fair performance appraisal.

3.3 Design System Performance Assessment

The project is established, should be familiar with and understand the business situation as soon as possible, gather information, from time to time with both organizations to discuss the performance evaluation team to analyze the organizational structure, business status, management status and other basic information.

Give full play to the advantages of human resources consulting projects, interviews and discussion a lot of internal employees, including management, middle, primary and some outsiders.

The release of the questionnaire survey is an effective collection, one of the methods of data collection, while the design of the questionnaire must be complete, scientific, rational, problem clear instructions to avoid ambiguity.

3.4 Design of System Performance Feedback

By evaluation of performance of the two sides reached consensus
To enable employees to recognize their achievements and benefits.
Pointed out that the staff areas for improvement.
Develop performance improvement plans.
A performance cycle, in consultation with the objectives and performance standards.

4 Performance Evaluation System Is Established

4.1 Evaluation Methods and Content

Table 2. Evaluation methods and content

Categories		Examination content	Appraisal cycle
Class A	Company Leadership	Job performance 100%	Year
Class B	Department Manager	Job performance 100%	Quarter
Class C	Head	Job performance 80%+ Performance 20%	Monthly
	Other production sector employees	Job performance 50%+ Performance 50%	
	Operations other employees	Job performance 70%+ Performance 30%	
	Other back office administration staff	Job performance 50%+ Performance 50%	

4.2 Assessment Relationship

Assessment as a direct charge employees who, with the result of justice, objectivity is responsible; direct supervisor for the second examination who has oversight of the evaluation results, guidance responsibilities and ensure that an assessment of the consistency between the evaluation criteria , As well as the relative fairness of the examination results.

Table 3. Assessment relationship

Category	Evaluation subjects	Class A assessment	Class B assessment
Class A	Board of Directors	Shareholders	
	Management team members	Board of Directors	
Class B	Department Manager	Charge of the department heads	President
Class C	Head	Department Manager	Charge of the department heads
	Other staff	Immediate supervisor or department manager	Department Manager

5 Examination Procedures

Results from the assessment and report on his work: the work of each of the first six days of January was the annual performance evaluation in a comprehensive summary based on the completion of annual performance and control self-assessment performance contract, to direct assessment of people, and a public report on his work.

Performance evaluation: evaluation of people performance person under examination was completed, combined with people's self-assessment by examination and debriefing the situation, to communicate with by assessment based on performance assessment, proposed the formation of assessment results.

Examination results validation: assessing the results of the Office of summary assessment, submitted to Review Committee approval, to determine the final examination scores and grades.

References

1. Cai, Z., Chang, Z., Wang, N.: Study on Manufacturing Enterprise Solution System. Computer Application Research 2, 22–26 (2005)
2. Ma, L., Wang, Y., Xia, J.: Analysis of Production Abnormity and Exploration of Corrective Ways in Workshop of Manufacturing Enterprise. Northeast Agricultural University · Social Science 1, 35–39 (2009)
3. Li, Y., Wang, G., Qiu, X.: Performance Evaluation of College Teachers. Higher Education Research (Wuchang) 7, 82–86 (2007)
4. Cai, Y., Lin, C.: Teacher Performance Evaluation Theory and Practice. Teacher Education Research 1, 36–39 (2005)
5. Li, S.: Analysis of Human Resource Information Management. Economic Forum 15, 50–53 (2006)

The Importance of Service Sector in Value-Added Generation Using Input-Output Analysis

Mohd Sahar Sauian, Nik Fatimah Nik Aznan, and Nurul Nisa' Khairol Azmi

Faculty of Computer and Mathematical Sciences
Universiti Teknologi MARA, 40450 Shah Alam, Malaysia
{Mshahar,nisa}@tmsk.uitm.edu.my, sots82@gmail.com

Abstract. The manufacturing sector had been the catalyst for growth in Malaysia since the eighties and the nineties. However, after the late nineties and post 2000, the service sector had become the major contributing sector to the growth of the Malaysian economy. In 2008, the service sector contributed 55% of the GDP and accounted for 52% of the overall workforce. This paper attempts to investigate the importance of this sector using two approaches of input-output analysis. The first approach is to use economic linkages analysis, in order to determine the appropriate key sub-sectors within the service sector. On the other hand, the second is to use multiplier analysis to analyze the ability of the niche sub-sectors to generate value-added in the economy. In essence, this paper is of benevolence to determine whether Malaysia is in the right track in enhancing her competitive niche in service industries in this global ICT era.

Keywords: Service sector, input-output analysis, economic linkage, multiplier analysis, value-added.

1 Introduction

The decades of the eighties and the nineties saw the emergence of the manufacturing sector as the most important sector in the Malaysian economy. It had surpassed the agricultural sector in its contribution to the gross domestic product. This was the results of the replacement of "import substitution" policy to the "export promotion" policy in the seventies. The policy was in fact a stride to enhance the manufacturing sector.

However, the post 2000 scenario saw the emergence of the service sector as the powerful sector that created tremendous wealth in the global economy. One of the major shifts to this scenario was the easier access to communication among countries through the use of ICT (information and telecommunication technology) in conducting trade of goods and services. Furthermore, after the year 2000, the growth of trade in services had grown at a faster rate compared to the growth of trade in goods. For instance, in 2007, the World Trade Organization (WTO) [1] had shown that trade in commercial services grew at 18% compared the growth of trade in goods of only 15%. In retrospect, most advanced countries today are competing to export commercial services throughout the globe. These include most of the senior members of the European Union, like Denmark, Sweden, Germany, United Kingdom and

M. Zhou (Ed.): ISAEBD 2011, Part III, CCIS 210, pp. 198–205, 2011.

Finland as well as other countries like Japan and the United States. Then, other middle-income to high-income developing counties, including Malaysia follow the same stride to enhance their service sector.

2 Malaysian Service Sector

Over the years, the service sector has been growing in its size and contribution to the Malaysian economy. According to the Malaysian Economic Report 2009 [2], the growth of service sector remained steady in all quarters of 2008. The overall expansion of all the service sectors in Malaysia was 9.7% in 2007 and 7.3% in 2008.However, the growth rate declined to only 2.0% in 2009. This rate of growth was still considered as fairly good because in 2009, Malaysia experienced a negative growth of (-1.75%) in the overall economy. Table 1 below shows the growth of the service sector between 2007 and 2009.

The table indicates that all sectors within the service sector experienced positive growth throughout the years 2007, 2008 and 2009. For instance, in 2007, real estate and business services sector as well as wholesale and business trade services grew with the largest and second largest growth of 18.2% and 12.5% respectively. In 2008, on the other hand, government services grew at 11.9% followed by wholesale and retail services at 9.8% and hotel and restaurant at 7.3%. Even in 2009, where the overall Malaysian economy experienced a negative growth, all services sector showed a positive growth, with the largest growth sector shown in hotel and restaurant services (5.7%) followed by real estate and business services (3.2%) and other services (2.8%).

Table 1. Annual Growth of Various Service Sectors in Malaysia 2007 to 2009

Year/Sectors	2007(%)	2008(%)	2009(%)
Transport and Storage	10.0	6.1	1.0
Communication	7.0	7.3	1.6
Finance and Insurance	11.1	7.7	0.4
Real Estate and Business Services	18.2	1.5	3.2
Utilities	3.9	2.1	0.2
Wholesale and Retail	12.5	9.8	1.0
Hotel and Restaurant	10.8	7.3	5.7
Other Services	5.0	4.9	2.8
Government Services	4.5	11.9	1.5
Total Services	9.7	7.3	2.0

Sources: Economic Report Malaysia 2009 and Department of Statistics, Malaysia 2009.

From the data and the growth trend of the service sector shown above, it is not surprising that the government has put an enthusiastic effort in emphasizing a greater focus on the service sector in planning for the economic development. In this regards, we can see out of 60 projects listed in the Economic Transformation Programmes (ETP) recently released by the government, 32 projects are from the service sectors [3].

3 Objectives

The main aim of this study is to analyze the importance of the service sector in the Malaysian economy. Thus the study has two-fold objectives. Firstly, it tries to determine the major sub-sectors of services that contribute to the economic growth in Malaysia and hence determine the economic linkages of the service sectors with other sectors in the economy. Secondly, it attempts to determine the income multipliers of the selected sub-sectors in the service industries.

4 Input-Output Framework of Analysis

The main methodological approach in this exercise is to use the input-output approach of analysis. This approach shows the relationship between the flows of the various sectors in the economy, whereby the relationship between the producers and the consumers as well as the interdependence among industries can be shown. It can also track the flow of commodity (goods and services) from one industry to another industry. The flow of commodities supplied and used is compiled systematically in the form of input-output table [4].

Basically, the input output table has four quadrants. The first quadrant is the intermediate input quadrant which is referred to as the heart of the input-output table [5].The second quadrant represents the final demand where it is considered as the output of the producing sectors, i.e the sectoral distribution of household expenditure, government expenditure, gross fixed capital formation and exports. On the other hand, the third quadrant shows the primary inputs quadrant, which consists of the sectoral distribution of wages, operating surplus, value-added, indirect taxes, subsidies and depreciation, while the fourth quadrant represents the primary inputs directly linked to final demand [6, 7,8].

The input-output tables describe the complex process of production, the use of goods and services and the way in which income and value-added products are generated within the various sectors of the economy, where the set of producers of similar goods and services forms a homogenous industry [9]. Through a set of tables during a period, the structural change in the economy and the specific sector's economic characteristics can be revealed.

In essence, the symmetric input-output table is a product or industry matrix describing the domestic production processes and the transactions in products of the national economy in detail. For example, a two-sector input-output table allows us to understand the industrial relationship between agriculture and the rest of the economy, thus highlighting the implication for structural and policy analysis [10].

Therefore, input-output analysis has multifarious applications. For instance, it offers a static view of the structural relationship among the different sectors in the economy (typically national or regional) for a certain period of time, generally a year. The relationship is expressed purely in monetary terms [11]. Other applications of input-output tables are determining the technical capability of production, labour productivity and comparing the technological standard of one country compared vis-à-vis other countries. Similarly, the study of economic linkages among the various sectors of the economy can easily be discovered.

5 Methodological Approaches

To be more specific the two methodological approaches that are utilized here are the economic linkages approach and multiplier analysis.

5.1 Economic Linkages Approach

In an interdependent economy, a sector is linked to its input and output sectors by its direct and indirect purchases and sales [12]. A sector's linkage through its direct and indirect purchases is called the backward linkage. On the other hand, a sector is said to be forward-linked to other sectors through its direct and indirect sales to them. Hirschman (1958) [13] stated the analysis of strengths of backward and forward linkages allowed us to identify the most important sectors in the economy.

Backward linkage or input provision is defined as an activity that employs significant amount of intermediate inputs from other activities for production purposes. Output utilization or forward linkage, on the other hand, is defined as an activity that caters for final demand but also induces attempts to utilize its output as inputs in other new activities.

Two common approaches to measure the strength of backward and forward linkages are the works of Rasmussen (1956) [14] and the Chenery & Watanabe (1958) [15]. Since the Chenery-Watanabe Approach of evaluating the impact of a sector to the overall economy is only confined to the direct linkage only, we resort only to the Rasmussen's approach as it considers both the direct and the indirect linkages.

For inter-industry comparison purposes, the linkage indices are normalized in such a way that their average value is unity. Based on Rasmussen's model, the measure of backward linkages is called the Power of Dispersion Index. It describes the relative extent to which an increase in final demand for a product of a given industry is dispersed throughout the total system of industries. The Power of Dispersion Index is defined as:

$$BL_i^{SW} = \frac{\sum_i B_{ij}^{SW}}{\left(\sum_i \sum_j B_{ij}^{SW}\right) / N} . \qquad (1)$$

Where: BL_j indicates backward linkage of service subsector in jth. sector
S indicates service subsector
W indicates other sector
N indicates number of sectors
B_{ij} is the ij^{th} element of the Leontief's inverse matrix.

The forward linkage index is measured using The Sensitivity of Dispersion Index. The index describes the importance of a given industry as a supplier of resources to other industries. It is defined as in equation 2 below:

$$FL_i^{WS} = \frac{\sum_i B_{ij}^{WS}}{\left(\sum_i \sum_j B_{ij}^{WS}\right) / N} \quad (2)$$

Where : FL_j indicates the extent of forward linkage of service in jth sector and S, W, N and B_{ij} as defined in equation 1, above.

5.2 Multiplier Analysis

Another approach in looking at the impact of services is through the use of impact analysis. This analysis is also known as multiplier analysis. Multiplier analysis measures the total change throughout the economy from one unit change for a given sector. For instance, for every one dollar of final demand for a product of a sector generates direct and indirect income to the economy as a whole. The relationship between the initial spending and the total effect generated by the spending is known as the impact of that sector to the economy as a whole

In this analysis, we use only the income multiplier because it is the simplest form of various multipliers. It is considered useful because it is expressed as a ratio of the sum of direct and indirect income change resulting from a unit change of final demand in that sector. The calculation is obtained by multiplying the rows of technical coefficients of the income in each sector by the column of the interdependence coefficients [16]. It should be noted that the multiplier value is less than unity.

The income multiplier is defined as:

$$\varepsilon = (I - A)^{-1} A_y^T \quad (3)$$

where $(I-A)^{-1}$ is the interdependence coefficient

A_y^T is the technical coefficients of income arising.

6 Data Sources

Most of the data used is based on the Input-Output table of Malaysia 2005, published in 2010 [17]. Other sources include the Economic Report Malaysia 2009, Department of Statistics Malaysia 2009 and Economic Transformation Programmes: A Roadmap for Malaysia 2010.

7 Results and Analysis

7.1 Economic Linkages

To determine the sectors that become the key sectors in contributing to the Malaysian economy, the backward and forward linkages are determined as mentioned in equations (1) and (2) respectively. Table 2 shows the results of the backward and forward linkages.

Table 2. Economic Linkages of Malaysian Industries and Service Industries 2005

Sectors	BL Index	FL index
1. Agriculture	0.85642	0.74666
2. Mining	0.65442	0.71881
3. Manufacturing	0.92120	2.91247
4. Utilities	1.05846	0.92398
5. Construction	1.03284	1.07770
6. Wholesale and Retail	0.94436	0.84251
7. Hotel and Restaurants	1.25620	0.77659
8. Transport & Storage	0.83848	1.02494
9. Communications	1.11892	0.70502
10. Finance & Insurance	1.11712	1.43089
11. Real Estate	1.33123	0.96913
12. Business Services	0.89041	0.95239
13.Education	0.81473	0.54101
14. Healthcare	1.07600	0.70439
15. Government Services	1.02042	0.65540

Source : Calculated from Input-Output Table Malaysia, 2005 (Published 2010).
Note: BL : Backward Linkage, FL: Forward Linkage.

From the above table 2, it shows that construction and engineering services as well as finance and insurance sectors show the key sectors in the economy as they have both the values of the backward and forward linkages greater than 1. This means that these two sectors are both good suppliers as well as good purchasers of inputs to other sectors in the economy. On the other hand, utilities, hotels and restaurants, communication, real estate, healthcare and government services have strong backward linkages (greater than 1) but weak forward linkages (less than 1). They are good suppliers of inputs or resources in the economy. However, transport and storage has a strong forward linkage but weak backward linkage. In essence, transport is a good user of inputs in the economy. Outside the service sector, manufacturing still holds the strongest forward linkage.

7.2 Results of the Multiplier Analysis

As we have discussed earlier the multiplier analysis signifies the ability of a given sector in generating final demand in the national economy. By looking at the service sectors which at least show a strong backward or a strong forward linkage, the following Table 3 depicts the calculated results of the income multiplier of selected and relevant service sub-sectors in Malaysia in 2005.

The result reveals that all the selected service sub-sectors give a modest to strong contribution to the impact of the increase in final demand to the increase in the entire economy. The multiplier effect ranges between 0.0754 (7.54%) to 0.4778 (47.78%). The highest value of the income multiplier within the selected nine sectors is healthcare services sub-sector showing the multiplier effect of 0.4778, followed by finance and insurance sub-sector of 0.3937, government services of 0.3885 and hotel and restaurant services sub-sector of 0.3617. It is therefore obvious that an increase of one unit final demand in finance and insurance sub-sector, for instance, will generate

0.3937 unit of output in that sector. Similarly, a unit increase of final demand in hotel and restaurant service sub-sector will generate an income of 0.3617 unit of output in that sector. This output is in fact the proportion of value-added generated from these sectors to the rest of the economy. We also notice here that hotels and restaurants as well as healthcare service sub-sectors show multiplier effects of more than 30% to the generation of output in the economy. In retrospect, these sub-sectors actually have strong relation to "tourism" which was not shown in the input-output table 2005.

Table 3. Interdependent coefficients, technical coefficients and income multiplier of selected service sub-sectors, Malaysia 2005

Major Service Sub-sectors	1	2	3	4	5	6	7	8	9
1. Utilities	1.2823	0.0171	0.1268	0.0148	0.0474	0.0245	0.0355	0.0400	0.0381
2. Construction Services	0.0610	1.0141	0.0675	0.0300	0.0425	0.0208	0.4834	0.0804	0.1492
3. Hotels/Restaurants	0.0073	0.0102	1.3320	0.0030	0.0073	0.0494	0.0340	0.0129	0.0523
4. Transport	0.0328	0.0636	0.0681	1.1352	0.1007	0.1370	0.0550	0.0300	0.0627
5. Communication.	0.0095	0.0219	0.0258	0.0200	1.0329	0.0314	0.0191	0.0156	0.0586
6. Finance & Insurance	0.0222	0.0588	0.0980	0.0963	0.4877	1.5628	0.0853	0.0287	0.0504
7. Real Estate	0.0059	0.0080	0.1550	0.0317	0.0658	0.0404	1.3346	0.0295	0.0477
8. Healthcare	0.0007	0.0015	0.0020	0.0006	0.0020	0.0012	0.0041	1.0157	0.0008
9. Govt. Services	0.0082	0.0097	0.0130	0.0056	0.0832	0.0117	0.0177	0.0129	1.0394
Technical Coefficients									
Compensation of Employees	0.0374	0.0719	0.2282	0.1241	0.0865	0.2263	0.0725	0.4469	0.3240
Income Multiplier (ε)	0.0754	0.1032	0.3617	0.1722	0.1933	0.3937	0.1797	0.4778	0.3885

Source; Calculated from Input-Output Table Malaysia, 2005 (published 2010).

8 Concluding Remarks

The exercise reveals that the service sector could give a benevolent impact to the rest of the Malaysian economy. Using the economic linkages analysis, we found out 2 service sub-sectors showed strong backward and forward linkages. On the other hand, 5 sub-sectors showed strong backward linkages but weak forward linkages, while other 2 sub-sectors showed strong forward linkages but weak backward linkages. Generally, it appears that the major service sub-sectors have above average linkages to the other sectors in the economy. It is obvious that they are still important sector in the Malaysian economy as they are either the supplier of inputs to the other sectors or the consumers from other sectors in the economy.

Using the multiplier analysis, we showed that at least nine service sub-sectors have significant impact on the economy as a whole. This was indicated by the modest to moderately high values of income multipliers of the nine selected sub-sectors.

This study also gives and affirmative note to laud the government effort in enhancing the service sector as a future catalyst for growth. Through the ETP programme, Malaysia is embarking to become an economy with high-income status. The role of service sector is becoming more prominent as the government is targeting about 65% of the GDP would be contributed by the service sector by 2020 as compared to about 56% in 2010.

References

1. World Trade Development. World Trade Organization, WTO (2008)
2. Malaysia Economic Report, Ministry of Finance, Malaysia (2009)
3. Economic Transformation Programme: A Roadmap for Malaysia, PEMANDU, Prime Minister's Department (2010)
4. Hj Ismail, F.: Structural Change of Agricultural Sector. Department of Statistics, Malaysia (2007)
5. Jensen, R.C., West, G.R.: Input-Output for Practitioners: Theory and Applications. Australian Government Publishing Service, Canberra (1986)
6. Miller, R.E., Blair, P.D.: Input-Output Analysis: Foundations and Extension. Cambridge University Press, Cambridge (2009)
7. O'Cornor, R., Henry, E.W.: Input-Output Analysis and Its Applications. Charles Griffin & Company Ltd., London (1975)
8. Sauian, M.S.: Input-Output Analysis: An Enthusiastic Approach in Securing Sectoral and Productivity Planning. In: Proceedings of the 9th International Conference in Statistical Sciences, ICCS-IX, Malaysia (2007)
9. Valadkhani, A.: Using Input-Output Analysis to identify Australia's High Employment Generating Industries. University of Wallongong, Australia (2003)
10. Pizzoli, E.: Agricultural Sector in an Input-Output Matrix: Micro-data Approach for Italian Case. In: Conference on Input-Output and General Equilibrium Modeling. Free University of Brussels (2004)
11. Lee, T., Mokhtarian, P.L.: An Input-Output Analysis of the Relationship between Communication and Travel Industry. University of California, Davies (2004)
12. Cai, J., Leong, P.S.: The Linkages of Agriculture in the Hawaiian Economy, Cooperative Extension Service. University of Hawaii (2002)
13. Hirshman, A.O.: The Strategy of Economic Development. Yale University Press, New Haven (1958)
14. Leatherman, M.: Inter-industry Linkages and the process of Internal Integration. Department of Applied Economics. University of Cambridge (1987)
15. Rasmussen, P.N.: Studies in Inter-sectoral Relation. North-Holland, Amsterdam (1956)
16. Chenery, H.B., Watanabe, T.: International Comparison of the Structure of Production. Econometrica 26, 487–521 (1958)
17. Input-Output Tables of Malaysia 2005. Department of Statistics, Malaysia (2010)

An Empirical Study of the Cultural Statements of Chinese State-Owned Enterprises

Jie Li

School of Management, Xiangfan University
Xiangyang, Hubei, China
lijielara@163.com

Abstract. As the pillar industry of national economy, China's large and medium-sized state-owned enterprises (SOEs) need to advance their management system further. A systematic strategy focusing on culture building is critical for the success of such a transformation. In order to evaluate the degree to which the cultural construction of SOEs has arrived and whether it can support the development of SOEs in the future, we made an empirical analysis of the cultural statements of top 39 SOEs according to Deal and Kennedy's cultural elements framework. The results showed that: (1) These SOEs' cultural statements are of good quality. (2) The cultural statements are most concerned about values and external environment. (3) The quality of cultural statements of traditional companies is prior to high-tech companies, while companies in secondary industry have superior cultural statements than those in service sector. (4) China SOEs' cultural statements consist of diversifying topics.

Keywords: Company culture, Cultural statement, Chinese state-owned enterprises.

1 Introduction

Since China's reform and opening-up in 1978, the environment in which Chinese state-owned enterprises operate has changed sharply. Especially in the 21st century, the large and medium-sized SOEs which are the pillar industry of the national economy have not only to bear the burden of the development of state national industry but also to face the competition from domestic industry and the challenge of economic globalization. All of these require SOEs to conduct management transformation to adapt the outside environmental changes and improve performance. Although the management transformation of SOEs has made remarkable achievements over the past thirty-plus years, many problems still exist in practical operations such as depending on government, serious administrative bureaucracy, lack of innovation and competition consciousness, etc. Therefore, China's SOEs need to further and deepen management changes to settle the conflicts between traditional management concepts, employees' deep-rooted "iron rice bowl" thoughts and rapid changes of external competitive environment, to insist the idea that customer is the center, expend the market, establish good credit image and improve competitiveness

M. Zhou (Ed.): ISAEBD 2011, Part III, CCIS 210, pp. 206–212, 2011.

outside, and to put people first, motivate staff's enthusiasm, initiative and creativity inside.

How to ensure the success of the transformation? Cameron (1994) put forward that one of the most critical factors leading to successful management changes is to incorporate systematic strategies focusing on changing the organization's culture and the attitudes and values of employees. Denison& Mishra (1995) and Schein (1990) pointed out that organizational culture is a key way to integrate internal efforts and processes and to accommodate them with external environment. It's clear that organizational culture has great impact on the success of enterprises' transformation and this view has been accepted universally. Thus it's worthwhile to research on the degree at which the cultural constructing procedure of SOEs has arrived and whether the present situation of the culture construction can support the development of SOEs in the future. Using empirical method, this paper provides a description of the present status of top 50 SOEs' culture since the reform and opening-up from the perspective of cultural statement and conduct a research on the relationship between the enterprise's characteristics and its culture.

2 Theoretical Review

A number of scholars have put forward their views on company culture (Allaire & Firsirotu, 1984; Hatch, 1993; Martin, 1992; Ott, 1989; Schein, 1985, 1990). However, there is little consensus with regard to a general theory of organizational culture. The enterprise culture connotation brought forward by domestic and overseas scholars can be roughly divided into two perspectives. The first is in a narrow sense, focusing on the category of consciousness which only includes ideas, values, believes, feelings of enterprises, etc. The second is in a general sense, emphasizing that enterprise culture is the accumulation of material and spiritual civilization during its start-up and developing process which includes two parts, i.e., hardware facilities or explicit culture and software or implicit culture. Related analysis of studies on this issue shows that most scholars recognize the spirit of enterprise as the core and soul of enterprise culture. Factors on spiritual level have the largest effect on enterprise management activities and employee behavior as a whole. Enterprise culture statement is the literal embodiment of enterprise spirit and an abstract concept on the practical level of enterprise culture.

As for what elements should be included in company cultural statement, different researchers have developed different models. Hofstede(1980) identified four dimensions of culture in his study of national influences: power distance, uncertainty avoidance, individualism vs. collectivism, masculinity vs. femininity. Deal and Kennedy suggested that the basis of corporate culture was an interlocking set of five cultural elements: enterprise environment, values and beliefs, rituals and ceremonies, heroic figures, the cultural networks. Edgar Schein's organizational model (1985) illuminated culture from the standpoint of the observer, described by three cognitive levels of organizational culture: artifacts, values, tacit assumptions. Daniel Denison's model (1990) asserted that organizational culture could be described by four general dimensions–mission, adaptability, involvement and consistency. O'Rielly, Chatman & Caldwell (1991) developed their Organizational Profile Model (OCP), a self reporting tool which made distinctions according seven categories: innovation, stability, respect for people, outcome orientation, attention to detail, team orientation, and aggressiveness. In this study, we applied Deal and Kennedy's five cultural elements as evaluating elements.

3 Methodology

3.1 Sample

The sample was obtained from the companies listed in the 2008 Top 50 Enterprises of China issued by China Entrepreneur Association (`http://www.cec-ceda.org.cn`). For the initial sample, 44 SOEs were selected. Cultural statements were found on the web sites of 39 firms which do business in 14 industries of chemical, electric power, finance and insurance, communications, steel, automobile manufacturing, transportation, construction, food, military, metallurgy, electrical appliance, IT and energy.

3.2 Objectives

First, to analyze the overall level of large and medium-sized SOEs' cultural statements and on which elements the firms generally emphasize. Second, to compare the differences of cultural statements of firms in its nature and industry. Third, to examine the uniqueness of China's SOEs' cultural statements.

3.3 Procedure

Webpage for each firm were searched for the culture statements including vision, mission, value, philosophy, spirit, figure, social responsibility, etc. We classified the structure and contents of the original culture statements in accordance with Deal and Kennedy's cultural elements. Based on the classifying, we analyzed and evaluated the quality and uniqueness of the cultural statements of these firms. The standard of quality evaluation is to examine whether Deal and Kennedy's cultural elements are included in them and how many elements are included. As for the uniqueness, we screened and analyzed the critical words of original statements, i.e., the phrases that had substantial connotations and reflect the firms' core values and unique features.

4 Results

For the constraints of space, we only discussed the specific results and neglected the name of each company.

Table 1 showed the frequency of cultural elements in the cultural statements of sample firms. The frequency of firms that include different numbers of cultural elements in their cultural statements was presented in Table 2.

Table 1. Frequency of cultural elements in the cultural statements

Cultural elements	Enterprise environment	values	Heroic figures	Rituals and ceremonies	Cultural networks
Frequency	70.5%	79.5%	31.8%	43.2%	54.5%

Table 2. Frequency of cultural elements sum in cultural statements

Number of cultural elements inclusion	0	1	2	3	4	5
Frequency	13.6%	6.8%	18.2%	25.0%	22.7%	13.6%

Table 3 showed the frequency of cultural elements containing respectively in the cultural statements of traditional and high-tech firms and table 4 indicated that the correlation between the sum of cultural element and the nature of enterprises is positive and highly significant. Table 5 showed at what degree firms of traditional and high-tech industry put attention on different evaluating elements.

Table 6 showed the frequency of cultural elements containing respectively in the cultural statements of enterprises in secondary industry and firms in service sector and table 7 indicated that the correlation between the sum of cultural elements and the nature of industry is positive and highly significant. Table 8 showed at what degree enterprises in secondary industry and firms in service sector put attention on different cultural elements.

Table 3. Frequency comparison of cultural elements sum between traditional and high-tech firms

Frequency	Cultural elements sum			
	2 and below	3	4	5
The traditional	35.1%	27.1%	24.3%	13.5%
The high-techs	57.1%	14.3%	14.3%	14.3%

Table 4. Chi-square tests of cultural element sum and the nature of firms

Chi-Square Tests

	Value	df	Asymp. Sig. (2-sided)	Exact Sig. (2-sided)	Exact Sig. (1-sided)	Point Probability
Pearson Chi-Square	3.069[a]	5	.689	.754		
Likelihood Ratio	3.312	5	.652	.829		
Fisher's Exact Test	3.049			.769		
Linear-by-Linear Association	.803[b]	1	.370	.437	.223	.068
N of Valid Cases	44					

a. 7 cells (58.3%) have expected count less than 5. The minimum expected count is .48.

b. The standardized statistic is -.896.

Table 5. Cultural element content comparison between traditional and high-tech firms

Frequency	Enterprise environment	Values	Heroic figures	Rituals and ceremonies	Cultural networks
The traditional	70.3%	81.1%	35.1%	45.9%	56.8%
The high-techs	71.4%	71.4%	14.3%	28.6%	42.9%

Table 6. Frequency comparison of cultural elements sum between firms in the secondary industry and service sector

Frequency	Cultural elements sum			
	2 and below	3	4	5
Secondary industry	34.5%	24.1%	24.1%	17.3%
Service sector	46.7%	26.7%	20.0%	6.6%

Table 7. Chi-square tests of cultural element sum and the industrial nature of firms

Chi-Square Tests

	Value	df	Asymp. Sig. (2-sided)	Exact Sig. (2-sided)	Exact Sig. (1-sided)	Point Probability
Pearson Chi-Square	1.814[a]	5	.874	.905		
Likelihood Ratio	1.872	5	.867	.902		
Fisher's Exact Test	2.053			.915		
Linear-by-Linear Association	.530[b]	1	.466	.483	.266	.061
N of Valid Cases	44					

a. 9 cells (75.0%) have expected count less than 5. The minimum expected count is 1.02.

b. The standardized statistic is -.728.

Table 8. Cultural element content comparison between firms in the secondary industry and service sector

Frequency	Enterprise environment	Values	Heroic figures	Rituals and ceremonies	Cultural networks
Secondary industry	65.5%	82.8%	37.9%	44.8%	58.6%
Service sector	80.0%	73.3%	20.0%	40.0%	46.7%

Through the statistical analysis of the phrases commonly used in the SOEs' cultural statements, we found that: (1) SOEs had great emphasis on "innovation" and the frequency of its occurrence is 12 which is the highest of all the key words. (2) "Responsibility, being pragmatic / seeking truth from facts / pursuing practical results, honor credibility, cooperation / team / unity" were phrases of high frequency of occurrence except for innovation. (3) Phrases such as "party building, serving the country / country" appeared many times in the cultural statements which to some extent reflected the intrinsic relations between SOEs and the Chinese government and the close ties between enterprise culture and the ideological and political culture, party culture of the Chinese government. Such situation also displayed SOEs' sense of national and social responsibility as the leading enterprises of China's economy. In addition, during the collection process of key words, we found that SOEs' cultural statements consisted of a number of different topics which reflects diversity of the trend.

5 Conclusions

According to the Deal and Kennedy's cultural elements framework, these top SOEs' cultural statements are in good quality. The number of elements included in the majority of the cultural statements is three or above. However, there are still some of top SOEs having no cultural statements and SOEs with complete cultural statements is very scant.

The results indicate that the cultural statements of China's top 50 SOEs are most concerned about values and enterprise environment, followed by cultural networks, rituals and ceremonies. A heroic figure is of the lowest concern.

The cultural statements of SOEs of different nature (traditional／high-tech) are at different levels. Overall, the quality of traditional companies' cultural statements is better than that of high-tech companies. The proportion of traditional SOEs with cultural statements and the inclusion of evaluation elements in their cultural statements are higher and the cultural statements are more normative.

The cultural statements of SOEs of different industry are at different levels and have different focuses. Generally, the quality of cultural statements of SOEs in secondary industry is better than that of in service sector. SOEs in secondary industry are more concerned about values while SOEs in service sector pay more attention to environmental factors.

Excellent Chinese SOEs' cultural statements are characterized by focusing on innovation, organizational orientation, blood relations with government and the intersection between SOEs' culture building and the ideological and political construction.

6 Limitations and Future Research Opportunities

Due to constraints of time and other objective factors, we only collected data in China's superexcellent top 50 SOEs which caused an issue regarding the generalization of our study findings. Thus, these results may or may not generalize to other SOEs and the sample size could be enlarged in the future researches.

Our research found that the content of China's SOEs' cultural statements is more diversifying than Deal and Kennedy's cultural elements. Thus, this framework may not be suitable for the study of Chinese companies or China's SOEs and the validity of the results reflecting the true level of China's SOEs' cultural statements would be discounted. Future studies may be necessary to build up a more appropriate model.

The method of data gathering was mainly scanning the official websites of companies, Baidu and other web pages to obtain information of cultural statements. For the convenience and simplicity of data processing using SPSS, deviation and non-comprehensive problem may exist in the classification of elements and selection of key words.

Although academic and practitioner publications have stressed the importance and value of enterprise culture, the real relationship between enterprise's performance and cultural statement is still puzzling and our study did not address this issue. Thus, the future research is needed not only to construct a proper model but also to examine the relationship between enterprise's performance and cultural statement.

References

1. Ralston, D.A., Terpstra-Tong, J., Terpstra, R.H., Wang, X., Egri, C.: Today's SOEs of China: are they dying dinosaurs or dynamic dynamos? Strategic Management Journal, 825–843 (2006)
2. Hansen, P.H.: Organization Culture and Organizational Change: The Transformation of Savings Banks in Denmark, 1965-1990. Enterprise & Society, 920–953 (2011)
3. Qu, Q.: A Comparison Between the Cultural Statements of Chinese and United States Companies. China Industrial Economy, 80–87 (2007)
4. Yuanli, R., Chong, S.: Cultural statement for Part of China Enterprises: An Empirical Study. Nankai Business Review, 64–68 (2005)

The Research on Income Effect of Service Industry Development in Northeast China

Tao Huang

Tao Huang, School of Management and Economy,
Shenyang Aerospace University, 110136, Liaoning, China
huangtao024@163.com

Abstract. In recent years, the service industry enjoys rapid development in Northeast China, where employment in modern sectors increases and traditional type decreases. This trend complies with the law of development of service industry. In this paper, data analysis method is used for investigation of income distribution effect in the service industry. With research on the mechanism of this effect, the conclusions are obtained, which indicate that the development of service industry tends to make income distribution fairer; the decreasing of the employment number of the traditional sectors greatly reduces the unfair level of income distribution, however, the modern sectors does not contribute to this significantly.

Keywords: Northeast China, Services Industry, Income Effect.

1 Introduction

In recent years, the rapid development of service industry becomes a strong impetus to the economy growth in China. And in Northeast China(as convention, only 3 provinces are considered in this paper: Heilongjiang, Jilin and Liaoning), according to the statistics data in 2009, added value of service industry was 207.43 billion RMB together, and its proportion in tertiary industry reached 38.67%. Beyond its impetus effect on economy growth, development of service industry also affected the income distribution by changing the employment structure. In 2009, employment from service sector accounted for 38.07% of the total in this region. Moreover, from all new employees, the service industry absorbed more than any other. Inevitably, above changes will have direct and indirect effects on the income distribution.

2 Development and Structure Changing of Service Industry in Northeast China

With the growth of economic output and per capita income, people's demand structure for goods and services will change, following the adjustment of output structure. However, this adjustment can only be achieved by re-configuration of input elements among all industries. Since labor force is the most important and active element, the

M. Zhou (Ed.): ISAEBD 2011, Part III, CCIS 210, pp. 213–219, 2011.

employment structure will change during the re-configuration. It happens because the rapid development of tertiary industry will attract more labor, which will change the distribution of labor within the industry.

2.1 Inside Composition Change of Service Industry in This Region

When employment in service industry increases, it will be decreasing in primary & secondary industry. Meanwhile, employment structure will be changing in each sector of service industry.

Table 1 shows the employment structure in Northeast China from 2003 to 2009. During this time, some of the traditional sectors suffered a downward trend in employment, such as transport-storage-logistics, wholesale-retail, etc. Employment in some of the modern sectors shrank too, such as finance, education, health-social security and social welfare, public administration and social organization. Some sectors had slight ups-and-downs, such as leasing and business services, research-technical services and geological prospecting, water conservancy-environment and public facilities management. Anyway, the employment proportion of a few industries was expanding year by year, such as information transmission, computer services and software industries.

Table 1. Service Industry Output Growth in Northeast China Font sizes of headings

Sector	2003	2004	2005	2006	2007	2008	2009
Transport, storage and logistics	6.03	5.44	4.84	4.70	4.43	4.14	3.80
	2.03	1.90	1.68	1.66	1.60	1.54	1.45
Wholesale and Retail trade	4.32	3.75	2.96	2.86	2.54	2.37	2.26
	1.45	1.31	1.02	1.01	0.92	0.88	0.86
Finance	2.63	2.38	2.40	2.32	2.32	2.31	2.26
	0.89	0.83	0.83	0.82	0.83	0.86	0.86
Leasing and Business Services	1.08	1.13	1.06	1.06	1.02	1.09	0.95
	0.36	0.39	0.37	0.37	0.37	0.40	0.36
Research, Technical Services and Geological Prospecting	1.57	1.51	1.49	1.51	1.52	1.52	1.49
	0.53	0.53	0.52	0.53	0.55	0.56	0.57
Water, Environment and Public Facilities	1.61	1.51	1.57	1.54	1.55	1.50	1.48
	0.54	0.52	0.54	0.54	0.56	0.56	0.56
Education	8.70	8.05	8.03	7.85	7.61	7.26	6.91
	2.93	2.80	2.78	2.77	2.74	2.69	2.63

Table 1. (*continued*)

Sector	2003	2004	2005	2006	2007	2008	2009
Health, social security and social welfare	3.47	3.17	3.27	3.24	3.17	3.14	3.01
	1.17	1.10	1.13	1.15	1.14	1.16	1.15
Public Administration and Social Organization	7.28	6.99	7.04	6.92	6.74	6.65	6.30
	2.45	2.43	2.44	2.44	2.43	2.47	2.40
Others (including info-transmission, computer services & software, culture-sports & entertainment, etc.)	63.30	66.07	67.34	68.00	69.12	70.01	71.54
	21.30	23.00	23.30	24.02	24.90	25.97	27.23

Remark 1. Data based on "China Statistical Yearbook". For every sector, top row is the share of employment in the service industry, and the other is the share in the whole tertiary industry.

In figures, employment proportion of transport-storage-logistics decreased from 6.03% in 2003 to 3.8% in 2009, and wholesale and retail sector from 4.32% to 2.26%. The declines are very large, nearly half. However, Table 2 shows a year-by-year increasing of the output value of these two traditional industries, indicating that they are still main fields absorbing many labors, but with a weakening status during economy growth.

Similar situation occurred for industries like finance, health-social security & welfare, public administration & social organizations in recent years. Table 2 tells that with declining of the proportion of employment, they all enjoyed output increasing. This means that although employment dropped, but the efficiency increased, and fewer employees can create more output value.

As stated previously, some industries have slight ups-and-downs in Table 2. This can be explained that they are underdeveloped industry in this region, which keeps them in a relatively stable level.

Table 2 also tells that the employment shares of information transmission, computer services & software and other emerging services sector are increasing, also with outputs growing, which indicates that they are the main driving-force for employment growth and development of service industry in Northeast China. Especially, led by Daqing, Harbin and Dalian, the rapid development of software outsourcing sector has made outstanding contribution to the service industry in this region.

The rising of modern sectors and the declining of the traditional ones, reflects the effort of Northeast China trying to upgrade and optimize the structure of employment in recent years. Employees' transfer from traditional to modern service sectors improves the labor efficiency, and further benefit the entire socio-economic growth and social development.

This also shows that the development of service industry has competition among sectors, which led to the expansion of modern advanced high skill & high income sectors to traditional low-skill & low-income peers. In fact, Table 1 illustrates a trend: during the expansion of modern advanced sectors, the employment of traditional sectors kept going down.

Table 2. Added Value of Each Sector of Service Industry in Northeast China (units: million)

Sector	2003	2004	2005	2006	2007	2008	2009
Transport, storage & logistics	1042	1057.7	1120.7	1216.01	1413.5	1566.4	1562.42
Finance	243.79	297.41	350.19	471.9	560.43	757.55	968.57
Business Services		142.56	174	216.3	257.9	288.5	325.5
Wholesale & Retail Trade	877.24	1026.81	1201.88	1406.8	1733.46	2233	2479.47
Accommodation & catering	273.75	321.73	367.55	415.88	479.79	570.97	697.53
Scientific Research, Technical Services	104.32	110.33	116.68	123.4	130.51	138.03	145.98
Real Estate	377.82	438.77	532.53	644.79	790.06	932.02	1106.59
Info-transmission, computer & software		181.7	366.52	432.5	474.9	539.1	581.5

Remark 2. Data based on "China Statistical Yearbook".

2.2 Output Growth of Service Industry in Northeast China

The developing trend of the output growth of service industry in the region can be seen in Table 3. Generally, this industry has kept growing, from 50.313 million RMB in 2003 to 120.19 million in 2009. However, its proportion in local GDP has no obvious increasing, which must be caused by the strategic policy that puts much favor on the Secondary Industry and the stage of industrialization. But in 2009, that proportion grew significantly. This can be explained by the policy favor and guide on service industry and its vigorous development, which can narrow the income gap.

Table 3. Service Industry Output Growth in Northeast China

Item	2003	2004	2005	2006	2007	2008	2009
Shares in GDP (%)	39.55	39.23	37.50	36.98	36.16	35.01	38.67
Output (million)	50.31	57.06	64.42	73.18	85.17	99.45	120.2

3 The Mechanism of Income Distribution Effect by the Development of Service Industry

3.1 The Role of Knowledge

Inevitably, the development of modern service industry will affect income distribution. In this process, the knowledge plays a bridge role. Knowledge greatly reduces the economy's dependence on natural resources, and realizes the increasing of marginal revenue. Beyond this, the concentration of knowledge in workers and production process, make them knowledge-based human capital and innovative production and development respectively. So, the combination of them turns to a multiplier to the output of knowledge-based production. Therefore, making knowledge as a element of production will bring workers higher income.

Modern service industry is characterized by higher technology and knowledge. So when absorbing labor, it has higher requirement on the labor's knowledge and skills. As a result, most of low-quality and low-skilled labor have to be employed in the low-threshold & low-paid traditional sectors. Due to the restrictions on labor quality, workers more likely prefer to traditional sectors of service industry rather than modern sectors during the labor transfer from primary & secondary industries to the tertiary. Considering the distribution of incomes inside service industry, traditional sectors offer lower salary. So, the labor transfer does improve employment, but hardly can raise the level of labor income and reduce income distribution inequities.

3.2 The Specialized Form

The division of labor and specialization lead to the separation of modern service sectors from traditional, and make it a single industry, which will break the old averaged distribution pattern, resulting in income disparity. Based on division of labor, specialization of production, and comparison of benefit difference, income distribution system must recognize income gap. This gap is allowed during economy development, and it is an objective reality and integral part of economic development. Hence, it is conducive to promoting economic growth. In fact, a relatively equitable income distribution system should recognize this gap. However, it is hardly to say that development of service industry in Northeast China has brought significantly widened income gap.

3.3 The Excitation Function

Beyond its fairness effect, income distribution also provides incentive function on efficiency. Under the conditions of modern enterprise system, human capital plays an increasingly important role during value creation. As a element of production, knowledge and technology are the result of innovation, and they are also the key to modern economic development. So it is necessary to to encourage innovation of knowledge and technology through income distribution system. Income distribution effect of the development of modern service industry is conducive to the formation of human capital, and the incentive on innovation and invention by labor. It also encourages individual workers to put additional investment to improve their human capital stock, in order to obtain more revenue. So workers can involve income distribution by their non-material elements: human capital. This means that the income distribution is based on the contribution of knowledge and technology to material wealth production. So, emphasizing the importance of knowledge in the whole society will conduct to long-term development of our economy. In the age of knowledge economy, human capital gains mainly come from knowledge, and knowledge comes from education, from the study of innovation, so this distribution effects will promote the development of education. Differences in income between people will inspire competition to seek a relatively high-income position. This competition, on the one hand, expands the quality supply of elements to high-yield sector. On the other hand, people working in the sector have to work harder to avoid being replaced by new entrants. Meanwhile, it also encourages enterprises to invest more innovation efforts in products and technology. With the deepening of the income distribution effect, it is obviously performing more and more incentive effect in China, besides its general function in every marketing economy. As to the incentive on individual effort by income differences, it sums up in three aspects: firstly, encourages people directly by improving working enthusiasm in current productive activities; secondly, stimulates people's effort in choosing or finding new position or other career consideration; thirdly, posts information on different positions and incomes, stimulating employment competition, and further leads to workers' competition in their human capital investment for developing their own qualities and professional skills.

The development of service industry, especially the modern sector, has brought changes in the distribution of income, which will produce incentive effect. This is because the income distribution is interest-oriented, and becomes impetus to maximize the benefits of any economic interest subject. Income distribution and redistribution provides material incentive for producers, consumers and government, stimulating the enthusiasm and creativity of each part, and improves the vitality and efficiency of economic activities. Change of the pattern of income distribution is conductive to the competition between involved parts for the quantity of economic interest and the quality of other interest. In the market of elements, in order to obtain higher returns, the competition will focus on high-income industries and sectors, which will make modern service industry more efficient through the survival of the fittest configuration of elements. Meanwhile, the transfer of elements from low-income sectors to high-income ones, the rising of modern service sectors and the shrinking of traditional sectors, also make the whole service industry to achieve more efficient configuration of elements. The realization of income distribution means achieving goals on material interests, which indicates that every part has done their jobs and got their slices. In turn, new goals on interests will attract and encourage every part to participate more actively in the economy activities, making which more efficient and dynamic.

4 Conclusions

The service industry in Northeast China has developed rapidly, with increasing of employment share of modern sectors and reducing of the traditional. This trend complies with the law of development for service industry. However, comparing with international level, it still falls behind. In fact, the absolute and relative output number of modern service industry is still lower than expectation.

As to Northeast China, the development of service industry tends to make income distribution fairer. The decreasing of the employment number of the traditional sectors greatly reduces the unfair level of income distribution, but the modern sectors does not contribute significantly.

Furthermore, it should be noticed that knowledge and skills have played a pivotal role between the development of modern service industry and the income distribution. And the education level of labor force in modern sectors in higher than traditional ones.

References

1. Liu, Z., Zheng, J.: Service Industry is Driving Yangtz River Delta, pp. 290–315. China Renmin University Press, Beijing (2008)
2. Zhang, S.: Research on the Employment Effect of Service Industry.China Financial & Economy Publishing House (2006)
3. Zhang, C., Cai, F.: Research on the Change Trend of Employment Elasticity. China Industrial Economy (2002)
4. Feng, H.: Research on Correlation Between Income Distribution and Differentiation of Urban Interest Groups. Management World 4, 142–143 (2006)
5. Gao, M.: Effect of Income Gap Between Individuals on Economy Growth. Pandeng 6, 26–29 (2003)
6. Zeng, F.: Discussion on Income Distribution and Effective Incentive. Xiangxiang Forum 17, 3 (2004)
7. China Statistical Yearbook (2003-2010)

The Analysis of Developing Mode of Rural Clean Energy: Using Xuzhou as an Example

Jingya Hao and Fuxing Zhu

Teacher, Economic and Trade Department,
Xuzhou Institute of Technology, 221008

Abstract. It is very important of the development and sustainability of clean energy to develop recycling economy and prompt development of rural production, life and biology. This essay firstly shows three rural cleaning energy modes that have been built in Xuzhou villages in Jiangsu province. Besides, it explains the functions of these three modes respectively in detail. Then, using statistic and calculated number, it analyses the present situation and problem of rural cleaning energy development in Xuzhou villages. Finally, it gives suggestions and measurements. And, it discusses channels of developing rural clean energy.

Keywords: Sustainable Development, Clean Energy, Mode.

Under the leading of sustainable development, basing on material cycle and energy transforms of natural biological system and using efficient and recycling utilization of resources as a center, biological cycling economy integrates clean production, comprehensive utilization of resources and its wastes, biological design and continuity into one body. Additionally, it harmoniously puts economic system into the material cycling process of natural biological system, raises efficiency of resources deployment, and realizes effective utilization of material resources and biological sustainable development.

Recently, Xuzhou government implements rural clean energy construction using rural biogas and straw gasification as the main content, turns rural "three wastes" (straw, excrement, rubbish) into "three usefulness" (fuel, feed, fertilization), leads villagers to organically link production with life, and cultivate with breed, realizes renewable increasing value and multistage utilization of agricultural resources, and prompts coordinative development of rural production, life and biology.

1 Rural Clean Energy Construction and Developing Modes

Since coming into the new century, as a big agricultural city, Xuzhou has exerted great efforts to implement rural clean energy construction, continually reinforced supporting forces, and formed recycling economic mode using biogas establishment and straw gasification as the channel. And, it also has developed agriculture and rural economy, prompted increasing agriculture effects and growing harvest, improved rural environmental conditions production and living, realized clean rural looking, and settled good fundament for establishing socialism new villages.

M. Zhou (Ed.): ISAEBD 2011, Part III, CCIS 210, pp. 220–226, 2011.

1.1 One Pond Three Changes Family Biogas Biological Mode

Using a farm family as a unit and utilizing techniques of biogas ferment, this mode puts human and livestock and poultry excrement, discards straws and organic rubbish into biogas pond for antioxidant ferment, and forms integration of change pen, toilet and kitchen. It makes simultaneous design and implement, mutually links biogas pond, pen and toilet, realizes that human and livestock and poultry excrement automatically go into the pond, and makes laboring breed produce conveniently. The biogas is used for energy of family ordinary living. Biogas slurry and biogas pit sediment are used for culturing fish, soaking seed, planting non-polluted vegetables and so on. That forms a non-pollution and non-rubbish benign recycling comprehensive utilization of biological mode. Xuzhou has have33,951 "one pond three changes" family biogas construction. In Xuzhou, there are 170 villages having hundreds of ponds. This constructing mode is an integration of economic, biological, and social effects, and is welcomed by farmers. This mode has three following functions.

First, it effectively improve rural biological environment. Through "one pond three changes", in village, livestock and poultry excrement, living dirty water and organic rubbish are put into biogas pond for decontaminating. That solves rural environmental healthy problem in the ground and living place. The clean and beautiful ground and living place and clear air improve producing and living conditions of farmers and healthy conditions of rural environment. Using biogas high-grade fuel changes rural traditional fire habit and improves farmer living quality.

Secondly, it promotes the agricultural effects and harvest. Each family builds underground biogas pond from 8 to 10 m3 .The square of livestock and poultry pen is not less than 12 m2 per family. The square of family toilet is not less than 2 m2 per family. Besides, each family also changes kitchen and net equipment and so on. Each family invests about 3,500 yuan. The output of biogas of each pond is about 350 m3 per year. Each family can save fee of living fuel that is up to 400 yuan. Output of biogas fertilizer is up to from 15 to 20 ton per pond in each year, which saves money for using fertilizer and pesticide to be 300 yuan. The implementation of "one pond three changes" can effectively enhance the development of farm aquaculture. It lets the revenue increase by more than 600 yuan per year (calculated by marketing 6 pigs per year). Furthermore, it makes comprehensive direct economic return per year be up to about 1,300 yuan. Based on calculating by 30-year using life, the cost per year is less than 120 yuan.

Third, it promotes the adjustment of agricultural structure. Through "one pond three changes", it directs farmers to link product, living, cultivation and breed, realizes renewable increasing value and multistage utilization, and boosts rural recycling economic development. Biogas slurry and biogas pit sediment contain organic matter, humic acid, micronutrients, variable amino acid, enzyme, beneficial microorganism, including elements such as nitrogen, phosphorous, potassium and so on. They can satisfy with growing demands of plants, have two functions of quick and slow effects. When they are put into gound, they will continue to ferment and release nutriment that can effectively improve soil, heighten grain output, and reduce around 25%of using quantity of fertilizer. They also can be used for feeding fishes, which let output increase 400 kilogram per hectare. And, they can be used to feed pig, which saving 15% feed. Biogas slurry can be sprayed to fruit trees and crops as fertilizer, which increases ability of disease and frost resistant. Biogas slurry and biogas pit sediment are good-quality organic fertilizer that make fruit and crops taste better and bigger, and save them be longer. They realize saving cost and increasing effects, and boosts farm aquaculture development and non-polluted vegetable production.

1.2 The Mode of Administrating Biogas of Livestock and Poultry Aquaculture

This mode is to large-scale livestock and poultry ground. According to the scale of breeding, it builds large-, medium-, and small-scale biogas administrating comprehensive utilizing construction, which use biogas antioxidant ferment technique to make excrement and urine in livestock and poultry aquaculture be through non-polluted treatment by anaerobic, oxic, solid-liquid separator system. This clean energy (biogas) can be used for product, living fuel and generating electric power. Biogas slurry and biogas pit sediment can be used for feeding fish, cultivating grasses, and providing high-quality organic fertilizer for producing non-polluted agricultural products, which forms resources totally recycling utilization and gains no pollution emission. Since 2002, Xuzhou has built 94 scaled biogas of livestock and poultry aquaculture administrating construction. Among them, there are 2big and medium generating power places. And, there are 92 medium and small comprehensive utilizing places. The content of pond is 14,000 m3. It deals more than 1,500,000 ton of livestock and poultry excrement per year. The output of biogas is up to more than 1,650,000 m3 per year. Through biogas of livestock and poultry aquaculture administrating construction, it not only solves the problem of excrement polluted environment in scaled livestock and poultry aquaculture, but also provides lots of high-quality organic fertilizer for agricultural production. That really solves restricting bottleneck of animal husbandry development, realizes biologic agricultural transformation that resources consumptive regular agriculture into resources cycling utilizing agriculture, boosts agricultural cycling economic development, and increases value in cycling.

1.3 The Mode of Straw Gasification Center Gas Provision

Using small town, administrative or natural village as a unit, through gasification unit of pyrolysis gasification reaction under lacking of oxygen, this mode transforms straw, grasses and other discarded materials into carbon monoxide, hydrogen, methane and other mixed combustibility gas. Then, it reduces ash, tar and other impurities from these gases. Next, it transits them into each family through gas holder and transiting net. Xuzhou has established 14 straw gasification center gas provision constructions in Yaoxi village in Ba Yiji town in Pizhou city, Sunzhuang village in Liuxin town and Dazhuang village in Maocun town in Tongshan district, and Mazhuang village in Qing Shanquan town and Quantai village in Dawu town in Jiawang district and so on. These can consume 8,000 ton village straw and other discarding materials, output 14,200,000 m3 straw combustibility gas per year, provide centre gas for 7,800 families. Through these, each family only spends about 20 yuan, which save 40% money than using carbon and 60% money than using liquefied petroleum. The technique of straw gasification is implemented, which lets straw have useful functions and big markets and gives new channels for utilizing village discarding straws. Recently, this mode has three following functions.

Firstly, it provides convenient, healthy, cheap, high-quality energy for farmers. Recently, the economy of villages in Xuzhou changes a lot. The level of living of farmers distinctively heightens. Under this situation, farmers urgently demands to gain convenient, healthy, cheap, high-quality living fuel and change the out-of-key situation that farmers fires grasses in the building. According to calculated results, straw per kilogram can output 2 m3 straw gas. The cost of gas provision is about 0.18 yuan/m3. The quantity of using gas per farm family is from 4 to 5 m3, which takes about 20 yuan per month. Through this, it realizes advanced mode that spends two covering whole village. It not only saves times for farmers, but also lets women in villages get out of the dirty kitchens.

Second, it develops cleaning energy that eases the presses from non-renewable energy. According to statistics, 80% farmers in economic developed region utilize carbon or liquefied gas as living fuel. So, totally utilizing and developing rural non-renewable energy can ease the presses of limitation of carbon and petroleum, and promise national economy to healthily continue to develop. Based on calculating, establishing a gasified station in a village that has 300 families can consume around 300 tons of straws per year, which produces 600,000 cm3 gases, replacing more than 200 tons carbon or 40 tons petroleum liquefied gas.

Thirdly, it reduces environmental pollution and improves rural biological environment. Recently, the quantity of straws increases, the straw has been a big polluted source. Firing straw has been a social effect. In summer and autumn per year, fire straw in the field and on the side of road cannot be prevented, which pollutes environment and arouses fire accident. The reason of this dues to that the channels of comprehensively utilizing straws does not be solved. The utilization of straw gasified technique provides good qualified fuel for farmers, realizes rural cooking gas net, promotes to utilize reasonably sources, reduces to the phenomenon of firing fuel and discarding, and protects rural biological environment.

As these modes are spread and applied, practiced and testified, it shows these modes not only provide cleaning energy for many farmers but also improve rural environment and promote agricultural sustainable development. Rural cleaning energy establishment has developed from small-scaled experimental exemplifying in the past to large-scaled centered connect and promote in the whole village, and expanded from unitary living region in the past to producing, biological, environmental healthy region. That has become a cleaning construction that improves rural producing living conditions, establishes an energy biological construction that saves resources and has a friend environment society, and a civilian construction that benefits farmers.

2 The Present Situation and Problem of Rural Cleaning Energy Development

Xuzhou is a big livestock city. The quantity of breeding livestock and poultry stands an advanced position in the whole province. The population of each kind of breeding farmers is up to 1,000,000 families, which puts dispersing and small-scaled breeding in thousands of families as the main part. According to statistics, the output of human and animal excrement of villages in the whole city is around 7,500,000tons per year. Most of them do not got the best effective utilization. Disorder stack, throw and emission not only pollute the environment, but also lose nutrients and wastes resources. Simultaneously, Xuzhou also is a big agricultural productive city. The total square of cultivated land is 6,095,100 hectare. The output of straws of each kind of agricultural product per year is more than 42,000,000tons. 50% of these are directly fired or discarded, which polluted the environment badly. At the present, Xuzhou has spread and applied family biogas in 33,951 families and straw gasified center gas provision in 7800 families, which does not reach 2.5% of farmers in the whole city. Using rural biogas and straw gasified establishment as a bond, resource cycling agricultural mode has guaranteed sources, which is the best entering point for applying agricultural cycling economic establishment, is a effective channel for solving the problems of biological protection, source wasting and so on, and has wide developing space and potential ability.

Recently, Xuzhou rural cleaning energy establishment has the following problems: First, the penetration rate in fitting farmers is low. The duty of spreading and applying is heavy. The propagation and leading, policy supports, standard management, technique training, and after-establishment service hurries to enhance. Second, the income of farmers is low. And, the poor farmers have difficulties in establishing ponds. According to the criterions of establishing "one pond three changes", average investment of a family is round 3,500yuan. Although the subsidy is around 1,500 yuan, farmer still needs to raise around 2,000yuan by himself or herself. So, the poor farmer has the financial problem to build pond. Third, total project subsidy fund directly is given to farmers. The serious shortage of managing rural energy and spreading works, ineffective application of implement management, technique training, property management net installment and so on, problems of paying more attention on establishing and paying less attention on managing, defective service system, and laggard technological service and so on lead to have difficult in managing farmer users and completely show comprehensively utilizing effects.

3 Suggestions and Measure

The establishment of rural cleaning energy construction is an effective channel of discovering energy, saving sources, improving rural healthy environment, heightening the living quality of farmers, increasing farmers' revenue and promoting sustainable development of rural economy, and an important measure of completely establishing well-off society, promoting socialism new village establishment. Since 2006, provincial committee and government put establishment of rural cleaning energy construction as the main content of rural new five practicing things. Besides, city committee and government put it in to ten projects of establishing new village and conclude it into assessment of "rural social career development". So, all levels of governments need to enhance propagating and leading, strengthen investing power and controlling quality of establishing construction , heighten subsidy standard, do technique training, establish healthy property service system and heighten comprehensive utilizing effects.

3.1 Unified Plan, and Step-by-Step Implication

We need to totally consider the changes of villages and rural residents, insist on unified plan and step-by-step implication, organize reasonably, protrude the main points, enhance the governmental supports, respect civilian ideas, create system, and keep the principle of combination of establishment and management. Under the premise of plan, we take actions that suit local circumstance and reasonably manage scale of establishing basing on the demands and financial ability of villagers, prevent having no direction, and steadily promote better and quicker development of Xuzhou rural cleaning energy establishment.

3.2 Fulfill the Working Responsibility, Carefully Organize and Imply

All levels of leaders and relative departments need to be good organizers, propagandists, and servers. They need to let rural cleaning energy establishment as the action of concerning, supporting and developing "three agricultures". They also need to enhance coordination among departments, conduct the lower level of government, implement level by level, and make sure all measures in practice.

3.3 Conduct Technique Training, Imply Specialized Construction

Towards the characteristics of strong specialization and high technique content of rural biogas construction establishment, we need to strengthen examining and training professional technique. We also need to pay more attention on training establishing standards of "one pond three changes", techniques of establishing ponds, conduction of safety of biogas pond, and comprehensively utilize biogas slurry and biogas pit sediment and so on. Additionally, we train some brilliant biogas producers and provide strong technique protection for construction.

3.4 Strength Conducting and Make Sure the Quality of Constructing

We need to track and conduct project fund, process organization, material purchase, quality guarantee, follow-up management and other implying process, and establish files relative materials. Furthermore, we strengthen to conduct the location and using situation of project subsidy fund, in order to make special fund for special use. We need to invite bid for choosing constructing group, establishing quality conductive group, and track and manage the whole process of construction.

3.5 Strengthen Establishment of System, Enhance After-Establishment Service

We shall add more staff, locate necessary fund, establish city technique training basis, town service station, village service net, and progressively realize "one technician in one village, one intellectual in one family". We need to organize special fund for supporting the establishment of service system, progressively realize "specialized service, marketed operation, and property managed management", make sure construction be steady, safe, effectively operated and make farmers get sustainable benefits.

3.6 Create the System of Operating, Heighten Comprehensive Effects

We need to create technique mode, positively research new products, new crafts, new technique, and new materials for rural cleaning energy construction, enhance exemplifying and spreading technique testing, increase science content, heighten the level of constructing. We also need to organically combine rural cleaning energy construction with rural environmental management, rural organization, polluted water administration, and biologically agricultural construction, heighten economic, biological, social effects of rural cleaning energy construction.

References

1. Xu, D.M.: The Research on Accelerating Rural Energy Modernized Establishment—Rural Energy Construction of Yanqing Town in Beijing. China Technology Investment, 13–14 (2007)
2. Gu, Y.S.: The Analysis of Cycling Utilization of Rural Discarding Materials—Using Zhejiang Jiaxing as an example. Biological Economy, 82–85 (2009)
3. Zhang, M., Lai, M.: The Research on Problems and Measures of Rural Biogas Development Construction. Anhui Agricultural Technology, 2108–2110 (2007)
4. Zhang, G.Z.: The Discussion on Discovering and Utilizing of Our Country's Rural Energy. Agricultural Modernization Research, 24–27 (1988)

Several Measures to Perfect Tax Administration by Law

Wenyi Dong

Shandong University at Weihai, Finance and Securities Research Institute,
Shandong Weihai 204209
dong_wenyi@yahoo.com.cn

Abstract. The basis of tax administration by law is to establish the perfect tax law system, and the taxation basic law is in the lead. Especially, making out the Special Taxation Preference Law plays an important role in standardizing the tax law. The key to the tax administration by law is to enforce the law strictly, and setting up the independent tax inspection institution is very important to standardization of tax law enforcement. The motivation of tax administration by law is to improve the evaluation of execution level of law, and it is necessary to establish an evaluation indicator system, the core of which is to measure the execution level of tax law. The evaluation index system and reduction of the tax plan rigidity are important factors of standardization of tax collection.

Keywords: Tax Law System, Independent Examination, Execution Level of Law, Special Preference Method.

In China, some outstanding problems of tax administration by law are as follows: firstly, tax law system and the foundation of tax administration by law are not complete; secondly, tax preference is so complicated that leads to executive inconvenience and constraint fatigue; thirdly, tax check is repeated and the independence and restraining forces are insufficient; fourthly, tax plan rigidity and tax administration by plan are serious. This paper argues that several measures to perfect law administration by law in China are strengthening and improving tax legislation construction; making out tax special preference method; setting up independent tax inspection institution and improving the evaluation of execution level of tax law.

1 Basic Thoughts of Strengthening and Improving Tax Legislation Construction in China

1) Perfect the tax law system

Using the other countries' experiences and practices for reference, China should adopt tax law system model of "the constitution add basic law add special law" under the national conditions. Tax legislation should be constructed as follow.

Firstly, supplement the clauses of the constitution about taxation and make the basic content of tax law as the principle provision. The constitution about taxation is too curt and only in the 56th regulation of the constitution refers that every citizen of the People's Republic of China has the tax liability according to the law. Therefore, it is necessary to explicitly stipulate the rights, the legislation scope, process and principles

M. Zhou (Ed.): ISAEBD 2011, Part III, CCIS 210, pp. 227–231, 2011.

of all levels of the legislatures; clearly stipulate the rights, obligations and range of taxpayers, etc.

Secondly, enact the taxation basic law as soon as possible. Yet there is no a taxation basic law in China and some the most fundamental and the most important issues of the tax law system do not get the identification by law, for instance, the definition, purpose, basic principles and components of taxation and tax law, tax legislative, tax law enforcement powers and so on, all of which are not got effectively rules and instructions thereby cause the misunderstanding of tax law. So it is important to through the taxation basic law to standardize and guide the whole tax law system, and explicitly stipulate the aspects according to the constitution to guide the other tax laws and regulations.

Thirdly, increase the lacking supposing regulations of tax law. Tax law system must be complete and have a reasonable structure. China used to pay more attention on the tax substantive law, while thinking little of some relevant supporting laws, and this situation causes a weak tax law enforcement and administration, besides, some methods to deal with problems lack legal basis. Therefore, China should make out the supporting laws as soon as possible, for instance, tax authorities law; tax agency law; tax violation punishment law; tax law enforcement authority security; tax administrative reconsideration and procedural law and invoice management law, etc.

2) Appropriately decentralize the tax legislative

In the case of local taxes legislative, according to the national conditions in China, it can consider dividing the local taxes into several situations, and treat them differently. For the local taxes which are need to be levied nationwide and have a greatly influence on the macroeconomic, the central government should stipulates the basic law and regulation and the measures for the implementation, while the local governments can stipulate the partial tax elements and partial collection methods in its power; for the local taxes which are need to be levied nationwide and have a less impact on the macroeconomic but have a greatly influence on the regional economics, the central just stipulates the basic law and regulation and measures for the implementation, and the powers including policy explanation, taxable items, tax rates adjusted, tax reliefs and tax administration can be decentralized to the local governments; according to the regional economic development, the local governments can levy some local taxes, put some local charges into the local taxation system and make out some relevant rules and regulations.

3) Improve the tax law grades

At present, most of the tax laws are interim regulations, only a few are passed by the state legislature, which will severely affect the validity of tax law level. So it is necessary to put forward some administrative regulations that are available proved by practice in China to the state legislature, and make them to the formal laws according to the tax legislative procedures, in order to improve the grades and effect of tax law, and change the chaotic situations of executive authorities, and then, the tax law can not be misused and abused. Primary and basic tax laws should be drafted and adopted by the state legislature; tax legislation by the authorized government must carry out under the NPC laws; as for the interim regulations, it is supposed to be made a deadline instead of being unlimited; these above aspects compose the goal mode of tax legislative in China.

2 Making out Special Taxation Preference Law

Taxation preference clauses are distributed to step-up method of each tax category. The problems caused by this are: the first is that the step-up method of some tax categories are made more complicated, for instance, enterprise income tax law and its regulations; furthermore, it is hard to understand the taxation content in step-up method of every tax category completely due to looking through variety of step-up methods and to avoid the appearance of deviations. Second, many taxation preference regulations are lack of stability in long run in China; some rules in regulations are specified, but no cancellation or announcement are made when later they are changed or amended, even there appears that taxation documents dominate the regulations or rules. The seriousness of taxation law is faced with challenge.

To overcome the weak normalization, bad transparency and hard operation caused by present taxation preference distributed to various step-up methods, in my opinion, a special taxation preference should be made out to show the guideline of national industrial policy and regional development policy only for the long-run stable content embodied by taxation system structure, for instance, the arrangement of object of taxation, incidence of taxation, choice of taxpayer and disparate tax rate system. And a great amount of taxation preference regulations should be focused on one special taxation preference regulation. This regulation should list national industrial policy and regional development policy, other policies related to taxation preferences, the sequencing of national industrial development and regional development so as to make people aware of taxation preference goal and the reason for taxation preference. Later on, the taxation preference way should be specified, including the form, degree and operating method of taxation preference, to make people know clearly about the specific content of taxation preference and how to handle. Meanwhile, when an item of taxation preference changes, all the laws (include the unchanged items) are supposed to be promulgated anew, or provide a revise, making sure the revise is the most comprehensive, most authoritative and most applicative. Moreover, the state derecognition and tax authorities and relevant departments being forbidden to carry out the tax reliefs beyond the taxation preference can play a certain role of the constraint in tax reliefs problems of exceeding the local governments and relevant departments powers.

3 Setting up the Independent Tax Audit and Investigation Institutions and Strengthening Supervision over Law Enforcement

The reform of the separation in China is always stagnant within the tax authorities. However, it causes many problems as follows. Firstly, it lacks of the mutual restraining forces and supervision power. The supervision and restriction of the same institution is far than that of an independent institution; secondly, it considers the tax check as the primary or the main approach to finish the taxation tasks. Tax check is not valued if the task is easy, to the contrary, when the pressure is heavy, the tax check will be aggravating; thirdly, tax check is repeated. Nowadays, all levels of auditing departments are basically only responsible for the departmental collection by taxes, but there are many inspections overlap; fourthly, some departments have their hands full to be investigated, and complain a lot.

Given the above problems, in my opinion, the key to fundamentally solve the problem is to improve the tax authorities setting and assignment of responsibility which are the basic and key issues. The setting of the tax authority should focus on the specialty, independence and mutual constraints to change thoroughly the comprehensive situation that one tax authority carry out all kinds of the tax administration woke, and build an independent tax authority with division of responsibility. The specific practice is to set up an independent tax inspection bureau, paralleling the National Tax Bureau and Local Tax Bureau. Tax inspection bureau should be directly managed by the state administration of taxation, breaking the administration division setting, and which is primary responsible for the supervision of activities between tax collectors and taxpayers and dealing with the tax cases. The responsibilities of the tax inspection bureau can be briefly summarized as follows: checking the implementation of the tax regulations and policy; tax inspection of the taxpayers; examination and approval of the auditorial report by the tax unit; acceptance the tax reporting and tax cases investigation, implement and processing; implementing measures of the taxpayers for violation of laws and disciplines; in charge of the tax administrative review and the examine and approve the tax reliefs and tax preference.

The independent tax inspection bureau plays a supervisory role in the taxpayers and tax authorities, which is a primary and independent part of the supervision and inspection system of tax collection. The supervision is an afterward monitoring to the taxpayers while restricts the tax authorities which is reflected indirectly by the audit of the taxpayers. Only the independent tax inspection bureau has the access to on-the-spot investigation in the companies, and which can either avoid the repeated check or strengthen the supervision and restriction of the tax administration, in this way, it can make sure the implement of the tax policy correctly, and also plays a certain role of containment in the interference of taxation working from the relevant administration department.

4 Handling the Revenue Plan Properly and Improving the Examination System about the Implementation of Tax Administration

The evaluation index can form a kind of motivation mechanism or punitive mechanism, which can influence the operation of mechanism and human behavior. Whereas the tax collection, a lawful administrative action, request can not depart form the law. So only the targets relative to revenue and the resulting motivation mechanism and punitive mechanism are designed according to the tax legal system it can reach a good effect.

1) The disadvantage of examining the taxation collection with single index.
Firstly, this practice violates the principle of tax legislation that can make the administrative decree have more power than law. To levy tax in accordance with the tax rate and the tax law is the foundation of the tax revenue activities. While the taxes levying based on the plan deviates basically from the requirements of law-based tax

which are the key representation on the dim of tax legislation consciousness and the idea of ruling by human.

Secondly, this practice agonists the tax law leading to increase or reduce casually. Due to the discrepancy of economy development in different areas, there is a certain gap between the revenue task ordered by the government and the revenue collected according to the tax law. Therefore, in order to accomplish the tasks, some tax authorities have to increase or reduce casually by themselves which against the tax law. To levy tax ahead of time or some taxes that should not be existed and the deficit spending often occurs in some areas whose economy is underdeveloped and revenue tasks is weighed. To the contrary, there has some tax sources left after accomplishing the tasks in that very year in some areas whose economy is developed and the revenue tasks is light. When the revenue is nearing completion, the grass-roots tax authorities sometimes conceal some tax sources for the purpose of using when the tasks increasing in the next stage or under a greater pressure which forms parts of outstanding taxes.

Thirdly, this practice breaks down the social morality and relaxes the taxation management. In cases of putting upside down the relationship between the administrative order and the tax legal system, whether developed regions or underdeveloped areas, falsification that not only cause the distortion of the statistics but also undermines the Party discipline are repeatedly arising. The reason why they practice fraud is that they want to gain rewards, ease the revenue tasks pressure increasing year by year based on the radix number. Meanwhile, evaluating the tax revenue work's stand or fall by the completion status of the revenue will surely make tax authorities pay much attention on tax revenue, but not tax management which is not conducive to the level of collection and management.

2) Building up a revenue assessment indictors system with a core of measuring the level of law-enforcement.

It can be used various indexes from multiple angles to the quality of collection and management by measuring the level of law-enforcement. The following respects should be on the list: the tax rate of registration and ignoring tax rate, tax returns filing rate and its real ratio, income taxes receiving rate and back tax rate, ratio of legality on tax-related documents and accuracy rate of tax law enforcement and the maintenance rate of tax administrative review and the winning rate of tax-related administrative litigation.

References

[1] Gao, B., Wu, X.: Outline of Legislative Regulation of Taxation. Taxation Research (2) (1999)

[2] Wu, B., Liu, Y.: Perfecting Taxation Legislation and Improving Taxation Executive Efficiency. Taxation Research (11) (1999)

[3] Tu, L., Wang, H.: Legislative Taxation Principles and Perfecting Chinese Taxation Legislation System. Taxation Research (12) (1999)

[4] Dong, W.: Thinking about the Construction of Tax Law. Journal of Dongbei University of Finance and Economics 61(1) (2009)

Based on Fishbone Diagram Analysis of Management 80s Employees Performance in Enterprise

Cheng Cheng[1] and Enyi Zhou[2]

[1] School of Management, Xi'an University of Architecture & Technology, PhD Student
[2] Professor of Xi'an University of Architecture & Technology
710055, Xi'an, China
chengcheng0403@163.com

Abstract. The development of enterprises has an important driving force on the development of the whole country, while the level of job performance of employees between the survival and development of enterprises. Facing of corporate development, take measures to control the work performance of employees, is important to enhance their level of development. Current 80s employees accounted for a large proportion, they are special of the generation, is a product of unique phenomenon of China's national conditions, as 80s has the strong features, the management of 80s should also have its unique. As the lack of management theory of 80s and the impact and collision in practical work, so that "how to manage the 80s"has become a problem that all business managers must solve. This paper analyzes working characteristics of the 80s employees and point out a range of factors that influenced their performance, draw fishbone diagram according to factors, using the basic principles of fishbone analysis proposed countermeasures of how to manage 80s for ease of enterprise manage generation y employees.

Keywords: Fishbone Analysis, 80s, Job Performance.

1 Introduction

80s refers to the people born between the 1980 and 1990, then Chinese family planning policy is birth control, their growth has distinctive characteristics of the times. Today 80s have started working one after another and gradually grew into the backbone of the social strata, how to understand and use them will determine the future of enterprise and society. However, many business managers find the management mode and method which has accumulated years are not applicable to the management of 80s staff. Scholars at home and abroad have a thorough study of 80s with the qualitative analysis, but hasn't a system with the use of fishbone analysis to analyze the management of 80s employees, companies need to find out the influencing factors of generation y job performance and given countermeasure through fishbone diagram, therefore, this paper has a practical significance for analyze the management of 80s and improving the management of enterprise human resource through the fishbone analysis.

M. Zhou (Ed.): ISAEBD 2011, Part III, CCIS 210, pp. 232–238, 2011.

2 Basic Principle of Fishbone Analysis

There will be a variety of business issues in the actual management process which require effective solutions. One effective way is fishbone analysis. The so-called fishbone analysis is a method by which discover root causes of the problem and through the appearance to perceive the essence. The characteristics of the problem are always subject to some factors, we find these factors through brainstorm and associate them with special values, together with them in accordance with the interrelatedness, consolidation of a structured and coherent, and graphics to mark the important factors called the fishbone diagram.

Using fishbone analysis with comprehensive system observation, investigation and analyze the factors which affect 80s' job performance that in order to find out the causality. As Figure 1: First of all is to find out the so-called major cause, and then require further decomposition, which is the reason, small reasons or less reason, their relationship said by the production lines with arrows to work out a solution.

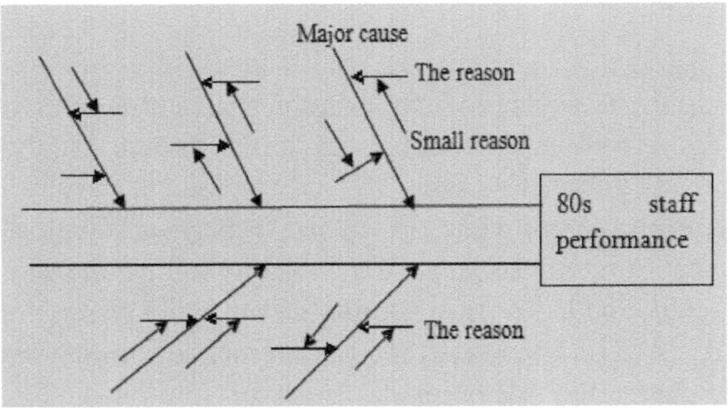

Fig. 1. Fishbone diagram

Here's analysis of the factors that affect 80s employees work performance, to find the possible measures that can optimal performance management of 80s.

3 Analysis of Influence Factors of Generation Y Employee Job Performance

Modern management and psychology studies have shown that factors affecting 80s job performance comes from three main areas: personal, organizational, and job, employee performance can be expressed in the following formula: P=f (I,O,T). This formula shows that staff performance is a function of three variables which are individual, organization and work. It is these three relatively independent factors influence and they interact with each other, culminated in the reality of staff performance, as shown in Figure 2.

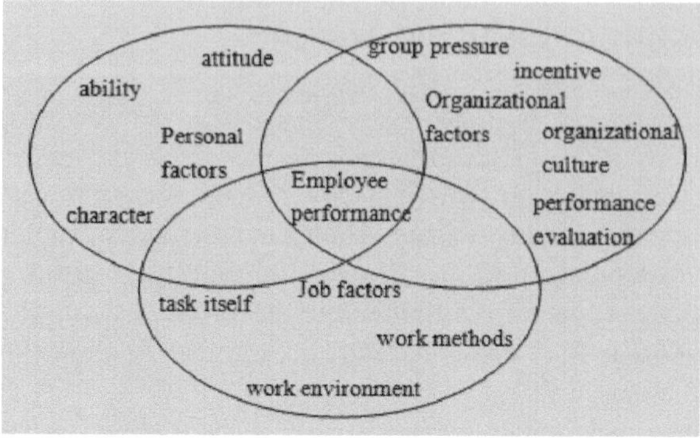

Fig. 2. Factors Affecting Employee Performance

3.1 Personal Factors

Personal factors include its ability, character and attitude of employees.

Ability factor

Ability is an individual psychological characteristics that individuals successfully completing certain activities and task. Individual through analyze and synthesize objective things, using knowledge and skills to complete an activity successfully, this is the ability. Generation y employees are trained to better education and have a higher degree mostly, according to surveys, the majority of generation y employees has adapted existing work and has a strong ability to work and professional quality, but the practical ability should be improved. At work practical ability includes planning of work content, organization of rational, finishing job on time and so on. These shortcomings will inevitably affect their performance and career development.

Character factors

80s are mostly one-child, they are used to passively accept their elders care and love, in the growing role of error prone and even have more psychological problems. Their lack of experience and peer interaction, without establishing good habits of cooperation and communication with others to solve the problem. If this habit to the work, it will produce a series of problems.

Attitude factors

Generation y have gone through 9 years of compulsory education, most of them in the school formal education is about 15 years, with higher education and degree, they adapted to the study, the examination of the growth mode, and lack of concern for the natural and social enthusiasm and participation. Therefore, when they join the work, they will experience the increased competitive pressure and the tension of interpersonal relationships, these are formed with the gap between their expectations, and non-adaptability, enthusiasm and dedication index of the work will be reduced.

3.2 Organizational Factors

Organizational factors including group pressure, motivating factors, performance evaluation, organizational culture factors and so on.

Group pressure factors

Group pressure has positive and negative double impact on employee performance. When employees find their work performance levels and groups that don't correspond, they'll have a psychological state of intense fear, fear of marginalization and neglect of the other members of the group, which led him to raise or lower the performance level of their work to make it consistent with the group. Facing the increasingly fierce competition, 80s' working pressure were greater than ever before, whether it is from society, family or business, they have more requirements and expectations on generation y. If they don't pay attention to release the pressure, it's possible to have a reverse psychology on work and affect performance.

Incentive factors

Incentive factors refer to the ability to have a stimulating effect on motivated behavior, thus mobilizing the positive factors, which closely linked with the job content. Incentives need to be improved or met, is often give employees an incentive to a large extent, generated a sense of job satisfaction, conducive to full and lasting mobilize the enthusiasm of the staff. For generation y, wages tend to become their first evaluation criteria of choice of occupation, therefore, they seek higher wages as one of the important goals, if you do not pay the incentive, which may affect 80s enthusiasm for work.

Performance evaluation factors

Performance evaluation is a process, it refers to control work targets or performance standards, use of certain evaluation methods, assessing the task completion of staff, the degree of fulfillment duties and development of staff, and feedback the above process of evaluation to employees. In the 80s' mind fair is very important, so evaluation must be open, fair, otherwise they will be affected the enthusiasm of the 80s staff.

Organizational culture factors

Organization culture is a unique cultural image consisting of the organization's values, beliefs, rituals, symbols and working styles. The core of enterprise culture is the spirit and values of enterprise, generation y attaches great importance to corporate culture, focusing on business opportunities. If the generation y thinks that organizational cultures do not meet with their values, they are likely to move on to another comparison which enterprise culture in line with their values, resulting in a higher turnover rate.

3.3 Job Factors

Job factors include the factor of the task itself, work methods factors, work environment factors and so on.

Factor of the task itself

Most of the generation y employees are active and innovative, dislike doing the dull and boring work. If the enterprise's work is challenging, it will mobilize their enthusiasm for work, on the contrary, generation y will cope with trouble. Therefore, whether the task meets the interests of generation y, has a far-reaching impact on the 80s' job performance.

Methods of work

Working methods refers to ways and means that people taken by in the process to achieve a certain purpose and effects in practice. Generation y employees most like flexible working hours system, their working methods are also maverick, if it's too well-behaved, will make them think the work is boring, thus affecting performance.

Work environment factors

Work environment not only includes the office of the natural environment, also includes cultural environment and the management mechanisms. Generation y considered the target of their work is to have better lives. They have high requirements on the work environment than ever before. They do not want to work under very harsh conditions, and do not want disharmony coexistence between people. Therefore, the work environment influences employee performance as much as other factors.

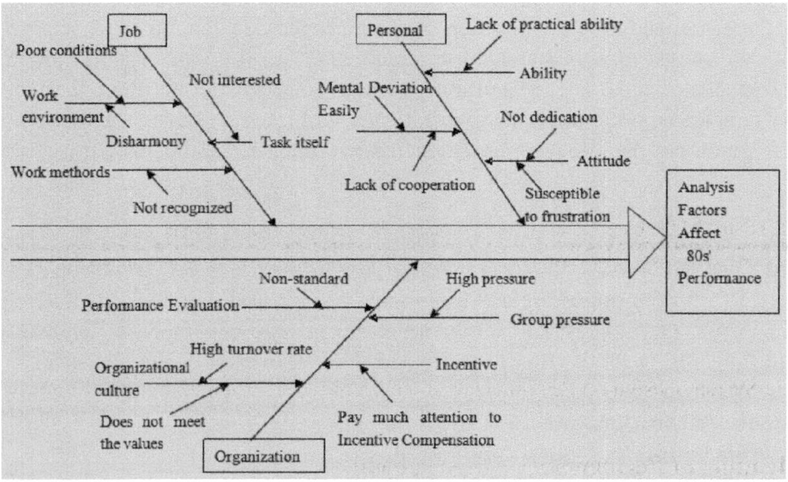

Fig. 3. Chart of analysis factors affect 80s' performance

Specific analyze the factors impact of the 80s' employee performance, came to an analysis chart, as shown in Figure 3.

4 Countermeasures to Improve the Generation Y Employee Job Performance

Based on the personal factors affect the 80s' performance, 80s staff may appears such problems as lack of practice ability and team cooperation spirit, and easily susceptible to frustration affect passion for work, under the conditions permit enterprise should train the 80s' by scientific, reasonable and comprehensive ability training, to training the 80s ability as a long-term investment in human capital, enterprise should not only to carry out training of professional knowledge directly related to the work, and to strengthening the education of 80s' moral, to enhanced organization cohesion. Enterprises should also pay special attention to the use and training of generation y workers ' capacity, and have a deep understanding of the 80s' characteristics, knowledge and skills in their possession at the time of assignment, use of personnel, making it from each according to his ability. While also organize more activities to promote team work, and concerns of employee emotion and mood swings in the work.

Based on the organizations factors influencing the generation y employee performance, generation y employees may arise resistance in work due to population pressure, excessive pursuit of wage to the neglect of other work factors, enterprise culture does not comply with the values make the turnover rate rise, generation y employees disappointment on enterprise due to the lack of credibility evaluation. For these possible problems, enterprises can improve the performance of the group level, take advantage of the group pressure on the positive effects of job performance to improve the generation y employees of individual job performance, while encouraging independent behavior of high performance employees. Enterprises should establish excellent incentive system and evaluating system, using incentives such as bonuses, promotions to stimulate staff to improve performance, thereby reducing the negative effects of population pressure on staff performance. Evaluation objectives clear, regular and institutionalized should be done in the evaluation, when making any decision about the employee fairness should be in the first place. In the area of enterprise culture, enterprise should encourage innovation, tolerance for failure, shoulder the responsibility of training staff responsibilities consistent with corporate culture.

Based on work factors influencing the generation y employees performance, generation y employees will not mobilize enthusiasm for work, not to play their own abilities, because disappointed on the working environment and the working methods were not recognized. On these issues, at the time of assignment, matching functions should be carried out by enterprise, enterprise should do position analysis for rational allocation of work, while take fully prepared for generation y employees completed working tasks, provide their employees with the tools needed to complete the task, and to provide sufficient time and a good environment, democratic management, building a people-oriented corporate culture, so as to improve the generation y employee's work performance.

5 Conclusion

The social environments for 80s' growth are more complex than ever, so that they have strong characteristics of the times, these characteristics far-reaching on generation y employee job performance. Enterprise management can draw fishbone diagram according to affect factors, and work out countermeasures table by fishbone analysis, full estimate of the possible problems in the process of generation y employees work, and precontrol to the factors, so that make the 80s' performance according to the company's development goals. Enterprises were seen negative factors influencing the generation y employees while also fully recognizing their strengths, on generation y employees to more tolerance, understand the pressures they face, give generation y employees more tips and help. For the factors affect the 80s' work performance, enterprise managers should used suitable of method let them avoid weaknesses, maximize their ability to play in work, provides space to play their own, let them know their importance in the workplace, understand the impact their work status is important for enterprise, let them see a bright enterprise prospects for the future, and enterprise can let them realize their dreams. To let the 80s has a sense of identity, consider themselves to be masters of enterprise, managers cannot depressed employee's personality excessively, enterprises in the proper occasion should let them show their personality freely, and take personality into the work. Enterprise managers should guide the 80s' thought varies in people, understanding of their work status at any time, make themselves into work wholeheartedly, gradually makes enterprise and 80s staff harmonious development and implementation win-win.

References

1. Swanson, R.A., Holton III, E.F.: How to Assess Performance, Learning and Perceptions in Organizations. China Renmin University Press, Beijing (2008)
2. Zheng, X.: Human Resources Development and Management. Science Press, Beijing (2009) (in Chinese)
3. Wang, Y., Liu, Y.: "80s" Students work values survey. Talent Development (05) (2009) (in Chinese)
4. Zhou, X.: "80s" value for their work performance of the direct and indirect effects. Productivity Research (9) (2010) (in Chinese)
5. Zhou, S.: 80s "professional view" analysis. Management World (4) (2009) (in Chinese)
6. He, K.: Based on a comprehensive evaluation of fishbone analysis and its application. Control and Decision (10) (2010) (in Chinese)
7. Wu, Y.: To create an effective way to maximize enterprise value - to reduce costs of the fishbone diagram analysis. Business Accounting (21) (2010) (in Chinese)

Visual System Design for Independent Safety Management in Petrochemical Enterprises

Ruisheng Yong, Hanbin Luo, and Dukui Guo

School of Civil Engineering & Mechanics, Huazhong University of Science & Technology(HUST), Wuhan 430074, China
lhblhb1963@vip.sina.com

Abstract. Safety is the lifeline for survival and development of petrochemical enterprises. In order to achieve independent safety management, this paper builds structural safety chain model for safety management of petrochemical enterprises according to safety chain theory, and analyzes demand for safe production information in petrochemical enterprises. Moreover, it employs visual management technology to provide safety information for the object, position, forms and application levels of management so as to enhance independent safety management. On this basis, safety visual management system for petrochemical enterprises is designed.

Keywords: independent safety management, safety chain, visual management, safety visual system.

1 Introduction

Petrochemical industry is vital to the development of national economy. However, it is a capital-intensive industry with complex technological processes and auxiliary system; as a high-risk industry, it also requires strict production conditions and daily operation maintenance. Owing to high-frequency accidents, safety is the lifeline for survival and development of petrochemical enterprises. Therefore, the goal of petrochemical enterprises is to improve safety management level and to achieve independent safety management.

Visual management is an important lean technology as well as a kind of management method on the spot. It focuses on expressing information in words, color, sound and image to help monitor and control personnel perceive the abnormal status quickly, so that they can take real-time measures to reduce or eliminate the hazards, thus greatly improving the safety level. The use of visual management technology can acquire knowledge, express and organize the knowledge better [1]. Based on visual technology, visualization decision support system can implement enterprises' information management better and improve their comprehensive competitive capability [2]. The information visualization model combined with whole life cycle theory can help the stakeholders grasp the omni-directional engineering information, which plays an important role in strengthening the management of the whole process of the construction project [3]. Meanwhile, visual management technology can improve the production efficiency at different stages and make sustainable improvement of management methods [4]. In addition, visual management has a positive effect on

M. Zhou (Ed.): ISAEBD 2011, Part III, CCIS 210, pp. 239–246, 2011.

identifying waste, ensuring employees to comply with operational standards and improving production efficiency [5].

Currently, there are many researches on visual management which mainly focus on function analysis. However, no systematic research has been done on its mechanism, object, observation point, information forms and degree, and the specific measures are not flexible too. Combined with the safety chain model, this paper analyzes safety information demands. On the basis of this, with visual management approach, safety visual subsystem is designed from two perspectives of person, environment, equipment and person, technology, management, providing guidance for independence safety management in petrochemical enterprises.

2 The Connotation and Characteristics of Independent Safety Management in Petrochemical Enterprises

Independent safety management is a comprehensive method involving modern management science, humanities, sociology, psychology and economics. It explores the causes of unsafe behaviors, the relationship between individual behavior and organizational behavior based on safety behavior theory and incentive efficiency theory. In addition, it focuses on effective guidance and control of personal and organizational behaviors, and emphasizes the subject of safety management actively allocating with other safety factors, thereby ensures safety management work in order.

Independent safety management is a high level of safety management; how to reach this stage is the goal that vast majority of petrochemical enterprises pursue. At present, safety management in most petrochemical enterprises at home is significantly different from independent safety management which emphasizes self-conscious and active management subject. This means the original passive participation in safety management turns into active participation, the original “want me to be safe” turns into “I want to be safe”, so that they give full play to the initiative and strengthen the role of prevention in advance. In order to arouse their initiative and enthusiasm, three requirements should be satisfied: firstly, personnel with strong safety consciousness; secondly, to obtain relevant safety information accurately and immediately and make decisions quickly; at last, the ability to handle crisis. In view of various risks, the main problems are how to analyze risk factors as well as relevant system elements, how to premeditate the elements demand at different phases and optimize the allocation of resources, and the safety chain model provides solutions to those problems.

3 Safety Chain Model and Principle Analysis of Visual Management

3.1 Establishment of Safety Chain Model

To realize independent safety management in petrochemical enterprises, mutual relationship of safety elements, the location and the coordinated elements have to be confirmed, then the hierarchical relevant factors and hazard sources are identified accurately. According to the safety chain theory, the elements of production system can be summed up as person, equipment, tools, environment, information, technology, management, the interaction between them makes up of different states of the system. In this system, person, equipment, tools and environment are the key hazard factors for prevention, and information, technology, management are supporting elements, playing an important role of stabilizing the system. In addition, the accident prevention process can be divided into five stages: pro-action, prevention, preparation, response and recovery [6], at each stage it is suggested that an appropriate action should be taken. Safety chain model can be constructed as follows based on the analysis and management methods:

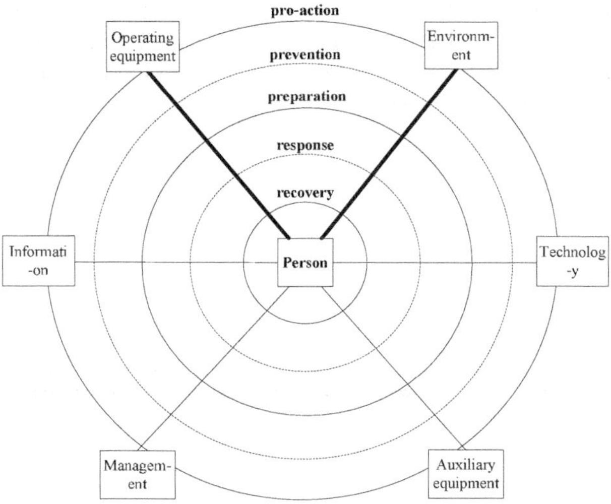

Fig. 1. Safety chain model

3.2 Safety Management Analysis Based on the Safety Chain Model

Safety chain model can not only cognize system elements clearly which are involved in independent safety management, but also identify the safety needs at different stages for the same elements, then propose the solutions to the problems from two-dimensional perspective. Detailed analysis is as following:

In operation, the personnel are not only active implementers in safety activities carrying out coordinative function, but also the purpose of the safety management locating in the center of the safety chain. It shows the concept of "person first" when ensuring person's safety. Human safety is closely related to other factors, and the most important factors are the status of operating equipment, auxiliary equipment and environmental safety conditions; the state of those elements will have a direct impact on the personnel's safety level, so it is the core target of HSE system. With subjective initiative, human should also employ technology, management, information to provide corresponding support so as to coordinate system elements and keep the system in balance.

From the perspective of dimension of safety chain process, the unsafe behaviors of people, the unsafe status of equipment, the unsafe conditions of the environment and t other elements vary over time, thus different forms of measures are required for different stages. According to the model, five concentric rings stand for five kinds of defense systems. If the current system fails, the later will start. From outside to inside, it indicates the aggravation of crisis and the increasing difficulty to deal with the problems. Therefore, a clear knowledge of accident status can be obtained in the model, thus enough attention will be paid to prevention and maximum safety can be achieved with minimize investment.

Overall, safety chain model can comprehensively analyze elements required and the performance of various elements at different stages of independent safety management in petrochemical enterprises, thus specific measures can be proposed. However, to achieve it not only safety information but also an appropriate way to express and display the information is required. In daily activities, we perceive things through senses of vision, smell, hearing, touch and taste. Among which the most commonly used is vision. Through vision, the size, shading, color, movement of external objects are perceived, and information important to the survival of all kinds of life is obtained. According to statistics, at least 80% of the outside information is obtained by the vision [7], so vision is one of the most important feelings for human beings and animals. Visual management method based on visual effect can meet this requirement and provide accurate information for managing subjects.

3.3 The Principle of Visual Management

Visual effect is not a simple function; it should coordinate all the systems associated with the visual sense when changing abstract things or process into image. From the perspective of time and space, it obtains various elements in the environment, understands those elements and forecasts their future status [8]. The results of prediction will directly affect people's judgment and decision, leading to their actions, so it can be expressed as objects – visual sense – recognition – judgment – action.

Visual management is an effective management approach; it employs intuitive images and various appropriate color information to organize the field production activities so as to improve the productivity. Taking visual signals as the basic means and openness as the basic principle, it is a "visible management". As a field management method, visual management can make anyone who gets to the place, even though he or she doesn't know the details, rapidly know the work ongoing, understand and judge whether it is under control, then evaluate the current operation status.

4 Design of Visual Management System for Petrochemical Enterprises

4.1 The Role of Visual Management for Achieving Independent Safety Management in Petrochemical Enterprises

Visual management is a scientific management method based on visual principles, involving achievements of management, physiology, psychology, and other disciplines [9]. As an effective technology in lean management, it provides a good means to gain the maximum effective output with minimum investment, which improves the production efficiency and increases valuation stream in production operation. Its functions are mainly as follows:

1) Identify and instruct important information; reveal the required elements in safety operation; detect errors or defects in advance; even though errors or defects do occur, rapid response and timely measures can help to establish and maintain standards of zero error, defect and waste so as to create a good environment for first-time-through-quality products or services.

2) Transfer hazards; promote communication within the company; create fast-response systems which comply with all work standards and deviation report so as to improve workplace safety and employees' health.

3) Keep track of the real-time status of equipment performance, confirm the operation process so as to improve the overall efficiency of the workplace and equipments and meet customers' expectations.

4) Provide real-time feedback information for participants in the production process; reduce unnecessary conferences and lower the total costs maximally.

Table 1. The design of visual management subsystem for person, equipment, environment

Subsystem name	Subsystem composition	Identification name	Identification position	Information form	Information levels
person, equipment, environment	personnel visual identification	special operation qualified visual identification	helmets, safety uniform	color and letter	pro-action/ prevention
		high-risk operation qualified visual identification	helmets, safety uniform	color and letter	pro-action/ prevention
		entrance visual identification	cards armband	color and letter	pro-action/ prevention
	the equipment visual identification	operation equipment instructions marking	production equipment , instrument	words and symbols	pro-action/ prevention
		fire equipment instructions marking	fire extinguisher, fire belt, alarm	graphics and letter	preparation/ response
		process visual identification	high pressure sprinkler, valve	words and symbols	prevention
	environment visual identification	outdoor visual identification	layout, duty board emergency figure	graphics / letter	prevention/ preparation
		indoor visual identification	evacuation identification, bulletin board, limited space	color/ symbols/ letter	prevention/ preparation
		the natural environment visual identification	vane, weather display screen	object/ display screen	prepare/ response

Table 2. The design of visual management subsystem for person, technology, management

Subsystem name	Subsystem constitute	Identifying name	Identifying position	Information form	Information levels
Person, technology and management	personnel visual identification	the content of this part is the same as table 1			
	technology visual identification	blind spot identification	corresponding maintenance place	letter	prevention
		sunstroke prevention, sampling points identification	corresponding facilities point	words and symbols	prevention/ preparation
		electrostatic release meter, isolation identification	electrostatic /energy concentration area	object/ graphics /symbols	prevention/ preparation/ response
		fire doors, cell phone ban identification	restricted Sites Zone	graphics and letter	prevention/ preparation
	management visual identification	prohibit identification	restricted Sites Zone	graphics/ letter	pro-action/ prevention
		warn identifications	dangerous equipment	graphics/ symbols	pro-action/ prevention
		oriented diversion identification	gateway, the channel, corridor	symbols/ blackboard/ display screen	pro-action/ prevention

4.2 Design of Safety Visual Identification System for Petrochemical Enterprises

In each aspect of petrochemical enterprises, on-site safety management is the most important task which involves many wide-range factors and complex process. According to the above analysis, it is concluded that the key element of safety management is the personnel, and the essential is to obtain information timely and accurately, which helps to increase safety management levels by improving safety behaviors. Specifically, the information that visual management system reveals are strictly selected. According to the needs of field safety management in petrochemical enterprises, with safety chain model, the object, position, information form and analytical hierarchy of visual management can be accurately identified. Based on the above ideas, safety visual identification system is designed for petrochemical enterprises respectively from the perspective of person, environment, equipment and person, technology, management, so as to promote the progress of independent safety management. Table 1 indicates the design of visual management subsystem from the perspective of person, equipment and environment, the object of system is just the goal of the HSE system.

Table 2 indicates the design of visual management subsystem from the perspective of person, technology and management. In this system, technology and management are supporting elements, which provide service for the HSE system. This subsystem is conducive to independent safety management for petrochemical enterprises.

5 Conclusions

Independent safety management is the goal of majority petrochemical enterprises to pursue. By establishing safety chain model, the paper analyzes the safety information in the production process from the perspectives of elements and processes, identifies the weak links and key elements from the complicated sites, predicts the safety status of the elements at different stages, and enhance the value of each element from the perspective of process, thus providing effective tools for safety management.

Visual management can make safety risk and potential safety problems in production process more intuitive and visible by means of various visual carriers, and make full use of visual warning. It not only strengthens the personnel's independent safety consciousness, but also improves enterprises' ability to evade, reduce and control risk. Furthermore, it regulates daily operational behaviors of the personnel and improves their ability to handle accidents. As a result, based on information demand identification for elements in the production process, by means of visual management, independent safety management level of petrochemical enterprises can be improved.

In the future research, interoperable safety visual system will be developed. It can share safety information and improve the level of independent safety management, not only for petrochemical enterprises, but also for other fields, such as construction projects.

Acknowledgements. This research was supported by PetroChina Ningxia petrochemical company.

References

1. Zhang, F.: The Application of Visualization Technology on Knowledge Management. In: 2008 IEEE International Conference on Intelligent Computation Technology and Automation, pp. 767–771. IEEE Press, Hunan (2008)
2. Zhang, W.-y., Zheng, N.: Research on Visual Decision Support System Based on Management of Petroleum Enterprise. In: Proceedings of the 2010 International Conference on Internet Technology and Applications, pp. 1–4. IEEE Press, Wuhan (2010)
3. Hu, W.: Visual Information Lifecycle Modeling for Effective Construction Management. In: 2008 International Conference on Information Management, Innovation Management and Industrial Engineering, pp. 163–166. IEEE Press, Taipei (2008)
4. Murata, K., Katayama, H.: Development of Kaizen case-base for effective technology transfer-a case of visual management technology. Int. J. Prod. Res. 48(16), 4901–4917 (2010)
5. Kim, D.H., Lee, J.H.: Mechanism, control, and visual management of a jumping robot. Mechatronics (UK) 18(10), 591–600 (2008)

6. Ten Brinke, W.B.M., Saeijs, G.E.M.: Safety chain approach in flood risk management. P. I. Civil Eng.-Munic. 161, 93–102 (2008)
7. Visual Management: Seeing clearly (2007), http://www.ad-esse.com/media/11662/visual_man.pdf
8. Zhou, N., Wu, J.: A Visualization Model for Information Resources Management. In: 12th International Conference Information Visualization, pp. 57–62. IEEE Press, London (2008)
9. The Lean Enterprise Memory Jogger (2002), http://www.qualitycoach.net/land/goalqpc/leanenterprise.pdf

FDI, China's Non-agricultural Employment and Urban-Rural Income Inequality

Dancheng Luo, Chunhui Gao, and Juan Zhou

Shenyang University of Technology, Shenyang 110870, China
Donna_luo@sina.com

Abstract. With the further development of economic globalization, the large flow of FDI to China had a tremendous impact on China's economic development. This article analyzed the impact of FDI and rural non-agricultural employment on the residents income distribution theoretically, and based on China's inter-provincial panel data from 1988 to 2009, using STATA10.0 software and establishing equations, we studied the direct and indirect effects of FDI and non-agricultural employment to China's urban-rural income inequality empirically. The results showed that an appropriate introduction of foreign direct investment could reduce urban-rural income inequality, however, the current non-agricultural employment expanded urban-rural income inequality.

Keywords: foreign direct investment, non-agricultural employment, China's urban-rural income inequality, panel data, SURE.

1 Introduction

Since reform and opening-up policy, China's foreign direct investment has constantly expanded, China's actual FDI is only 1.258 billion US dollars in 1984 and by 2002, and FDI has increased to 52.74 billion US dollars, which made China exceed the United State to become the country absorbing the most FDI. The data from China's Ministry of Commerce shows that actual foreign direct investment (FDI) increased by 10.17 percent over the same period in 2009, reaching 20.359 billion US dollars. Although FDI has driven the flow of capital, labor, technology, management and other elements, and has played a positive role in China's economic development, but we can not afford to ignore its negative impact on China's economic security and social stability, the income distribution is one of the problems, which is caused by its different regional distribution and advantages of regional resources. In 1978, the per capita disposable income of urban resident is 2.57 times more than the rural per capita net income. Since 1986, the income gap between urban and rural residents has expanded each year, the ratio of urban-rural income reached 3.27: 1 in 2009.

Clearly, the relationship of FDI, non-agricultural employment and China's urban-rural income inequality are complex and uncertain. Through what channels foreign capital influence urban-rural income gap, and what the conduction mechanism is? Did the non-agricultural employment increase the income of the farmers and effectively ease the urban-rural income inequality? Under what conditions, the introduction of

M. Zhou (Ed.): ISAEBD 2011, Part III, CCIS 210, pp. 247–253, 2011.

foreign capital is considered reasonable? Research on these issues is of great significance in promoting China's economic development, optimizing the structure of employment and alleviating income inequality. Therefore, we analyze the effect of FDI and non-agricultural employment to the income distribution theoretically, and based on China's inter-provincial panel data from 1988 to 2009, using STATA10.0 software and establishing equations, the article studies the direct and indirect effects of FDI and non-agricultural employment to China's urban-rural income inequality empirically.

2 Theoretical Analysis of FDI and Labor Flow to Affect China's Urban-Rural Income

Based on the framework of H-O-S theory and the background of international flow of production factors, let's suppose the host country has two sectors (sector 1 and sector 2) and two kinds of workers (L1, L2): sector 1 is the urban sector, which uses the labor and capital as production factors, sector 2 is the rural sector, which use rural workers and land; $\overline{L_1}$ displays urban workers, $\overline{L_2}$ represents the rural laborers, and rural laborers is abundant, the labor market is perfectly competitive. On the assumption that FD1 only enter sector 1, so, before we introduce FDI into sector 1, production of urban and rural sectors can be denoted by Cobb-Douglas production function with unchanged scale income:

$$\overline{Y_1} = T_1 \overline{K_1}^{\alpha} \overline{L_1}^{1-\alpha}, \quad \overline{Y_2} = T_2 \overline{G_2}^{\beta} \overline{L_2}^{1-\beta} \tag{1}$$

Among them, $\overline{L_1}$、$\overline{L_2}$ show the number of workers in the two sectors before economy opening up, urban sector employs some city workers and migrant farmers; $\overline{K_1}$、$\overline{G_2}$ express the capital owned by the urban sector and the land possessed by the rural sector; T_1、 T_2 denote production technology coefficient of the two sectors; $\overline{Y_1}$、$\overline{Y_2}$ display the initial output of the two sectors. Here, we use the value of the products to measure actual profits; the profits of urban sector can be expressed as follows:

$$\overline{\pi_1} = T_1 \overline{K_1}^{\alpha} \overline{L_1}^{1-\alpha} - R\overline{K_1} - \overline{W_1 L_1} \tag{2}$$

Here, R is capital interest rate for the host country; $\overline{W_1}$ expresses the labor wage of urban sector. Assume that the host country's labor market is fully competitive market, the demand function of the urban sector elements:

$$\overline{K_1} = \frac{\alpha \overline{Y_1}}{R}, \overline{L_1} = \frac{1-\alpha}{\overline{W_1}} \overline{Y_1} \tag{3}$$

By (3), we have the formula:

$$\overline{W_1} = \frac{1-\alpha}{\alpha} * \frac{R\overline{K_1}}{\overline{L_1}}, \quad \overline{W_2} = \frac{1-\beta}{\beta} * \frac{\eta \overline{G_2}}{\overline{L_2}} \tag{4}$$

In (4), η denotes the return rate of the land; $\overline{W_1}$、$\overline{W_2}$ express respectively initial wage rates of city workers and rural laborers. Therefore, before opening up, the average income of urban and rural laborers is as follows:

$$\overline{AR_1} = \overline{W_1} = \frac{1-\alpha}{\alpha} * \frac{R\overline{K_1}}{\overline{L_1}} \tag{5}$$

$$\overline{AR_2} = \overline{W_2} = \frac{1-\beta}{\beta} * \frac{\eta\overline{G_2}}{\overline{L_2}} \tag{6}$$

On the assumption that Capital only enters the host country's urban sector and the labor market is perfectly competitive, the interest rate of capital is unchanged. After FDI enters the host country, the rural labor force flows in sectors as follows:

$$L_1 = \overline{L_1} + L_{2L},\ L_2 = \overline{L_2} - L_{2L},\ K_1 = \overline{K_1} + K \tag{7}$$

L2L shows the rural laborers flowing from the rural sector into the urban sector, K1 displays the capital owned by the urban sector after opening up; L1、L2 express the number of workers in the two sectors. And after capital enters the, the increase of capital will be more than that of labor force, then wages for the two sectors is:

$$W_1 = \frac{1-\alpha}{\alpha} * \frac{R_1\left(\overline{K_1} + K\right)}{\overline{L_1} + L_{2L}} > \overline{W_1}, \frac{\overline{K_1} + K}{\overline{L_1} + L_{2L}} > \frac{\overline{K_1}}{\overline{L_1}} \tag{8}$$

$$W_2 = \frac{1-\beta}{\beta} * \frac{\eta\overline{G_2}}{\overline{L_2} - L_{2L}} > \overline{W_2} \tag{9}$$

After opening up, the average income of urban and rural laborers is:

$$AR_1 = W_1 = \frac{1-\alpha}{\alpha} * \frac{R_1\left(\overline{K_1} + K\right)}{\overline{L_1} + L_{2L}},\ AR_2 = \overline{W_2} + \frac{W_1 * L_{2L}}{L_2} \tag{10}$$

Based on the above analysis shows: When $\frac{AR_1}{AR_2} = \frac{\overline{AR_1}}{\overline{AR_2}}$, that is, $\frac{\overline{W_2}}{\overline{W_1}} = \frac{\overline{L_1}}{\overline{L_2}} * \frac{\overline{K_1} + K}{\overline{L_1} * K/L_{2L} - \overline{K_1}}$, urban-rural income inequality did not changed; when $\frac{AR_1}{AR_2} > \frac{\overline{AR_1}}{\overline{AR_2}}$, that is, $\frac{\overline{W_2}}{\overline{W_1}} > \frac{\overline{L_1}}{\overline{L_2}} * \frac{\overline{K_1} + K}{\overline{L_1} * K/L_{2L} - \overline{K_1}}$, urban-rural income inequality expanded; when $\frac{AR_1}{AR_2} < \frac{\overline{AR_1}}{\overline{AR_2}}$, that is, $\frac{\overline{W_2}}{\overline{W_1}} < \frac{\overline{L_1}}{\overline{L_2}} * \frac{\overline{K_1} + K}{\overline{L_1} * K/L_{2L} - \overline{K_1}}$, urban-rural income inequality narrowed.

Under the perfectly competitive conditions, the prices of final products are equivalent to the cost of production:

$$\overline{P_1} = \overline{W_1}A_1 + R_1B_1,\ \overline{P_2} = \overline{W_2}A_2 + \eta_2B_2 \tag{11}$$

In (11), A_1、A_2 represent labor input coefficients of the two sectors; B_1、B_2 show capital investment coefficient of urban sector and land input coefficient of the rural sector; P_1、P_2 are initial product prices in the two sectors; actual outputs of the urban sector and the rural sector are Q_1、Q_2 respectively; EP_1Q_1、FP_1Q_1 express the interests assigned to the urban and rural labor force in the urban sector respectively. Therefore, the average income of city workers and rural workers is:

$$AR_1 = EP_1Q_1/\overline{L_1} = EQ_1(W_1A_1 + R_1B_1)/\overline{L_1} \tag{12}$$

$$AR_2 = \frac{P_2Q_2 + FP_1Q_1}{\overline{L_2}} = \frac{(W_2A_2 + \eta_2B_2)Q_2 + FQ_1(W_1A_1 + R_1B_1)}{\overline{L_2}} \tag{13}$$

$$E + F = 1, 1 > E > F > 0$$

$$\frac{AR_1}{AR_2} = E\frac{1}{\frac{P_2Q_2/\overline{L_2}}{P_1Q_1/\overline{L_1}} + F\frac{\overline{L_1}}{\overline{L_2}}} \tag{14}$$

$$\ln\frac{AR_1}{AR_2} = \ln\frac{EL_R}{FL_U} - \ln\left(\frac{L_RP_2Q_2/L_R}{FL_UP_1Q_1/L_U} + 1\right) \approx \beta_0 \ln\frac{E}{F} + \beta_1 \ln\frac{L_R}{L_U} - \beta_2 \ln\frac{P_2}{P_1} - \beta_3 \ln\frac{Q_2}{Q_1} + \beta_4 \ln Q \tag{15}$$

The above analysis shows that both FDI and the flow of rural labor force in urban areas increase the average income of rural and urban residents, but due to many other factors, the effects of FDI and the China's rural non-farm employment to urban-rural income inequality is uncertain, the following part studies their impacts on China's urban-rural income inequality empirically.

3 Empirical Analysis of the Impacts of FDI and Rural Non-agricultural Employment on China's Urban-Rural Income Inequality

3.1 Model and Data

The above factors may not only directly affect China's urban-rural income inequality, but indirectly affect the income distribution by other channels, single equation OLS analysis could not inspect this complex relationship, so we use equations:

$$\begin{cases} UBR = f(PGDP, PGDP^2, FDI, NRE, TRADE, CAP, EDU, FZR, MAR, ALR) \\ PGDP = f(FDI, NRE, TRADE, CAP, EDU, FZR, MAR, ALR) \\ NRE = f(PGDP, PGDP^2, FDI, TRADE, CAP, EDU, FZR, MAR, ALR) \\ TRADE = f(PGDP, PGDP^2, FDI, NRE, CAP, EDU, FZR, MAR, ALR) \end{cases}$$

We use the panel data with time span from 1988 to 2009 and the cross section is China's 31 provinces, municipalities and autonomous regions. It includes four equations, namely the urban-rural income inequality decision equation (UBR), per capita income decision equation (PGDP), the rural non-farm employment decision equation (NRE) and trade (TRADE) decision equation. UBR represents the income gap between urban and rural areas of the 'i'th provinces in the year of t, which expressed by the ratio of urban per capita disposable income to rural per capita net income ; per capita income (PGDP) and the square term ($PGDP^2$)are used to examine the impact of economic growth on the urban-rural income inequality ; FDI donates the actual value of FDI; NER is the proportion of population of rural non-farm employment in rural areas; TRADE displays the ratio of import and export trade to GDP; CAP expresses the fixed assets investment of each province; EDU expressed that the number of students enrolled in colleges and universities, representing the human capital of all regions; FZR represents proportion of the added value of the first section each province; MAR expresses degree of the market opening, displayed by the ratio of state-owned and collective-owned workers to total number of workers; ALG shows the agricultural labor productivity in every province.

3.2 The Estimated Results and Illumination

In order to control the residual relativity among the equations, we use the seemingly unrelated regression estimates (SURE), that results are displayed in table 1. Based on the above model of the regression equation, we provide further explanation of the regression results in econometric model in detail:

(1) In income distribution decision equation (UBR), the estimated coefficient of "PGDP" is notable and that of its squared term is negative ,which indicate that with the increase of China's per capita GDP, the urban-rural income inequality would increase after declining, that is, the Kuznets's inverted-"U" theory is applicable to China's economic practice. FDI and the income gap between urban and rural areas is negatively correlated, from the value perspective, FDI increases by 1%, the income gap between urban and rural will decline by 0.19 percent. At present, attracting foreign investment has played a positive role in narrowing China's urban-rural income inequality. But estimated coefficient of rural non-farm employment is significantly positive, that is, the current flow and migratory model of rural surplus labor force can not improve the urban-rural income inequality. From a long-term point of view, although economic growth will narrow the urban-rural income inequality, China's material and human capital accumulation exacerbated income inequality. In addition, as reflected in the equations, improving labor productivity of the first industry and releasing the surplus rural labor force effectively, we can reduce the urban-rural income inequality.

(2) In Income decision equation (PGDP), the estimated coefficients of FDI and the rural non-farm employment are significantly negative, which shows that the introduction of the current FDI and the transfer of surplus labor force can not effectively promote income growth? Human capital, improvement of labor productivity in the first industry, upgrading of the industrial structure and the further opening of the market are greatly promoting China's economic growth, but in the

equation, coefficients of physical capital and trade liberalization is not significant. All of these factors will indirectly impact the urban-rural income inequality by affecting their income.

Table 1. Estimated results of equations

	SURE estimation			
	UBR	PGDP	NRE	TRADE
PGDP	2.8241		-0.52787	6.17366
	(2.41**)		(-0.53)	(3.73*)
PGDP2	-0.15459		0.11383	0.37351
	(-1.88***)		-1.81***)	(3.6*)
FDI	-0.19838	-0.03456	-0.06195	0.320956
	(-5.95*)	(-3.52*)	(-2.07**)	(8.3*)
NRE	0.30639	-0.27207		-0.01544
	(4.68*)	(-17.71*)		(-0.18)
TRADE	0.092388	-0.0153	-0.01171	
	(2.04**)	(-1.13)	(-0.29)	
CAP	0.003573	0.37501	0.99127	0.020872
	(0.03)	(14.23*)	(11.69*)	(0.15)
EDU	0.165138	0.16436	0.3864	0.7864
	(2.18**)	(4.78*)	(5.96*)	(9.11*)
FZR	0.705645	-0.55921	-1.413	-1.01735
	(4.41*)	(-15.77*)	(-11.26*)	(-5.12*)
MAR	-1.76718	-1.27709	-3.3385	-1.4573
	(-3.18*)	(-9.96*)	(-7.32*)	(-2.14**)
ALR	-0.60788	0.493625	1.1173	0.0731
	(-5.18*)	(24.54*)	(12.26*)	(0.48)
C	-7.75131	8.815135	14.53397	37.7485
	(-1.47)	(27.9*)	(3.55*)	(5.86*)
R-sq	0.629	0.9357	0.6443	0.752
RMSE	0.3229	0.1501	0.2986	0.2086
Obi	291	291	291	291

(3) In rural non-farm employment (NRE) decision equation, the inflow of FDI, added value of the first industry and increasing employment in the state-owned and collective units will significantly inhibit the flow of rural surplus labor force, but the enhancement of human capital and labor productivity in the first industry will effectively promote the flow of rural labor force. Similarly, estimated coefficient of trade liberalization is not significant, because of the system and institutional reasons; rural residents still can not fully share the benefits and welfare of trade.

(4) In the trade liberalization (TRADE) decision equation, the estimated coefficient of FDI was significantly positive, which indicates the introduction of foreign capital promotes China's trade growth; increase of Human capital and the further opening of Chain's market effectively force the development of trade liberalization. But to a

certain extent, increasing the value of the first industry has reduced the volume of trade; this may be because manufactured goods in China's export products accounts for absolute advantage. What's more, the estimated coefficient of material capital and labor productivity in the first industry is not significant; they didn't have much impact on trade liberalization.

4 Conclusion

(1)Theoretical analysis shows that in the open economy, FDI and the flow of rural labor force to urban areas increase the average income of urban and rural residents, but because such factors as the urban-rural population ratio, the interests shared by migrant farmers in the urban sector, product prices of the two departments and the actual production of two departments, the impact of FDI and China's rural non-farm employment on urban-rural income inequality is uncertain.

(2)In the income distribution decision equation, China's introduction of foreign capital has played a positive role in reducing the urban-rural income inequality, and because of problems in structure and system, the flow of rural surplus labor force has not improved the urban-rural income inequality. To a certain extent, it has played the role of deterioration. Per capita GDP has a "inverted-U" type relationship with urban-rural income inequality, increase of the first industrial productivity effectively mitigate the urban-rural income inequality, but accumulation of the material and human capital expanded the urban-rural income inequality.

(3)In Rural non-farm employment decision equation, improving human capital can significantly promote the flow of rural surplus labor force, and education and training for farmers have more important role in engaging in their non-farm employment. But the impact of trade liberalization on rural residents is not significant, which shows that China's rural areas still can not fully share the benefits and welfare of trade.

References

1. Borenzstein, E., Gregorio, J., Lee, J.-W.: How Does Foreign Investment Affect Economic Growth? Journal of International Economics 45, 115–135 (1998)
2. Bhandari, B.: Does Foreign Direct Investment Affect US Income Inequality? (2004) (forthcoming)
3. Choi, C.: Foreign Direct Investment and Income Convergence. Applied Economics, 1045–1049 (2004)
4. Feenstra, R.C., Hanson, G.H.: Foreign Direct Investment and Relative wages: Evidence from Mexico's maquiladoras. Journal of International Economics (42), 371–393 (1997)

An Empirical Study on the Relationship between China's Food Trade and Economic Growth in Food Industry

Dancheng Luo and Chunhui Gao

Shenyang University of Technology, Shenyang 110870, China
Donna_luo@sina.com

Abstract. The study is focused on the relationship between food trade and Economic Growth in food industry in China. First, we review some theories of foreign trade promoting economic growth, which is considered as theoretical basis of studying the paper. Then, we introduce the general situation about the food trade and the food industry since the reform and opening-up of China. On the basis of these, it make an Empirical Study on the relationship between trade and Economic Growth in food industry by using a mass of data: by using Co-integration model to analyze the relationship between the export and import of food and economic growth of food industry; by using Feder model to find out an indirect enhancive function to the growth of its food industry through externality effects on other sectors; by using Panel Data model to compare the extent of the influence on the local food industry. Finally, it presents some suggestions to improve international trade's positive influences on economic growth of food industry in China from the government and the foodstuff corporation aspects.

Keywords: International Trade; Food Industry; Economic Growth; Empirical Study.

1 Introduction

With the developing of domestic food industry Modern production, its industry structure has been optimized, especially since the 90's of last century, annual growth rate of China's food industry is 10.4%, it Promoted international competitiveness of China's food industry to further. In the 21st century, the development of domestic economic promotes food consumption to a new stage, and with China's accession to WTO, the scale of food imports and exports also expanded. Whether the growth rate of China's food import is faster than food export? Speed up or slow down the speed of China's food import and export, whichever is more conducive to the further development of the food industry, how will specific to the Province in China? In addition, food foreign trade is through which kind of mechanism to promote the development of food industry, these are worth our considering.

In this paper, the relationship between food foreign trade and economic growth in food industry will be studied, while external economic model will be introduced to examine external economic benefits of food export sector to other non-food industrial export sector in food industry. It can be said, to some extent, this paper will makes up

M. Zhou (Ed.): ISAEBD 2011, Part III, CCIS 210, pp. 254–259, 2011.

for lack of micro-level studies, it can be regarded as a modest contribution to the largest industry in China---food industry economic.

2 Current Status of Food Foreign Trade and Food Industry Economic Growth

2.1 Overview of China's Food Foreign Trade Development

Food import and export is very important strategic issue, which related to people's livelihood and China's exports. When we draw up China's food export development strategy, we must not only master the changes in international market, more importantly, we should take the domestic population, production, consumption, distribution and other aspects into account, particularly the history and current situation of food import and export. This paper mainly studied the great changes of China's total food size, trade structure and other field.

Table 1.

	Food Import and Export Trade				All merchandise import and export trade			
Year	Export Value	Import Value	Import and Export Value	Net Exports Value	Export Value	Import Value	Import and Export Value	Net Exports Value
1980	31.23	32.02	63.25	-0.79	181.19	200.17	381.36	-18.98
1981	30.72	39.34	70.06	-8.62	220.07	220.15	440.22	-0.08
1982	30.83	44.39	75.22	-13.56	223.21	192.85	416.06	30.36
1983	30.62	32.38	63.00	-1.76	222.26	213.90	436.16	8.36
1984	34.86	25.27	60.13	9.95	261.39	274.10	535.49	12.71
1985	40.33	18.81	59.24	21.62	273.50	422.52	696.02	-149.02
1986	46.81	20.02	66.83	26.79	309.42	429.04	738.46	-119.62
1987	50.37	30.55	80.92	19.82	394.37	432.16	826.53	-37.79
1988	61.99	41.91	103.90	20.08	75.16	552.75	1027.91	-77.59
1989	65.45	52.69	118.14	12.76	525.38	591.40	1116.78	-66.02
1990	71.12	44.74	115.86	26.38	620.91	533.45	1154.36	87.46
1991	79.05	37.18	116.23	41.87	719.10	637.91	1357.01	81.19
1992	91.68	39.10	130.78	52.58	849.40	805.85	1655.25	43.55
1993	95.05	29.53	124.58	65.52	917.44	1039.59	1957.03	122.15
1994	115.12	50.14	165.26	64.98	1210.06	1156.14	2366.20	153.92
1995	117.78	91.31	209.09	26.47	1487.80	1320.84	2808.64	166.96
1996	119.49	78.66	198.15	40.83	1510.48	1388.33	2898.81	122.15
1997	127.71	63.08	190.79	64.63	1827.92	1432.70	3251.62	404.22
1998	117.95	54.58	172.53	63.37	1837.09	1402.37	3239.46	434.72
1999	113.61	51.94	165.55	61.67	1949.31	1656.99	3606.30	292.32
2000	131.43	60.99	192.42	70.44	2492.03	2250.94	4724.97	241.92
2001	137.61	61.51	199.12	76.1	2660.98	2435.53	5096.51	225.45
2002	157.03	72.5	229.53	84.53	3255.96	2951.7	6207.66	304.26
2003	186.65	94.5	281.15	92.15	4382.28	4127.6	8509.88	254.68
2004	202.26	139.16	341.42	63.1	5933.26	5612.29	11545.55	320.97
2005	239.31	135.41	377.7	103.90	7619.53	6599.53	14219.06	1020.02
2006	272.89	149.71	422.60	123.18	9689.36	7914.61	17603.97	1774.77

Since the reform and opening up, China's food foreign trade gained rapid development. Table 1 shows that, in 1980, China's food import and export value is 6.325 billion dollars, in 2006, it reaches 42.26 billion dollars, an increase of 5.68 times, the average annual rate is 7.6%, export value increases from 3.123 billion dollars to 27.289 billion dollars, an increase of 7.74 times, the average annual rate is 8.7%, import value increased from 3.202 billion dollars to 14.971 billion dollars, an increase of 3.68 times, the average annual growth rate is 6.1%.

As we can see from Table 1, China's food foreign trade gains a greater degree of development, however, compared with the overall development of China's foreign trade, the develop pace and scale of foreign trade is seriously lagging behind.

3 Empirical Study on the Influence of Food Foreign Trade to China's Food Industry Economic Growth——Cointegration Model Income Inequality

3.1 Data Processing

In this paper, food exports Value (EX) and imports Value (IM) reflect the situation of China's food foreign trade, the food industry added value (Y) reflects economic growth of food industry. In order to eliminate heteroscedasticity existed in data, we respectively take the logarithm of the three variables to get LnY, LnEX, LnIM, the corresponding difference sequences are DlnY, DlnEX, DlnIM.

3.2 Stationary Test

We use the ADF test methods to test the Stability of time series data, respectively test the level value and the first difference of each variable, the results shows that lnY, lnEX and lnIM are unstable at the 5% significance level, and the first difference DlnY and DlnIM are also unstable at the 5% significance level, but DlnY, DlnEX and DlnIM are stable at 10% significant level, so LnY, LnEX and LnIM belong to I (1) Sequence, there may be cointegration in them.

Table 2. ADF test result of Time serial

variable	Test form (C,T,K)	ADF statistics	1% critical value	5% critical value	Conclusion
LnY	(C,T,1)	0.56	-4.42	-3.62	Unstable
LnEX	(C,T,1)	-2.94	-4.42	-3.62	Unstable
LnIM	(C,T,2)	-2.32	-4.44	-3.63	Unstable
DlnY	(C,0,1)	-2.99	-3.77	-3.00	stable
DlnEX	(C,0,1)	-3.12	-3.77	-3.00	stable
DlnIM	(C,0,1)	-2.95	-3.77	-3.00	Unstable

3.3 Cointegration Test

As we can see from the stability test, time series LnY, LnEX and LnIM are the first single series, maybe, there is a stable linear combination in them, which reflects a long-term stable relationship in variables, that is cointegration relation. In this paper, maximum likelihood estimation is adopted to test the cointegration of time series. Therefore, before cointegration test, we should determine the vector autoregressive model, maintain a reasonable degree of freedom, so that the model parameters have a strong explanatory power, while eliminate autocorrelation of errors, we use the SIC, SC information criteria and LR statistic as the test standard for selecting the optimal lag orders, so we get VAR (4) model as the optimal model. The overall test result of VAR (4) model is in Table 3.

Table 3. ADF test result of VAR model

Determinant Residual Covariance	6.78E 07
Log likehood	56.90231
Akaike Information Criteria	-3.590231
Schwarz Criteri	-2.544712

The overall test result of VAR (4) model shows that the log-likelihood function value of overall model is big enough (56.90), AIC and SC are very small (-3.59 and -2.54), indicating that the explanatory power of model is strong. Cointegration test carries out gradual test from testing the cointegration relationship is not exist in variables, the determined of lag period is according to unconstrained VAR model. Owing to the maximum lag of VAR model is 4, so the lag is 3 in cointegration test, test result is in table 4.

Table 4. ADF test result of cointegration test

Eigenvalue	Likelihood value	5% significance level critical value	1% significance level critical value	the number of assuming cointegration equation
0.9350	54.35	29.68	35.65	None
0.6200	19.01	15.41	20.04	At most 1
0.0868	2.62	3.76	6.65	At most 2

As we can see from Table 4, 54.35>29.68,19.01<20.04, there is only one cointegration relationship at 1% significance level, the cointegration formula is following:

$$LnY = 2.882 + 0.289 LnEX + 0.171 LnIM + \mu$$

t = (3.305) (4.095)

R^2=0.995 S.E.=0.059 DW=2.349 F=1231.655 AIC=-2.679 SC=-2.482

The fit goodness of this equation is 0.995, indicating that this model is significant. From the cointegration equation, we can see, in the long run, there is a positive correlation between China's food industry economic growth and food exports and imports, the export output elasticity is 0.289, the import output elasticity is 0.171.

3.4 Causality Test

The result of cointegration test shows that there is a long-term equilibrium relationship between China's food import and export and food industry economic growth, but whether this relationship is a causality, it requires further validation. In this paper, Granger test method based on VAR model is adopted, the test result is in table 5. When P is smaller, it shows that rejecting original hypothesis and the probablity of first type error is smaller, so the probability of rejecting null hypothesis is greater. There are one-way causal relationship between LnEX and LnY, LnY and LnIM, LnIM and LnEX, indicating that, for the food industry, food exports can promote economic growth in the short term, and food industry economy growth directly promotes the growth of food imports; for food import and export, the export can not immediately promotes the growth of import in the short term, food exports indirectly promote the growth of imports through promoting food industry economic growth, which requires a process.

Table 5. The causality between variable

Original hypothesis	F statistic	P value	Conclusion
LnEX does not Granger Cause LnY	2.345	0.099	Reject oiginal hypothesis
LnY does not Granger Cause LnEX	2.499	0.114	Do not reject original hypothesis
LnIM does not Granger Cause LnY	0.433	0.733	Do not reject original hypothesis
LnY does not Granger Cause LnIM	3.137	0.057	Reject original hypothesis
LnIM does not Granger Cause LnEX	2.225	0.037	Reject original hypothesis
LnEX does not Granger Cause LnIM	2.178	0.133	Do not reject original hypothesis

4 Conclusion

(1) There is a strong correlation in exports, imports and economic growth, though each is non-smooth, cointegration relationship exit in them. China's food import and export commonly promote food industry economic growth, but the promoting role are relatively small, export growth rate increases 1%, food industry economic grows 0.289% ; in import growth increases 1%, food industry economic grows 0.171%. This may be related to the composition of food import and export, for a long time, the export situation of China's Initial processed raw materials food is good, the domestic

traditional staple foods, such as frozen seafood, canned vegetables, fruits, they have certain competitive advantage in international market, while the competitive advantage of our deep processed food is relatively weak, and suffered "anti-dumping ", "green barriers " and other unfavorable factors from import country. With the elevate of domestic food supply capacity, food imports is far less than exports, so the promoting role of food imports to food industry economic growth is less than exports. However,for food export and import, they should be encouraged in China, so we can accelerate food exports and imports, to better promote the development of food industry.

(2) Causality test shows that there is one-way causal relationship between food exports and food industry economic growth, there is one-way causal relationship between food industry economic growth and import growth, and between import growth to export growth. So food export promotes economic growth in the short term, it is just in line with our development of export-oriented economy. Exports means adding into the international market competition, it will motivate the raise of technology level, guide our food industry enterprises to be market-oriented constantly, update product mix, and improve the efficiency of enterprise. But in the short term, food industry economic growth is not the reason of food export growth, it is mainly due to China's current food industry structure is not reasonable, and the level of technical equipment is not high, which hinders forming scale effect of economic growth on export growth, food industrial economy growth can promote the size and development level of food companies, and expand the demand for foreign food and raw materials. A large part is processing trade in foreign food trade structure, and imports of many raw materials, as soybeans and edible vegetable oil, is mainly in order to meet the need of export processing, so it is easy to be understood import growth contributed to export growth.

References

1. Irwin, D.A., Tervio, M.: Does Trade Raise Income? Evidence from the Twentieth Century. Journal of International Economics (5), 1–18 (2002)
2. Frankel, Romer: Does Trade Cause Growth? American Economic Review (89), 379–399 (1999)
3. Bayoumi, T., Coe, D.T., Helpman, E.: R&D Spillovers and Global Growth. Journal of International Economics 47(2), 399–428 (1999)
4. Romer: Idea Gaps and Object Gaps in Economic Development. Journal of Monetary Economics (32), 543–574 (1993)
5. Coe, Helpman: International R&D Spillovers. European Economic Review 39(5), 859–887 (1995)
6. Sachs, Warner: Economic Reform and the Process of Global Integration. Brooking Papers on Economic Activity (1), 11–18 (1995)
7. Sala-I-Martin: I Just Run Two Million Regressions. In: American Economic Association Paper and Proceedings, vol. (87), pp. 178–183 (1995)
8. Slaughter: International Trade and Labor Demand Elasticities. Journal of International Economics (54), 27–56 (2001)

A New Approach to Achieve e-Inclusion with ICT Education in Rural Taiwan

Chih-Hong Huang and Yi-Ting Huang*

Graduate Institute of Design, National Taipei University of Technology
No. 1, Sec. 3, Chung-Hsiao E. Rd., Taipei, 10608, Taiwan
evie.ting.huang@gmail.com

Abstract. With regards to the applied education of ICT tools in rural Taiwan, past studies on digital opportunity and digital divide have somewhat overlooked the purpose and requirements of e-learning, as well as suitable teaching materials and teaching methods. This study analyzes the case of PunCar Action, and employs participant observation and in-depth interviews to explore key factors that affect information application learning in rural communities, namely how communities learn to apply ICT tools. Research results show that PunCar Action's "flexible teaching materials with an emphasis on communication" and "localized teaching methods" are the key to its successful ICT education in rural Taiwan.

Keywords: Digital Divide, ICT Education, PunCar Action, Rural Community.

1 Introduction

Over ninety percent of all households in Taiwan owned a computer in 2010, with internet penetration rate reaching 82.8% [1]; it seems that an extraordinary accomplishment had been made in digitization. Yet, even today digital divide remains an issue in remote areas of Taiwan. Government policies often neglect usage barriers of emerging technologies in remote areas; the government has constructed information hardware, popularized the broadband network and provided instructions for basic internet skills, but has not made effort to enhance practical applications [2]. This is the core issue with closing the last mile of digital divide between urban and rural areas.

1.1 Status Quo of Digital Divide in Taiwan

According to the "World Information Society Report 2007" published by the International Telecommunication Union, in the Digital Opportunity Index (DOI), which analyzes the information society's development status and trends using three sub-indexes "Infrastructure," "Opportunity" and "Utilization," Taiwan

* Corresponding author.

M. Zhou (Ed.): ISAEBD 2011, Part III, CCIS 210, pp. 260–268, 2011.

ranked 7th out of 181 countries around the world [3], moving up from 10th place in 2006.

However, even though Taiwan has made an exceptional performance in information technology, it is still like other advanced countries in that it faces the issue of "digital divide." In the dissemination process of ICT(Information and Communication Technology), it is inevitable that the time new technologies are introduced to different groups will cause them to develop varying levels of intimacy with information equipment, as well as different levels of proficiency in internet utilization, and is most significant among different age groups, geographical locations and social status. Studies show that the gap between urban and rural areas has always been a main cause of uneven distribution of information resources [4,5]. Using Taiwan as an example, under the effects of both age and geographical location, Taipei City residents in the ages of 51-64 years old have the highest internet prevalence rate (68.0%), while residents in Changhua County, Yunlin County, Chiayi County, Tainan County/City and Pingtung County in the same age group have the lowest internet prevalence rate (17.9%) [6].

1.2 Introduction to the PunCar Action

"PunCar Action" is Asia's first digital divide project that keeps real-time records and utilizes versatile Web2.0 technology services. The project is implemented by the non-profit organization -Association of Digital Culture, Taiwan (ADCT) and targets rural communities and social welfare organizations; the project offered its first ICT education course in May 2008 [7]. The founders of PunCar Action, Hsu Ting-Yao and Hsu Tzu-Han, were famous young bloggers that grew up in the Taipei metropolitan area. They had rich digital knowledge and skills and passion. With the idea to "let Otaku teach residents of rural communities how to use the computer," they borrowed money to buy a van (in Chinese van is literally bread car, in which Pun is the Taiwanese for bread, thus the name Pun-Car), and installed information equipment in the van. The PunCar carried volunteer lecturers and systematically carried out a digital education tour around Taiwan, disseminating new knowledge of information technology and the status quo of its applications. "PunCar Action" is a display of the originality of Taiwan's youth; this knowledge implementation action won the "digital community" award in the 2010 ARS Electronica in Linz [8].

This study analyzes the diverse courses on life applications of the internet offered by PunCar Action in its mobile information classroom, as well as intergeneration learning records. The courses were offered according to requirements of each rural community in Tainan in 2010. This study then generalizes operation procedures for using e-inclusion principles and learning models to implement life applications of the internet in remote areas, and uses results to find key factors that affect a community's success in learning applications of ICT Tools.

(a) (b)

Fig. 1. The PunCars and its information equipments. (a) Digital divide action car (Left: Fourth PunCar; Middle: First PunCar). (b) Information equipment in PunCar.

2 Methodology

This study employs case interview and participant observation which conducted in-depth interviews with the execution team and students of PunCar Action, visited communities to learn their requirements, and participated in tour courses. The research method also uses evidence and literature for support, and analyzes the courses and operation procedures of PunCar, comparing its curriculum and teaching methods to the requirements of residents in rural communities.

The scope of this study is as follows:

(1) The background, targets and implementation status of PunCar Action.
(2) Operation procedures and content of teaching materials and methods of PunCar Action.
(3) Motivation and requirements of rural communities for learning ICT Tools.

The duration of this study's survey was from June 2010 to December 2010; the geographical area selected was mainly rural communities in Tainan, Taiwan; subjects of in-depth interviews include PunCar lecturers, PunCar project implementation personnel, PunCar students and community cadres.

3 Results

3.1 Analysis of Tour Lectures by PunCar

From Metropolitan trotted Villages by Puncar with Otaku. Implementation of PunCar Action began in May 2008 in rural communities around Taiwan. The PunCar (Fig.1(a)) was equipped with information equipment (Fig.1(b)) and carried volunteer lecturers, systematically carrying out a digital teaching tour around Taiwan. PunCar Action teaches senior citizens and immigrant brides in rural communities how to use the computer, search for information online and set up blogs to promote their community features.

PunCar directly faces the most difficult last mile issue of digital divide, and thus sends people and resources to remote areas that need them via the PunCar (see Table 1).

Table 1. PunCar Action tour record (up to the end of 2010)

Implementation unit	Association of Digital Culture, Taiwan
Starting date	May 17th, 2008
Total lectures	276
Total teaching hours	828 hours
Average number of students per lecture	15
Number of volunteer lecturers	34
Average number of lectures at each community	6.5
Total number of students	4,028
Average age of students	53.2 years old
PunCar Action Van	Replaced four vans
Total mileage	72,000 Km

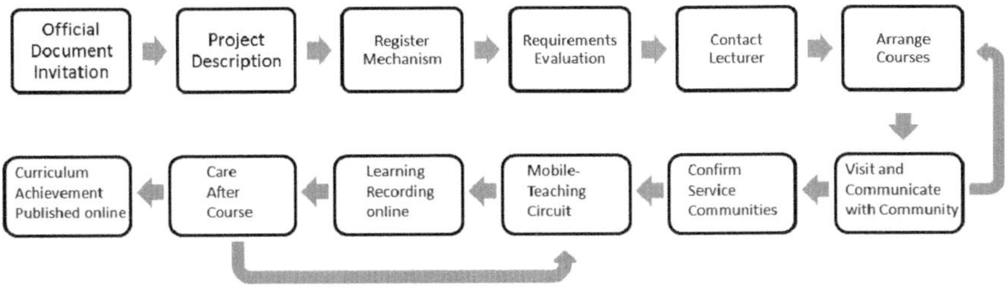

Fig. 2. PunCar Action service process

Service process that emphasizes on communication lays the best foundation for planning teaching materials and teaching methods

Community representative Ms. Lin: In the past, education and information agencies have also taught senior citizens how to use the computer, but maybe the materials were too hard, courses moved too fast, or were just plain boring, so elders often weren't able to understand and apply what was taught. This made them even more afraid of computers and the internet.

In the service process of PunCar (Fig. 2), the most important parts are the 2-3 visits to the registering community to communicate requirements, and arranging courses after the requirements evaluation, including the arrangement of suitable lecturers. Each lecture is recorded on blog, and after class lecturers and volunteers provide assistance to students either face to face or online, adjusting contents of the next class if necessary.

Director Gimi Wu of the PunCar south Taiwan center: After driving PunCar on a tour of over two hundred courses, I found that 'communication' was an intangible but immense cost. Yet, it was the only way to provide quality courses. If the framework of digital divide does not demand the existence of communication, then pursuing "what to learn" and "how to learn" will be deemed unnecessary.

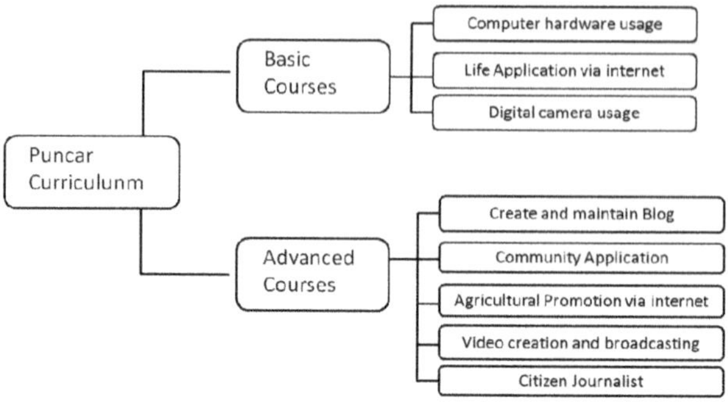

Fig. 3. PunCar curriculum

3.2 ICT Education Curriculum Design for Rural Communities

Slime Hsu, founder of PunCar Action: For a long time rural communities have relied not on digitization, but rather on passion and connections between people. Is digitization necessary to them? What benefit can e-learning provide to them?

PunCar student Mr. Ho (62 years old): I took the computer course for elders offered by the community before. At the time, they immediately taught us how to use e-mail, but I had no one to write to. So going to class was like pursuing fashion, and it wasn't before long that I had forgotten everything they taught about computers and the internet.

PunCar courses are divided into basic courses and advanced courses (as shown in Fig. 3): Basic courses consist of 2–3 classes, and mainly aim to guide residents to come in contact with computers, so they are not afraid of computers and develop an interest in learning ICT. The majority of course contents are on life applications via the internet, including going online to browse the news, weather report, make a hospital appointment, buy train tickets and use Skype. Advanced courses are adjusted according each community's requirements in terms of number of classes and contents; there are generally 4–7 classes; students learn advanced internet application skills, and join together to create and maintain a blog on community features.

PunCar's ICT courses uses a great number of freeware as its teaching platforms, e.g. Google map, Blogger, Picasa, YouTube, etc., allowing rural community residents to come in contact with digital information via the cheapest, most easily acquired ICT tools. In addition, before the community's curriculum ends all results are published on the community blog.

PunCar student Ms. Juan (30 years old, immigrant bride from Vietnam): PunCar teachers taught me how to make phone calls using Skype. It is a lot cheaper to make phone calls using internet phone. In class I learned how to search for Ho Chi Minh City using Google map, and was very glad to see my hometown.

(a) (b)

Fig. 4. Localized teaching methods (a) PunCar lecturer holding an elderly student's hand to use the mouse. (b) Community students practicing how to use a digital camera.

Community representative Mr. Chang: Our community is very beautiful and has many features. Through PunCar's blog class, community residents can go online to edit and record every thing that goes on in the community, and it has drawn everyone even closer together...

3.3 Dynamic Teaching Method That Is Easier to Understand for Senior Citizens and Immigrant Brides

Due to the majority of its students being senior citizens and immigrant brides, the ICT teaching method of PunCar Action for rural Taiwan includes slow and patient communication during interactive teaching, and step by step guidance when operating computer hardware (Fig. 4); this makes them feel more at easy with ICT tools. Teaching features of PunCar Action include using local dialects (Southern Taiwanese dialect) for teaching and using easy to understand terms instead of technical terms (e.g.: using open the box instead open the window). Another feature is the experience interactive teaching method; for example, the lecturer and volunteers hold the hands of elderly students to click on the mouse, so that students become familiar with the feeling and the cursor's corresponding movement.

PunCar Student Mr. Lee (62 years old): Classes taught by young PunCar teachers are very interesting, and we can understand better because they teach in Taiwanese. Retired senior citizens in the community gather together to learn how to use things on the internet; we ask the teacher whenever there is something we don't understand; there is no need to feel embarrassed. Now, I can post photos onto the blog, it is very interesting...

PunCar Lecturer C. L. Hsu: After understanding the thoughts of the elderly, I teach them how to use ICT tools, starting out from their point of view when telling them to click this and click that, and gradually explaining how these actions are different from their habits.

4 Discussion

Although PunCar Action initially aimed to "reduce digital divide," this study discovered that the digital mobile classroom of PunCar Action that visited rural communities in 2010 had already conformed to principles established by "e-Inclusion" [9]. The project implemented information education by "establishing a society without information barriers, so that people with different levels of education, gender, age and living in different areas will enjoy the same opportunity to come in contact with and use information, creating a society without discrimination."

PunCar Action uses a qualitative in-depth teaching method (average 15 students per class and 6.5 classes per community) to enhance e-learning for the elderly (average age of students was 53.2 years old), and allowed students to jointly write about cultural features of their community on a blog to develop a consensus in the community. Here this study will further discuss two aspects of ICT education in rural communities, "course contents" and "teaching methods."

4.1 Rural Community ICT Education: Course Contents

Curriculum planning begins with "requirements communication". "Communication" is an important link in the operation process of PunCar Action. Before planning course contents for a specific community, several visits must be made to the community, local groups and local leaders, in order to plan suitable e-learning teaching materials and consolidate the common needs of rural community residents. Accumulating over 300 teaching tours, PunCar Action built its basic and advanced courses based on its experiences, and then adjusts the weight of each course according to the requirements of each community. Lecturers and volunteers provide after-class guidance to see what necessary adjustments need to be made; all courses are based on the needs of its students.

Contents of basic courses on e-learning must be based on convenient life applications. Digital skills are a tool and a means. Its purpose is to allow rural community residents to go online to make a doctor's appointment, purchase a train ticket, talk with children working in other cities via video conference, use digital cameras to take photos and then upload the photos to share with family and friends. Basic courses thus focus on teaching rural community residents how to make life more convenient, turning the computer and internet into a means for making life more convenient, and an effective tool for connecting with family and friends.

Contents of advanced courses on e-learning are based on community life. To let rural community residents learn more advanced ICT applications, PunCar Action selected communities with the closest relationships and taught elders and immigrant brides how to set up a blog; contents of the blog are adjusted according to the features of each community. Students learned new digital skills in the process of setting up and editing their community blog; the blog enhanced residents' identification and sense of achievement in e-learning.

4.2 Rural Community ICT Education: Teaching Methods

Teaching method gives consideration to students' individual differences. The average education level of senior citizens and immigrant brides in rural communities is junior high school, and their main occupations are farmers and housewives. Therefore, the teaching method must be suitably adjusted according to students' individual differences. In this study the teacher-student ratio of PunCar Action is an average of 1 lecturer and 2–3 volunteers to 15 students. During class students operate the ICT tools themselves and give feedback as a means for verifying that they are familiar with the usage of ICT tools (includes hardware and software).

Community learning groups and experience interactive teaching using local dialects. Rural community students form community learning groups as a result of community clustering; the homogeneity of such community learning groups (age, familiarity with each other, similar schedules, time of contact with ICT tools) allow them to overcome their fear of using digital software and hardware. At the same time, the use of local dialects and interactive teaching method removes the lecturer's authority and allows lecturers to draw near to students. This study also summarizes three features of PunCar Action:

(1) **Brings "cheap" information equipment into courses:** The internet environment is set up using computer equipment of community centers, churches or temples together with laptops, digital cameras and network equipment provided by PunCar. With regards to software, freeware offered online are used as the main teaching platform.
(2) **"Friendly" teaching of ICT tools applications:** Intergeneration education is adopted to eliminate digital divide between urban and rural areas, adjusting the roles between "teachers" and "students" [10]. The primary goal is to remove senior citizen's fear of computers and the internet; thus courses are taught in local dialects, students experience using computers, instructions are given at a slower pace, and themes are related to the community. This friendly teaching method allows rural community residents to gain a sense of familiarity and achievement with using ICT tools.
(3) **Offers tour courses in nearby areas:** Daily activities of senior citizens and immigrant brides in rural communities are mainly at the community center. For this reason the mobile classroom of PunCar selects places near to home for the convenience of community residents. This reduces their fear of ICT tools by creating a relaxed environment, and accumulates community learning groups' passion for learning to use ICT tools in a pressure free environment.

5 Conclusions

Key factors of PunCar Action's success in providing digital education to rural communities include "flexible teaching materials" and "localized teaching methods," which were created and adapted to the needs and opinions of senior citizens and new immigrants after clarification and communication. In terms of PunCar Action's teaching material and teaching method design, themes that are able to arouse rural community residents' passion for ICT learning must be closely related to "daily life applications and requirements" and "consensus developing in the community."

In summary, based on this study's analysis of ICT education among rural communities in Taiwan, mobile intergeneration ICT education models with high penetration ability, such as PunCar Action, that emphasize on interpersonal communication, informational application and residents' requirements are indeed beneficial to closing the last mile of digital divide.

References

1. FIND, 2010 Survey of current state and level of demand on household broadband in Taiwan. Institute for Information Industry, Taipei (2011)
2. Tseng, S.F.: Integration Policy Research of Networking Society Development. RDEC, Taipei (2007)
3. ITU, World Information Society Report (2007), `http://www.itu.int/net/home/index.aspx`
4. Parker, E.B.: Closing the digital divide in rural America. Telecommunications Policy 24(4), 281–290 (2000)
5. Graham, G.: Bridging urban digital divides? Urban polarization and information and communication technologies (ICTs). Urban Studies 39(1), 33–56 (2002)
6. RDEC, Executive Yuan: 2010 Individual/Household Digital Divide Survey, Taipei (2010)
7. PunCar Official website Information, `http://puncar.tw`
8. The ARS Electronica Information, `http://new.aec.at/news/en`
9. ITU "World Summit on the Information Society (WSIS)–Elac 2007: Access and Digital Inclusion" presented in the WSIS meeting (November 2005)
10. Salinas, A., Sanchez, J.: Digital inclusion in Chile: Internet in rural schools. International Journal of Educational Development 29, 573–582 (2009)

The Internationalization Strategy and Overseas-Listings: A Case Study of ZTE Co., Ltd

Hong Xu

School of Business Administration,Zhejiang Gongshang University,
18# Xuezheng Street, Xiasha Higher Education Park, Hangzhou, Zhejiang, China(310018)
College of Economics and Management, Zhejiang Normal University,
688# Yingbin Road, Jinhua, Zhejiang, China(321004)
xhong@zjnu.cn

Abstract. This paper, with a case study of ZTE Co., Ltd, examined the impacts of the firm's overseas-listings on its internationalization's degree in terms of performance dimension, structure dimension and attitude dimension respectively, trying to explore the relationship between the firm's overseas-listings and its internationalization strategy. Finally, conclusions were acquired that overseas-listings did contribute to enhance the firm's degree of internationalization, and turned out to be part of the firm's internationalization strategy.

Keywords: Overseas-listings; Performance dimension, Structure dimension, Attitude dimension, Degree of internationalization.

1 Introduction

Chinese firms' activities of financing overseas could be dated back to Citic Pacific's going public through a shell in Hongkong capital market in 1990. However, properly defined activities of listing overseas began with Qingdao Beer Co.,Ltd, who listed on the stock exchange of Hongkong limited in 1993. During the subsequent 20 years, Chinese corporations experienced 4 climaxes of overseas-listings. Up to February 28th, 2011, the number of Chinese corporations listed overseas totaled 473[1], making the overseas-listing an important financing form. The overseas-listing refers to the activities that a firm lists its equity shares on one or more foreign stock exchanges rather than on its domestic stock exchange. Chinese corporations have been performing overseas-listings in two forms, that is, the direct overseas-listings and the indirect overseas-listings. Considering the complexities in judging the foreign affiliates, it is difficult to define the indirect overseas-listings precisely. In view of this, this paper only focuses on the direct overseas-listings.

Because of relative proximities in geographical location, culture and system, Hong Kong turns out to be one of the primary destinations for Chinese corporations' direct

[1] The number of Chinese listed corporations totaled 67 on NYSE, 188 on NASDAQ, 43 on London stock exchange, 12 on Stock Exchange of Singapore and 163 on Hong Kong Exchange. Data were collected from www.nyse.com, www.nasdaq.com, www.londonstockexchange.com, www.sgx.com and www.hkex.com.hk respectively.

M. Zhou (Ed.): ISAEBD 2011, Part III, CCIS 210, pp. 269–277, 2011.

overseas-listings. Up to February 28th, 2011, 130 China Mainland-incorporated corporations listed on the main board of Hong Kong Exchange with the total market value of HK$ 5,108,625,600,000, occupying 24.73% of the total market value of Hong Kong Stock Exchange's main board. In addition, 33 China Mainland-incorporations listed on the start-up market of Hong Kong Exchange with the total market value of HK$ 17,353,070,000, occupying 13.30% of Hong Kong start-up market's total value[2]. Accordingly, this paper only focuses on Chinese corporations listed on Hong Kong Exchange's main board.

Why do corporations list abroad? In essence, overseas-listing is a type of firms' financing activities, and the academia currently tends to explain the motives driving firms to list abroad in terms of financing scales and capital costs. One set of literatures have developed the explanations for motives of overseas-listings in terms of financing scales. Liche(2003) claims that the primary purpose of overseas-listings is to acquire capital; Cui Yuansen(2004) highlights the financing motives of overseas-listings by Chinese mainland-incorporated corporations; and Yin Xianrong(2006) portrays the overseas-listings by Chinese mainland-incorporated corporations as a market-oriented choice for maximizing corporations' value. Another set of literatures have developed the explanations for overseas-listings in terms of decreasing the capital costs from different standpoints, including the Market Segmentation Hypothesis, the Liquidity Hypothesis, the Investor Recognition Hypothesis and the Bonding Hypothesis. Market Segmentation Hypothesis was first put forward by Stapleton and Subrahmanyam in 1977 as a prevalent explanation for overseas-listings. It is claimed that the market segmentation always exists, constraining corporations' financing activities, while the overseas-listing turns out to be a solution to alleviate the negative effects of market segmentation. Two seminal studies of this literature are Foerster and Karolyi (1999) and Miller(1999). Foerster and Karolyi (1999) examine weekly abnormal returns for two year before and after the U.S.-listing by foreign corporations through establishing an ADR program. The result shows that the firms who list in U.S. through ADR issuance eventually experience an unexpected increase in their stock prices, of about 10% in the year before the listing. However, this unexpected increase is followed by a decrease of 9% in the year after listing. Miller (1999) finds that the corporations from the emerging markets with the relatively higher degree of market segmentation earn the higher positive average abnormal returns than the corporations from developed markets with relatively lower degree of market segmentation do. These findings support the Market Segmentation Hypothesis, confirming that overseas-listings can lower the costs of capital for corporations. Overseas-listing can also be explained by a liquidity argument. Amihud and Mendelson (1986) claim that overseas-listings can enhance the stock's liquidity so as to decrease the capital costs, because over-listings would help companies to get access to more investors, leading to a higher volume. Following that, Foerster and Karolyi (1998), Domowitz, Glen and Madhavan (2004) study the impact of foreign firms' listing on U.S. exchanges on the costs of security transactions, and generally find that spreads decrease and trading volume increases following the listing, both of which reflect an increase in liquidity. Bonding Hypothesis can be dated back to the introduction of Law and Finance Theory. Coffee (1999,2002) was the first one to

[2] Data are from the website of Hong Kong Exchange (http://www.hkex.com.hk).

point out that corporate governance matters for overseas-listing firms, the so-called "bonding" hypothesis. He argues that firms with poor corporate governance in their home countries or regions tend to list their securities on the stock markets located in countries or regions with more rigorous governance standards. "Bonding" to more rigorous governance standards boosts investors' confidence as well as improves the access to capital, which, in turn, lowers the cost of capital and increases the value of the firm. In terms of the information asymmetry and agency costs, Stulz (1999) points out the significant impacts of corporate governance on the capital cost, that is, overseas-listings can decrease the equity costs through improving some forms of corporate governance mechanism such as improving legal systems, regulating the information disclosures and so on. Reese and Weibach (2002) study the sequel financing following the firm's overseas-listing, and find that the foreign firms increase equity financing after their listing on U.S. capital market, especially for those firms from countries or regions with poorer investor protection. Their findings support Coffee's Bonding Hypothesis from another standpoint.

To sum up, the limits of current literatures are to merely explain the firms' listing overseas as a type of financing activities, rather than to deeply explore the relationships between the firm's overseas-listing and its other basic economic activities. Accordingly, there lack the literatures on the motives of overseas-listings in terms of corporate strategy. In fact, the firm's overseas-listing not only does with its financing activities, but also closely relates with its strategy of overseas expansion. For those firms who are planning to tap into overseas markets, listing overseas undertakes part of responsibilities for the firm's strategic development. Considering that, this paper's discussion over the link between the firm's overseas-listing and its internationalization strategy can further enrich the current theories on the overseas-listing's motives, being theoretically significant. At the same time, due to the Government's deregulation efforts, Chinese firms are expanding overseas more and more quickly. Under such a practical background, whether the firm's overseas-listing and its overseas expansion can complement each other is a practical issue, which deserves analyzing.

2 The Overseas-Listing and the Internationalization Strategy: A Theoretical Analysis

The firm's internationalization strategy is a set of development plans during the firm's international operation, targeting to enhance the firm's competitiveness and its adaptive capacity to the environment. The firm's internationalization strategy will affect its internationalization progress greatly, and eventually determine its future development. The internationalization strategy takes the forms of exports, foreign direct investments (FDI), cross-border mergers and acquisitions (M&A). By its very nature, export is the result of the firm's operating activities, while FDI and cross-border M&A fall in the firm's investing activities. Then, how about the overseas-listing? In nature, it is a type of financing activities. According to the financial management principles, the scale and efficiency of the firm's financing activities determine the scale and efficiency of its investing activities, and all kinds of assets formed through investing activities provide the foundation for the firm's operation.

Thereby, the scale and efficiency of the firm's financing activities determine its operating activities ultimately. Based on that, this paper believes that the firm's listing overseas will affect the internationalization strategy's implementation through the two approaches as below. Firstly, the overseas-listing can decrease the capital cost according to the financial motives theory of overseas-listing, which will bring more investment projects with positive net present value for the firm, and eventually expand its investment scale with a better investment return, especially benefiting its FDI and cross-border M&A. Secondly, once the firm lists its shares on foreign markets, the consumer recognition for the firm's products and services will be reinforced, which enlarges the customer segments in foreign markets with a great increase in the firm's export to this country or region, and improves the firm's operation eventually. Thus it can be seen that overseas-listing performs a significant role in the firm's fulfillment of its internationalization strategy.

In order to quantify the impacts of the firm's overseas-listing on its fulfillment of internationalization strategy, we must first quantify the results of the firm's internationalization strategy. The results of internationalization strategy have many dimensions, among which, the degree of internationalization turns out to be the most intuitive dimension. This paper follows Sulivan(1994)'s indicator system, which tries to measure the degree of internationalization in terms of performance dimension, structure dimension and attitude dimension. Detailed descriptions for each indicator are included in table 1.

To conclude, we put forward a hypothesis for testing, that is, the firm's listing overseas is beneficial to enhance its degree of internationalization.

Table 1. The indicator system for measuring the degree of internationalization[3]

Variable	Descriptions
FS	$\frac{\text{overseas sales}}{\text{total sales}} \times 100\%$
FENA	$\frac{\text{longterm equity investments overseas}}{\text{net assets}} \times 100\%$
FETA	$\frac{\text{longterm equity investments overseas}}{\text{total assets}} \times 100\%$
FH	$\frac{\text{the number of overseas subsidiaries}}{\text{the number of all subsidiaries}} \times 100\%$
PDD	psychological distribution degree of international operations
CN	The number of foreign countries or regions where the firm operates

3 An Overview of ZTE Co., Ltd

Up to December 31st, 2010, 64 China mainland-incorporated firms out of 130 firms listing on the main board of Hong Kong Exchange cross-listed on the A share market in China mainland. Most of these cross-listing firms performed IPOs on the H share

[3] Referring to Wang Fusheng, Sun Nina,Wang Hongmei(2009). Empirical analysis of the relationship between the Chinese listed companies' degree of internationalization and operating Performance.

market and then came back to the A share market. To separate the overseas-listing's impacts on the firm's internationalization degree, as well as to take the data availability into account, this paper plans to include the firms who list on the A share market first and then list on the H share market in the testing sample. Considering this standard, the sample includes China Merchants Bank Co.,Ltd, The Pacific Securities CO., LTD, China Minsheng Banking Co., Ltd, ZTE Co.,Ltd, Shandong Chenming Paper Group Co., Ltd and Metallurgical Corporation of China, Ltd. After excluding financial firms and the firms with the time interval between its A-share listing and H-share listing shorter than 1 year, only two firms (ZTE Co., Ltd and Shandong Chenming Paper Group Co., Ltd) remain in the sample. After further removing Shandong Chenming Paper Group Co., Ltd, who listed on Hong Kong, New York and London markets at the same time, only ZTE still remains in the sample for analysis. The process of sampling reflects the randomness to ensure the universal applicability of the conclusions in this paper.

Founded in 1985, ZTE is China's largest listed telecom equipment public company, who listed on the Shenzhen Stock Exchange (A share: 000063.SZ) on October 6th, 1997 and Hong Kong (H share: 0763.HK) Exchange on December 9th, 2004.ZTE Corporation is a leading global provider of telecom equipment and networking solutions operating in more than 140 countries, servicing 59 of the world's top 100 telecom operators. The company has 15 global R&D centers in the U.S, France, Sweden, India and China. It employs 25,000 researchers around the world, developing new and innovative products covering more than 30,000 issued and pending patents. ZTE's products and solutions can be found in over 140 countries, servicing 59 of the world's top 100 telecom operators.[4]

4 Case Analysis

ZTE issued 160,151,040 H shares in December, 2004, and listed these shares on the main board of Hong Kong Stock Exchange on December 9th,2004, which made it the first A share firm listing on the main board of Hong Kong Stock Exchange. Following related laws and regulations, the state-owned shareholders underweighted the state-owned share by 1,384,590 shares, which amounted to about 0.9% of total amount of H-share issuance. After that, ZTE Holdings Co., Ltd still holds 44.1% of ZTE's total shares, remaining as the biggest controlling shareholder. Foreign investors hold 18.6% of ZTE's total shares. To some extent, ZTE's listing on H share market facilitates its decentralization, diversification and internationalization in its ownership structure, which provides it with a better and broader capital operating platform, accelerating its internationalization progress.

With an eye to the macro-situations, we can never neglect the fact that China joined in WTO on December 10th,2001. Among the WTO legal documents related with China, *Agreement On Basic Tele-communications, General Agreement On Trade In Services, Information Technology Agreement And Agreement On Trade-related Aspects of Intellectual Property Rights, Trips* all deal with the communication industry, which forced China to deregulate its communication market. With the

[4] Information is from the website of ZTE Co., Ltd (http://wwwen.zte.com.cn).

deregulations, great changes take place in our communication industry. On one hand, foreign competitors penetrated into China's communication industry, making the competitions more dramatic. On the other hand, China's communication operators could enter the communication markets of about 130 countries or regions as well, achieving better development chances. Accordingly, we set the time zone between 2002 and 2009 as the time window for the following analysis.

4.1 Overseas-Listing and Internationalization Degree: In Terms of Performance Dimension

The performance dimension measures the firm's performance on overseas markets, as well as its dependence on overseas markets. Figure 1 shows that ZTE's FS indicator hung about the level of 10% before 2004, and then increased to the level of 21.56% in 2004. Afterwards, this indicator remained a steady growth, reaching its summit of 60.57% in 2008. In view of this, ZTE's overseas listing does have a positive impact on its performance dimension of internationalization degree.

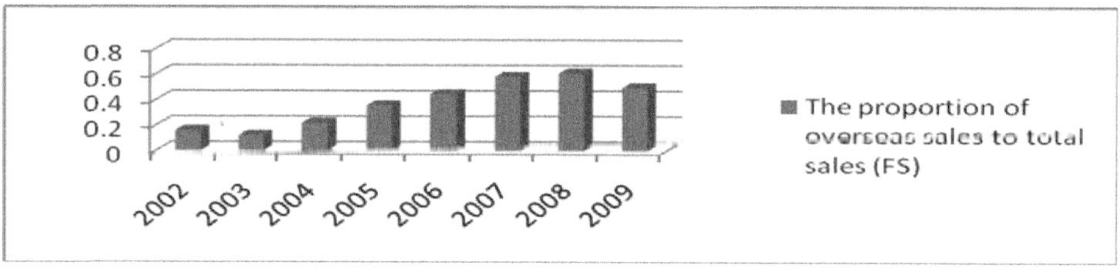

Fig. 1. ZTE's proportion of overseas sales to total sales (2002-2009)[5]

4.2 Overseas-Listing and Internationalization Degree: In Terms of Structure Dimension

The structure dimension describes the characteristics of overseas resources held by the firm, which can be measured by three indicators, the proportion of overseas equity investment to total net assets (FENA), the proportion of overseas equity investment to total assets(FETA) and the proportion of the number of overseas subsidiaries to the total number of its subsidiaries(FH). A slight difference exists between FENA and FETA, that is, FENA describes the distribution of the firm's equity capital overseas, while FETA measures the deployment of assets to foreign markets in terms of investment. Up to December 31st, 2007, ZTE had 106 holding subsidiaries with 65[6] of them located overseas, and its long-term equity investment overseas totaled

---

[5] Data are from ZTE's annual financial reports of 2002 to 2009.

[6] According to ZTE's financial reports, only the subsidiaries that ZTE holds their shareholding ratios of 50% and above are included in ZTE's consolidated financial statements. This paper follows this standard to determine the statistical range of holding subsidiaries. In view of the fact that since 2008 the list of ZTE's holding subsidiaries is not given in its financial statements, our statistical time span ends on December 31st, 2007.

Table 2. ZTE's overseas subsidiaries and its long-term equity investment overseas[7]

Year	Number of subsidiaries overseas	Total number of subsidiaries	Long-term equity investment overseas (Unit: RMB Yuan)
2001	4	11	75405550
2002	9	26	102572058
2003	16	35	126562570
2004	21	47	182986581
2005	37	69	213641371
2006	46	84	248276627
2007	59	102	260482265

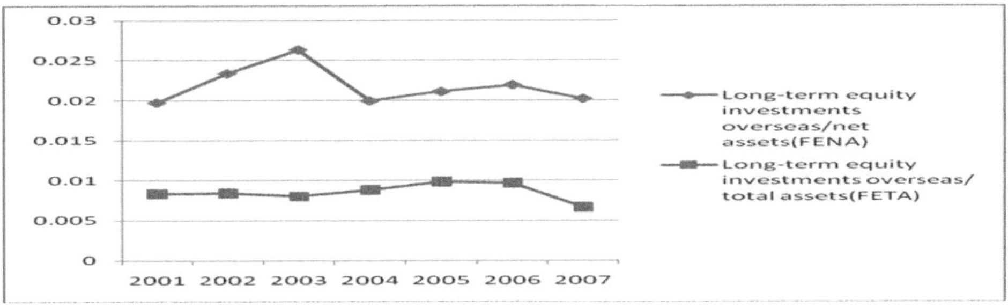

Fig. 2. ZTE's FENA indicator and FETA indicator (2001-2007)

¥260482265[8]. Detailed information is given in Table 2.Based on the data in Table 2, FENA indicator, FETA indicator and FH indicator are calculated and summarized in Figure 2 and Figure 3 as below.

As shown in Figure 2, during the period of 2001-2007, FENA indicator reached its peak in 2003 with the level of 2.631%, and then experienced a transient decline in 2004 and ascended to 2.1% in 2005. Subsequently, FENA indicator remained stable at a relatively high level. However, FETA indicator's peak arrived in 2005 with the level of 0.8909%. After comparing and analyzing, we find that the trend of FETA is in accord with our previous expectation, while the trend of FENA does not. In Figure 3, FH indicator increases from the level of 26.36% in 2001 to the level of 53.62% in 2005, and keeps a steady growth during the following 2006 and 2007 with the peak level of 57.84% in 2007[9].

In summary, two indicators (FETA and FH) out of the three indicators experienced an evident increase around 2005, basically supporting our expectation. Thus, it's relatively safe to say that, the firm's overseas-listing is beneficial for enhancing the degree of internationalization in terms of structure dimension.

---

[7] Figure 2 is complied based on ZTE's annual financial reports.

[8] The overseas long-term equity investments include equity investments on subsidiaries and equity investments on affiliates. Amount of equity investment is calculated by currency converter using the historical exchange rates and historical costs.

[9] Data are from ZTE's annual reports.

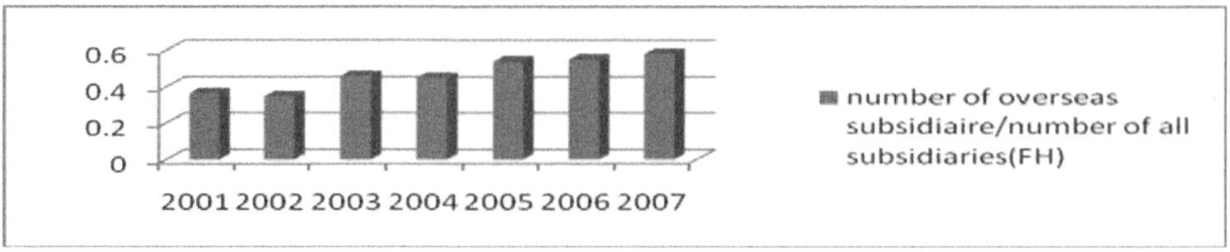

Fig. 3. ZTE's FH indicator (2001-2007)

4.3 Overseas-Listing and Internationalization Degree: In Terms of Attitude Dimension

The attitude dimension reflects the management's inclination and tendency towards overseas operation, which is measured as psychological distribution degree (PDD) and the number of countries or regions where the firm's subsidiaries operate (CN). John (1977) claims that the psychological distance between the firm's home country and its overseas operation destination is positively correlated with its degree of internationalization. The psychological distance involves the factors disturbing information flows between the firm and market, such as language, culture, political system, education, economic development, and so on, which is often used to evaluate the investor's social familiarity with the overseas markets.[10] With other conditions unchanged, the further the firm's psychological distance is, the higher its degree of internationalization is. Following this perspective, Sulivan (1994) divides global countries and regions into 10 districts based on Ronen(1985)'s results of global nation cluster analysis[11]. Under this framework, if the firm has overseas operation in one of these 10 districts, 1 is given to its value of PDD indicator, and so on.

Table 3. The cluster analysis on ZTE 's global operations and its PPD scores(2002-2007)[12]

Clusters \ Year	2002	2003	2004	2005	2006	2007
ARAB				0.1	0.1	0.1
NEAR EASTERN				0.1	0.1	0.1
NORDIC		0.1	0.1	0.1	0.1	0.1
GERMANIC				0.1	0.1	0.1
ANGLO	0.1	0.1	0.1	0.1	0.1	0.1
LATIN EUROPEAN		0.1	0.1	0.1	0.1	0.1
LATIN AMERICAN		0.1	0.1	0.1	0.1	0.1
FAR EASTERN		0.1	0.1	0.1	0.1	0.1
INDEPENDENT	0.1	0.1	0.1	0.1	0.1	0.1
OTHERS	0.1	0.1	0.1	0.1	0.1	0.1
PDD scores	0.3	0.7	0.7	1	1	1

[10] John Jan, Erik Vahlne. The Internationalization Process of the Firm- A Model of Knowledge Development and Increasing Foreign Market Commitments [J]. Journal of International Business Studies, 1977,(4):23-32.

[11] Ronen, Smcha, Oded Shenkar. Clustering Countries on Attitudinal Dimensions: A Review and Synthesis [J]. Academy of Management Review, 1985,10(3):35-54.

[12] Data are from ZTE 's annual reports.

Up to December 31st, ZTE holds 15 R&D centers and 107 subsidiaries and affiliates all around the world. The cluster analysis on ZTE's overseas operations and PPD scores are described in Table 3. According to the rough statistics, the number of overseas countries or regions ZTE operates increased from 8 in 2002 to 50 in 2007, with its greatest increasing rate of 66.67% in 2005.[13]

Based on the cluster analysis and PDD evaluation, ZTE 's listing on Hong Kong Exchange in the end of 2004 did have the positive effects on its internationalization strategy in terms of PDD and CN.

5 Conclusions and Discussions

In final summary, the firm's overseas-listing decision has a positive impact on its degree of internationalization in terms of the performance dimension, the structure dimension and the attitude dimension basically, especially measured by the performance dimension and the structure dimension. Therefore, the previous hypothesis is verified that the firm's overseas-listing enhances its internationalization degree, which confirms the link between the firm's overseas-listing and its global strategy. However, this paper only provides a specific firm's descriptive analysis and simple statistics, and the future quantitative works based on large samples will be done to further confirm the hypothesis of this paper.

References

1. Sullivan, D.: Measuring the Degree of Internationalization of A Firm. Journal of International Business Studies 25(2), 325–342 (1994)
2. Merton, R.: Presidential Address: A Simple Model of Capital Market Equilibrium with Incomplete Information. Journal of Finance 42, 483–510 (1987)
3. Miller, D.: The Market Reaction to International Cross-listings: Evidence from Depositary Receipts. Journal of Financial Economics 51, 103–123 (1999)
4. Coffee, J.: Racing Toward the Top?: the Impact of Cross-Listings and Stock Market Competition on International Corporate Governance. Working Paper. Columbia Law School (2002)
5. Errunza, V., Miller, D.: Market Segmentation and the Cost of Capital in International Equity Markets. Journal of Financial and Quantitative Analysis 35, 577–600 (2000)
6. Foerster, S., Karolyi, G.: The Effects of Market Segmentation and Investor Recognition on Asset Prices: Evidence From Foreign Stocks Listing in the U.S. Journal of Finance 54, 981–1013 (1999)

[13] The increasing rates are 62.5% in 2003, 38.5% in 2004, 66.67% in 2005, 26.7% in 2006 and 31.6% in 2007 respectively. Data are from ZTE 's annual reports.

Research on the Warning System of Regional Scientific and Technological Progress

Zhiping Wu[1], Xu Xu[2,*], and Zhenjie Hong[1]

[1] School of Mathematics and Information Science, Wenzhou University,
[2] Oujiang College of Wenzhou University, Wenzhou University,
325035 Wenzhou, China
{373914774,493103722,544561084}@qq.com

Abstract. Scientific and technological (S&T) progress is a determinate factor for economy development. Based on the macroeconomic development situation China facing, this paper sets up a monitoring model and a warning model to master regional S&T dynamic development and provides data support for macro-management effectively. The warning model analyses and evaluates the condition of S&T progress in recent decade in 11 cities of Zhejiang. When the evaluation indexes lag behind the other compared cities, the warning model will ring alarms. The government and researcher will pay more attention to the S&T development to promote a healthy development of regional economy.

Keywords: S&T progress, regional, warning model.

1 Introduction

The level of S&T progress is a relative index which reflects the relative intensities of S&T development in the economic and social backgrounds. Currently, with the rapid development of China economy, the investment in S&T development has constantly increased from country and local governments, the condition of S&T progress has concerned by people from all walks of life, so constructing a complete and effective warning system has its reality and necessity. When the level of regional S&T progress is out of line with economic development, it means the S&T development has happened alerts. Warning is the process that searches, analyzes, evaluates, alarms to the deciders and controls alerts according to the alert-degrees [1]. After determining alert-limits, when the level of evaluation regional S&T progress appears recession, stagnant and unsteady states compared with the previous years and the other compared cities, the warning system sounds alarms timely and searches for deep reasons.

More attention has been paid on the warning mechanisms about macro-economic and traditional enterprises, burgeoning areas such as knowledge management, network organization and urban construction are also involved, but the warning system of level of regional S&T progress remains to be constructed. This paper

* Corresponding author.

M. Zhou (Ed.): ISAEBD 2011, Part III, CCIS 210, pp. 278–285, 2011.

explores a warning system that consists of a monitoring model and a warning model, evaluates the level of regional S&T progress and provides decision support for regional management.

2 Monitoring Model

Monitoring is the process that selects, normalizes, aggregates and evaluates the indexes that represent the level of S&T progress. The construction of the monitoring model is the core of the warning system and affects the validity of the warning system directly.

2.1 Monitoring Index Construct and Normalization

Referring to statistical bulletins of 11 cities in Zhejiang from year 2000 to 2009 and Zhejiang Statistics Yearbook, this paper constructs a monitoring indexes system which involves many aspects such as industry, agriculture, patent, achievement, talents and education based on statistics methods and the index design principles of systematicness, operability and warning. The indexes system is designed with three-framework structure, including 4 indexes of class 1, 9 indexes of class 2 and 28 indexes of class 3, as shown in table 1.

The normalization of indexes is the method that eliminates the dimension influence of index statistics through mathematical transformation. The indexes are divided into benefit-types and cost-types. The larger evaluation values of benefit-type indexes are, the better, such as per capita GDP; the smaller evaluation values of cost-type indexes are, the better, such as Engel coefficient. The normalization process is also a positive process. The interval spans of indexes are huge and the computations are relatively large, so this paper adopts formula (1), the evaluation values are controlled at a range between 40 and 100.

$$F_{ij} = \begin{cases} \dfrac{X_{ij} - \min\limits_i(X_{ij})}{\max\limits_i(X_{ij}) - \min\limits_i(X_{ij})} \times 60 + 40 & \text{if } X_{ij} \text{ is benefit} - \text{type} \\ \dfrac{\max\limits_i(X_{ij}) - X_{ij}}{\max\limits_i(X_{ij}) - \min\limits_i(X_{ij})} \times 60 + 40 & \text{if } X_{ij} \text{ is cost} - \text{type} \end{cases} . \tag{1}$$

In formula (1), F_{ij} : the evaluation value of index j in area i ; X_{ij} : the statistic of index j in area i ; $\max\limits_i(X_{ij})$: the maximum of the statistic of index j in all areas; $\min\limits_i(X_{ij})$: the minimum of the statistic of index j in all areas.

2.2 Setting Weights for Monitoring Indexes

The monitoring indexes are given corresponding weights according to the characteristics of multi-goal and multi-level structures and different effects in S&T progress. The indexes are too complex and the computations of paired comparison matrixes by Analytical Hierarchy Process (AHP) are large, so we improve and expand the AHP to Fuzzy Analytic Hierarchy Process (FAHP). The method minimizes the influence of subjective factors to evaluation results and improves the accuracy and rationality. The two steps are as follows:

(1) Identify the problem, establish analytic hierarchy tables;

(2) Construct fuzzy judgment matrixes $w=[w_{ij}]_{n*n}$ in terms of binary contrast principle of indexes importance, of which

$$w_{ij}=\begin{cases}1 & \textit{if} \text{ index } i \text{ is more important than index } j;\\ 0.5 & \textit{if} \text{ index } i \text{ is as important as index } j;\\ 0 & \textit{if} \text{ index } i \text{ is less important than index } j\end{cases}$$

The detailed solving processes are seen in reference [2]. When fuzzy judgment matrixes satisfy with consistency checking, compute the corresponding weights of the monitoring indexes by combining hedge operator and relative membership relational table of quantitative scale [3], as shown in table1.

2.3 Comprehensive Evaluation Model As a Case of 11 Cities in Zhejiang

The comprehensive evaluation values are aggregated by normalization values and corresponding weights of all levels monitoring indexes. The calculative process of comprehensive evaluation values $f(V^t)$ in area V in year t are as shown in formula (2), the areas that sort forward are advanced units of level of S&T progress after sorted in descending order.

$$f(V^t)=\sum_{i=1}^{4}\sigma_i\sum_{j=1}^{n_i}\omega_{ij}\sum_{k=1}^{n_{ij}}\rho_{ijk}P_{ijk}(V^t)\ . \qquad (2)$$

In formula (2), σ_i :the weight of 1-class index i $(i=1,\cdots,4)$; n_i :the number of factors under 1-class index i $(i=1,\cdots,4)$; ω_{ij} :the weight of factor j under 1-class index i, it meets $\sum_{j=1}^{n_i}\omega_{ij}=1(i=1,\cdots,4)$; n_{ij} :the number of indexes under factor j of 1-class index i $(i=1,\cdots,4)$; ρ_{ijk} :the weight of index k under factor j of 1-class index i, it meets $\sum_{k=1}^{n_{ij}}\rho_{ijk}=1(\ i=1,\cdots,4)$; V^t :the statistic of index k under factor j of 1-class index in area V in year t ; $P_{ijk}(V^t)$:the normalization value of V^t .

Considering the incomplete information on partial monitoring indexes of the level of S&T progress, this paper disposes the data by the following principles. (1) When partial index values in few special years are not collected, but the information around this year is integrated, the missing data are fixed completely by the interpolation method. (2) When partial index values in early years are not collected, the missing data are fixed completely by the time series method and the regression method. The estimate value is accepted if the error is in the reasonable range after testing the error, otherwise, the index is abandoned. The comprehensive evaluation values of 11 cities in Zhejiang are aggregated from year 2000 to 2009 with the two mentioned principles in table 2.

Table 1. Monitoring Indexes System and Weights

1-class index	2-class index	weight	3-class index	weight
Environment of S&T progress Weight: 0.18	Economic development level	0.55	Per capita GDP	0.29
			Per capita retail sales of consumer goods	0.12
			Per capita total investment in fixed assets	0.24
			Per capita total value of imports & exports	0.19
			Per capita disposable income of urban residents	0.16
	Awareness of S&T innovation	0.45	Applications for patent per million population	0.45
			The ratio of government funds for technology by local government to fiscal expenditure	0.55
Input of S&T activities Weight: 0.27	Human resources in S&T activities	0.45	Personnel engaged in S&T activities per 10,000 population	0.40
			Trained personnal resources per 10,000 population	0.33
			Scientists and engineers engaged in S&T activities per 10,000 population	0.27
	Financial resources of S&T activities	0.55	The ratio of total input for technology to GDP	0.23
			The ratio of expenditure for technological development of enterprises to prime operating revenue	0.19
			Per capita expenditures for science popularization activities	0.16
			Per capita expenditure for education	0.13
			The ratio of funds for education to local finance expenditure	0.10
			The ratio of expenditure for R&D to GDP	0.19
Output of S&T activities Weight: 0.33	Output level of S&T activities	0.40	Information level	0.40
			Approval indexes of patents per 10,000 population	0.33
			Approvals for invention per million population	0.27
	Marketization of tech results	0.33	Output rate of new industrial product	0.55
			Agricultural productivity	0.45
	High-tech industrialization	0.27	The ratio of the added value of high-tech enterprises to the added value of industry	0.55
			The ratio of high-tech enterprises to industrial enterprises above designated size	0.45
Technology promotes development Weight: 0.22	Economic development	0.55	Contributing rate of the three industries	0.38
			Engel Coefficient	0.31
			Urbanization level	0.31
	Environmental development	0.45	Electricity consumed by industrial sector per unit GDP	0.55
			Green area coverage rate in developed zone	0.45

Indexes source: Statistical Bulletins of 11 cities in Zhejiang from year 2000 to 2009 and Zhejiang Statistics Yearbook.

Table 2. Comprehensive Evaluation Values of Level of S&T Progress

City \ Year	2000	2001	2002	2003	2004	2005	2006	2007	2008	2009
Hangzhou	86.60	83.29	83.75	85.27	86.53	86.17	89.02	88.30	88.41	86.60
Ningbo	77.21	80.57	76.86	74.13	77.26	72.58	76.04	75.74	74.18	71.47
Wenzhou	65.42	65.49	61.19	58.09	62.29	60.81	59.72	59.35	60.06	58.24
Jiaxing	66.70	66.89	64.13	64.34	67.84	68.38	67.26	69.94	70.54	69.58
Huzhou	62.42	63.77	62.64	60.79	62.23	65.51	62.75	64.86	67.72	63.96
Shaoxing	65.71	66.18	69.77	68.43	71.19	69.05	71.93	73.82	75.05	69.30
Jinhua	63.84	61.28	64.97	63.01	63.76	66.18	64.79	63.25	61.45	61.48
Quzhou	49.31	47.10	51.10	53.00	49.14	52.39	48.76	51.96	49.67	51.12
Zhoushan	64.25	63.14	67.86	62.55	63.95	61.19	64.94	68.54	67.58	65.73
Taichow	64.59	66.90	66.84	65.83	66.43	65.62	64.74	67.48	70.11	67.89
Lishui	86.60	83.29	83.75	85.27	86.53	86.17	89.02	88.30	88.41	86.60

Data source: Calculated by formula (2) according to Statistical Bulletins of 11 cities in Zhejiang Province from year 2000 to 2009 and Zhejiang Statistics Yearbook.

3 Warning Model Construct——As a Case of Wenzhou

The emphasis on warning system is to construct a warning model, which monitors all factors of the level of S&T progress, forecasts the alerts caused by the decline, makes the alert status return to normal timely and improves the alert processing power. The warning model is constituted of warning indexes, alert-limits, signals and risk states.

3.1 Warning Model Construct Based on Lateral and Longitudinal Comparison

Warning indexes must be determined firstly. After analyzing the comprehensive evaluation values of the level of S&T progress in 11 cities of Zhejiang province from year 2000 to 2009, we find that the relationships between the data of current year and the previous years are close, the comparability of these data are greater among the areas on the same layer in the horizontal comparison, and the growth rates of the monitoring indexes are calculated compared with the previous year. The level of S&T progress of Wenzhou is on the third or fourth layer, Jinhua, Quzhou and Lishui are on the same level as Wenzhou after calculated. Construct a warning indexes system in view of the foregoing and set the weights of the compared cities on the same level and the data over the years, as shown in table 3. The 2-class index values are the aggregation of the difference between the values of 3-class index in the monitoring indexes system, then the weights of corresponding indexes and the differences are aggregated so as to judge whether the level of regional S&T progress in year t happens alerts.

The calculation formula of comprehensive evaluation value of Wenzhou in year t in warning indexes system is:

$$Cev(W^t) = \lambda \sum_{l=1}^{3} \alpha_l (f(W^t) - f(B_l^t)) + (1-\lambda) \sum_{l=1}^{3} \beta_l (f(W^t) - f(W^{t-l})) \quad . \tag{3}$$

Table 3. Warning Indexes System

1-class index	Weight	2-class index	Weight
Compared cities	0.55	Indexes of Jinhua	0.40
		Indexes of Quzhou	0.33
		Indexes of Lishui	0.27
Data over the years	0.45	Indexes of the year *t*-1	0.40
		Indexes of the year *t*-2	0.33
		Indexes of the year *t*-3	0.27

In formula (3), $f(W^t)$:the comprehensive evaluation value of Wenzhou in year t in the monitoring indexes system; $f(B_l^t)$:the comprehensive evaluation value of the compared city which ranks l in year t in the monitoring indexes system, the calculation formula refers to formula (2); λ :the weight of compared cities in 1-class indexes in warning indexes system; α_l :the weight of compared city of the importance ranks l in 2-class indexes in warning indexes system; β_l :the weight of index of the year $t-l$.

Determine the limit of no alert of the comprehensive evaluation values of the warning indexes according to the principles of majority, half and mean [4], and then determine the limits of light alert, medium alert, heavy alert and giant alert according to the similar principles, as shown in table 4. Classify the alerts of the level of S&T progress of Wenzhou in year t based on the comprehensive evaluation values of the warning system, as shown in table 5.

Table 4. Alert-limits of Comprehensive Evaluation Values of Warning Indexes

Alert	No alert	Light alert	Medium alert	Heavy alert	Giant alert
Limit	$[1.92, +\infty)$	$[0.48, 1.92)$	$[-0.86, 0.48)$	$[-2.37, -0.86)$	$(-\infty, -2.37)$

Table 5. Alerts and Comprehensive Evaluation Values of Warning Indexes

Year	2003	2004	2005	2006	2007	2008	2009
Cev(W)	-1.17	4.47	2.53	2.20	1.58	3.03	1.25
Alert	Heavy alert	No alert	No alert	No alert	Light alert	No alert	Light alert

3.2 Alert Analysis

When the warning model appears light alert or above, the inside reasons of the decline of the level of S&T progress are searched gradually by FAHP based on the positive or negative indexes. The steps are as follows: (1) Determine the alerts based on alert-limits after searching the indexes of class 1 in warning indexes system. If the index values of class 2 are negative, it means the evaluation area is lagging behind the other compared cities. (2) Find the indexes of negative value in class 3 of the monitoring indexes system step by step. (3) The alert sources are found in the monitoring indexes of class 3. The alert-limits of the warning indexes of class 2 are determined with the principles of majority, half and mean, as shown in table 6.

Table 6. Alert-limits of the Warning Indexes of Class 2

Single	Alert	Alert-limit	Risk state
Green light	No alert	[0.100)	The development is basically stable and the decline signs are not obvious
Blue light	Light alert	[−10, 0)	There are some gaps between Wenzhou and the other compared cities, we should sound alarms
Yellow light	Medium alert	[−20, −10)	The gaps between Wenzhou and the other compared cities are big, we should pay more attention to the lagging indexes
Orange light	Heavy alert	[−40, −20)	The gaps between Wenzhou and the other compared cities are prominent, we should pay highly attention to the lagging indexes
Red light	Giant alert	(−100, −40)	The gaps between Wenzhou and the other compared cities are huge, we should adjust the S&T policies immediately

Table 5 shows that alerts appeared in the years 2003, 2007 and 2009, no alerts appeared in year 2004, 2005, 2006 and 2008. The reasons are that the gaps of partial monitoring indexes are widening between Wenzhou and the advanced cities, but the gaps are shrinking between Wenzhou and the backward cities. The growth rates of the data over the years are lower than the rates of the other advanced cities. As a case of the year 2009, the separations of hysteretic indexes in the warning system are as follows:

Light alerts: per capita total investment in fixed assets, applications for patent per million population, trained personnal resources per 10,000 population, the ratio of total input for technology to GDP, approval indexes of patents per 10,000 population, agricultural productivity, output rate of new industrial products, the ratio of high-tech enterprises to industrial enterprises above designated size, contributing rate of the three industries;

Medium alerts: green area coverage rate in developed zone, urbanization level.

4 The Evaluation and Improvement of Warning Model

With reference to other existing achievements and experiences in warning mechanism, this paper explores the warning system of the level of regional S&T progress for the first time. The monitoring model we construct provides data support for the warning model. Further construct the warning model and classify the alerts by alert-limits. When regional S&T development is unbalanced, the warning system sounds alarms and reminds the decider to search the lagging indexes effectively. The warning system also has positive impacts on regional S&T development.

With the development of S&T activities, the monitoring indexes of the level of regional S&T progress have different weights at different periods, but the data aren't updated in real-time in this paper. In order to remove the negative effect, the group FAHP can be used to adjust the weights objectively. As the space is limited, this paper doesn't adopt the time series model and regression model to predict the advance indexes of the level of S&T progress. Finally, extensive data should be simulated, compared and repeatedly verified in order to determinate the limits of the warning system more accurately.

Acknowledgments. The authors acknowledge the financial support of the Project of Soft Science of Zhejiang (No.: 2010C35048), the Cultural Project of Wenzhou (No.: Wyk10009), the Project of Science & Technology of Wenzhou (No.: R20090065), Scientific Research Fund of Zhejiang Provincial Education Department (No.: 20070534) and the Innovation Fund of Wenzhou University (No.: 3160601010955).

References

1. Wenhao: Research on Indicator System of Setting up Chinese Financial Safety Section. Master Degree Paper of DongBei University of Finance and Economics (2003)
2. Zi, H., Liu, Y.: The Application of Fuzzy Analytic Hierarchy Process in the Sustainable Development of Regional Lakes Resources. Modern Construction of Pearl River, 2008 5, 5–8 (2006)
3. Wang, X., Zhaobin, et al.: Mining Method Choice Based on AHP and Fuzzy Mathematics. Journal of Central South University (Science and Technology) 39, 875–880 (2008)
4. Ma, Y., Baiyong, Cheng, W.: Analysis of Early Warning Systems Theory and Demon Stration of China's Export Trade. Commercial Research 1, 31–34 (2010)

Research on Regional Competitiveness—Based on Comparison between Wenzhou and Shaoxing

Xu Xu[1], Mengmeng Lin[2,*], Ying Jin[1], and Jingru Jia[2]

[1] Oujiang College of Wenzhou University, Wenzhou University,
[2] School of Mathematics and Information Science, Wenzhou University,
325035 Wenzhou, China
{373914774,948038726,573940050,825111024}@qq.com

Abstract. On account of construction idea of cluster competence GEM model, this paper establishes a regional competitiveness SAVPC model that can be evaluated in multi-angle (Strength system—Ability system—Vitality system—Potential system—Charm system), which will be beneficial for raising comprehensive evaluation value in consideration of balanced development of evaluation index. All original indexes are standardized according to data types as benefit type, cost type and ideal point type etc. First-level index and second-level index set weight by Analytic Hierarchy Process. Due to tremendous quantity of three-level index Entropy Method is applied to conduct objective empowerment, and SAVPC model is applied to make analysis and comparative research on competitiveness in Wenzhou and Shaoxing from 2003 to 2009. It can be shown from the research that regional competitiveness in the two areas rises steadily year by year. Because rise speed of Shaoxing in Ability system, Vitality system and Potential system is higher than that of Wenzhou; comprehensive competitiveness in Shaoxing catches up with and surpasses that in Wenzhou after 2007.

Keywords: Competitiveness, Entropy method, Wenzhou, Shaoxing.

1 Introduction

Regional competitiveness is a concept with definite and visualized meaning which cannot be grasped easily. Regional competitiveness can be regarded as an ability to attract and strive for resources reflected in development process of a region competing with other regions and an ability to continuously form regional competitive edge through optimizing and reasonably allocating existing resources so that the region can gain sustainable, comprehensive and coordinative development. The stronger the regional competitiveness is, the more strategic resources the region can gain, and then it can optimize and allocate resources more effectively so that economy and society develop faster. Regional competitiveness is a composite result of multiple abilities in a region, whose core is to create competitive advantage. In the thesis, the author plans to

* Corresponding author.

M. Zhou (Ed.): ISAEBD 2011, Part III, CCIS 210, pp. 286–294, 2011.

establish competitiveness evaluation model to analyze and compare competitiveness with Wenzhou and Shaoxing as an example.

2 Regional Competitiveness Evaluation Index System Design

Regional competitiveness is a complete and organic systematic institution, which can be estimated and measured through choosing and establishing a whole set of index system. Index design is a key factor for studying success or failure. There should be solid theory to support setting and choosing any measure index, otherwise, explanatory ability of index won't be strong. In current study references, there still many problems existing in choosing index, which are shown in metrizability and comparability of index data. Furthermore, internal relations and understanding hierarchy between indexes are insufficient. In the thesis, an evaluation system is established by explaining regional competitiveness from multiple levels and starting from the index system.

2.1 Index System Design Principles

In the thesis, the author strives for overcoming disadvantages in current research while choosing index keeping to the following four principles.

First is representativeness. Each index chosen in the index system can at least reflect certain basic characteristics of regional competitiveness in some aspects approximately to some extent and in a certain period.

Second is metrizability. All chosen indexes must be metrical and can gain date practically. Although some indexes are available in theory, they are lack of data source; or although data can be gained, the reliability is rather low; we would rather be lack of index so as to avoid subjective judgment replacing objective measurement. Data mainly comes from various different statistical indexes, expert assessment and evaluation is complemented in individual situation while using survey data in short of statistical data.

Third is comparability. From practical situation of regional development, index setting should not only comply with generality among regions but also reflect that regional competitiveness is a dynamic developing process, so that indexes have vertical comparability to broaden applicable scope of index system.

Fourth is understanding hierarchy. Because the index system is multi-level and multi-element compound, setting of indexes must subdivided gradually according to height of level and importance of function.

2.2 The Establishment of Index System

According to the evaluation purpose, task and evaluation objects of the regional competitiveness, we will determine several indicators that can fully reflect it, then constitute evaluation index system, which is the basis for comprehensive evaluation. This paper is aimed to find out the indexes meet the requirements, from the aspects of regional Strength system, ability system, Vitality system, potential system and charm system as a whole. The evaluation index system is established as shown in table 1.

Table 1. Evaluation index system of regional competitiveness

1-class indexes	2-class indexes	Weight	3-class indexes	Weight
Strength system Weight: 0.39	Developmental Level	0.42	GDP	0.3547
			GDP growth rate	0.2710
			Fiscal revenue	0.3743
	Economic Strength	0.27	Gross fixed investment volume	0.2988
			Per capita total retail sales of consumer goods	0.3403
			Number of above designated size industrial enterprises	0.3609
	Growth Performance	0.20	Per capita disposable income of urban residents	0.4877
			Per capita net income of rural residents	0.5123
	Infrastructure	0.11	Per capita households electricity consumption	0.3641
			Gross domestic volume of waterway passenger traffic and highway passenger traffic	0.3172
			Gross domestic harbor cargo throughput	0.3188
Ability System Weight: 0.23	Industry Gathered	0.30	Gross industrial output value	0.3353
			Investment in fixed assets	0.3233
			Investment from foreigners	0.3414
	Innovation Ability	0.54	Proportion of science and technology and exploration industry employment	0.4678
			Proportion of investment in science and technology of the GDP	0.5322
	Public Services	0.16	Number of inventions owned by per 10,000 persons	0.3128
			Number of doctors owned by per 10,000 persons	0.3443
			Total collections in public libraries per 10,000 persons	0.3429
Vitality system Weight: 0.21	Enterprise Vitality	0.40	Total profits of industrial enterprises	0.3494
			Proportion of above designated size industrial enterprises invested by foreigners or investors from Hong Kong, Macao and Taiwan	0.2654
			Proportion of tertiary industry of the GDP	0.3851
	Population Structure	0.40	Proportion of the employed population	0.3695
			Proportion of tertiary industry employment	0.3634
			Number of staff and workers	0.2671

Table 1. *(continued)*

	Information Efficiency	0.20	Number of Internet subscribers	0.5233
			Informatization level statistical values	0.4767
Potential System Weight: 0.08	Resource Sustainability	0.59	Sown area of farm crops	0.5360
			Loan balance(year-end)	0.4640
	Human Resource	0.41	Proportion of primary and secondary school students of the total	0.4111
			Number of college students per 10,000 persons	0.5889
Charm System Weight: 0.09	Tourism Atmosphere	0.16	Domestic tourists	0.5134
			International tourists	0.4866
	Public Culture	0.30	Theaters, cinemas and music halls owned by per million persons	0.5243
			Proportion of culture, sport and entertainment industry employment	0.4757
	Public Satisfaction	0.54	Average wages of fully employed staff and workers	0.3568
			Savings deposit balance of urban and rural residents(year-end)	0.3443
			Mass happiness index	0.2989

Note:3-class indexes weight are calculated by the related data of "Zhejiang Statistical Yearbook", "Wenzhou Statistical Yearbook" and "Shaoxing Statistical Yearbook" according to the listed steps in 2.3.

2.3 The Determination of Index Weight

2.3.1 Calculation of 1-Class Indexes Weight and 2-Class Indexes Weight

Analytical hierarchy process (AHP) is a method used for making decisions on some complex and fuzzy problems, especially for those difficult to be fully quantitative analyzed. In this paper, AHP is adopted to determine the weight of 1-class indexes and 2-class indexes. Firstly, we should construct the pairwise judgment matrix of 1-class indexes, as illustrated in table 2.

Table 2. Pairwise judgment matrix

	S	A	V	P	C	Geometric Mean
S	1.00	2.00	2.00	4.00	4.00	2.30
A	0.50	1.00	1.00	3.00	3.00	1.35
V	0.50	1.00	1.00	3.00	2.00	1.25
P	0.25	0.33	0.33	1.00	1.00	0.49
C	0.25	0.33	0.50	1.00	1.00	0.53

Note: S—Strength system, A—Ability system, V—Vitality system, P—Potential system, C—Charm system.

According to the calculation steps of AHP[1], 1-class indexes weight can be obtained. After consistency checking, CR=0.04868<0.1, so the result can be accepted.

Similarly, we can get the 1-class indexes weight values according to the AHP method, the fact that their consistency rate are all less than 0.1 pushes them through the consistency check.

2.3.2 Measure and Calculation of 3-Class Indexes weIght

(1) relativity analysis

Linear correlation degree can be divided into the following situations: when $|r| \geq 0.8$ it regarded to be related to high degree; when $0.5 \leq |r| < 0.8$, it regarded to be related to moderate degree; when $0.3 \leq |r| < 0.5$, it regarded to be related to low degree; when $|r| < 0.3$, correlation degree between variables is weak, which can be regarded as uncorrelated. The flowing conclusion can be gained through relevant analysis of SPSS towards initial 3-class indexes and by original data of Shaoxing and Wenzhou: if 3-class indexes data in all systems don't reach moderate correlation, it can be used to explain 2-class indexes; if there are few 3-class indexes with high correlation at the same time, which have certain persuasion to explain 2-class indexes, it should be kept because these indexes have different features.

(2) Positiveness and standardization of 3-class indexes

Because all 3-class indexes have different dimensions (for example, units of total industrial output value and employed population weight are different with great difference in data scope), we must conduct standardization and positiveness to all index data. In case of the corrupt practice that the standardization method that moderate high mark is too high while low mark is too low is generally in the theory circle (the highest mark is 1, the lowest mark is only 0) and in order to ensure goodness of standardized data, the minimum adjusting parameter B is introduced in standardization process, the following model is established:

$$f(v_{ij}^{t})=\begin{cases} \dfrac{v_{ij}^{t}}{H}, & v_{ij}^{t} \text{ is the qualitative language evaluation index value of level } H \\ \dfrac{H-B}{H}\cdot\dfrac{v_{ij}^{t}-\min\limits_{t} v_{ij}^{t}}{\max\limits_{t} v_{ij}^{t}-\min\limits_{t} v_{ij}^{t}}\cdot\dfrac{\max\limits_{t} v_{ij}^{t}}{u_{ij}}+\dfrac{B}{H}, & v_{ij}^{t} \text{ is the benefit type rational index value} \\ \dfrac{H-B}{H}\cdot\dfrac{\max\limits_{t} v_{ij}^{t}-v_{ij}^{t}}{\max\limits_{t} v_{ij}^{t}-\min\limits_{t} v_{ij}^{t}}\cdot\dfrac{u_{ij}}{\min\limits_{t} v_{ij}^{t}}+\dfrac{B}{H}, & v_{ij}^{t} \text{ is the cost type rational index value} \\ \dfrac{H-B}{H}\cdot\left(1-\dfrac{|v_{ij}^{t}-u_{ij}|}{\max\limits_{t}|v_{ij}^{t}-u_{ij}|}\right)+\dfrac{B}{H}, & v_{ij}^{t} \text{ is the ideal point index value of } u_{ij} \end{cases} \tag{1}$$

In the above formula: v_{ij}^{t} : year t, evaluation value of index i in factor j ; $f(v_{ij}^{t})$ standardization value of v_{ij}^{t} ; v_{ij}^{t} is divided into 3 types, among which the larger the benefit type rational index value is, the better it is, while the smaller the cost type rational index value is, the better it is, the closer the ideal point index value is, the better it is. u_{ij} is ideal value of index i in factor j ; H : progression of qualitative language evaluation index. Seven-level evaluation system is applied in the thesis:

$H = 7$, among which: very good=7, good=6, fair=5, moderate=4, a little bad=3, bad=2, very bad=1. $\max_t v_{ij}^t$ and $\min_t v_{ij}^t$ is the maximum value and the minimum value of v_{ij}^t in evaluation circle respectively. B: the minimum adjusting parameter.

(3) Entropy Method

Entropy Method[2] (Entropy Method) is a kind of objective empowering method. Given that there are n schemes need evaluating and m evaluation indexes, forming original index evaluation matrix $V = (v_{ij})_{n \times m}$, then the following treatment is made according to formula (1) :

The first is to confirm property of three-level index; the original index evaluation matrix should be positive and standardized by formula (1) according to t. Because the index number is tremendous according to time sequence, the benefit type index is standardized by formula (2) .

$$f(v_{ij}) = c_1 \times \frac{v_{ij} - \min v_{ij}}{\max v_{ij} - \min v_{ij}} \times c_2 + c_3 \tag{2}$$

Given that $H = 7$, $B = 4.2$, $c_1 = 0.4$, $c_2 = \frac{\max v_{ij}}{u_{ij}}$, $c_3 = 0.6$ in formula (1) . In consideration of complexity measured and calculated at ideal point, make simplified treatment, get the maximum index value over the years only 92% of ideal value, namely $c_2 = 0.92$. And so forth the cost type index etc. Next, weight of index i in factor j can be calculated: $p_{ij} = f(v_{ij}) / \sum_{j=1}^{n} f(v_{ij})$; thirdly, entropy value of index i in factor j can be calculated: $e_j = k \sum_{i=1}^{N_i} p_{ij} \ln p_{ij}$ •among which $k = 1/\ln N$; Finally, weight of entropy value of index i in factor j can be calculated: $\omega_j = (1-e_j) / \sum_{j=1}^{N_i} (1-e_j)$.

(4) Entropy Method determines 3-class indexes weight

Among original data of relevant indexes of regional competitiveness in Wenzhou and Shaoxing from 2003 to 2009, except that happiness index comes from massive questionnaire in the two regions, other data all comes from various yearbooks and official websites. As for individual missing data, the evaluation value can be gained through known data interpolation, regression forecasting or time sequence forecasting, 3-class indexes weight of regional competitiveness can be confirmed according to 3-class indexes weight algorithm---Entropy Method. Furthermore, in the 3-class indexes, except that the happiness index is language evaluation index (from 1 score to 7 scores), other indexes are all benefit type indexes. The large the index value is, the better it is. Standardize all original data by formula (1) - (2) , then the three-level index weight based on data in Wenzhou and Shaoxing can be gained by

Entropy Method. It can be inferred by testing data in different places the there is no obvious difference in all weights, thus, the 3-class indexes weight takes average value of measured and calculated value of the two samples, which is shown in the last row in table 1.

2.4 Evaluation Model Construction of Regional Competitiveness—SAVPC Model

Two Canadian scholars Padmore and Gibson (1998) have made improvement to Diamond Model[3] of Potter based on his research, who establishes GEM model (groundings-enterprises-markets, for short of GEM model)[4] suitable for cluster competitiveness evaluation form quantitative angle. In concrete evaluation and calculation process, they scored 6 factors involving in GEM model with cluster competition in worldwide scope form 1 to 10 and established experience formula to calculate gross scores of certain industrial cluster competitiveness. In the thesis, the author mirrors partial thinking and principles of GEM evaluation model to improve subjective marking to quantitative evaluation of statistical data, and establishes brand-new regional competitiveness evaluation model SAVPC model.

Regional competitiveness is determined by five 1-class indexes, in consideration of good regional competitiveness of all indexes with balanced development, if one index value is small in five 1-class indexes in one city, although other four indexes are large, they can weaken whole residence-comfort degree greatly, thus, SAVPC model doesn't apply traditional simple method of weighted mean. All 2-class indexes have complementary relation with the whole residence-comfort degree, which can effectively evaluate 3-class indexes after weighting. According to 5 1-class indexes, 15 2-class indexes and 39 3-class indexes, the evaluation model of regional competitiveness is established as follows:

$$SAVPC(t) = 100\left\{\prod_{i=1}^{5}[\sum_{j=1}^{M_i}\rho_{ij}\sum_{k=1}^{N_{ij}}\omega_{ijk} f(v_{ijk}{}^{t})]^{a_i}\right\}^{\frac{1}{5}} \tag{3}$$

Among which $\sum_{j=1}^{M_i}\rho_{ij} = 1; \sum_{k=1}^{N_{ij}}\omega_{ijk} = 1, (i = 1,2,3,4,5;\ j = 1,2,\cdots,15); \sum_{i=1}^{5} a_i = 5;$ a_i is adjusting parameter of the model, namely revision weight parameter of 1-class indexes. According to characteristics of the model and weight of 1-class indexes, we can suppose $(a_1, a_2, a_3, a_4, a_5) = (1.943,1.143,1.053,0.413,0.448)$. $f(v_{ij}{}^{t})$ is evaluation value of 2-class indexes after standardization; ω_{ijk} is weight of the 3-class index k of 2-class indexes j under 1-class index i ; ρ_{ij} is weight of 2-class index j under 1-class index i .

According to construction and design method of SAVPC model, it can be thought that: over 90, the regional competitiveness is very good; 80-90, the regional competitiveness is good; 70-80, the regional competitiveness is fair; 60-70, the regional competitiveness is a little bad; 50-60, the regional competitiveness is bad; below 50, the regional competitiveness is very bad.

3 Comparative Study on Regional Competitiveness in Wenzhou and Shaoxing

Over the past 30 years since the reform and open up, Wenzhou has created a developing road suitable for local practice under disadvantageous natural resource, location and original economic basis and an area with the fastest economic growth and the most vigorous privately-owned economy in China, whose economic and social development has won achievements attracting worldwide attention. From 1978 to 2009, total output value in the whole city rose from 1322 million Yuan to 2.52788 billion Yuan, ranking the 3rd place after Hangzhou and Ningbo. However, its GDP per Capita in Wenzhou was only 32,595 Yuan in 2009, ranking the 9th in 11 cities in Zhejiang Province. While its brother city Shaoxing has developed gradually and surpassed Wenzhou in the primary industry and secondary industry with rising rank of all indexes, which showed fierce regional competitiveness. In this paper, Wenzhou and Shaoxing City, as the research objects, have good comparability.

According to the formula (1) - (3), firstly, calculate the value of all 2-class indexes, then the 1-class indexes and finally the SAVPC value of the index system, as shown in table 3.

Table 3. SAVPC value of the index system

Year	Strength System		Ability System		Vitality System		Potential System		Charm System		SAVPC Value	
	WZ	SX	WZ	SX	WZ	SX	WZ	SX	WZ	SX	WZ	SX
2003	63.23	66.41	65.17	62.34	64.21	61.57	79.58	65.55	69.01	66.06	65.61	64.32
2004	66.66	69.02	72.41	73.80	70.18	68.07	77.81	68.96	72.04	75.96	70.04	70.48
2005	72.05	71.69	78.60	72.83	79.16	66.64	74.53	73.05	74.34	75.66	75.39	71.30
2006	77.83	78.39	89.01	78.75	81.09	74.80	72.32	79.56	77.96	77.99	80.47	77.76
2007	85.77	85.99	84.17	84.46	79.55	78.99	71.67	80.04	79.61	83.05	82.27	83.36
2008	89.89	90.37	82.12	83.38	84.15	83.00	75.23	88.68	80.92	82.82	84.77	86.33
2009	92.57	89.82	83.60	91.92	89.08	92.39	77.22	94.78	86.56	85.34	87.85	90.82

Note: WZ—Wenzhou, SX—shaoxing. The data listed are calculated by the related raw data according to "Zhejiang Statistical Yearbook", "Wenzhou Statistical Yearbook" and "Shaoxing Statistical Yearbook".

It can be seen in table 5 that comprehensive evaluation values of Wenzhou and Shaoxing in Strength system, Ability system, Vitality system, Potential system and Charm system have been rising year by year. Comprehensive regional competitiveness in Wenzhou rose from 65.61 scores to 87.85 scores from 2003 to 2009, while that in Shaoxing rose from 64.32 scores to 90.82 scores. Regional competitiveness in two regions has been raised greatly with obvious fast speed. To put in detail, except that the evaluation value of Charm system in both cities has made no distinction of rank over the years, Wenzhou has surpassed Shaoxing in Strength system a little, while in Ability system, Vitality system and Potential system, Shaoxing surpassed Wenzhou; especially in Ability system and Potential system, Wenzhou has been developing from superior position in 2003 to inferior position in 2009 with an obvious distance with Shaoxing, which has been also a major reason for Wenzhou to fall behind Shaoxing in comprehensive competitiveness since 2007.

Acknowledgments. The authors acknowledge the financial support of the Project of Soft Science of Zhejiang (2010C35048), the Cultural Project of Wenzhou (Wyk10009), the Project of Science & Technology of Wenzhou (R20090065), Scientific Research Fund of Zhejiang Provincial Education Department (Y200906547) and the Science and Technology Innovation Program for Undergraduates of Zhejiang province. The authors are also very grateful to the strong support of Professor Zhu Kangdui.

References

1. Wang, Xu, S.: The theory of analytic hierarchy process. China renmin university press, Beijing (1990)
2. Xie, C., Zhong, Z.: Entropy method and its application in comprehensive evaluation of bank's performance. China Soft Science 9(22), 810–811 (2002)
3. Porter, M.: National competitive advantage. polity press, Beijing (2002)
4. Tim, P., Hervey, G.: Modeling system of innovation: A framework for industrial cluster analysis in regions. Research Policy 26, 635–641 (1998)

The Construction and Management of Trust Mechanism of Virtual Team: Based on Lifecycle Analysis

Yanchun Zou, Man Huang, and Yingyuan Wu

Business School, Guangzhou University
Guangzhou, China

Abstract. Virtual team refers to a new formation of team with a common goal and it relies on information technology as its working media, over time limits, space distance and organization boundary. With the integration of the world economy and the rapid development of information technology, more and more organizations are using virtual team as a working model. In virtual team management, trust mechanism management become important, since the construction and maintenance of trust mechanism will effectively affect the success of virtual team. This research studies virtual team based on life cycle model—corresponding methods of constructing and managing trust mechanism under different life stages are proposed, which aim to provide practical strategies for effective management for virtual team.

Keywords: virtual team, Trust mechanism, Life cycle.

1 Introduction

Peter Drucker predicted on future enterprise as the following: today's work is done by different functional departments, will be completed by some special "task-oriented team" tomorrow. Functional departments will serve as enterprise resource, technology and personnel's base and product standards providers and existence, and by the group to manage projects from start to push to the market process.

Virtual team as a product of knowledge economy and information technology, it is one of the most important organizational forms. At present, the domestic and international academic field has formed basic consensus toward virtual team—they regard virtual team as a brand new formation of team with common goal, which relies on information technology as its working media, and span time limits, space distance and organization boundary. The application of internet and computer provides the material basis of virtual team; the world economic integration and globalization accelerated the development process of virtual team; the emergence of knowledge workers for provides human resources support.

Since its unique organization form of virtual team, most scholars concur that trust mechanism should be the key for virtual team management. Virtual team should have trust relations as a basis, and then can let members in the team bring out their advantages in order to accomplish the cooperation. This research studies virtual team

M. Zhou (Ed.): ISAEBD 2011, Part III, CCIS 210, pp. 295–301, 2011.

based on life cycle model—corresponding methods of constructing and managing trust mechanism under different life stages are proposed, which aim to provide practical strategies for effective management for virtual team.

2 The Connotation of Virtual Team Trust Mechanism

Trust is a complicated social psychological phenomenon, psychologists Rotter regard a person's life experiences and views on humanity would make the formation of degree of trust and belief toward other people. Management experts Stephen .P. Robbins views the trust is between team members of their respective integrity, personality characteristics and working ability. At present, more accepted from for understanding trust is: trust is the fairness, reliability and faith for individuals or groups, regardless of whether they have the ability to monitor others behavior, believe that the other party will perform specific expected behavior, and put themselves at undefended state.

By synthesizing various aspects, this paper proposes three key elements of virtual teams:

Trust subject. Virtual team members are the first element of trust formation. Their personal knowledge, ability, background, personal factors will become the key for whether they could be trusted.

Trust object. Virtual members need common task for trust goal, that is, it is the common goal for all the members.

Trust approach. Trust approach refers to the approach which built to construct trust relationship among trust subjects. For example, members use internet as the approach to understand each other's personal reputation and field advantage, corresponding psychological identity can be made although they have never met.

3 The Life Cycle Model of Virtual Team and Key Tasks in Each Stage

This paper proposed the following virtual team life cycle model and various stages of key tasks on the basis of this analysis as below.

Graph 1. The life cycle model of virtual team

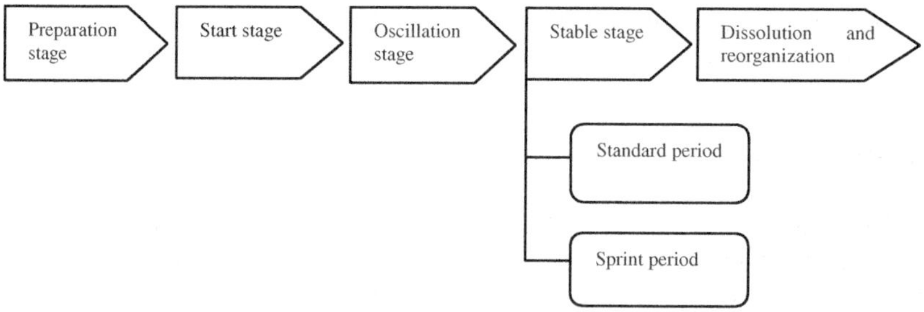

Life cycle	Key tasks
Preparation stage	choose members, task design, compensation system, technical selection, organization fusion
Beginning stage	start work, familiar with team members, clear objectives, setting team work rules, staff training
Oscillation stage	solve conflicts, standardize agenda, incentives, knowledge management
Stable stage	summary previous experience, knowledge management and incentive measures, complete the task
Dissolution and reorganization stage	performance assessment appraisal, commitment, team recombined

Fig. 1. Key tasks of virtual team in each stage

4 Construction and Management of Trust Mechanism in Different Lifecycle Stages

Based on the proposed virtual team life cycle model and relevant literature reviews, Corresponding methods and strategies of constructing and managing trust mechanism under different life stages are proposed.

4.1 Trust Mechanism in the Preparation Stage

The most important job in preparation stage is to select team members. Virtual team member's personal skills and knowledge to complete the task must satisfy the requirements, while the combination of all individuals to produce coordination effect, namely 1 + 1 + 1 > 3 effect. Aiming at this stage, this paper suggests the following:

First, it is important to select the high tendency of trust members in virtual team. The trust is the tendency to trust in the relatively stable personality factor, the difference in having individual interpersonal trust, early life experience makes people establish the preliminary to others the general concepts. High credibility of virtual team member's trust will benefit the establishment of the trust. The related credibility test software or assessment measurements can be used to test the trust tendency among the candidates. Meanwhile, studies have found that those with virtual team work experience with those are not, are relatively have faster heterogeneity Therefore, former experiences is the important factor when choosing members.

Secondly, establishing clear task allocation and incentive distribution system. Clear task allocation can help members to build their orientation, and foster members of each division to understand factors of instability. In addition, there is usually a divergence of interests, which hinders member's collaboration. Hence, establishing a clear interest distribution system can let members know virtual team insiders interests is consistent, does not exist the overall interests of the differences.

4.2 Trust Mechanism in the Start Stage

Start stage is the beginning of virtual team, the main tasks including: team members get to know each other, description of team goal, and regulation of internal.

Hold face-to-face forums. This is to make the team members to establish the first impression in the early stage. Let members know each other and to get to know the team, the division within the conflict can reduce the operating process. Symposium on the virtual team can task and goal, division of labor, the system to members account etc.

Develop short-term training program. Training can enhance virtual team member's trust tendency, improve their work skills, and improve the recognition, vision of cultural understanding each other, so as to promote the communication between members. Training courses include: strengthening the training of members, enhance trust tendency of Shared vision, enhance the training objective identification of cultural understanding training etc.

Remind for substance. It refers to a virtual team can use material objects to remind members that they are in the team. It eliminates loneliness and anxiety, can strengthen members' sense of collective and trust. Material objects include: collective photo, collective memorial value items, collective video etc.

4.3 Trust Mechanism in the Oscillation Stage

Whether it is the traditional team or the virtual team, they have to undergo break-in stage, and must get through effective management mechanism to smooth the transition. The main auxiliary team includes: the objective between environment and members, and conflicts between members. The former refers to the members of the team of the procedure, the system within and working conditions restrict the objective environment does not agree with or not adapt to the conflicts caused. The latter is due to the differences of the members of the conflict, for example: cultural clashes. At this time, member needs the proper guidance mechanism; this paper has the following Suggestions.

According to the objective environment and produced between members of the conflict, the team through "a core can help a few" form to accelerate members of their familiarity with the team environment. Virtual team organization can form as below:

Graph 2. The organizational structure of virtual team

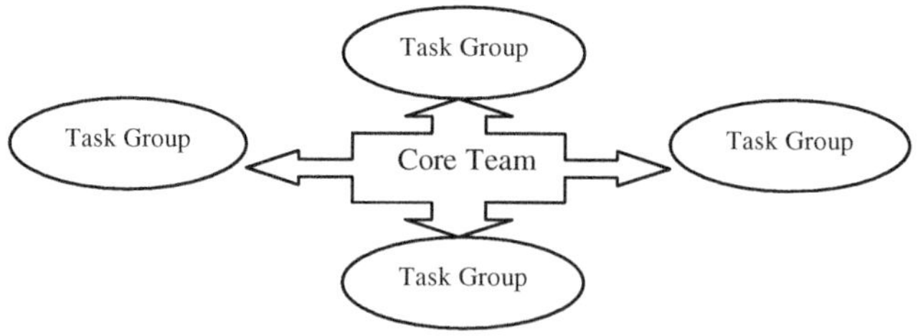

The core personnel are those senior staff with better cooperation experience, familiar with the operational mechanism and with high tendency of trust. They are responsible for providing timely resolution methods for different task groups the conflicts happen.

At the same time, establishing the efficient communication mechanism is the key to reduce risk of conflict; virtual team can establish an effective mechanism through the following ways:

Fulfill the role of information technology media. Through the phone, email, chat rooms, online bulletin boards, regular briefing, members of the public information exchange personal space and various forms to increase the number of member's communication.

Pay more attention to informal communication. Informal communication can best practiced through emotional communication between members of the party by travelling, celebration dinner, individual special events, such as marriage etc.

Improve the effectiveness of the official communication. Compared with the face-to-face communication, there is a problem by using media communication—the effectiveness of the communication error is difficult to solve, especially in different culture backgrounds. Hence, team members' standards toward media response should be standard, in order to reduce consensus between different regional cultures which produced obstacles. Reply to standard should consider the following elements: in what way after an acceptance due records and instant reply whether; to solve the problem of how to temporarily unable to answer, for example, can be simple reply after formally reply to the agreed time, etc.

4.4 Trust Mechanism in the Stable Stage

When virtual team entered the development of stable stage, it can be differentiated into two phases: the former part of stable stage— from the fierce oscillation into a leveled off stage, can be called standard period stage. And the second half time is sprint period, this phase commonly occur in team members when it is nearing completion of task before work efficiency is very high, the team have the collective sense of pride and problem solving process will encourage each other to help. Performance of virtual teams of each stage will peak at this stage, but trust still need the appropriate mechanism to maintenance. This stage in this paper has the following advices:

Summaries experience and form in-depth consensus. After oscillation stage, virtual team internal conflict decrease, but does not exclude the potential conflict will suddenly erupted. Virtual team needs to solve the conflicts summarize experience, including: institutional processes, team management, members of conflict, task process, etc. Put this experience through various channels to every member communicated through the Internet, for example: a summary released, face-to-face meetings, written documents as the problems and solutions form statement clearly.

Sublimate foundation trust relationship. Sprint period is t the golden period of the whole life cycle. Task progress and human relations are in the development peak. Team leader need to pay special attention to the trust between members to promote task progress and team performance in this phase. Trust is a mode of operation and material capital different spiritual resources, trust and its use, and the more people is proportional to the use of resources, trust will be more secure, if you don't use it, trust will dry up. Virtual team should notice to use crisis core means such as target motivation incentive and stimulate between members of team members centripetal force, through between a high level of trust and cooperation to promote team combat effectiveness.

4.5 Trust Mechanism in the Dissolution and Reorganization Stage

The main task of this phase is to stable hearts and feeling of members', and to avoid anticlimactic phenomenon. The core personnel of the team should be actively arrange the parties undertake each member's work, and the key is to fulfill the agreement such as cash commitment and to enhance the team members to the virtual team of trust, improve work enthusiasm. This paper has the following Suggestions:

Maintain the fair distribution of incentives. Virtual team dissolved stage to avoid in the distribution of interests conflict because the trust between members of destruction. The main measures to maintain trust is the guarantee of fair distribution of interests of the members, the reasonable cash commitment, etc. Interest distribution should and the specific performance appraisal members and combining the performance of evaluation criteria should be work, work behavior and characteristics of the organic unity. Members the work product completed work include: the quality of the finished product, submit time, customer satisfaction, and use of the cost, etc. Work behavior index includes: team in activities, the degree of efforts to complete the task. Members of the indicators include: characteristics of commitment, care for members, co-operative, etc.

Disband the former team meaningfully. After the first four stages of cooperation, virtual team members have established trust relations, however, when the members foreseen when the team is dissolved, trust relationship will be dissolved by the negative impact at this stage, members' innermost feelings respectively is: both the sadness, and including separation for the achievements and feel proud and proud. If this mood does not back to normal in a short time, it will affect the new job. Therefore, at this stage, in order to maintain the trust relationship, core team can arrange the necessary review meeting, celebration dinner, the collective travel and other activities. So, the trust relationship between members will further deepen cooperation for the next opportunity to continue playing good foundation.

Restructure virtual team based on early success. In a virtual team before completion of the tasks, both members of the former team have to evaluate and maintain, or add new members. The restructuring of the virtual team is team development and team to complete the needs of different tasks. At this stage, the new virtual team each core members of staff should assess to arrange task and new members of the distribution of future, in order to maintain a formed before the life cycle motivation and satisfaction. Have accumulated trust relationships before as basis, restructuring of the virtual team will run more efficiently.

To sum up, this paper researches the trust mechanism based on virtual team in the life cycle model, however the discussion is just a tip of the iceberg. The future direction of the research and research method will further developed. We hope there will be more effective management paths of trust mechanism analysis of future virtual team, and make the virtual team can be adopted by more enterprises.

References

1. Peters, L.M., Manz, C.C.: Team Performance Management Identifying tecedents of virtual team collaboration 13(3/4) (2007)
2. Ubell, R.: Virtual team learning. Development and Learning in Organizations 25(1) (2011)

3. Xiao, W.: Virtual team organization and management analysis of typical problems. Journal of Modern Management Science (February 2006)
4. Song, Y.: On the basis of human resource management of virtual team based on trust. Journal of Academic Exchanges (January 2007)
5. Bao, G.X., Qing, S.: Construct high performance the knowledge team strategy. Journal of Chinese Science (April 2010)
6. Pedro, S.R.: Virtual team management life cycle model. Analysis Technology Management Innovation (December 2006)
7. Tang, Y.N.: Virtual team study: reviews, analysis and prospects. Word-Occurrence Frequencies (February 24 ,2006)
8. He, Y.: Virtual team management: core problem. Journal of Enterprise Management and Information Technology (2002)
9. Cheng, J.L.: Foreign virtual team present research situation and development trend of modern management. Science (2006)
10. Hu, M.: Multinational virtual team challenges and countermeasures: a case analysis. Journal of Modern Management Science (2006)
11. Ma, Y., shenzhen: Trust in the virtual team. Progress Psychological Science (2) (December 2004)
12. Deng, J.S.: Virtual team life cycle. The trust management study. Journal of Sun Yat-Sen University (2004)
13. Virtual team at Nike the theory and case. economic management press, beijing (2003)
14. Zhang, X.L., Bao, G.X.: Based on service scientific virtual enterprise trust mechanism study. Business Research (2011)

Ordering Policy for Deteriorating Items with In-Transit Deterioration and Permissible Delay in Payments

Fangjie Chen, Tao Jia, and Yi Zheng

Department of Industrial Engineering, School of Management,
Xi'an Jiaotong University, Xi'an, 710049, P.R. China
{fangjie.chan,zhengyi}@stu.xjtu.edu.cn, jiatao@mail.xjtu.edu.cn

Abstract. In the classical deterministic models of inventory replenishment policies for the deteriorating items, the in-transit deterioration is seldom considered. However, in practices, the length of lead time has a significant impact on the extent of deterioration of the fresh items. The paper proposes an inventory model in which products deteriorate in both in-transit and on-hand period with different deterioration rates under permissible delay of payment. Different facets of the permissible delays in payment were discussed. It is proved that there exists unique optimal ordering cycle to minimize the annual cost under every scenario. Numerical examples were conducted to illustrate the effectiveness of the proposed model. Results show that the optimal ordering cycle is affected by the length of lead time and the deterioration rates, as well as the credit period.

Keywords: deterioration rate, transportation time, delay payments.

1 Introduction and Literature Review

Deteriorating items widely exist in our daily life, such as fruits, vegetables, seafood, etc, which will damage, spoil, decay or vaporize during their delivery and storage stage. People's appetite for high quality deteriorating items is continually upgrading rapidly, so it's more and more popular a topic to study the replenishment policy for deteriorating inventory systems. Ghare and Schrader [1] firstly proposed a no-shortage model for an exponentially decaying inventory with constant decaying rate. Covert and Philip [2] extended the constant deterioration rate to a two parameter Weibull distribution. Then, researchers started to consider other factors, like trade credit, for deteriorating inventory replenishment problem. Aggarwal and Jaggi [3] introduced trade credit to a deteriorating inventory model. They assumed that interest was earned on the revenue received within trade credit, and that interest was charged beyond this period. Based on Aggarwal and Jaggi's model, Chuang and Liao [4] assumed that delay in payments should depend on the ordering quantity and incorporated discounted cash-flows approach. Chang and Dye [5] dealt with a varying deterioration rate problem, and proposed an inventory model with partial backlogging rate under the condition of permissible delay in payments. Chang et al. [6] gave an algorithm to find the optimal solution for deteriorating inventory model with permissible delay in

M. Zhou (Ed.): ISAEBD 2011, Part III, CCIS 210, pp. 302–309, 2011.

payments. Liao [7] further analyzed Chang et al.'s model and provided an accurate and rapid algorithm.

Lead time is the length of time between the time when an order is placed and when it is actually available for customers. [8] The length of lead time will affect the policies of ordering, distribution and storage, and it should be taken into consideration. Liao and Shyu [9] developed an inventory model in which piecewise linear function was used between crashing cost and the length of lead time. Ben-Daya and Raouf [10] extended Liao and Shyu's model by considering both lead time and the order quantity as decision variables, and assumed that lead time could be reduced at the expense of an additional cost. Besides, the effect of lead time control was incorporated in the joint economic lot sizing problem (JELP). Goyal [11] was the first proponent for introducing a deterministic JELP model with the assumptions of infinite production rate and lot-for-lot considering customer's order time. Yang [12] built an JILP model with lead time crashing decision, where crashing cost and the length of lead time follow a power function, thus the relationship between time value and the length of lead time was considered. Chen et al. [13] established a JELP model with nonlinear lead time crashing cost and lost sales. In the existing literatures of deterministic inventory replenishment models, in-transit deterioration is seldom considered. In practical situations, however, it plays an important role in making inventory replenishment decisions. So, taking the in-transit deteriorating cost into account for the lot size decision making problem has theoretical and realistic significance.

We extend Chang's [5] inventory model by considering in-transit deterioration with the assumption that the ordering cost is a linear function of transportation time [14], and formulate an inventory model for deteriorating items with in-transit deterioration and permissible delay in payments. The goal of this paper is to find the unique optimal solution to minimize the total annual cost. Numerical example is given to illustrate the impact of in-transit deterioration on optimal inventory policy and total annual cost.

2 Mathematical Model

The fundamental assumptions and notations used in the study are as follows:

(1)There exists a lead time t_d before the goods arrive at retailer. During t_d goods deteriorate at the rate of $\theta_1 (0 \le \theta_1 < 1)$, and the deteriorated cost is carried by retailer.

(2)The demand rate of the on-hand inventory is a constant α, and the deteriorating rate is a constant $\theta_2 (0 \le \theta_2 < 1)$ during the sales cycle.

(3)The supplier provides the retailer a fixed credit period M. Within the period M, the retailer can use the sale revenue to earn the interest with an annual rate I_e. However, beyond M, the product still in stock is assumed to be financed with an annual rate I_r, where $I_r \ge I_e$.

(4)Carrying cost per unit per year is h, unit purchase price is c, fixed transportation cost per shipment is F, order processing cost per unit time is u, transportation cost per unit is S, order quantity from the vendor is Q_0, and reorder cycle is T which is decision variable.

(5)Shortages are not allowed.

During the sales cycle T, the inventory level $I(t)$ gradually decreases owning to demands and deterioration, and it could be represented by

$$\frac{\mathrm{d}I(t)}{\mathrm{d}t} = -\theta_2 I(t) - \alpha \ . \tag{1}$$

With the boundary condition $I(T)$=0, the solution of (1) is given by

$$I(t) = \frac{\alpha}{\theta_2}[\mathrm{e}^{\theta_2 (T-t)} - 1] \ . \tag{2}$$

Then the scheduled receipt quantity for each cycle is

$$Q = I(0) = \frac{\alpha}{\theta_2}(\mathrm{e}^{\theta_2 T} - 1) \ . \tag{3}$$

During the transportation time t_d, the inventory level decreases due to deterioration only, thus we have differential equation as

$$\frac{\mathrm{d}I_1(t)}{\mathrm{d}t} = -\theta_1 I_1(t) \ . \tag{4}$$

Considering the boundary condition $I_1(t_d) = Q = \alpha(\mathrm{e}^{\theta_2 T} - 1)/\theta_2$, the solution of (4) is

$$I_1(t) = \frac{\alpha}{\theta_2}(\mathrm{e}^{\theta_2 T} - 1)\mathrm{e}^{\theta_1 (t_d - t)} \ . \tag{5}$$

Let t=0 in (5), the actual order quantity from the vendor is

$$Q_0 = I_1(0) = \frac{\alpha}{\theta_2}(\mathrm{e}^{\theta_2 T} - 1)\mathrm{e}^{\theta_1 t_d} \ . \tag{6}$$

Ordering cost per cycle consists of the fixed transportation cost and time-related order processing cost [14], thus it could be represented as $F + ut_d$.

Deteriorated cost per cycle (including deterioration in transit and on-hand) is

$$c(Q_0 - \alpha T) = c\frac{\alpha}{\theta_2}(\mathrm{e}^{\theta_2 T} - 1)\mathrm{e}^{\theta_1 t_d} - c\alpha T \ .$$

Holding cost in transit per cycle is $h\int_0^{t_d} I_1(t)dt = h\frac{\alpha}{\theta_1\theta_2}(\mathrm{e}^{\theta_2 T} - 1)(\mathrm{e}^{\theta_1 t_d} - 1)$.

Holding cost on-hand per cycle is $h\int_0^{T} I(t)dt = h\frac{\alpha}{\theta_2^2}(\mathrm{e}^{\theta_2 T} - \theta_2 T - 1)$.

Purchasing cost per cycle is $cQ_0 = c\frac{\alpha}{\theta_2}(\mathrm{e}^{\theta_2 T} - 1)\mathrm{e}^{\theta_1 t_d}$.

Freight cost per cycle is $SQ_0 = S\frac{\alpha}{\theta_2}(\mathrm{e}^{\theta_2 T} - 1)\mathrm{e}^{\theta_1 t_d}$.

The sales revenue could earn interest within the fixed credit period *M*; meanwhile, the product still in stock is financed beyond *M*.

Considering the interest earned in the case of $T \le M$, it can be expressed as $cI_e[\int_0^T \alpha t dt + \alpha T(M-T)] = cI_e \alpha T(M - T/2)$, and in the case of $M < T$, it can be expressed as $cI_e \int_0^M \alpha t dt = cI_e \alpha M^2/2$.

Beyond the fixed credit period, in the case of $T \le M$, there is no interest to pay, when $M < T$, the interest payable is $cI_k \int_M^T I(t)dt = cI_k \frac{\alpha}{\theta_2^2}[\mathrm{e}^{\theta_2(T-M)} - \theta_2(T-M) - 1]$.

Hence, in the case of $T \le M$, the average relevant cost per year is

$$\begin{aligned}\pi_1(T) = {} & \frac{F+ut_d}{T} + c\frac{\alpha}{T\theta_2}(\mathrm{e}^{\theta_2 T}-1)\mathrm{e}^{\theta_1 t_d} - c\alpha + h\frac{\alpha}{T\theta_1\theta_2}(\mathrm{e}^{\theta_2 T}-1)(\mathrm{e}^{\theta_1 t_d}-1) \\ & + h\frac{\alpha}{T\theta_2^2}(\mathrm{e}^{\theta_2 T} - \theta_2 T - 1) + (c+S)\frac{\alpha}{T\theta_2}(\mathrm{e}^{\theta_2 T}-1)\mathrm{e}^{\theta_1 t_d} - cI_e\alpha(M - \frac{T}{2}).\end{aligned} \tag{7}$$

In the case of $M < T$, the average relevant cost per year is

$$\begin{aligned}\pi_2(T) = {} & \frac{F+ut_d}{T} + c\frac{\alpha}{T\theta_2}(\mathrm{e}^{\theta_2 T}-1)\mathrm{e}^{\theta_1 t_d} - c\alpha + h\frac{\alpha}{T\theta_1\theta_2}(\mathrm{e}^{\theta_2 T}-1)(\mathrm{e}^{\theta_1 t_d}-1) \\ & + h\frac{\alpha}{T\theta_2^2}(\mathrm{e}^{\theta_2 T} - \theta_2 T - 1) + (c+S)\frac{\alpha}{T\theta_2}(e^{\theta_2 T}-1)e^{\theta_1 t_d} \\ & - cI_e\frac{\alpha M^2}{2T} + \frac{cI_k\alpha}{T\theta_2^2}[e^{\theta_2(T-M)} - \theta_2(T-M) - 1].\end{aligned} \tag{8}$$

3 Solution Analysis

Case 1: $T \le M$

Now, to minimize average total inventory cost per unit time, take the first and second derivation of $\pi_1(T)$ with respect to *T*, we have

$$\begin{aligned}\pi_1' = {} & -\frac{F+ut_d}{T^2} - \frac{c\alpha(\mathrm{e}^{T\theta_2}-1)\mathrm{e}^{\theta_1 t_d}}{T^2\theta_2} - \frac{h\alpha(\mathrm{e}^{T\theta_2}-1-T\theta_2)}{T^2\theta_2} \\ & - \frac{(c+S)\alpha(\mathrm{e}^{T\theta_2}-1)\mathrm{e}^{\theta_1 t_d}}{T^2\theta_2} - \frac{h\alpha(\mathrm{e}^{\theta_1 t_d}-1)(\mathrm{e}^{T\theta_2}-1)}{T^2\theta_1\theta_2} \\ & + \frac{h\alpha(\mathrm{e}^{\theta_1 t_d}-1)\mathrm{e}^{T\theta_2}}{T\theta_1} + \frac{h\alpha(\mathrm{e}^{T\theta_2}-1)}{T\theta_2} + \frac{(2c+S)\alpha\mathrm{e}^{T\theta_2+\theta_1 t_d}}{T} + \frac{1}{2}cI_e\alpha.\end{aligned} \tag{9}$$

and $\pi_1''(T)=\dfrac{f_1(T)}{T^3\theta_2^{\ 2}\theta_1}$, where

$$\begin{aligned}f_1(T)=&2c\alpha\theta_2^{\ 3}e^{T\theta_2+\theta_1t_d}T^2\theta_1-2h\alpha\theta_2e^{T\theta_2}-2h\alpha\theta_1+2\theta_2^{\ 2}\theta_1ut_d-2h\alpha\theta_1T\theta_2e^{T\theta_2}\\&+2h\alpha\theta_1e^{T\theta_2}+\alpha\theta_2^{\ 3}e^{T\theta_2+\theta_1t_d}T^2\theta_1S+h\alpha e^{T\theta_2}T^2\theta_2^{\ 2}\theta_1-4c\alpha e^{T\theta_2+\theta_1t_d}T\theta_2^{\ 2}\theta_1\\&+2h\alpha\theta_2+2h\alpha\theta_2e^{T\theta_2+\theta_1t_d}-2\alpha e^{\theta_1t_d}\theta_2\theta_1S+2\theta_2^{\ 2}\theta_1F-4c\alpha e^{\theta_1t_d}\theta_2\theta_1\\&+4c\alpha e^{T\theta_2+\theta_1t_d}\theta_2\theta_1-h\alpha\theta_2^{\ 3}e^{T\theta_2}T^2+h\alpha\theta_2^{\ 3}e^{T\theta_2+\theta_1t_d}T^2+2h\alpha e^{T\theta_2}T\theta_2^{\ 2}\\&-2h\alpha e^{T\theta_2+\theta_1t_d}T\theta_2^{\ 2}-2h\alpha\theta_2e^{\theta_1t_d}+2\alpha e^{T\theta_2+\theta_1t_d}\theta_2\theta_1S-2\alpha e^{T\theta_2+\theta_1t_d}T\theta_2^{\ 2}\theta_1S.\end{aligned}\tag{10}$$

Taking the derivative of $f(T)$ with respect to T, we get

$$f_1'(T)=h\alpha\theta_2^{\ 4}e^{T\theta_2}T^2(e^{\theta_1t_d}-1)+\alpha\theta_2^{\ 3}e^{T\theta_2}T^2\theta_1(2c\theta_2e^{\theta_1t_d}+\theta_2e^{\theta_1t_d}S+h)>0\ .\tag{11}$$

So $f(T)$ is increasing function of T in the interval $(0,+\infty)$. Moreover from (10) we know that $\lim_{T\to0}f_1(T)=2\theta_2^{\ 2}\theta_1ut_d+2\theta_2^{\ 2}\theta_1F>0$. Thus we can conclude that $\pi_1''(T)>0$. So, $\pi'(T)$ is increasing function of T in the interval $(0,M]$. Obviously, $\lim_{T\to0}\pi_1'(T)<0$, and we easily know that:

Theorem 1: If $\pi_1'(M)>0$, there exists a unique value of T_1^* in interval $(0,M]$ which minimizes $\pi_1(T)$. If $\pi_1'(M)\le0$, $\pi_1(T)$ is increasing in interval $(0,M]$, and the optimal solution T_1^* is obtained on the bound $T_1^*=M$.

Case 2: $M<T$

To minimize average total inventory cost per unit time, we take derivation of $\pi_2(T)$ with respect to T, and we have $\pi_2'(T)=\dfrac{f_2(T)}{2T^2\theta_2^{\ 2}\theta_1}$, where

$$\begin{aligned}f_2(T)=&2h\alpha\theta_1-2h\alpha\theta_2-2\theta_2^{\ 2}\theta_1ut_d-2h\alpha\theta_2e^{\theta_1t_d}+2cI_k\alpha\theta_1e^{\theta_2(T-M)}(T\theta_2-1)\\&-2\theta_2^{\ 2}\theta_1F+2cI_k\alpha\theta_1+cI_e\alpha M^2\theta_2^{\ 2}\theta_1+2h\alpha\theta_2e^{T\theta_2}-2cI_k\alpha\theta_1\theta_2M\\&+4c\alpha e^{T\theta_2+\theta_1t_d}\theta_2\theta_1(T\theta_2-1)+4c\alpha e^{\theta_1t_d}\theta_2\theta_1+2h\alpha e^{T\theta_2+\theta_1t_d}\theta_2(T\theta_2-1)\\&+2h\alpha T\theta_2e^{T\theta_2}(\theta_1-\theta_2)+2\alpha e^{\theta_1t_d}\theta_2\theta_1S+2\alpha e^{T\theta_2+\theta_1t_d}\theta_2\theta_1S(T\theta_2-1).\end{aligned}\tag{12}$$

Taking the derivative of $f(T)$ with respect to T, we get

$$\begin{aligned}f_2'(T)=&2cI_k\alpha\theta_1T\theta_2^{\ 2}e^{\theta_2(T-M)}+4c\alpha\theta_2^{\ 3}e^{T\theta_2+\theta_1t_d}T\theta_1-2h\alpha\theta_2^{\ 3}e^{T\theta_2}T\\&+2h\alpha\theta_2^{\ 3}e^{T\theta_2+\theta_1t_d}T+2h\alpha\theta_1T\theta_2^{\ 2}e^{T\theta_2}+2\alpha\theta_2^{\ 3}e^{T\theta_2+\theta_1t_d}T\theta_1S>0.\end{aligned}\tag{13}$$

So, $f_2(T)$ is increasing function of T in interval $[M,+\infty)$ and obviously $\lim_{T\to+\infty}f_2(T)=+\infty$ .Similarly to Case 1,we easily get that:

Theorem 2: If $\pi_2'(M) < 0$, there exists a unique value of T_2^* in interval $[M, +\infty)$ which minimizes $\pi_2(T)$. If $\pi_2'(M) \geq 0$, $\pi_2(T)$ is increasing in interval $[M, +\infty)$, and the optimal solution T_2^* is obtained in the bound $T_2^* = M$.

4 Numerical Analysis

To illustrate the results of the proposed model, we consider an inventory item with the following characteristics: A=400, c=30, α=50, h=4, θ_1=0.4, θ_2=0.2, t_d=0.5, S=2, u=100, M=0.6, I_e=0.05, I_k=0.08. The optimal ordering cycle is obtained at T^*=0.8659, and the optimal total relevant annual cost $\pi(T^*)$=3355.75. Comparatively, if the deterioration rate θ_1 during lead time is not considered, the optimal ordering cycle and total annual cost are T^*=0.9332 and $\pi(T^*)$=2482.61 respectively. So, in order to control in-transit deterioration, the retailer has to purchase less quantity of goods which decreases the cycle time T. We carry out sensitivity analysis of θ_1, t_d, M in Table 1 to 3.

Table 1. Optimal solutions under different θ_1

θ_1	0.1	0.2	0.3	0.4	0.5
T^*	0.9094	0.8949	0.8804	0.8659	0.8514
π	2.77e3	2.96e3	3.15e3	3.36e3	3.57e3

As is shown in Table 1, with the increasing of θ_1, the retailer's optimal ordering cycle T^* is shortened. So, to decrease deterioration loss during lead time, retailer will decrease ordering quantity and increase ordering frequency.

Table 2. Optimal solutions under different t_d

u	t_d	0.1	0.3	0.5	0.7	0.9
100	T^*	0.8807	0.8739	0.8659	0.8567	0.8466
	π	2.60e3	2.96e3	3.36e3	3.78e3	4.23e3
1000	T^*	0.9655	1.0949	1.1929	1.2690	1.3285
	π	2.70e3	3.24e3	3.79e3	4.37e3	4.98e3

From Table 2, the total relevant cost increases with the increasing of lead time t_d. The effect of t_d to the optimal ordering cycle T^* is complex. On one hand, with the increasing of t_d, retailer will shorten ordering cycle and decrease ordering quantity to reduce deterioration loss during lead time. On the other hand, as the increasing of t_d will increase ordering cost F+ut_d, retailer will extend ordering cycle to decrease average ordering cost (F+ut_d)/T. So, the tradeoff between the deteriorating cost and the ordering cost during lead time must be taken into consideration, and the decision is strongly related to specific set of parameters. When u=100, the optimal decision is to decrease ordering cycle as t_d increases; while when u=1000, the increasing of t_d, however, lead to the increasing of the optimal ordering cycle.

It can be viewed from Table 3 that with the increasing of trade credit M, the optimal ordering cycle T^* is increased so that retailer is increasingly financed, thus the average total relevant cost is decreasing.

Table 3. Optimal solutions under different M

M	0.2	0.4	0.6	0.8	1.0
T^*	0.8569	0.8608	0.8659	0.8721	0.8746
π	3.40e3	3.37e3	3.36e3	3.34e3	3.32e3

5 Conclusion

This paper discusses a deterministic deteriorating inventory replenishment model with in-transit deterioration and permissible delay in payments. It is proved that there exists a unique optimal solution to minimize total cost per year under every scenario. Numerical example indicates that retailer's optimal decision differs from the policy of the non in-transit spoilage replenishments model. In practices, enterprises can further cut down the total average cost by introducing cold-chain cars which may reduce in-transit deterioration. Taking the tradeoff between the investment of cold-chain cars and the in-transit deteriorating cost into consideration can be a direction for future research.

Acknowledgments. The authors would like to thank anonymous referees. This work was supported by the National Natural Science Foundation of China (Grant No. 70871097).

References

1. Ghare, P.M., Schrader, G.F.: A model for exponentially decaying inventories. Journal of Industrial Engineering 14, 238–243 (1963)
2. Covert, R.B., Philip, G.S.: An EOQ model with Weibull distribution deterioration. AIIE Transactions 5, 323–326 (1973)
3. Aggarwal, S.P., Jaggi, C.K.: Ordering policies of deteriorating items under permissible delay in payments. The Journal of the Operational Research Society 46, 658–662 (1995)
4. Chung, K.J., Liao, J.J.: The optimal ordering policy in a DCF analysis for deteriorating items when trade credit depends on the order quantity. International Journal of Production Economics 100(1), 116–130 (2006)
5. Chang, H.J., Dye, C.Y.: An inventory model for deteriorating items with partial backlogging and permissible delay in payments. International Journal of Systems Science 32(3), 345–352 (2001)
6. Chang, C.T., Ouyang, L.Y., Teng, J.T.: An EOQ model for deteriorating items under supplier credits linked to ordering quantity. Applied Mathematical Modelling 27, 983–996 (2003)

7. Liao, J.J.: A note on an EOQ model for deteriorating items under supplier credit linked to ordering quantity. Applied Mathematical Modelling 31(8), 1690–1699 (2007)
8. Tersine, R.J.: Principles of inventory and materials management, pp. 24–56. North-Holland, Amsterdam (1982)
9. Liao, C.J., Shyu, C.H.: An analytical determination of lead time with normal demand. International Journal of Operations and Production Management 11, 72–78 (1991)
10. Ben-Daya, M., Raouf, A.: Inventory model involving lead time as a decision variable. The Journal of the Operational Research Society 45(5), 579–582 (1994)
11. Goyal, S.K.: An integrated inventory model for a single supplier-single customer problem. International Journal of Production Research 15(1), 107–111 (1976)
12. Yang, M.F.: Supply chain integrated inventory model with present value and dependent crashing cost is polynomial. Mathematical and Computer Modeling 51, 802–809 (2010)
13. Chen, Z.G., Xu, Y., Wang, Y.: Integrated vendor-buyer cooperative inventory model with nonlinear lead time crashing cost. System Engineering Theory and Practice 3, 64–70 (2008)
14. Huang, C.K., Tsai, D.M., Wu, J.C., Chung, K.J.: An integrated vendor–buyer inventory model with order-processing cost reduction and permissible delay in payments. European Journal of Operational Research 202, 473–478 (2010)

Evaluation and Risk Analysis on Henan Agricultural Products Processing Enterprises

Rui Wang, Keqin Su, Yawei Wang, and Baosong Liang*

Department of Information and computational Science
Henan Agricultural University
Zhengzhou, China
liangbaosong@sohu.com

Abstract. Risk analysis and evaluation is the key problem in risk management, the outcome of assessment directly affects business policy and enterprises development. This article mainly studies qualitative issues in quantitative analysis on risk problems among present agricultural products processing enterprises by applying a simple and flexible decision-making method, the fuzzy analytic hierarchy process method, through analyzing the total level weight, we obtain the weight in each level relatively to the main goal, and then get the order to all risk factors for Henan agricultural products processing enterprises so as to help enterprises to make sound countermeasures correspondingly.

Keywords: agricultural products processing enterprises, fuzzy-AHP method, fuzzy matrix, risk.

1 Introduction

Henan as a famous agriculture province home and abroad fiercely needs to develop farm produce processing industry in the present situation, only the farm produce processing industry is well promoted can it enhance the province agricultural products and the products manufactured in the market competitiveness. To farm produce processing industries, the changeable internal and external environment always keep the production in a lot of uncertainty which makes enterprises face a grave risk. Therefore, to ensure a good development for farm produce processing industries, it is quite necessary to present a comprehensive analysis on Henan agricultural products processing enterprises [1].

In this paper, we mainly study the risk problem in Henan agricultural products processing enterprises, after giving a corporate existence of risk factors, we analyze the total level weight to obtain the weight in each level that is related to the main goal with the fuzzy-AHP method, and then we get the orders to risk factors for Henan agricultural products processing enterprises so as to help industries to make sound countermeasures correspondingly.

---

* Corresponding author.

M. Zhou (Ed.): ISAEBD 2011, Part III, CCIS 210, pp. 310–316, 2011.

2 Sources of Risk for Henan Agricultural Products Processing Enterprises

In this paper, we mainly consider two kinds of agricultural products processing enterprises, risks that are not directly related to the production process and risks that are related to the production process.

2.1 Risks Indirectly Related to Production Process

Risks indirectly related to production process mainly contain eight types:

1) Natural risk. Natural hazards denote the uncertainty brought to agricultural products processing enterprises in the production and operation process under environmental change.

2) Policies risk. The formulation or adjustment of national policies and laws will affect the construction, operation and development of agricultural products processing enterprises, which just form the policy risk.

3) Economic risk. Economic risks include risks derived from the investment, lending policy change, interest rate and exchange rate fluctuations in financial market that are exerted on the agricultural products processing enterprises and market for agricultural products processing by our country, and risks from a global economic development, our economic growth and unemployment.

4) Industry risk. In industries, other enterprises growth, distribution and strategy may have great impact on a certain enterprise, which forms the business risk.

5) Organization risk. The organization risk denotes risks issued from the relationship inharmonious in enterprise.

6) Human resource risk. Human resource risks denote the risk in staff configuration, reward design and staff training to agricultural products processing enterprises.

7) Decision risk. The agricultural products processing enterprises may produce a big loss in schemes choosing as a result of the inadequacy of information and experience limitations in decision-making, this is a decision risk..

8) Client risk. The principal product for some enterprise is mainly suitable for pregnant women, so the enterprise may face a single client risk.

2.2 Risks Directly Related to Production Process

Risks directly related to production process contain five types:

1) Raw material risk. The agricultural products processing enterprises mainly use the agricultural products as the main raw materials, while, farm prices may change frequently with season and climate that often causes a high price of manufactured goods with low profits.

2) Product species risk. Agricultural products should make appropriate adjustment to its own strength and customers' requirement.

3) Scale risk. Enterprise risk is in direct ratio to the scale of production, and the common risk factors from production are generally related to assessment methods and estimation credibility of production scale, and the deviation between the production scale and mean value of the previous scale.

4) Technical risk. Technology risk comes mainly from enterprise technical innovation. Technological innovation is an activity with potential effectiveness and high-risk, and it is impossible to make fully prediction to technology outcome transformation, which form the technology risk.

5) Maintenance risk. To ensure the production continued stability and security, the agricultural products processing enterprises have to make regular maintenance and repair to produce processing equipment that needs a lot of expenses.

Through risk analysis on agricultural products processing enterprises, we establish the appraisal target system for agricultural products processing enterprises [3], as shown in figure 1.

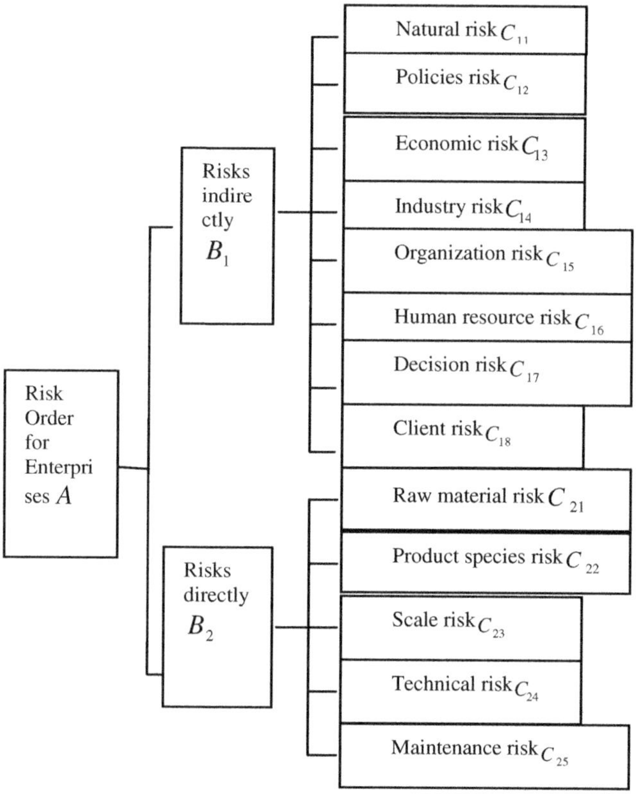

Fig. 1. The appraisal target system for agricultural products processing enterprises

3 Fuzzy-AHP Method

Fuzzy-AHP method is an analysis combining fuzzy consistent relationship and fuzzy consistent matrix in fuzzy set theory. The fuzzy consistent matrix [4] - [5] plays a key role in this method. The definition and steps are given as follows.

3.1 Concepts and Properties

Definition 1. Let the Fuzzy matrix be $R=(r_{ij})_{n\times n}$, then R is called a fuzzy complementary matrix for $r_{ij}+r_{ji}=1(i=1,2,\cdots n;j=1,2,\cdots n)$.

Definition 2. Let the Fuzzy matrix be $R=(r_{ij})_{n\times n}$, then R is called a fuzzy consistent matrix for $r_{ij}=r_{ik}-r_{jk}+0.5$ $(i=1,2,\cdots n;j=1,2,\cdots n)$, $\forall k$.

Definition 3. Let the fuzzy consistent matrix be $R=(r_{ij})_{n\times n}$, then i is as important as j for $r_{ij}=0.5$; j is more important than i for $0\le r_{ij}<0.5$, and the smaller r_{ij} is, the more important it denotes; i is more important than j for $0.5<r_{ij}\le 1$, and the larger r_{ij} is, the more important it denotes.

Theorem 1. Let the Fuzzy matrix be $R=(r_{ij})_{n\times n}$, if R is also a fuzzy consistent matrix, then

1) $r_{ii}=0.5$ $(i=1,2,\cdots n)$, $r_{ij}+r_{ji}=1(i=1,2,\cdots n;j=1,2,\cdots n)$;

2) The sum for the $i-th$ row and the $i-th$ column in R is n, and the matrix left after removing any row and the corresponding column is still a fuzzy consistent matrix;

Theorem 2. Fuzzy consistent matrix constructed by fuzzy complementary matrix: Suppose $R=(r_{ij})_{n\times n}$ is a fuzzy complementary matrix, then $S=(s_{ij})_{n\times n}$ is a fuzzy consistent matrix, where $r_i=\sum_{k=1}^{n} r_{ik}$ $(i=1,2,\cdots n)$ and $s_{ij}=\frac{r_i-r_j}{2n}+0.5$.

3.2 Steps for Fuzzy-AHP Method

Steps for Fuzzy-AHP Method are given as follows:

1) Construct the hierarchy model. Through analysis, we determine the target, appraisal indexes and lay all index factors, here, the upper layer is the main goal; the middle layer is relevant factors to the objective and the lower layer is the strategy.

2) Establish the priority relationship matrix. For convenience, according to the importance between different layers to construct a matrix like this: denote $r_{ij}=0.5$ when i is as important as j; $r_{ij}=0$ when j is more important than i, and $r_{ij}=1$ when i is more important than j, then the matrix is a fuzzy complementary matrix.

3) Find the fuzzy consistent matrix, see theorem 2.

4) A hierarchy sort. Use the fuzzy consistent judgment matrix to calculate the order of importance of factors in a layer, and then make the unitary processing, that is, $T_i^k = \frac{T_i}{\sum_{i=1}^{n} T_i}$ where $T_i = \left(\prod_{j=1}^{n} s_{ij}\right)^{\frac{1}{n}}$.

5) A hierarchy total sort. Based on hierarchy sort, we obtain a synthesis matrix of index factor corresponding to the objective, that is, get superiority coefficients of these schemes, $x_i = \sum_{k=1}^{n} \omega_i T_i^k \ (i = 1, 2, \cdots n)$, and $x_1 > x_2 > \cdots > x_m$ just show the order of superiority with scheme 1, scheme 2, $\cdots$, scheme n.

4 Application of Fuzzy AHP Method in Henan Agricultural Products Processing Enterprises

According to some agricultural products processing enterprise in Henan province, we make risk analysis on the basis of the risk identification; then the risk is divided into different levels, such as the goal layer, principle layer and scheme layer.

1) Through risk analysis for agricultural products processing enterprises, we establish an appraisal target system for agricultural products processing enterprises.

2) Construct the priority relationship matrix. Denote $A-B$ matrix for priority relationship between layer 1 and layer 2, correspondingly, we have matrices between layer 2 and layer 3, like $B_1 - B_{11}, B_{12}, \cdots B_{18}$, $B_2 - B_{21}, B_{22}, \cdots B_{25}$, see table 1-table 3.

Table 1. $A-B$ priority matrix

A	B_1	B_2
B_1	0.5	0.5
B_2	0.5	0.5

Table 3. $B_2 - C_{21}, C_{22}, \cdots C_{25}$ priority matrix

B_2	C_{21}	C_{22}	C_{23}	C_{24}	C_{25}
C_{21}	0.5	1.0	0.5	0.5	0.5
C_{22}	0.0	0.5	0.5	0.0	0.5
C_{23}	0.5	0.5	0.5	0.0	1.0
C_{24}	0.5	1.0	1.0	0.5	1.0
C_{25}	0.5	0.5	0.0	0.0	0.5

Table 2. $B_1 - C_{11}, C_{12}, \cdots C_{18}$ priority matrix

B_1	C_{11}	C_{12}	C_{13}	C_{14}	C_{15}	C_{16}	C_{17}	C_{18}
C_{11}	0.5	0.0	0.0	0.0	0.0	0.0	0.0	0.0
C_{12}	1.0	0.5	0.0	0.0	0.5	0.0	0.0	0.0
C_{13}	1.0	1.0	0.5	0.5	0.0	0.0	0.0	0.5
C_{14}	1.0	1.0	0.5	0.5	0.0	0.0	0.0	0.5
C_{15}	1.0	0.5	1.0	1.0	0.5	0.5	1.0	1.0
C_{16}	1.0	1.0	1.0	1.0	0.5	0.5	1.0	0.5
C_{17}	1.0	1.0	1.0	1.0	0.0	0.0	0.5	1.0
C_{18}	1.0	1.0	0.5	0.5	0.0	0.5	0.0	0.5

3) Find the fuzzy consistent matrix, see table 4-table 6.

Table 4. $A-B$ fuzzy matrix

A	B_1	B_2
B_1	0.5	0.5
B_2	0.5	0.5

Table 6. $B_2-C_{21},C_{22},\cdots C_{25}$ fuzzy matrix

B_2	C_{21}	C_{22}	C_{23}	C_{24}	C_{25}
C_{21}	0.500	0.700	0.550	0.400	0.650
C_{22}	0.300	0.500	0.400	0.250	0.500
C_{23}	0.450	0.600	0.500	0.350	0.600
C_{24}	0.600	0.750	0.650	0.500	0.750
C_{25}	0.350	0.500	0.400	0.250	0.5 00

Table 5. $B_1-C_{11},C_{12},\cdots C_{18}$ fuzzy matrix

B_1	C_{11}	C_{12}	C_{13}	C_{14}	C_{15}	C_{16}	C_{17}	C_{18}
C_{11}	0.500	0.406	0.375	0.375	0.125	0.125	0.187	0.281
C_{12}	0.594	0.500	0.406	0.406	0.219	0.219	0.281	0.375
C_{13}	0.625	0.594	0.500	0.500	0.312	0.312	0.375	0.469
C_{14}	0.625	0.594	0.500	0.500	0.312	0.312	0.375	0.469
C_{15}	0.875	0.781	0.688	0.688	0.500	0.500	0.563	0.659
C_{16}	0.875	0.781	0.688	0.688	0.500	0.500	0.563	0.659
C_{17}	0.813	0.719	0.625	0.625	0.437	0.437	0.500	0.594
C_{18}	0.719	0.625	0.531	0.531	0.344	0.344	0.406	0.500

4) Find the weight of all risk factors to a fuzzy consistent matrix.
Through calculation, all factor weights are respectively provided as follows:
$\omega_0 = (0.5, 0.5)$, for B layer respect to A layer;

$\omega_1 = (0.0683, 0.0917, 0.1157, 0.1157, 0.1669, 0.1669, 0.1504, 0.1244)$ for C layer respect to B_1 layer;

$\omega_2 = (0.2246, 0.1537, 0.2005, 0.2628, 0.1585)$ for C layer respect to B_2 layer.

5) Make the unitary processing, we obtain the relative weight of all risk factors corresponding to the objective:

$$\omega = (0.0342, 0.0459, 0.0579, 0.0579, 0.0835, 0.0835, 0.0752, 0.0622, 0.1123, 0.0769, 0.1003, 0.1314, 0.0793)$$

In light of weight factors contrast, we get the order of risk for some agricultural products processing enterprises, that is, technical risk, raw material risk, scale risk, organization risk, human resource risk, maintenance risk, product species risk, decision risk, client risk, industry risk, economic risk and natural risk.

5 Conclusions

As the result of numerous and complicated risk factors affecting agricultural products processing enterprises, the risk evaluation becomes more difficult, in this paper, with the fuzzy AHP method, we mainly study the level of risk factors of agricultural products processing enterprises in Henan province, from the angle of risks indirectly and directly related to production, we firstly establish the risk of appraisal target system, and then apply the fuzzy AHP method to get the order of risk so that it provides an effective quantitative assessing approach for objective assessment of the risk problems, and thereby promotes enterprises to make right strategies accordingly.

References

1. Luo, Y.: The present situation and prospects for farm produce processing industries in China. Food Industry and Technology 5, 7–9 (2005)
2. Qi, X., Yang, J., Wang, W.: A study of risk resources and control mechanisms for agricultural products processing enterprises growth. Modern Scientific Management 11, 87–88 (2008)
3. Wang, K.: Risk assessment studies on agricultural products processing enterprises based AHP method. Chinese Agricultural Mechanization 5, 76–79 (2006)
4. Chen, X.: The Application of fuzzy AHP method in Scheme orefered aspect. Computer Engineering and Design 10, 1847–1849 (2002)
5. Chen, Y., Zhou, S.: The application of fuzzy AHP method in college teaching. Technology Evaluation 8, 115–116 (2008)

Affective Variables and Listening Comprehension in College English Classrooms

Jun Ren

Department of Foreign Languages, Beijing Union University
No. 97, North Fourth Ring Road (East), Chaoyang Dist., Beijing, China
nancyren.2007@yahoo.com.cn

Abstract. Affective variables play an important role in foreign language students' classroom performance. This paper explores major affective variables that affect the process of listening in college English classrooms and provides some suggestions on how to improve listening comprehension proficiency.

Keywords: affective variables, listening comprehension, suggestions.

1 Introduction

The reforms of college English examinations raise new questions for teachers. It is of great importance for teachers of English to reflect on the teaching process and find better ways to enhance learners' listening proficiency. Many students have difficulty in listening comprehension when learning English. For one thing, some of them may not build a solid foundation of English language learning; and for another, they lack self-confidence. In this paper, we will discuss the role of affective variables in the listening process and some suggestions will be made to improve listening proficiency based on the monitor theory.

2 Theories on Affective Variables

As one of the major second language learning theories, the monitor theory developed by S. Krashen has achieved great popularity among second language teachers. It is well-known that this theory consists of five hypotheses, in which the affective filter hypothesis plays an imperative role when researchers discuss the relationship between affective variables and second language acquisition. Krashen puts forward that different affective variables act to impede or facilitate the delivery of input, and a low or weak affective filter that allows the input in is necessary for learners to acquire a second language. The core of this theory lies in two factors: comprehensive input and the strength of the filter. (Le, 1999) Among four basic language skills, listening seems to have closer relationships with different affective variables, such as motivation, attitude and personality.

Motivation is generally considered as some kind of driving force, the incentive, the need or the desire that the learners feels to learn the second language. According to

M. Zhou (Ed.): ISAEBD 2011, Part III, CCIS 210, pp. 317–321, 2011.

Gardner, Lambert and Dulay et al., there are three types of motivation, that is, integrative motivation, instrumental motivation and social-group-identification motivation. (Wang, 1990) Learners with an integrative motivation are really interested in the target community. The purpose of learning the target language is to communicate with people from that community and keep in touch with the culture. Learners with an instrumental motivation are more concerned with utilizing the language to find a good job, improve their social status and obtain some qualifications. And these two types of motivation are frequently mentioned as major causes of learning a foreign language. Learners who have a social-group-identification motivation not only wish to participate in the social or cultural life of the target language, but also want to become members of the target language community, such as the immigrants.

Another affective variable is attitude, which is closely related with motivation. Attitudes towards a language show what people feel about the speakers of the target language and the language community as a whole. They can be positive or negative feelings towards the language.

Individual personality traits strongly influence the language learning process. Researchers hold different views about the classifications of personality. Generally the major dimensions include anxiety, extroversion and introversion, self-confidence, empathy and inhibition. It is accepted by lots of researchers that self-confidence and empathy tend to facilitate language learning, while inhibition has a detrimental effect on language acquisition.

Anxiety can be harmful or helpful. Though some researchers suggests that language anxiety was facilitating in some ways, such as keeping students alert, most research shows negative relationships between anxiety levels and language performance.

The differences between extroversion and introversion lie in that the former is sociable and likes to take chances and make decisions, while the latter tends to be quiet and plan things carefully in advance. It is not clear whether extroversion or introversion is directly related to success in language learning, but we can organize different types of activity that are appropriate for different learners.

Discussions on affective variables may help teachers to understand problems arisen in the course of listening comprehension and find solutions to them.

3 Applications of Affective Variables in Listening Comprehension

Different from learning other skills, listeners can not keep the listening materials under control, that is to say, the difficulty or speed of the language input is not controlled by the learners. Due to the characteristics of the listening course, learners need to memorize what they have heard as quickly as possible, which requires the combination of both short-term memory and long-term memory. And affective variables play a crucial part in this course. Compared with other forms of exercises, lots of students find it especially hard to do listening exercises. It may result from learners' weak cognitive competence, however, we should also notice the role of affective factors played in the listening practice. As mentioned earlier, if the affective filter in the listening course can be lowered, learners can take in more comprehensive language input. We will discuss it from the following four aspects.

3.1 On the Role of Students

We should take learners' individual differences into account and have a better understanding of the personality of every student. For extrovert students, they enjoy excitement, like to make friends, and are eager to try new and unpredictable experiences. They are less afraid of making mistakes and more willing to guess compared with students of the introvert type, who do not make friends easily and tends to be quiet. Therefore, with the help of teachers, learners should know what type of personality they have and adopt different learning strategies that meet their needs. Extroverts may do better in speaking than introverts, but it is not always the same case in listening. The former can be encouraged to predict answers and be reminded of the mistakes they made; and the latter has the tendency to care more about others' view of themselves, so it is necessary for instructors to consider the factor and be more tolerant to these students' mistakes so as to lower anxiety levels.

In addition to teaching basic language skills and vocabulary in listening, the instructors should also help students to build confidence by encouraging learners instead of criticizing or correcting them frequently. Each time learners get praised, they will feel a little confident about their learning. On the contrary, if every tiny mistake is corrected, they will be less confident and feel uncertain about the language output.

3.2 On the Role of Teachers

As teachers, they need to be aware of what kind of roles they will play in the whole course of listening. They guide students and organize listening activities in which different learning strategies can be used. To stimulate the motivation, they should encourage students to find self-satisfaction in a listening task well done and give opportunities for cooperative learning. That requires teachers to raise questions suitable for students at different levels to give satisfactory answers. Cooperative learning can lower learners' anxiety to some extent, so it is suggested that teachers find proper forms of exercises to practice listening, for example, group discussion or report may achieve better results than answering questions orally. (Arnold, 2004)

To enhance listening teaching efficiency, it is crucial for teachers to cultivate the culture awareness in students to hold a positive attitude towards the language. Introduction of Western culture enables them to learn to appreciate the language and people who speak the language. Instead of learning listening skills purely, understanding of cultural differences may broaden their horizon so as to trigger the intrinsic motivation.

In addition, before doing listening exercises, teachers can introduce some listening skills to the students. For example, taking a quick look at the question and the analysis of four choices before listening can help them to predict the context. Moreover, the introduction of background information of materials is necessary for students to do well in listening practice.

3.3 Choices of Listening Materials and Learning Activities

To arouse learners' interests in listening, teachers may choose teaching materials closely related to their lives, such as current events and campus life. Listening materials should be comprehensible input. According to Krashen's monitor theory, teachers need to avoid choosing materials that are too difficult to be understood. For example, the speed of the given materials is supposed to be appropriate. The new words, the length and the content of the text should be neither too difficult nor too long. And the literary style and themes can also be taken into consideration. Teachers have to be familiar with their students and find suitable materials for them to practice.

Various types of activities can also be designed to stimulate students' motivation and lower anxiety. Students may be involved in content-based activities related to their interests, which help focus their attention on meanings and purposes. Cooperative learning and discussions help introverts to relax and enhance learning proficiency. More challenging and open questions are good for extroverts to take risks.

3.4 The Learning Environment

An easy learning environment is necessary for learners to achieve better results in language learning. It involves various aspects, such as the relationship between the teacher and students, group dynamics and teaching aids, etc.

A harmonious relationship between the teacher and students facilitates learning. Teacher should create an equal and friendly environment in the classroom. When teachers listen to students carefully and communicate with them frankly, it will be easier to find problems and help students to lower the affective filter. It also requires teachers to learn to appreciate their students and observe advantages in their learning process. On the other hand, students will at the same time accept what the teacher instructs and develop a good relationship with him. On the contrary, if the teacher does not have a positive attitude towards his students and the course he teaches, it is hard to believe that he can gain positive responses from his students.

The learning environment is also determined by group dynamics, which includes factors such as cooperation between students and the degree of individual involvement, the order and discipline in the classroom, students' relationships with their classmates and the teacher, to name just a few. A good class environment allows teachers and students to produce a beneficial interaction, while a class that is bored or simply not learning can hardly participate in listening activities. Thus it is necessary for teachers not only teach language points but also guide their students to take a correct attitude towards learning so as to get every individual involved in the class.

With the help of different kinds of teaching aids, teachers can make students become more interested in listening. Multimedia computers provide teachers with more flexibility to design the listening contents. Music, movies and many other factors can be integrated into the listening materials, which not only transmit large amount of information to students, but also make the process of teaching and learning become more vivid and fruitful.

4 Conclusion

As mentioned earlier, the teaching and learning process of listening at the college level is strongly influenced by affective variables. In addition to what the paper has discussed, there must be some other factors that facilitate listening. As a tentative exploration of this area, this paper provides suggestions from four aspects, hoping that language teachers pay attention to the issue and find more solutions to problems that arise in the process of listening.

Acknowledgments. The work is supported by the program of "The Cultivation of Non-English Majors' Autonomous Learning Competence from the Metacognitive Perspective".

References

1. Arnold, J.(ed.): Affect in Language Learning. Beijing Foreign Language Teaching and Research Press, Beijing (2000)
2. Elkhafaifi, H.: Listening comprehension and anxiety in the Arabic language classroom. The Modern Language Journal (2005)
3. Horwitz, E.K., Young, D.J. (eds.): Language Anxiety: From Theory and Research to Classroom Implications. Prentice Hall, Englewood Cliffs (1991)
4. Le, M.Y.: Applied Linguistics. Nanjing Normal University Press, Nanjing (1999)
5. Wang, C.M.: Applied Psycholinguistics. Hunan Educational Press, Changsha (1990)

Using English Learning Strategies to Improve Reading Proficiency at the College Level

Jun Ren

Department of Foreign Languages, Beijing Union University
No. 97, North Fourth Ring Road (East), Chaoyang Dist., Beijing, China
nancyren.2007@yahoo.com.cn

Abstract. After a brief overview of language learning strategies and individual factors that affect the reading process, this paper discusses the relationship between the use of English learning strategies and reading comprehension at the college level. As effective strategy use facilitates reading, some reading strategies and pedagogical implications are then discussed in the paper.

Keywords: language learning strategies, the reading process, individual factors, reading strategies.

1 Introduction

Reading may probably be thought of as the most prominent input among the four language skills that most college students of English as a foreign language need to acquire. They can not only obtain a large amount of information from reading, but also develop the overall language competence. Reading comprehension is essential not only in academic learning in all subject areas but also to professional success and indeed to lifelong learning. (Dreyer and Nel, 2003)

Understanding of the reading process will contribute to the improvement of reading proficiency. Due to increased attention to the learner and learner-centered instructional models of teaching, there are growing interests in learning strategies among language researchers. The paper will discuss the reading process from the cognitive, affective and social side of learning. Learning strategies and individual differences including learning styles and affective variables will be illustrated. And it also provides reading strategies to help enhance reading proficiency of college students.

2 On Learning Strategies

Teachers and researchers have attached great importance on learners' factors in teaching a second language since the mid-1970s. Rubin (1975) and Stern (1975) described "good" language learners in terms of personal characteristics, styles and strategies, which aroused other researchers' interests in identifying characteristics of "successful" language learners. Numerous studies have been carried out on the use of

M. Zhou (Ed.): ISAEBD 2011, Part III, CCIS 210, pp. 322–326, 2011.

learning strategies. Researchers hold different views towards the classifications and defining of learning strategies. A dictionary definition of strategy refers to "a clever plan or method; the art of employing plans towards achieving a goal". Oxford defined learning strategies as specific actions, behaviours, steps, or techniques that students employ-often consciously-to improve their progress in internalizing, storing, retrieving, and using the second language. (Grenfell and Harris, 1999) Michael O'Malley and Anna Chamot proposed that there were three types of learning strategies in the field of second language acquisition: metacognitive strategies, cognitive strategies and socioaffective strategies. (Brown, 2002) Andrew D. Cohen provides a detailed classification related to language learning and language use strategies. With regard to the use of materials, strategies include four subsets: retrieval strategies, rehearsal strategies, cover strategies and communication strategies. Chamot and Oxford pointed out that learning strategies can be divided into three domains: cognitive strategies, metacognitive strategies, and communication strategies according to whether they are cognitive, metacognitive, affective or social. (Cohen, 2000) Oxford identified six major groups of second language learning strategies, which were probably one of the most prominent classifications. These learning strategies include cognitive strategies, metacognitive strategies, memory strategies, compensatory strategies, affective strategies and social strategies. (Oxford, 1990)

A better understanding of these strategies contributes to enhance students' overall language competence. Many researchers have carried out studies on the effectiveness of using learning strategies in the process of language learning. Take for example, effective listening skills through monitoring, elaboration, and inferencing are found by O'Malley, Chamot, Kupper, and Anderson identified forty-seven different reading strategies. (Brown, 2002)

In the Chinese context, English learning is thought of as an indispensable part of college education. Teachers are more concerned about how to help students, especially those inexperienced learner, to achieve success in their language performance. To probe into the question of employing learning strategies in reading, we need to analyze the process of reading.

3 The Process of Reading Comprehension

Analysis of the process of reading can not be separated from individual differences, one of the most important factors that have impact on the reading process. Two major factors that we focus on in the paper are learning styles and affective factors. Learning styles might be thought of as "cognitive, affective, and physiological traits that are relatively stable indictors of how learners perceive, interact with, and respond to the learning environment" according to Keefe. We will mainly discuss learning styles from the following aspects: field dependence and field independence; reflectivity and impulsivity. Field independence is closely related to classroom learning that involves analysis, attention details, mastering of exercises, drills, and other focused activities. And lots of studies have provided the evidence. One the other hand, primarily field-dependent persons will be successful in learning the communicative aspects of a second language because of their empathy, social outreach, and perception of other people. (Brown, 2002) Thus this may be used to illustrate why some students tend to perform better than others when given a reading task. Field-independent people are born with the potential of perceiving particular and relevant items, and they counter little difficulty in concentrating on the content of classroom activities related to reading. Therefore, students should be guided to understand which type they belong to in order to realize their preferences.

The second type of learning styles deals with reflectivity and impulsivity. The two styles sometimes are hard to be distinguished from the personality of a person. Studies have shown that children who are conceptually reflective tend to make fewer errors in reading than impulsive children; however, impulsive persons are usually faster readers. And reflective students were slower but more accurate than impulsive students in reading. (Kagan 1965; Goodman 1970; Doron 1973)

Affective factors include motivation, ambiguity tolerance, and anxiety. Motivation can be divided into intrinsic motivation and extrinsic motivation. Students are intrinsically motivated when learning is a goal in itself and extrinsically motivated when learning is done for the sake of rewards, such as grades or praise. The purpose of participating reading tasks reflects the motivation of participants. As it is generally accepted by many researchers that intrinsic motivation correlates more closely with language learning success than extrinsic motivation, design of the reading course can take this factor into account and trigger students' intrinsic motivation as fully as possible.

Tolerance of ambiguity also differs among different students. Some students are relatively open-minded in accepting information that contradicts their own beliefs, while others are more close-minded to reject items that are contradictory or slightly incoherent with their existing system. The process of reading requires students to take in a lot of information, which may seem familiar or unacceptable. Thus the degree of ambiguity tolerance partly influences the reading speed and accuracy.

Reading is affected by anxiety, as was proved by Saito, Y., Horwitz, E. K, and Garza, T. J. in 1999. Their study found that students' reading anxiety levels increased with their perceptions of the difficulty of reading in their foreign language learning. Though there has been little discussion of anxiety and foreign language reading, teachers should be aware of this phenomenon and pay attention to students' affective side in the process of reading.

4 On Reading Strategies

Keeping those factors in mind, teachers should help learners choose effective strategies to enhance reading proficiency. In this paper, we do not distinguish strategies from skills. Although there are some subtle differences, the two terms are often interrelated with each other. Devine and Flavell divided reading strategies in two major categories: cognitive and metacognitive. Cognitive strategies aid the reader in constructing meaning from the text. Metacognitive strategies are strategies that function to monitor or regulate cognitive strategies. That is to say, skimming a text for key information involves using a cognitive strategy, while assessing the effectiveness of skimming for gathering textual information would be a metacognitive strategy. Here we can find the similarities between this classification with learning strategies.

Reading strategies are closely related to learning strategies, whether we notice it or not. The following are some learning strategies that can be employed in the process of reading. Students can use cognitive strategies to manipulate the reading materials, for example, through reasoning, or analysis. Metacognitive strategies are used to plan and evaluate the overall process. Compensatory strategies may be the most frequently used strategies, such as guessing from the context, when learners encounter new words. And affective strategies are adopted when learners feel anxious in reading. Using deep breathing or positive self-talk help them manage their emotions.

We can also use some specific strategies or skills to guide reading, for example, find the topic sentence of each paragraph. The topic sentence that summarizes the main idea is often the first or last sentence of the paragraph; grasp the superficial meaning and deep meaning of a given passage; make guesses from the context; and pay attention to the signal words, words of providing definitions, retelling and indicating transition. Skimming and scanning are two key skills that teachers often emphasize in reading comprehension.

To increase language learning proficiency, some researchers and teachers have provided instructions that help learners learn how to adopt more relevant and powerful learning strategies. Positive effects of strategy instruction emerged for proficiency in speaking and reading. (Ehrman, Leaver, Oxford, 2003) It is important to design and carry out strategy training programs to achieve learning success. Language teachers should give first priority to arouse students' interests in reading when carrying out reading strategies training. Introduction of the Western culture contributes to a better understanding of background knowledge. And a wide range of reading also needs to be encouraged.

5 Conclusion

On the basis of understanding the reading process and learning strategies, the paper discusses the use of English learning strategies. In addition to what we have mentioned in this paper, there remain some questions for language teachers to answer. To what degree the use of English language strategies can influence the reading proficiency? Are there any other strategies that have impact on the reading process? Empirical studies and reading strategy training can be carried out in this area in the future.

Acknowledgments. The work is supported by the program of "The Cultivation of Non-English Majors' Autonomous Learning Competence from the Metacognitive Perspective".

References

1. Brown, H.D.: Principles of Language Learning and Teaching. Foreign Language Teaching and Research Press, Beijing (2002)
2. Cohen, A.D.: Strategies in Learning and Using a Second Language. Foreign Language Teaching and Research Press, Beijing (2000)

3. Dreyer, C., Nel, C.: Teaching Reading Strategies and Reading Comprehension Within a Technology-enhanced Learning Environment. System 31 (2003)
4. Ehrman, M.E., Leaver, B.L., Oxford, R.L.: A Brief Overview of Individual Differences in Second Language Learning. System 31 (2003)
5. Grenfell, M., Harris, V.: Modern languages and Learning Strategies in theory and practice. Routledge, London (1999)
6. Oxford, R.L.: Language Learning Strategies: What Every Teacher Should Know. Newbury House, New York (1990)
7. Saito, Y., Horwitz, E.K., Garza, T.J.: Foreign Language Reading Anxiety. The Modern Language Journal 83 (1999)

Consumer Private Product Complaint Ripple Effect: A Theoretical Analysis

Jiacan Wu, Shan Li, and Wei Li

Dept. of Marketing, School of Business, Sichuan University, Chengdu 610064, China
{b091020,lishan}@stu.scu.edu.cn

Abstract. Consumer complaint behavior (CCB) attracts increasing attention from most marketing scholars recently, but there are still few research focus on consumer private product complaint behavior (CPPCB) with its interpersonal influence and the influence on the brand of product to company. We attempted to analyze the influence caused by CPPCB. Through interview method and theoretical analysis based on word-of-mouth (WOM) and spillover effect, this study indicates that CPPCB could generate negative influence which can reach far beyond its proximate impact on the product. Then we introduce the CPPCB ripple effect construct and define it as the transverse effect which enlarges the influencing scale and the longitudinal effect which generates negative consumer perception from product brand to company brand. The paper proposes the CPPCB Ripple Effect Model (CRE Model) and provides some suggestion to companies on minimizing the negative influence caused by CPPCB.

Keywords: Consumer private product complaint behavior, Ripple effect, Transverse effect, Longitudinal effect.

1 Introduction

Consumer complaint behavior (CCB) has received increasing attention from researchers and practitioners alike Ngai [1]; Jones [2]; Stephens [3]; Singh [4]; Day [5, 6] in the last 34 years. As one basic form of CCB, consumer private complaint behavior (CPCB), according to CCB classifications proposed by researchers (Davidow & Dacin [7]; Singh [4]; Day & London [5], is harmful behavior to companies by its privacy and uncontrollability. What's more, a neglected area in CPPCB is the binary potential effect.

Redress seeking or voice responses is the most direct complaint behavior to companies. Most researchers and practitioners prove that the direct complaint behavior is the best opportunity for communicating with customers and creating loyal customers by taking some measures in good time (Blodgett [7], Spreng [8], Tax & Brown [9], Estelami [10]). The other public complaint behavior is the third party responses. Customers seek redress by the third party but not by themselves. Although it is very harmful, companies could take some specific measures as reaction (e.g. public announcement and so on). Taking no action is private, but we could consider that it could, in the best, be harmful in short time and limited scale.

M. Zhou (Ed.): ISAEBD 2011, Part III, CCIS 210, pp. 327–334, 2011.

Hence, the objectives of this study are:

1. To define CPPCB
2. To analyze the ripple effect of CPPCB
3. To construct the model of CPPCB ripple effect

2 Review of Literature

2.1 Concept of Consumer Complaint Behavior

Researches on CCB began from 70s in last century. Several definitions have been proposed. Jacoby and Jaccard [11] suggests that consumer complaint behavior is generally related to the emotional reactions of dissatisfied consumers due to a product and/or service failure.

Singh [4] supposes that CCB is conceptualized as a set of multiple (behavioral and nonbehavioral) responses, some or all of which are triggered by perceived dissatisfaction with a purchase episode.

The considerable agreement about the conceptual meaning of consumer complaint behavior is the CCB phenomenon is drived by some feelings or emotions of perceived dissatisfaction (Day [12]; Landon [13]).

2.2 Classification of Consumer Complaint Behavior

We could realize by the CCB concepts that CCB responses generally are considered to fit into two broad categories, behavioral and nonbehavioral. Behavioral responses focus on the consumer's actions that convey an "expression of dissatisfaction" (Landon [13]). And of course, consumer's behavioral responses could not be towards to the sellers directly, but also to the manufacturers and retailers, etc. While some consumers take behavior responses, the others take nonbehavioral ones (Day et al. [6]). For example, it should be considered as legitimate CCB responses when consumer forgets about a dissatisfying episode and does nothing. Sometimes, consumer will not do behavioral responses because of timing, financial cost or physical cost, but which doesn't mean consumer is satisfied.

With a review of CCB literature, we find Day [5, 14] and Singh [4] proposed their representative CCB taxonomies. The first CCB taxonomy is advised by Day and Landon [5]. They suggest that CCB should be classified in a two-level hierarchically. In the first level, CCB could be distinguished behavioral response from nonbehavioral response. In the second level, behavioral response could be classified with public action and private action. The public response including seeking redress, legal action and complaining to public. The private response includes two typical action, boycotting and word-of-mouth communication with friends (see Fig. 1).

Then, Day [14] modifies the classification at the second level. He noted consumers complain to achieve specific objectives with their various "explanations" for complaint action they take. Day proposed that the complain motive can be used to classify behavioral CCB into three broad categories: redress seeking, complaining and personal boycott.

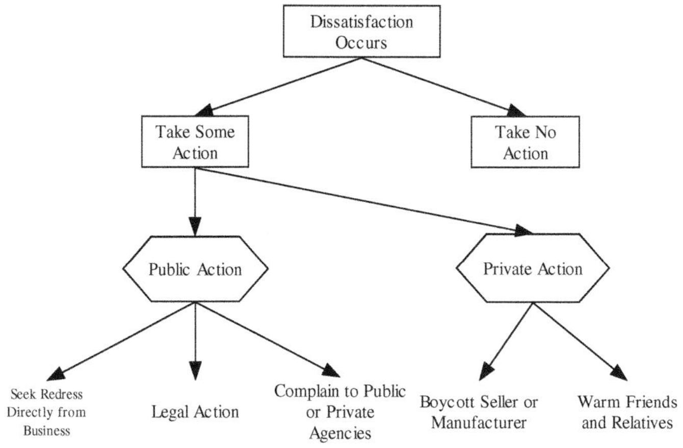

Fig. 1. Day and Landon's classification of CCB

Singh [4] conducts his study with 4000 questionnaires sending out and posed his proposed taxonomy of CCB responses (see Fig. 2). By confirmatory analysis, he argues that CCB responses could be classified into three categories.

1. Voice responses. It is a direct complaint behavior including seeking redress from seller and no action, etc.
2. Private responses. It is an indirect complaint behavior including word- of-mouth communication, etc.
3. The third party responses. It means taking legal action, etc.

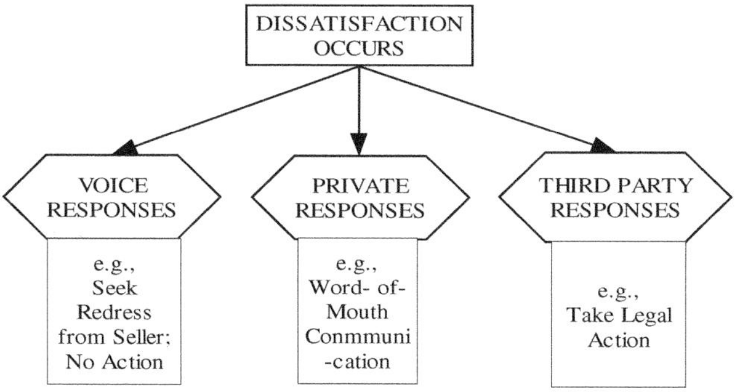

Fig. 2. Singh's Taxonomy of CCB Responses

We consider that Singh's CCB taxonomy is concise for his classification is in one-level hierarchy. We believe that, by the action appearance but not consumer's motive is more scientific, because consumer's motive is far beyond the three ones suggested by Day [14] but always in the three types advised by Singh [4]. Hence, we choose Singh's CCB taxonomy as theoretical basis.

2.3 Consumer Private Product Complaint Behavior

We could learn it from the concepts of CCB given by researchers that CCB origin from dissatisfaction due to product and/or service failure. So, we can think that there are three situation in which CCB could happen.

1. Product Failure. Consumers complain about the product they purchased but not about the service sellers or manufacturers supplied at all.
2. Service Failure. Consumers complain about the service the sellers supplied but not about the product they purchased at all.
3. Product and Service Failure. Consumers complain about not only the product they purchased but also the service sellers or manufacturers supplied.

We consider that consumer's private complaint behavior due to product failure is Consumer Product Private Complaint Behavior (CPPCB).

2.4 Word-of-Mouth

Word- of- mouth (WOM) behavior has received few attention from researchers. From a marketing perspective, Dichter [15] proves that WOM communication is a major type of advertising and advanced the principle of WOM advertisement. Arndt [16] describes WOM communication as simply "oral, person-to-person communication between a perceived non-commercial communicator and a receiver regarding a brand, a product, or a service". Westbrook [17] considers WOM communication "consist of informal communications directed at other consumers about the ownership, usage, or characteristics of particular goods and services and/or their sellers". Some scholars believe that only positive and not negative WOM is used to inform others about new products rather than existing products and it has limited influence. On the other hand, some scholars hold opposite view. Marsha [18] proves that the negative WOM is one basic type of CCB responses and it has a great influence on the other consumers. Nancy and Kevin [3] propose that WOM communication has a strong ripple effect which could help companies create more loyal customer.

Hence, we could think that WOM could have a big and far power of influence but not a limited one on other related people directly or indirectly.

2.5 Spillover Effect

Spillover effect on brand has received a increasing attention from marketing researchers recently. Spillover refers to the phenomenon in which information influences beliefs that are not directly addressed in a communication (Ahluwalia, Unnava and Burnkrant [19]). Research has documented spillover not only from one attribute to another of the same brand (Ahluwalia, Unnava, and Burnkrant [20]) but also from one product to another within a brand family (e.g., Balachander and Ghose [21]; John, Loken, and Joiner [22]).

In one of the few studies to examine this phenomenon in a consumer research setting, Lutz [23] finds that spillover effects explain more variance in attitude change than do changes in beliefs that are addressed by the message. This study is meaningful because it shows the importance of spillover, but we could still know little about the conditions under which spillover will occur or the role played by commitment in moderating spillover effects through it. With experimental research, Ahluwalia [20] shows the importance of spillover effect of marketing communication and finds: first, negative information but not positive information spills over to attributes that are associated with the target attribute but not mentioned in the message when consumers are not familiar with a brand; second, both positive and negative information spill over when consumers like a brand; third, when consumers are committed to a brand, negative information spillover is minimized, but positive information spills over more freely to other associated but unmentioned attributes. Roehm and Tybout [24] identifies conditions under which a brand scandal spills over and negatively affects attitudes and beliefs about the product category and competing brands with three experiments and supplies responding suggestion by examining factors that may enhance or reduce the likelihood of spillover effects. Haizhong Wang [25] classifies spillover effect with transverse spillover effect and longitudinal spillover effect and analyzes dissymmetric spillover effect with experimental method by flagship and non-flagship product.

CCB is a kind of information broadcasting on some product or service. Thus, we consider that spillover effect exists in CCB.

3 Theoretical Analysis

Many big companies own several product categories, and of course, many product brands by multiple-brand strategy. As a matter of fact, consumer could always associate company brand with limited products. The flagship products have the stronger relationship with company brand than the other products because they are always the leading roles of products. On the contrast, non-flagship products are at the margin of product mix, so they have a weak relationship with company brand so that consumers can't realize it is the company products that they are.

When product but not service dissatisfies consumers, according Singh's point (1988), they could make public complaint responses, private complaint responses or the third party complaint responses. When they choose private complaint responses, it means that their complaint about the product will be broadcasted by WOM communication basically to their closest relatives and/or friends, and then to their relatives' and/or friends' closest relatives and/or friends and keep up like that. This is the CPPCB ripple effect, but not the only one, or rather, it is the transverse effect of the CPPCB ripple effect.

The other one is the longitudinal effect of the CPPCB ripple effect. When consumers are dissatisfied with some products, according our survey and deep interviews, they would not only make complaint about the products, but also attempt to make complaint about the companies which own the products brand. But the point is whether they could realize the connections between the products and companies or not. As to the flagship product, they are always famous product, dissatisfied consumers are easy to make complaint on from the products to the companies, and then even doubt on all the company products quality. For the non-flagship product, they are not remarkable products, consumers may need to take a lot of time to investigate the companies which own the product brands if they want to know, so the consumers are inclined to make a product complaint only.

4 CPPCB Ripple Effect Model

Based on the theoretical analysis, we propose the CPPCB Ripple Effect Model (CRE Model) (see Fig.3).

Remark 1. *In the figure,* P_i *denotes the* i *th person* $(i = 1, 2, \ldots, n)$.

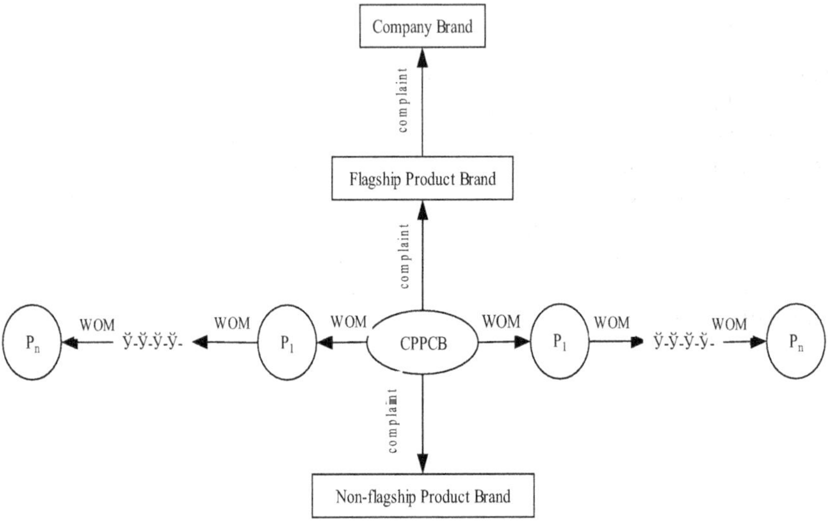

Fig. 3. CPPCB Ripple Effect Model (CRE Model)

5 Conclusion and Implication

The study generally found that CPPCB has a ripple effect composed of transverse effect and longitudinal effect. Based on above, we could learn that CPPCB is the most uncontrollable and harmful to companies in some sense. So, one feasible management method for companies is to create chances for consumer voice response or the third party response as possible as they could so that reduce the possibility of CPPCB. That means companies should encourage dissatisfied consumers to feedback their opinions directly by multiple reward measures and convenient friendly after sale service. Another feasible measure is attempting to persuade dissatisfied consumers to make the third party response. It's obvious that companies should make effective reaction with their rational public relationship management techniques.

Acknowledgements. This study is supported by "Research on Customer Loss Prediction and Supervision System: Based on competitive dynamic Bayesian", Chinese Social Science General Project of Ministry of Education (09XJC630007).

References

1. Ngai, E.W.T., Heung, V.C.S., Wong, Y.H., Chan, F.K.Y.: Consumer Complaint Behaviour of Asians and Non-Asians about Hotel Services: An Empirical Analysis. European Journal of Marketing 41, 1375–1391 (2007)
2. Jones, D.L., McCleary, K.W., Lepisto, L.R.: Consumer Complaint Behavior Manifestations for Table Service Restaurants: Identifying Sociodemographic Characteristics, Personality, and Behavioral Factors. Journal of Hospitality & Tourism Research 26, 105–123 (2002)
3. Stephens, N., Gwinner, K.P.: Why don't some people complain? A cognitive-emotive process model of consumer complaint behavior. Journal of the Academy of Marketing Science 26, 172–189 (1998)
4. Singh, J.: Consumer Complaint Intentions and Behavior: Definitional and Taxonomical Issues. Journal of Marketing 52, 93–107 (1988)
5. Day, R.L., Landon, E.L.: Toward a Theory of Consumer Complaint Behavior. In: Symposium on Consumer and Industrial Buying Behavior, pp. 425–437. North-Holland, New York (1977)
6. Day, R.L., Klaus, G., Thomas, S., Fritz, S.: The Hidden Agenda of Consumer Complaining. Journal of Retailing 57, 86–108 (1981)
7. Blodgett, J.G., Anderson, R.D.: A Bayesian Network Model of the Consumer Complaint Process. Journal of Service Research 2, 321–338 (2000)
8. Spreng, R.A., MacKenzie, S.B., Olshavsky, R.W.: A Reexamination of The Determinants of consumer satisfaction. Journal of Marketing 60, 15–32 (1996)
9. Tax, S.S., Brown, S.W., Chandrashekaran, M.: Customer Evaluations of Service Complaint Experiences: Implications for Relationship Marketing. Journal of Marketing 62, 60–76 (1998)
10. Estelami, H.: Competitive and Procedural Determinants of Delight and Disappointment in Consumer Complaint Outcomes. Journal of Service Research 2, 285–300 (2000)
11. Jacoby, J., Jaccard, J.J.: The Sources, Meaning and Validity of Consumer Complaining Behavior: A Psychological Review. Journal of Retailing 57, 4–24 (1981)
12. Day, R.L.: Modeling Choices Among Alternative Responses to Dissatisfaction. Advances in Consumer Research 11, 496–499 (1984)
13. Landon, E.L.: The direction of consumer complaint research. Advances in Consumer Research 7, 335–338 (1980)
14. Day, R.L.: Research Perspectives on Consumer Complaining Behavior: Theoretical Developments in Marketing. In: Lamb, C., Dunne, P. (eds.), pp. 211–215. American Marketing Association, Chicago (1980)
15. Dichter, E.: How Word-of-Mouth Advertising Works. Harvard Business Review 44, 147–162 (1966)
16. Arndt, J.: Word-of-Mouth Advertising and Perceived Risk: Perspectives in Consumer Behavior. In: Kassaijian, H., Robertson, T. (eds.) Glenview, Illinois (1968)
17. Westbrook, R.A.: A Rating Scale for Measuring Product/Service Satisfaction. Journal of Marketing 44, 68–72 (1980)
18. Richins, M.L.: Negative Word- of- Mouth by Dissatisfied Consumers: A Pilot Study. Journal of Marketing 47, 68–78 (1983)
19. Ahluwalia, R., Burnkrant, R.E., Unnava, H.R.: Consumer Response to Negative Publicity: The Moderating Role of Commitment. Journal of Marketing Research 37, 203–214 (2000)

20. Ahluwalia, R., Unnava, H.R., Burnkrant, R.E.: The Moderating Role of Commitment on the Spillover Effect of Marketing Communications. Journal of Marketing Research 38, 458–470 (2001)
21. Balachander, S., Ghose, S.: Reciprocal Spillover Effects: A Strategic Benefit of Brand Extensions. Journal of Marketing 67, 4–13 (2003)
22. John, D.R., Loken, B., Joiner, C.: The Negative Impact of Extensions: Can Flagship Products Be Diluted? Journal of Marketing 62, 19–32 (1998)
23. Lutz, R.J.: First-Order and Second-Order Cognitive Effects in Attitude Change. Communication Research 2, 289–299 (1975)
24. Roehm, M.L., Tybout, A.M.: When Will a Brand Scandal Spill Over, and How Should Competitors Respond? Journal of Marketing Research 43, 366–373 (2006)
25. Wang, H.Z., Chen, Z.X., Yin, L.: The Impacts of Corporate Message Portfolio: The Vertical and Horizontal Spillover Effects. Nankai Business Review 12, 84–89 (2009)

Applied Research of Ant Colony Clustering Algorithms in Healthcare Consumer Segments

Qi Wen Jiang and Jing Wang

School of Economics and Management, Southeast University,
Nanjing 210096, China
jqw_ais@yahoo.com.cn, wangjing880220@hotmail.com

Abstract. The aim of this paper was to introduce a new method to healthcare markets and analyze the value difference of different market segments. Data clustering is an important data mining technology in engineering and technology. Ant colony optimization algorithm, which is an emerging bionics evolutionary algorithm, has strong robustness and adaptability. Clustering method based on ant colony algorithm has been widely applied in many fields. Market segmentation is the basis of hospitals' market understanding and service management strategy making. This paper classified healthcare customers into three groups based on ant colony clustering algorithm. The experimental results validate the algorithm's efficiency in healthcare market segmentation. This paper also provide data basis for Chinese hospitals to further improve the efficiency and effectiveness of healthcare services.

Keywords: ant colony algorithm, clustering, consumer segments, healthcare.

1 Introduction

Currently, most market segmentation is achieved through clustering. Cluster analysis classifies a set of observations (data) into two or more mutually exclusive unknown clusters so that objects within a cluster are more similar to each other than they are to objects in other clusters [1]. Cluster analysis can not only be used as independent data mining tools to discover some in-depth information of data distribution in the database, but can also serve as a preprocessing step of data mining algorithms. It has now been widely used in financial data analysis, spatial data processing, satellite image analysis and automatic detection in medical images [2]. In the area of customer segmentation, clustering methods such as K-Means, SOM (Self-Organizing Maps), BIRCH have been widely used. Chen et al. indicated that K-Means has the best segment results among the above three methods [3]. As for the healthcare market segments, Cayirli proposed patient classification to arrange out-patient appointment scheduling problem, where he classified the customer as "New" and "Return" patients [4]. Bosch and Dietz considered that in outpatient clinics there are pre-registered patients and new patients who just come in [5]. By using interest-value-based segment method, Zhang et al. segmented customers in public hospitals into six categories according to characteristics of customers' demand for healthcare service [6].

M. Zhou (Ed.): ISAEBD 2011, Part III, CCIS 210, pp. 335–342, 2011.

In 1991, Marco Dorigo et al. introduced a new optimization method ---ant colony algorithm [7]. The earliest model (Basic Model) to explain the ant's behavior of piling corpses was proposed by Deneubourg. Based on BM, Lumer and Faieta presented a formula to measure the similarity between two data objects and designed the LF algorithm for data clustering [8]. Later on, Monmarché introduced a mixed clustering method and suggested that each unit, equivalent to a cluster item, should be placed with more than one object [9]. Meanwhile, a variety of improved ant colony clustering algorihtms have been proposed and applied in different fields [10] [11] [12].

Current studies on healthcare market segmentation at home and abroad only focus on the general description. Lack of procedural system analysis methods and deficiency in analysis tools lead to difficulty in solving the practical problem of healthcare customer segmentation. This paper applied ant colony clustering algorithm to healthcare market to obtain effective and feasible segment groups.

2 Description of Ant Colony Algorithm

When dealing with a large number of samples, traditional clustering algorithm often faces problems like slow clustering, easily falling into partial optimal solution and other issues, thus results in the difficulty getting the best cluster outcome. Additionally, the algorithm itself involves the selection of the number of clusters K, of which the sensitivity directly affects the results of clustering. However, cluster analysis based on ant colony algorithm is similar to the foraging behavior of ant colonies, that is, ants recognize the skin odor (label) produced by other ants and compare it with their own neuron template to distinguish from friend and foe. Ant template is obtained at an early age and updates as they grow up, while label is determined by the chemical substances produced from continuous exchange between ant nests and its own genome. The phenomenon that the odor (label) is identified and shared by every ant in the same nest is called "community circle", which is also the basic principles of chemical recognition system [13].

Define $Lable_i$ as the nests property of ant i, and assume that ant i belongs to no nest at first, so $Lable_i = 0$. Then the label keeps on changing until each ant is to find the most suitable nests for their own. When two ants (i and j) meet, template determines whether they belong to the same nest or not. Define $Template_i$ as the accepted threshold of each ant, which is determined by the genes $Genetic_i$ of ant i and equals to half of the average and maximum similarity. When different ants meet, accepted threshold $Template_i$ is dynamic. We modify it according to equation (1)

$$Template_i \leftarrow \frac{\overline{sim(i,j)} + Max(sim(i,j))}{2} \tag{1}$$

Where, $Sim(i,j)$ means the gene similarity between ant i and j.

In order to ensure the robustness of the nest, evaluation factors M_i is to reflect the size of the nest ant i belongs to, M_i^+ represents the level of ant i accepted by nests. When t=0, ant doesn't belong to any nest, so $M_i^+ = 0$. When two ants of the same label (except 0) meet or two ants accept each other, M_i^+ increases, and vice versa. Parameters convert according to equation (2) and (3)

$$x \leftarrow (1-\alpha)x+\alpha \qquad x \in \{M_i, M_i^+\} \tag{2}$$

$$x \leftarrow (1-\alpha)x \qquad x \in \{M_i, M_i^+\} \tag{3}$$

Where, $\alpha \in (0,1)$, and it is easy to prove that M_i and M_i^+ take values in the interval [0,1). Parameter α accesses a very small number and determines the increase or decrease in M_i and M_i^+.

The process of clustering is to simulate ant's behavior of building nests, recognize ants within the hole and transform the nests. Investigated the case of two ants i, j meet:

When two ants do not belong to any ant nest, determine whether they belong to the same nest according to their similarity $Sim(i, j)$ and accepted threshold $Template_i$ and $Template_j$. They established the initial nest marked by $Lable$, and the accepted relationship is defined as

$$(Sim(i, j) > Template_i) \wedge (Sim(i, j) > Template_j)) \tag{4}$$

1) Assume ant i does not belong to any nest while j belongs to some nest, if they can accept each other, which means they are of the same label value, then ant i joins the nest of ant j.

2) If two ants belong to the same nest and accept each other, increase the evaluation factors M_i, M_j, M_i^+ and M_j^+ according to equation (2).

3) If two ants belong to the same nest but mutually exclusive, then modify M_i and M_j, M_i^+ and M_j^+, according to equation (2) and equation (3) respectively. Reduce the nests acceptance level of ant x with smaller accepted value to make $Label_x$, M_x and M_x^+ close to 0.

4) If two ants belong to different nests but can accept each other, then reduce the value of M_i and M_j first. Change the classification of ants y which accounts for a smaller portion of ant nests, allowing them to choose a more suitable nest.

No changes will be made except for the above case, and repeat above steps to achieve the most reasonable classification at last. To prevent nests being too small and hence reducing the efficiency of clustering, we assume delete threshold of nests be P_{del}. After completion of ants meeting $2m$ times at random, examine comprehensively the average value $\overline{M^+_{cluster}}$ of acceptance level M_i^+ of each ant within nest S and the proportion (β) of ants within nests to all ants. Define $P_{cluster} \leftarrow (1-\beta)\overline{M_i^+} + \beta N_{cluster}$, if $P_{cluster} < P_{del}$, then delete nest S. Calculate the nest acceptance level M_i^+ of ant in each nest respectively, and assume the value of delete threshold is θ_a. If M_i^+ is less than θ_a, then remove ant i from where it is now to make sure the structure of ants nests is tight rather than large or loose. Repeat random encounters between ants until they find the best nest, which means the nests each ant belongs to will not change any more.

Ant colony clustering process is as follows:

```
Input ants' Genetic        // Input attribute value Genetic of each ant
for (int i=0; i<m; i++)
{ Label_i = 0 ;  M_i = 0 ;  M_i^+ = 0 ; }        // Initialize the ants attributes
for (int i=0; i<m; i++)
    {  for (int j=0;  j<m;  j++)
         {compute Sim(i, j)}                    // Calculate similarity
    }
for (int K; K< Nb_Iter /2m ; K++)
    {  for (int k; k<2m; k++)
         {  random i , j
       compute Template_i and Template_j    //Calculate accepted threshold
            Apply the cases (1)-(5)
         }
      for all identified clusters
      compute P_cluster = (1 - β) mean(M_i^+) + βN_cluster
      if ( P_cluster < P_del )
        remove all i witch belong to the cluster
      for (int i=0; i<m; i++)
         {  if ( M_i^+ < θ_a )
           assign the ant to the most similar ant j,
which L_j ≠ 0 and M_j^+ > θ_a
         }
      }
```

3 Application and Analysis

We conducted survey on demand and perception for healthcare services in Nanjing public hospitals and 928 effective questionnaires were collected. Based on the sample data, we use MATLAB7.1 to determine the weight value of healthcare customers and cluster customer's evaluation based on ant colony clustering algorithm as well. After clustering, the average attribute value of *Genetic* within each nest represents ants nests' *Centre* value, and we calculated *Genetic* attributes deviation and variance of each ant from the nest center, removes the ants with deviation more than twice the variance, and re-random encounters between ants until the attribute value *Label* of ant nests does not change any more, so that we can get a scientific and reasonable segmentation. When using ant colony clustering algorithm, parameter α is used to increase or decrease the value of M and M^+, where α must be very small in case of rapid fluctuation of M and M^+ values and volatility of clustering results affected by initial encounters. In calculation, take the number of ant as 10, 15, 16, take

$\alpha = 0.1$ or $\alpha = 0.2$, iteration times as 2000, 10000, 20000, 50000, 100000, and analyze clustering results separately, as shown in Table 1. β value represents the weights of $\overline{M^{+}_{cluster}}$ and $N_{cluster}$, which is for evaluation of the nest's robustness. Let β be 0.2, delete threshold of nest P_{del} and delete threshold of ant θ_a be 0.1 respectively.

Table 1. Taking tables of incremental ant colony clustering

Number of ants	α	Iteration number	Results
10	0.1	Iteration number is 2000, 10000, 20000, 50000, 100000	When the number of ants is 16, $\alpha = 0.1$, iteration number is 20000, better results are achieved.
	0.2		
15	0.1		
	0.2		
16	0.1		
	0.2		

Conclusion: When the number of ants is 16, $\alpha = 0.1$, iteration number is 20000, the difference between each group is big enough to have better clustering results, but as the iteration number increased to 100000, calculation is meaningless due to too much time is wasted.

Based on ant colony clustering analysis, this article divided healthcare customers into three categories, and demographic characteristics of healthcare customers in each group is shown in Table 2.

Table 2. Demographic characteristics of each healthcare customer segments

Characteristics of healthcare customers		Number and percentage of each customer groups of sample customers[1] (%)			Frequency	Percentage of the sample (%)
		1	2	3		
Gender	male	159	130	127	416	44.8
		38.2	31.3	30.5		
	female	214	160	138	512	55.2
		41.8	31.3	27.0		
Age	Under 18	1	8	9	18	1.9
		5.6	44.4	50.0		
	18-29	69	54	44	167	18.0
		41.3	32.3	26.3		
	30-44	96	84	74	254	27.4
		37.8	33.1	29.1		
	45-59	116	79	75	270	29.1
		43.9	29.3	27.8		
	Over 60	91	65	63	219	23.6
		41.6	29.7	28.8		

[1] The numbers of 3 kinds of customer segments accounts for the total sample 928 are 373, 290, 265, and the percentage of 3 groups of total sample is 40.2%, 31.3%, 28.6% respectively.

Table 2. *(continued)*

Education Level	Primary and below	24 35.3	19 27.9	25 36.8	68	7.3
	Secondary	75 38.3	61 31.1	60 30.6	196	21.1
	Higher/Post-secondary	116 42.6	75 27.6	81 29.8	272	29.3
	College/University	134 39.8	121 35.9	82 24.3	337	36.3
	Post-graduate	24 43.6	14 25.5	17 30.9	55	5.9
Economic Income	Below RMB 500	21 32.3	21 32.3	23 35.4	65	7.0
	RMB500-999	31 31.3	30 30.3	38 38.4	99	10.7
	RMB1000-1999	134 42.4	98 31.0	84 26.6	316	34.1
	RMB2000-3999	129 39.4	99 30.3	99 30.3	327	35.2
	Above RMB 4000	58 47.9	42 34.7	21 17.4	121	13
Occupation	Workers	91 44.2	57 27.7	58 28.2	206	22.2
	Farmers	26 26.5	23 23.5	49 50.0	98	10.6
	Professional soldiers	3 27.3	2 18.2	6 54.5	11	1.2
	Civil servants and staff members of institutions	78 43.8	51 28.7	49 27.5	178	19.2
	Staff members of enterprises	84 42.9	71 36.2	41 20.9	196	21.1
	Freelancers	29 31.5	31 33.7	32 34.8	92	9.9
	Others	62 42.2	55 37.4	30 20.4	147	15.8
Payment Method	Full payment	78 29.4	90 34.0	97 36.6	265	28.6
	Partial payment	252 45.7	172 31.2	128 23.2	552	59.5
	Non-payment	43 38.7	28 25.2	40 36.0	111	12
Origin	City	287 44.0	204 31.3	161 24.7	652	70.3
	Town	53 34.2	48 31.0	54 34.8	155	16.7
	Country	33 27.3	38 31.4	50 41.3	121	13

According to ant colony clustering results and demographic characteristics of healthcare customers, this paper labeled the three customer categories as priority-oriented service, economy-oriented service, and security-oriented service. The following analysis of basic characteristics and the type of services requested by healthcare customers, as well as corresponding healthcare service strategies can all be used as baisic input for hospitals to provide better healthcare services.

(1) *Customers with Priority-Oriented Service.* Most of them are highly educated urban population with higher income, especially those over 45 years old who have a certain social security. With higher purchasing power, they are willing to pay as long as the disease can be cured and pay more attention to the ways and other aspects of healthcare services. Apparently a variety of healthcare services are in high demand among these customers who are not concerned about medical expenses but focus on the core needs to be met. Compared to price of healthcare services, this customer group is more sensitive to time and quality, they are eager to have access to non-basic medical services (special services) besides those basic health services. Therefore, if hospitals can adjust service capacity and provide such customers with high-quality healthcare resources to meet their needs, the *Priority-Oriented Service* customers will be the most valuable group for the hospitals.

(2) *Customers with Economy-Oriented Service.* Middle-aged customers with middle income are the main body of this group, and most of them are workers, staff members in enterprises and companies with an education background above high school. They pay partial or all the expense on their own and the services they request are of good quality and moderate costs. The fact that most healthcare customers belonging to this group results in the even distribution of basic features. They have a high level of demand in all aspects with strong economic sense. Though having capacity to cover the expense, they cannot recognize the reasonableness of medical expenses. They hope to get maximum perceived value at least perceived cost to obtain the most affordable medical services. This customer group is sensitive to prices, time and quality, and they demand a small number of special services besides basic healthcare services while considering perceived cost. Therefore, hospitals should try to turn part of these customers into valuable groups by stengthening propaganda and guidance to enlarge valuable customers scale.

(3) *Customers with Security-Oriented Service.* Basically, urban population of 45 years old and over and rural population regardless of age and education are all in this customer group. They are mainly professional workers, farmers and freelancers with an average monthly income below 1,000 Yuan, whose education level are below high school. They are of poor economic conditions but have to pay partially at their own expense. Compared with time and quality, they are more sensitive to the price, and what they need is the basic healthcare services and security protection mechanism to cure the disease. However, services provided by hospitals at present have exceeded the level of this group needs, especially in terms of service value. Hospitals can transfer the excess capacity of healthcare resources and services to other target customers to reduce service costs.

Experimental results show that ant colony clustering algorithm can achieve better clustering results when clustering large amounts of data. Hospitals can treat healthcare customers of common characteristics and similar medical needs as one market segment. Combined with its own resources such as scale, strength and technical features, hospital management can choose one, several or all of the segments as their target market.

4 Conclusion

This paper applied ant colony clustering algorithm to healthcare market segmentation. Ant colony clustering process we presented ensures a scientific and a reasonable market segments. Characterized by high-efficiency, self-organization and dynamic, ant colony clustering algorithm is suitable for high-dimensional and complex data clustering. We have demonstrated that ant colony clustering algorithm can achieve best clustering results in healthcare customer segments. We also propose that hospitals should make the best of each customer's demand for healthcare service and develop relevant marketing strategies to further improve its competitive advantage. Threshold setting is critical to clustering, so possible dynamic adjustments to improve the quality of ant conoly algrithm is an important direction for future research.

References

1. Chen, M.S.: Data Mining: an Overview from a Database Perspective. IEEE Transactions on Knowledge and Data Engineering 8(6), 866–883 (1996)
2. Ramosa, G.N., Hatakeyamab, Y., Donga, F., et al.: Hyperbox Clustering with Ant Colony Optimization (HACO) Method and Its Application to Medical Risk Profile Recognition. Applied Soft Computing 9(2), 632–640 (2009)
3. Chen, Z.-p., Hu, Y.-z., Gu, X.-d.: Applied Research of Clustering Algorithm in Telecom Consumer Segments. Computer Applications 10, 2566–2569 (2007)
4. Cayirli,T.: Scheduling Outpatient Appointments Using Patient Classification: A Simulation Study. In: Proceedings-Annual Meeting of the Decision Sciences Institute, pp. 2195–2200 (2002)
5. Bosch, P.M.V., Dietz, D.C.: Minimizing Expected Waiting in a Medical Appointment System. IIE Transactions 32, 841–848 (2000)
6. Zhang, D.-l., Liu, Y., Shen, Q.-l.: Medical Market Segmentation of Management Strategy Based on Customer Value. Chinese Hospital Management 27(2), 31–33 (2007)
7. Dorigo, M., Colorni, A., Maniezzo, V.: Distributed Optimization by Ant Colonies. In: European Conference on Artificial Life, pp. 134–142. Elsevier Publishing, Paris (1991)
8. Lumer, E., Faieta, B.: Diversity and Adaptation in Populations of Clustering Ants. In: Proceedings of the Third International Conference on Simulation of Adaptive Behavior, pp. 501–503. MIT Press, Cambridge (1994)
9. Monmarche, N., Venturini, G., Slimane, M.: On How Pachycondyla Apicalis Ants Suggest A New Search Algorithm. Future Generation Computer Systems 16(8), 937–946 (2000)
10. Liu, X.-y., Fu, h.: An Effective Clustering Algorithm with Ant Colony. Journal of Computers 5(4), 598–605 (2010)
11. Han, Y.-f., Shi, P.-f.: Image Segmentation Based on Improved Ant Colony Algorithm. Computer Engineer and Application 18, 5–7 (2004)
12. Biswal, B., Dash, P.K., Mishra, S.: A Hybrid Ant Colony Optimization Technique for Power Signal Pattern Classification. Expert Systems with Applications 38(5), 6368–6375 (2011)
13. Zaharie, D., Zamfirache, F.: Dealing with Noise in Ant-based Clustering. IEEE Congress on Evolutionary Computation 3, 2395–2401 (2005)

Research on the Transition of Resource-Based Cities Based on Circular Economy: To Take the City of Yulin in Shanxi Province as an Example

Xirong Wang and Juan Wei

College of Management, YuLin College, YuLin, Shanxi, 719000, China
wangxirong2004@163.com

Abstract. The development of resource-based cities confronts plenty of difficulties so transition is inevitable. Although there are some problems during the rapid economic growth in Yulin, circular economy which is developing actively there has laid the foundation for its transition and transition superiority is formed. To achieve the transition of Yulin successfully, we should give full play to the leading role of government, establish the consciousness of circular economy, rely on science and technology, improve the credit and carry out protective development.

Keywords: circular economy, resource-based cities, the transition, the city of Yulin.

1 Introduction

The city of Yulin in Shanxi province, Erdos in Inner Mongolia and Dadong in Shanxi province are the three big coal cities all over the country, which are typical resource-based cities. Natural resources in Yulin especially mineral resources are rich and ShenFu Coal Field in it is one of the seven biggest coal fields in the whole world. And Yulin also has the biggest mono-block gas field in Chinese continent, which has been verified, and has the reputation of "Kuwait in China". At present, Yulin has the problems like environmental pollution and ecological crisis in varying degrees caused by out-of-order development and extensive development. Besides, what course to follow if it can't continue to rely on resources also makes economic growth of Yulin complicated and confusing. Behind the temporary prosperity and growing GDP, it requires urgently finding out the routes for scientific development of energy economy and establish reasonable industrial model in Yulin. Only to get rid of the dependence on resources, develop circular economy and achieve the transition successfully can Yulin improve the competitiveness increasingly and avoid resource exhaustion.

2 The Problems behind Rapid Economic Growth of Yulin

After ten-year construction, energy and chemical industry base in Yulin has become the gathering place for well-known enterprises and important projects, new growth

M. Zhou (Ed.): ISAEBD 2011, Part III, CCIS 210, pp. 343–349, 2011.

pole in Shanxi and one important energy exporting place all over the country, which has been a major support for regional economy. The financial revenue of Yulin is growing steady. In 2008, the total revenue is 22,120,000,000 Yuan, which is the second in the whole province. At the same time, its growth rate of GDP is the first in Shanxi six years in succession. The economic development in Yulin has made positive contribution to state and local finance. However, there are also some problems behind rapid economic growth.

2.1 Out-of-Balance Industrial Structure

The industrial development in Yulin is out-of-balance under the developmental model of energy and chemical industry base which is driven by resources mainly. The development for mineral resources in Yulin pushes manufacturing industry and other industries aside and the development of fine chemical industry and downstream industries of energy and chemical industry lags behind seriously. Within the city, non-energy and chemical industry has been marginalized gradually and equipment manufacturing industry and light industry decline rapidly. As a result, economy of energy is outstanding and industrial structure is out-of-balance seriously. Furthermore, the proportion of primary industry and tertiary industry takes up a small part while the situation of second industry is opposite. This unreasonable industrial structure leads to high price of commodities in Yulin which is even higher than the average of the whole province.

2.2 Ecological Environment Is Getting Worse and Worse

As Yulin develops and transports resources outside on a large scale, wasting of resources, over-exploitation of resources, environment pollution and ecological disruption and other phenomena are serious. The large-scale development for energy and chemical industry base in Yulin has caused the collapse of earth's surface, the damage of groundwater system, the decline of water table, the cutoff of surface water, the shrink of wet land's areas, vegetation deterioration, exacerbating soil erosion and increasing pollution of "three wastes". At the same time, the length of service of coal mine is shortened because of over-exploitation and the waste of coal resources is also serious because of low rate of recovery and associated deposits don't carry out stereoscopic exploration and development.

2.3 Increasing Bottleneck Restriction

Land, environmental carrying capacity and water have been three major bottlenecks for base construction. Usually, important projects need large land, environmental carrying capacity and water consumption. At present, the land index for projects of energy and chemical industry base has been brought into the whole city's deploy uniformly so that land for construction run short gradually. Besides, the transaction procedures of land acquisition are complicated and sluggish, which have influenced the progress of projects seriously. Moreover, it is distinct for rigid growth of environmental carrying capacity of important projects. According to current planning projects to measure and calculate, the sum of pollution discharge in the whole city in 2015 will double based on that in 2005 so new projects has hardly environmental carrying capacity on the promise of "two reduction" for sulfur dioxide and chemical oxygen demand. In addition, according to water consumption of planning projects to measure and calculate, the water supply can only meet the demand in short term while for long it has to transfer water from Yellow River.

2.4 The Absence of Local Participation in the Development

According to the principle of centralized development on large scale of projects, central and provincial enterprises take up the main body in the development of energy and chemical industry base early. And in following attracting investments extensively, the government implements different preferential policies to domestic and foreign enterprises so that local government and enterprises are enslaved to policies, capital, technology and other factors and not able to participate in the development and construction really. For those reasons, the development model that central and provincial enterprises and foreign capital take up the main body of development is formed. Central and provincial enterprises and foreign capital always occupy mineral resources with largest areas and best quality and have the priority for water supply while local enterprises are outshone pale by comparison. At present, the sum of coal resources allocation which has been defined is 49,167,000,000 tons while local place only takes up 17.23%. Oil and gas resources are owned mostly by Chang Qing and Yan Qing Group. This kind of development model can result in not only the outflow of enormous profits made in base construction but the absence of local government and enterprises' participation in the base development, which restricts the coordinated growth of regional economy.

2.5 The Absence of Benefit Balance Mechanism

The benefit distribution mechanism in Yulin is not reasonable. In terms of lengthways distribution of benefit, among government, enterprises and residents, the proportion of disposable income of the government is rising; so far as crosswise distribution of benefit is concerned, the revenue departs from tax fund seriously, which results in irrational revenue transition among regions. In 2007, the revenue transition of coal, oil and natural gas three kinds of mineral resources, which is caused by head office and branches and trans-regional operation, is 5,510,000,000 Yuan and the revenue transition of them which is caused by non-market pricing of resource products is 7,282,000,000 Yuan; in point of benefit distribution among province, city and county, the proportion of disposable income of the governments of city and county is declining. Moreover, it also exits problems like the overlap of management function, administrative division and extent of authority, which bring about the unsuccessfulness of management system and the disunion between powers of office and right of property.

2.6 The Enlargement of the Gap between the Rich and the Poor

The financial revenue of Yulin is raising steady in recent years. In 2008, its sum of financial revenue, 22,120,000,000 Yuan, is the second in whole province. Among 12 counties and districts in Yulin, there are two key counties included in the provincial plan for poverty alleviation through development and nine key counties included in the national plan for poverty alleviation through development. The poverty-stricken population of Yulin is the largest in whole province and 35% of all administrative villages in Yulin have not got rid of poverty. And the per-capita net income of rural residents is still lower than the average of whole province. Although Yulin has abundant resources and local financial income is raising rapidly, the speed to overcome poverty far lags, which contrasts with the rapid growth of the economy in Yulin distinctly.

3 Advantages of the Transition of Yulin Resource-Based City

The transition of resource-based cities is one huge and complicated economic social system engineering. To start this engineering, we have to have sufficient conditions and do comprehensive and careful preparatory work. Yulin is a resource-based city in growth stage so its transition can be smooth and successful only under proper conditions.

3.1 Comparative Advantage—The Basic Condition for the Transition of Yulin

The comparative advantage of Yulin is abundant natural resources like coal, oil, natural gas and salt and development time for natural resources is till short so that resources there are not on the edge of exhaustion. Besides, the quality of coal resource in Yulin is excellent. At present, Yulin takes energy and chemical industry as leading factor, works up high-tech industry, builds up industrial estates and pilot circular economy. Those advantages are not owned by resource-exhausted cities. Yulin is one resource-based city in growth stage so its transition cost is low.

3.2 Advantage of Late Development —The Special Advantage of Yulin's Transition

The advantage of late development of late-development cities contrasts with early-development ones, which is also a comparative advantage. Compared with resource-exhausted cities, Yulin is late-development city so that it can give full play to study effect, that is, to learn, use for reference and absorb the experience and lessons from early-development cities. Therefore, Yulin can learn from the developmental experience and lessons of early-development cities gotten by long-term practice and huge cost in order to know what to do and what not to, avoid frustration and reduce transition cost. Compared with southeast coastal cities, Yulin is backward so it can give play to introduction affect, like to introduce advanced management experience and technology to support the transition of it.

3.3 Political Advantage—The Unique Advantage of Yulin's Transition

Yulin is one national energy and chemical industry base so the nation supports the development and transition of Yulin. At the same time, Yulin also is an experimental city for circular economy among the second batch in China. National policies are making a major effort to it and support Yulin to develop circular economy and protect and manage the environment. Besides, the government of Yulin also makes implementation programs of experimental city for circular economy so as to provide policy security for the development of circular economy in Yulin and support the transition in terms of policy.

4 The Ways for the Transition of Resource-Based City Yulin

Yulin, in the west of China, is a typical burgeoning resource-based city in growth stage which is developing rapidly. It is developing booming based on resources and in the best stage for the transition. If it doesn't transit until resources exhaust, it is inevitable to spend much more cost. The stage now is the best one for resource-based city Yulin to transit so the government is supposed to be the leading role in the process of transition and achieves the transition of Yulin through various ways.

4.1 To Set Up the Consciousness of Circular Economy So as to Improve the Transition

Based on the foundation of cyclic utilization for materials, circular economy is an advanced economic model which pursues more economic profit, less resources consumption, lower environment pollution and more labor employment as well as is the fundamental reform for traditional growth model "mass production, mass consumption, mass waste". It is necessary to publicize the meaning and advantages of circular economy by various means to draw attention of every level department of party and government and the masses; it is supposed to popularize the knowledge and law relevant to circular economy widely in many ways to guide people for scientific and civilized consumption; it is necessary to summarize and extend the experience of circular economy both in this locality and other places carefully and to strength people's consciousness of resources, energy conservation and environmental protection through demonstration by example. In point of Yulin, there are also some enterprises and units which are done well in circular economy. The government of each city and county should value and summarize the experience, sum up some development models of circular economy which are suitable for local situations and then spread them in a certain area.

4.2 To Express the Leading Role of Government in Transition

Yulin is now in a good developmental period based on resources. Its economy grows quickly, which is the first seven years in succession in Shanxi province. Resources play an important role in the growth of GDP in Yulin. Although there exits some problems like out-of-balance industrial structure, ecological environment deterioration, resource exhaustion and increasing social instability factors, on the other hand, it is inevitable for government to pay for pushing forward the transition. The government of Yulin is the framer and designer for the transition of Yulin, the maker for the transition policies, the integrated player for transition resources, the coordinator for transition profit and the leading role to push forward the transition. Therefore, only if the government determines to motivate the transition of Yulin, it can be successful step by step.

4.3 To Make Relative Policies to Carry Out Protective Development

From a current situation point of view, one important reason why the utilization of energy exploitation is low in Yulin is that resources are occupied free at first and the compensation is pretty low after the exploitation. Therefore, it has to advise financial and revenue departments of our country to make and implement relative preferential policies to support the transition: first it has to change the measurement basis of resource tax, that is, to turn the levy based on enterprise's output to the one on recoverable reserve of resources distributed to enterprises so as to urge enterprises by profits to improve mining rate of resources by all manner of means; second it is supposed to adjust the levy ways for resource tax as soon as possible. The government can link the levy of revenue with rate of recovery of resources and environmental recovery and confirm corresponding standards of levy. For some economic behaviors like cyclical utilization for wastes and the improvement for environmental quality, government can encourage them by tax abatement, subsidy, supplement interest for loan and other incentive policies in order to make enterprises obtain profits in the development of circular economy and implement protective exploitation for energy consciously; third it has to increase current levy standard of resource tax; forth it should support to build wastes disposal plants.

4.4 To Achieve the Transition Based on Science and Technology

Technology content in traditional industries of Yulin is pretty low so it is necessary to bring in advanced science and technology and depend on technological innovation to improve and reform traditional industries and alter the current situation of high energy consumption, high pollution and high cost; it has to bring in advanced technologies and support burgeoning hi-tech industries to turn the superiority of resources to steady one through advanced technologies. At the same time, we should strengthen diversification development which doesn't depend on resources and start from advanced technology at the beginning; it is supposed to depend on technological innovation to develop featured industry and activate characteristic resources at local area, which will play an important role to push the economic growth of Yulin; we should broaden fields of resources development and elongate the chain of resource industry, which is the major direction for structure diversification. Moreover, to cultivate new economic growth points for the city is a key measure for Yulin to achieve the transition of economic structure and avoid resource's exhaustion and city's decline.

4.5 To Improve the Management of Credit to Support the Development of Circular Economy

To reform the management of credit, on the one hand, Yulin should give full play to "window guidance" of People's Bank of China, guide financial institutions to adjust credit structure as well as carry out various macro-control policies of the nation actively, increase credit input for key resource projects and enterprises, the introduction of advanced technologies home and abroad, the research and extension of science and technology achievements, the down-stream processing using new energy and renewable energy and the upgrade of key technologies. On the other hand, each financial institution should give full play to own advantages to support the development of circular economy on the basis of ensuring the quality of credit. Besides, they are also supposed to carry out different policies of macro-control and industry, which favor energy SMEs that are with high technological content and can drive the economic growth in local area and projects which research and extend new energy. Those means can improve the healthy development of regional energy industry.

References

1. Liang, J.: The Coupling of Energy Industry and Circular Economy in Shanbei and the Basic Features of its Industrial Model. Journal of Socialist Theory Guide (5) (2007)
2. Shi, W.: Research on the Development of Circular Economy of Resource-based Cities—Take Yulin as an Example. Master's Thesis of Northwest University (2007)
3. Zhang, S.: Developing Stages of Recycling Economics and Corresponding Government Policy. Journal of Xi'an Jiaotong University (Social Sciences Edition) (9) (2004)
4. Shi, G.: Ways of the development of circular economy of the city of Yulin. Sanqin Daily (February 5, 2007)
5. Li, D.: The introduction of the promotion of enterprise's competitiveness of resource-based cities (regions) in Heilongjiang Province. Commercial Research (22) (2005)
6. Wei, W.: Ponder over the development of circular economy in the city of Yulin (EB/OL), http://www.yldrc.gov.cn
7. Su, Z.: Tell on industry transition of resource-based cities—take Tongchuan as an example. Coal Economic Research (8) (2007)

Research on the Effect of Independent Director System on Shareholder's Interest Conflicts in Public Company

Jifeng Chen, Lianghua Chen, and Xiaoqian Cheng

School of Econmics and Management, Southeast University, Nanjing 211189, China
{Chenjifenggnj,drinktea41}@163.com, lianghua_c@vip.163.com

Abstract. In China, the independent director system has a history of practice of ten years. On the implementation effect, opinions are widely divided. Through a game theory analysis on public company's policy to employ independent directors and independent directors' strategies when faced with interest conflicts between majority and minority shareholders, conclusions were drawn. Nowadays, to give full play to the independent director system, independence of the independent directors should be ensured first, which calls for outside interference. Independency of independent directors subjects to the degree of perfection of the independent director system. On the stage of appointing independent directors, situations should be analyzed and approaches be made to ensure that the independent directors do their duties, so that shareholders' benefits can be protected.

Keywords: independent director system, major shareholders, principal agent, shareholders' interest risk.

1 Introduction

In the early 20th century, modern corporate system witnessed a profound change: equity of a company was highly decentralized and ownership and operation right had a high degree of separation. Social division of labor made operation more professional and complicated, which led to the occurrence of professional managers. However, highly decentralization of equity made it hard for shareholders to supervise company's managers directly and effectively. The independent director system was exactly a remedy for the defect of the existing corporate governance structure and an effective measure to control and balance the authority of executive directors and managers. The independent director system was based on principal-agent theory, which was the mainstream economic theory in the west, and developed gradually with separation of proprietary rights and management rights. So the core of principal-agent problem was how to ensure utmost consistence of the interest of principal and agent's and maximum compatibility between them.

The most prominent problem that faces listed companies is interest conflicts between all shareholders and managers under the condition of equity separation and high degree of separation of proprietary and management rights. In China, most of the listed companies' ownership is of high degree of centralism and shows a typical

M. Zhou (Ed.): ISAEBD 2011, Part III, CCIS 210, pp. 350–358, 2011.

phenomenon of Ownership Structure of state-owned shares because most of them were reformed from state-owned enterprises. Many troubles exposed in public companies also presented the seriousness of controlling and large shareholders occupying small shareholders' interest maliciously (Yongxiang Sun, Zongmin Tang et al.). To solve this issue, functional organizations and scholars used for reference of the experience of western countries and put independent director system in force in public companies of China in August, 2001. We tried to explore function mechanism of the system in shareholders' interest conflicts in the context of Chinese public company.

2 Essentials of Establishing Independent Director System Mechanism in Corporate Governance

The independent director system was originated in the United States. While in China, the listing of "Qingdao beer" （168, hk） in Stock Exchange of Hong Kong Ltd was considered the first application. The independent director system went through 10 years from being used initially to being established by law now. By analyzing independent directors' practice when taking part in corporate governance in Chinese listed companies, we knew that effective independent director governance mechanisms should include three aspects of independency, dynamic mechanism and guarantee mechanism. Independency consists of not only externality but also property of part-time, which means independent directors in general are from outside the company, and have their main business so that they can make fair decisions in favor of all stakeholders' benefits. Dynamic mechanism is a system of incentive constraint which includes reputation and incentive and restriction of payment. Guarantee mechanism refers to that independent directors should have enough specialized knowledge, capacity, time and energy to participate in corporate governance. Independence is the precondition to establish the independent director system.

The goal of implementation of the independent director system is to protect the interests of all the shareholders. In listed companies where equity is of relative or a high degree of centralism the interest's inconsistency of all the shareholders leads to interest conflicts between major and minority shareholders. Minority shareholders expect that independent directors can not only solve insiders control problem but also prevent major shareholders' violation of their interest. Many cases currently available demonstrate that independent directors' role played in protecting shareholders' interest is unsatisfactory. This paper studies on independent directors' choice in shareholders' interest conflicts in China by using game analysis.

3 Game Analysis of Independent Director System in Interest Conflicts among Shareholders

Game theory assumes that men are economic men of limited rationality who maximize their own interests in the face of given constraints. Accordingly the process of independent directors preventing interest distribution risk among shareholders is actually a game in which independent directors, shareholders and market regulators are players. From the perspective of game theory, effectiveness of independent director system actually depends on the result of the game among independent directors, shareholders and market regulators. Risk arising from independent directors system's precaution of interest inconsistency among shareholders is defined as shareholders' interest risk. This article aims at analyzing function of independent director system and finding out required condition of independent director system's preventing shareholders' interest risk. We divided the operation of independent director system into two phases of employment and post-employment. For independence is a prerequisite for the system as referred before, independent directors are divided into two groups of strong and weak independence. Also, because of large shareholders' expropriation of minority shareholders' interest which arises from the problem of principal - agent and difference of stakeholders' objective function major shareholders are divided into types of occupation and non-occupation. First discuss the satisfaction of independent director system's independence condition required in preventing shareholders' interest risk in the phase of employment.

3.1 Game Analysis between Large Shareholders and Independent Directors in the Phase of Employment

In China's securities market, there exist two types major shareholders who occupy or not occupy other shareholders' interest especially minority ones' and two groups independent directors of strong and weak independence. The two types of shareholders are called aggressive and non-aggressive for short. The listed companies generally follow the provisions of the Commission to employ a certain proportion of independent directors to avoid huge losses (L). Game between major shareholder and independent director is under the state of perfect information. We will analyze it by divide it into four types as follows:

(1) Static game analysis of employing independent directors in the type of listed companies with aggressive major shareholders

This game mainly deals with how aggressive major shareholders (through the listed company) and the employees would make rational choices when they don't know actions of opposing party. For convenience, we made the following assumptions:

Assumption 1: In the stock market in China, major shareholders could get extra benefits (r) in addition to normal benefits (R) by expropriating other shareholders' profits especially minority shareholders'. And if candidates for independent directors of listed companies were employed, regardless of strong or weak type of independence they would pay the effort cost (C), which includes time and risk cost. Then they would get normal benefits of the pay and prestige (W).

Assumption 2: If the major shareholders employed independent directors of strong independence through the listed company, their aggressiveness would easily be disclosed by independent directors and be imposed a fine (F) by regulatory authorities. We set the probability of disclosure and fine as P_1.

Assumption 3: If the major shareholders employed independent directors of weak independence through the listed company, they would gain an income of comradeship(S) because of the relevance between two sides. The probability of investigated and treated by regulatory authorities is P_2. For the relevance between the two sides, $P_1 \geq P_2$. Then payoff matrix of the two is shown in Figure 1.

		Independent director	
		Weak independence	Strong independence
Major shareholder	Employ	$(R+r-P_1*F, W-C)$	$(R+r+S-P_2*F, W-C)$
	Not employ	$(R-L, 0)$	$(R-L, 0)$

Fig. 1. Payoff matrix of two players in occupying type listed companies

When $R+r+S-P_2*F \geq R+r-P_1*F$, namely $S+F*(P_1-P_2) \geq 0$, major shareholders would employ independent directors of weak independence. Assume that the policy is mandatory, $L \geq R$, $W-C \geq 0$, then the only Nash Equivalence exists(employ, weak independence).

(2) Static game analysis of employing independent directors in the type of listed companies with non-aggressive type major shareholders

This game mainly deals with how non-aggressive major shareholders (through the listed company) and the employees would make rational choices when they don't know actions of opposing party. For convenience, we made the following assumptions:

Non-aggressive major shareholders couldn't get extra benefit (r). If the major shareholders employed independent directors of weak independence through the listed company, they would gain an income of comradeship(S) because of the relevance between two sides. However, they couldn't get that if they employed independent directors of strong independence. Then payoff matrix is shown in Figure 2.

		Independent director	
		Weak independence	Strong independence
Major shareholder	Employ	$(R, W-C)$	$(R+S, W-C)$
	Not employ	$(R-L, 0)$	$(R-L, 0)$

Fig. 2. Payoff matrix of two players in non-occupying type listed companies

Because $R+S \geq R$, the only Nash equilibrium exists (employ, weak independence).

(3)Dynamic game analysis of employing independent directors in the type of listed companies with aggressive major shareholders

The two players of this game are large shareholders and candidate group of independent directors. In this dynamic game, major shareholder takes the initiative, because independent directors are appointed by them (through the listed company).

The game process is divided into three phases. In the first stage aggressive major shareholders issue (or not issue) demand information of employing independent directors. If not issue, the game ends; in the second stage, candidate group of independent directors (including two types of strong and weak independence) issue (or not issue) applying intention. If they have no intention, the game ends. In the third stage major shareholders employ (or do not employ) independent directors (including two types of strong and weak independence). Thus, we can obtain extensive form of dynamic game as shown in Figure 3.

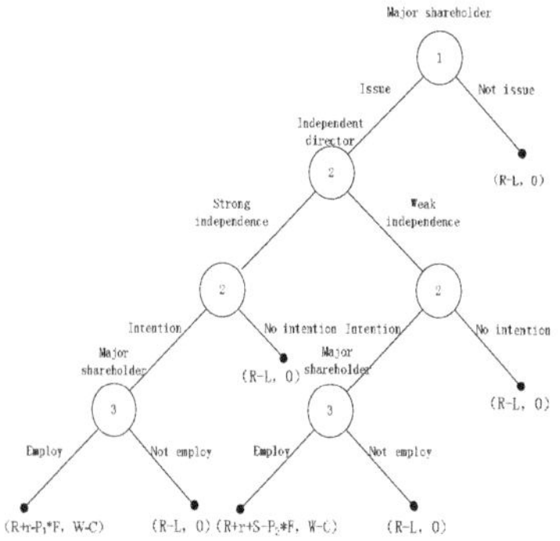

Fig. 3. Dynamic game between independent director and major shareholder in occupying list companies

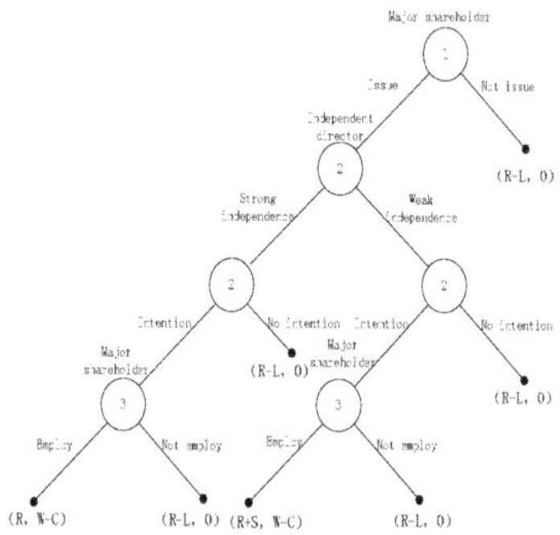

Fig. 4. Dynamic game between independent director and major shareholder in non-occupying list companies

When $R + r + S - P_2 * F \geq R + r - P_1 * F$, namely $S + F * (P_1 - P_2) \geq 0$, large shareholders would employ independent directors of weak independence. As referred before, $P_1 - P_2 \geq 0$, $S \geq 0$, and $R - L \leq 0$, $W - C \geq 0$, the only Nash Equivalence exists(employ, weak independence).

(4) Dynamic game analysis of employing independent directors in the type of listed companies with non-aggressive major shareholders

The two players of this game are non-aggressive large shareholders and candidate group of independent directors. In this dynamic game, major shareholder takes the initiative, because independent directors are appointed by them (through the listed company). The game process is similar to that in (3). Thus, we can obtain extensive form of dynamic game as shown in Figure 4.

Because $R + S \geq R$, $R - L \leq 0$, the only Nash Equivalence exists(employ, weak independence).

The result of the game is: all independent directors of strong independence will be cleared out. So, in practice, interference from outside is indispensable to ensure the admitted independent directors' independence which ultimately depends on the degree of perfection of related system.

3.2 Game Analysis between Major Shareholders and Independent Directors after Employment

(1) Static game analysis of required conditions of independent directors' preventing shareholders' interest risk (after employment)

We assumed that large shareholders and independent directors of the company were rational economic man. Furthermore, we made the following assumptions:

Assumption 1: In perfect stock market of China, major shareholders had two strategies of occupying or not occupying other shareholders especially minority shareholders, and independent directors had countermeasures of fulfilling or unfulfilling responsibility to prevent occupying behavior.

Assumption 2: In perfect stock market of China, major shareholders could get extra benefits (r) in addition to normal benefits (R) by expropriating other shareholders' profits especially minority shareholders'. And if independent directors didn't fulfill responsibility to prevent the shareholder's occupying behavior, they could obtain certain extra benefits (w) besides normal interest (W). Independent directors fulfilling responsibility would pay the effort cost (C) and extra pay(c) for suffering from major shareholders' obstruction even dismissal.

Assumption 3: In perfect stock market of China, supervision system exists outside companies. Independent directors and major shareholders may be investigated and treated for their seriously unfulfilling responsibility and occupying behavior. They could suffer from reputation losses and fines. Just set probability of non-independent directors' been investigated as P_3, they paid a F_3 fine and bore some reputation damage (D). Major shareholders should pay a penalty (F_4) if found occupied minority shareholders' interest. The probability of major shareholders' being investigated was P_4. Because the impact of major shareholders occupying behavior was worse than that of independent directors unfulfilling responsibility, $P4 \geq P3 \geq 0$. Then the payoff matrix of the two players is shown in Figure 5:

		Independent director	
		Fulfill responsibility	Unfulfill responsibility
Major shareholder	Occupy	$(R+r-P_4*F_4, W-C-c)$	$(R+r-w, W+w-C-P_3*F_3-L*P_3)$
	Not occupy	$(R, W-C)$	$(R, W-C-L*P_3)$

Fig. 5. Payoff matrix of major shareholder and independent director after employment

Obviously, mixed strategy equilibrium rather than pure strategy Nash equilibrium exists in this game. Just set the probability of independent directors unfulfilling responsibility as p_3 and the probability of major shareholders' occupation behavior as p_4. Now calculate revenue function of independent directors in the game:

First, expected profit function of independent directors taking strategy of fulfilling responsibility:

$$p_4 * (W - C - c) + (1 - p_4)(W - C) = W - C - p_4 * c \quad \text{Equation (3-1)}$$

Second, expected profit function of independent directors taking strategy of unfulfilling responsibility:

$$\begin{aligned} &p_4 * (W + w - C - P_3 * F_3 - L * P_3) + (1 - p_4)(W - C - L * P_3) \\ &= W - C - P_3 * L + p_4 * (W - P_3 * F_3) \end{aligned} \quad \text{Equation (3-2)}$$

$p_4 = (P_3 * L)/(W + c - P_3 * F_3)$ is the Nash equilibrium of major shareholders adopting strategy of occupation.

Again, calculate return functions of major shareholders:

First, expected profit function of major shareholders taking strategy of occupying:

$$\begin{aligned} &(1 - p_3) * (R + r - P_4 * F_4) + p_3 * (R + r - w) \\ &= (R + r - P_4 * F_4) + p_3 * (P_4 * F_4 - w) \end{aligned} \quad \text{Equation (3-3)}$$

Second, expected profit function of major shareholders taking strategy of occupying:

$$(1 - p_3) * R + p_3 * R = R \quad \text{Equation (3-4)}$$

$p_3 = (P_4 * F_4 - r)/(P_4 * F_4 - w)$ is the Nash equilibrium of independent directors adopting strategy of unfulfilling responsibility.

(2) Dynamic game analysis of required conditions of independent directors' preventing shareholders' interest risk (after employment)

For convenience, we made further assumptions as follows:

Assumption 1: The dynamic game process was divided into two phases. Firstly major shareholders took the initiative and there were two strategies of occupying or not occupying in the strategy space. Secondly there were two strategies of fulfilling responsibility or unfulfilling responsibility for independent directors after major shareholders' action. The game ended after independent directors' action.

Assumption 2 and 3 were the same as in the static game analysis after employment. Expansion equation of this game is illustrated in Figure 6:

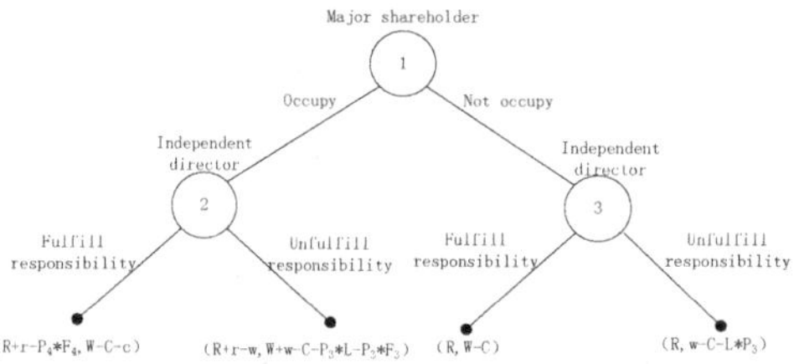

Fig. 6. Dynamic game between independent director and major shareholder after employment

Subgame-perfect Nash equilibrium of game above would be solved by using backward induction below.

First consider the decision node③. Independent directors would get income of $W - C$ if they choose to fulfill responsibility and get income of $W - C - L * P_3$ if they don't fulfill responsibility. However, $W - C - (W - C - L * P_3) = L * P_3 \geq 0$, so on the decision node③they would choose to fulfill responsibility.

Then examine the decision-making node②. In the decision-making node②, independent directors would get income of $W - C - c$ .If they choose to fulfill responsibility and get income of $W + w - P_3 * L - P_3 * F_3$ if they don't fulfill responsibility. And there were two cases separately:

$$\text{Firstly } W - C - c > W + w - P_3 * L - P_3 * F_3 \quad \text{Equation (3-5)}$$

This represents that on decision node②the expected value of independent directors fulfilling responsibility is large when the punishment $(P_3 * L + P_3 * F_3)$ is larger than the sum of total cost and extra benefits namely $(C + c + w)$ from major shareholders for unfulfilling responsibility.

$$\text{Secondly, when } W - C - c < W + w - P_3 * L - P_3 * F_3 \quad \text{Equation (3-6)}$$

Namely $P_3 * L + P_3 * F_3 < C + c + w$, this represents that the punishment $(P_3 * L + P_3 * F_3)$ is less than the sum of total cost and extra benefits $(C + c + w)$ from major shareholders for unfulfilling responsibility. So independent directors won't fulfill the responsibility on decision node②.

Finally, analyze the decision node①. Major shareholders take action on the node ①: Occupy or not occupy. Major shareholders know that if they choose not to occupy, independent directors would choose to fulfill responsibility on decision node ③and got earnings (R). When major shareholders choose to occupy, under the condition of equation (3-5), independent directors would choose to fulfill responsibility .Then major shareholders' income would be $R + r - P_4 * F_4$. Under the condition of equation (3-6), independent directors won't fulfill responsibility on decision node ②and get earnings $(R + r - w)$. The results are as follows:

If the formula (3-6) holds, for $r > w$, then $R + r - w > R$, major shareholders' expected payoff would be large. Their rational choice on decision-making node ①is occupying, then this game's sub-game Nash equilibrium is (occupying, unfulfilling responsibility).

If the formula (3-5) holds, two cases exist:

$$\text{Case 1, if } R + r - P_4 * F_4 > R \quad \text{Equation (3-7)}$$

Equivalently, when $r > P_4 * F_4$, the benefits (r) exceed the losses $(P_4 * F_4)$ if major shareholders choose to occupy. Their rational choice on decision-making node ①is occupying, then this game's sub-game Nash equilibrium is (occupying, fulfilling responsibility).

$$\text{Case 2, if } R + r - P_4 * F_4 < R \quad \text{Equation (3-8)}$$

Equivalently, when $r < P_4 * F_4$, the benefits (r) are less than the losses $(P_4 * F_4)$. Obviously, their rational choice on decision-making node ① is occupying, then this game's sub-game Nash equilibrium is (not occupying, fulfilling responsibility).

To sum up, under different conditions, different sub-game Nash equilibriums exist in the dynamic game.

4 Conclusion

In the discussion above, this article analyzed required conditions of independent director system preventing interest distribution risk among shareholders effectively in the two phases of employment and post-employment.

(1) In the phase of employment, the results of market game show that all independent directors of strong independence and adherence to the "principles" will be cleared out. Therefore, in practice, interference from outside is indispensable to ensure the admitted independent directors' independence which ultimately depends on the degree of perfection of related system.

(2) In the phase of post-employment, firstly, independent directors will select strategy of fulfilling responsibility only when $p_4(W + c - P_3 * F_3) \leq P_3 * L$ in static game analysis of independent directors' preventing shareholders' interest distribution risk (after employment). Secondly, independent directors will select fulfilling responsibility as the strategy if $W - C - c > W + w - P_3 * L - P_3 * F_3$ in dynamic game analysis of independent directors' preventing shareholders' interest distribution risk (after employment). But independent directors' strategy is not necessarily able to stop large shareholders' act of occupying. Additional conditions are needed: independent directors will fulfill responsibility if $R + r - P_4 * F_4 > R$. If $r > P_4 * F_4$, large shareholders will occupy; if $r < P_4 * F_4$, they will not. In practice, in order to prevent major shareholders from occupying the interests of minority shareholders, shareholding pattern of relative concentration or high concentration should be changed fundamentally. Moreover, supervision should be enhanced over listed companies. Once violations are discovered, punishment must be far greater than their illegal income so that independent director system can really protect the interests of all shareholders.

References

1. Zhang, W.: Game Theory and Information economics. Shanghai Sanlian Press, Shanghai (1996) (in Chinese)
2. Guo, Y.: The Arrangement of Independent Board Director and Protection of the Interests of Small Stockholders. Research on Financial and Economic Issues 222, 36–39 (2002) (in Chinese)
3. Fan, R., Han, M.: Game Theory. Wuhan University Press, Wuhan (2006) (in Chinese)
4. Feng, G., et al.: Empirical study of ownership concentration change in Chinese listed companies. Economic Research Journal 8, 12–18 (2002)
5. Sun, Y.: Corporate governance structure: theoretical and empirical study. Shanghai People's Press, Shanghai (2002)
6. Tang, Z., et al.: Empirical Analysis on the expropriation in Chinese listed companies. Economic Research Journal 4, 44–50 (2002)

Analysis of Construction a Three-Dimensional Simulation Tour System of Wudang Mountain Based on CRM

Xiangling Kuang[1,2], Peng Yan[1], Fengzhou Gan[1], Shuai Zhu[1], and Zengping Cheng[1]

[1] Dept. of Information Management, School of Economics and Management, Hubei University of Automotive Technology, Shiyan 442002, China
[2] School of Management, Xian University of Architechture and Technology, Xian 710055, China
{kuangxiangling,woniu-dream,ganfengzhou1989}@163.com, 1160479615@qq.com, thinkpad.ibm@gmail.com

Abstract. The three-dimensional simulation tour system is in a low development level in domestic, and its commercial mode is still unclear. This paper takes the Wudang Mountain Tourism E-Commerce Sites as the object, builds a three-dimensional simulation tour system combining culture, game and business as an integration which based on CRM conception. The three-dimensional simulation of tour system, as the center, also contains malls of the inside& outside-system, CRM data analysis system of visitors, call center and other main function modules. This construction can improve the network client stickiness, create a new business model and serve customer better.

Keywords: CRM, Wudang Mountain, three-dimensional simulation tour system, travel e-commerce, scheme.

1 Introduction

Virtual tour has become an important mode of travel e-commerce in developed countries, but as to China, it's still in its infancy. The three-dimensional simulation tour system is the main part of virtual tour. This paper analyzes the current situation, and constructs a three-dimensional simulation of tour system, malls of inside &outside system, CRM data analysis system of visitors, call center and other major function modules, and presents a preliminary scheme in building travel e-commerce sites which considers the three-dimensional Wudang Mountain simulation tour system as the center and also considers the CRM concept as the basic thought.

2 Analysis of the Current Situation

2.1 Analysis of the Current Situation of the Virtual Tour System

Virtual tour system is a virtual reality system platform oriented the tourism which using three-dimensional GIS, virtual reality and network technology [1]. The three-dimensional simulation tour system is one of its components. The online virtual tour

M. Zhou (Ed.): ISAEBD 2011, Part III, CCIS 210, pp. 359–364, 2011.

can enhance the online virtual tourists' capability of travel information-gathering, so that it can realize booking and purchasing of tourism products finally. Now the virtual tour and virtual shopping are very popular in the world. The number of virtual tourism websites has account for nearly 60% of its tourism websites in America; nearly 10% of the European tourism market has been established on the basis of network virtual tourism. Instead, the development of virtual tour system in China is not always as what we like [2]. Because the virtual tourism of China doesn't have a long history, and it has also been restricted in the condition of hardware and software, and the settings of its system functions are in a lower level which are not enough in both depth and width. Also the business model as it concerns, is singleness,. The construction level of most of the virtual tour business websites has been delayed seriously [3].

2.2 Analysis of the Current Situation of Wudang Mountain Tourism E-Commerce Sites

As a famous taoist mountain, Wudang Mountain, in 1994, was already in the name list of the world cultural heritage. But the images and functions of the official website, Wudang Mountain Tourism E-Commerce Sites [4] cannot be compared to that of the other website of famous mountains such as Huangshan Mountain or Mount Tai. They can not match its laureate of "World Cultural Heritage". In recent years, the municipal government carried out a series of key-construction in Wudang Mountain [5]. With the rapid growth of tourist' number of Wudang Mountain, the construction of e-commerce platform is lagging far off the development of Wudang Mountain scenic area and of Wudang Mountain tourism, which is rapid, so the re-design and re-orientation of Wudang Mountain Tourism E-Commerce Sites are imminent. From the view of designing, the functions of the website are comparatively singleness as they are only for providing several basic functions such as introduction of tourist attractions, travel information, tourism-related products, and tickets reservation of Wudang Mountain, which is not only unable to show the profound cultural connotations of the Wudang Mountain entirely, but also cannot properly serve tourists and the internet better. The profit model of the website is single. At present, it has only one business module--tickets reservation system, and it is mainly targeted at the objects for travel agencies, and the individual visitor service is not keep up with it. Because the website functions are not that perfect, therefore the customer-oriented service is not that sound. A call center has not been set up, and without a group for handling customers' complaint and the emergency, it cannot implement the whole solution scheme for all the phases of tourism. The website has a lower viscosity to the potential young visitors for lacking of entertainment and interesting programs.

3 Analysis of Construction

3.1 Analysis of System Target

The re-design and re-location of the website need to consider the target such as expanding internet market, constructing new business models and promoting network traffic and so on.

Expanding Internet Markets

The current customers of Wudang Mountain are mostly in middle-aged and elderly population. Source markets of the customers are: Shiyan, Wuhan, Xiangfan, Beijing, Guangzhou, Shandong, Fujian and Taiwan. The market composition has no more changes as shown in table 1 in the period from 2005 to 2009.

Re-design and re-orientation of the website will take it into account which can help to complement the traditional market, to nurture and develop customer group, to expand remote network markets.

Table 1. The statistics table of tourist source from 2005 to 2009

Year	Customers (million)	The main intermediate market	The main remote market
2005	0.73	Wuhan, Shiyan, Xiangfan and the other nearby area	Beijing, Guangzhou, Taiwan and so on
2006	0.84	Shiyan, Wuhan, Xiangfan and the other nearby area in Hubei	Beijing, Guangzhou, Shandong, Taiwan and so on
2007	1.02	Shiyan, Wuhan, Xiangfan, Nanyang, Zhengzhou	Beijing, Guangzhou, Shandong, Fujian, Taiwan and so on
2008	1.22	Shiyan, Wuhan, Xiangfan, Nanyang, Zhengzhou, Xian and so on	Beijing, Guangzhou, Shandong, Fujian, Taiwan, Chongqing and so on
2009	1.60	Shiyan, Xian, Wuhan, Xiangfan, Nanyang, Zhengzhou and so on	Beijing, Guangzhou, Shandong, Fujian, Taiwan, Chongqing, Jiangsu, Zhejiang and so on

Construction of a New Business Model

The current main operating business model of the website is mainly about the tickets reservation income while being without any other business model. The re-design and re-orientation of the website should be considered to create a new business model and improve the profitability.

Improve the Website Traffic

In the current situation, the website traffic is not high, viscosity of the website is not strong and neither data collection nor analysis of customers has been developed. Website designing must focus on how to improve website traffic, how to enhance client stickiness, and how to increase the number of registered users, concerning the data preparation for customers' data analyzing and network marketing.

3.2 Functional Module Design

The following several functional modules are designed, a relationship among various modules is shown in figure 1 below. The design is according to the targets above, is drawn on the function of the core module of a three-dimensional simulation tour system of virtual tour websites at home and abroad and is integrated CRM concept and overall business ideas. A three-dimensional simulation tour system is the core of the connection to the system. A CRM data analysis system of visitors is the foundation of the entire system. A call center is a converter which transfers virtual internet service into a real service.

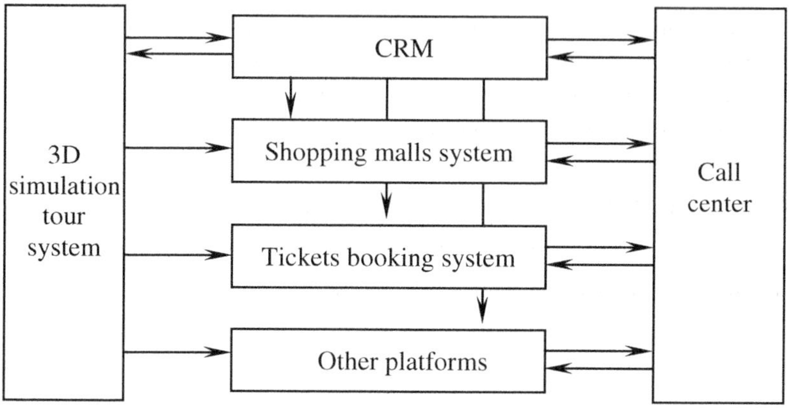

Fig. 1. The relation figure of modules

Function and Design of the Three-Dimensional Simulation Tour System

A three-dimensional tour system will be developed through surveying and mapping real scenes in Wudang Mountain and through using three-dimensional simulation design. It leads tourists to visit and game system by application of image-based simulation in form, blending historical stories and legends related to Wudang Mountain into the game plot, drawing on the process design of the game, and expanding the story plot. In the system tourists can be virtually equipped by props and equipments whose prototypes are special local specialties of Wudang, the local brands, herbal medicine of Wudang Mountain or discoveries of the ancient utensils around it, and then select the plot of the game to travel from after set a role category. In the course of the virtual travel, tourists can gain points or rewards by completing several small tasks, link to malls of inside & outside system, and exchange points. Perhaps they may get local specialties of Wudang Mountain, Wudang Mountain souvenirs, free tickets such as of Wudang Mountain scenic spot, hotel discounted, exhibitions discounted, and performances discounted or other practicality rewards. Within a certain scope, the higher point players gain, the lower discount tickets discounts. The player can achieve real rewards in the malls of inside &outside system, or claim rewards in Wudang Mountain with related information.

Function and Design of Malls of Inside &Outside System

With embed internet shopping of tourists into the three-dimensional simulation tour system, inside the system, the platform of online mall is developed or outside the system, shopping mall and flagship stores group are registered in order to sale Wudang Mountain tourism products, Wudang Mountain and peripheral special local products.

On one hand shopping mall system is designed to become an online commercial city for purchasing Wudang tourism products, realize "one-stop shopping", on the other hand docking with the three-dimensional simulation tour system and changing points into awards for tourists is realized.

Function and Design of CRM Data Analysis System of Visitors and of the Call Center

A CRM data analysis system of visitors is established based on data collecting from registered visitors in various modules of the basic personal information, on-line trading habits, and personal hobby data. The basic data sources include visitor registration information of the three-dimensional simulation tour system, the buyer registration information and trade records of malls of inside &outside system, customer information of e-booking system, registration information of forums, blogs, post bars, terms and other platforms and information from call center which can service customers the whole process that is before, in the middle of and after their visit, as shown in figure 2. Through data analysis and data mining in tourists' database, service demand standards of different age phrases, different social levels, and different customer service can be worked out. These standards can be applied reversely to those function modules such as the three-dimensional simulation tour system, malls of inside &outside system, e-booking system, scenic spots service, visitors' follow-up services, other portfolios of marketing platform and call center services.

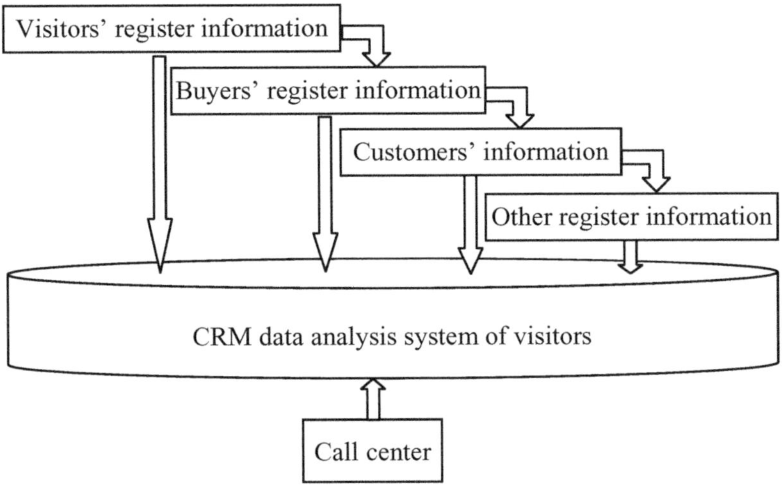

Fig. 2. The data source of CRM data analysis system of visitors

4 Conclusions

The overall scheme is original in conception to connect the Wudang Mountain three-dimensional simulation tour system with e-business and it designs a new business model. The application of CRM idea accurately grasps the tourist psychology. The style of combining cultural, business with game tour will enhance client stickiness and raising the Wudang Mountain reputation. The scheme got a nod assent from the Wudang Mountain government departments.

5 Future Work

After the three-dimensional simulation tour system frame construction, the next step will be the implementation and operation process during which there are still many problem worth studying. In addition, construction of comprehensive virtual tour website based on the three-dimensional simulation tour system will be studied further.

Acknowledgments. This work was supported part by the 11th five-year plan project of education science in Hubei province, China(2007B309), a higher education research project of Hubei University of Automotive Technology(J200719) and two quality engineering projects of Hubei University of Automotive Technology(SJ200905, SJ201022).

References

1. Jiang, W., Luan, R., Zhu, X.: Design and Realization of Virtual Tourist Landscape Based on VRML_ArcGIS. Geographical Research, 1715–1723 (2010)
2. Lu, Z.: Study Review about Foreign Network Virtual Tourism: Retrospect and Prospect. Tourism Tribune, 83–89 (2009)
3. He, X.: Analysis and Strategy of Virtual Tour Advantages. Market Modernization, 82–83 (2007)
4. Wudang Mountain Tourism E-commerce Sites, http://www.wds369.com.cn
5. Jing, Z., Hu, Z., Li, X., Li, W.: Strategy Plan of Tourist Function Building for Shiyan City. Journal of Hubei Automotive Industries Institute, 54–58 (2010)

Study on the Effect of Self Consistency and Congruence, Locus of Control and Coping Style on Loneliness of Impoverished Undergraduates

Jinhui Ye[1] and Qin Zou[2]

[1] School of Psychology, Jiangxi Normal University, Nanchang.330022, Jiangxi, China
[2] Student-Working Department, Jiangxi Agricultural University, Nanchang.330045, Jiangxi, China
yjhzou@yahoo.com.cn, zouqinjcw@126.com

Abstract. Purposes: To investigate influence of self consistency and congruence, locus of control and coping style on loneliness. **Methods:** 330 impoverished undergraduates were measured by the UCLA loneliness scale (UCLALS), the self consistency and congruence scale (SCCS), the Internality, Powerful Others and Chance Scale (IPCS), the Trait Coping Style Questionnaire (TCSQ). **Results:** There is main significant effect in the loneliness of different gender and only-child or none-only-child of the impoverished undergraduates ($P<0.01$). And there is no significant interactive effect between gender and only-child or none-only-child in the loneliness of impoverished undergraduates ($P>0.05$). The loneliness of impoverished undergraduates is significant correlated with self inconsistency, self agility, self stiffness, internality, powerful others, chance, positive coping style and negative coping style ($P<0.05$, or $P<0.01$). Regression analysis shows that self inconsistency, self agility, self stiffness, internality, powerful others, chance, positive coping style and negative coping style can effectively predict the loneliness of impoverished undergraduates (β=0.286, 0.156, -0.176, -0.165, 0.140, 0.175, -0.263, 0.170), and it can explain the total variance of 41.2%. **Conclusions:** Self inconsistency, self agility, self stiffness, internality, powerful others, chance have direct impact on the impoverished undergraduates' loneliness and indirect impact on it through positive coping and negative coping.

Keywords: Loneliness, Impoverished Undergraduates, Self Consistency and Congruence, Locus of Control, Coping Style.

1 Introduction

Loneliness is a negative emotional experience when individual social network in quality or quantity appears defect [1]. Foreign scholars' research indicates that loneliness has a certain effect on a person's health. Bennett, et al finds that lack of self-esteem, social support and close friends is prone to emotional and social

M. Zhou (Ed.): ISAEBD 2011, Part III, CCIS 210, pp. 365–371, 2011.

loneliness [2]. Self consistency and congruence theory is one of the most important ideas in Rogers' personality theory, it closely contacts to mental health. It refers to the self internal coordinated and the coordination between self and experience. If individual experiences the large gap of self and experience, it will make him anxiety or nervous, and such is an inconsistency state [3]. Locus of control is from Rotter's social learning theory of the social psychology that locus of control is about personal character, action and ending the relationship between events generalization expectations [4]. Many foreign studies show that locus of control has a lot of influence on a person's mental. Blanchard and Irion find that youth use the internal control in avoiding danger, hostile reaction, and powerful others is advantageous to old man to solve elderly problem and self-control, but opportunities are correlated with the old man's self control [5]. Coping is the important factor of psychological stress process, and it has relationship with events nature and results. It is a strategy that a person makes cognitive and behavior efforts to change events situation or adapt individual mood when he face the stress events. Many domestic scholars put it applied to the group stress level and psychosomatic health. Among undergraduates, coping styles has mutual influence on parents' upbringing, personality traits, and locus of control [6]. Impoverished undergraduates are of a special group, and under the market economy they appear in the intriguing social hotspot and focus. Therefore, this research hypothesizes self harmonious, local of control and coping styles both direct impacts on the loneliness of impoverished undergraduates and through coping styles they had indirect impact on the loneliness.

2 Methods

2.1 Participants

Participants were 330 impoverished undergraduates from universities of Jiangxi province, the efficient percentage of participants is 94%. Their age range is from 18 to 23 years old (*M*= 20 years, *SD*=1.91), there are 170 males, 160 females, 130 only-child persons, 200 non-only-child persons.

2.2 Measures

UCLA loneliness scale (UCLALS) [7]. The UCLA loneliness scale contains 20 items, using 4 grading. The higher the score is, the stronger individual loneliness is. The scale have good reliability and validity. In the present study, the alpha coefficients is 0.84.

Self consistency and congruence scale (SCCS) [8]. The Self consistency and congruence scale contains 35 items, using level 1~5 score (i.e. from completely doesn't accordance with to completely accordance with), including three subscales of self inconsistency, self agility and self stiffness. The alpha coefficients of three subscales and total scale are 0.81, 0.85 0.89, 0.84.

Internality, powerful others and chance scale (IPCS) [9]. The internality, powerful others and chance scale contains 24 items, using - 3 (very disagree) - + 3 (very agree) seven score, including three subscales: internality, powerful others, chance. The scale have high reliability and validity. The measurement of the three subscales and total alpha coefficients are 0.84, 0.83, 0.86, and 0.88.

Trait Coping Style Questionnaire (TCSQ) [10]. The trait coping style questionnaire contains 20 items, including two subscales negative coping and actively coping, using level 1 ~ 5 rating. The questionnaire has good reliability and validity. The measurement of the two subscales and total alpha coefficients are 0.81 and 0.84 0.80.

2.3 Procedure

The investigation time was in June, 2010. The questionnaire-conducting adopted an anonymous way. Before the test, the participants were instructed as how to use questionnaire according to the instruction by the host and then were officially measured in about 30 minutes. Statistical data processing and analysis was used by SPSS 18.0.

3 Results

3.1 Analysis of Variance on Loneliness of Different Gender, and Only-Child or None-Only-Child of Impoverished Undergraduates

Table 1 shows that there is main significant effect in the loneliness of different gender and only-child or none-only-child of impoverished undergraduates (P <0.01). And there is no interaction effect on loneliness between gender and only-child or none-only-child of impoverished undergraduates (P > 0.05).

Table 1. Analysis of variance on loneliness of different gender, and only-child or none-only-child of impoverished undergraduates

	Squares	*df*	Mean square	*F*	*P*
Gender	91.12	1	91.12	9.03	0.00
Only-child or none-only-child	95.82	1	95.82	9.04	0.00
Gender×Only-child or none-only-child	21.48	1	21.48	2.81	0.09

3.2 Descriptive Statistics and Correlation Analysis of Each Variable

Table 2 shows that the impoverished undergraduates of loneliness is significant correlated with self inconsistency, self agility, self stiffness, internality, powerful others, chance, positive coping and negative coping (P <0.05, or P <0.01).

Table 2. Descriptive statistics and correlation analysis of each variable (*r*)

Variables	*M*±*SD*	Self inconsistency	Self agility	Self stiffness	Internality	Powerful others	Chance	Positive coping	Negative coping
Self inconsistency	49.12±7.41	-							
Self agility	40.32±7.09	0.43**	-						
Self stiffness	19.62±3.78	0.32**	0.24**	-					
Internality	29.71±6.12	0.35**	0.18**	0.25**	-				
Powerful others	18.76±6.44	0.11*	0.28**	0.36**	0.24*	-			
Chance	22.12±7.71	0.26**	0.23**	0.27**	-0.22**	0.22**	-		
Positive coping	22.52±5.24	0.26**	-0.45**	0.41**	0.23**	-0.12*	0.25**	-	
Negative coping	30.11±5.11	0.20**	0.20**	-0.34**	0.35**	0.20**	0.38**	-0.23**	-
Loneliness	38.08±4.54	0.37**	0.21**	-0.24**	-0.33**	0.12*	0.23**	-0.13*	0.24**

Note. * $P<0.05$, * * $P<0.01$.

3.3 Regression Analysis of the Mediating Role of the Influence on Coping Styles among Self Harmonious, Local of Control and of Loneliness of Impoverished Undergraduates

In order to test the mediating role of intermediary variable, it must verify the following three regression equations: regression equation of intermediary variable for independent variables; regression equation of the dependent variable for independent; regression equations of the dependent variable for the independent variable and intermediary variable. A regression model, must meet the following three conditions: independent variables must affect intermediary variables; dependent variables must affect independent variable; intermediary variable must affect dependent variable [11]. From the correlation analysis, we can see that the loneliness of impoverished undergraduates is significant correlated with self inconsistency, self agility, self stiffness, internality, powerful others, chance, positive coping style and negative coping style ($P<0.05$, or $P<0.01$), thus we can do intermediary role test. Took total score as the dependent variable and took self inconsistency, self agility, self stiffness, internality, powerful others, chance as independent variables make layer regression. Controlling gender effects, with self inconsistency, self agility, self stiffness, internality, powerful others, chance as a second layer, and with positive coping and negative coping as the third prediction variables, we built multivariate regression equation. Through the multivariate linear regression analysis, the results show that on the second layer, self inconsistency, self agility, internality, powerful others and chance can positively forecast the loneliness, and self stiffness can negatively forecast the loneliness. On the third layer, negative coping can positively forecast the loneliness and positive coping can negatively forecast the loneliness, between them which influence is positive coping (β= - 0.263). When positive coping and negative coping are into third layer, the whole equation of the explanatory power of first layer is from increased 18.9% to 41.2 percent ($\triangle F$ = 56.175, $P<$ 0.001), and increases 20.3%

respectively. This shows self inconsistency, self agility, self stiffness, internality, powerful others, chance have direct and indirect impact on the impoverished undergraduates' loneliness through positive coping and negative coping (see table 3).

Table 3. Regression analysis of the mediating role of the influence on coping styles among self harmonious, local of control and of loneliness of impoverished undergraduates

	Variables	β	t	R^2	$\triangle R^2$	F	$\triangle F$
First layer	Gender	0.12	3.91**	0.04	0.02	9.46**	9.46**
Second layer	Gender	0.10	2.59**	0.19	0.17	35.47***	47.83***
	Self inconsistency	0.37	7.89***				
	Self agility	0.25	6.12***				
	Self stiffness	-0.27	-6.65***				
	Internality	-0.29	6.99***				
	Powerful others	0.24	5.70***				
	Chance	0.26	6.35***				
Third layer	Gender	0.09	1.99*	0.41	0.31	49.35***	56.18***
	Self inconsistency	0.29	6.54***				
	Self agility	0.16	4.33***				
	Self stiffness	-0.18	-4.84***				
	Internality	-0.17	-4.51***				
	Powerful others	0.14	3.80***				
	Chance	0.18	4.78***				
	Positive coping	-0.26	6.30***				
	Negative coping	0.17	4.65***				

Note. * $P<0.05$, * * $P<0.01$, * * * $P<0.01$.

4 Discussion

Research shows that there is main significant effect in the loneliness of different gender and are significant differences between male and female impoverished undergraduates. Due to the expectations differences of men and women in society, some pressure such as employment, marriage and study make men more likely to experience loneliness. There is main significant effect in the loneliness between only-child and none-only-child of the impoverished undergraduates ($P<0.01$). Only-child impoverished undergraduates came from city, and they can easily obtained social support, but the none-only-child children impoverished undergraduate mainly come from the countryside, they obtain less social support opposite, and can't adapt the urban environment change well and feel much lonely. The none-only-child's social interaction skills may be lower and it may cause loneliness deeper reasons [12].

This study find that self inconsistency, self agility, powerful others, chance, positive coping and negative coping are positively correlated with the loneliness of impoverished undergraduates, and self stiffness, internality are negatively correlated with the loneliness of impoverished undergraduates. Because of fear of social benefit and taboos, impoverished undergraduates emerge self inconsistency, and thus appear loneliness. Previous studies also find that that loneliness is negatively correlated with internality, but it is positively correlated with powerful others and chance [13]. Adopting positive coping style way to deal with, the individual experiences less loneliness. And use negative coping styles, individual pay more attention to the inner negative emotional experience. This research is consistent with the results of previous studies [14].

This study uses intermediary effect testing methods between variables examined mechanism of action and finds the mechanism of action. The results find that self inconsistency, self agility, self stiffness, internality, powerful others, chance directly affected loneliness of impoverished undergraduates. Self inconsistency, self agility, self stiffness, internality, powerful others, and chance indirectly affect loneliness of impoverished undergraduates through positive coping and negative coping. Positive coping and negative coping directly affect loneliness of impoverished undergraduates. The higher is self internal coordination and the coordination between the self and experience, the less is self stereotype and individual experience of loneliness, the higher is health level [15]. The study finds that the intermediary role indirectly achieves mainly through individual positive coping and negative coping. Local of control would affect loneliness of impoverished undergraduates, but this effect indirectly achieves mainly through individual positive coping and negative coping. Impoverished undergraduates like to pay attention to and concentrate on external, most belong to external control people, tend to take success and failure on others and opportunity, few believe in yourself and sure of your ability. Facing with Psychological problems or psychological contradictions, they like to put failure and success attributed to external factors or external influence.

5 Conclusion

There is main significant effect in the loneliness of different gender and only-child or none-only-child of the impoverished undergraduates ($P<0.01$). And there is no significant interactive effect between gender and only-child or none-only-child in the loneliness of impoverished undergraduates ($P>0.05$). The loneliness of impoverished undergraduates is significant correlated with self inconsistency, self agility, self stiffness, internality, powerful others, chance, positive coping style and negative coping style ($P<0.05$, or $P<0.01$). Regression analysis shows that self inconsistency, self agility, self stiffness, internality, powerful others, chance, positive coping style and negative coping style can effectively predict the loneliness of impoverished undergraduates (β=0.286, 0.156, -0.176, -0.165, 0.140, 0.175, -0.263, 0.170), and it can explain the total variance of 41.2%. Self inconsistency, self agility, self stiffness, internality, powerful others, chance have direct impact on the impoverished undergraduates' loneliness and indirect impact on it through positive coping and negative coping.

This study aims to cause society and universities for their attention to impoverished undergraduates, and provides guidance for universities that they carry out psychological health education.

References

1. Rokach, A.: Determinants of loneliness of young adult drug users. The Journal of Psychology 6, 613–630 (2002)
2. Bennett, P., Norman, P., Moore, L., Murphy, S., Tudor-Smith, C.: Health locus of control and value for health in smokers and nonsmokers. Health Psychology 2, 179–182 (1997)

3. Rogers, C.R.: A theory of therapy, personality, and interpersonal relationship as developed in the client-centered framework. In: Kosh, S. (ed.) Psychology: A Study of Science, pp. 184–256. McGraw-hill, New York (1959)
4. Rotter, J.B.: Application of asocial learning theory of personality. Holt, Rinehart and Winston, New York (1972)
5. Blanchard-Fields, F., Irion, J.C.: The relation between locus of control and coping in two contexts: Age as a moderator variable. Psychology and Aging 2, 197–203 (1988)
6. Shen, X., Huang, L., Zhu, Y.: A study on contributing factors of coping styles in college students. Chinese Journal of Behavioral Medical Science 1, 67–69 (2002)
7. Liu, P.: The UCLA loneliness scale. Wang, X., Wang, X., Ma, H.: Rating scales for Mental Health (Reset and Enlarged Edition). Chinese Mental Health Journal, 286–287 (1999)
8. Wang, D.: Self consistency and congruence scale; Wang, X., Wang, X., Ma, H.: Rating scales for Mental Health (Reset and Enlarged Edition). Chinese Mental Health Journal, 314–317 (1999)
9. Xin, Y.: The internality, powerful others and chance scale; Wang, X., Wang, X., Ma, H.: Rating scales for Mental Health (Reset and Enlarged Edition). Chinese Mental Health Journal, 333–334 (1999)
10. Jiang, Q.: Trait Coping Style Questionnaire. X. Wang., X. Wang., H. Ma.: Rating scales for Mental Health (Reset and Enlarged Edition). Chinese Mental Health Journal, 122 (1999)
11. Kenny, D.A., Bolger, N., Korchmaros, J.D.: Lower level mediation in multilevel models. Psychological Methods 2, 115–128 (2003)
12. Luo, G., Ruan, J., Lou, C., et al.: Investigation and analysis of the feeling of loneliness among college students. Journal of Zhe jiang University (Sciences Edition) 3, 113 (1999)
13. Tong, H.: Loneliness depression anxiety and the locus of control. Chinese Journal of Clinical Psychology 3, 196–197 (2001)
14. Buskirk, A.M.V., Marshall, P.D.: The relationship between coping style and loneliness in adolescents: can "sad passivity" be adaptive. The Journal of Genetic Psychology 2, 145–157 (1991)
15. Wang, C., Cong, Z.: Clinical therapy, pp. 86–89. People's Military Medical Press, Beijing (2001)

Evaluation on the Efficiency of Financial Governance of Listed Companies under Split Share Structure Reform

Shaofeng Zheng[1] and Qinghua Huang[2]

[1] School of Economics and Management, Northwest A & F University, 710021Yangling
[2] Economics Department, Northwestern Polytechnical University, 710129 Xi An City, Shaanxi Province, China
nflhua@sina.com

Abstract. The split share structure reform is a major institutional change of China's capital market, which has a long and great influence on China's capital markets and listed companies. In order to measure the impact of financial governance on share reform of listed companies, by the use of DEA, calculation and evaluation of the efficiency of financial governance, the paper clearly indicated the main factors that affect the financial governance: Institutional ownership, the largest shareholders, creditors, executive compensation, independent directors, which influence the efficiency of financial governance from the financial governance structure and mechanisms, therefore, they should be the starting point to improve financial governance efficiency.

Keywords: split share structure reform, financial governance, efficiency evaluation.

Split share reform is a major institutional change of Chinese capital market. Stock reform on listed companies' has made financial governance undergo a fundamental change. In order to measure the impact of split share structure reform on financial governance of listed companies, we select the relevant factors setting up input-output model, by using DEA, calculating and evaluating of the efficiency of financial governance, the paper tries to find factors which influence corporate performance and growth.

1 Construction of DEA Model of Financial Governance

DEA is a nonparametric method that directly uses sample data, by which we establish the appropriate non-parametric DEA input-output optimization model. DMUs with a finite number of input and output data form the production possibility set, by seeing whether it falls on the front surface of the production possibility set, we can determine whether a DEA DMU is efficient or not.

We assume there are n DMUs, they can be compared. All input-output data of DMUs are given in the form of a matrix.

M. Zhou (Ed.): ISAEBD 2011, Part III, CCIS 210, pp. 372–377, 2011.

Table 1. Data matrix

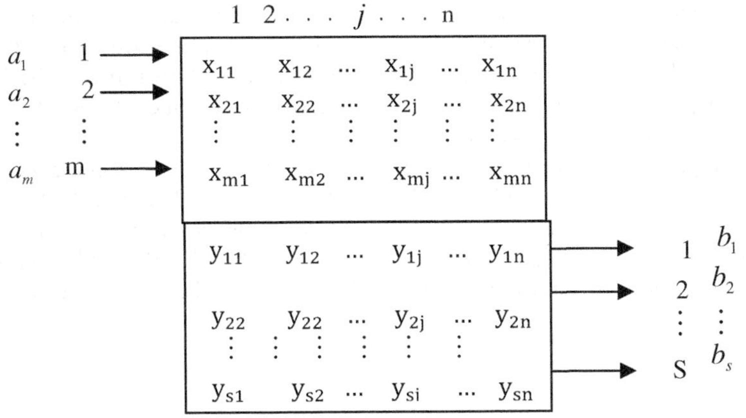

DMU is denoted by DMU_j $1 \le j \le n$, j= 1, 2... n. x_{ij} Is the input elements of DMU_j to the element i, x_{ij}>0. y_{rj} Is the output of DMU_j to the output r, y_{rj}>0. a_i Is the input weight of the input i, i=1,2,..., m. b_r Is the output weight of the output r, r=1,2,...,s.
We simplify above-mentioned variables to the vector form:

$X_j = (x_{1j}, x_{2j}, \cdots, x_{mj})^T$, j=1,2,...,n. $Y_j = (y_{1j}, y_{2j}, \cdots, y_{mj})^T$, j=1,2,...,n.
$a = (a_1, a_2, \cdots, a_m)^T$, $b = (b_1, b_2, \cdots, b_m)^T$

X_j is the input vector of DMU_j, Y_j is the output vector of DMU_j, j= 1,2, ..., n. Input and output data are actual value, and must be non-negative; v and u are respectively the weight vector of m types of input and s kinds of output.

For weights $a \in E^m$ and $b \in E^s$, the efficiency evaluation index of DMU_j ($1 \le j \le n$) is:

$$f_j = \frac{a^T Y_j}{b^T X_J}, \quad j=1,2,\ldots,n \tag{1}$$

Select the appropriate weights a and b, such that $f_j \le 1$, j=1,2,...,n. Efficiency f_j is input-output ratio under the evaluation index weights a and b, while input is $a^T X_j$, output is $b^T Y_j$. When f_j= 1, DMU_j is considered to be optimal efficiency. When f_j<1, DMU_j is not optimal, and there is room for improvement.

When calculating the efficiency of DMU_{j0}, we need to establish the evaluation index of DMU_{j0} as the objective function, to all decision-making unit (j = 1,2, ..., n) ,the efficiency index as the constraint, so we get the fractional programming, which is the DEA model.

$$\begin{cases} \max \quad \dfrac{b^T Y_0}{a^T X_0} = V_P \\ \dfrac{b^T Y_0}{a^T X_0} \leq 1, \ j = 1, \cdots, n \\ a \geq 0, b \geq 0 \end{cases} \tag{2}$$

As to establish input-output variables of DEA model, we selected two variables as output, respectively is ROA, AIR; at the same time, we select 10 variables as input, respectively are: the largest shareholding ratio (F share), the proportion of institutional ownership (JP), the equilibrium of shareholders (ER), the proportion of tradable shares (LP), debt ratio (DTAR), stock dividend per share (SDPS), the amount of M & A (AM), Executive Compensation (SM), the proportion of managerial ownership (MP), number of independent directors (NIE). Model indicates the company's financial management efficiency from the view of all company stakeholders.

In the real world, returns to scale are variable because of various factors. Therefore, we choose the variable returns to scale (VRS) in the DEA model. Also, we calculate the constant returns to scale (CRS) of the DEA technical efficiency. We compare the DEA constant returns to scale technical efficiency (CRSTE) and the DEA variable returns to scale technical efficiency (VRSTE), the scale efficiency can be obtained (SE).

$$SE = CRSTE / VRSTE \tag{3}$$

In addition, in order to remove scale efficiency, we must research returns to scale in the case of constant input. So we select the output-oriented DEA model.

2 Financial Governance Analysis of Measurement Data

Split share structure reform launched in 2005, to the end of 2008, the majority had been finished. The paper selected those listed companies who had achieved full circulation by the end of 2008 as samples. Excluding some unusual samples, we got 70 samples. At the same time, we construct a virtual decision making unit U, that the amount of their investment decisions take the maximum among the 70 samples above, while output take the minimum value, which makes U to be the least efficient decision making unit. Through the comparison on the amount of input and output among 71 decision making units, we find the relative efficiency of each decision unit, and sort it. By analysis the surplus, we could find factors which affect the efficiency of financial management, and the ways to improve financial governance efficiency.

70 decision-making units, 2 output variables, the 10 input variables, 6 time scale (from 2004 to 2009) of the input and output values, total of 2982 data, constitute a set of panel data. In order to avoid differences between these variables affecting the efficiency of analysis, input-output data had been standardized. Because of the characteristics of DEA method, so standardization would not affect the efficiency of the final evaluation.

The paper used the DEAP software to calculate DEA model established above. By sorting constant returns to scale technical efficiency (CRSTE), variable returns to scale technical efficiency (VRSTE) efficiency and scale efficiency (SE) respectively, we get orders of DMUs.

3 Financial Management Efficiency Evaluation

According to the previous theoretical analysis, CRSTE effective decision-making units indicate that economy is efficient. Economic efficiency is consisted with technical efficiency and allocation efficiency, while VRSTE measure the output of decision making units under the established minimum investment, which is a pure technical efficiency; SE measures input resources optimal ratio being allocated. In order to achieve CRSTE effective, any decision making unit must be both SE effective and VRSTE effective.

ROA and AIR are output variables, which measure the efficiency of the company's overall financial governance. In the model, there are 71 DMUs, of which 28 DMUs are CRSTE effective, 58 DMUs are VRSTE effective, 30 DMUs are SE effective. 28 CRSTE effective DMUs must also have complete SE and VRSTE, and constant scale returns. 58 VRSTE effective DMUs, excluded the front 28 DMUs, the remaining 30 DMUs are the pure technical efficiency. But due to the unreasonable allocation of factor inputs, it doesn't get scale efficiency. It can be improved by adjusting the scale efficiency of factor inputs to achieve the overall economic efficiency, so there are 30 DMUs belongs to increasing scale returns. The other two are neither CRSTE effective DMUs, nor VRSTE valid. Though technical invalid lead to economic invalid, the allocation of resources can still be optimal.

In the Model, the mean of VRSTE is greater than that of SE. Most companies can control the input and output elements of financial governance to achieve the technical efficiency, irrational allocation of resources leading to inefficient, and ultimately affects economic efficiency. Most of corporate finance is inefficient or ineffective governance not due to inadequate investment, but due to the unreasonable ratio of inputs and lack of appropriate mechanisms for protection.

4 Surplus Analysis of Financial Management

When efficiency of DMU is not optimal, it means inefficient Outputs under unit input, or outputs inefficient under unit input, which means the lack of pure technical efficiency. Slack variables are used to measure these circumstances. not enough output is called Output slack, as overdone input is named input slack, or surplus.

Since the paper is to establish investment-oriented DEA model, among the 10 input variables, any invalid decision making unit must have some of the variables are surplus. Through the analysis of these inputs' surplus, we can find the main factors that impact financial governance.

To make all DMUs have a uniform standard of comparison, the largest input and minimum output of all DMUs set forms the 71st DMU. Accordingly we can see that the 71st policy-making must be the least efficient units, investment far exceeds the actual need, resulting in diminishing marginal utility, and so the decreasing scale returns. We will remove the 71st surplus decision unit in the later.

From the view of company, the efficiency of financial governance is most affected by the options structure, including institutional shareholders, the largest shareholder, the proportion of circulation shares and equilibrium of shareholders as major factors. Indicating a higher proportion of circulation shares together with relatively lower institutional support share, while the dominance of the bigger share ratio has not been a fundamental change, so there is no check and balance to achieve equity, which shows that an irrational ownership structure cause the imperfections of financial governance structure. Second, corporate financial governance is influenced by the capital structure, including debt ratio as the major factor. High debt ratio means increased financial risk, and while corporate creditors who provide substantial development funds are not involved in the corporate financial governance, capital structure imperfections leading to an irrational financial governance structure. Finally, corporate financial governance is also affected by the incentive and restraint mechanisms, including mergers and acquisitions, independent directors and executive compensation, which are the main factors. Because these markets are underdeveloped leads to acquisition can not be an effective constraint on executive, and the independent director system has not played an important role in corresponding constraints, while the unreasonable executive salary structure leads to ineffective incentive. The imperfections of incentive and restraint mechanisms lead to the defects of financial governance. In addition, dividends per share and executives holding stocks also have impact on financial governance.

5 Conclusion

Considering efficiency evaluation and surplus analysis, we can find that the following factors are the main factors which affect financial governance of listed companies: (1) institutional ownership; (2), the largest shareholder; (3) creditors' governance; (4) executive compensation, (5) independent director. They impact efficiency of financial governance from the financial governance structure and financial governance mechanisms respectively. Therefore, they should be the start point to improve corporate financial governance.

Acknowledgments. The paper is subsidized by Humanities and Management Science Found of NWPU (RW2009015& RW200822).

References

1. Banker, R.D., Charnes, A., Cooper, W.W.: Some Models for Estimating Technical and Scale Inefficiencies in Data Envelopment Analysis. Management Science 30, 1078–1092 (1984)
2. Berglof, Erik, Von Thadden.: Short-Term versus Long-Term Interests: Capital Structure with Multiple Investors. Quarterly Journal of Economics 109, 1055–1084 (1994)
3. Bhagat, S., Black, B.: Board Independence and Long-Term Firm Performance. University of Colorado working paper (2000)

4. Charnes, A., Cooper, W.W., Lewin, A.Y., Seiford, L.M.: Data envelopment analysis: theory, methodology and applications. Kluwer Academic Publishers, Boston (1995)
5. Zhang, R.: Outline of Financial Management Efficiency. Financial Theory and Practice 7, 43–47 (2009)
6. Ding, S.: Empirical Analysis on Split Share Reform Effect. Economic Theory and Economic Management 1, 54–59 (2007)

Research on the Impact of Divisions' Lobbying Activity on Efficiency of Internal Capital Market in Diversified Enterprises

Da-Qin Wu[1], Mei Cai[2], Yun Zhou[1], and Liang-Hua Chen[1]

[1] School of Economy and Management, Southeast University, Nanjing 210096, China
[2] School of Economics and Management, Nanjing University of Information Science and Technology, Nanjing 210044, China
wdq575fc@163.com, lianghua_c@vip163.com

Abstract. Investment decision-making effectiveness depends on the effectiveness of capital allocation, which is affected by division lobbying activity. This paper firstly analyzes the result of division manger's lobbying activity in capital allocative decision-making using game theory. The result shows deviations from efficient investment decision-making (under-investment) under the conditions of information asymmetry. Division manger's lobbying activity is either exacerbating the deviation from the effective investment (under-investment and excess investment), or making up for the information asymmetry (effective investment). Despite previous literatures, this paper shows that division mangers' lobbying activities in capital allocation decision-making may not always result in negative consequences (under-investment and excess investment), but also may have positive results (effective investment).

Keywords: efficiency of ICM, diversified enterprise, lobbying activity.

1 Introduction

Capital allocation is, firstly operated by external capital marketed (ECM) between enterprises, then finished by internal capital market (ICM) between different divisions in diversified enterprises. Capital allocation is of great importance in the internal capital market, [1][2][3]because of imperfect financial market and serious information asymmetry about investment opportunities among enterprises[4][5][6] (for example, in China). Finding out ways to improve efficiency of internal capital markets is an important subject for corporate finance both in theory and in practice. In diversified enterprises, divisions act as both the executives of business decisions, and the applicants of investment decisions, which inevitably have impact on decision-makers'(headquarter) judgment of investment opportunities, supervision and cost of capital, resulting in affection on the efficiency of internal capital market. Therefore, it is necessary to investigate how divisions' behavior affects the efficiency of internal capital market.[7][8]

From domestic and foreign literature about efficiency of internal capital market, we can conclude that so far there has been little literature concerning division impaction

M. Zhou (Ed.): ISAEBD 2011, Part III, CCIS 210, pp. 378–386, 2011.

on efficiency of ICM. [8][9]Only a small number of research concentrated on the problem of agency(Scharfstein and Stein,2000), lobbying activity(Meyer et al,1992) and holding efforts of other division, all of which came to the conclusion that divisions' activity was negative for the efficiency of ICM. [10]Some scholars proposed to prevent division lobbying activity, from views of supervision, fame, compensation, the restructure and capital structure etc., to improve the efficiency of internal capital markets. [11][12][13]In this context, we show that it is to some extent unilateral to take division lobbying activity as bad behavior, which is common in domestic and foreign literature. With the model in Section 2, we prove that under the condition of information asymmetry, headquarters need the division lobbying activity to obtain more information for capital allocation decisions, so as to improve the efficiency of internal capital markets. Therefore, this paper introduces factors of division lobbying activity into capital allocation model concerning capital configuration in diversified enterprises. The focus of this paper is to analyze effects of division lobbying activity on the efficiency of ICM, with the tool of game theory.[14]

The remainder of the paper is organized as follows: Section 2 outlines the model of capital allocation in diversified enterprises. Section 3 introduces the factor of division lobbying activity into model, and analysis its impaction on the efficiency of ICM under various condition. Section 4, Section 5 presents empirical study. Conclusions and recommendations are discussed in Section 6.

2 A Model of Capital Allocation

2.1 Overview

The information received by division i、CEO and shareholders are represented by information set $\Omega_i, \Omega_i^H, \Omega_i^w$. Define θ, η, v as revenue allocation ratio in division investment decision-making. We assume that the three information sets are subject to $\Omega_i^W \subseteq \Omega_i^H \subseteq \Omega_i$ .Declaration funds, approved funds, approval probability, and return of not applying for project are represented by $C_i, N_i, \omega_i, \Delta_i$ .Denote $\vartheta(p_i), e(p_i)$ as information quality function and effort cost function for project p_i which, for convenience, are expressed by ϑ_i, e_i in later equations. Let L, M be numbers of approved project and departments, notice that $L \le M$. The cost of shareholders' funds is represented by rN , with N being available for opportunity cost of other investment.

2.2 Model Construction

Efficiency of ICM is essentially concerned with ways to arrange funds in various groups under the condition of information asymmetry, as a result of group hierarchy level and structure of complexity. The agent, owning information superiority, can take the advantage, while client who own control rights can inspire and supervise for themselves when subjective condition permits. Therefore, the efficiency of ICM is game between client and agent under condition of asymmetric information. In this game, principal and agents action influence on the results of the game, which reflect the interest and costs of principal and agents. Therefore, the capital allocative model is a balanced decision-making process by client and agent (shareholders, group headquarter and divisions), whose constraints are listed as follows respectively.

$$\omega_i \theta E_{\Omega_i} f(\vartheta_i, e_i, N_i) - e_i - \Delta_i \geq 0 \tag{1}$$

$$\sum_{i=1}^{L} \eta E_{\Omega_i^H} f(\vartheta_i, e_i, N_i) - \sum_{i=1}^{L} H_{ei} \geq 0 \tag{2}$$

$$\sum_{i=1}^{L} v E_{\Omega_i^W} f(\vartheta_i, e_i, N_i) - r_W N \geq 0 \tag{3}$$

Under the conditions above, allocation decision-making in ICM can be performed only when expected total income of headquarter ($E_{\Omega_i^H} f(\vartheta_i, e_i, N_i)$) is larger than the sum of net income of division i ($E_{\Omega_i^H} \theta f(\vartheta_i, e_i, N_i)$),net income of headquarter ($E_{\Omega_i^H} \eta f(\vartheta_i, e_i, N_i)$),net income of shareholders($E_{\Omega_i^H} v f(\vartheta_i, e_i, N_i)$)and capital cost(rN_i). So the capital allocation decision model can be written as follow:

$$E_{\Omega_i^H} f(\vartheta_i, e_i, N_i) - E_{\Omega_i^H} \theta f(\vartheta_i, e_i, N_i - E_{\Omega_i^H} \eta f(\vartheta_i, e_i, N_i - E_{\Omega_i^H} v f(\vartheta_i, e_i, N_i) - rN_i \geq 0, i = 1,2\cdots, M \tag{4}$$

2.3 Fundamental Assumptions

Our model is based on the following assumptions.

(a) The total income of the project is comprised of expected income of actual information and income resulting from division lobbying activity.

(b) Divisions obtain more opportunity, because divisions own private information about the project more than other subjects.

(c) When divisions own more actual information, they expect more income with the advantage of their information opportunity.

(d) It is a concave function between the cost of division effort and the amount of project actual information.

(e) Division lobbying activity improves expected income of the headquarter, and meanwhile increases the cost of other division's investment project.

3 Impact of Divisions Lobby on Capital Allocation in ICM

For headquarter, division i 's expected income and cost is changed by lobbying activities of divisions, which, consequently, influences the efficiency of ICM. In this section, we analyze impact of division lobbying activity on the efficiency of ICM under different circumstances.

3.1 All Divisions Do Not Lobby

In this case, capital allocative model equation (1) can be written as follow:

$$E_{\Omega_i^H} f(\vartheta_i, e_i, N_i)(1-\theta-\eta-v) - rN_i \geq 0 \tag{5}$$

As $\Omega_i^H \subseteq \Omega_i$,expected net income of division i is taken into consideration by headquarter in project capital allocative decision, so we have:

$$E_{\Omega_i} f(\vartheta_i, e_i, N_i)(1-\theta-\eta-v) - rN_i \geq E_{\Omega_i^H} f(\vartheta_i, e_i, N_i)(1-\theta-\eta-v) - rN_i, i=1,2\cdots,M \tag{6}$$

Which means expected net income of headquarter is lower than the actual income in division i project, resulting in insufficient investment in high effective investment project.

3.2 Division i Does Not Lobby, While Other Divisions Lobby

In this case, capital allocation of projects in division i is influenced by other divisions' lobbying activity, which makes headquarter reduce expected income or increase financial cost. So equation (1) may be written as follow:

$$E_{\Omega_i^H} f(\vartheta_i, e_i, N_i)(1-\theta-\eta-v) - (r + r_{j\neq i} N_i) \geq 0, i = 1,2\cdots,M \tag{7}$$

As $\Omega_i^H \subseteq \Omega_i$, and expected income of division i is $E_{\Omega_i} f(\vartheta_i, e_i, N_i)(1-\theta-\eta-v) - rN_i$, so we have:

$$E_{\Omega_i} f(\vartheta_i, e_i, N_i)(1-\theta-\eta-v) - rN_i \geq E_{\Omega_i^H} f(\vartheta_i, e_i, N_i)(1-\theta-\eta-v) - rN_i, i=1,2\cdots, M,$$

note that $E_{\Omega_i^H} f(\vartheta_i, e_i, N_i)(1-\theta-\eta-v) - rN_i > E_{\Omega_i^H} f(\vartheta_i, e_i, N_i)(1-\theta-\eta-v) - (r_{j\neq i} + r)N_i, i = 1,2\cdots,M$.So we get:

$$E_{\Omega_i} f(\vartheta_i, e_i, N_i)(1-\theta-\eta-v) - rN_i > E_{\Omega_i^H} f(\vartheta_i, e_i, N_i)(1-\theta-\eta-v) - (r_{j\neq i} + r)N_i, \geq 0, i = 1,2\cdots,M \tag{8}$$

Which means expected income of headquarter is lower than expected income of actual information. Under the condition of headquarter expecting constant income, lobbying activity of other divisions may increase expected financial cost of the headquarter, which means severe insufficient investment.

3.3 All Divisions Lobby

In this case, lobbying activity of division i may increase the expected income of project investment in division i evaluated by headquarter, $r_i E_{\Omega_i^H} f(\vartheta_i, e_i, N_i)$ (r_i is income coefficient of division influence on headquarter).Then expected income of headquarter can be expressed by $E_{\Omega_i^H} f(\vartheta_i, e_i, N_i)(1+r_i)$. Lobbying activity of other division will increase expected financial cost of headquarters, which can be denoted by $r_{j\neq i} N_i$ (the same as Case 2),equation(1)may be written as follow:

$$E_{\Omega_i^H} f(\vartheta_i, e_i, N_i)(1 + r_i - \theta - \eta - v) - (r + r_{j \neq i} N_i) \geq 0, i = 1,2\cdots, M \tag{9}$$

As $\Omega_i^H \subseteq \Omega_i$, $E_{\Omega_i} f(\vartheta_i, e_i, N_i)(1-\theta-\eta-v) - rN_i$, $E_{\Omega_i^H} f(\vartheta_i, e_i, N_i)(1+r_i-\theta-\eta-v)-(r+r_{j\neq i})N_i$ represents net income of division i in a information symmetry project. Their size relation represents the degree of influence on headquarter decision-making by division lobbying activity(See table 1, line 2, column 2).

3.4 Division i Lobbies, While Other Divisions Do Not Lobby

In this case, lobbying activity of division i increases expected income of project investment in division i evaluated by headquarter, which is denoted by $r_i E_{\Omega_i^H} f(\vartheta_i, e_i, N_i)$,so equation (1) can be written as follows :

$$E_{\Omega_i^H} f(\vartheta_i, e_i, N_i)(1 + r_i - \theta - \eta - v) - rN_i \geq 0 \tag{10}$$

Analyzed above, size relations between $E_{\Omega_i} f(\vartheta_i, e_i, N_i)(1-\theta-\eta-v) - rN_i$ and $E_{\Omega_i^H} f(\vartheta_i, e_i, N_i)(1+r_i-\theta-\eta-v) - rN_i$ can be replaced by size relations between $r_i E_{\Omega_i^H} f(\vartheta_i, e_i, N_i)$ and $E_{\Omega_i} f(\vartheta_i, e_i, N_i) - E_{\Omega_i^H} f(\vartheta_i, e_i, N_i)$. In that case, all the results can be divided into three cases (See table 1, line 3, column 2).

Table 1. Results of division lobbying activity

	Division i lobbies	Division i no lobby
Other divisions lobby	its result may be divided three cases: ① $\tau > 0$, Capital configuration indicates under-investment for effective investment. ② $\tau = 0$, Capital configuration indicates effective investment. ③ $\tau < 0$Capital configuration shows over-investment for ineffective investment.	Serious insufficiency for effective investment
Other divisions lobby	its result may be divided three cases: ① $\kappa > 0$, Capital configuration indicates under-investment for effective investment. ② $\kappa = 0$, Capital configuration indicates effective investment. ③ $\kappa < 0$, Capital configuration shows over-investment for ineffective investment.	Insufficiency for effective investment

Notes: Set $\tau = [E_{\Omega_i} f(\vartheta_i, e_i, N_i) - E_{\Omega_i^H} f(\vartheta_i, e_i, N_i)](1-\theta-\eta-v) - r_i E_{\Omega_i^H} f(\vartheta_i, e_i, N_i) + r_{j\neq i} N_i$, $\kappa = [E_{\Omega_i} f(\vartheta_i, e_i, N_i) - E_{\Omega_i^H} f(\vartheta_i, e_i, N_i)](1-\theta-\eta-v) - r_i E_{\Omega_i^H} f(\vartheta_i, e_i, N_i)$.

4 Data and Parameter

4.1 Data

This paper empirically analyzes the impact of division lobbying activity on the efficiency of ICM, taking jiangyin FR Group in Jiangsu as an example. Jiangsu FR Group is a state-owned large comprehensive machinery manufacturing enterprise with a long history of more than 50 years. In 2004, it was transformed from a privatized company into a big diversified manufacturing enterprise. The majority of its stock is private equity, and is transacted in Shenzhen stock market. FR Group runs in several industries, mainly including: cables, optical fiber, memory metal, electronic manufacturing and trading, intelligent electronics, software information and modern service industries, etc. The data needed is from the following sources: some from company's financial database listed in CCER(Sinofin), other data, such as project budgets of FR Group, financial data and financial cost rates through field research and interview by project team. We take cables division as division i when doing empirical research.

4.2 Parameter Selection

Parameter is selected in accordance with following criteria: (1) r is internal cost of capital. FR Group sets r amount lower than interest ration in ECM, which is 90% of loan interest ratio calculated in weighted average method in the same year. (2) N_i is approved amount of capital, which comes from actual investment project. (3) θ,η,ν is expected revenue ratio of division, headquarter, shareholder in division i project respectively. They are calculated with data from 2004-2009 annual report about assessment and profit distribution. (4) $E_{\Omega_i} f(\vartheta_i, e_i, N_i)$ and $E_{\Omega_i^H} f(\vartheta_i, e_i, N_i)$ are expected income of the project for division i and headquarter respectively. They are calculated with data of project income from feasibility report and average income ratio of prior three years. (5) We see all projects in Division as a virtual project in the same year. (6) r_i is income level of cables division with lobbying activity. (7) c_i is effort cost of cables division with lobbying activity.

5 Empirical Analysis

Now we select actual data of cables division in Jiangsu FR Group during 2004-2009, and build model of four different situations depending on whether divisions lobby or not. The results are listed as following (See table 2).

From the results of four different circumstances in table 2,we can come to the following conclusions:

(1) There is under-investment and severe under-investment in the year 2004 and 2009. The expected income of the FR Group was one million Yuan less than the cables division in 2004, and $130+8000r_{j\neq i}$ less in 2009.

Table 2 Results of cables division under different circumstances in FR Group (ten-thousand Yuan)

Simulation Cases	expected net income of cables division	expected income of FR Group
all divisions lobby (2004)	150	50
division i lobbies, while other divisions do not lobby(2005)	260	$(r_i + 0.1)X$
all divisions lobby (2007)	240	$(r_i + 0.1)X - r_{j\neq i}N_i$
division i does not lobby, while other divisions lobby (2009)	180	$-r_{j\neq i}N_i + 0.1X$

(2) In the year 2005, when cables division lobbies and other divisions do not lobby, net income gap of project between cables division and FR group is $550.2 - 2754r_i$. Only when $r_i = 0.1998$, so that the net income gap is 0 can there be best allocation efficiency. When $r_i < 0.1998$,so that $550.2 - 2754r_i < 0$, cables division gets over-investment. When $r_i > 0.1998$, so that $550.2 - 2754r_i > 0$, cables division gets under-investment.

(3) In the year 2007, net income gap of project between cables division and FR group is $411.4 - 1968r_i + 13000r_{j\neq i}$. When $411.4 - 1968r_i + 13000r_{j\neq i} > 0$, cables division gets under-investment. When $411.4 - 1968r_i + 13000r_{j\neq i} = 0$, cables division meets effective investment. When $411.4 - 1968r_i + 13000r_{j\neq i} < 0$, cables division gets over-investment.

Comparing actual ratio of income-investment with the average income ratio of prior three years, we find two results:

(1) In the year 2004,2005,2007 and 2009, the gap between actual investment ratio and average income ratio of prior three years was 0.5% ,0.14%, -7.53% and 4.9% respectively, which clarified that there was effective investment in 2005 when the gap was the smallest. There was under-investment and severe under-investment in 2004 and 2009, while in the year 2007 there was over-investment.

(2) FR Group had more free cash flow in the year 2004 and 2009, which resulted in less money to invest in project(2.31,1.48 billion respectively), and consequently leading to under-investment and severe under-investment. In 2007, there was little free cash flow (only 0.76 billion), which demonstrated more capital to invest in projects, so that there was over-investment. In 2005, FR Group got effective investment with a free cash flow is 0.97 billion (See Table 3). The four cases simulate results above are verified by actual situation.

Table 3. Actual investment, income of feasibility report, average income ratio of prior three years and free cash flow of Cables division in FR Group (billion Yuan)

Fiscal Year	Income of feasibility report	Actual investment	Ratio of investmet (%)	Average invest ment *ratio* of prior three years (%)	Free cash flow of FR Group
2004	0.1495	1.5011	9.96	9.13	1.48
2005	0.3274	2.511	13.04	13.12	0.97
2007	0.2060	1.337	15.41	17.93	0.76
2009	0.1006	0.8	12.57	10.64	2.31

Note that free cash flow=all the cash flow−cash flow of next year−cash flow for investment of next year. If a project is thought as promising, it will own more cash flow, which makes the free cash flow smaller, and vice versa.

6 Concluding Remarks

(1) Division's manager, who own information superiority ,have the power to influence final decision of the headquarter through its behaviors, such as its lobbying activity. Therefore, its behavior is of great importance for the efficiency of ICM
(2)A lot of literatures take the view that lobbying activity of divisions is a "bad" behavior. This paper proves it is actually a neutral action through model construction and analysis. Lobbying activity may not always be negative; sometimes it may have a positive effect on efficiency of capital allocation.
(3)Under what circumstances does lobbying activity of divisions have positive effects? The answer is when net income of divisions lobbying activity equals income gap resulted from information asymmetry of the project between headquarter and divisions. It is positive impact on the efficiency of ICM for divisions to lobby.
(4) Under what circumstances does lobbying activity of divisions have negative effects? The answer is when net income of divisions lobbying activity does not equal income gap resulted from information asymmetry of the project between headquarter and divisions. It is negative impact on the efficiency of ICM for divisions to lobby in two aspects as follows. Firstly, when net income of divisions lobbying activity exceeds income gap resulted from information asymmetry of the project between headquarter and divisions, it is over- investment. Secondly, when net income of divisions lobbying activity is less than income gap resulted from information asymmetry of the project between headquarter and divisions, it is under-investment.

Acknowledgements. The authors would like to thank the referee and the editor for their helpful comments and suggestions to improve the earlier version of the paper.

References

1. Roig, R.A.: Relative efficiency of the internal capital market in a multi-division firm. Case Western Reserve University (2008)
2. Brusco, S., Panunzi, F.: Reallocation of corporate resources and managerial incentives in internal capital markets. European Economic Review 49, 659–681 (2005)

3. Rajan, Raghuram, Henri, S., Luigi, Z.: The cost of diversity: the diversification discount and inefficient investment. Journal of Finance 15(1), 35–80 (2000)
4. Wulf, J.M.: Influence and Inefficiency in the internal capital market: Theory and Evidence. Columbia University (1999)
5. Rovetta, B.: Investment policies and excess returns in corporate spin-offs: evidence from the US market. Fin. Mkts Portfolio Mgmt 20, 287–307 (2006)
6. Lundstrum, L.L.: Firm Value, Information Problems and the Internal Capital Market. Review of Quantitative Finance and Accounting 21, 141–156 (2003)
7. Laux, V.: On the value of influence activity for capital budgeting. Journal Of Economic Behavior & Organization (65), 625–635 (2008)
8. Wulf, J.: Influence and inefficiency in the internal capital markets: theory and evidence. Working Paper, The Wharton School University of Pennsylvania (2002)
9. Ahn, S., Denis, D.J.: Internal capital markets and investment policy evidence from corporate spinoffs. Journal of Financial Economics 71, 489–516 (2004)
10. Siddiqi, M.A., Warganegara, D.L.: Using spinoffs to reduce capital mis-allocations. Review of Quantitative Finance and Accounting 20, 35–47 (2003)
11. Billett, M.T., Mauer, D.C.: Diversification and the value of internal capital markets: The case of tracking stock. Journal of Banking & Finance 24, 1457–1490 (2000)
12. Burch, T.R., Nanda, V.: Divisional diversity and the conglomerate discount: evidence form spinoffs. Journal of Financial Economics 70, 69–98 (2003)
13. Bernardo, A.E., Luo, J., Wang, J.J.D.: A theory of socialistic internal capital markets. Journal of Financial Economics 80, 485–509 (2006)
14. Zhang, W.-y.: Game and information economics. Shanghai people's press (1996)

The Mediating Role of Knowledge Acquisition in Network Munificence and Innovation

Mangui Wu

Zhejiang Gongshang University, Xuezheng Street 18#, Xiasha High Education District
310018, Hangzhou, China
wumangui@gmail.com

Abstract. Drawing on the organizational learning and network literature, we posited that knowledge acquisition play a mediating role in network munificence and innovation performance. Hierarchical regressions of data from 183 firms revealed that all three dimensions of network munificence (partner diversity, mutual trust and knowledge reservation) were positively related to a firm's knowledge acquisition, and knowledge acquisition mediated the relationship between mutual trust and knowledge reservation on one side, and innovation performance on the other. These findings suggest that firms should pay attention to learning capability building as well as network building.

Keywords: network munificence, knowledge acquisition, innovation performance.

1 Introduction

Innovation originates from the combination and restructuring of knowledge. If appropriate institution for knowledge sharing is installed, organization's network can turn into a unique channel for knowledge acquisition (hereafter KA), and provide raw materials for innovation (Lane & Lubatkin, 1998). Therefore, network has been considered a major infrastructure for innovation. However, extant literatures tend to assume a direct effect between network characteristics and innovation performance (hereafter IP), and few papers have studied the role of KA in the relationship between network characteristics and IP. This paper intends to fill this gap.

2 Literature Review and Hypothesis

The term "munificence" has been widely used to denote the availability of resources opportunities present in the environment. Zhang (2009) suggested that besides relational patterns and structural characteristics, networks are different in munificence. He distinguished three dimensions of network munificence (hereafter NM): Partner diversity, trust and knowledge reservation.

Partner diversity reflects the degree that partners belong to different industries. Networks consist of diversified partners can better facilitate KA for several reasons.

M. Zhou (Ed.): ISAEBD 2011, Part III, CCIS 210, pp. 387–392, 2011.

First, when network partners operate in different industries, they are less likely to involve in learning competition, and their will of knowledge sharing increases (Mowery et al., 1996). Second, as the diversity of network partners increases, the degree of knowledge heterogeneity increases as well, and this will speed up the process of knowledge transfer and expand the scope of knowledge exchange (Cohen & Levinthal, 1990). Thirdly, contact with a large number of members of different industries can increase the firms' opportunity of "learning by doing" and improve its knowledge integration capability (Zahra & Irleand, 2000). Therefore:

H1a: Partner diversity of a firm's network is positively related to its KA.

Sharing information and know-how with other organizations in the network always entails risk. Proper institutions must be in place to prevent free-riders. Dyer and Singh (1998) found that the trust relationship among network partners is an effective mechanism to prevent free-riding activities in knowledge sharing. This is because trust can reduce the necessity for knowledge authentication and evaluation, cut the time spent on bargaining and supervision, and help partners focusing more on information processing and exchange. In China, the slack law enforcement makes knowledge transfer and exchange even more risky. As a rational choice, Chinese firms tend to pass important information only among trusted partners (Li & Zhang, 2007). Therefore, solid trust among network partners will increase KA by promoting learning and expanding the scope of knowledge transfer. Formally stated:

H1b: Mutual trust among network partners is positively related to its KA.

Stuart (2000) suggested that network partners are of different value. Those who have more know-how, stronger innovation capability and more solid market foundation are of higher value, they bring more learning opportunities to the host firm. Partnering with such firms could also function as a signal, sending favorable messages about the host's quality and reputation to the outside world. For firms that lack tracking records, partnering with high-profile companies is like an endorsement of competitiveness, and can help them get access to resources. Therefore:

H1c: Knowledge reservation in a firms' network is positively related to its KA.

Innovation is the result of combining and restructuring of knowledge. With knowledge acquired from suppliers and buyers, a firm can foresee opportunities brought by the changing commercial environment, launch products that best suit customers' potential needs (Cohen & Levinthal, 1990), assess the commercial value of scientific findings (Wiklund & Shepherd, 2003), shorten R & D cycle (Dyer & Singh, 1998), maintain technological uniqueness and product differentiation (Zahra & Ireland, 2000). Therefore:

H2: A firm's KA from its network is positively related to its IP.

H1a through H1c assume a relationship between NM and KA, H2 assumes a relationship between KA and IP. These relationships imply that NM might impose its influence on a firm's innovation through KA. Therefore, we propose:

H3: KA mediates the relationship between NM and IP.
H3a: KA mediates the relationship between partner diversity and IP.
H3b: KA mediates the relationship between network mutual trust and IP.
H3c: KA mediates the relationship between knowledge reservation and IP.

3 Methods

3.1 Sample

With help from government agents that are in charge of economic issues, we delivered and collected 250 questionnaires from companies in Changsha, Xiamen, Shenzhen and Ningbo (100% response rate). After deleting questionnaires with severe missing data, we had 183 (73.2%) valid questionnaires. Sample firms covered 4 industries, including machinery (65, 35.5%), electronics (47, 25.7%), software (55, 30%) and pharmaceutical (16, 8.8%). These firms aged 6.08 years on average, with the maximum 10 years and minimum 2 years. They hired 265 employees on average, with the largest company hiring 1200 and smallest one 28.

3.2 Variables and Measures

Innovation performance. Measurement scale was adopted from Rindfleisch (2001). The scale consists of 9 items, measuring a firm's product innovation, process innovation and speed of innovation. Typical questions included "Compared with other firms in the industry, our products are very innovative."

Network munificence. Four items adopted from Zhang's (2009) research measured partner diversity. Typical questions included "Our network partners are from a variety of industries." Four items taken from Gupta & Govindarajan (2000) measured knowledge reservation. Typical questions included "Our network partners possess technological expertise." Four items taken from Levin & Cross' (2004) scale of trust measured mutual trust among partners.

Knowledge acquisition. Yli-Renko's (2001) scale of knowledge were slightly modified and adopted to measure KA. Typical questions included "We learned a lot of technological know-how through network partners."

4 Results

Table 1 showed the means, standard deviations and inter-correlations of all variables.

We used hierarchical regression to test the mediating effect. The mediating variable (KA) was first regressed on independent variables (Model 1), and then the dependent variable (IP) was regressed on independent variables (model 2). At last, KA was imported as mediating variable (Model 3). Results are shown in Table 2.

Model 1 indicates that partner diversity ($B=0.129$, $p<0.05$), mutual trust ($B=0.303$, $p<0.01$) and knowledge reservation had positive effect on KA, supporting H1a, H1b and H1c. In model 2, all dimensions of NM had significant effect on IP, as previous literatures had rightly supposed and tested. In model 3, two findings are notable. First, the coefficient of KA was significant ($B=0.343$, $p<0.001$), supporting H2. Second, when KA was introduced into the equation, the power of explanation of the model marked a significant increase ($\Delta R^2=0.085$, $p<0.001$), supporting H3. However, when checking closely whether KA mediated the relationship between specific dimensions of NM and IP, we found that only the coefficients of mutual trust and knowledge reservation decreased significantly. The first shrank from B=0.320 (p<0.001) to B=0.219 (p<0.05), and the second from B=0.208 (p<0.05) to B=0.105(p>0.05). These results indicate that H3b and H3c were supported while H3a was not.

Table 1. Discriptive Statistics and Correlations (n=183)

	Mean	SD	1	2	3	4	5	6
Age	6.08	2.23						
Size	264.67	251.10	.291**					
Partner Diversity	2.31	.63	.067	.021				
Mutual Trust	3.44	.69	.126	.256**	.239**			
Knowledge reservation	3.55	.59	.130	.125	.201**	.367**		
KA	3.10	.57	.058	.052	.267**	.411**	.424**	
IP	2.71	.58	.028	.014	.432**	.192**	.149*	.243**

*p<.05; ** p<.01.

Table 2. Results of Hierarchical Regression Analysis

	Model 1	Model 2	Model 3
Age	-.001	-.031	-.025
Size	-.034	.133*	.151**
Partner Diversity	.129*	.271***	.223***
Mutual Trust	.303***	.320***	.219**
Knowledge Reservation	.296***	.208**	.105
KA			.343***
R^2	.291***	.415***	.500**
Adjusted R^2	.267	.395	.480
ΔR^2			.085***

* p<.05; ** p<.01; *** p<.001.

5 Discussion

Researches of organization learning show that the learning effect of a firm depends on the teacher firm's willingness to share knowledge. In a network of firms, if the members aggregate in the same industry, they might engage in learning competitions and this might hinder the process of knowledge transfer. Our research demonstrates that if a firm builds a network of more diversified partners, they might be more willing to share knowledge, hence positively impact the KA of the host firm.

Both structural and relational perspective of network suggests that trust among network partners is the foundation for knowledge transfer. Our research supports this view. This is partly because high levels of trust decreased the risk of being taken advantage by other network members, minimized the time and cost for knowledge screening, and in turn improved the efficiency of learning and KA.

Network could be seen as a reservoir of knowledge whose volume depends on how much network members could contribute. Our study reveals that when network consists of partners who have expertise in technology, marketing or processing methods, it has more value to the host firm in terms of KA. It's natural that willingness of sharing matters, but in the business world, networking with a grudging yet wealthy partner might be more practical than a generous yet poor one.

The most interesting finding is that network does not affect a firm's innovation performance directly. KA plays a mediating role between these two variables. A firm might have a magnificent network, but if it does not work diligently to absorb the knowledge embedded in the network, the network might be nothing more than an expensive furnishing. Simply put, the paper shows that firms should not only focus on network building, but also pay close attention on improving their learning capability, and this is the real magic that works on innovation.

References

1. Baron, R.M., Kenny, D.A.: The moderator-mediator variable distinction in social psychological research: Conceptual, strategic, and statistical considerations. Journal of Personality and Social Psychology 51(6), 1173–1182 (1986)
2. Cohen, W.M., Levinthal, D.A.: Absorptive capacity: A new perspective on learning and innovation. Administrative Science Quarterly 35, 128–152 (1990)
3. Dyer, J.H., Kale, P., Singh, H.: How to make strategic alliances work. Sloan Management Review 42(4), 37–43 (2001)
4. Gupta, A., Govindarajan, V.: Knowledge flows within multinational corporations. Strategic Management Journal 21(4), 473–496 (2000)
5. Lane, P.J., Lubatkin, M.: Relative absorptive capacity and interorganizational learning. Strategic Management Journal 19, 461–477 (1998)
6. Levin, D.Z., Cross, R.: The strength of weak ties you can trust: The mediating role of trust in effective knowledge transfer. Management Science 50(11), 1477–1490 (2004)
7. Li, H., Zhang, Y.: The role of managers political networking and functional experience in new venture performance: Evidence from China's transition economy. Strategic Management Journal 28, 791–804 (2007)
8. Mowery, D.C., Oxley, J.E., Silverman, B.S.: Strategic alliances and inter-firm knowledge transfer. Strategic Management Journal 17, 77–91 (1996)
9. Rindfleisch, A., Moorman, C.: The acquisition and utilization of information in new product alliances: A strength-of-ties perspective. Journal of Marketing 65(2), 1–18 (2001)
10. Stuart, T.E.: Interorganizational alliances and the performance of firms: A study of growth and innovation rates in a high-technology industry. Strategic Management Journal 21(8), 791–811 (2000)
11. Subramanian, A., Nilakanta, S.: Organizational innovativeness: Exploring the relationship between organizational determinants of innovation, types of innovations, and measures of organizational performance. International Journal of Management Science 24(6), 631–647 (1996)

12. Thompson, V.A.: Bureaucracy and innovation. Administrative Science Quarterly 10, 1–20 (1965)
13. Tsai, W.: Knowledge Transfer in Intraorganizational networks: Effects of network position and absorptive capacity on business unit innovation and performance. Academy of Management Journal 44(5), 996–1004 (2001)
14. Wiklund, J., Shepherd, D.: Knowledge-based resources, entrepreneurial orientation, and the performance of small and medium-sized businesses. Strategic Management Journal 24, 1307–1314 (2003)
15. Yli-Renko, H., Autio, E., Sapienza, H.J.: Social capital, knowledge acquisition, and technology-based firms. Strategic Management Journal 22, 587–613 (2001)
16. Zahra, S.A., Ireland, R.D.: International expansion by new venture firms: International diversity, mode of market entry, technological learning and performance. Academy of Management Journal 43, 925–950 (2000)
17. Zhang, R.X., Wu, M.G.: Dynamic network capability, network quality and innovation performance. Journal of Lanzhou University 37(2), 107–114 (2009)

Post-Merger Integration Management

Yongmei Cui[1] and Yifei Zhang[2]

[1] Doctor, Deputy Director of Center of China Merger and Acquisition(CCMAR), Beijing Jiaotong University
[2] Graduate of Center of China Merger and Acquisition(CCMAR), Beijing Jiaotong University

Abstract. Post-merger integration gets across the phases of decision-making, implementation, take-over, assessment and other links. In integration work, it is crucial to the company adhere the principle of integrated reforming. Through the integration, first the simples preform the purpose of perfect industrial chain and optimize the allocation of resources. Then, after the enterprises realize stable development, do the further reforming measure. Basic on M&A Integration theory and Project Management, this paper describes a system of the analysis of post-merger integration, which is the whole process of and dynamic integration.

Keywords: M&A process, post-merger integration, integration team, post-merger integration of the "four stages" management model.

1 Introduction

M&A is not a simple amendment, but a revolution involving in various aspects interest. Post-merger integration (PMI) refer that M&A enterprises arrange the overall systemic enterprise resource, such as assets, human resources, management system, organization structure, cultural factors, after obtained ownership of the target company's assets, equity or management control. PMI is required, since the necessity of PMI is some kinds of risk brined by M&A and the purchaser expects to meet the acquisition effect and to avoid the trap of mergers and acquisitions (Zhang Jinxing etc., 2005).

After a preliminary investigation, the following ways could do the best to integration. First, M&A occurred in two enterprises which have the similar main business. Second, the companies do internal restructuring. For example, treat the central enterprise integrating SASAC thought there are three points. First, Policy guide M&A between the power-and-power states own enterprise power-and-power. Second, common central state own enterprise incorporated into performance of outstanding achievement of enterprises. Third, research institutes merge into industry group.

In M&A, the company focuses more on the M&A transaction process. Most companies rely heavily on the strategic plan of enterprise's senior manager or on the business docking, to solve problems in the integration process. In most case, such performance for the integration lacks of clear rules and norms (Cui Yongmei etc., 2009). A research by Boston Consulting Group showed that less than 20% of the M&A business has taken integration issues into consideration or has developed integration plans. However, it has a direct negative impact on post-merger corporative

M. Zhou (Ed.): ISAEBD 2011, Part III, CCIS 210, pp. 393–399, 2011.

performance and management strategy, thus even affecting the company's future survival. So as soon as possible to consider integration issues for mergers and acquisitions businesses, it is possible that enterprise can find out problem and identify risks in advance. From the perspective of integration, it will also help to achieve the acquisition and trade.

The study by Haspeslagh and Jemison (1991) showed that PMI is divided into two parts: communication and implementation. Pritchett, along with others, (2005) proposed the "five-stage integration process," including the design phase, evaluation phase, start phase, the management phase and final phase. Based on such view, a successful integration need the well communication, the analysis to the feasibility of the integration, the construal of the match of two sides and the in-depth analysis of the potential risk, which indicates that integrated management should be started before the formal takeover. Meanwhile, the integration process should be set as a series of steps, which aims to organically combine the two sides. (Qiu Hongsheng etc, 2006).

2 PMI Management

Unlike the general project, the most significant difference of the integration is that when the integration is done, the management organization will be dissolved and will be gradually transited to the daily management. This feature is similar to project management, so the project management idea will be applied to the integration management in this paper.

Project management stressed the importance to conduct a whole and all-around process of planning, organization, control and leadership due to specific norms, in a certain period, within the budget. Integration stresses that in a specific period, we should recreate the value of every department and service influenced by the integration process under the basement that we should systematically take the profit of the stakeholder into first consideration. During the integration, professional project management methods can us with the integration of the overall planning and control, with the effective contribution of time and resources, with focusing on the main concern and with the management of the risks in advance.

The practice of GE Capital Company shows PMI should begin at M & A preparation and throughout the enterprise management process. While there are clear beginning and ending time boundaries between integration stages, in fact, we can not distinguish integration from M&A at all stages. These stages should be mutual connection, between mutual infiltrations (see Fig.1.).

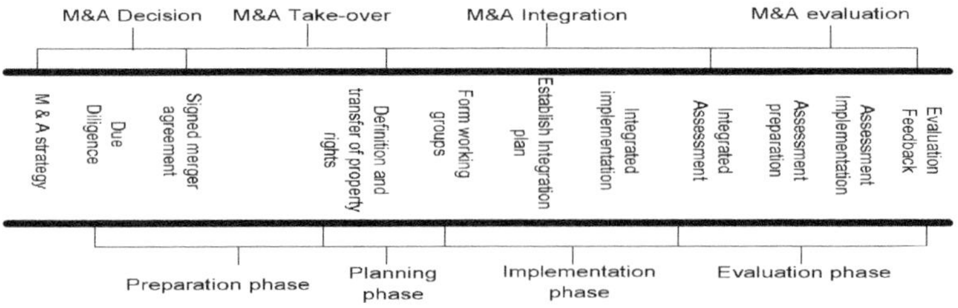

Fig. 1. Whole Process of PMI Model

3 Management Model Application

M&A, dynamic and development process, with the changing of potential factors which influence the M&A risk, puts in force dynamic flow control. Thus, M & A process is divided into several sub-processes and research the risk of every sub-processes, in order to control the potential risk and ensure the smooth integration.

Based on the above theoretical analysis, in this paper, the integration process will be divided into preparation, integration planning, implementation and integration of audit and evaluation of integrated four stages (see table 1).

Table 1. PMI "four stages" management model

	Preparation phase	**Planning phase**	**Implementation phase**	**Evaluation phase**
Period of time	From due diligence to signed a merger agreement	From Industrial and commercial registration to take-over	From official take-over	Stage or fully completed integration
Personnel	Integration steering committee, integrated manager, M&A team	Integration steering committee, Management group,	Same as Planning phase	Internal audit department
Target	Formulation of a preliminary integration plan	Formulation of a formal integration plan	Synergistic effect and realize M&A	Integrated Performance measure
Major work	Established PMI management organization, Perfected integration working constitution, Match Analysis, constituted integration plan	Communicated with executive, Formulation of a formal integration plan	Human Resource Integration, Financial Integration, Business Integration, Legal Integration	Determine the content of assessment and Identified the main assessment, build up evaluation model, Implemented evaluation program, PMI Exchange and learning

4 Integration Preparation Phase

M&A practice in China, many enterprises focus on M&A negotiations and transactions in stead of focus on post-merger integration which in a large extent decides success or failure of M&A and corporate strategy. Inappropriate choice of integration strategy and highly integration costs lead to mergers and acquisitions fail (Du Jianyao, 2008).If the two simply can not enhance the core competitiveness through the integration and create synergies between the business combinations, this transaction is not necessary to retain. Thus it is important to consider integration problem as early as possible in success PMI. Preparation stage means the start of integration, which is the basis for the success of integration.

(1) Start-stop points. Comprehensive predecessor studies, integration preparation phase should begin in due diligence, in which stage both parties of M&A already produced intention. Since this phase the corporation starts to prepare for integration, especially appointed integrated manager, established PMI team. PMI team utilize internal and external due diligence to comprehensively assess status of target company in order to posit integration goals and potential resource value.

(2) Select and engage Integration manager. Integration is a very complex task. McKinsey research shows that inappropriate candidates for the integration manager and who failed to participate in the integration process as soon as possible are poor integration of the important reasons. Integration manager who posit in the central of the integrated system is not only the team leader, but also the team coordinator. Integrated manager involve in integration from the due diligence phase, full-time participation, but do not need comment on his deal.

(3) Match Analysis. Using due diligence information, definitude match standard from the point of integration about analyzing the feasibility of transaction. Based on improving core competitiveness and realizing M&A motivation, merged enterprise should analyze M&A from stratagem, culture, business, human resource, finance and so on.

(4) Preliminary integration plan. After due diligence, basic on project management, management group analyze the situation, nail down clear integration objectives, identify critical path, analysis estimated cost of resources and risk. Specially attend to integrate demarcation.

4.1 Planning Phase

From the means of point of view, integration is to integrate the operation of reallocation of resources. From the aim of point of view, integration is to maximize the outcome of the operation. These must be through the integration of plan establishes the planning implementation. Integrated plan of PMI that security integration smoothly provides strategic and policy, which include strategic integration plan, business integration plan, cultural integration plan, human resource integration plan and financial integration plan etc. Integrated plan stage to improve the organization and the appropriate principles, a clear one, the corresponding post and duties and to improve efficiency of communications in order to ensure the orderly conduct of integration.

Integrated plan which plays the role of general programme is propitious to improve efficiency. In the other hand, plan, based on limited information, have to modify for the sake of adapting variational reality. So company should pay attention to the point as follows.

(1) Principle. Aims disassemble. Integration involved in almost every department and field of the company, so the integrated manager should consider various factors Interlaced.

(2) Mode. Generally there are two ways to established integrated plan. First, integrated team, unilaterally, develop integration plans though the result of due diligence. Second, integrated team and Target Company discuss the plan together. In the integration planning process, you can force the appropriate use of external experts, but their advice should not be a dominant factor in the integration planning.

(3) High-level support. In integration process, high-level that plays a crucial role, especially early in the integration, provide strong support to promptly resolve problems and risks.

(4) Full range of communication and feedback mechanism. If you do not advance with key stakeholders to communicate effectively, even after careful planning and cooperative relations, integration could collapse.

4.2 Implementation Phase

Integration of the implementation phase will integrate the plan into reality. In this stage, integration will generally involve management and staff changes, and the integration of related fields such as financial, operational, organizational culture.

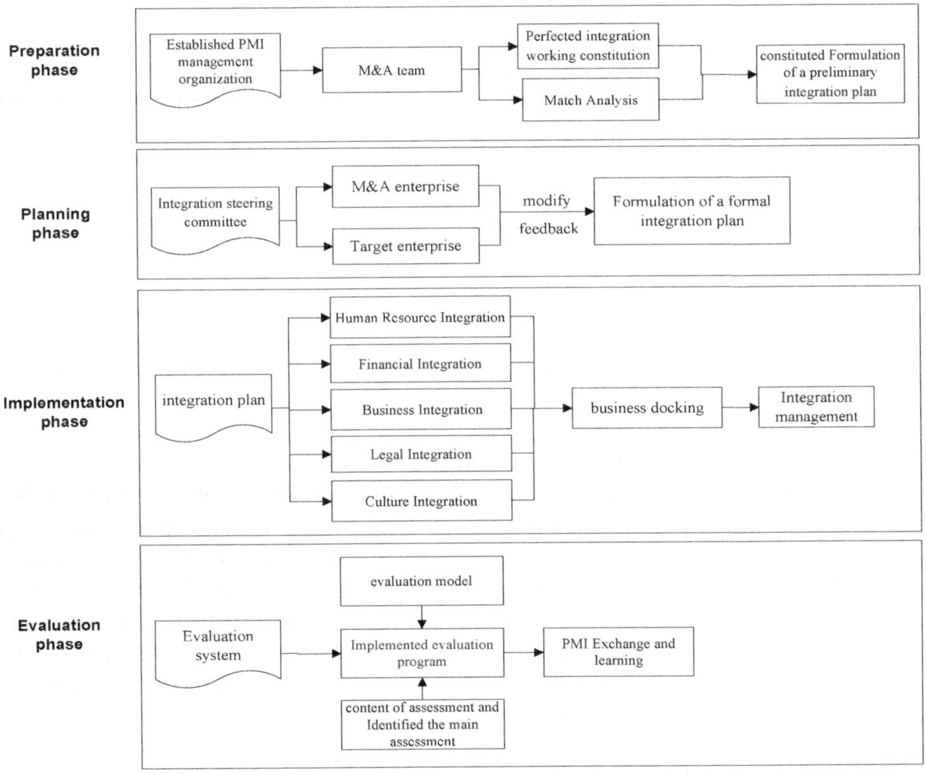

Fig. 2. Integration phases

(1) Coordination of various departments. Integration does not independently perform which involve in some interrelated departments. Integration between relevant departments involved in the integration is not independent. The lack of any one would lead to decrease the overall value of the company. At the same time, enterprises should also establish channels of top-down and bottom-up decision-making pass to report feedback channels.

(2) Concerned about the integration of stakeholders. Resolve personnel problems, in other ways, can play a catalytic role. The decision-making of the management structure, key people, reporting relationships, layoffs should be determine and perform as early as possible.

(3) The combination of management and integration. Enterprises in the integration process will face a wide range of adjustment. Thus, it is that the related department operation ability, mergers between both sides department cooperation ability take a great influent to operating performance.

4.3 Evaluation Phase

The research on integrated evaluation is still in its infancy. PMI evaluation refers to the whole process of enterprise integration. In integrated evaluation phase, the company should set up evaluation team that led by internal audit staff. Evaluated team measure whether the objective of integration activities achieve integration goals. So company should pay attention to the point as follows.

(1) Evaluation of the development of indicators. Integration of aspects involved in broad and faced diversified risks. Thus evaluation should be set for a particular method and indicators, which always consist of Index measures and results indicators.

(2) Integrated exchange and experiential learning. Integration of the feedback process of implementation should be recorded by the acquisition of both parties to form complete information.

5 Conclusion

First, in this paper, the thinking of "the whole process of PMI", throughout the phase of decision-making, implementation, take-over and evaluation, will be conducive to the sustainable development of the successful implementation and integration.

Second, construction of the merger integration of the "four stages" management model for the successful implementation of the integration after M&A provides standard operating guidelines.

Third, using project management, PMI program construct PMI team that play key role for the success of integration.

References

1. Aspeslagh, P., Jemison, D.: Managing Acquisitions: Creating Value through Corporate Renewal. Free Press, NewYork (1991)
2. Pritchett, P., Robinson, D., Clarkson, R.: After the Merger. Machinery industry press, Beijing (2005)

3. Luo, J., Cui, Y., Zhang, Q.: Internal Control and Risk Management in Enterprise Merger and Acquisition. Dalian Press, Dalian (2010)
4. Qiu, H., Chen, L.: M&A defining battle- Integration to create value. China Planning Press, Beijing (2006)
5. Agrawal, A., Jeffe, J.F., Mandelker, G.N.: The Post-merger Performance of Acquiring Firms: A Reexamination of an Anomaly. Journal of Finance, (47) (1992)
6. Xu, B.: Post-merger integration and synergy. Journal of Beijing Institute of Technology (8), 71–74 (2000)
7. Gao, L.: Post-merger integration management - Based on Empirical Analysis of Chinese Listed Companies. Management World (12), 107–114 (2003)
8. Zhang, J., Wang, F., Zhang, Q.: Review of M&A Integration. Commercial Research (9), 111–114 (2005)
9. Cai, B.: Integration is Key for the Success of Enterprise M&A. China Business and Market (11), 45–48 (2006)
10. Gao, C., Tang, G.: Multiple cases study on integrated management control systems: theoretical analysis and innovation in Chinese companies. Accounting Research (8), 68–75 (2007)
11. Du, J.: Issues of Enterprises Merger and Acquisition. Reformation & Strategy 11(3), 105–107 (2008)
12. Li, S., Liu, Y.: How Does the Post Merger and Acquisition Integration Affect Firms Performance? Based on the Study of China LPG Industry. Nankai Business Review (4), 154–160 (2010)
13. Xu, C., Zhou, W.: Identification by Stages and Systematic Control of Business M&A Risk. Science & Technology Progress and Policy (6), 62–64 (2004)
14. Xu, J., Zhao, B.: The Risks Analysis of M&A. Science Technology and Industry (10), 17–20 (2006)
15. Cheng, Z.: How to engage in merger and integration of GE. Sino-Foreign Management (1), 56–57 (2001)

Application of Relationship Marketing in Customer Management of Travel Agency in China

Yang Zhao

Tourism & Cuisine School of Harbin Commercial University,
150076, Harbin, China
Economic & Management School of Northeast Agriculture University,
150030, Harbin, China
zhaoyang99@126.com

Abstract. The application of relationship marketing in customer management of travel agency is helpful to solve the problems caused by weak tourism marketing. The method of keeping the long-term good relationship with the customer in the fierce travel market competition is the key of managing advantage for travel agency. On analysis of the significance for application of relationship-marketing in customer management of Chinese travel agency, the paper puts forward the principles for application of relationship marketing in customer management. It states the basic methods for application of customer-centric relationship marketing in detail, in order to reduce marketing cost and increase profits of travel agency in China effectively.

Keywords: Relationship marketing, customer management, customer satisfaction.

1 Introduction

The term "relationship marketing" was first used in the United States in 1983 when Leonard Berry presented a paper entitled simply "Relationship Marketing" at the American Marketing Association's Services Marketing Conference. It originated in Europe in the 1980s, where businesses quickly began to use the strategy. Since its introduction to North American universities, relationship marketing has been widely discussed and has begun to be applied to various North American industries.[1] Don E.Schultz pointed out in his IMC (Integrated Marketing Communications) that relationship marketing was the key to the future marketing. Relationship marketing is generally thought to establish and develop a long-term relationship through which the exchange between parties with relations would be optimized. It is defined as a form of marketing developed from direct response marketing campaigns which emphasizes customer retention and satisfaction, rather than a dominant focus on sales transactions.

In the tourism sector, it is most evident in resort marketing, where repeat customers are relatively common and there are more opportunities to communicate with the client. In other words, relationship marketing refers to developing a detailed understanding of

M. Zhou (Ed.): ISAEBD 2011, Part III, CCIS 210, pp. 400–406, 2011.

what your clients want from a holiday and working to fulfill these wants in the tourism industry. There has been transaction marketing in operation of travel agency in China. Application of relationship marketing in customer management of travel agency in China is to observe tourist enterprises in social economic environment based on system theory, by which travel agency marketing is considered as an interact process with customer, other tourist companies, tourist suppliers, tourist distribution, government and social organization. The theory of relationship marketing is applied in customer management of travel agency in China to form customer relationship marketing in order to ensure the customer satisfaction and create customer loyalty.

2 Significance for Application of Relationship Marketing in Customer Management of Travel Agency

Relationship marketing emphasizes cultivating customer satisfaction and loyalty. It may improve profits of the company by enhancing corporate value. Application of relationship marketing to establish and develop long-term relationship between customer and travel agency has the following advantages: first, it can promote tourist loyalty. The problem of customer loss has been the persistent ailment in travel industry. Many travel agencies have to struggle for tourist resource by low-price competition, which causes the result that, neither side gains in the price war. Relationship marketing can promote tourist loyalty by enhancing their satisfaction and cultivating their trust. Second, it can enhance the advertisement effect of the tourists. "The satisfied customer is the best advertisement."[2] Customers with high satisfaction are willing to introduce the travel agency they trust to others, which plays a big role in recommendation. Besides, comparing with advertised customers through other means, the tourists that are introduced to the company have higher loyalty and consumption. Third, relationship marketing is helpful to reduce marketing cost and increase profits. High loyalty and good recommendation effect can reduce service cost of travel agency and increase average profit per tourist. Research indicates that the fee of maintaining a loyal customer is only 20% of that of attracting a new customer; when the rate of repeat customer up by 5 percentage points the profit increases by 25%—125%. That means relationship marketing is the good solution for problems in travel agency marketing.

3 Principles for Application of Relationship Marketing in Customer Management of Travel Agency

Relationship marketing is a core tool and tactic used within the tourism industry. A relationship marketing program, designed to optimize the customer experience and make marketing more efficient, can help travel agencies more effectively turn leads into sales and establish repeat business. But its application has some principles and rules to abide by.

3.1 Principle of Customer Delivered Value

Customer delivered value (CDV) refers to the difference between total customer value (TCV) and the total customer cost (TCC), which is expressed in formula as

$$CDV = TCV - TCC$$

To observe principle of CDV allows travel agency to evaluate the supply from every competitor in order to make clear the target positioning of its own supplement. Besides, by increasing the supplement of product, service, working staff and image value, the travel agency with delivered value at a disadvantage can improve total customer value or reduce the price, decrease the cost of customer's time and energy to reduce total customer cost.

3.2 Principle of Customer Satisfaction

Customer satisfaction with tourist product is decided by two factors: one is the quality level of tourist resources that is natural formed; the other is service quality, which is determined by expectation and feelings of customer. Their relationship is as follows:

$$\text{Customer Satisfaction} = \frac{\text{Customer Service Experience}}{\text{Customer Expectation}} \mathbf{X}\ 100\%$$

The higher the expectation for value is, the bigger the purchasing desire is. From this point of view, travel agency should strengthen the efforts to improve information transformation for raising expectation of customers. In customer's mind, tourism means to buy leisure with money instead of family living, especially not to buy suffering. Therefore, customers pay much more attention to the quality of tourism service and prefer to obtain maximal satisfaction, which is one of the most important standards for tourists to pay, and even exceed the price element to be the priority. As a result, service becomes the effective competition tool for travel agency to win new customers and maintain old ones when the quality, function and price of tourist products are quite similar.

Though a satisfied customer seldom buys the same tourist product, he may be interested in other kinds of the products. Besides, reutilized trade reduces the costs of transactions, which makes travel agency easier to obtain tangible profit. On the other hand, a satisfied customer is the best advertisement that is more effective than media means, and he will be highly engaged in operation of travel agency and provide extensive information and suggestions.

3.3 Principle of Customer Profitability

The task of marketing is not only to establish customer relationships, but also to maintain and enhance them in order to improve customer profitability. Relationship marketing involves attracting, developing and keeping relationship with customers, whose core principle is to create "real customer". The so-called real customer means those that are satisfied with tourism service, and will keep loyalty in a period of time to repurchase more products. They are the customers that have low sensitivity to product price and will make advantageous advertisement for travel agency. There may be 20 %– 40 % customers of travel agency who are not beneficial, it is necessary to analyze customers. The quantity buying customers demand meticulous service and biggest discount, which may reduce the profit of travel agency; intermediate buying customers demand good service and normally buy in full payment, which is much profitable; "purchase piecemeal" customers may pay in full payment and accept only lowest service, but the cost fee with them reduces profit of travel agency. Therefore, most profitable customers are not quantity buying and small buying ones, but the intermediate buying group instead. Profitability emphasizes customer lifetime value instead of one certain trading profit. There are many factors influencing profitability, including the size of demand feature, bargaining ability of customer, price sensitivity of customer, geographical position and concentrative degree of customer, and so on.

4 Basic Methods for Application of Relationship Marketing in Customer Management of Travel Agency

Because the world economy has entered the new stage of "service economy period", travel agency' operation must be customer-centric both directly and indirectly, with tourist behavior as both the starting point and the ultimate goal of marketing. Tourists are no doubt to be one of the most precious resources. But, because of interaction between service staff and tourists and the influence of emotions in process of service enjoyment and evaluation by tourists, service is not always satisfied by tourists as what the operators of travel agency have expected. Furthermore, tourists select travel agency by chance, and it makes travel agency spend recurring costs to advertise, promote and attract customers.

In order to establish relationship with satisfied customer, customer-centric idea is the first step, which means to do everything in terms of customers' interests and to consider of their ambition, and the cost they are willing to pay for. Quality first and the best service is service essentials of travel agency, with "honesty and prestige" as the basic principle. Thus, it is requested to pay attention to their aspiring of culture and knowledge, to provide warm-hearted service to establish their mental trust and to ensure more satisfaction, in order to improve total purchase value of customer. At the same time for serving customers, travel agency may obtain respect and reward inevitably. In view of realization of satisfying customer's real demands, travel agency should do as follows:

4.1 Specific Method According to Three-Stage System of Relationship Marketing

The relationship on first stage prefers to increase financial benefits depending on customer relationship, which is the lowest level of relationship marketing. For marketing on this stage, it is helpful to establish preference of customer by preferential price and prize. In recent years, many foreign tourist companies promote "rewarding plan for those who always make a trip" to reward repeaters with complementary holiday, and discount. But such plan can not meet the needs of tourist really, which is quite easy to be copied by competitors and is difficult to maintain differentiation from other travel agency's product so as not to create loyal customer.

The relationship on second stage is to increase social interests together with financial benefits in additional. On this circumstance, the importance of price will not be ignored, but social relationship between travel agency and customers is emphasized. Travel agency should find out the demand and willingness of individual customer by keeping contact with customers initiatively, and try to make its service individualized and personalized for enhancing relationship. At this stage, marketing among people and that between travel agency and individual customer are combined together by establishing customer organization.

The relationship on third stage requires the travel agency to enhance the structure bond with financial and social benefits in additional. It is the highest level of relationship marketing. The travel agency is required by structural relationship during customer management for the service that is valuable to related customers but can't be obtained through other resources. Such individualized service is normally provided to customer according to his special needs by increasing technology investment, taking advantage of high-tech achievements, collecting customer demands in time, designing service system. Thus, customers may obtain more consumption benefits and higher value in use, through which they may keep close relationship with travel agency. There are two advantages in establishing good structural relationship with customers, the first is to improve their satisfaction, and the second is to build of higher customer switching cost.

4.2 Introducing CS Strategy on the Basis of CI

CI (Customer Identification) is a strategy, programme and means of certain enterprise to implement organization image design, spreading and management. CS (Customer Service) Strategy is customer-centric, which puts forward operation and management policy on the basis of customer demands combining with its own characteristics. It focuses on customer and puts forward "Customer is the God". It achieves a consensus with customers by suitable explanation and communication in order to make customers satisfied. [3]

CS strategy firstly regards customers as the most valuable property, because the profit of travel agency comes from customers and the survival, development and expansion depend on customers. Therefore, the travel agency with a large number of customers is sure to have exuberant vitality. Even if intangible assets are lost, it still can rejuvenate through its loyalty customers. Secondly, CS strategy creates loyal customer for travel agency. Loyal customers are the most stable tourist resource for travel agency, which reflects competitive strength of it. The introduction of CS Strategy on the basic of CI may combine customer management and travel agency management effectively, which reflects customer-centric policy.

For example, GZL (Guangzhilv) International Travel Service Ltd. took the lead in introducing CI in travel agency industry of China from May, 1994, which got great succeed together with CS strategy based on customer satisfaction, by improving essential rules and regulations, unifying standard management, perfecting guiding service, and so on. The new brand "GZL" swept the whole tourist industry in China with profit growth of 41% of that year, which was called as "GZL Effect".

4.3 Establishing and Improving Customer Database

Customer data is the important property of travel agency that should collect data from a number of sources. These data are verified, cleaned, integrated and stored on computers, often in data warehouses or data-marts. They are then used for marketing purposes such as market segmentation, targeting, offer development and customer communication. Depending on database, periodical survey of customers' satisfaction can be implemented to collect their feedback of product and service, and their criticisms and suggestions to travel agency. The travel agency can generalize and analyze different kinds of information to know the reason of customers' deviation from the company. Besides, the customer data can be used to produce customized products and services. It also can be used by people management (human resources) to recruit and train staff for the front-line jobs that interface with customers. It can be used by research and management to focus new product development.

4.4 Providing Individualized Service Oriented by Information Technology

The intermediary position of travel agency in tourism industry makes it quite important for travel agency to collect information, transmit information and use information comprehensively, which means that travel agency has natural dependence. Tourist product has the special features of comprehensiveness and intangibility that require travel agency to grasp tourist information in time so as to improve customer value by satisfying different demands of tourists.[4] Thus, carrying out relationship marketing with information technology is the inevitable choice for travel agency. Thereby, network technology and new data processing provide strong technological support for relationship marketing of travel agency. The network provides effective communication channel between travel agency and customer, which not only reduce the marketing cost but also make travel agency more responsive to feedback of customer and market. On the other hand, travel agency can identify customers' demands effectively and classify different customers so as to improve old products or develop new product according to the feedback and evaluation of customers. In this way, the travel agency can satisfy personalized demand of customers and improve their satisfaction and loyalty for guaranteeing application of relationship marketing.

4.5 Emphasizing After-Sale Service

According to a systematic survey made by American magazine Travel Agent on the reasons of the customers who don't visit specific travel agency any more, more than 68% shows that the travel agency pays less attention to after-sale service and is less active to gain repeat customers. Generally speaking, the tourists who are not satisfied with service during the trip will choose the method of "only once, no more time" to solve the problem. There may be only one among ten customers to complain to the travel agency after the trip. Therefore, active after-sale tracking service can not only abate customer's discontent but also avoid them to choose other travel agency, and even make closer relationship with customer through communicating for solving problems.

The common methods of after-sale service for travel agency include telephone greetings and return visit. That is to make a phone call to the customer on the second day after the trip. By doing this, first, it can make tourists to feel that they are concerned by travel agency and to feel grateful; second, travel agency may know something about service provided by different departments during the trip; third, travel agency can obtain some information about emergency and tourists' dissatisfaction during the trip in time. Thus, the management of travel agency may take the initiative and handle things appropriately in advance.

5 Concludes

The travel agency can not survive and develop with customers. The common customer, satisfied customer and loyal customer may bring different profits to travel agency. At present, marketing has developed into relationship marketing that focuses on establishing and maintaining long-term and satisfied relationship with customers instead of traditional marketing that is limited within transaction trade activity of travel agency, which emphasizes customer-centric idea and requires establishing long-term interacted cooperation relationship. In the present buyer's market, in order to avoid keen competition, the basic approach of obtaining operating advantage for travel agency is to create value for customer and to make customer satisfied. Chinese tourism industry has entered the customer-dominated age; tourist enterprise must equip itself with scientific, advanced customer theory in order to stabilize and increase tourist resources for improving economic profits, and to promote development of Chinese tourism. Therefore, only when travel agency in China takes customer satisfaction in priority and implements relationship marketing properly, can travel agency industry in China resolve dilemma and develop healthily.

References

1. Berry, L.: Relationship Marketing. American Marketing Association, Chicago (1983)
2. Ren, S., Wen, Z.: Thoughts of Relationship Marketing of Travel Agency in China. Modern Business 8, 123–124 (2007)
3. Shi, Y.: The Four Key Strategies of Personalized Customer Marketing. Innovation Technology 10, 46–47 (2006)
4. Ma, L.: Research on Relationship Marketing of Travel Agency Based on Information Technology. Modern Business Trade Industry 23, 60–61 (2009)

The Empirical Study on the Intraday Interaction Relationship between Stock Index Futures and Stock Index

Xiaoxue Liu and Cuiping Dong

School of Economics, Beijing Technology & Business University,
P.R. China, 100048
liuxiaoxueabc@126.com

Abstract. This paper examined the lead-lag relationship between Hushen 300 stock index futures and spot markets in China. We employed an AR(1)-EGARCH(1,1) model to estimate the volatility and Granger Causality Test to explain the casual relationship. Empirical results confirm that the fluctuation of stock index futures price is higher than the stock index. The returns and risk of stock index futures and stock index have a negative correlation. There is an asymmetric effect in both Stock index futures and stock markets. Stock index futures returns and returns volatility lead the stock index. Our results are helpful to traders, speculators and financial managers dealing with Chinese stock index futures.

Keywords: Hushen 300 Stock Index Futures, Stock Index, Intraday Interaction Relationship.

1 Introduction

In spite of their relatively short history, the stock index futures market has become a popular topic of discussion and debate in China since it was listed in April 16, 2010, while at the same time it has led to a controversy over the relationship between futures and spot prices. The intraday interaction relationship illustrates how well the two markets are affected, and how fast one market reflects new information from the other. If feedback between futures and spot exists, then it is possible that investors may use past information to predict prices (or returns) in the future [1]. Recent papers examining are at variance with the price discovery role and the lead-lag relationship between futures and spot prices, but a majority of studies indicate that futures market has a price discovering role [2]. Also, when a bi-directional causality exists between the two markets, then futures and spot have an important discovery role. Price discovery refers to the impounding of new information into the price [3].

In this paper, we examine the intraday interaction relationship between futures markets and spot markets using data from China. The following section will give an exposition of the literature review, whereas the data is presented in section three, in section four multivariate empirical specifications are presented and discussed. Section five present the result and some concluding remarks.

M. Zhou (Ed.): ISAEBD 2011, Part III, CCIS 210, pp. 407–413, 2011.

2 Literature Review

The subject of intraday interaction relationship between futures and spot markets are attractive topics for analysts, financial economists, investors and traders. The principal problem is which market reacts first though futures and spot markets react to the same information. A great many of empirical results show that futures prices lead spot prices, and includes information about spot prices [1,2,3]. The similar study [4] which examines the link between information and volatility suggests that the index of futures trading reduces volatility asymmetries and improves the quality and speed of the flow of information. In addition, the intraday volatility patterns in both markets show strong persistence and predictability [5], and we find little reason to expect that the introduction of new stock index futures contracts in emerging nations will destabilize stock markets [6]. In general, the futures price leads the stock index [7]. Further, Abhyankar [8] examines the relationship between futures and spot returns using 5-minute returns on the FTSE 100. He finds that the futures returns lead the spot returns by 15-20 minutes.

However, due to the asymmetry of volatility and other external conditions, the impact of *good news* and *bad news* on futures and spot markets is different, so the lead-lag relationship is different as well. The similarity of paper [9] indicates that in the pre-ITSA period, the options market leads the stock market for negative surprises but for positive surprises the stock market leads. C. W. J. Granger [10] proposes a simple two-variable model, namely Granger Causality Test, to study the causal relationship. In this study we follow this approach.

3 Data

The data used in this study were obtained from "Wenhua Information Database". It provided the Hushen 300 index and index futures closing prices for the period July 21, 2010-March 24, 2011. The high-frequency intraday time series are partitioned into five-minute intervals. Since the Hushen Stock Exchange closes at 3:00 p.m., 15 minutes earlier than the futures market, futures price observations after that time are removed. Futures prices recorded before the Hushen Stock Exchange opens are also excluded. Removing no records of transactions and those which do not match, we have 7756 set of observations, of which the futures data are chosen from active trading contact. Figure 1 shows that stock index futures prices and stock index prices with different time to maturity follow the almost same stochastic trend, and move

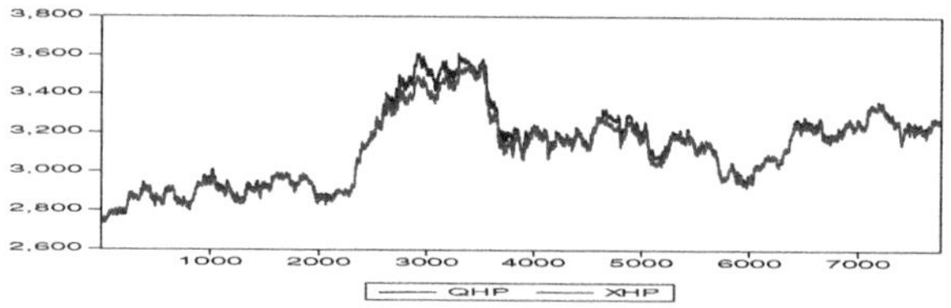

Fig. 1. Stock Index and Stock Index Futures Prices Every 5 Minutes

proportionally over time, but the volatility of futures prices are much higher. (QHP is defined as closing stock index futures prices; XHP is defined as closing index prices).

4 Empirical Specification

4.1 Decision of Returns and Preliminary Statistics

Returns in period *t* is defined as,

$$R_t = \ln(P_t) - \ln(P_{t-1}) . \tag{1}$$

Where P_t and P_{t-1} are the closing prices in period t and $t-1$, and they are transformed to natural logarithms. Table 1 describes that futures returns fluctuations are slightly higher than spot's, similarly to the earlier studies in this paper; the skewness of futures and the spot returns series are all positive, and their kurtosis values are greater than 3; JB statistic values of both returns series are higher, and they are statistically significant. It indicates empirical distributions with heavy tails and sharp peaks at the center compared to the normal distribution.

Table 1. Basic Statistical Analysis of Stock Index Futures and Stock Index Returns

Series	SD	Skew	Kurt	J-B	Prob
Spot returns	0.0020	0.1104	8.7123	10559.28	0
Futures returns	0.0021	0.9750	18.4319	78179.05	0

In addition, we know from figure 2 and 3, futures and spot markets returns trends show that there are relatively larger fluctuations after large fluctuations, and there are relatively smaller fluctuations after small fluctuations. This series is called Volatility Clustering, and models of ARCH can describe the characteristics of the time series.

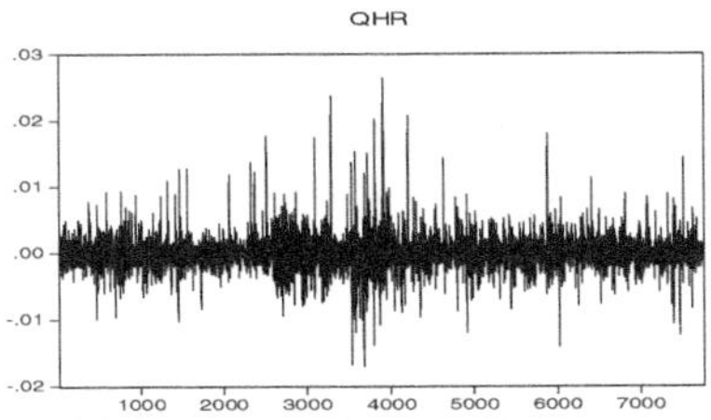

Fig. 2. Futures Returns Trend

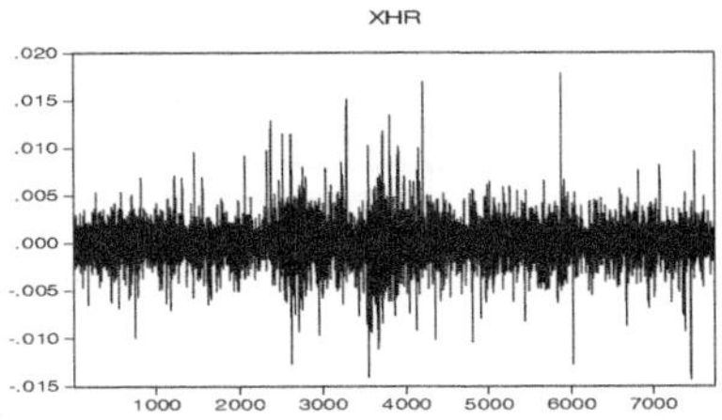

Fig. 3. Spot Returns Trend

4.2 Estimates of Returns Volatility and Preliminary Statistics

4.2.1 Estimates of Volatility

We consider volatility estimators that are based upon three ways—the square of returns, the method of OHLC [11], the model of GARCH(1,1). The model of

GARCH–EGARCH can describe a wide range of asymmetric effect of price volatility in financial markets, and imitate most of volatility of financial time series [12]. Therefore, we employ the model of AR(1)–EGARCH (1,1) to estimate the volatility of stock index futures and stock index returns. We posit the following model for the joint processes governing the index futures and stock index returns:

$$R_t = a + b\hat{\sigma}_t + \hat{u}_t \qquad \text{(Mean Equation)} \tag{2}$$

$$\ln(\sigma_t^2) = \alpha_0 + \sum_{i=1}^{q} \alpha_i \left[\frac{u_{t-i}}{\sigma_{t-i}}\right] + \sum_{i=1}^{q} r_i \left[\left|\frac{u_{t-i}}{\sigma_{t-i}}\right| - u\right] + \sum_{i=1}^{p} \lambda_j \ln(\sigma_{i-j}^2) \qquad \text{(Variance Equation)} \tag{3}$$

From the evidence in Table 2, the negative parameter "b", as well as it is insignificance at the 0.01 level, which is in mean equation of futures and spot, indicates that the greater the risk, the smaller the expected returns of stock index futures and stock index, that is returns will be a decrease of 0.0605% and 0.0437% on average when the expected risk of stock index futures and stop markets has a increase of 1%.

All parameters of stock index futures and stock index in Variance Equation is significant at the level of 0.01, and all leverage coefficients "c(5)" are negative, which imply that *bad news* elicit a larger response than *good news* of an equal magnitude, and both markets have an effect of leverage. Furthermore, the effects of both markets returns are 0.0332 (0.0643+(-0.0311)) and 0.0296 (0.0534+(-0.0238)) times When both markets are shocked by *good news*, instead are 0.0954 (0.0643-(-0.0311)) and 0.0772 (0.0534-(-0.0238)) times.

Table 2. Empirical Results of AR(1)–EGARCH (1,1) Model

	Futures Volatility Model			Spot Volatility Model		
	Coefficient	Z-Statistic	Prob.	Coefficient	Z-Statistic	Prob.
	Mean Equation			Mean Equation		
a	0.0001	1.2625	0.2068	0. 0001	0.9334	0.3506
b	-0.0605	-1.1897	0.2342	-0. 0437	-0.7315	0.4645
	Variance Equation			Variance Equation		
c(3)	-0.1946	-15.6816	0	-0.1429	-11.031	0
c(4)	0.0643	31.8331	0	0.0534	21.1926	0
c(5)	-0.0311	-16.7809	0	-0.0238	-13.1179	0
c(6)	0.9877	993.1517	0	0.9917	997.1263	0

4.2.2 Residual Test

AR(1)–EGARCH(1,1) models are tested with LM (Lagrange multiplier tests) , and we obtain the probability of 0.1502 (futures) and 0.2429 (spot), which implies that they are statistically insignificant, with no ARCH effects. Consequently, we confirm that the choice of model lags is appropriate, and there is no residual information which is not used.

4.2.3 Basic Statistics of Volatility

We employ above AR(1)–EGARCH(1,1) model to estimate the basic statistics of volatility of both markets, and table 3 indicates that fluctuations of futures returns volatility are slightly greater than the spot, which can be confirmed from the variance; The skewness values of futures and spot returns volatility are all positive, and their kurtosis values are greater than 3; JB statistic values of both returns volatility are higher, and they are statistically significant. It indicates empirical distributions with heavy tails and sharp peaks at the center compared to the normal distribution.

Table 3. Basic Statistical of Stock Index Futures and Stock Index Returns Volatility

Series	SD	Skew	Kurt	J-B	Prob
Spot Volatility	1.95E-06	2.0465	8.3630	14706.87	0
Futures Volatility	2.18E-06	1.8805	7.7662	11910.89	0

4.3 Casual Relationship Test

First, the time series properties of the data must be investigated before conducting any econometric analysis, and this is done with Augmented Dickey Fuller (ADF) test. In this article ADF results argue that returns and returns volatility series in both markets are stationary in levels. Thus, they don't need to be done with Cointegration Test (long-run relationship). Second, we apply a Granger Causality Test to study the lead-lag relationship between futures and spot markets. In particular, to account for relationship of them felicitously, we select different lags to observe.

Table 4. The Granger Causality Test of Returns and Returns Volatility

lags (time /m)	H_0: spot does not Granger Cause futures				H_0: futures does not Granger Cause spot			
	returns		volatility		returns		volatility	
	F	Prob.	F	Prob.	F	Prob.	F	Prob.
1(5)	1.146	0.284	7.162	0.0075	1415.970	9E-285	57.223	4E-14
2(10)	0.313	0.731	8.506	0.0002	767.360	9E-305	258.207	3E-109
3(15)	3.930	0.008	7.010	0.0001	527.012	0	174.542	2E-109
4(20)	1.333	0.255	18.092	8E-15	400.678	0	139.369	3E-115
5(25)	1.953	0.082	15.248	6E-15	319.439	0	111.092	1E-113
6(30)	1.897	0.077	12.847	2E-14	266.471	0	93.782	4E-114
7(35)	1.571	0.139	11.839	4E-15	232.521	0	80.929	7E-114
8(40)	1.442	0.173	10.294	2E-14	204.387	0	70.906	4E-113
9(45)	1.295	0.234	9.917	3E-15	181.846	0	63.391	8E-113
10(50)	1.224	0.270	8.847	1E-14	164.344	0	57.029	7E-112
11(55)	1.216	0.271	8.292	1E-14	149.402	0	51.887	4E-111
12(60)	2.072	0.016	7.710	2E-14	137.153	0	47.426	6E-110
15(75)	1.724	0.040	7.499	7E-17	109.999	0	38.347	1E-108
20(100)	2.075	0.003	5.869	1E-15	82.936	6E-307	29.783	7E-109

The Granger Causality Test results of both markets returns reported in table 4 indicate that futures returns lead spot returns evidently, which can conclude from F-Statistics and Probability values at the 0.05 significance level, and spot returns lead futures returns by 15 minutes. Moreover, changes in futures returns lead changes in spot in most cases, especially when lag length is 1 and then F-Statistic values are 1415.97 at its maximum. The decreasing trend of futures F-Statistic with lags increasing suggests that influence of changes in futures returns on the spot is weakening, and it can be defined as the influence is strongest when futures returns changes 10 minutes later. We can obtain the conclusion from Kawaller [13], Fleming [14] and Hans R. Stoll [15].

The Granger Causality Test results of volatility in both markets are almost the same with the returns, but the futures volatility changing 5 minutes later has an effect on spot, and mainly 10 minutes later.

5 Conclusion

This paper examines the intraday interaction relationship between returns changes and returns changes volatility in stock index futures and stock index markets in China. Using an AR(1)-EGARCH(1,1) model to estimate the returns volatility, and Granger Causal Test to argue the lead-lag relationship of both markets. we confirm that (i) the fluctuation of stock index futures price is higher than the stock index; (ii) returns and risk of stock index futures and stock markets are asymmetry; (iii) both markets exist an asymmetry effect, that is their responses become larger when *bad news* occurs than *good news*; (iv) returns and returns volatility of stock index futures lead the stock index.

The introduction of stock index futures contracts and, in particular, as a hedging instrument in China, the preparatory course has been almost four years though its short listing history. Thus, the futures market being the leading indicator of the stock market is not by chance. While the immature technology, knowledge and investment techniques for Chinese index futures investors compared to other developed countries, the strengthening risk awareness of stock markets traders after global financial crisis and the system of appropriate investors of participation in stock index futures contribute to the asymmetry effect of futures and spot markets. Our results are of guiding significance for traders, speculators and financial managers dealing with Chinese stock index futures, and provide them with important insights into the stock index futures trading-stock market intraday interaction relationship, as the stock index futures market leads to new channels of information which are uniformed in stock market.

Acknowledgments. This work is supported by Scientific Research Base of Beijing Municipal Education Commission-Science and Technology Innovation Platform-Research Base of Beijing Futures and Bulk Commodity Markets.

References

1. Floros, C., Vougas, D.V.: Lead-lag Relationship between Futures and Spot Markets in Greece: 1999–2001. International Research Journal of Finance and Economics 7, 168–174 (2007)
2. Asche, F., Guttormsen, A.G.: Lead Lag Relationships between Futures and Spot Prices. The Research Council of Norway 2 (2002)
3. Tse, Y.: Price Discovery and Volatility Spillovers in the DJIA Index. Journal of Futures Markets 19, 911–930 (1999)
4. Alexakis, P.: On the Effect of Index Futures Trading on Stock Market Volatility. International Research Journal of Finance and Economics, 7–20 (2007)
5. Chan, K., Chan, K.C., Andrew Karolyi, G.: Intraday Volatility in the Stock Index and Stock Index Futures Markets. The Review of Financial Studies 4, 657–684 (1991)
6. Gulen, H., Mayhew, S.: Stock Index Futures Trading and Volatility in International Equity Markets. The Journal of Futures Markets 20, 661–685 (2000)
7. Antoniou, A., Garrett, I.: To what Extent did Stock Index Futures Contribute to the October 1987 Stock Market Crash? Economic Journal 103, 1444–1461 (1993)
8. Abhyankar, A.: Linear and Nonlinear Granger Causality: Evidece from the U.K. Stock Index Futures Market. Journal of Futures Markets 18, 519–540 (1998)
9. Mitchell Conover, C., Peterson, D.R.: The Lead-lag Relationship between the Option and Stock Markets Prior to Substantial Earnings Surprises and the Effect of Securities Regulation. Journal of Financial and Strategic Decisions 12, 41–52 (1999)
10. Granger, C.W.J.: Investigating Causal Relations by Econometric Models and Cross-spectral Methods. Econometrica 37, 424–438 (1969)
11. Garman, M.B., Klass, M.J.: On the Estimation of Security Price Volatilities From Historical Data. Journal of Business 53, 67–78 (1980)
12. Nelson, D.: Conditional Heteroskedasticity in Asset Returns: A New Approach. Econometrics 59, 347–370 (1991)
13. Kawaller, I.G., Koch, P.D., Koch, T.W.: The Temporal Price Relationship between S&P 500 Futures Prices and the S&P 500 Index. Journal of Finance 5, 1309–1329 (1987)
14. Fleming, J., Ostdiek, B., Whaley, R.E.: Trading Costs and the Relative Rates of Price Discovery in Stock, Futures, and Option markets. Journal of Futures Markets 16, 353–387 (1996)
15. Stoll, H.R., Whaley, R.E.: The Dynamics of Stock Index and Stock Index Futures Returns. Journal of Financial and Quantitative and Analysis 25, 441–468 (1990)

Teenagers' Sports Consumption Status and Restricted Factors in Southwest China

Lizheng Gong, Jiong Luo, Yan Tang, and Li Peng

School of Physical Education, Southwest University, Tiansheng Road. 2, 400715, Beibei, Chongqing, China
gonglizheng@gmail.com, {Luojiong,tyww,plmzs}@swu.edu.cn

Abstract. This study attemps to analyze the investigation on sports consumption of 3500 teenagers in southwest China and to provid teenagers with proper consumption guidance, government with policy suggestions and enterprises with sell strategies. Speeding up the socio-economic development, enhancing the incomes of households of both rural and urban residents and decreasing the economic pressures of families are the key ways of promoting the sports consumption level of teenagers. Teenagers' sports consumption types should be paid close attention to especially their "practical demand" and "random demand" of sports consumable. To raise the correct sports values of teenagers, to guide the correct sports policies of schools, to optimize the fitness environment for teenagers, to enhance their training of fitness knowledge, to strengthen the construction of fitness instructors teams and to ease teenagers' homework pressures are important prerequisites for the prosperous of the teenagers' sports consumption market in west China.

Keywords: Southwest China, teenagers, sports consumption, restricted factors.

1 Introduction

According to the data, teenagers between 13 and 17 years old in big cities such as Beijing and Shanghai, 30.1% wear Nike shoes and 23.6% wear Lining shoes. [1, 2] This fact obviously shows that teenagers are the main consumers in sports consumption market. With the progressive growth of the national economy and steady enhancement of living level in China, especially after the Beijing Olympic Games in 2008, the teenaagers sports consumption demands and the sports industry in China have been experiencing an unparalleled development. Besides, some data show that in the past ten years, there is a durative downtrend in the corporeity of Chinese teenagers. The conceptions and atmospheres of fitness have not yet formed in teenagers' minds. The preference of one-side pursuit of being admitted to schools of a higher level is still undue and the students in primary schools and high schools are suffering from the burdensome schoolwork pressures. [3,4,5,6]

It is acknowledged that the sports consumption behaviors of teenagers are directly or indirectly concerned with their fitness and teenagers' sports consumption behaviors are restricted by individual psychological factors and many other social factors. [7,8,9,10]

M. Zhou (Ed.): ISAEBD 2011, Part III, CCIS 210, pp. 414–420, 2011.

Therefore, in July, 2010, the National Science and Technology department supporting plan again draws out 10 million Yuan research funds to intend to discuss "the key technologies for strengthening the physical fitness of teenagers" hoping to find the basic reason and effective strategies. This research paper, supported by the National Science and Technology plan, starts with the sports consumption behaviors of teenagers of southwest area and the restricted factors. By analyzing of the present state and restricted factors, this research attempts to find the key factor that restricts the sports consumption of teenagers in southwest of China in order to effectively explore the sports consumption market of teenagers in the western area of China in the future, to grasp the teenagers' sports consumption features and to offer correct guide to the teenagers. This research on one hand provides significant references for the macro-control of the local government and the policy-making of the enterprises and businesses. On the other hand, it provides certain important basis for the forming the best patterns of strengthening teenagers' fitness and health.

2 Method

2.1 Participants

According to the general demand of national science and technology supporting plan, the primary schools and high schools in Chongqing are selected to be the representatives for the accessorial topics in southwest region of China. The reasons of the selecting are: 1) Chongqing is the only "province (municipality)" in China that is authorized by the state council to establish for the first time the "national comprehensive reform trial area for coordinating urban-rural"; 2) Chongqing is typical mountin city with "big city and countryside", wildly varies in the development of different regions and serioius contradictions in dual conspicuous structures between urban and rural.

2.2 Sampling Method

According to the implementation of the science and technology supporting plan, this research uses the stratified cluster sampling method: elementary school group 1(grade 3), elementary school groups 2 (grade 5), junior high school group (grade 2) and senior high school group (grade 2). The proportion of male and female should be as close as possible. Each community is divided into two categories of the traditional features schools and non-characteristic schools. Regarding schools in the Chongqing urban district and nearby regions as the research objects, the Bureau of Education of each region carries out the survey and investigation on the detailed proceedings of the sports curriculum delivered in middle and primary schools. On condition that the survey result meets the requirement of the seminar, the aimed inquired organizations and the sample size shall be decided in the way of random sampling, and then the aimed inquired organizations and detailed sample acquirements shall be decided sequently, also in the way of random sampling.

2.3 Questionnaire

Uses "situation and influencing factor of Young people's physical training and sports consuming behaviors" questionnaire which is designed by the technical support plan topic-based group in or der to provide fixed answer questionnaire law with recycling, which means filling in front and takes back immediately. Altogether provides questionnaire 3500, rejection invalid questionnaire 203, the valid returns-ratio is 94.2%. The questionnaire are composed of two parts, The first part is the present situation of young people's physical training, which is consist of 26 major terms and 18 minor terms, the content includes the understanding young people have towards physical training, physical training's participation inside and outside of school, school and family's participation in students' physical training, students' fitness conditions, sports expense and other aspects; The second part is the reasons that prevent the young people from participating in the physical training using " five points "meter form formulates, and consist of 21 questions.

2.4 Reliability Test of Questionnaire

Based on Delphi law, the questionnaires, designed by the technical support plan, are above suspicions in their validities. In order to obtain its testing validities in western area, for two times we have made the attempt to investigate at two schools in Beibei District, Chongqing. Around two time-gap 15 days, the objects of the questionnaire give similar responses for both of the time and the reliable coefficient is up to 0.87.

2.5 Mathematical Method

Use SPSS16.0 to provide a statistics analysis on all collected data. A one-way ANONA, crosstabs analysis, factorial analysis and logistic regression analysis are adapted in this study. The significance level s is set at the .05 level for all analyses.

3 Results

3.1 Analysis of Restriction Factors of Teenagers' Sports Consumption

3.1.1 The Extraction and Naming of Sports Consumption Restriction Factor

This research firstly will study the 21 questions by means of factorial analysis. To test the original variable 21 under the examination of KMO, its value equals to 0.701>0.5, which achieves the basic requirements of factorial analysis. According to the Bartlett Test, the chi-squared X^2=71.21, P<0.01, further affirmed that the 21 causal variables are suitable for the factorial analysis.

The principal components analytic method obtain 6 components which characteristic roots is in turn 9.002, 2.614, 2.062, 1.670, 1.321 and 1.011 (all the characteristic roots are bigger than 1); the degree of their variation explain to the 21 origional variables are 36.59%, 10.62%, 8.38%, 6.79%, 5.37% and 4.11%. The progressive contributions achieve at 71.86%>70% (achieves the basic requirements for social science research).

Table 1. statistical table of differences in the score of restriction factors on sports consumption of teenagers in varied schools and grades

(note 1: The single factor variance analysis, Letter "a" stands for elementary school, "b" for junior high school "c" senior high school, "P_{ab}*" for marked difference between elementary school and junior high school, "*" for statist significance. Other similar symbols have the similar meanings. Note 2: factor 1: family economic pressure fac factor 2: fitness habit and method factor; factor 3: fitness interest and value orientation factor ; factor 4: school sp policy factor ;factor 5: fitness environment and instruction factor ;factor 6: schoolwork pressure factor.

	Elementary schoo	Junior high school	Senior high schoo	T test (G-H)
factor 1	-0.0423±0.9401	0.2857±0.9324	-0.2175±1.122	P_{ab}* P_{ac}* P_{bc}*
factor 2	0.1905±0.9390	-0.2196±0.9923	-0.070±1.0564	P_{ab}* P_{ac}* P_{bc}
factor 3	-0.0681±1.028	-0.1037±0.9044	0.2624±0.9886	P_{ab} P_{ac}* P_{bc}*
factor 4	0.0231±0.9574	0.2298±0.9132	-0.2964±1.100	P_{ab}* P_{ac}* P_{bc}*
factor 5	0.2360±0.9578	-0.1602±0.9739	-0.3513±0.983	P_{ab}* P_{ac}* P_{bc}*
factor 6	0.1674±1.0713	-0.0981±0.9129	-0.2662±0.8433	P_{ab}* P_{ac}* P_{bc}

3.1.2 Analysis on Restricted Factor Scores of Different Grades Teenagers

The SPSS software automatedly generates the scores of the 6 common factors. All the 21 questions are endued with Li Kete five scoring levels of offering five options "very fitful/much, somewhat, not sure, not very /much, do not" separately evaluating from 1 score to 5 scores. Therefore, the lower the factors are scored, the bigger the economic pressures are (the worse the supports are showed), which means a worse habits and methods of fitness, an inproper sports policy, a less fitness interests and value oriented, a worse fitness environment and instructions and a heavier schoolwork pressures.

Table 1 displays that: among the students in different grades, 6 general factors appear to have the following characters: The family economic support for students varies remarkably from the elementary schools, junior high schools and senior high schools. Junior high school students get the strongest family economic support, and then come to the elementary school pupils, but the senior high school students get less economic support form their families. The fitness interests and value orientation factors are clearly different in different grades. The elementary pupils are the worst and senior high school students are the best in this factor. The differences exist in school sports policies of different grades. The junior high school students are enjoying the best sports policy while senior high school students are experiencing the worst sports policy. The fitness habits and methods are so difference that the elementary pupils have the best fitness habits and methods while junior high school sutents have the worst fitness habits and methods. Different grades have different fitness environments and instructions. elementary pupils have the best fitness environments and instructions and senior high school students have the worst fitness environments and instructions. The schoolwork pressures of different grades vary from each other. Students in grade three of senior high school have the heaviest schoolwork pressures and elementary pupils have the most minimal schoolwork pressures.

3.2 Correlation Analysis between Teenagers' Extracurricular Sports Consumption Behaviors and Restricted Factors

3.2.1 Construction of the Polynomial Categorical Logistic Regression Model

Taking the relationship between consumption sum and its six restriction factors as an example, the way of model constructing is absolutely the same as that of the other 4 models. Take consumption sum as effect variable Y, and classify it into 5 standards, i.e. "under 100 RMB", "100-200 RMB", "200-300 RMB", "300-400 RMB" and "above 400 RMB", assuming their corresponding probabilities are respectively P_1, P_2, P_3, P_4, P_5 and comply with the condition $P_1+P_2+P_3$ $P_4+P_5=1$, on account of these probabilities, the independent objects of observation whose quantity is 'n' are distributed to their own categories, and the distribution of these objects in the category whose quantity is J comply with polynomial distribution. Six impeding factors the independent variables are marked as X_k (K=1,2,3......6) αj and bjk respectively represent constant and explaining variable parameters of the j type, Polytomous Logistic Model could be presented in the graphs below :

$$\ln\left(P_j/P_J\right) = \alpha_j + b_{j1}X_1 + b_{j2}X_2 + b_{j3}X_3 + b_{j4}X_4 + b_{j5}X_5 + b_{j6}X_6$$

In the graphs, X_1, X_2, X_3, X_4, X_5 and X_6 are 6 general factors. The introduction of OR (Odds Ratio) into the regression model when OR > 1 shows that this factor is favorable factor, if OR < 1, it shows that such a factor is a unfavourable one; if OR=1, it proves that such factor has nothing to with the dependent variable.

3.2.2 Analysis of the Odds Ratio of General Factor to the Results of Sports Consumption Behavior

Table 2 displayed: the two models of consumption desire and consumption frequency are both influenced by 6 constraint factors, the odds rations OR_1="consume willingly"/"consume unwillingly " and OR_2="consume frequently "/"never consume" are successively 1.734, 1.322, 1.315, 1.471, 1.377, 1.719 (correspondingly the 6 values of P are all less than 0.05) and 1.615, 1.520, 1.401, 1.469, 1.389, 1.360 (correspondingly the 6 values of P are all less than 0.05), in other words, when the values of other factors remains, as the economic pressure reduces one unit value, then the number of teenagers who are willing to spend money on sports will increase 1.734 times as many as the original one, and the number of people who frequently spend money on sports will increase 1.615 times as many as the original one. The influential force of other constraint factors upon the model can be explained in the same way.

Consumption type model is constrained by fitness habit and method factor、fitness interest and value orientation factor、school sports policy factor and fitness environment and instruction factor, the odds ration OR_3="reality need"/"random need" are successively 1.715, 1.492, 1.323, 1.703 (correspondingly the 4 values of P are all less than 0.05), obvious fitness habit and method have the greatest influence over consumption type model, while school sports policy has the least influence, consumption model is constrained by fitness habit and method factor、fitness interest and value orientation factor and school sports policy factor (correspondingly the 3 values of P are all less than 0.05), the odds ratio (OR_4="deserving consuming"/"deserve little") are successively 1.688, 1.588, 1.531; the consumption sum model is seemly influenced only by economic pressure factor, the odds ratio (OR_5="above 400 RMB"/"under 100 RMB") is 1.833, that is, when the value of other constraint factor remains, as the economic pressure reduces one unit value, in half a year the number of people whose sports consumption sum that is above 400RMB will increase as 1.833 times as many as that of the former period.

Table 2. Statistical parameter table from the 6 general factors influences on model 1-5 (odds ratio Exp(b)=OR)

Note: Model 1: consumption desire; Model 2: Consumption type ; Model 3: consumption worthness; Model 4: consumption frequency ; Model 5: the consumption sum;

	Model 1:		Model 2:		Model 3:		Model 4:		Model 5:	
	Exp(b) P值	P	Exp(b) P	P	Exp(b) P值	P	Exp(b) P值	P	Exp(b) P值	P
factor 1	1.734	.000 ; *	1.019	.774	.960	.373	1.615	.008;*	1.833	.000 ; *
factor 2	1.322	.000 ; *	1.715	.000 ; *	1.668	.000 ; *	1.520	.001 ; *	1.027	.541
factor 3	1.315	.009 ; *	1.492	.008 ; *	1.588	.030;*	1.401	.001;*	.868	.159
factor 4	1.471	.000 ; *	1.323	.000 ; *	1.531	.006 ; *	1.469	.005;*	1.026	.804
factor 5	1.377	.000 ; *	1.703	.000 ; *	0.988	.588	1.389	.005 ; *	1.079	.118
factor 6	1.719	.000 ;	1.066	.612	1.022	.002▯	1.360	.006;*	1.133	.192

4 Conclusion

As discussed previously, the study draw some conclusions as follows: (1) By the method of Principal Component Analysis, six influential factors can be extracted from numerous factors which restrict the sports consumption behavior of teenagers in the southwest region, namely, economic pressures, fitness custom and method, fitness interest and value orientation, school sports policy and fitness conditions and instruction and academic pressure. (2) The fitness custom and method, the fitness interest and value orientation and school sports policy 3 factor's influences more extensively, which occupy the remarkable level in 4 models, and the runner-up is the economic pressures factor, which achieves the remarkable level in 3 models, while the academic pressure factor influence is relatively narrow, which only achieves the remarkable level in 2 models; In the perspective of influence dynamics, the economic pressure factor is most strong, in 3 models, whose OR average value approximately is 1.73, and the runner-up is the fitness custom and method and academic pressure, while the fitness interest and value orientation, the school sports policy and fitness conditions and instruction and other factor influence dynamics is relatively slightly weak. (3) compared with general schools, the traditional school posses better school sports policy, better physical training consciousness and value orientation and more superior fitness conditions and instruction, while have no difference in the fitness custom and method and academic pressure two aspects, But students in the traditional school have high economic pressures than that in the general school, and the deeper reasons are to be probed in further discussion. Among students in different grades, the elementary student has the best fitness custom and method, the most superior fitness conditions and instruction, and the smallest academic pressure. The junior high students earn the biggest economic support (economic pressures to be smallest) and best school sports policy. The high-school students have the best fitness interest and value orientation, but the biggest economy and academic pressure, most unfair sports policy, worst fitness custom and method and most disadvantageous fitness conditions and instruction.

References

1. Non-brand, Non-sports–Analysis on The Present Statue of High School Students Sports Shoes Consumption, http://www.efu.com.cn/topic/555/
2. Chu, Y., Song, L.: A Study of High School Students Consumption of Sports Goods and the Influential Factors. Journal of Physical Education Institute of Shanxi Teachers University (2), 37–39 (2007)
3. Dai, Y., Xu, C., Liu, Y.: Effect of Exercise and Diet Intervention on the Physical Fitness of Obese Women during Weight Reduction. Chinese Journal of Sports Medicine 27(6), 715–718 (2008)
4. Liu, W., Chang, C., Zhao, X., et al.: Effect of School-Based Supervised Exercise Intervention on Body Mass Index and Glucolipid Metabolism in Chinese Obese Adolescents. Chinese Journal of Sports Medicine 27(3), 329–333 (2008)
5. Deng, H.: Development in Social Psychological Factors And Teenager Hypertension Research. Journal of Nurses Training 24(2), 150–152 (2009)
6. Zhang, f., Liu, Y., Wang, J., et al.: Investigation and Analysis of Middle School Students Mental Health Status in Wuxi City. China Journal of Health Psychology 14(4), 382–384 (2006)
7. Hou, J., Liu, J.: Statistical Analysis on Development State of Chinese Teenagers (EB/OL) (2005), http://www.cys.org.cn
8. Shi, W.: A Research on Urban Residents Structure of Consumer Psychological Expectations and Its Influencing Factors. Psychological Science (3), 426–429 (2003)
9. Lin, J., Cong, H.: A Review on the Research Work of Sports Consumption in China. Journal of Sports and Science 2, 34–35 (2001)
10. Ma, Y., Ouyan, L.: An investigation and analysis of the Chinese residents' sports consumption. Journal of Wuhan Institute of Physical Education (3), 10–12 (2002)

Study on the Index-Evaluation System of Local Public Goods Supply: A Case of Beijing

Hui Liu

School of Public Finance and Taxation, Capital University of Economics and Business, No.121 Zhangjialukou Huaxiang, Fengtai District, Beijing, China,
liuhui314@126.com

Abstract. In modern society, the supply level of public goods has become the important landmark to measure the civilization and progress of the region. In order to effectively measure the level of local public goods supply, it is necessary to found a set of supply system, including some empirical, quantitative, scientific indicators. This paper focuses on the index-evaluation system, which is used to measure local public goods supply. First, according to the supply of public goods related researches, index-evaluation basis is drawn. Subsequently, the index system of local public goods supply is designed, including principles and contents. Basis on this, the level of Beijing public goods supply is tested by comparing the core indicators in index-evaluation system. The findings of this paper provide valuable reference for the improvement of public goods supply in Beijing.

Keywords: local public goods, index-evaluation system, core indicators.

1 Introduction

With the economic and social development, public goods has become an integral part of social life. No matter public education and public health, or social security, environmental protection, public security, fire protection, etc., invariably affect the quality of people's life and social development. The supply level of public goods has become the important landmark for the measure of civilization and progress of the region. In order to effectively measure the level of local public goods supply, it is necessary to establish a set of evaluation system, which is designed with empirical, quantitative and scientific indicators.

Index-evaluation is a useful method to judge the objective reality. Index itself is a specific, measurable, behavior-oriented evaluation criterion which determines the assessment content on the basis of the measurable or observable request. As one of common assessment methods, the index-evaluation system of public goods supply is a quantified and logical framework. Through the analysis on various indicators, the regional level、 status and overall capacity of the current supply of public goods are evaluated. At the same time, it is also used to simulate and predict the level of the

M. Zhou (Ed.): ISAEBD 2011, Part III, CCIS 210, pp. 421–427, 2011.

supply of local public goods within a certain controlled span time in future. Thus, local residents will be provided the channel of understanding and grasping of the regional development and welfare improvement. Furthermore, local residents can also determine the working directions for suppliers of public goods.

The remainder of this paper is organized as follows: Section 2 is literature review. Section 3 puts forward the evaluation index system formation. Discussion and conclusion of Beijing example are presented in section 4.

2 Literature Review

At present, developed countries have higher ability and more experience to supply public goods, but domestic just starts to concern about public service and public goods, and the study on measuring and evaluating the level of local public goods is fairly rare. However, there are some useful foreign literatures, which related to the indicators to measure public goods supply, such as competitiveness indicators system, sustainable development indicator system, the modern index system, and human development indicator system (United Nations Development Program, 2001[1]; World Bank (WB), 1995[2]). Meanwhile, some experts in China also have established sustainable development indicators system, government performance evaluation index system, index system of the government's public supply, and urban competitiveness indicator system related to the supply situation of regional public goods (Tanxiang Chen, 2008[3]; Junpeng Li, 2004[4]; Xing Ni, 2007[5]).These are the necessary basic conditions to prepare for the establishment of index-evaluation system of local public goods supply.

The above researches are contributed much to study the index system of local public goods supply, however, some limitations are also existed.

- From the content points of current views, the designs of index system are not unified owing to different research purposes. Most index-evaluation systems not only lack the appropriate theoretical basis, but also do not form the standardized assessment framework.
- Existing related indicator systems may be more suitable for developed countries and regions, which do not reflect the situation in developing countries and regions; they may focus on possible future development potential of countries and regions, but do not reflect the status of the existing level of development.
- Most studies emphasis on the supply of government level, market-oriented supply of public goods may be neglected.

Therefore, it is necessary to establish the index-evaluation system reflecting the status and capacity of local public goods supply, which uses the combined qualitative and quantitative research methods. This is exactly the focus of the research topic.

3 Formation of Index - Evaluation System

3.1 Determination of the Supply Scope of Local Public Goods

Theoretically, there are a variety of ways to provide public goods: the government supply, private supply, supply of public and private jointly. Actually, the current supply structures of local public goods are composed of government supply and market-oriented (including private and third sector) mixed supply [6].

Table 1. Composition of public goods supply

Intensities	Supply mode	The principle of supply	Examples of public goods
Purely operating	Market-oriented supply	It follows the supply principles of market-based, supplemented by government; the fees can cover the cost. However, it must be controlled to ensure the interests of consumers.	Toll roads, city gas, urban water supply, culture, sports organizations, rural power, rural water conservancy facilities
Quasi-operating	Jointly supply where government provide subsidies to attract market investment	Government should guarantee the basic needs of the residents; projects have the social characteristic which can be compensated by the market process	Urban health, radio, television, stadium, exhibition halls, subway, light rail, buses, solid waste disposal, sewage treatment, rural public transport, postal service and telecommunications.
Non-operating	Government supply	It complies with the social contract based on a fair, public, and social vision.	National defense, fire fighting, epidemic prevention, judicial services, basic research, basic education in rural areas, health insurance, special care.

Note: It is summarized on the basis of related materials.

3.1.1 The Defining Scope of the Financial Supply of Local Public Goods

In 1954, Paul Samuelson, who is a famous American economist, published public expenditure of pure theory, which gives us the classic definition for public goods [7]. Namely, public goods has the characteristic of non-competitive and non-exclusive. Because two properties can result in the market failure of public goods supply, the government supply of public goods is inevitable. Public finance is the foundation and the core of the public goods supply.

The supply of public goods should be mainly undertaken by central and local governments who make budget arrangement from the mandatory tax revenue. Public products mainly include security, macro economic control, income distribution, basic education, equal basic medical epidemic prevention system, infrastructure construction, environmental protection, basic research, etc.

3.1.2 The Defining Scope of the Market Supply of Local Public Goods

However, most public goods in real life is quasi-public goods, or mixed public goods except for national defense, diplomacy and other rare public goods. The quasi-public goods has the characteristics of incomplete non-competitive and non-exclusive, so it does not necessarily lead to the failure for market supply [8].

Recently, with continuous development of market economy in China, the public goods supply through market mechanism has become more and more common. Large private capital has begun to enter into public goods supply in various fields, including transportation, water, electricity, coal, environmental sanitation, technology development and education. All those have become the irresistible trend. However, it should be noted that the provision of public goods is currently the main body of local government in China; the market supply has just started.

3.1.3 The Defining Scope of the Supply of Local Public Goods

Combined with above analyses, the supply scope of the local public goods includes the contents of three categories in accordance with the characteristics of different suppliers and operating intensity. These are: purely operating category of public goods, quasi-operating category of public goods and non-operating category of public goods; it can be shown in table1.

3.2 The Design of Index System of Local Public Goods Supply: The Principles and Contents

3.2.1 The Design of the Principles of Index-Evaluation System

As a standard of characterization and measurement, the index system has the following features: (1) It is composed of a set of core indicators, which should be as little as possible to facilitate the strategic control of operations; (2) as one of important local public goods supply, the government supply can reflect real and potential level of local public goods supply; (3) Leading indicators and lagging indicators are combined, dynamic index combining with static index, which can optimize the process of local public goods supply and provide specific guidance for practice.

According to above assumptions, the design of local public goods supply mainly follows four principles: sophistication, particularity, integrity and practicability.

3.2.2 Construction of Index-Evaluation of Local Public Goods Supply

On the basis of international public supply relevant measure index systems, Index-evaluation system of local public goods supply is composed of 9 categories and 42 indicators which is named general index, which is shown in table 2.

For the convenience of comparison, 42 indicators can be simplified 10 core indicators: social security spending/GDP, adult illiteracy rate, higher education enrollment rate, infant mortality, forest coverage, R&D expenditure/GDP, persons drinking safe water / total population, the number of bed per thousand persons, private investment/the total domestic investment, and fiscal expenditure/GDP.

Table 2. The index-evaluation system of the local public goods supply

Index-evaluation system of local public goods	General Index
Indicators of social security category	Three guarantees number(medical insurance, pension insurance and unemployment insurance), urban unemployment, spending of pension and social assistance welfare, social security spending/GDP, net income of rural households per capita
Indicators of public health category	Infant mortality, average expectancy lifetime, the average practitioners per thousand, the number of bed per thousand persons, the number of health technicians, health expenses
Indicators of environmental category	Investment in environmental protection/GDP, industrial wastewater discharge compliance rate, forest coverage, compliance rate of centralized water quality, the average of regional environmental noise, industrial sulfur dioxide emission rate
Indicators of public science and technology	Expenditures for S & T activities, R&D expenditure / GDP, the approval patent (case), the number of research with international advanced level
Indicators of public order category	Mortality rate of production and traffic accident, detection rate of criminal cases, funding for public security agency
Indicators of public administration category	Administrative expenses/ fiscal expenditure, administrative population, penalty income and administrative fees
Indicators of education and culture category	State education budget, adult illiteracy rate, TV coverage, higher education enrollment rate, entering rate of junior middle school graduates, public library collection, social donations and fund for running school
Indicators of public utilities	Persons drinking safe water / total population, urban maintenance cost, the number of gas residents, the total tap water supply, the total mileage of highway
Indicators of public investment	Agricultural expenditure, private investment/the total domestic investment, expenditure for technology promotion

4 The Case of Beijing

4.1 International Comparison of the Public Goods Supply in Beijing

After choosing 10 core indicators to measure local public goods supply, we compare the public goods supply level between Beijing and some high-income countries, middle-income countries, low-income countries, and average level in the world. The result is shown in table3.

4.2 The Index Level of Public Goods Supply in Beijing

If we regard the public goods supply in the high-income countries as a market average level of developed countries, the 10 core indicators as the key factor can be used to measure the public goods supply condition in Beijing. Here are the specific performances: we suppose that public goods supply level of developed country is preferred and its reference value is set 100, so, the index level of public goods supply in Beijing can be obtained; it can be shown in table 4:

Table 3. International comparison of the public goods supply

Items	High-income countries	Middle-income countries	Low-income countries	World average level	Beijing
Social security spending / GDP(1996)	16	12.5	6.2	14.5	1.93
Adult illiteracy rate (1998)	1.7	14.5	28.5	16	3.9
Higher education enrollment rate (1999)	62	12	8	14	59
Infants mortality (1999)	6	31	77	54	3.49
Forest coverage (2000)	26.1	32.9	26.8	29.7	36.4
R&D expenditure / GDP (1997)	2.81	≠	≠	≠	5.5
Persons drinking safe water / total population (2000)	99	81	76	81	99
The number of beds per thousand persons (1998)	7.2	3.4	1.3	3.3	6.62
Private investment / the total domestic investment (1999)	79.2	74.8	53.7	76.0	50 (1997)
Fiscal expenditure / GDP	30.2	20.5	17.0	27.9	23.2

Note: ① Beijing indicator is the data of 2009; ② expenditure-GDP ratio is regarded as foreign central government expenditure. **Source:** Beijing Statistical Yearbook of (2010); World Bank: "World Development Indicators 2001".

Table 4. The index level of the public goods supply in Beijing

Items	High-income country	Beijing	Realization degree %
Social security spending / GDP(1996)	16	1.93	12.1
Adult illiteracy rate (1998)	1.7	3.9	43.6
Higher education enrollment rate (1999)	62	59	95.2
Infants mortality (1999)	6	3.49	129
Forest coverage (2000)	26.1	36.4	136
R&D expenditure / GDP (1997)	2.81	5.5	156
Persons drinking safe water / total population (2000)	99	99	100
The number of beds per thousand persons (1998)	7.2	6.62	91.9
Private investment / the total domestic investment (1999)	79.2	50 (1997)	63.2
Fiscal expenditure / GDP	30.2	23.2	76.8
	100	90.36	90.36

4.3 Brief Conclusions

According to the standard of the World Bank Report 2007, the areas in 2005 whose per capita gross domestic income more than $10066, are considered high-income level countries and regions. In 2010, the per capita GDP in Beijing is more than 10,335 U.S. dollars; it has exceeded the average of middle-income countries and regions. The demand of Beijing residents for public goods of residents gradually moves towards diversification and high-quality. Through the international comparison and measurement, the findings can be illustrated by the data:

- Compared with other countries, the index level of public goods supply in Beijing is in higher level and regions. The index level is 90.36, which is close to the level of 100 high-income countries and regions. The capacity of public goods supply in Beijing exceeds that in middle-income countries and regions.
- By testing 10 core indicators, it can be found that the index level in Beijing has basically overtaken that in high-income countries and regions, including infant mortality, forest coverage, R&D expenditure/GDP, persons drinking safe water / total population, and the number of beds per thousand persons.
- For some indicators such as private investment / the total domestic investment and fiscal expenditure / GDP, the index level of Beijing remains to be further improved. Especially, the indicator of social security spending / GDP is obviously low, which is looked forward to be further improved.

Acknowledgments. The research is supported by National Social Science Foundation of China (N0.10CGL077), and by "Middle-aged backbone teacher" Project and social science program of Beijing education commission.

References

1. United Nations Development Programme: Human Development Report 2001. China Financial and Economic Press (2003) (in Chinese)
2. World Bank: World Development Indicators 2001. China Financial and Economic Press (2002) (in Chinese)
3. Chen, T.: The government Performance Evaluation System Approach - Investigation on the Governance Process. Wuhan University Journal (Philosophy and Social Sciences) (1) (2008) (in Chinese)
4. Li, J.: The Chinese Government Supply of Public Goods of International Comparative Study. Chinese Public Administration (6) (2003) (in Chinese)
5. Ni, X.: Selection and Design of the Local Government Performance Evaluation. Wuhan University Journal (Philosophy and Social Sciences) (2) (2007) (in Chinese)
6. Fan, L., Shi, S.: Public goods supply mechanism: role boundary changes and influencing factors. Modern Economic Science (1) (2006) (in Chinese)
7. Samuelson, P.A.: The Pure Theory of Public Expenditure. The Review of Economics and Statistics 36(4), 387–389 (1954)
8. Ye, W.: Urban Public Goods Supply in the Market, and Improve Efficiency of Public Services. Jiangxi Social Science (4) (2004) (in Chinese)

Fiscal Equalization in Corporate Taxation — A Way of Limiting the Harmful Tax Competition in the EU

Adina Trandafir and Luminita Ristea

Spiru Haret University, 32-34 Unirii Street, 900532 Constanta, Romania
atrandafir04@yahoo.com, luminita.ristea@crgnexia.ro

Abstract. EU endeavored in harmonizing and coordinating taxes in order to eliminate or limit the harmful tax competition that affects most Member States companies. Tax base equalization seems to be the right way towards fiscal equalization. However, tax competition is the result of the worldwide mobility of tax bases, companies and financial assets. This mobility was not generated only by technological innovations in transport and telecommunication, but was mostly influenced by political decisions such as liberalization and deregulation. This paper addresses the issue of eliminating harmful tax competition through fiscal equalization, by adopting the CCCTB system. Under these circumstances, tax competition would be limited only to the tax rates applicable in the 27 EU Member States.

Keywords: fiscal coordination, fiscal competition, corporate tax rate competition, common consolidated corporation tax base.

1 Introduction

The risk of harmful tax competition among major industrialized countries seems to be acknowledged, as suggested by attempt of the European Commission (1997) and the OECD (2001) to organize an international coordination to counter the negative effects of this competition. The potential sources of inefficiency arising from tax competition are well known since the seminal paper of Zodrow and Mieszkowski (1986). Negative fiscal externalities emerge from the independent government's competition for mobile tax base through reductions of tax rates. Each government ignores the positive effect on other government's budgets of its tax base outflows in response to higher taxes. For this reason, tax rates and the provision of local public good tend to be too low from an efficiency viewpoint[1]. The well documented description by Devereux, Griffith and Klemm (2002) on the development of source-based capital income taxes over the last two decades reveals a picture close to this scenario. Faced with this risk of harmful tax competition, many observers argued that member states should agree on a tax harmonization policy to avoid tax competition. According to the traditional literature on tax competition, by raising their tax cooperatively all jurisdictions would benefit from an increase in the level of public services. Sinn (1990) as well as Tanzi

[1] See literature in this field like Wilson (1999) as well as Wilson and Wildasin (2003).

M. Zhou (Ed.): ISAEBD 2011, Part III, CCIS 210, pp. 428–434, 2011.

and Bovenberg (1990) among others highlighted the importance of harmonizing tax rates via collective agreements between the European governments. However, the efficiency of tax harmonization is far from clear-cut. For instance, Baldwin and Krugman (2004) analyzed tax competition among countries with different population sizes and imperfect competition and trade costs and got to the conclusion that harmonization may not be desirable, due to the fact that peripheral countries may lose some advantages generated by their initial low tax, while core countries, where taxes are higher, may have to inefficiently reduce public service levels. In addition, using a similar pattern, Ottaviano and Van Ypersele (2003) show that when a differential tax rate, inferior to the one obtained under tax competition, is in place, the overall welfare is minimized. This suggests that, if tax harmonization is avoided, tax rates setting is imperative.

In Section 2, this paper approaches the fiscal equalization from a theoretical point of view, presenting the current state of knowledge. In Section 3, this paper presents the way the EU approaches the fiscal equalization in order to eliminate the harmful effects of tax competition that corporations operating on the Internal Market face.

2 Fiscal Equalization – A Theoretical Approach

Some theoretical works have shown that adequate fiscal equalization may reduce the tax competition and can lead to efficient tax rates[2]. Many countries have adopted equalization systems in order to correct different problems associated with fiscal decentralization (Canada, Germany, Denmark among others, as well a large number of developing countries). In its more standard form, an equalization scheme sets a per-capita transfer to each government equal to the difference between its tax capacity and the capacity of all regions, multiplied by an average tax rate. Such a system is often implemented to serve both equity and efficiency objectives. On one hand, equalization and transfers are meant to offset disparities among regions regarding the ability to provide public goods. On the other hand, as Smart (1998) shows, equalization grants represent strong incentives for local governments to increase their tax on elastically supplied and immobile tax bases. Indeed, negative effects of a higher tax rate on a region's tax base are partly compensated by higher equalizing transfers that reduce the marginal cost of public funds. In addition, Köthenbürger (2002) and Bucovetsky and Smart (2002) show that with traditional tax competition models, horizontal fiscal externalities can be corrected within such system. Boadway and Hayashi (2001) and Esteller-Moré and Solé-Ollé (2002) who have studied provincial governments in Canada have proved that equalization weakens tax competition between local governments. Considering these theoretical and empirical results and the fact that equalization preserves some fiscal sovereignty, it is to be considered that the fiscal equalization has the ability to mitigate the international tax competition. Indeed, existing literature on equalization works that presents a basic tax competition model seems not to be able to describe two main characteristics. The first one is that the EU is an imperfectly integrated economic space. Even though regional trade agreements have produced significant effects, Member states are not perfectly

[2] See Boadway, 2003, for a survey.

integrated. For instance, Head and Mayer (2000) estimate positive border effects in Europe which could be considered as positive transaction costs between European countries. The basic tax competition models do not allow focusing on this feature since they ignore trade costs (Zodrow, 2003). In addition, evidence suggests that economic activities are not evenly distributed among developed countries[3]. This reveals unequal natural advantages between regions and it also indicates that some agglomeration externalities due to increasing returns are at work when firms locate. By assuming that firms face perfect competition and constant returns, a basic tax competition model does not allow addressing this point and the way it may affect tax competition[4]. Literature shows that, whatever the nature of competition and the degree of economic integration, fiscal equalization may increase tax rates. Two fiscal equalization systems are able to reduce tax rates differences. In other words, fiscal equalization may lead to more efficient tax rates and spatial allocation of tax bases. This result proves that local governments can (or are aware that they can) manipulate the average tax rate. Otherwise, fiscal equalization is not able to modify the gap in tax rates.

3 The European Fiscal Equalization Scheme in Corporate Taxation

On March 16, 2011, the European Commission proposed a common system for calculating the tax base of corporations operating in the EU. Proposal for a common consolidated corporations tax base (CCCTB) would mean that companies could benefit from a "one-stop-shop" for filing tax returns and would be able to consolidate all profits and losses incurred throughout the EU. This way, Member States could maintain full sovereign right to determine their own tax rates. The European Commission believes that the only way to systematically address the obstacles that companies face when operating in more than one Member State in the Internal Market is to provide them with a consolidated tax base for their activities at EU level. This represents a first step in the fiscal equalization in the field of direct taxation in the EU, because establighing the level of tax rates is currently a national sovereignity. Each Member State has its own corporate tax system that is significantly different from that of the other states, both in terms of tax rates and tax bases. In addition to these differences, other aspects regarding income tax are also different in each Member State. See below the key characteristics of corporate tax systems in the European Union.

The tax rates shown in the table below are significantly different in the 27 EU Member States. The lowest nominal tax rate (10%) is recorded in Bulgaria and Cyprus. They are followed by Ireland, with a rate of 12.5%, Latvia, Lithuania 15%, and Romania 16%. The average EU 27 nominal rate is 22%. The highest nominal corporation tax rate is recorded in Malta (35%), followed by France (33.33%), Belgium (33%) and Spain (30%).

---

[3] See the survey of Combes and Overman, 2004, for the European space.

[4] Note that, according to the Starrett's theorem, a perfect competition model with trade costs cannot explain the uneven distribution of economic activities, except if technological externalities are introduced.

Table 1. Combined and nominal tax rates in the EU 27

Member State	*Combined rate (%)	Nominal rate (%)
Austria	25	25
Belgium	33,99	33
Bulgaria	10	10
Cyprus	10	10
Czech Republic	19	19
Denmark	25	25
Estonia	21	21
Finland	26	26
France	33,33	33,33
Germany	29,8	15
Greece	23	23
Hungary	20,62	19
Ireland	12,5	12,5
Italy	27,5	27,5
Latvia	15	15
Lithuania	15	15
Luxembourg	28,59	21
Malta	35	35
Netherlands	25,5	25,5
Poland	19	19
Portugal	26,5	25
Romania	16	16
Slovakia	19	19
Slovenia	20	20
Spain	30	30
Sweden	26,3	26,3
United Kingdom	28	28
Average EU27	**23**	**22**

Source: Own elaboration from: http://ec.europa.eu/taxation_customs/taxinv, 2011.
**) Combined share is made up of statutory rate, local rate and surcharges apply.*

Combined rates include the local nominal rate; the central authority receives a percentage of the profit share owed to local authorities and certain surcharges. The biggest difference is recorded in Germany, where the nominal rate is 15% and the combined rate is 29.8% (it includes 14% local incumbent). In Belgium a 3% crisis surcharge that benefits only the central authorities is included in the combined rate of 33.99%. In Hungary, the combined rate of 22.62% includes, in addition to the nominal rate of 19%, a 2% local rate. Luxembourg charges a combined rate of 28.59%, which includes the nominal rate of 21%, a profit share of 7.5% (which applies in Luxembourg-City) and a 4% solidarity surcharge to finance unemployment fund. Portugal levies a local income tax of 1.5%, which added to the 25% nominal rate determines a combined rate of 26.5% which is above the EU 27 average (which is 23%).

Elschener and Vanborren (2009) analyzed the evolution of the effective average tax rate (The Average Effective Tax Rate (EATR) is, in fact, the relevant rate for the analysis of discrete investment choices, such as location selection; EATR is calculated for 15 different investment types - five assets, each one being funded from three sources; EATR is a measure of present value of taxes paid and is expressed as a proportion of net present value of the income stream, less the initial cost of investment), using the Devereux and Griffith (1999, 2003) methodology and they reached the following conclusions: the average EU-27 EATR is 22.3%, but there are considerable dispersion between the Member States EATR levels. The lowest EATR level is recorded in Bulgaria (8, 8%) and the highest one in Germany (35.5%). In the EU15, EATR (26.3%) is considerably higher than in the 12 new EU Member States (where the average EATR is 17.4%). There may be more reasons for variances between actual tax levels. One of them could be the size and the economic development that can lead to higher levels of the EATR for larger countries. For most countries, EATR is slightly below the statutory tax rates. In some countries, EATR is higher than statutory tax rates. In Ireland, real estate taxes are very high compared to income taxes. France imposes a tax on business (*Taxe professionnelle*) for fixed assets. Cyprus applies a special tax on financial assets. Only in Belgium, Estonia and Italy, the average actual rates are considerably lower than the statutory tax rates. This is mainly due to a specific tax regime for financial assets or differences in tax treatment depending on funding. In Italy, the local tax of 4.25% does not apply to financial assets, leading to a lower EATR. In Britain, EATR reaches 29.3%, in Spain 34.5%, in Ireland 14.4% and in Malta 32.2%.

In order to minimize differences between the corporate tax systems operating in the EU, the Commission proposed the introduction of Common Consolidated Corporation Tax Base system, on March 16, 2011.

Common consolidated corporations' tax base (CCCTB) is a single set of rules that companies operating in the EU could use to calculate their taxable profits. In other words, a company or a qualified group of companies should follow only one set of rules when calculating the taxable base - the EU's rules and not the different ones that apply in the Member States where they operate. In addition, using CCCTB, groups may submit a single consolidated tax declaration for their entire activity in the EU and the consolidated group's taxable profits would be divided among individual companies through a simple formula, so that each Member State can then tax the corporate profits with the tax rate they choose.

The CCCTB would be optional, allowing companies that felt that they would truly benefit from this harmonized system to opt-in, while other companies could continue to work within their national systems. This is a common sense approach, as it means that companies that have no intention of expanding beyond their national borders, and therefore will only ever work within one system, do not have to shift needlessly to a new tax system. The Commission also believes that a compulsory CCCTB would disagree with the principle of subsidiarity, as it would mean that EU measures were introduced to cover both purely domestic, as well as EU-level activities. Companies would have to opt-in for the CCCTB for a minimum of five years (to avoid opting in and out for tax planning purposes).

In addition, various criteria that a company must meet to be eligible for the CCCTB system are detailed in an annex to the proposal (e.g. type of corporate tax rules that it must be in place; type of company). Another crucial aspect of the CCCTB is consolidation, because it means that a company's cross-border activity within the

EU will be fully recognized. Also, consolidation would eliminate the need for a complex transfer pricing system that is currently in place for cross-border intra-group sales. Given that transfer pricing is one of the most burdensome and expensive aspect of corporate taxation for enterprises, its elimination will significantly benefit companies and groups within the EU. Another positive aspect of the CCCTB is that it can make the EU a much more attractive market for foreign investors. For example, at the moment, companies operating in third-countries such as the USA or China only have to deal with one national tax system. This is compared to a European system of 27 different sets of rules, which creates far more complexity and costs. A single set of rules for the corporate tax base and a one-stop-shop system for filing tax returns, would make the EU a much easier place for foreign firms to invest in. Many third-countries have already indicated to the Commission that the CCCTB would help to make the EU a more interesting market for foreign investments.

4 Conclusions

Fiscal equalization is more than desirable in the Internal Market of the EU. This may help to reduce the gap between tax rates that operate in the 27 national systems, and, also can eliminate or limit more other differences between fiscal systems. Fiscal equalization is as necessary as it is desirable in the EU. The adoption of the CCCTB system by companies which operate in more than one Member State provides the following advantages:

- the CCCTB would make things far cheaper and simpler for businesses by creating one set of rules for calculating the tax base of a company or group and by setting up a one-stop-shop system for filing tax returns.

- the CCCTB would allow the consolidation of profits and losses at EU level, and would enable cross border activities of businesses to be fully taken into account and would avoid over taxation.

- for businesses operating cross border in the EU, the CCCTB unequivocally translates into savings in compliance time and costs. It is estimated that the current compliance costs could be reduced by 7%, which is equivalent to a saving of €0.7 billion across the EU.

- the CCCTB would be optional, allowing companies that felt that they would truly benefit from this harmonized system to opt-in, while other companies could continue to work within their national systems. This is a common sense approach, as it means that companies that have no intention of expanding beyond their national borders, and therefore will only ever work within one system, do not have to shift needlessly to a new tax system. The Commission also believes that a compulsory CCCTB would disagree with the principle of subsidiarity, as it would mean that EU measures were introduced to cover both purely domestic, as well as EU-level activities.

- the CCCTB opens up the possibility of expansion within the EU for SMEs that may, up to now, have thought is too costly and complicated to do so.

- overall, CCCTB offers a better environment for research and innovation than foreseen in the current corporate tax systems of most Member States.

- the CCCTB can also make the EU a much more attractive market for foreign investors

Tax competition is aggravated by the tax base mobility. By establishing a common system for determining taxable income, the tax competition in the EU will be determined taking into consideration the profit rates and there will be no hidden elements to distort the tax base and to emphasize the harmful effects of tax competition. And over all, states would retain sovereignty in setting their tax rates.

References

1. Devereux, M., Griffith, R., Klemm, A.: Corporate tax income reforms and international tax competition. Economic Policy, 451–495 (2002)
2. Köthenbürger, M.: Tax competition and fiscal equalisation. International Tax and Public Finance 9, 391–408 (2003)
3. Ottaviano, G.I.P., Tabuchi, T., Thisse, J.F.: Agglomeration and trade revisited. International Economic Review 43, 409–436 (2004)
4. Sinn, H.W.: Tax harmonization and tax competition in Europe. European Economic Review 34(2-3), 489–504 (1990)
5. Smart, M.: Taxation and deadweight loss in a system of intergovernmental transfers. Canadian Journal of Economics 31, 189–206 (1998)
6. Tanzi, V.Y., Bovenberg, A.L.: Is there a need for harmonization capital income taxes within EU countries? European Economic Review 34(2-3), 473–489 (1990)
7. Wilson, J.: Theories of tax competition. National Tax Journal 52, 269–304 (1999)
8. Wilson, J., Wildasin, D.: Tax competition: bane or boon? Journal of Public Economics 88, 1065–1091 (2003)
9. Zodrow, G., Mieszkowski, P.: Pigou, Tiebout, property taxation and the underprovision of local public goods. Journal of Urban Economics 19, 356–370 (1986)
10. Combes, P.P., Overman, H.G.: The spatial distribution of economic activities in the European Union. In: Henderson, V., Thisse, J.F. (eds.) Handbook of Urban and Regional Economics. Elsevier-North-Holland, Amsterdam (2004)
11. Bucovetsky, S., Smart, M.: The efficiency consequences of local revenue equalization: tax competition and tax distortions. Mimeo (2002)
12. Ottaviano, G., Van Ypersele, T.: Market access and tax competition. CORE Discussion Paper (2003)
13. European Commission, Towards tax co-ordination in the European Union: a package to tackle harmful tax competition. Communication from the European Commission COM (1997) 495 final (1997)
14. OECD, Towards global tax co-operation: progress in indentifying and eliminating harmful tax practices, OECD, Paris (2001)

Industrialized Development Strategy and Chinese Rural Land System

Zheng Li

China Univeristy of Geosciences (Beijing), 100083, Beijing, China
lizheng63@vip.sina.com

Abstract. From the perspective of path selection of national industrialized development strategy and adopting historical analysis and institutional cost analysis, this paper gives an explanation to the determinants, causes of Chinese rural land system from 1950s to 1970s and the effects of land system on rural property relationships, political relationships and social relationships. The results indicate that state power in the path selection of the industrial development strategy is the ultimate determinant of Chinese rural land system design. The institutional cost determined by rural population and peasantry resistance is the root cause of many changes in Chinese rural land system. Each change in rural land system will have a great impact on rural property relationships, political relationships and social relationships. This impact will lay a foundation for China to accomplish the goal of economic liberalization, political democratization and contractual relationships.

Keywords: Rural Land System, Institutional Cost, Industrialized Development Strategy, China.

1 Introduction

The land system in rural China has changed drastically over the past decades. Such rapid, frequent and drastic evolution of an institution within such a short timeframe in the most populous country is rarely seen in the human history of institutional change, providing a classic case for the study of institutional changes. This paper discusses the change in the rural land system in China from 1950s to 1970s.

The rural land system in China since the 1950's underwent many institutional changes from peasant land ownership, collective ownership of land by the combining of ownership and use rights and state ownership of land. Most previous studies attributed the aforesaid frequent institutional changes to Marxist public economy theory. These explanations, however, often ignore the fact that the rural land system in China never established public ownership in a real sense but has long retained the partial private land property rights of peasants, and also ignore the multidimensional value that the rural land system has in traditional Chinese society. This makes it very difficult for existing theories to establish an analytic framework for complete explanation of the changes in the rural land system in China. Over the past years, although some research findings began adopting North's "institutional change theory"

M. Zhou (Ed.): ISAEBD 2011, Part III, CCIS 210, pp. 435–442, 2011.

citation needed to address these issues and made considerable progress (Zhou, 1995), most existing findings only explain the regular pattern of rural land system change in part of the historical period using this theory, and such theory itself is considerably deficient when used to explain the decision making process and social impact involved in land system change (Hayami, 1997).

This paper demonstrates the inherent causes of different institutional arrangements in the land system in rural areas in different historical periods and builds an analytic framework for change in the rural land system in China from the perspective of path selection in the national industrialization development strategy. The central argument in this paper is that the rural land system in China reflects the inherent requirement of the national industrialization development strategy for institutional design in rural areas. Each change in the rural land system represented both a process during which the national will rebuilt the property, political and social relations in rural areas according to the requirements of industrialization development strategy and a process of game playing between national government power and peasants' power regarding land property relations in rural areas.

2 The Design of Rural Land System

Industrialization is the ultimate goal of development for the new China. To this end, choice of suitable development strategy became the top-priority topic. Under the then historical conditions, the central government finally chose heavy-industry-first development strategy that can enable the country to realize industrialization within a short timeframe (Lin et al., 2003). However, the fact that heavy industry is capital-intensive one that has very limited capacity to take in labor was exactly opposite to the resource endowment situation of the newborn China where capital was highly scarce and labor was relatively sufficient. This led the central government to leverage the administrative power to artificially lower the prices of raw materials, capital and labor required for industrial production, enhance the national capability of capital accumulation, and limit migration of agricultural population to industrial population through a series of institutional arrangements, thus realizing reintegration of the nation's resource endowment and creating conditions for development of heavy industry. This became a logical starting point of the second significant change of rural land system in China. This change of rural land system was realized through three institutional arrangements of land collectivization, production socialization and urban-rural separation.

2.1 Land Collectivization

Although the land reform unleashed the peasants' enthusiasm about production, the motivating role of the peasant land ownership disappeared within a short timeframe due to the technical, capital and production condition constraints, as a result of which the grain production entered a stage of stead development since 1952. Coupled with the very limited capabilities of individual peasants to cope with natural disasters, many peasants had to consider the possibility of realizing mass production through participation in agricultural cooperatives (elementary agricultural producers' cooperatives) and agricultural mutual-aid teams after being allocated land lots. Meanwhile, along with the year-on-year growth of grain output in the early days of the founding of new China, the central government started considering further expanding the coverage of procurement quotas of farm produce so as to ensure sufficient supply of raw materials to heavy industry. This practice, however, met strong resistance from the peasants at the very outset, resulting in the "unified purchase and sale" policy being brought up to the agenda (Du, 2005). As such, the Agricultural Cooperative Movement that emerged gradually after the founding of the new China began changing from a spontaneous act of peasants under the government-led pilot scheme to an act dominated and driven by the government and a corresponding "unified purchase and sale" policy was gradually set up. The Agricultural Cooperative Movement marked the complete substitution of peasant land ownership by collective ownership of rural land. Peasants' associations were subsequently replaced by agricultural cooperatives, which became the basic economic and political organization in rural China at that time.

Agricultural cooperatives to a certain extent met the peasants' requirements for increased agricultural capital and technology input and realization of mass production, reversed the stagnant grain output landscape during this period and enabled successful implementation of the "unified purchase and sale" policy in support of the nationwide industrialization drive. Along with the advent of the Great Leap Forward and the People's Commune Movement in 1958, however, this situation was radically broken up.

People's Commune represented the development of agricultural cooperative but it transcended the development of productivity level. Its fundamental starting point originated from the need to shift the collective ownership of rural land directly to state ownership of rural land in order to realize the direct governmental control over all production factors in rural areas like resources (including land), capital and labor. Correspondingly, the political relation in rural areas shifted from "state-peasants' association-peasant" structure to "state-collective (cooperative, People's Commune)-peasant" structure and further to "state-peasant" structure. This was the head-on collision between the state power and peasants' power that had never happened before in Chinese history. Meanwhile, it also meant that the state had to assume the responsibility for daily life and agriculture production of all peasants in the country while "purchasing" all land property rights of peasants. Although a state as a violent organization can create any form of property rights, it can never get rid of the constraint of institutional cost (North, 1990). Practices prove that People's Commune could at most and narrowly assume the agriculture production and social security functions granted by the collective ownership of rural land given its institutional design, but by no means can afford the same functions resulting from state ownership of rural land, otherwise the strong resistance from the peasants would be inevitable. This is also the basic reason why the repeated attempts of People's Commune to directly shift to the aspiration of communism all fell through. So, the People's Commune system that was followed for many years thereafter had to be brought back onto the track of continuing to maintain the collective ownership of rural land, a track that is far away from its original intention. Under the influence of institutional cost, the political relation in rural China was finally fixed at the "state-collective-peasant" structure. However, even this discounted People's Commune was sufficient to meet the institutional arrangement required for the heavy-industry-first development strategy, which not only provided enormous land resources for industrialization drive free of charge but also paved the way for production socialization and urban-rural separation.

2.2 Production Socialization

Since People's Commune is the continuation and development of agricultural cooperative, it means that People's Commune will undertake both the economic and political functions at the same time, that is, organizing agricultural production activities and carrying out day-to-day management in rural areas. In fact, People's Commune not only shouldered economic and political functions but also assumed social security function in rural areas from the very outset, yet the very foundation for its existence was the collective ownership of rural land characterized by high degree of combination of land ownership and land use right.

In the early days of the founding of new China, land was still the most fundamental and important production factor for peasants. The reason all peasants, especially the middle-class peasants and poor peasants, gained access to land within a short period of time was totally because of the Land Reform Movement lead by Chinese communists. Since the land property rights of peasants was obtained through the direct administrative intervention of the state power, the land property rights incorporated the element of state power from the very beginning. When the state power deems it necessary to reclaim the land property rights, it can naturally make it happen through administrative coercive power, which peasants can hardly resist (Zhou, 1995). As the land system in rural areas shifted from individual to collective, not only peasants lost the production basis of income generation that they had always been relying upon, the market mechanism's role in regulating land and agricultural produces also disappeared as a result, forcing peasants back into People's Commune in order to sustain their production activities and mere subsistence. Production activities conducted at the People's Commune not only realized the complete communization of production materials but also excluded independent production activities of peasants. Highly centralized and unified mode of production helped the central government directly control production activities and distribution of agricultural produces in rural areas through the People's Commune system and "unified purchase and sale" policy without regard to the cost element according to the heavy-industry-first development strategy on the one hand; on the other hand, the state could totally transfer the organizing agricultural production activities, day-to-day management of peasants and social security affairs (such as education and medical care) to the People's Commune and bear only low control costs. Meanwhile, with the dual constraint of the People's Commune and "unified purchase and sale" policy, due to the radical abolition of market mechanism, collectivized land resources can be used free of charge, prices of agricultural produces can be seriously distorted and labor resources subjected to unified allocation, all of which undoubtedly provided sufficient sources, capital and labor for the nationwide development of heavy industry in a long-term, effective and low-cost manner. This is also the primary reason the accumulation of industrial capital in China has been relying upon agricultural surplus. From 1953 to 1983, the scissors difference in prices between industrial goods and agricultural products resulting from the "unified purchase and sale" policy alone amounted to as high as 600 billion to 800 billion Yuan (Wu, 2001).

2.3 Urban-Rural Separation

Giving top priority to the development of heavy industry means all social capital and resources need to be concentrated in urban industry districts while the outflow of capital and resources to rural areas is minimize. With the constraints of land collectivization and production socialization, labor became the only factor that likely allows the capital and resources to flow into rural areas.

With peasants deprived of land property rights, moving to urban industry districts would become the only option for most of peasants if participation in collectivized agricultural production activities would not more beneficial for them than participation in urban industrial production activities. Due to the very limited capability of heavy industry to take in labor, however, the significantly increased population of labor would instead reduce the industrial input-output ratio and affect the continuous improvement of the nation's level of industrialization. Meanwhile, in the planned economy, migration of a large number of rural laborers into cities would inevitably result in tension in distribution of agricultural products in urban areas and increase the urban demand for agricultural products, thus further aggravating the burden of supply in rural areas and forcing more peasants to seek a livelihood in cities. This vicious cycle is obviously detrimental to the successful implementation of the heavy-industry-first development strategy. For this reason, it is necessary to tie peasants up with agricultural production activities through certain institutional arrangements in order to effectively thaw the aforesaid paradox. This gave birth to the urban-rural household registration system.

Urban-rural household registration system is an institutional expression of urban-rural separation. In the era of planned economy, urban-rural household registration system was not only closely related to people's employment and livelihood but more tightly connected with welfare and even clothing, food, shelter and weans of travel, which radically eliminated the possibility that peasants will seek a livelihood in cities. The migration of rural surplus labor to cities could be possible only under the planned and organized arrangement of the central government. The urban-rural household registration system eventually provided effective support for successful implementation of land collectivization and production socialization.

The trinity of institutional arrangements of land collectivization, production socialization and urban-rural separation represented the institutional design that the state will adopted for rural areas after choosing the heavy-industry-first development strategy, which were closely connected with and indispensable to each other. Land collectivization serves as the foundation for the existence of production socialization and urban-rural separation, not only providing free land resources for the nation's industrialization drive but also depriving peasants of the right to independently engage in agricultural production. Under the urban-rural separation, peasants had no choice but participate in People's Commune to simply sustain their very subsistence; production socialization was the ultimate goal of land collectivization and urban-rural separation, which not only could support successful implementation of the "unified purchase and sale" policy but also assumed all economic, political and social security functions in the rural areas; Urban-rural separation was an important prerequisite to land collectivization and production socialization in that it not only effectively prevented free flow of rural labor and ensured input of agricultural labor but also significantly reduced the consumption of agricultural products resulting fro free flow of labor.

3 The Effect of Rural Land System

These institutional arrangements undoubtedly represented attempt of the heavy-industry-first development strategy to rebuild the property, political and social relations in rural China.

3.1 Reconstruction of Property Relations

The head-on collision between state power and peasants' power regarding rural land property rights led to a situation where the land property rights reform involved change only from private land ownership to collective ownership of rural land without going further to state ownership of rural land. The collective ownership of land was indisputably more suitable for the actual level of development in the rural China at that time than state ownership of land. Meanwhile, even during the People's Commune period, the state gave tacit consent to the existence of a small portion of private property rights of land and market mechanism in rural areas by appropriately retaining the private plot and small-scale farm produce markets in addition to the socialized production system. This to a certain extent addressed both the agricultural production requirements and the peasants' needs during this period, weakened the adverse impact of the "unified purchase and sale" policy on lives of peasants and greatly cushioned the conflict between the state and peasants on land property rights. Meanwhile, it was exactly this negligible existence of private property rights and market mechanism that significantly increased the leverage of peasants' power in the process of game playing with the state power at the later stage of the People's Commune (Zhou, 1995).

3.2 Reconstruction of Social Relations

Agricultural Cooperative Movement and People's Commune Movement ultimately and radically destroyed the root of agnatic relation, affiliation and geographic relation in traditional Chinese society. In the crusade against landlords as part of the Land Reform Movement, many peasants showed more or less hesitation and sympathy towards landlords in their villages but little sympathy to landlords from outside their own villages (Huang, 2006), indicating the Chinese peasants, despite of the baptism of Land Reform Movement, were still under profound influence of traditional agnation, affiliation and geographic affinity. After the agricultural cooperative movement and the People's Commune Movement, however, peasants were enabled to establish production linkage, trade and social relations within a broader scope as the means of agricultural production rapidly went beyond the boundaries of family and village, thus greatly weakening the effects and constraints of traditional agnation, affiliation and geographic affinity. The previous social relations based on agnation, affiliation and geographic affinity collapsed, giving way to social relations based on production and economic activities. This enabled Chinese peasants to be released from the traditional social relations and gradually become individual right holders with independent economic sense and capability. In the following economic system reform, it was these independent individual right holders that became an important driving force behind construction of social relations based on contractual relation under the market economy conditions.

It should be admitted that the aforesaid institutional arrangements did produce positive impact on China's agricultural production. Between 1958 and 1978, the country's grain output rose from 197.65 million tons to 304.77 million tons, a rise of 54.20%; per unit area grain output increased from 1,548.8 kg/ha. to 2,527.3 kg/ha., a 63.18% rise, a figure that could be even higher if such factors as private plot are allowed for. However, along with the explosion of rural population in the country between 1960's and 1970's, the institutional cost of People's Commune began skyrocketing, so was the institutional cost of the state for further implementation of the People's Commune system and "unified purchase and sale" policy. From 1958 to 1978, the rural population in the country rose from 560.17 million to 803.20 million people, a shocking rise of 43.39%. During the same period, the index of expenditure used by the state to control rural economic system rose from 3.52 to 5.75, a 63.35% rise (Zhou, 1995). The growing institutional cost aggregated the conflict between the state and peasants on land property rights instead of effectively thawing the same. Till the reform and opening-up, modes of production like "contracting production quotas to individual households" and "contracting work to individual households" emerged covertly to different degrees in many rural areas across the country, and the scope of previously tacitly approved private ownership of rural land became so insufficient to meet the peasants' needs that more and more peasants began resisting the People's Commune system. Meanwhile, the trinity of institutional arrangements confined most of rural population in agricultural production activities, which not only made it very difficult to effectively improve the agricultural productivity but also significantly delayed the urbanization process, with the living standard of peasants rarely improved. As the drawbacks of the heavy-industry-first development strategy surfaced, these trinity of institutional arrangements based on this strategy became very difficult to sustain. A new change of the rural land system in new China was brewing.

4 Conclusion

This paper provides a systematic review of the change in the rural land system in China from 1950s to 1970s. Classic theories maintain that ideology is the primary reason the Chinese communists and government have always stipulated public ownership of rural land. Despite this perception, this paper demonstrates the inherent cause of different institutional arrangements designed for the rural land system in different historical periods from the perspective of path selection of the national will in relation to industrialization development strategy; that is, the institutional design of the rural land system in essence reflects the institutional arrangement of the national industrialization strategy in rural areas and the choice of specific development strategy inevitably entails the choice of a suitable rural land system. Meanwhile, since the rural land system is also the foundation for all institutional designs in rural areas in the context of the national industrialization development strategy, its economic, political and social implications have gone far beyond the reach of ideological explanation. Every process of change in the rural land system both represented the process during which the national will rebuilt the property, political and social relations in rural China according to the industrialization development strategy and at the same time involved the process of game playing between state power and peasants' power regarding rural land property rights.

The huge rural population ultimately means that the rural land system is a key issue affecting China's industrialization process from beginning to end. Beyond all questions, against the background of the irreversible movement of Chinese society towards economic liberalization, political democratization and contractual relationships, the continuous change in the rural land system will pave the way for realization of these objectives.

References

1. Chinese State Grain Administration: China Grain Development Report 2009. Economic Management Press, Beijing (2010)
2. Chinese State Statistics Bureau: China Statistical Yearbooks. China Statistical Publishing House, Beijing (1999-2009)
3. Du, R.: Important Decision of System Change in Rural China. People's Press, Beijing (2005)
4. Hayami, Y.: Development Economics: From the Poverty to the Wealth of Nations. Oxford University Press, Clarendon Press, Oxford (1997)
5. Huang, R.: The Revolution and Rural Areas: Study on the Rural Land Ownership 1949-1983. Shanghai Academy of Social Sciences Press, Shanghai (2006)
6. Lin, J.Y., Cai, F., Li, Z.: The Chinese Miracle: Development Strategy and Economic Reform. The Chinese University of Hong Kong Press, Hong Kong (2003)
7. North, D.: Institutions, Institutional Change, and Economic Performance. Cambridge University Press, Cambridge (1990)
8. Wu, L.: Scissors Movement in China: 1949-1978. Researches in Chinese Economic History 4, 5–11 (2001)
9. Zhou, Q.: China's Rural Reform: the Changes between State and Land Ownership. Social Sciences in China (6) (1995)

An Empirical Study on the Relationship between Equity Ownership Structure of Chinese Fund Management Company and Fund Performance

Xuerong Wang and Qingqing Xie

Nanjing University of Finance and Economics, School of Accounting,
P.R. China, Nanjing, Jiangsu Province

Abstract. In order to analysis the relationships between equity ownership structure of Chinese fund management company and fund performance, this paper takes 121 open-end funds from 50 fund management companies in china for the period of 2008–2009 as a sample and applies a regression experimental analysis models. We find that equity ownership by the first major stockholder in fund management companies has a significantly positive effect on fund performance. It is also found that equity ownership by securities companies has a significantly positive effect on fund performance. There are some differences between the conclusions in this article and other related literatures' conclusions.

Keywords: Equity Ownership Structure, Fund Performance, Empirical study.

1 Introduction

The securities investment fund is an investment instrument operated by fund manager in order to achieve capital appreciation. By the development of about ten years, the securities investment funds have become the most important institutional investors in China, influencing all aspects of securities market and becoming the focus of the market. According to the data of Wind Database, by the December 31, 2009, the number of fund management companies in China has reached 60.These 60 fund management companies manage more than 500 open-end funds in the market and the assets under management reach about 2.68 trillion. In 2009, with the stock market's strength, China's fund industry has experienced a revival and the formation of a new industry structure. In all types of securities investment funds, open-end fund's number has reached 527; accounting for 94.6% of the number of all funds.

Although the open-end funds all achieve good profits in 2009, performances of the open-end funds differ obviously. How do fund management companies' shareholder structures affect fund performances? This paper conducts an empirical study on the relationship between Chinese fund management companies' equity ownership structures and fund performances and tries to answer the above question.

M. Zhou (Ed.): ISAEBD 2011, Part III, CCIS 210, pp. 443–449, 2011.

2 Literature Review

Western developed countries' researches on fund performance began in the 1950s. Most relevant researches show that fund management companies' equity ownership structures have effect on the fund performances. Shleifer and Vishny (1986) found that a certain degree of equity ownership concentration can limit the ability of the management to pursue private interests and monitoring the behavior of managers, ultimately beneficial to fund performance improvement. Barclay, Holderness and pontiff (1993) studied closed-end funds performance and found a positive effect of shareholder structures of owning more than 5% share on closed-end funds' discount rate. They concluded that the major stockholders' pursuing of various personal interests can hinder the maximization of fund performances. But Demsetz(1983) got the different conclusion. He thought that there is no correlation between the fund management companies' equity ownership structures and fund performances, while the fund management companies' equity ownership structure is the result of the internal selection for the organization to achieve a balance.

For the Chinese market, Zhang (2008) conducted an empirical study on the relationship between Chinese fund management companies' equity ownership structures and fund performances, respectively taking the open-end funds and closed-end funds as the sample. The conclusion indicated that the relationship between Chinese fund management companies' equity ownership concentration degree and fund performance is not obvious, but equity participation of foreign capital is beneficial to the improvement of the fund performance. He (2005) found that equity ownership by securities companies has a significantly positive effect on fund performance. For domestic researches, there is a problem that sample size is small. Otherwise, the study period of the funds of sample is short is another problem. In studies abroad, the study period of the funds in the sample is over ten years and the observations of the sample are big. Only in this way, the empirical conclusion of high accuracy and can better reflect the mutual fund performance. Yet the domestic researches on fund performance restricted by the current situation. Currently, the operation time of the open-end funds in domestic market is short and the number of the open-end funds is small.

3 Hypothesis Development

Equity ownership concentration or the existence of large shareholders can create incentives on the company's operating to a certain extent. As the manager is the direct representative of the controlling shareholder interests of the operators are in line with the interests of shareholders. For a company of dispersed equity ownership, interests of the operators are often not consistent with the interests of shareholders. Therefore, managers may harm the interests of the shareholders. Meanwhile, in the situation of dispersed equity ownership the supervision of the manager will be a problem. Shareholders will have the "free rider" incentive, not willing to supervise the managers. For fund management companies, concentration of equity ownership will promote the function of corporate governance mechanism and improve the level of operating and managing fund assets, ultimately improving the fund performance. The reasoning leads us to hypothesize that:

H1: Degree of ownership concentration has a positive effect on fund performance, other things being equal.

Securities companies are engaged in the securities business and have a deep understanding of China's capital market. Securities companies can provide fund management companies strong supports in making investment decisions. These supports can help fund management companies grasp the trend of the market more accurately and make more rational investment decisions, ultimately improving the fund performance. We hypothesize that:

H2: Equity ownership by securities companies has a positive effect on fund performance.

Foreign investment institutions can bring domestic fund management companies more advanced concepts. Foreign shareholders' mature experience in asset management will help domestic fund management companies control investment risk better and improve the fund performance. We hypothesize that:

H3: Equity ownership by foreign shareholders has a positive effect on fund performance.

4 Research Design

4.1 Sample Selection

Our sample included open-end funds in Chinese market. We applied the following restrictions: (a) A fund should have been established for two years at the end of 2009 in order to ensure that its performance is not significantly affected by new establishment. (b) A fund should mainly invest in stocks and is the type of open-end. (c) A fund management company /year should not have missing data. The above criteria yielded a usable sample of 242 observations, representing 121 funds from 50 domestic fund management companies for the period of 2008–2009.

4.2 Variables

4.2.1 Dependent Variable

In this article, unit net value growth is used as a measure of fund performance. Because for investors funds' unit net value growth is the most important criterion they care about. It is defined as follows:

$$ZZL = (AAV_t - AAV_{t-1}) / NAV_{t-1}$$

Where, NAV_{t-1} is unit net value of the fund at the end of period t-1, AAV_t is unit accumulative net value during period t, ZZL is the unit net value growth during period t.

We also use Sharpe index as an alternative performance measure. Sharpe index not only considers the fund's systematic risk, but also consider the fund's non-systematic risk. Sharpe index is defined as follows:

$$SHARPE = (r_p - r_f) / \delta_p$$

Where, r_p is the expected return rate of the fund, r_f is the risk-free rate of return, δ_p is the standard deviation of return rate.

4.2.2 Independent Variables

In our study, we choose these three independent variables: degree of ownership concentration of fund management companies、equity ownership by securities companies and foreign equity ownership. We measure the degree of ownership concentration by the percentage of shares held by the first major stockholder (i.e. JZD). Equity ownership by securities companies is measured by the percentage of shares held by securities companies (i.e. ZQ). We use the dummy variable (i.e. HZ) to measure the equity ownership by foreign shareholders. HZ equals 1 if the fund management company has the foreign shareholder and 0 otherwise.

4.2.3 Control Variables

The control variables in our article include the asset size and the year dummy variable. We measure fund size (SIZE) as the natural logarithm of a fund's net asset at the end of the year. Year dummy variables (YEAR) are included to control for changes in macroeconomic environment common to funds over the sample period. YEAR equals 1 if the year is 2009 and 0 otherwise.

4.3 Models

On the basis of the analysis above, we establish multiple-regression models, as follows:

Model 1: $ZZL(SHARPE) = \alpha_0 + \alpha_1 JZD + \alpha_2 HZ + \alpha_3 SIZE + \alpha_4 YEAR + \varepsilon$
Model 2: $ZZL(SHARPE) = \alpha_0 + \alpha_1 ZQ + \alpha_2 SIZE + \alpha_3 YEAR + \varepsilon$

5 Empirical Results

5.1 Descriptive Statistics

In order to accurately reveal the characteristics of Chinese fund management companies' equity ownership structures, we conduct descriptive statistics of the variables and analyze basic information. Table 1 shows the descriptive statistics of dependent variables、independent variables and control variables in our paper. The descriptive statistics include Minimum、Maximum、Mean and Standard Deviation of the observations.

5.2 Correlation Analysis

Table 2 reports the calculated Pearson correlation coefficients between variables. The results suggest that HZ has significant and negative correlation with ZQ, but exhibit no significant correlation with JZD. Table 2 also shows a high positive correlation between JZD and ZQ (0.206). All the remaining correlations between the independent variables are relatively low. Pearson correlation coefficients of independent variables are lower than 0.4, so there is no serious co-linearity problems.

Table 1. Descriptive statistics

	N	Minimum	Maximum	Mean	Standard Deviation
2009					
ZZL	121	33.2%	116.08%	71.7437%	15.309279%
SHARPE	121	0.149	0.448	0.306	0.04881
JZD	121	0.2	1	0.503	0.162755
ZQ	121	0	1	0.3365	0.284596
HZ	121	0	1	0.5289	0.501238
SIZE	121	-1.68	5.6727	4.027	0.948243
2008					
ZZL	121	-66.42%	-30.7%	-50.01%	5.6698%
SHARPE	121	-0.3466	-0.144	-0.271	0.03326
JZD	121	0.2	1	0.5126	0.1702
ZQ	121	0	1	0.3484	0.305389
HZ	121	0	1	0.5289	0.501238
SIZE	121	-0.16185	5.2766	3.6059	0.993456

Table 2. Pearson correlation coefficients of variables

	JZD	ZQ	HZ	SIZE	YEAR
JZD	1				
ZQ	0.206**	1			
HZ	0.071	-0.358**	1		
SIZE	-0.064	0.133*	-0.075	1	
YEAR	-0.029	-0.02	0.00	0.213**	1

*Significance at 10%, **Significance at 5%, *** Significance at 1%.

5.3 Regression Results Analyses

Table 3 displays the results of regression model 1 used to test H1 and H3. Results shows that both the Adjusted R^2 is over 0.9 in two measures of fund performance, indicating a significant simulation degree. From the F test, we can find that the equation is statistically significant at the1 percent level. The coefficient on JZD variable is 18.686 and significant at the 1 percent level using ZZL as dependent variable. The coefficient on JZD variable is 0.068 and significant at the 1 percent level using SHARPE. H1 is supported by the positive and significant coefficients of JZD in regressions using both ZZL and SHARPE as measures of fund performance. The results show that, for Chinese fund management companies, concentration of equity ownership is able to promote the function of corporate governance mechanism and improve the level of managing fund assets, ultimately improving the fund performance.

Table 3 displays the results of regression model 2 used to test H2. Results also indicate a significant simulation degree and the whole equation is statistically significant. The coefficient on ZQ variable is 7.048 and significant at the 1 percent level using ZZL as performance measure. When using SHARPE, the coefficient on ZQ variable is 0.021 and significant at the 5 percent level. Therefore, H2 is supported by the positive and significant coefficients of ZQ in regressions using two measures. The coefficient of HZ is positive, but not significant. So H3 is not supported by the results of regressions. The results show that, securities companies can provide fund management companies strong supports in making investment decisions. These supports can help fund management companies grasp the trend of the market more accurately and make more rational investment decisions, ultimately improving the fund performance.

Table 3. Regression Results of model

	Results of model 1		Results of model 2	
	ZZL	SHARPE	ZZL	SHARPE
JZD	18.686*** (4.319)	0.068*** (4.302)	7.048*** (2.815)	0.021** (2.323)
HZ	-0.679 (-0.472)	-0.001 (-0.269)	1.015 (1.334)	0.001 (0.207)
SIZE	1.478** (1.992)	0.002 (0.783)	0.967	0.98
Adj-R^2	0.968	0.981	2330.84	3913.29
F	1820.16	3084.28	0.000	0.000
Sig.	0.000	0.000	242	242
N	242	242	ZZL	SHARPE

6 Conclusions

Through our study, we gain conclusions as follows: (1) Degree of ownership concentration of Chinese fund management companies have a positive effect on fund performance.(2)Equity ownership by securities companies has a positive effect on fund performance.(3) The development of foreign investors as shareholders of Chinese fund management companies generates insignificant impacts on fund performance.

By the regression analysis, we get policy suggestions as follows: firstly, keeping degree of ownership concentration of fund management companies is important. In Chinese market, we should emphasize the important role of controlling shareholders on fund governance mechanism. Secondly, regulatory efforts in promoting the development of domestic security companies as shareholders seem to have generated positive impacts on fund performance and so should be carried on.

Acknowledgements. This paper is supported by the National Nature Science Foundation of China(No.71071072).

References

[1] Barclay, M., Holderness, C., Puntiff, J.: Private Benefits from Block Ownership and Discounts on Closed-end Funds. Journal of Financial Economics (33), 263–291 (1993)
[2] Demesetz, H.: The structure of ownership and the theory of the firm. Journal of Law and Economics (26), 375–390 (1983)
[3] He, J.: Demonstration between Securities Investment Fund Governance Structure and Performance. Management Review (7), 49–44 (2005)
[4] Jensen: The Performance of Mutual Funds in the period 1945-1964. Journal of Finance (23), 132–136 (1968)
[5] Lipton, Lorsch: A Modest Proposal for Improved Corporate Governance. Business Lawyer (1), 19–36 (1992)
[6] Morck, R., Shleifer, A., Vishny, R.W.: Management Ownership and Market Valuation: An Empirical Analysis. Journal of Financial Economics (20), 293–315 (1998)
[7] Tufano, P., Sevick, M.: Board structure and Fee-setting in the U.S Mutual Industry. Journal of Financial Economics (46), 321–355 (1997)
[8] Yu, L., Wang, B., Fan, Z.J.: Study on Stock Investment Funds' Performance Evaluation. Transaction of Shanghai University of Science and Technology 27(2), 167–171 (2005)
[9] Yermack, D.: Higher Market valuation of Companies with a Small Board of Directors. Journal of Financial Economics 40(2), 185–211 (1996)
[10] Zhang, B.: A Research on the Relationship between the Ownership Structure and Performance of Fund Management Company in China. Journal of Taiyuan Urban Vocational College (1), 1–4 (2008)

Evolutionary Game Analysis on Real Estate Overestimation Problem

Lining Jiang, Wentian Cui, and Haihua Hu

School of Management, Xi'an Jiaotong University, Xi'an, 710049, China
lining.jiang@stu.xjtu.edu.cn

Abstract. This paper develops an evolutionary game model with real estate appraisers and government supervisors to study the real estate overestimation problem in the mortgage background. By analyzing two groups' evolutionary stable strategies (ESSs), we find that appraisers' high rewards and/or light punishments from overestimating, government supervisors' inefficient supervision, or the poor self-discipline of appraisal industry, can directly encourage appraisers to overstate the property value while the government performs no supervision. And supervisors' small reputation loss as well as the big monitoring cost can indirectly inspire appraisers' over appraisal by inducing government's controls to be extinct. This paper quantitatively analyzed the effects of the government supervision and self-discipline of appraisal industry, which extends the traditional model to be more realistic and practical.

Keywords: real estate appraisal, overestimation, evolutionary game, evolutionary stable strategy.

1 Introduction

Before a mortgage is approved, real estate appraisal is required to provide a reference for the property value. And government supervisors take charge of the fairness of appraisers' stated values to insure that the mortgagee can recover the face value of the loan with the collateral while the mortgagor fails in the mortgage. However, overestimations are prevalent in practice: the appraiser can get more incomes by overstating the property because his commission is closely related to this appraisal value; and the mortgagee and/or mortgagor often encourage the appraiser to overestimate so that a higher loan can be induced, which can benefit all of them in a short term [1]. If most appraisal values are higher than their true worth, it is likely to result in bubbles in real estate market and systematic financial risks [2,3]. Then, the problem emerges that what are the conditions under which the overestimation occurs in the long run? How to solve it?

We intend to investigate the problem with the evolutionary game theory because it is overwhelmingly suitable to solve our problem rather than orthodox methods. The traditional economic methods and game theories suppose all players are fully rational and they can take the optimal actions in every process. Moreover, the players have the common knowledge of each others' rationalities and have clear awareness of the rules

M. Zhou (Ed.): ISAEBD 2011, Part III, CCIS 210, pp. 450–457, 2011.

of the game. Such strict assumptions are difficult to meet in reality. At least one player has bounded rationality and can reach the optimal action only after repeated game process, which are the very assumptions made in evolutionary game theory [4]. Besides, by analyzing the developing trend and the stability of a given strategy, evolutionary game theory can help to forecast the long term tendency and explain a lot of widespread social and economic phenomena. Apparently, it can accomplish our task smoothly.

The rest of the paper is organized as follows. In section 2, we discuss the relationship between our paper and the current literature. In section 3, we give some descriptions of our model. In section 4, we analyze the model to define the conditions under which the overestimation will arise. In section 5, some conclusions are made.

2 Literature Review

The real estate overestimation study origins from Martin [3], who points out the over appraisal of assets can lead to financial risks and analyzes the factors resulting in over appraisals qualitatively. Before Martin, literature about real estate appraisal focused on emphasizing its fairness [5], as well as on improving its accuracy [6,7]. Following Martin's research, many scholars apply game theory to real estate appraisal analysis. Rudolph [8,9] considers the adverse selection problem that bad appraisers will derive out good ones by claiming a higher value. And he finds mandatory appraiser licensing and appraisal standards, for example, FIRREA standards, can improve the appraisal quality. Finch et al. [10] confirm Rudolph's findings by arguing that the appraisers' long-term reputation can act as a strong signal that he has the ability to provide a good appraisal. These studies all lead us to explore the effect of self-discipline in property appraisal. Moreover, they all assume players having full rationality, which ignores the phenomena that sometimes players make mistakes. We will make the assumption that players have bounded rationality so that we can consider a more realistic scenario.

The developing appraisal market also draws many researchers to conduct surveys in order to discover whether the appraisers suffer pressures from mortgagee or mortgagor to overestimate [11-13]. The survey results show nearly 80 percent appraisers sustain such pressures [12]. But these surveys do not address whether these pressures do good or harm to each game party. Gwin and Maxam [1] answered this question. They delineate the conditions under which the appraiser's subjective judgment, with or without the pressure from others, actually makes all of the players better or no worse off. However, the above literature attaches no importance to the government' supervision. But Hu [14] and Jiang [15] find this factor plays an important role in preventing the appraiser's overestimation in the short term. So, our paper will discuss whether the supervision is effective in the long run.

As to evolutionary game theory, it has been widely used in many fields to analyze what percentage of the player population would prefer a given strategy, or the change of the possibility to select a specific strategy [16]. In our model, we follow the former rule to search the conditions under which the overestimation strategy will be chosen.

In general, our paper is different from the current literature in the assumption of the degree of players' rationality. We assume that the players have bounded rationality, which is supported by a mass of real life experience [4]. Another difference of our work from the existing papers is that the effect of self-discipline in property appraisal industry and governmental supervision are analyzed quantitatively.

3 The Model

In our model, the appraisal market consists of two player groups. They are the appraisers denoted by A and the government supervisors denoted by B .The appraisers have two strategies to choose from: overestimation and fair appraisal [3], denoted by O and F respectively. Their proposed appraisal value is the reference to close a real estate mortgage. Because they can gain rewards v ($v > 0$) from an overstated value [1], the appraisers often have incentives to over appraise the property. The government supervisors take charge of the fairness of the appraisal value. We assume the cost of such a supervision is c_1 ($c_1 > 0$), which is generated from taking inspection and finding evidence [2]. The government supervisors also have two strategies: supervision and no supervision [9], denoted by S and N respectively. When they select supervision, the chance to find overestimation is p_1 ($p_1 \in [0,1]$). Because there can be a sudden increase in property value, which can disguise the overstated part of the true worth, all overestimations may not be fully discovered [15]. Once the over appraisal is caught, the appraisers will face a penalty noted by f ($f > 0$). This penalty acts as the revenue of the government supervisors. If they do not monitor, the chance to find overestimation is p_2 ($0 \le p_2 < p_1$), which depends on the self-discipline of the real estate appraisal industry [15]. The higher the self-discipline is, the larger the discovery chance is. If the overestimation is found by self-discipline and the government performing no supervision, the government supervisors will suffer a reputation cost denoted by c_2 ($c_2 > 0$). If we use $\pi^i(a,b)$ to represent the player i 's payoff while appraisers select strategy a and government choose strategy b , ($i = A,B$, $a = O,F$, $b = S,N$), the two parties' payoffs under different situations are as follows:

$$\pi^A(O,S) = v - p_1 f \text{ , } \pi^B(O,S) = -c_1 + p_1 f \text{ ;}$$
$$\pi^A(O,N) = v - p_2 f \text{ , } \pi^B(O,N) = -c_2 + p_2 f \text{ ;}$$
$$\pi^A(F,S) = 0 \text{, } \pi^B(F,S) = -c_1 \text{; } \pi^A(F,N) = 0 \text{, } \pi^B(F,N) = 0 \text{.}$$

We summarize the payoffs in Table 1.

Table 1. Payoff bi-Matrix

		Government Supervisor (B)	
		Supervision (S)	No Supervision (N)
Appraiser (A)	Overestimation (O)	$v - p_1 f, -c_1 + p_1 f$	$v - p_2 f, -c_2 + p_2 f$
	Fair Appraisal(F)	$0, -c_1$	0,0

4 Evolutionary Stable Strategies

Suppose among the appraisers, a proportion of x ($x \in [0,1]$) chooses the overestimation strategy and the other selects fair appraisal. Among the government supervisors, the ratio of those taking supervision strategy is y ($y \in [0,1]$) and the other ($1-y$) population performs no supervision.

4.1 Appraisers' Evolutionary Stable Strategies

Denote the appraisers' expected payoff with overestimation strategy as u_{Ax}, and that with fair appraisal as u_{An}, and the average expected payoff of the appraiser population is $\bar{u}_A$. The appraisers' expected payoffs with different strategies are expressed as follows:

$$u_{Ax} = y(v - p_1 f) + (1-y)(v - p_2 f) \tag{1}$$

$$u_{An} = 0 \tag{2}$$

$$\bar{u}_A = xu_{Ax} + (1-x)u_{An} = x[y(v - p_1 f) + (1-y)(v - p_2 f)] \tag{3}$$

The appraisers' duplicative dynamic equation with overestimation strategy is

$$F_A(x) = x[u_{Ax} - \bar{u}_A] = x(1-x)[(v - p_1 f)y + (v - p_2 f)(1-y)] \tag{4}$$

Let $F_A(x) = 0$, we can get the possible stable states as follows: $x_1^* = 0$, $x_2^* = 1$, and $y^* = \dfrac{v - p_2 f}{f(p_1 - p_2)}$ when $0 \le \dfrac{v - p_2 f}{f(p_1 - p_2)} \le 1$.

Theorem 1: If the proportion of government supervisors with supervision strategy is y ($y \in [0,1]$), the appraisers' Evolutionary Stable Strategies (ESSs) are as follows:

(1) If $p_2 f < v < p_1 f$, (a) all x ($x \in [0,1]$) are stable states but not ESS when $y = \dfrac{v - p_2 f}{f(p_1 - p_2)}$; (b) ESS is $x_1^* = 0$ when $y > \dfrac{v - p_2 f}{f(p_1 - p_2)}$; (c) ESS is $x_2^* = 1$ when $y < \dfrac{v - p_2 f}{f(p_1 - p_2)}$.

(2) If $v \le p_2 f < p_1 f$, ESS is $x_1^* = 0$.

(3) If $v \ge p_1 f > p_2 f$, ESS is $x_2^* = 1$.

***Proof*:** According to Gintis [4], x^* is an ESS if and only if $F'(x^*) < 0$.

Because $F_A'(x) = (1-2x)[(v - p_1 f)y + (v - p_2 f)(1-y)]$, there are three cases to discuss:

(1) If $p_2 f < v < p_1 f$, it must be that $y \in [0,1]$.

(a) If $y = \dfrac{v - p_2 f}{f(p_1 - p_2)}$, $F_A^{'}(x) = 0$. All x ($x \in [0,1]$) are stable states but not ESS.

(b) If $y > \dfrac{v - p_2 f}{f(p_1 - p_2)}$, we can get $(v - p_1 f)y + (v - p_2 f)(1 - y) < 0$, which indicates $F_A^{'}(x_1^*) < 0$, $F_A^{'}(x_2^*) > 0$, so ESS is $x_1^* = 0$.

(c) If $y < \dfrac{v - p_2 f}{f(p_1 - p_2)}$, we can get $(v - p_1 f)y + (v - p_2 f)(1 - y) > 0$, which indicates $F_A^{'}(x_1^*) > 0$, $F_A^{'}(x_2^*) < 0$, so ESS is $x_2^* = 1$.

The proofs of (2) and (3) are similar to that of (1). □

Theorem 1 indicates that if the income from overestimation is equal to its expected penalty (in (1) (a)), neither of the two strategies is overwhelming and there is no ESS. If the reward from over appraisal is less than its penalty (in (1) (b) or (2)), the fair appraisal strategy is selected. On the contrary (in (1) (c) or (3)), the over appraisal strategy will arise. From theorem 1, we can delineate the conditions under which the overestimation will be dominant. We find that the high rewards of overestimation, its light punishment, the inefficient government's supervision, or the poor self-discipline of appraisal industry, can directly encourage over appraisal.

4.2 Government Supervisors' Evolutionary Stable Strategies

Similar to 4.1, we suppose the government supervisors' expected payoffs with supervision and without supervision strategy are respectively denoted by u_{By} and u_{Bn} , and the average expected payoff of this group is $\overline{u}_B$. All the payoffs can be expressed as follows:

$$u_{By} = x(p_1 f - c_1) - c_1(1 - x) \tag{5}$$

$$u_{Bn} = x(p_2 f - c_2) \tag{6}$$

$$\overline{u}_B = y[x(p_1 f - c_1) - c_1(1 - x)] + (1 - y)[x(p_2 f - c_2)] \tag{7}$$

The government supervisors' duplicative dynamic equation with supervision strategy is

$$F_B(y) = y[u_{By} - \overline{u}_B] = y(1 - y)[(p_1 - p_2)fx + c_2 x - c_1] \tag{8}$$

Let $F_B(y) = 0$, we can get the possible stable states as follows: $y_1^* = 0$, $y_2^* = 1$, and $x^* = \dfrac{c_1}{(p_1 - p_2)f + c_2}$ when $0 \le \dfrac{c_1}{(p_1 - p_2)f + c_2} \le 1$. Similar to Theorem 1, we can get the theorem 2.

Theorem 2: If the ratio of appraisers with overestimation strategy is x ($x \in [0,1]$), the government supervisors' ESSs are as follows:

(1) If $0 < c_1 \leq (p_1 - p_2)f + c_2$, (a) all y ($y \in [0,1]$) are stable states and there is no ESS when $x = \frac{c_1}{(p_1 - p_2)f + c_2}$; (b) ESS is $y_2^* = 1$ when $x > \frac{c_1}{(p_1 - p_2)f + c_2}$; (c) ESS is $y_1^* = 0$ when $x < \frac{c_1}{(p_1 - p_2)f + c_2}$.

(2) If $c_1 > (p_1 - p_2)f + c_2$, ESS is $y_1^* = 0$.

Theorem 2 shows that for the government supervisors, if the expected payoff with supervision is equal to that with no supervision (in (1) (a)), there is no ESS. If the expected payoff with supervision is bigger than that without it (in (1) (b)), the supervisors will carry out supervision strategy. On the contrary, no supervision strategy is preferable (in (1) (c) or (2)). From theorem 2, we find both the significant reputation loss and the few supervision cost can inspire the government to perform a supervision.

4.3 The Market's Evolutionary Stable Strategies

Since $x^* = \frac{c_1}{(p_1 - p_2)f + c_2}$ and $y^* = \frac{v - p_2 f}{f(p_1 - p_2)}$, we can use 2-dimentional planes to show the duplicative dynamic relations between the appraisers and government supervisors, as shown in Fig.1.

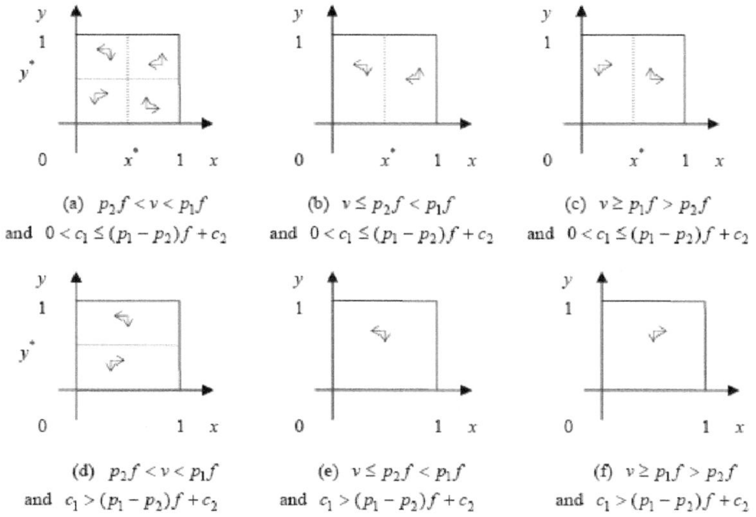

Fig. 1. These are duplicative dynamic relationships between two player groups under different conditions

Through the duplicative dynamic transformations in Fig.1., we can get the market's ESSs in Theorem 3.

Theorem 3: If the proportion of appraisers with overestimation strategy is x ($x \in [0,1]$), and that of the government supervisors with supervision strategy is y ($y \in [0,1]$), the market's ESSs in the 2-dimentional plane are:

(1) If $p_2 f < v < p_1 f$ and $0 < c_1 \le (p_1 - p_2)f + c_2$, there is no ESS.
(2) If $v \le p_2 f < p_1 f$, ESS is $(0,0)$.
(3) If $v \ge p_1 f > p_2 f$ and $0 < c_1 \le (p_1 - p_2)f + c_2$, ESS is $(1,1)$.
(4) If $c_1 > (p_1 - p_2)f + c_2$, ESS is $(1,0)$.

From Theorem 3, we know: (1) when $0 < c_1 \le (p_1 - p_2)f + c_2$ and $p_2 f < v < p_1 f$ (Fig.1 (a)), neither player has an overwhelming strategy and their strategy selections are interdependent. As a result, there is no ESS. (2) When $v \le p_2 f < p_1 f$ (Fig.1 (b) and (e)), appraisers' income from overestimation can not offset their penalties. No matter which strategy government supervisors choose, appraisers will stick to fair appraisal. Under such conditions, fewer and fewer supervisors will choose supervision in the long run until there is no supervision. (3) When $v \ge p_1 f > p_2 f$ and $0 < c_1 \le (p_1 - p_2)f + c_2$, (Fig.1 (c)), appraisers' expected penalty is too low relative to their income while performing overestimation strategy, so that they will choose to overstate the property value no matter what strategy the supervisors take. In this situation, more and more supervisors will choose supervision in the evolutionary term until all of them supervise. (4) When $c_1 > (p_1 - p_2)f + c_2$ (Fig.1 (d) and (f)), government supervisors' expected penalty is higher than their expected income. As a result, they will prefer no supervision strategy. Then, more and more appraisers will implement overestimation in the aforesaid situation until they all choose this strategy.

5 Conclusions

In this paper, we incorporate the government supervision and self-discipline of appraisal industry into traditional models, and consider real estate overestimation problem in the mortgage situation with evolutionary game theory. The results show that high rewards and/or light punishment from overestimation, inefficient government's supervision, and/or poor self-discipline of the appraisal industry, can directly facilitate appraisers' preference of over appraisal. And government supervisor's small reputation loss and his large supervision cost can indirectly give rise to appraisers' overestimation by inducing governments to drop monitoring.

According to the above results, several measures can be taken to normalize the real estate appraisal market. From the mortgage market aspect, we can construct a more regulatory competing circumstance, in which the reward of unfair appraisal is no longer appealing. From the appraisal industry aspect, there is no doubt that a strict industrial self-discipline is needed. Maybe an appraisal association can be helpful to attain this goal. From the government supervision aspect, one important task the government should take is to build a professional supervision schedule to cut down his monitoring cost. Also, the government could put a rigorous punishment on the appraiser with overestimation in order to prohibit his overstating action.

There are several directions to continue. First, the model could be extended to involve the quantitative effect of the mortgagee or mortgagor. Second, some empirical research should be performed to verify the evolutionary trends obtained in this paper. Finally, the question whether the appraisal-warrant mechanism [15] will still work to prohibit overestimations in the evolutionary process needs to be answered.

Acknowledgments. The authors gratefully acknowledge the support of the Doctoral Fund of Ministry of Education of China (No. 20100201110043, 20100201120050).

References

1. Gwin, C.R., Maxam, C.L.: Why Do Real Estate Appraisals Nearly Always Equal Offer Price? A Theoretical Justification. Journal of Property Investment & Finance 20, 242–253 (2002)
2. Qi, J.: The Real Estate Mortgage Risks and the Counter Measures. China Real Estate 4, 61–62 (2002) (in Chinese)
3. Martin III, V.: Appraising the Profession. Mortgage Banking 5, 61–66 (1991)
4. Gintis, H.: Game Theory Evolving. Princeton University Press, Princeton (2000)
5. Kochin, L.A., Parks, R.W.: Vertical Equity in Real Estate Assessment: A Fair Appraisal. Economic Inquiry 20, 511–532 (1982)
6. Carbone, R., Longini, R.L.: A Feedback Model For Automated Real Estate Assessment. Management Science 24, 241–248 (1977)
7. Varian, H.R.: A Bayesian Approach to Real Estate Assessment, in Studies in Bayesian Econometrics and Statistics in Honor of Leonard J. Savage. North Holland, Amsterdam (1975)
8. Rudolph, P.M.: Will Bad Appraisals Drive Out Good? The Appraisal Journal 62, 363–366 (1994)
9. Rudolph, P.M.: Will Mandatory Licensing and Standards Raise the Quality of Real Estate Appraisals? Some Insights From Agency Theory. Journal of Housing Economics 7, 165–179 (1998)
10. Finch, J.H., Fogelberg, L., Weeks, S.: The Role of Professional Designations as Quality Signals. The Appraisal Journal 67, 143–146 (1999)
11. Lentz, G.H., Wang, K.: Residential Appraisal and the Lending Process: A Survey of Issues. Journal of Real Estate Research 15, 11–39 (1998)
12. Smolen, G.E., Hambleton, D.C.: Is the Real Estate Appraiser's Role Too Much to Expect? The Appraisal Journal 65, 9–17 (1997)
13. Worzala, E.M., Lenk, M.M., Kinnard, W.N.: How Client Pressure Affects the Appraisal of Residential Property. The Appraisal Journal 66, 416–427 (1998)
14. Hu, Z.: The Problems and Countermeasures in Real Estate Appraisal Industry. China Real Estate 3, 43–47 (1998) (in Chinese)
15. Jiang, L., Cui, W.: Game Analysis and Mechanism Design in Real Estate Mortgage Loan. Forecast 28, 43–47 (2009) (in Chinese)
16. Morrison, W.G.: Instincts As Reflex Choice: Does Loss of Temper Have Strategic Value? Journal of Economic Behavior and Organization 31, 335–356 (1996)

The Research of e-Commerce Site Evaluation Based on AHP and Cluster Analysis Means

Wenyan Pan and Kefei Wang

Jilin Business and Technology College
Changchun, China

Abstract. We combined the status of our business e-commerce website with Its Evaluation of the type, analyzed that the traditional evaluation means is not suitable for e-commerce system of this new business model, put forward the principle based on subjective evaluation and objective evaluation, constructed the content and index system of e-commerce evaluation. Used the Delphi method with AHP to subjectively evaluated e-commerce website, combined AHP with cluster analysis objectively evaluated, proposed a more suitable content and e-commerce website evaluation index system under the current business environment, and thus make the analysis conclusions more objective and more scientific.

Keywords: e-commerce website, evaluation means, cluster analysis.

1 Introduction

With the rapid development of Internet, many enterprises attach great importance to the construction and use of e-commerce sites.However, business owners need to know the site where the successes and weaknesses in order to find further improvements.Solve these problems must use the appropriate method to evaluate the site.For a long time,the e-commerce sites evaluation are not scientific and objective on theoretical study , formulate the situation of a great differentiated evaluation of the site , e-commerce Web site evaluation is based on certain evaluation meanss and index the contents to evaluate operation status and quality of work.Evaluation of activities to promote e-commerce site by the overall level and quality improvement, thereby promoting the development of electronic commerce[1-2].This paper intends to analyze business e-commerce Web site evaluation studies, and propose a set of business conditions for the current evaluation of enterprise content and e-commerce site index system and method.

2 The Status of Domestic and Foreign Enterprises e-Commerce Site, Type, Evaluation Means

2.1 The Status of Enterprises e-Commerce Site

At this stage the nature of the Internet site in accordance with the main divided into corporate websites, commercial websites, education and research sites, government

M. Zhou (Ed.): ISAEBD 2011, Part III, CCIS 210, pp. 458–463, 2011.

websites, personal websites and other public service websites. Enterprises including manufacturing, IT industry, wholesale and retail trade, catering, consulting services and so on. July 2010, according to data released by CNNIC, nearly 234 million global Web site, a total of 2.79 million kinds of sites, the largest number of corporate websites, accounting for about 70.8%.

The real value of enterprise e-commerce site through the online trading and business activities, and to reduce operating costs, improve efficiency reflected. Mainly in two aspects: First release of information; The second function is the core of e-commerce. However, the "2010 China Internet Survey Report the number of information resources" provided by the data, enterprises engaged in information dissemination is still the main function of the site. The real commercial value of the after-sales service / technical support to 28.2%; Users Online Enquiry / Complaint 16.6%; Online sales (B2C) 33.8%; Internet sales between enterprises (B2B) 20.6%; Online purchases accounted for 6.1% of the tender, that corporate e-commerce website development and use of the progressive attention[3-4].

2.2 Types of Enterprises e-Commerce Website Evaluation

On the view of current practice, there are several types of e-commerce website evaluation. According to the organizers of site evaluation activities, enterprises e-commerce website can be divided into sectors of official or unofficial evaluation agencies, the business of rating agencies, all kinds of consulting research firms and related media. Various types of e-commerce website rating agencies have their own evaluation meanss, evaluation, and serve different purposes

2.3 Evaluation Means of Enterprises e-Commerce Site

There are many enterprises e-commerce website evaluation meanss to be used , from the acquisition of required evaluation data view, currently, there are following methods:

2.3.1 Web Site Traffic Statistics

Web traffic statistics are statistics and analysis of site traffic through specific software. CNNIC is traffic statistics agencies that currently have certain influence site, the center's third-party certification system regularly launch site traffic website ranking of the industry, generally have weekly rankings, the monthly rankings. However, indicators of domestic and international traffic on the site definition is not consistent with the definition of domestic approach to each site are different, which to some extent, limit the authority of the domestic Web site traffic ranking and consistency.

2.3.2 Expert Evaluation

Expert evaluation is the use of the established procedure to wither on the experts to invest, relying on expert knowledge and experience through comprehensive analysis by experts, and to judge the issue. Expert assessment method has the advantages of collective wisdom, you can site a comprehensive evaluation of all options, but its limitations are obvious, for example, the number of experts is limited, representative not comprehensive enough; Individual influence of authority figures or words may be more about the expert evaluation of the results, thus affecting the fairness of the evaluation results.

2.3.3 Survey

Survey is a commonly used method of investigation, sample surveys and online forms. The main drawbacks of this form of cheating is human existence possible. In addition, removing the invalid questionnaires, take more manpower.

3 Enterprises e-Commerce Site Evaluation Process

We combined AHP with hierarchical cluster analysis method for objective evaluation of e-commerce site to determine the index weights each layer, in a prominent objective assessment of the weight of the principle, the use of expert evaluation and subjective evaluation questionnaire score, thereby enabling the analysis concluded more objective and more scientific.

3.1 Contruct Enterprises e-Commerce Site Evaluation Index System

Evaluation index system is the basis for e-commerce system, this article through e-commerce model for in-depth study of the integration of existing types of articles, e-commerce system evaluation based on the principle of building a Web site design

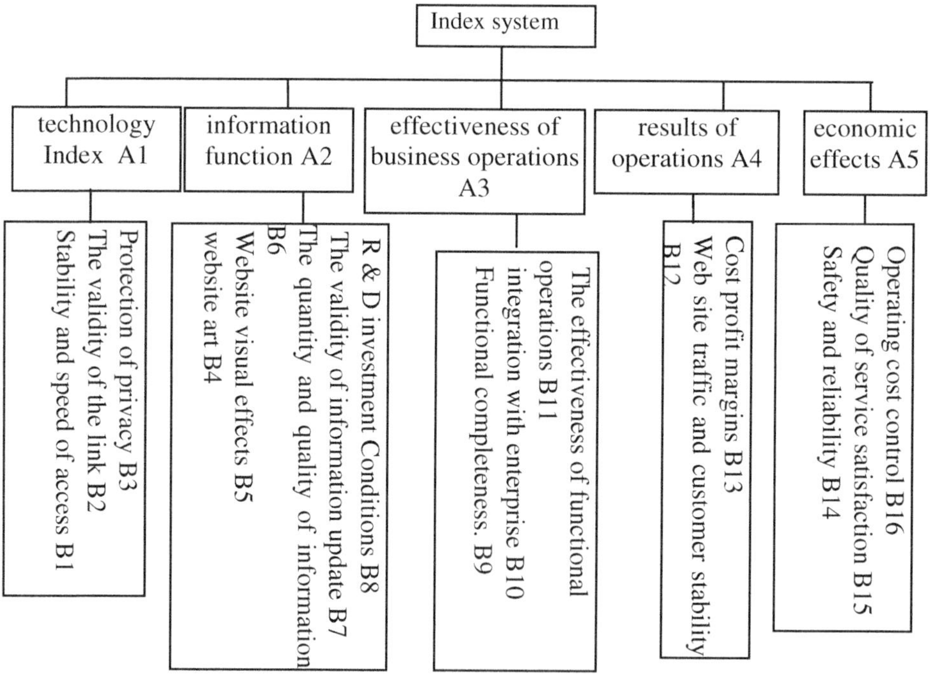

Fig. 1. Enterprise e-commerce website evaluation index sysytem

specifications, site information, features, sites effectiveness of business operations, results of operations, logistics and distribution of electronic payment and the five-level indicator system, building the evaluation system shown in Figure 1.

3.2 The Study Process of e-Commerce Website Evaluation Means

3.2.1 Combined AHP with Cluster Analysis Construct Evaluation System

Based on the Index System of former, calculated the weight of the index system as follows.

First: we constructed pairwise comparision matrix,caculated the matrix,determined the relative weight. When comparing the factors, AHP uses pairwise comparison.

Second: computed synthesis weight,then sorted it.as the previous level A includes m factors A1, A2, ... A5, the level of total ranking weights were a1, a2, ..., a5, the next level of B n factors, including B1, B2, ..., B16, which for factor in the level of single-sort Ai weights were b1j, b2k, ..., b5i, the right sort at this time the total value of B-level Σa1b1j ... Σa5b5i,here,j=3,k=5,......i=2.

3.2.2 Cluster Analysis Optimize the Results of AHP to Access to Each Layer Weights

Cluster analysis is an important application of fuzzy set theory, the main ambiguity is the real problem which by mathematical means to achieve certain classified and analyzed[5].

Classical clustering methods can be roughly divided into two categories: hierarchical clustering and non-hierarchical clustering method.In addition, this year to develop a series of intelligent clustering methods can be classified as a new category. First, the hierarchical analysis of multi group of experts on the index system to determine the weight and the corresponding weight matrix, and then by hierarchical clustering method shown in Table1 (parts) data analysis:

Table 1. Weights of determine layer(parts)

Experts number	Website technology	Information function	effectiveness of business operations	results of operations	Payment and Logistics
1	.198600	.388000	.089000	.075800	.239100
2	.181300	.089900	.180000	.359600	.178900
3	.095100	.263300	.043900	.182800	.391800

The results generated by cluster analysis and found that the number is divided into categories is difficult to determine is reasonable, in order to determine the number into the appropriate categories, and named for each category, but also on the clustering results for further analysis.

3.3 Evaluation Conclusion

According to F values, the F value of doing normalized index by five percentage weight in the evaluation, then the proportion by weight class from 4 to extract the effective number of experts.

Table 2. K-means cluster analysis

	Cluster			
	1	2	3	4
Website Technology	.098636	.113950	.143360	.451800
Information function	.344803	.092000	.256820	.243631
effectiveness of business operation	.160500	.180230	.079553	.124827
results of operations	.094175	.318650	.082300	.101675
Payment and Logistics	.248720	.294310	.434560	.126817

Effective means to take the weight of experts as the final evaluation of the index weight, and so, for the next layer of the evaluation index weights determined.

In accordance with the above method to obtain electric automobile project feasibility assessment model of the layers of the weight W1 ... ... W16.

Finally, most experts score the Delphi method, and data processing by experts score the indicators of the project data X1 ... ... X16.

$$A=WX=(W_1, W_2, ...W_{16})(X_1, X_2, ...X_{16})^T \quad (1)$$

A is the final score of the project 's feasibility evaluation, investors can refer the project evaluation conclusion to the project investment decisions or adjustments.

4 Conclusion Analysis

In this evaluation, the first is to establish a comprehensive evaluation index system of weighted;Then the combination of subjective and objective, to determine the weight assignment evaluation of science and rationality, while the expert scoring and survey were screened using the Delphi method to ensure the validity of data, and finally the use of AHP method to process their data draw scientific conclusions.

Business e-commerce sites for future evaluation of theoretical research and practical applications remain to be further strengthened, first, it is necessary to strengthen the site evaluation principles, contents and methods of research, to make assessment results more reasonable.

The second is to develop e-commerce sites for businesses neutral third-party evaluation of institution-building and management, through the evaluation activities, and promote the overall level of enterprise e-commerce website and quality improvement.

References

1. Wang, W.: The study of e-commerce websit evaluation and application analysis. Information Technology 21, 20–26 (2003)
2. Yong, P., Dong, K.: E-commerce website Reliability evaluation model. Information 7, 12–15 (2007)
3. Li, Y., Tang, S.: E-commerce website evaluation. Library Theory and Practice 1, 33–35 (2006)
4. Huang, P., Wang, Z.: E-commerce. Evaluation of Jinhua e-commerce D Industry Site Based on AHP 1, 26–29 (2011)
5. Wei, J., Sun, Y., Su, N.: Interdisciplinary research based on Cluster analysis. Journal of The China Society for Scientific and Technical Information 6, 1066–1073 (2010)

Urban Ecological Assessment: Indicator System and Model Construction*

Jing Zhu[1], Chao Yu[2], and Xihong Li[1]

[1] Shandong Institute of Business and Technology, Yantai, Shandong, 264005
[2] Haidu College Qingdao Agricultural University, Laiyang, Shandong, 265200

Abstract. The aim of this paper was to facilitate the future development of urban complex, and enhance the sustainability of the civilizing process at the social and national level. On the basis of the primary characteristics of the ecological civilization, this paper discusses the fundamental principles for the evaluation of ecological civilization. We have developed six categories,forty assessment criteria and the corresponding evaluation index model.

Keywords: the evaluation of ecological civilization, index system, evaluation index model.

1 Introduction

Urban cities are the center of economy, politics, culture and population in a certain social system. It is the natural driving force for the condensation of physical capital, human capital, social capital, technological progress and environmental resources, which make it the primary carrier of civilization and the main feature, and become a major social and ecological civilization thrusters. Therefore, the existent major problems of scientific evaluation of the level of urban ecological civilization will contribute to expand the urban development process on the future direction of civilization and exemplary role. For this, the great effort for establishing cities in the index system of ecological civilization and the index model will be offered by the author.

2 Principles of Evaluation

The future of civilization as the dominant form of ecological civilization to create the basis of industrial civilization is higher than the corresponding material, spiritual and political outcomes. It is not a new vision of society, but also is a overcome the drawbacks of the development model of industrial civilization. Therefore, the practice of measuring the effect of urban ecological civilization, the main indicators, selected on the basic principles should be mainly adhered to the following parts[1]:

* **Fund Project:** Ecological Civilization and Environmentally-friendly Government Innovation, stemming form Social Science Programme of Shandong Province of China, NO: 10DZZJ02.

M. Zhou (Ed.): ISAEBD 2011, Part III, CCIS 210, pp. 464–471, 2011.

2.1 Policy Value

First, the selected indicators should reflect the environmental dimensions of urban ecological environment faced by the basic pressure and the dynamic improvement of the ecological environment or ecological construction, ecological management. Secondly, from the natural - economic - social - political point of view reflects the complex systems of the city complex development. Finally, the boundary should have a particular application or application areas, the concept of simple, easily expressed and understood, can provide some basis of comparison for people.

2.2 Facilitating Investigations and Measures

First, indicators measuring the corresponding data obtained from a professional database can also be measured from the scene. Second, the cost of access to data should be as reasonable as possible. Finally, the data will have to concern about the reliability, validity, trying to have full support and quality assurance documentation, can be regularly updated.

2.3 Facilitating Further Research and Analysis

To promote the analysis of the data obtained after the process of selecting indicators should also be concerned with the current theoretical basis of the compatibility of science and technology, whether of general standards and legal international consensus, and whether existing ecological models, economic models and social progress are closely associated.

3 Evaluation Index System

Because civilization is a complex ecological system concept, its measure is also designed from the perspective of the system concept. Evaluation factors should include both environmental factors, but also should include human activities. Human activities include social, economic, political; include the ecological improvement of ecological environment, ecological safety; technology is the interaction between man and the primary means of Ecology. Also based on the United Nations Millennium Ecosystem Assessment and OECD organizations in ecological construction planning, evaluation of ecological modernization index set of reference, the author of Cities in the evaluation of ecological civilization factor from subsystem point of view summarized in the following six categories: ecological technology, ecological economy, ecological social, ecological and political, ecological improvement, ecological safety. Indicators of the 6 large-scale system further subdivided into 40 specific indicators. Specific evaluation system shown in Table 1[2].

Table 1. Evaluation Index System of Urban Ecology

Index Classification	Number	Index name	Units	Formula
Ecological Technology	1	The proportion of environmental research institutions	%	Environmental protection and scientific research units (number) ÷ total number of research units (home)
	2	The proportion of scientific research institutions Environmental Assessment	%	Number of research units involved in environmental impact assessment (home) ÷ total number of research units (home)
	3	The proportion of environmental engineering institutions	%	Environmental engineering units (number) ÷ total number of engineering units (home)
	4	The proportion of project evaluation of the institutional environment	%	Number of research units involved in environmental impact assessment (home) ÷ total number of research units (home)
	5	The proportion of environmental patents	%	Annual environmental Patent (item) ÷ total number of annual patent (pieces)
Ecological Economy	6	Decoupling of industrial and pollution	Kg / million	BOD (kg) ÷ industrial value added (million)
	7	Industrial energy density	Kg oil / element	Industrial energy consumption (kg oil) ÷ industrial added value (dollars
	8	The proportion of material economy	%	Industry and agriculture value added (million) ÷ GDP (million)
	9	The proportion of organic agriculture	%	Organic agricultural land (acres) ÷ total agricultural land (acres)
	10	The proportion of circular economy	%	Identified circular economy enterprises (number) ÷ total number of enterprises (companies)
	11	Environmental loan ratio	%	Environment construction to support the annual loan amount (yuan) ÷ total loan (million)
	12	Environmental loan ratio	%	Environment protection for the insured year (million) ÷ annual total insured amount (million)
	13	Environmental standard ratio	%	Environmental standards through the certification of enterprises (number) ÷ total number of enterprises (companies)
	14	Green Eco-tourism	%	Number of environmental compliance tourist area (a) ÷ total number of tourist areas (a)
Ecological Society	15	the proportion of green communities	%	Green Community (unit) ÷ total number of communities (a)
	16	The proportion of green schools	%	Green community recognized that national and provincial green community. Green Schools (a) ÷ total number of schools (a)
	17	Clean rate of traffic	%	Green schools found that national and provincial green schools. The number of vehicle environmental testing of vehicles (Department) ÷ total number of vehicles registered motor vehicles (Department)

Table 1. *(continued)*

	18	Utilization of clean energy	%	Clean energy use (tce) ÷ total final energy use (tce)
	19	Rate of the green logo merchandise	%	Green logo merchandise up (piece) ÷ total number of goods up (cases)
	20	The level of urbanization	%	Urban Population (person) ÷ total population (person)
	21	Population longevity	%	Population aged 65 and above (person) ÷ total population
Ecological politics	22	The proportion of government environmental assessment	%	Number of government agencies involved in environmental assessment (home) ÷ total number of government agencies (home)
	23	Investment-GDP ratio of government environmental	%	Annual environmental investment (million) ÷ total GDP that year (million)
	24	The proportion of eco-Forum	%	Any government other than government-sponsored participants will be eco discussion (time) ÷ seminar hosted by the Government the total number of (time
	25	Public satisfaction rate of environmental protection	%	Equivalent to the national "city test" the public on environmental satisfaction rate of the corresponding data
Ecological improvement	26	Air quality compliance rate% (annual daily air pollution index API ≤ 100 the number of days the proportion of total annual number of days)	%	API ≤ 100 the number of days (days) ÷ number of days throughout the year (days)
	27	Functional area of urban water environment quality compliance rate of	%	Frequency section, followed by certification standards, and (sub) ÷ certification section to monitor the overall frequency (times)
	28	Area coverage city noise standards	%	Urban area noise standard (square axioms) ÷ urban built-up area (sq. km)
	29	Utilization of industrial solid waste disposal	%	Then the use of industrial solid waste disposal volume (tons) ÷ then the total industrial solid waste generated (tons)
	30	The emissions of key industrial enterprises, standard rate	%	Stability of key industrial enterprises of industrial wastewater discharge standards, industrial smoke and industrial dust, industrial sulfur dioxide volume and (t) ÷ key industrial enterprises discharge industrial wastewater, industrial smoke and industrial dust, industrial sulfur dioxide, total (tonnes)
	31	Hazardous waste disposal rate	%	Medical hazardous waste and industrial hazardous waste disposal (tons) ÷ medical hazardous waste and industrial hazardous waste volume (tons)
	32	Centralized sewage treatment rate	%	Urban sewage treatment plant sewage treatment capacity (million tons) ÷ total amount of urban sewage discharge (tons)
	33	Harmless treatment rate of garbage	%	Life garbage treatment capacity (million tons) ÷ total waste generated (tons)
	34	Green coverage	%	Into the area green coverage area (square kilometers) ÷ total area of built (km)
	35	Rate of biodiversity loss	%	Higher number of threatened plant and animal species (species) ÷ total higher plant and animal species (species)
	36	Recovery rate of degraded land	%	Rehabilitation of degraded land area (acres) ÷ the total area of degraded land (acres)

Table 1. (*continued*)

Ecological security	37	Food (food) safety factor	%	Sampling qualified food species (species) ÷ Total current sampling food type (species)
	38	Resources (water) security rates	%	The drinking water sources and the amount of water quality standards (million tons) ÷ the quantity of water of drinking water sources, and (tons)
	39	Rate of energy security	%	Renewable energy (tons of standard coal) ÷ total current energy production (tons of standard coal)
	40	Rate of environmental security	%	Year were not natural disasters (person) ÷ total population of not (person)

4 Index Model

If the development of ecological modernization, ecological civilization as the primary means of evaluation system of ecological modernization can be the original model, the corresponding level of civilization come to urban ecological evaluation index model. Basis of this model should be able to calculate the corresponding index for Urban Ecology[3].

$$\mathbf{ECI} = (\mathrm{ETI} \times \mathrm{EEI} \times \mathrm{EGI} \times \mathrm{EPI} \times \mathrm{EII} \times \mathrm{ESI})^{1/6}$$

$$\mathbf{ETI} = (\textstyle\sum T_i) \;/\; N_T \qquad (i = 1, 2, 3, \ldots\ldots N_T)$$

$$\mathbf{EEI} = (\textstyle\sum E_j) \;/\; N_E \qquad (j = 1, 2, 3, \ldots\ldots N_E)$$

$$\mathbf{EGI} = (\textstyle\sum G_k) \;/\; N_G \qquad (k = 1, 2, 3, \ldots\ldots N_G)$$

$$\mathbf{EPI} = (\textstyle\sum P_u) \;/\; N_P \qquad (u = 1, 2, 3, \ldots\ldots N_P)$$

$$\mathbf{EII} = (\textstyle\sum I_v) \;/\; N_I \qquad (v = 1, 2, 3, \ldots\ldots N_I)$$

$$\mathbf{ESI} = (\textstyle\sum S_w) \;/\; N_S \qquad (w = 1, 2, 3, \ldots\ldots N_S)$$

The figure, ECI index for the Urban Ecology, ETI for the ecological technology index, EEI ecological economic indicators, EGI for the eco-social indicators, EPI index for the ecological politics, EII for the ecological improvement index, ESI for the ecological security index.

4.1 Index of Ecological Technology

Ti as indicators of ecological science and technology index, i for the index number of ecological technology, NT to participate in the evaluation of ecological indicators of

$$T_i = 100 \times i_{\text{actual value}} \quad (\text{Positive indicators}, \; 0 \leq T_i \leq 100)$$

$$E_j = 100 \times j\text{actual value} \quad (\text{Positive indicators}, \; 0 \leq E_j \leq 100)$$

$$E_j = 100 \times j_{\text{baseline value}} \div j_{\text{actual value}} \quad (\text{Inverse index}, \; 0 \leq E_j \leq 100)$$

$$G_k = 100 \times k_{\text{actual value}} \quad (\text{Positive indicators}, \; 0 \leq G_k \leq 100)$$

$$P_u = 100 \times u_{\text{actual value}} \quad (\text{Positive indicators}, \; 0 \leq P_u \leq 100)$$

$$I_v = 100 \times v_{\text{actual value}} \quad (\text{Positive indicators}, \; 0 \leq I_v \leq 100)$$

$$I_v = 100 \times v_{\text{baseline value}} \div v_{\text{actual value}} \quad (\text{Inverse index}, \; 0 \leq I_v \leq 100)$$

$$S_w = 100 \times w_{\text{actual value}} \quad (\text{Positive indicators}, \; 0 \leq S_w \leq 100)$$

Fig. 1. Urban Ecological index model

the total number of science and technology, Ti range is greater than or equal to 0 and less than or equal to 100, i actual value is the actual value of the index i.

4.2 Ecological Economic Indicators

Ej for the ecological and economic indicators index, j number of ecological and economic evaluation indices, NE to participate in the evaluation of the ecological economic indicators of the total number, Ej the range of greater than or equal to 0 and less than or equal to 100, j actual value is the actual value of the index j , j baseline value for the specific reference value for 2002 available world's advanced level of ecological modernization at current exchange rate average converted value (the average high-income countries by 2002, the average index $ 1 exchange conversion value 8.277 yuan), where original 6 baseline value was 5.9, converted to 0.71; where original 7 baseline value was 0.19, converted to 0.02; 8 baseline value of 28 (because the ratio of the value, without conversion).

4.3 Index of Ecological Society

G_k as indicators of ecological community for the first K index, K index number for the ecological community, N_G to participate in the evaluation of the total number of eco-social indicators, G_k range greater than or equal to 0 and less than or equal to 100, K actual value is the actual value of the index K number.

4.4 Index of Ecological Politics

Pu is the first eco-political indicators index U, U index numbers for the ecological politics, NP to participate in the evaluation of the total number of eco-political indicators, Pu range greater than or equal to 0 and less than or equal to 100, U actual value is the actual value of the index U.

4.5 Improvement Index of Ecology

IV for the ecological improvement of the first indicators of the index V, V index number for the ecological improvement, NI to participate in the evaluation of the ecological improvement of the total number of indicators, IV range greater than or equal to 0 and less than or equal to 100, V actual value is the actual value of the index, the specific values of V baseline value was the year of the world's advanced level of ecological modernization (high-income countries, the average of the index), where 35 baseline value is 9 (because the proportion of value, without conversion).

4.6 Security Index of Ecology

Safety Sw ecological indicators of the index w, W for the ecological security assessment index number, NS to participate in the evaluation of the total number of ecological security, Sw range greater than or equal to 0 and less than or equal to 100, W actual value is the actual value of the index W.

5 Conclusion

Special attention on ecological civilization for it is a complicated system should be paid by the society. Except for the improvement of the ecological environment, the ecological and economic changes may gradually become the first choice of economic development, but "civilization"in the term of " ecological civilization", is not simpe to economic development eco-efficiency standards, it is also essential to the interpretation of social or even political significance. Therefore, the Urban Ecological evaluation should focus on the content of social and political aspects of civilization. Moreover, with the weakness of the restriction power at the technical level, the guidance at the organic level or the effect, the issues of social security become more and more serious. The particularity of different countries and social historical circumstance will make how to maintain the regional characteristics of ecological civilization construction, to develop their competitive potential as a serious issue in the eductional circle.

References

[1] See OECD, OECD Environmental Outlook, Paris (2001)
[2] On the correlation between indicators, indicators of validity and other issues, remains to be further research. Indices system here only preliminary results of research or design

[3] Where exponential model of urban ecological civilization to ecological modernization index model, but I made adjustments and processing. Also be noted that, where the concept of positioning in the broad index index, including comparative relative number, intensity, relative number, relatively few structures and so on. Especially in the narrow concept of dynamic index of the relative number remains to be further in-depth study, where only preliminary results of research or design. See the China Modernization Strategic Research Group, Chinese Academy of Sciences Research Center of Modernization of China: "China Modernization Report, - Ecological Modernization", p. 314 (2007)

Asymmetric Information Game Analysis of the Energy-Saving Building Market and the Policy

Qian Li[1], Miaomiao Liu[1], and Hongliang Ma[2]

[1] Xi'an University of Architecture and Technology, 710055
[2] Shaanxi Vanda Northwest Engineering Design Institute, 710082

Abstract. Aiming at the problem of "market failure" in the domain of energy efficiency buildings, the principle of asymmetric information is discussed through the economic theory. Then an adverse selection game model of the real estate developers and the energy-saving product manufacturers is brought up in the energy-efficient product market, drawing a conclusion that developers in the consumer class tend to buy some non-energy-saving building product. Through the analysis of the model and the practical examples, a solution - signal display is put forward towards the whole building energy market adverse selection problem. However, the government in providing signals to the platform can not fully grasp the authenticity of the signals provided by the building energy regulation sector and the energy-saving manufacturers and developers. Therefore, it is necessary for the government to carry out the building energy regulation sector re-regulation.

Keywords: energy efficiency in buildings, information asymmetry, signal shows, government regulation, adverse selection model.

1 Introduction

In economics, the competitive market for the resource allocation is efficient, but in reality, in Chinese building market, housing consumers in the process of purchase and use are difficult to understand the energy-saving function, and it is also hard for the developers to grasp the timely and accurate information. At this time, the market information- asymmetrical questions make market have no efficiency, and this is the typical information asymmetry. In this case, signals is an effective way to solve the problem of information dissymmetry thought the game model in economics. But due to the information signal display will bring huge cost to the party displaying the information, therefore, the government and building energy regulation department's game analysis and solving are finally given.

2 Analysis of Information Asymmetry

2.1 Information Asymmetry Theory

Information asymmetry theory is important in information economics, which says one party knows more information than the other party [1]. In the failing building market,

M. Zhou (Ed.): ISAEBD 2011, Part III, CCIS 210, pp. 472–478, 2011.

there often appears adverse selection in the asymmetric information, namely, in saving energy department, the real estate developments tend to choose the worse performance of the energy-saving products, at the same time, the housing consumers will choose the energy-consuming house in the housing market.

2.2 The Cause of Information Asymmetry in the Building Energy Efficiency Market

In reality, market buyers and sellers usually have the different quality of information. Reasons about the information asymmetry are as follows:

Firstly, from the view of the national economic environment, and compared with more maturely western economic markets, Chinese market economy system is still in an unceasing improvement of process, and the market order needs to be regulated [3].

Secondly, consumers' energy knowledge is limited. Every consumer has different social background and knowledge level. The ability of obtaining information and understanding information of each person is not identical or not even. According to the public awareness survey of the less-energy-type buildings and the public buildings on the construction ministry web site in July, 2006, about 74% of the respondents cannot clearly tell the difference of the energy-efficient building and the energy-saving building. Considering the people joining to answer the questions are mostly the professionals who browse the construction website, it can be expected that there will be a high proportion of the average consumers who cannot distinguish them.

Finally, attainting building information also has its cost. From the viewpoint of the access to the information, China does not establish a system of the building products authentication and energy information disclosure, leading consumers always to be at a disadvantage in acquiring the energy-saving information, and making the costs of gaining consumer's information arise.

3 Adverse Selection Model

3.1 Analysis of Adverse Selection Game Model

In the information economics literature, participants having private information will often be called "agent", and the ones not having private information are referred to as "client" in game. Accordingly, Adverse selection model in the energy-saving product market is that the quality information of the energy-saving product is held in the hand of the manufacturers, but the real estate developers don't fully grasp the products' quality information. [7] Assuming quality Q is the only elements to decide how many investments developers will input. In market, quality of the energy-saving product differs. Therefore, different product has different quality effect. Transaction price between developers and manufacturer is P_2, and poor quality of energy-saving product manufacturers is P_3. P_1 says developers can inherit the highest price of good quality products, $P_3 \leq P_2 \leq P_1$.

Setting the market has two kinds of different quality of products, the good quality Q_1 and the poor quality Q_2, $0 \leq Q_2 \leqq Q_1 < \infty$. If developers understand the probability of the good one Q_1, the quantity of energy-saving product provided by the developers

Table 2.1

	Developer (energy-saving)	Developer (energy-consuming)
Consumer (adequate information)	￥5500	￥4725
Consumer (adequate information)	￥5500	￥5500 or ￥4725

is the function S(Q) of its quality Q, and the price function provided by the manufacturers is for P_j (Q), and developers choose P_k (Q) for its price function. At this time, when the energy department product's quality problem is not the private information, namely, the information is open, the developers will make a deal with the manufacturers at the quality price of the energy saving products. That is:

$$P_j\,(Q)=P_k(Q) \tag{2-1}$$

Therefore, all energy-saving products can clinch a deal. According to the first theorem of Welfare economics, if there is no asymmetric information, distribution realized by the market competition is Pareto optimality. Knowable, such market reaches Pareto optimality. Assumingly, in the energy department product market, when developers' information is insufficient, developers will give the same price level P* to all energy department products, this price level is equal to the average price P(Q) of all products in the energy saving market, k is for the amount variable of the average price P. Energy-saving product manufacturers' satisfied supply is grouped by z:

$$Z(P)=\{\ P:S\ (P)\ \leq k\ \} \tag{2-2}$$

$$W\ (P)=\begin{cases} 0\,(t>P) \\ [0,\infty)\,(t=P) \\ \infty\,(t<P) \end{cases} \tag{2-3}$$

Among them, t is for the expected value the one that developers provide for manufactures, and supplies equal needs under the balanced requirements. According to type (2-2) and type (2-3), only when t = P, the equation W (P) = Z (P) can be established, namely, the equilibrium price is equal to the expected value of the products' quality provided by the manufacturers. But this equilibrium is not Pareto Optimality. Assuming ratio of good-quality product for energy saving is X, ratio of poor-quality product is 1 - X, when developers think percentage of the good quality product is higher, they are willing to pay the highest price expectations for:

$$E(P)=P_1X+P_3(1-X) \tag{2-4}$$

Supposing a developer's expectation is greater than or equal to P2, the energy department product of market share is for:

$$E(P)=P_1X_1+P_3(1-X1)\geq P_2 \tag{2-5}$$

$$X_1 \geq \frac{P_2-P_3}{P_1-P_3} \tag{2-6}$$

At this point, all of the energy-saving product can clinch a deal, apparently, the energy goods are excessive and the developers can't tell the poor-quality ones from the market apart. In order to buy less poor-quality products in the energy saving department market, developer's expectation for the good ones will decline. When the expectation is greater than or equal to P_4, there is $P_3 \leq P_4 \leq P_2 \leq P_1$, market share of the energy department product is for:

$$E(P)=P_1X_2+P_3(1-X_2)\geq P_4 \tag{2-7}$$

$$X_2 \geq \frac{P_4-P_3}{P_1-P_3} \tag{2-8}$$

Comparing with X_1 and X_2, it can be seen the ratio of the good-quality products steps down. At this time, the price of energy-saving products is P2, and price of the energy-saving products which is higher than P4 can exit to the market. Similarly, as developers' price expectations continue to decline, there will be $X_1 \geq X_2 \geq X_3 \geq \ldots$. Finally, the energy-saving products of good qualities will gradually exit to building market, and only the poor qualities ones left.

In the building energy-saving products market, the real estate developers in consumer phase hope their energy department products do not exceed their expectations, causing the good energy-saving department manufacturers to withdraw from the market. Similarly, in the architecture energy-saving residential market, psychological demands of the purchase consumers is also to hope to buy houses within their expectations. Thus, through game model analysis of the real estate developers and consumers in the building energy-saving residential market of Xi'an city, psychology demands of the buyers and market trends can be concluded.

3.2 Game Model Case Analysis of the Real Estate Developers and Consumers

There are two kinds of energy-saving residents housing in Xi'an residential market, average turnovers of consumers and developers are ¥5,500 and ¥4725. Consumers can take the energy-saving good housing for the highest average ¥ 7,000. and developers can afford the energy-saving residential for the minimum average ¥4,000.

Situation1: When consumers get sufficient information, if developers can provide the energy-saving resident, both parties will clinch a deal with the average price of ¥ 5,500; if developers offer the energy-consuming residence, they will clinch a deal with the average price of ¥4725.

Situation2: When consumers get deficient information and developers can provide the energy-saving resident, both parties will clinch a deal with the average price of ¥ 6,000; if developers provide the energy-consuming residence and the sellers can hardly distinguish the energy-saving resident in the market, consumers only rely on their bargaining power to give the energy department product a price value, then all valence of the final deal is ¥4725 or ¥5,500.

Assuming the proportion of the energy-saving resident is X, and the ratio of it is 1-X, then consumers are willing to pay the highest price expectations for: E(P)=7000X +5000(1-X). If consumers hold an optimistic attitude to the energy-saving resident, setting the expectations are equal to or higher than the ¥5,500, then all of the residents will be sold, and all the average transaction is for ¥5,500, and all developers will benefit. However, if proportion of the energy-saving resident is too much, consumers' market expectations will decline to ¥4725, even below¥4000. At that time, developers won't sell their energy-saving houses so that the energy-saving ones will gradually exit to the building market of Xi'an. As Figure 2.1 shows:

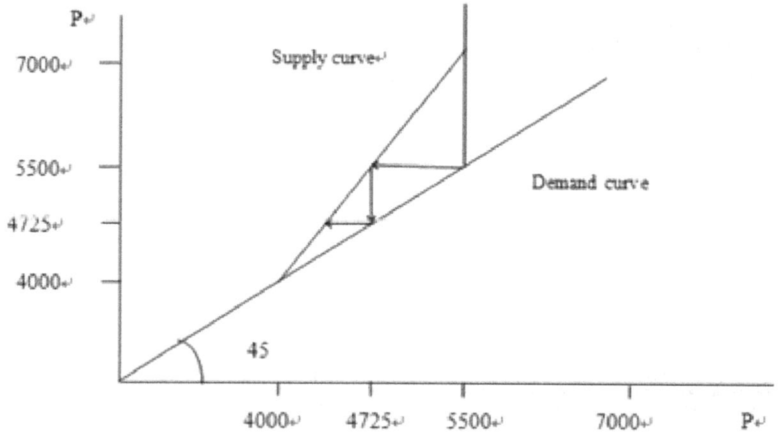

Fig. 2.1. Building energy-saving market doesn't exist

Predictably, adverse selection behavior under the information asymmetry makes Pareto optimality trading cannot come true, and eventually leads to market failure.

3.3 Government Regulation of Information Asymmetry

In the building market, information asymmetry of both buyers and sellers will often cause the energy-consuming department products to become the dominate ones. However, most consumers - developers hope to base price on quality in the market, and good energy-saving developers are reluctant to be expelled from the market by the energy-consuming products. In order to make the potential consumers find and believe they sell the good energy-saving products, building energy regulation department should provide a transaction platform -- using the "signals" method, to let the energy-saving product manufacturers show their energy-saving information to the others without information by taking the observed action. Now trading Pareto can be improved. Here, to use the energy-saving product after-sales service as an example.

Assuming the energy-saving product of good qualities on the marginal utility of developers is C1 and poor-quality one is C2, to developers, there is C1 > C2. Expenses spent for the product post-sale service is D, the transaction price between developers and manufactures is influenced by the products' quality, and function of the transaction price is M (Q), to set: M(Q1)=C, and M(Q2)=C2

At this time, the optimal profit for developers is:

$$M(Q1)\text{-}D > M(Q2)\text{-}D \tag{2-9}$$

Namely, the cost developers spend on the good-quality products does less than the poor-quality ones, so developers will choose manufacturers having the product after-sales service, and it is easy to distinguish the good-quality product manufacturers from the poor-quality ones through the signal display of the after-sales service. Obviously, building energy efficiency after-sale service is a kind of very effective signal display, making building energy efficiency manufacturers sell their products and letting developers buy the needful products. Therefore, the solution to the adverse selection is that manufacturers having good-quality products should offer signals to the market actively. But under the building regulation, energy-saving regulation department may not fully grasp the information. One reason of the government's failing regulation is that the building regulation department cannot get complete information of the building market, and the building producers and developers. Therefore, information incompletion makes the government produces deviation of the building energy-saving information identification, analysis and processing process, and lets the government make wrong decisions, or even far from the regulation of target.

4 Re-regulation of the Energy-Saving Building Government

From the whole analysis, the government regulation is essentially in the multiple entrust - agency relationship. Because the goal is not consistent between the government and the building regulation departments, the government cannot fully understand motives of the building regulation department; it is likely to lead to moral hazard or adverse selection. Therefore, the government must design an incentive mechanism in advance to respond to the department information and behaviors, taking measures such as punishment or reward, eventually to make the behavior of the regulation department's goals coincide in the maximum of their behavior targets and ensuring interests of the social public.

Assuming the risk of the building energy-saving regulation department is neutral, its utility function is for: U(a,b)=a-C(b).Among them, *a* shows duty salary, *b* shows power abuse or not, and C (a) says the cost function. Here C '> 0, C' '> 0, and C (0) = 0. If b takes two values, b = 0 says power abuse; *b* = 1 says no power abuse. *p* shows the probability of the discovery of power abuse, *F* is fines after the discovery. If the regulation departments choose not to abuse their power, their salary is a, and extra revenue brought by power abuse is C(w). *W* is for rights of the regulation department, more rights bring more extra income (C '(w) > 0). Therefore, expected return of power abuse is for: $P(a_0)$-F+(1-p)[a+C(w)]. Income of not abusing power is for wage *a*, and the constraint conditions are for:

$$a \geq p(a_0\text{-}F)+(1\text{-}P)[a+C(w)] \qquad (2\text{-}10)$$

$$a \geq (a_0\text{-}F)+(1\text{-}p)C(w)/p \qquad (2\text{-}11)$$

Obviously, if a_0, F and ($p < 1$) are given, the larger right w of the building energy regulation department is, the higher the wages should be, otherwise, he will be to look for the opportunity of corruption. Through the solving of the model, the government finds the method to restrict the corruption, which is as follows: to raise wages w, to increase punishment F, and to strengthen supervision and improve p.

Because writers' level is limited, only theoretically making the quantitative and qualitative analysis to problem of the building market information asymmetry and the government regulation, in practice, it still needs further discussion and study.

References

1. Mo, T.: Public Economics, pp. 130–135. Traffic University Press, Shanghai (2005)
2. Zhang, J.: Senior Microeconomics, pp. 171–172. Qinghua University Press, Beijing (2005)
3. Lai, M.: The Information Economics. Beijing University Press, Beijing (2006)
4. Ma, Y.: Regulation Economics, pp. 169–170. Economic Management Press, Beijing (2008)
5. Wu, Y.: Playing the Role of the Government's Public Management Functions and Advancing Building Energy Saving, 12–15. Building (2003)
6. Sun, P., Bo, Y.: Asymmetry Analysis and Countermeasures of the Building Market. Journal of University of Electronic Science and Technology, 89–93 (2008)
7. Xie, Z.: Economy Game, vol. 1. Fudan University Press, Shanghai (2002)
8. Spulber, D.F.: Control and Market Translation, pp. 387–390. People Press, Shanghai (1999)

Network Credit Ethics Absence Impact on the Development of E-Commerce Healthy Ecology

Ming Chen and Meihong Zhu

Zhejiang Water Conservancy and Hydropower College,
No. 583, Xue Lin Street, Xia Sha in HangZhou, China, 310018
{Chenming,zhmh}@zjwchc.com

Abstract. Development of e-commerce is changing the human society, economy and traditional culture very quickly. Network credit ethics, with the development of the Internet, is getting more and more important to build a harmonious e-commerce environment. False discount, inauthentic number of group purchase frequently exposed by the media, scandals happened in Alibaba, Taobao recently. Above these, we must resolve credit crisis in e-commerce industry. Based on the comparative analysis of Website credit information service system both at home and abroad, Summarized and list the dishonesty phenomenon of e-commerce, We made a conclusion about the absence of website credit ethics in China, Proposed how to build the website credit ethics system well. In conclusion, Whole society should work together to guarantee the credit problems of e-commerce, so that make the e-commerce ecology better in China.

Keywords: Network credit ethics, Credit information, E-commerce, Network credit rating system, Third-party credit platform.

1 Introduction

In 2010, internet users in China reached 457 million, in many network applications, online shopping made the fastest growing, meanwhile, with online shopping, spawned a lot of fraud and illegal network crimes, shop infringement, selling fake products and complaints have soared, consumers must face the fake commodity, network fraud, quality is not guaranteed, information disclosure and other bad credit events happened, the famous industry Alibaba B2B, C2C have also broken credit crisis, all above these,directly led to the whole e-commerce industry face the "credit crisis ".

In the early development of e-commerce, credit, payment and logistics are the three big problems baffled the e-commerce development, with the rapid development of logistics industry, logistics issues has greatly improved, payment security also has a certain extent solution because of the emerge of the third-party payment platform in China, but e-commerce development lack credibility, This is still a big problem, It hasn't been cured effectively. However, the credit problems run through the whole e-commerce activities, its radiation intensity can not be underestimated.

M. Zhou (Ed.): ISAEBD 2011, Part III, CCIS 210, pp. 479–485, 2011.

Essentially, the network credit crisis is a network cultural crisis, a network ethics crisis. E-commerce in China is still in the early development stages, the network ethics and main value system are still in the making, the e-commerce lack the general trust. The ethic meaning would be revealed in this network credit crisis research.

2 The Network Credit Ethics Situation both at Home and Abroad

2.1 Compare the Network Credit Information Services both at Home and Abroad

Most of the large credit information services bases are gathered in the United States. Almost all of the credit information services company has a large and comprehensive database. As strong support, they not only provide good quality services, develop new markets, but also are powerful to process credit information into the services products.

Some U.S. credit information agencies already have a long history. Which provide network credit information services as following: credit agencies, third-party online credit certification, e-commerce Rating sites.but China has not yet established a social credit service system, in particular, the credit intermediation services Develop slowly, the development of web-based credit information service is also affected. So, the old contradiction has not yet been resolved, to build our online credit information service will must face more complex and serious problems. For the network credit information services, there is a big gap between China and developed countries.

2.2 The Status of Chinese Credit System Regulated by Government

As the important part of improving market economy, building the credit system of e-commerce is gradually concerned by more departments and enterprises, many cities gradually released some laws and norms for the credit system, relevant government agencies are also continue to explore the field of credit legislation, but, compared to the overall demand for the development of e-commerce industry, it is still not enough.

1. The real-name authentication
In July 2010, the first regulation for online transaction, "the network behavior of commodity trading and related services Interim Measures" is formally implemented.

It put forward the real-name authentication for seller, not only helpful to protect buyer's interests, strengthen supervision, but also laid the foundation for the future tax.

2. Credit certification
Recently, as a new electronics consuming models, the consumer group together to make group purchase, through which they can get the lower discount, since this model emerged, group purchase is rapidly expanding. However, The web sites for group purchase are too much, some good and some bad ,and credit issues abound.

For regulate group purchase market through Internet, in the October 29, 2010, Chinese first "e-credit certification rules" released on a trial.

3. The service specification
Early April 2011, "third-party e-commerce trading platform services specification" is released. it is helpful to create a fair, honest and safe trading environment.

2.3 Analysis about the Chinese Credit Rating System by C2C Platforms

According to a large number of documents, we list the existing credit rating problems in China by the case C2C platforms, as follow:

1. The diversification of the credit rating system.

In China,there are some more active C2C e-commerce platforms, such as Taobao, eBay, paipai and baidu youa, they made their own credit rating criterias and only fit for their own platform. different platforms, different standards, so it is difficult to intercommunicate. And resulted in duplication construction and less effect.

2. Emerging the phenomenon of credit sensationalization.

C2C platform has low barriers to start business, easy to set up a simple shop, but it is not easy to get profit in an increasingly competitive e-commerce environment today.

Currently, The word "Brushes credit" is very popular, It seems that credit is depend on “brushed”. Indeed, the credit rating system is designed simply. many sellers think that the middle comments and negative feedback will affect the business, so they always pursue good feedback. consequently, they are unscrupulous to increase their credit rating by fraud. Under this kind of background,”brushing” platform which pollute the credit environment of e-commerce more emerged.

3. The credit rating is long-term cumulative.

The consumers only concerned about the seller's current credit to determine if they should do shopping. But according to the credit history provided by C2C platform, you can not be told whether the seller used the cheap commodity to accumulate credit and used the current "high credit" to do the high-end commodity fraud eventually.

4. The evaluation is not based on commodity attributes.

Compared with the small commodities trading, the good comments from high-tech products should be higher. because it maybe includes the seller provide buyers a variety of professional support, delivery and distribution requirements are also higher.But in the actual e-commerce transactions, there is no any e-commerce site make the evaluation based on commodity attributes.

5. It is difficult to discriminate the real evaluation from fake.

Sellers treasure rating very seriously, because that is the shops sign for good and bad. So, if buyers make a neutral or a negative comment, they will do everything possible to please buyers change it. This would produce a variety of network disputes, or the sellers would find ways to hide the true evaluations or forge evaluations.

3 The Causes of the Network Credit Ethics Absence

E-commerce is a kind of young network economy, when new social revolution come, people are often more focus on just the development, and ethical issues are often ignored or covered up.

3.1 Incorrect Information Worship and Incorrect Network Technology Concept

First of all, the information worship caused the network ethical issues. And many websites are free for people, both useless and useful information are produced and spreaded at the same time. Everybody can become the information creators and disseminators, they don't need think about paying, most of them have less ethical responsibility. They don't care if they damage the normal business order and pollute the Network environment. Secondly, some hacker opinions made network ethical issues. They insist they only enter into other's computer systems and find vulnerabilities, but not with intention to damage the system, what they do is to promote scientific and technological progress. But whatever, it is immoral and a violation Behavior to enter anybody's computer systems without authorization. Third, network Technocratic opinion is the important reason for network ethical issues. In the online world, many people are blind to pursue the development of network technology, as for the consequences of its practical application, not within the scope of their consideration, ignored the resulting social issues, the rapid development of network technology made us not attend to social and moral issues in time.

Now it is not just sociological or network technology issue, it is also a difficult ethical issue.

3.2 Imbalance of the Network Credit Ethics Is Motivated by Chasing the Interests

Pursuit of profit made ethical issues raised.

Emergence of e-commerce has reduced the transaction costs, increased profits, and has resulted in materialism. In e-commerce, you don't need to know intermediaries and the transaction identity of each other, this make e-commerce transactions just pursue the maximization of profit, no love each other, just interests entirely. so that companies take improper means to simply pursue the interests.

3.3 Not-Timely Supervision and Management Resulted in the Credit Ethics Absence

The traditional law has less applicability for Internet, and don't play a mandatory role in the network, meanwhile the network laws and regulations have lagged far behind. So that enterprises and individuals are fearless to face the traditional laws in e-commerce activities. On the other hand, they don't know whether or not their actions are correct.

In the network, even if some people gave up moral constraints and made bad ethical things, they also have opportunity to escape moral condemnation, because the internet makes him anonymous. Driven by unfair interests and commercial profit, some people flout the law and ethics and do everything what they want in this free space. Therefore, triggering a series of ethical issues.

Absence of network credit ethics not only affects the people's trust and confidence in e-business models, but also directly affects the healthy development of e-commerce itself.

4 Solutions for Network Credit Ethics Absence

4.1 Strengthen the Construction of Network Credit Information Services

In order to solve the credit crisis, E-commerce industry should start from the establishment of the network credit system. As parts of a social credit system construction, government, industry, business, consumers and the media all should be moral to work together to establish a truly worthy trust e-commerce credit system with the protection of the law.

1. Construct open third-party credit services organizations

It Can be a non-profit organization established by the government, also can be profit agency established by individuals, The open standard third-party service organizations do the network credit research, technology development, e-commerce website rating and so on to build e-commerce enterprise credit management system.

2. Gradually establish complete and open credit information databases

Incomplete credit information database hinder the development of credit information services. Some professional business information owned by government departments and agencies are not opened to public. Some databases have been built generally have small-scale, the network credit information is incomplete.

The demand for credit due to the information asymmetry, the current network credit information service agencies and various departments are independent each other, the one person credit information may be scattered in different credit systems. On the one hand, Waste of network resources, reducing the efficiency of credit management in this regard; the other hand, these each closed credit systems can not be established to a complete social credit system, the credibility of e-commerce is also greatly affected. Due to the lack of information exchange mechanism, one person make a fraud on one website may still cheat on another website.

3. Establish penalty mechanisms to dishonesty

It has two basic functions: First, eliminating the credit transaction information asymmetry. Secondly, blacklist will block dishonesty transaction into the web again.

4.2 Improve E-Commerce Credit Rating Rules

Improving credit rating rules can guarantee more reliable credit rating information. Then build a more reliable network business environment. Here, for the case of C2C online shopping platform, there are some advices as following:

1. The real-name authentication mechanism

First, the biggest problem in the certification is that all the third-party e-commerce platforms don't need buyers do real-name authentication. This is indeed a important risk, there would happen fraudulent online transactions and fake credit evaluation. If violate a treaty, the buyer can re-entered by change a new ID, or many sellers register as buyer for self-trading, do self-help praise or any other ways to obtain a higher credit rating and favorable rates, make the network credit distortion. It is recommended that the buyer also be made a real name authentication.

Secondly, the enterprise business certification content is not enough. Currently, certification for the online enterprises in Platform is limited to the "authenticity" aspect, but there are many certification elements can be brought, such as product category, productivity, product quality, reputation, and many other aspects, and all these projects must have credibility and execution by the participation of government.

2. Standard the credit rating system.

At present, every platform often developed their own credit rating criteria, different platforms, different standards, and most of them only fit for their own platform, there is no platform interoperability, resulted in duplication and ineffective. Therefore, it is urgent to form common standards in the industry to avoid some undesirable speculations, to avoid illegal operation in another website after the deception in one website. In addition, this requires the support and participation of the government.

3. Design scientific credit rating rules

Currently, credit parameters are too simple to accurately reflect the real level of network transaction credit, good or bad.

The American credit risk management expert Professor Altman's Z score model can solve "not real credit rating" phenomenon,as following:

Different commodity attributes set different weights, give a score according to every attribute, then do every " score × weight "and add together to get a total score. Then mark the credit levels according to the total acore.

$$Z = x1 \times a1 + x2 \times a2 + x3 \times a3 + x4 \times a4. \quad (1)$$

Note: x1, x2, x3, x4(every attribute score); al, a2, a3, a4 (respective weight)

To some extent, solve the phenomenon above mentioned: using high credit scores gotten by low-end commodities in short time to do high-end commodites fraud.

4.3 Government Coordinate and Supervise, Improve the Network Legal System

In order to create a healthy development environment of e-commerce, encourage more enterprises and individuals to participate in the e-commerce activities, the government departments should strive to build e-commerce credit system.

As a sector work for credit coordination and supervision, we should first straighten out the system deviation and comply with the international trend to establish the market-oriented network credit service system. Of course, taking into account current relatively weak market conditions, the government should play an active role, but also must prevent excessive involvement from monopoly hazards in the construction of network credit system.

4.4 Strengthen Education of the Network Credit Ethics

In fact, China has not established even basic business ethics.

To eliminate the e-commerce credit crisis, strengthen moral education is the fundamental strategy.

We can strengthen the network credit ethics education through schools, community, third-party e-commerce platforms, particularly focus on the college network ethics education. C2C platform may be a good platform for employment and entrepreneurship, the platform can solve some employment problems effectively. But, the third-party e-commerce platform can't do the training covered a large range and fragmentary. Its power is so small, and network credit ethics is not independent of traditional ethics, so government must join in.

Currently, college student access to the internet in China is beyond the 85%. Online world also makes some students spiritual emptiness, misconduct, or even loss of integrity. Therefore, strengthen the university network credit ethics education is necessary, the credit concept and ethics education is essential.

Meanwhile, the network credit ethics should be further expanded training professionally, make up a huge credit talent gap, speed up the national credit system construction and development.

5 Conclusions

Ethics construction of network credit system is a long-term project. It is unrealistic that the credit building depended on certain individual, a company and a department. Whole society should work together to establish a set of network credit rating, inspection, complaint system, so that the credit problems of e-commerce can be guaranteed. Companies and individuals will be more self-discipline on ethics, our e-commerce will show more strong vitality, e-commerce ecosystem will develop healthier, consumers and society will be benefited more.

References

1. Jeff, M.: Business Ethics and Social Responsibility, vol. (1). posts&telecom press, Beijing (2007)
2. Trevino, L.K., Nelson, K.A.: Managing Business Ethics, vol. (1). Publishing House of Electronics Industry, Beijing (2010)
3. Wang, W., Sun, J., Zhang, Y.: Network Credit Information Service System in China. Information and Documentation Services (01) (2007)
4. Bi, Q., Qi, Z., Bai, Y.: Model of e-business credit information services. Information Science (11) (2007)
5. Duan, H.: Online credit monitoring: rather be dredged than be blocked. Western Forum (09) (2009)
6. Shen, Q.: Risks Hidden in online shopping, For business, how to say "no". Network & Computer Security (01) (2010)
7. Chen, X.: U.S. credit service system study group, The experience of the U.S. credit service and enlightenment. Macroeconomic Research (1) (2005)
8. Chen, W.: Comparative Study of Network Ethics Education between American Schools and China School. Chinese Journal of Moral (12) (2009)
9. Zhu, G.: Network ethical issues lives in Digital state. Commercial Times (06) (2008)
10. Third-party credit monitoring: the basis way to order e-Commerce, http://tech.hexun.com/2011-03-15/127945915.html
11. China release "third-party e-commerce transaction platform service norms", http://miit.ccidnet.com/art/32559/20110413/2362065_1.html

Rational Thoughts of Fair Value and Governance Research in Accounting

Pengfei Zhao

School of Accounting, Zhejiang Gongshang University, Associate Professor of Accounting, Xiasha University Town Xuezheng Street 18,310018, Hangzhou, China
zpfyy123@sina.com

Abstract. The great challenge of financial crisis triggered thinking in the accounting profession. Fair value accounting is not a thermometer; or just an inaccurate thermometer. As the bias between theoretical concepts and application environment, fair value is not always fair; firms reporting unrealized losses and gains under fair value accounting may strengthen the economic pro-cyclical effect. So it is not strange that Fair Value Accounting is regarded as the Wrong Scapegoat for financial Crisis. Owing to providing more useful information to investors than the alternatives, fair value accounting can't be repealed and will be continuously improved in the future both conceptual and practical. Effective method to improve Fair value accounting is to maintain the joint development of accounting and financial innovation, including the improvement of standards and reporting System, strengthening supervision and extensive disclosure.

Keywords: Financial Crisis, Fair Value, Defects, Coordination, Governance.

1 Introduction

As one of the methods of accounting measurement and the objective being pursued by accounting profession before the global financial crisis, fair value has suffered an unprecedented challenge and almost Suspended by the U.S. SEC. Facing being criticized, the IASB Chairman, David Tweedie said: "Fair value Accounting is only a thermometer", but his responsibility sounds so pale and weak. People began to rethink fair value, FASB, IASB and other accounting standard's organization have also realized that fair value was not perfect; and it would encounter failure and embarrassment when it was applied in a non orderly market, just as in financial crisis. Within nearly six months since October 2008, the U.S. FASB has successively issued several FASB Staff Positions (FSPS), which increased the flexibility of fair value application, disclosing extra information out statement, reducing disclosure cycle to improve the timeliness and doing other thing to improve fair value theory and accounting system. And IASB has almost taken the same pace with FASB. Further, it brought the accounting academia to study fair value accounting's theory in-depth, such as the cyclical effect and its generating mechanism etc. And many results have impacted capital regulation.

M. Zhou (Ed.): ISAEBD 2011, Part III, CCIS 210, pp. 486–492, 2011.

The author agrees with those views and conclusions of FASB, IASB and other academic institutions about fair value, but in the meantime, the author thinks that the answer to the fair value accounting being regarded as the scapegoat for this financial Crisis is the bias between theoretical concepts and application environments. FAS157 defines fair value as "the price that would be received to sell an asset or paid to transfer a liability in an orderly transaction between market participants at the measurement date." And since 2009, IASB has almost accepted all ideas from FASB about value fair measurement.

The author thinks fair value was fundamental value, intrinsic value or theoretical value, but not market price. FASB and IASB defined fair value as "the price that would be received to sell an asset or paid to transfer a liability" should be a helpless Choice, as fair value was theoretical and virtual, and to recognize it very difficult in practice. So FASB and IASB emphasized that market price must be a price to be used in an orderly transaction between market participants at the measurement date, otherwise, the fair value may be an unfair price. Before the financial crisis, on account of market optimism and excess liquidity, markets exhibit "bubble prices" that far deviate from fundamental values and these market prices may not correspond to the future cash flows most likely to be received or paid. At this time, it is obviously inappropriate that market price is regarded as fair value, and firms reporting unrealized gains under fair value accounting may yield adverse feedback effects that caused further booms of market prices and increased the overall risk of the financial system. For example, the distribution of future cash flows on an asset might include some very low probability but very high loss severity future outcomes that reduced the fair value of the asset (Stephen G. Ryan, 2008). On the contrary, after the financial crisis breaking out, market prices are seriously depressed by market pessimism and illiquidity compared to fundamental values, so at the time, market price was not fair value and can't reflect and represent its real value, when firms reporting unrealized losses under fair value accounting might yield adverse feedback effects that caused further deterioration of market prices and increased the overall risk of the financial system. For the existing of complicated financial environment compared to the concept, sometimes, measuring fair value fairly is very difficult; and the controversy on the fair value in practice will be long-term.

2 Fair Value Is the Best Choice in Accounting Measurement due to Its Solid Theoretical Foundation

At the end of june2009, the US FASB had improved fair value accounting on the whole. There were some internal factors why the fair value accounting could get rid of the fate of almost being suspended by The US SEC. Recently, the rapid financial innovation has largely changed the accounting environment --frequent and substantial fluctuation in price, the traditional historical cost accounting strongly suffered from the unprecedented challenges—the information reflected to users was always quite different from the reality, which led users to make wrong decisions and suffered from economical losses. Being close to the reality in information disclosure, fair value helps accounting profession to realize the objective of financial reporting--decision usefulness, and widely accepted by accounting industry.

2.1 The Same Accounting Objective with the Mainstream Accounting Made Fair Value Measurement Recognized Widely in Theory

The current mainstream view of accounting objective is "decision-usefulness", which emphasizes that the most important task for accounting is to provide useful accounting information for outside user to make a decision about the enterprise, such as investor, creditors etc. Today, under the environment of highly developed capital market and increasingly fragmented ownership structure, the market price is one of the most important means for investors to constrain company's senior managers. Measuring company's assets and liabilities at fair value can provide more relevant information for investors, which improving the usefulness of accounting information. Fair value accounting information has played an important role in securities trading in modern capital market. We can say, as long as the accounting objective of "decision-usefulness" was still being recognized, the position of fair value accounting would be difficult to be weakened, it was the support of investors and other users of information that the fair value was not be repealed in financial crisis.

2.2 Financial Innovation and Economic Development Needs Fair Value Accounting

In order to hedge risks, Enterprises and investors have done a lot in financial innovation, and many derivative financial instruments and other complex financial products have been produced continuously. Derivative financial instruments are a series of contracts that have not been fulfilled or ongoing; but are not what has occurred in the past transaction, and often with great leverage. Traditional historical cost accounting can only measure transactions that have occurred in the past time, and poorly recognize and measure derivative financial instruments. As a measurement attribute for nearest the future cash flow, fair value have better relevance than historical cost. Today, we believe that fair value is only scientific measurement attribute for derivative financial instruments, and with the continuous development of financial markets and innovation, fair value accounting must be improved gradually both in theory and practice.

Despite the contradiction between theory and reality, today, fair value accounting is still an inevitable choice; we should pay attention to its application environment. Prior to the implementation of new accounting standards in 2006, fair value had been applied in china, but due to lack of normative and mature mechanism, fair value was abused to carry out earnings management by some companies and finally had been abandoned. When fair value accounting was applied again in china in 2006, we should create a good environment for fair value, including paying attention to market establishing, improving market operation mechanism and regulation etc.

3 Defects Analysis of Fair Value Information in Financial Crisis

3.1 The More Relevant Characteristic of Fair Value Is Hardly Reflected When Fair Value Itself Is Not Fair

Theoretically, fair value accounting reflected the actual situation of assets or liabilities in measurement date better compared to historical cost accounting, and help information users to understand the entity's financial position and potential outcomes better. However, practically, it is difficult to determine whether fair value is more relevant compared to historical cost accounting. U.S.FAS157 creates a hierarchy of inputs into fair value measurements: Level 1- Level 3, from most to least reliable, Level 1 inputs is unadjusted quoted market prices in active markets for identical items and regarded as the most reliable measurement attribute. However, according to the definition of fair value at home and abroad, even if market price is an irrational price produced by the irrational pricing behavior, such as speculation and other non-rational control, it is still accepted as fair value unless obvious evidences indicate that the transaction is forced to act. So, if a firm applies level 2 or level 3 inputs into fair value measurements, especially level 3, how to ensure fair value not being manipulated by firm's senior manger is a problem. FAS157 sensibly required considerably expanded disclosures for level 3 fair value measurements, but is it enough?

3.2 Fair Value Accounting Strengthened the Pro-cyclical Effects due to Non-rational and Orderly Market, and Further Exacerbating the Volatility of Financial Markets

Plantin etc all (Plantin ET all, 2007), Allen and Carletti (Allen and Carletti, 2008), Pengfei Zhao (2008) and other studies have shown that fair value accounting has a cyclical effect, which increasing the volatility of the financial statements and financial markets. The fair value of assets or liabilities usually demands a rational and orderly transaction market, but in fact, market is usually not so mature and perfect in reality, so the fair value is not always fair. Under the environment of economic prosperity and excess liquidity, the assets prices usually tend to be overestimated, and the same as the profit and equity. As the consequence, the relevance of accounting information at fair value decreased, and fair value even became a catalyst to further promote financial speculation with greatly blowing bubble. When the bubble burst, the market price of assets would gradually tumble back to the normal level or more lower level, corporate assets at fair value would shrunk dramatically, and profits dropped significantly, equity substantially reduced, or even became negative by recognizing unrealized losses, and company was forced to continue funding to escape the financial risk, if funding falls into difficulty to sustain the lowest capital demand, the financial crisis would inevitably occur. On the contrary, under the environment of economic recession and credit crunch, the price of assets was often severely underestimated, anod the profit and equity also, the relevance of accounting information at fair value was low and brought investor into more pessimistic financial environment. So, when markets were illiquid and irrational, fair value was a poorly defined notion involving hypothetical transaction prices that could not be measured reliably, it was difficult to draw a conclusion that fair value was more relevant than historical cost accounting in practice. Based on the above-mentioned shortcomings, when the financial crisis broke out; Wall Street bankers had the finger at fair value for the "culprit" of financial crisis.

3.3 Recognizing Unrealized Gains and Losses of the Volatility of Fair Value Violated the Conservatism Principle Adhered to Consistently by the Accounting Profession

When assets or liabilities were accounted at fair value in reporting date (measurement date), and firms further recognized the volatility of fair value into profit or loss, it would undoubtedly affect the quality of profits and equity, in particular to the quality of profit information, as these unrealized gains and losses may not correspond to the future cash flows most likely to be received or paid, maybe reversed with greater than 50% probability. According to No21 and N31 of "Accounting Standards for Enterprises - Basic Standards"(2006) of china, highly similar to International Financial Reporting Standards, one of the important conditions for income and assets recognized in accounting is that economic benefits ("with the resource-related") likely flow into the enterprise. Under strange fluctuations in financial markets, by recognizing unrealized gains and losses, fair value accounting creates volatility in firms' owners' equity and net income that likely not correspond to the cash flows that would ultimately be realized, how to accurately judge "likely" really was a problem, we subjectively assumed to be "very likely " (likely) was not rational. Recognizing and reporting unrealized gains and losses in the financial statements violated the Conservatism principle which the accounting profession consistently adhered to, and the Conservatism principle was usually considered improving the quality of the financial reporting, this is why the Conservatism principle has been strengthened in the accounting system reform in china, and why accounting standards around the world continue to implement conservatism principles (Xinshu Mao, Deming Dai, 2008).

4 Consideration on Accounting Governance after the Financial Crisis

Accounting should be held responsibility for information disclosers in financial crisis mainly due to defects in accounting standards and the absence of regulatory, which help reduce transaction risk by appropriate accounting treatment and disclosure system. Accounting governance may be solved mainly from both improving the accounting standards and ensuring strict implementation. The author believed that the financial crisis at least has provided the following information for accounting governance:

4.1 Improving Accounting Standards and to Maintain the Joint Development between Accounting and Financial Innovation

The reason why accounting suffered from accusations in the global financial crisis is mainly due to fair value accounting standards being abused in a non orderly market. Regulating accounting treatment and improving information disclosure system were the foundation and the guarantee to fulfill and exempt from the responsibility for accounting profession. As the old Chinese saying goes: "No rules, No standards", rule is the regulation of modern society. It is impossible to fulfill accounting responsibilities if there is no perfect system of accounting standards and regulation. Therefore, advancing with the times, to maintain the joint development between accounting and financial innovation, impproving accounting standards and ensuring their implementation is the first step in the accounting governance. After the financial crisis, US FASB acted quickly and issued several revised announcements of accounting standards, such as FAS157-3 etc. IASB and the European Union took the same action also.

4.2 In Face of the Frequent Fluctuations in Price and Highly Leveraged Financial Transactions, the Financial Reporting Should Be Disclosed Online

The traditional disclosure of accounting information was on a regular basis with releasing behind and showed lag effect, which greatly diminished the usefulness of accounting information, especially for derivative financial instruments which are very sensitive to market volatility. According to the traditional way of accounting information disclosure, the fair value measurement can only reflect the past period and the past point of information, with its decision-making function greatly weakened. With the development of modern information technology, in contrast to periodic accounting, information disclosure environment has greatly changed; real-time financial reporting disclosure can greatly shorten the interval of accounting information disclosure and to improve the timeliness of accounting information. For example, we may change the financial reports disclosure of listed companies from quarterly to monthly cycle, even shortened to half a month, ten days or less. In financial crisis, if financial institutions could disclose their financial position, operating results and cash flow information online, whoever, including regulators and investors, creditors and other information users, would have taken different behaviors and financial risk also would be distributed within a certain time rather than focusing on the tsunami-class erupted into global crisis. The financial crisis prompted the United States FASB improved the timeliness of information disclosure.

4.3 Improving Accounting Information Disclosure System to Avoid Being Manipulated by Enterprise Sensor Managers

As the producer and supplier of financial reporting, corporate management must be supervised completely by the authority's supreme body--General meeting of shareholders or the shareholders due to the conflicts of interests among Stakeholders and information asymmetry. Namely, there must be strict visa procedures among the manufacturing of accounting information, audit supervision and disclosure to avoid accounting information being manipulated by the corporate management. In particular, financial derivatives are often subtle, and the company's audit control system of financial report must be set up and strengthened, and led by top management. Improving accounting information disclosure system can help to fulfill the accountability.

4.4 Richening and Increasing Disclosure of Off Balance Sheet Information Should Be Required Strongly

Beaver, the U.S. accounting expert, had ever discussed the accounting issues for semi-strong efficient market: a company should disclose as much information as possible, rather than focusing on the disclosure form, including both the accounting statements and off-balance sheet disclosure. As accounting statements information is always limited, the off-balance sheet disclosure can added some extra information, such as Conditions assumed, judging to the trend of price and other information on business management so that stakeholders can be fully aware of business and implied transaction risks. The fact of inadequate information disclosure has resulted in the reduction both the decision usefulness and oversight functions of accounting information, adding off balance sheet information disclosure would become a mandatory disclosure requirement in order to perform the accountnotability better in a complex accounting environment. FASB, IASB and the European Union had recognized and taken some ways to strengthen off-balance sheet disclosure requirements as an important complement. The combined form for accounting statements and off-balance sheet disclosure would be the future direction of accounting information disclosure.

References

1. FASB: Summary of Statement No. 157 —Fair Value Measurements, http://www.fasb.org
2. IASB: IAS32: Financial instruments: Presentation, http://www.iasb.org
3. Mao, X., Dai, D.: A theoretical analysis of earnings conservatism: Based on the change of china accounting System. Accounting Research 9 (2008)
4. zhao, P.: Inspiration on the application of fair value measurement in the sub-prime crisis. Finance and Accounting Monthly 9, 5–6 (2008)
5. PRC Ministry of Finance, Accounting Standards for Enterprises - Basic Standards (2006), http://www.casc.gov.cn
6. Ryan, S.G.: Fair Value Accounting: Understanding the Issues Raised by the Credit Crunch (2008), http://www.uic.edu/

Agent Behavior Choice on Civil Business in China's Military Industry: A Multitask Agent Analysis

Lei Liu and Yenan Zhou

International Business School of Shaanxi Normal University,
Xi'an, 710062, Shaanxi, China
drliulei@263.net, largo2929@163.com

Abstract. Agent's behavior choice affects civil business performance in military industry. We built a multitask agent model to analyze agent behavior choice in China's military industry on civil business. We find that because of the rigidity nature, the volatility of military task intensity and the volatility of fixed salary, the agent's efforts on civil business would be inadequate and lack of persistence and stability, meanwhile, the agent is inclined to choose conservative strategy.

Keywords: Multitask, Military industry, Civil business, Military task.

1 Introduction

With the general adoption of the market principle and deepen reformation, civil businesses have become an indispensible support of sustainable development, and a key force for further progress of China's military industry.

Performance of civil business of military industry is signally affected by agent's behavior choice. While the existence and development of China's military industry originates from the national security need and the military tasks serve as a material base, military tasks are a primary task for the military industry. Meanwhile, with the accession of civil business, the agent of China's military industry undertakes multitask of civil business and military task. However civil business and military task endowed with diverse task features and motivations. Related researches(Laffont and Tirole, 1988, 1991; Holmstrom and Milgrom, 1991; Dewatripont et al., 2000; Bond and Gomes, 2009)showed that difference in task features and motivations brought about multitask agent problems.

Based on arguments above, we built a multitask agent model with military task and civil business to analyze the agent's behavior choice on civil business in China's military industry. We find that because of the rigidity nature, the volatility of military task intensity and the volatility of fixed salary, the agent's efforts on civil business would be inadequate and lack of persistence and stability, meanwhile the agent is inclined to choose conservative strategy.

2 Issue Description and the Model

Referred to Holmstrom and Milgrom(1991), we define the model as follows: The agent of military industry undertakes two tasks: military task and civil business, J and M .

M. Zhou (Ed.): ISAEBD 2011, Part III, CCIS 210, pp. 493–498, 2011.

We write $t=(t_1,t_2)$ for the agent efforts vector, where t_1, t_2 respectively for the agent's efforts on military task and civil business. We write $J(t_1)$, $M(t_2)$ for performance of military task and civil business, where $J(t_1)$ and $M(t_2)$ are strictly increasing concave, i.e., $J'=\frac{\partial J(t_1)}{\partial t_1}>0$, $M'=\frac{\partial M(t_2)}{\partial t_2}>0$, $J''=\frac{\partial^2 J(t_1)}{\partial t_1^{\,2}}<0$, $M''=\frac{\partial^2 M(t_2)}{\partial t_2^{\,2}}<0$. The agent chooses his efforts allocation on the two tasks.

We write $C(t)$ for cost function, where $C(t)$ is strictly increasing convex. We make further assumptions that agent's efforts on the two tasks are homogeneous, i.e., $C'=\frac{\partial C(t)}{\partial t_1}=\frac{\partial C(t)}{\partial t_2}>0$, $C''=\frac{\partial^2 C(t)}{\partial t_1^{\,2}}=\frac{\partial^2 C(t)}{\partial t_1 \partial t_2}=\frac{\partial^2 C(t)}{\partial t_2^{\,2}}<0$.

While military tasks of China's military industry originate from national security needs, and its nature is obviously different from that of civil businesses. Civil businesses originate from civil needs and emphasize on financial affairs. Generally speaking, military tasks are the primary job to the agent, in other words, military tasks have a nature of rigidity.

Based on the assumptions above, referred to modeling ideas of Holmstrom & Milgrom(1991), Bond & Gomes(2009), we build linear revenue function on condition that the agent succeeds with the rigid military task: $S(t)=\alpha_1 J(t_1)+\alpha_2 M(t_2)+\beta$, where α_1,α_2 respectively denotes agent's payoff proportion of military task and civil business, where β denotes agent's fixed salary, agent actual income $w=S(t)-C(t)$. While if military task is unfinished, agent's payoff $S(t)=0$. We write p for possibility of success of military task, thus the agent expected income is

$$w=[\alpha_1 J(t_1)+\alpha_2 M(t_2)+\beta]p \quad . \tag{1}$$

We can claim that incentive model above corresponds with China's reality of military industry agent.

In our model, the intensity of military task along with the agent efforts allocation determines the possibility of success in the rigid military task. We assume that the agent's effort on military task is increasing concave in the possibility of success in military task, while the intensity of military task is decreasing concave, i.e., $\frac{\partial p}{\partial j}<0$, $\frac{\partial^2 p}{\partial j^2}>0$, $p'=\frac{\partial p}{\partial t_1}>0$, $p''=\frac{\partial^2 p}{\partial t_1^{\,2}}<0$. Here, the intensity of military task includes two dimensions: the quota difficulty and the R&D difficulty of the military task.

We write U for agent utility, $E(U)$ for expected utility. The agent is assumed to be risk neutral , i.e., $E(U)=U(E)$. That means Max $E(U)$ equals Max $E(w)$ .Thus, the agent's problem could be described as follows.

$$\text{Max } E(w) = [\alpha_1 J(t_1) + \alpha_2 M(t_2) + \beta]p - C(t) \tag{2}$$

$$\text{s.t. } E(w) \geq \overline{E} \ .$$

where $\overline{E}$ denotes the agent's minimum payment.

3 The Agent Efforts Allocation Choice Analysis

Based on the analyses above, the agent chooses his efforts allocation to maximize his utility, i.e.,

$$\frac{\partial E(w)}{\partial t_1} = \frac{\partial\{[\alpha_1 J(t_1) + \alpha_2 M(t_2) + \beta]p - C(t)\}}{\partial t_1} = 0 \ .$$

$$\frac{\partial E(w)}{\partial t_2} = \frac{\partial\{[\alpha_1 J(t_1) + \alpha_2 M(t_2) + \beta]p - C(t)\}}{\partial t_2} = 0 \ .$$

We simplify the two equations. Throughout the paper, we repeatedly make use of the following equations of maximization conditions as follows:

$$\alpha_1 J'p + [\alpha_1 J(t_1) + \alpha_2 M(t_2) + \beta]p' - C' = 0 \ . \tag{3}$$

$$\alpha_2 M'p - C' = 0 \ . \tag{4}$$

We next analyze how the rigidity nature, the volatility of military task intensity and the volatility of fixed salary affect the agent efforts allocation choice as follows.

3.1 The Rigidity Feature of Military Task

To analyze what the rigidity feature of military task brings about to the agent efforts allocation, we compare the agent effort allocations on two conditions that the military task is with or without the rigidity feature.

On condition that military task is endowed with rigidity

If military task is endowed with rigidity, (3) minus (4) , we get:

$$\alpha_1 J' - \alpha_2 M' = -\frac{[\alpha_1 J(t_1) + \alpha_2 M(t_2) + \beta]p'}{p} \ .$$

For the rigidity of military task, i.e., $j > 0$, and $p < 1$, $p' > 0$, we get $-\frac{[\alpha_1 J(t_1) + \alpha_2 M(t_2) + \beta]p'}{p} < 0$, thus

$$\alpha_2 M' > \alpha_1 J' \ . \tag{5}$$

(5)says: on condition that military task is endowed with rigidity, marginal payoff on civil business is greater than marginal payoff on military task.

On condition that military task is not endowed with rigidity

If military task is not endowed with rigidity, we can say that military task and civil business are homogenous to the agent. Thus, the agent's problem could be described as follows

$$\text{Max } w = \alpha_1 J(t_1) + \alpha_2 M(t_2) + \beta - C(t)$$

$$\text{s.t. } w \geq \overline{E} \ .$$

Maximization conditions: $\alpha_1 J' - C' = 0$, $\alpha_2 M' - C' = 0$. Thus we get:

$$\alpha_2 M' = \alpha_1 J' \ . \tag{6}$$

(6) says: on condition that military task is not endowed with rigidity, marginal payoff on civil business equals marginal payoff on military task.

Compare (5) with (6), we conclude that, on condition that military task is endowed with rigidity and that other factors remain equal, as $J(t_1)$ and $M(t_2)$ are strictly increasing concave ,the agent would input more efforts on military business, while input less efforts on civil business. Then we have proposition 1.

Proposition 1. Because of the rigidity feature of military task, the agent would input less effort on civil business.

3.2 Intensity Volatility of Military Task

Based on equation(4), we write $\mho = \alpha_2 M'p - C'$, then $\mho = 0$ if the agent maximize his utility.

$$\text{By} \frac{\partial(\alpha_2 M'p)}{\partial j} < 0 \ , \ \frac{\partial C'}{\partial j} = 0 \ , \text{ we get: } \frac{\partial \mho}{\partial j} < 0 \ . \tag{7}$$

That is, when the military task intensity j undulates, the inherited efforts allocation would be no longer the agent optimum choice, i.e., $\mho < 0$, and the agent would rearrange his efforts allocation.

$$\text{By} \frac{\partial(\alpha_2 M'p)}{\partial t_2} < 0 \ , \ \frac{\partial C'}{\partial t_2} > 0 \ , \text{ we get:}$$

$$\frac{\partial \mho}{\partial t_2} = \alpha_2 p \frac{\partial M'}{\partial t_2} - \frac{\partial C'}{\partial t_2} < 0 \ . \tag{8}$$

By(7)and(8), we have propositions 2, 2a, 2b, as follows.

Proposition 2. When the military task intensity undulates, the agent would adjust his efforts on civil business t_2 in the opposite direction that the task intensity is going to maximize his utility.

Proposition 2a. When the military task intensity increases, the agent would decrease his efforts on civil business to maximize his utility.

Proposition 2b. When the military task intensity decreases, the agent would increase his efforts on civil business to maximize his utility.

3.3 Fixed Salary

(3)minus(4), we get $(\alpha_2 M' - \alpha_1 J')p - [\alpha_1 J(t_1) + \alpha_2 M(t_2) + \beta]p' = 0$.

We write $\pi = (\alpha_2 M' - \alpha_1 J')p - [\alpha_1 J(t_1) + \alpha_2 M(t_2) + \beta]p'$, then $\pi = 0$ if the agent maximizes his utility.

By $[\alpha_1 J(t_1) + \alpha_2 M(t_2) + \beta] p' > 0$, we get:

$$\frac{\partial \pi}{\partial \beta} = \frac{\partial \{(\alpha_2 M' - \alpha_1 J')p - [\alpha_1 J(t_1) + \alpha_2 M(t_2) + \beta]p'\}}{\partial \beta} < 0 . \tag{9}$$

That is, when the fixed salary β undulates, the inherited efforts allocation would be no longer the agent optimum choice, i.e., $\pi < 0$, and the agent would rearrange his efforts allocation.

By $\frac{\partial(\alpha_2 M' - \alpha_1 J')}{\partial t_2} < 0$, $\frac{\partial p}{\partial t_2} = 0$, $\frac{\partial [\alpha_1 J(t_1) + \alpha_2 M(t_2) + \beta]}{\partial t_2} > 0$, $\frac{\partial p'}{\partial t_2} = 0$,

we get:

$$\frac{\partial \pi}{\partial t_2} = \frac{\partial \{(\alpha_2 M' - \alpha_1 J')p - [\alpha_1 J(t_1) + \alpha_2 M(t_2) + \beta]p'\}}{\partial t_2} < 0 . \tag{10}$$

Based on(9)and(10),we have proposition 3, 3a, 3b.

Proposition 3. When the agent fixed salary β undulates, the agent would adjust his efforts on civil business t_2 in the opposite direction that the fixed salary β is going to maximize his utility.

Proposition 3a. When the agent fixed salary β increases, the agent would decrease his efforts on civil business t_2 to maximize his utility.

Proposition 3b. When the agent fixed salary β decreases, the agent would increase his efforts on civil business t_2 to maximize his utility.

4 Conclusions

Civil businesses have become a key force for further progress of military industry, and its performance is signally affected by the agent's behavior choice. Based on actual features of incentive system in China's military industry, we built a multitask model to analyze behavior choice of the China's military industry agent. We have conclusions summarized as below. First, because of the rigidity feature of military task, the agent would input less effort on civil business. Second, if the military task intensity undulates, the agent would adjust his efforts on civil business in the opposite direction to maximize his utility. Third, if the agent fixed salary undulates, the agent would adjust his efforts on civil business in the opposite direction to maximize his utility.

That means, because of the rigidity nature, the volatility of military task intensity and the volatility of fixed salary, the agent's efforts on civil business would be inadequate and lack of persistence and stability. Meanwhile, since China's military tasks originate from national security need, the intensity of military tasks is signally affected by state security strategy as well as national security environmental factors in politics, economics, military affairs, et al., therefore the intensity of military tasks are definitely endowed with uncertainties. For the purpose of mitigating possible risks that military task may bring about in the future, the agent is inclined to choose conservative strategies as a rational choice.

However, the results of this study should be interpreted in light of two limitations. First, this study focused on a general case that China's military industry undertakes multitasks of military task and civil business. Since there are some civil businesses independent of military tasks, such as in some low-tech industries, our results are therefore limited to the main situation but not all the cases in civil businesses in China's military industry. Second, this study is a theoretical analysis, and lack of empirical test support. Future research needs to examine whether the results accord with public companies controlled by China's military industry, and provisional data is in favor of our hypothesis.

References

1. Bond, P., Gomes, A.: Multitask principal–agent problems: Optimal contracts, fragility, and effort misallocation. Journal of Economic Theory 144, 175–211 (2009)
2. Dewatripont, M., Jewitt, I., Tirole, J.: Multitask agency problems: Focus and task clustering. European Economic Review 44, 869–877 (2000)
3. Holmstrom, B., Milgrom, P.: Multitask principal–agent analyses: Incentive contracts, asset ownership, and job design. Journal of Law, Economics and Organization 7, 24–52 (1991)
4. Laffont, J.J., Tirole, J.: Repeated auctions of incentive contracts, investment and bidding parity. Rand Journal of Economics 19, 516–537 (1988)
5. Laffont, J.J., Tirole, J.: Provision of quality and power of incentive schemes in regulated industries. In: Barnet (ed.) Equilibrium Theory and Applications: Proceedings of the Sixth International Symposium in Economic Theory and Econometrics, pp. 161–196. Cambridge University Press, Cambridge (1991)

On the Persistence of the Over-Reaction of Merger and Acquisition Announcements: Evidence from the U.S. Stock Market between 2003 and 2007

Emilia Țițan, Daniela Todose, Alexandra Țițan, and Mihaela Covrig

The Bucharest Academy of Economic Studies, Department of Statistics and Econometrics, Piata Romana, 6, 010374, Bucharest, Romania
{emilia.titan,daniela.todose,mihaela.covrig}@csie.ase.ro, alexandra_titan@yahoo.com

Abstract. The purpose of this paper is to examine how the M&A announcements affect the wealth of the investors in the case of the acquiring firms and if there is any persistent over-reaction. There is an extensive amount of studies written about M&As and their impact on both the short term stock returns and the long term performance of the stock prices, but the period starting in 2003 and ending in 2007, between two financial crisis, is in none of them analyzed. The paper points out the implications of the size of the acquirer and the method of payment that the bidding firm uses in the case of different types of M&As. Our results indicate that the over-reaction of the stock prices at M&A announcements is persistent, but only in the long-run.

Keywords: M&A (merger and acquisition), over-reaction, wealth effect, short term reaction, long term reaction.

1 Introduction

Mergers and acquisitions (abbreviated M&As in the rest of the paper) are a controversial subject in the financial literature. At one extreme are the studies that argue that managers pursue their own interest on the prejudice of the wealth maximization of the shareholders and that M&As appear as a willingness of the managers to increase the size of the company, because managers' salaries are positively correlated with the size of the company. At the other extreme are the beliefs that the stockholders earn positive abnormal returns from M&As using some private information about the capital markets.

The purpose of this paper is to examine how the M&As announcements affect the wealth of the investors in the case of the acquiring firms and if the over-reaction of these transactions is persistent or not. Over-reaction can be defined as a price change that exceeds the change in valuation [1]. It can appear as a positive change in the stock price as well as a negative change. After a period of time, the stock prices reverse themselves. The phenomenon of over-reaction can exist on a short period (few days) or on a longer horizon, for example one or two years. For over-reaction to be persistent, a condition would be that the results are significantly distinct from zero.

M. Zhou (Ed.): ISAEBD 2011, Part III, CCIS 210, pp. 499–505, 2011.

The period that will be analyzed starts in January 2003 and ends in December 2006, a period between two financial crises. We chose to examine the US stock market because it experienced a much higher value and dynamics of M&As.

Our paper can be viewed as an extension of the studies [7] and [5]. The first paper examines the effects that mergers have on the returns of the acquiring companies on a large sample of mergers from Anglo-Saxon and Non-Anglo-Saxon countries between 1981 and 2002 with a main focus on the evolution of the stock prices for the US acquiring firms. They found that the stock prices have a statistically positive performance in all the cases they analyzed, which is translated into persistent over-reaction of stock prices on the long-run. On the other hand, in [5], the authors analyze the relationship between the post-acquisition returns and the mode of acquisition (mergers or tender offers) and the means of payment (cash, stock or mixed) in the case of US acquirers between 1970 and 1989. They found that the acquirer firms that pay for their acquisition with cash tend to obtain positive and persistent abnormal returns in the five years following the acquisition, whereas the bidding firms that use stock as a mean of payment tend to have negative and significant abnormal returns.

The differences between these two studies and our paper lie in the classification of the M&As according to the three distinct groups of variables that influence the cumulative abnormal returns of the acquiring firms: the type of M&A, the method of payment and the firm size. In addition, we will study the period between 2003 and 2007 which is in none of them analyzed.

Our results indicate that the over-reaction of the stock prices at M&A announcements is persistent, but only in the long-run. Also, it is shown that the domestic M&As overperform the cross border transactions. In the short run, the stock prices usually positively but insignificantly over-react to the M&A announcements. In the long run they have large negative and significant values, being a sign of persistent over-reaction.

The paper is organized as follows: Section 2 provides an overview of the M&A transactions, highlighting the most important characteristics of cross-border and domestic M&As, as well as the wealth effects. Section 3 explains the methodology and data used in our paper. Section 4 presents our main results for the post-acquisition performance of the acquiring firms' stock prices and Section 5 concludes.

2 The M&A Transactions and the Wealth Effects

Mergers and acquisitions are terms usually used as synonyms, but, in fact, there is a clear distinction between the two. In a merger, the manager of the bidding company negotiates directly with the manager of the target company and the results are sent to the target's board of directors and voted by the target's board of shareholders. In this case, a new entity can appear [4]. In [9], an acquisition is defined as an event in which a firm purchases the shares of another one. It has as a result the transformation of the acquired company into a subsidiary of the acquirer.

In the case of cross-border M&As, the acquiring company must take into account some important characteristics like the differences in political and economic environment, culture, accounting techniques, tax rules and so on, which are different from the case of domestic M&As. Post-merger performance can be affected by the method of payment used by the acquirer company. There is some evidence which shows that a company that pays with cash tends to have a better post-merger performance than an all-equity bid [8]. The acquirer's size is also very important. Usually, small companies acquire small targets, the value of the transaction and the gains are also, in absolute terms, relatively smaller than in the case of larger companies. But, it has been shown that, in the majority of the cases, the small acquirers outperform the large ones in the sense that, while the small firms have small but positive abnormal returns, the large acquirers tend to have negative gains [6].

The evidence on the short term performance after a merger or acquisition is controversial. The results are sensitive to the analyzed period and also to the event window used to estimate the abnormal returns (ARs). The evidence for the acquiring companies is mixed. Some studies find positive and insignificantly distinct from zero cumulative abnormal returns (CARs) for domestic M&As, while other observe negative and significant stock returns. In [3], it is shown that the (CARs) in the case of the cross-border M&As, are usually positive, while the results for domestic transactions are negative. On average, bidder companies realize negative and significantly distinct from zero CARs.

Comparing the returns for domestic mergers and cross-border M&As, it can be seen that, in the case of the target firm, the stock prices in the first days following the announcements are smaller in the case of the cross-border M&As than in the case of domestic transactions. For the bidder companies, the studies show the opposite results. The CARs are larger for the cross-border M&As than for the domestic ones.

For the short-term horizon, there are very distinct results for the M&As reaction depending on the method of payment. For instance, if we analyze the ARs obtained by the bidder companies, we observe differences between the findings of different authors. For example, in [2] the results for the cash payments are positive and insignificantly distinct from zero, but M&As that have equity as the mean of payment tend to be followed by a decrease in the returns, having CARs negative and significant. In [10], it was found that acquirers paying for the target firms with pure cash and pure equity tend to have insignificant negative ARs in the first 5 and 10 days after the announcement. These results are contradicted by other studies showing that the bidding company will have insignificant and positive ARs in the case the transaction is paid with cash, and positive and significant CARs otherwise.

3 Data and Methodology

We are interested to examine the long run effects of the M&As announcements. But, there can exist information that prove the existence of ARs only in the first few days after the announcement date and, after this short period, the stock prices could revert to the normal values. This is the case of a scenario in which the capital market is efficient and all the information about the future costs and benefits of a merger or acquisition are incorporated into the stock price at the time of the announcement, so we will also analyze the ARs of the stocks in the short run.

We will test the efficient- market hypothesis (EMH), the same theory tested also in [5], and the stock price over-reaction hypothesis. The EMH assumes that financial markets are "informational efficient", meaning that markets have the capacity to reflect instantaneously any information into the stock prices. Market efficiency requires that at the moment of a M&A, there are equally chances that the stock price of the acquiring firm will be greater than expected as lower than expected. If the acquirers' stock prices are not reacting immediately after the announcement, we will conclude that the EMH does not hold. The stock market over-reaction hypothesis states that a stock price usually reverses itself after the stock price rapidly increased or decreased. If this hypothesis holds, then investors can construct profitable investment strategies and their profits can be very high. We follow two methodologies: first, to analyze the short run reaction of the stock prices of the acquiring firms following the announcement date, and second, to test, for the same set of companies, the long-run reaction. The sample consists of 140 M&As from January 2003 until December 2006, with acquirer a US firm and the bidder traded on NYSE, AMEX or Nasdaq.

For the short horizon, we compute the CARs, and the buy-and-hold abnormal returns (BHARs) of the acquiring firms for the long run analysis. We estimate the expected return of each acquirer included in the sample, using a market model:

$$E(R_{it}) = \alpha_i + \beta_i R_{mt} + \varepsilon_{it} , \quad (1)$$

where $E(R_{it})$ = the expected return on stock i at time t, R_{mt} = the return on the market portfolio at time t.

We will measure the effect of M&A announcements on the acquirer's stock price by calculating the ARs over different event windows: (-1;1), (-3;3) and (-5;5) days. For doing this, we will need a measure of the AR, which is:

$$AR_{it} = R_{it} - \left(\alpha^{OLS} + \beta^{OLS} R_{mt}\right) , \quad (2)$$

where: AR_{it} = the abnormal return for stock i at time t, R_{it} = the actual return on stock i at time t, and α^{OLS} and β^{OLS} are the ordinary-least-squares estimates of the market model parameters. After computing the ARs for each stock i, we determine the average AR during time t. Now, we can calculate the CAR as follows:

$$CAR_t = \sum_{t=1}^{T} AR_t \ . \quad (3)$$

We will compute the CARs through time, only for one security, and across securities. For the aggregation, we need to sum up the CARs for all the securities:

$$\overline{CAR}(\tau_1, \tau_2) = \frac{1}{N} \sum_{t=\tau_1}^{\tau_2} CAR_i(\tau_1, \tau_2) \ . \quad (4)$$

In the end, CARs will be used in the statistical t-test, for the whole sample to find whether CAR_ts are statistically different from zero. It will be computed for each category that is analyzed (type of M&A, acquirer's size and means of payment):

$$t_{CAR} = \frac{CAR_{t_1,t_2}}{\frac{\sigma_{CAR_{t_1,t_2}}}{\sqrt{N}}}, \qquad (5)$$

where: $\sigma_{CAR_{t_1,t_2}}$ is the standard deviation of the CAR during event window, and N is the number of observations included in the sample.

In order to measure the long-horizon reaction of firm's stock prices to M&A announcements, we take into account a post-announcement window of at least one year and calculate the BHARs, as they accurately take into account the wealth effects of the long-term investors:

$$BHAR_{i,\tau} = \prod_{t=1}^{\tau}(1+R_i) - \prod_{t=1}^{\tau}(1+E(R_i)) . \qquad (6)$$

Finally, we compute the average *BHAR*, using the following formula:

$$\overline{BHAR_\tau} = \frac{1}{N}\sum_{i=1}^{t} BHAR_{i,\tau} . \qquad (7)$$

4 Empirical Results

The average CARs to the bidding firms are shown in Table 1 in which we have also indicated the number of observations that formed the sample and the values for the *t*-test applied to the average returns obtained in our analysis.

The announcements of M&As are, for the short-run analysis, in all the cases, associated with insignificant CARs. The BHARs have both significant and insignificant values, for a one-year period, while for the two-year period, all the returns for the bidding firms are statistically significant. This is a proof of the market over-reaction and violation of EMH. As it concerns the sign of the average CARs, for the overall sample of M&As, the results indicate positive short-term CARs and negative long-term returns to the bidding companies. In contrast, for a longer period of time, it can be observed that the majority of the BHARs are significant at a 5% significance level. For a window of two years, the *t*-test is -6.98, which means that the BHAR is negative and significant. For the long-run examination, we obtained negative and significant results for domestic M&As while, in the case of cross-border M&As, the BHARs are insignificant for the first year data, but significantly distinct from zero at the level of 5% for a two-year period.

The differences generated by the size of the acquirers are evident: while the short-run results for all the categories are negative and insignificant, the long-term results are negative and significant for all the cases except of medium and small size firms for the first year, which are negative but insignificant. A conclusion can be obtained from these results: the small acquirers overperform the large ones. Finally, for the acquirers that pay with different means of payment, we obtained negative and insignificant short term results for cash and shares, while, for "mixed" category, the CARs are positive and also insignificant. About the long-run results, we can say that in all the cases the *t*-test showed that the stock returns are negative and significantly distinct from zero, with the exception of one year BHAR for the "shares" category which has positive and insignificant result.

Table 1. Cumulative abnormal returns to the bidding firms for each of the analyzed categories

		(t-5;t+5)	(t-3;t+3)	(t-1;t+1)	(t;t+250)	(t;t+500)
All mergers	N	140	140	140	140	113
	CAR|BHAR	0.0057	0.0023	0.0075	-0.1435	-0.8634
	t-test	*0.1815*	*0.0760*	*0.2754*	*-1.8524*	***-6.9826****
Domestic	N	70	70	70	70	57
	CAR|BHAR	0.0197	0.0224	0.0157	-0.2624	-1.0563
	t-test	*0.4274*	*0.4983*	*0.3756*	*-2.8970**	***-5.8004****
Cross-border	N	70	70	70	70	56
	CAR|BHAR	-0.0084	-0.0179	-0.0007	-0.0245	-0.6669
	t-test	*-0.2009*	*-0.4771*	*-0.0222*	*-0.2017*	***-4.0264****
Large	N	48	48	48	48	39
	CAR|BHAR	-0.0041	-0.0025	-0.0034	-0.1937	-0.4628
	t-test	*-0.1202*	*-0.0773*	*-0.1091*	*-2.3065**	***-3.0506****
Medium	N	55	55	55	55	44
	CAR|BHAR	-0.0039	-0.0061	-0.0071	-0.1203	-0.8316
	t-test	*-0.0910*	*-0.1454*	*-0.1905*	*-0.9831*	***-4.7530****
Small	N	37	37	37	37	30
	CAR|BHAR	0.0326	0.0210	0.0432	-0.1127	-1.4307
	t-test	*0.4190*	*0.2842*	*0.6444*	*-0.6144*	***-4.7788****
Cash	N	74	74	74	74	57
	CAR|BHAR	0.0134	0.0020	0.0079	-0.1754	-0.6840
	t-test	*0.3735*	*0.0637*	*0.2804*	*-2.1166**	***-5.0847****
Shares	N	30	30	30	30	27
	CAR|BHAR	-0.0072	-0.0047	0.0101	0.0668	-1.0672
	t-test	*-0.0802*	*-0.0534*	*0.1230*	*0.2952*	***-3.3095****
Mixed	N	36	36	36	36	29
	CAR|BHAR	0.0005	0.0086	0.0045	-0.2530	-1.0262
	t-test	*0.0108*	*0.1991*	*0.1330*	*-2.1291**	***-4.4598****

*t-test is significant at the 5% level based on a two-tailed test; **t-test is significant at the 5% level, but insignificant at the 1% level based on a two-tailed test.

Also, we have found that the positive returns for the domestic M&As, in the case of the three short-time event windows, are split up into positive and insignificantly different from zero results of the medium and small acquirers and negative ARs for the large acquirers. For the cross-border M&As, the situation is reversed.

The method of payment is another variable entitled to explain the results obtained for the cross-border M&As. More precisely, the negative short-run results can be explained by the same sign results in the case of the acquirers that paid with shares or another mixed method, while the cash category has positive and insignificant CARs.

5 Conclusions

The results obtained indicate that the investors have a positive, but insignificant reaction in the first days of the announcement in the case of domestic M&As which is an evidence of better performance of the domestic compared to cross-border M&As. Also, positive CARs exist, in the short-run, when the acquirers are small companies and when the means of payment are cash or mixed. For the rest of the categories, there appear to be a negative reaction of the investors. All the positive figures tend to be reversed after a longer period of time, when the calculated BHARs have negative values, a sign for the market over-reaction after the announcement.

The large and negative long-term ARs are inconsistent with the EMH. The results suggest that the stock returns of the acquiring firms are usually underestimated. The over-reaction hypothesis is sustained by our results, but only in the long run.

References

1. Duran, A., Caginalp, G.: Overreaction diamonds: Precursors and aftershocks for significant price changes. Quantitative Finance 7, 321–342 (2007)
2. Franks, J., Harris, R., Titman, S.: The Postmerger Share-price Performance of Acquiring Firms. Journal of Financial Economics 29, 81–96 (1991)
3. Goergen, M., Renneboog, L.: Shareholder Wealth Effects of Domestic and Cross-border Takeover Bids. European Financial Management 10, 9–45 (2004)
4. Jensen, M.C., Ruback, R.S.: The Market for Corporate Control: The Scientific Evidence. Journal of Financial Economics 11, 5–50 (1983)
5. Loughran, T., Vijh, A.M.: Do Long-Term Shareholders Benefit From Corporate Acquisitions? Journal of Finance 52, 1765–1790 (1997)
6. Moeller, S.B., Schlingemann, F.P., Stulz, R.M.: Wealth Destruction on a Massive Scale? A Study of Acquiring-firm Returns in the Recent Merger Wave. Journal of Finance 60, 757–782 (2005)
7. Mueller, D.C., Yurtoglu, B.B.: Corporate Governance and the Returns to Acquiring Firms' Shareholders: An International Comparison. Managerial and Decision Economics 28, 879–896 (2007)
8. Myers, S., Majluf, M.: Corporate Financing and Investment Decisions when Firms Have Information that Investors Do Not Have. Journal of Financial Economics 13, 187–221 (1984)
9. Sudarsanam, S.: Creating Value from Mergers and Acquisitions - The Challenges. Prentice Hall, Englewood Cliffs (2003)
10. Travlos, N.G.: Corporate Takeover Bids, Methods of Payment and Bidding Firms Stock Returns. The Journal of Finance 42, 943–963 (1987)
11. Voineagu, V., Țițan, E., Şerban, R., Ghiță, S., Boboc, C., Pele, D., Todose, D.: Econometric Theory and Practice (Teorie şi practică econometrică). Meteor Press Publishing House, Bucharest (2007)

An Empirical Research on the Relationship between Corporate Social Responsibility and Performance in Beijing-Tianjin-Hebei Region: A Case Study of Listed Companies in Shanghai and Shenzhen Stock Exchanges

Xu Hong[1], Weidong Li[2], and Xihuai Yang[1]

[1] School of Business Administration, Northeastern University, Shenyang City, Liaoning Province, China
[2] Foreign Language Department, Northeastern University at Qinhuangdao, Qinhuangdao, Hebei Province, China

jenna_qhd@tom.com, {leewd1225,jenna_qhd}@163.com

Abstract. According to Stakeholder Theory, the author of the article conducted a research on the influence of corporate social responsibility (CSR for short) on its performance by using the Structural Equation Modeling (SEM for short). On the basis of the research results of available literatures, setting up an assumptive Conceptual Model indicating the relationship between the factors of corporate social responsibility and the factors of its performance, selecting the annual report data of 138 listed companies in Beijing-Tianjin-Hebei region in the 5 consecutive years from 2005 to 2009 as research sample, the author conducted hypothesis testing through the Structural Equation Modeling. The result is that CSR for creditors has a positive effect on a company's performance. CSR for shareholders has the same effect on financial performance rather than on operating performance. Generally speaking, CSR causes great effects on a company's performance, the more responsibility for stakeholders, the better a company's performance.

Keywords: Stakeholders, CSR, Performance, SEM, Beijing-Tianjin-Hebei region.

With the increasing promotion companies have played to the rapid economic development, the matter of CSR has accordingly come into being since 20th century, because a company causes a negative effect on the society out of its profit creation [1]. For the definition of CSR has been enriched, a company's status advances on a gradual basis [2]. In recent years, CSR philosophy has drawn wide attention and been attached more importance to, which is proved by the event that China Corporate Social Responsibility Summit held in the Great Hall of the People awarded 17 outstanding companies in terms of their social responsibility in 2010. The Beijing-Tianjin-Hebei region is in the core area of the Bohai Sea District as well as Northeast Asia, and also is a main home for high-tech and heavy industry. So, in order to realize constant sustainable development, it is of great significance to study the relationship between CSR and a company's performance in the region.

M. Zhou (Ed.): ISAEBD 2011, Part III, CCIS 210, pp. 506–513, 2011.

1 The Theoretical Basis of the Study

Corporate social responsibility means that a company fulfills various positive obligations and duties for its stakeholders via its regulations and behavior. It is beneficial response to market and stakeholders, and an overall index for a company's operational objectives [3]. A company is supposed to take responsibility to maintain and foster public interests, when maximizing profits for shareholders [4].

CSR philosophy was derived from the United States in the early of 20th century as a result of American special system, then urbanization and the mergence of modern companies [5]. Thereafter, many a scholars held heated discussions and in-depth researches, and Stakeholder Theory which was concluded in the western countries after1960s came to become striking. Compared with traditional Shareholder Primacy, Stakeholder Theory emphasizes that a company's progress fail to come true without the participance and devotion from all stakeholders including those who are affected directly or indirectly by a company's operation such as shareholders, creditors, government, employees, clients and suppliers, not simply was confined to the main benefit body [6].

2 Research Hypothesis and Research Design

2.1 Research Hypothesis

Available literatures show that the fulfillments of CSR not only can meet stakeholders' interests, but also boost a company's performance, and then maximize profits of shareholders. The following research hypotheses are put forward in the view of definition of a company's social responsibility:

Hypothesis 1: CSR for shareholders is positively correlated with a company's performance.

Hypothesis 1a: CSR for shareholders is positively correlated with a company's financial performance.

Hypothesis 1b: CSR for shareholders is positively correlated with a company's operating performance.

Shareholders are the foundation as well as core for a listed company, and play a role of agents. As investors, shareholders are offered such rights as getting profits, making decisions and appointing corporate leaders in order to promote economic development and improve the efficiency of resource allocations. The main concern from shareholders is the rate of return on investment. Thus, the action that a company takes social responsibility does good to increase credibility and ability to finance which lays a constant and stable financial foundation for a company's development.

Hypothesis 2: CSR for creditors is positively correlated with a company's performance.

Hypothesis 2a: CSR for creditors is positively correlated with a company's financial performance.

Hypothesis 2b: CSR for creditors is positively correlated with a company's operating performance.

Creditors are among important stakeholders for a company. Creditors take more risks because more and more companies are run in gearing, and the gearing ratio and size are enlarged. A company's debt disputes and crises have a bad influence on its fame and reputation, and worsen its operation and profits. So, a favorable credit relationship between a company and its creditors will boost value of creditors and the company itself.

Hypothesis 3: CSR for government is positively correlated with a company's performance.

Hypothesis 3a: CSR for government is positively correlated with a company's financial performance.

Hypothesis 3b: CSR for government is positively correlated with a company's operating performance.

In the market economy, government regulation is a crucial factor to manage economy when the market fails to do so. Government offer corporations public services, share benefits and finance their organs via revenue. When public interests are met, government will provide better public services, such as perfecting market mechanism, improving infrastructure. Government is among stakeholders and its public benefits have a strong connection with a company's performance.

2.2 Model Building

The evaluation system of CSR has a broad definition including a lot of qualitative and quantitative indexes. The paper focuses on financial index [7]. According to the above hypothesis and the structural equation model, as is shown in Figure 1, the conceptual model of the study is presented. The model is used to investigate the connectivity between CSR and a company's performance on the basis of Stakeholder Theory. The arrow starts from CSR for stakeholders and ends with a company's financial and operating performance, which indicates the relationship between the two.

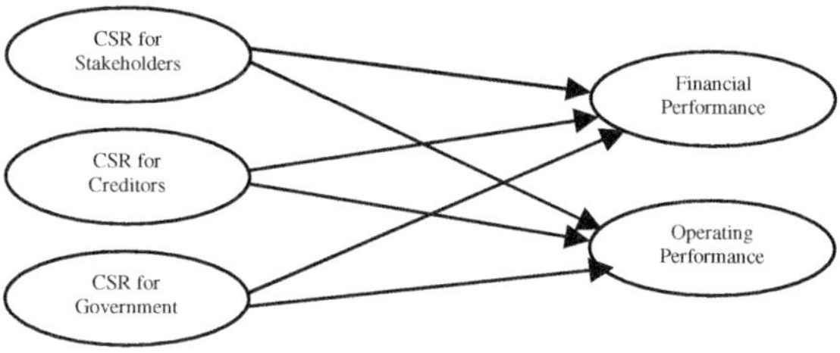

Fig. 1. The Conceptual Model of CSR and Performance

2.3 Sample Selection

The paper studies those companies listed in the Shanghai and Shenzhen Stock Exchanges from 2005 to 2009 on the basis of their mean financial figures. By the end of 2009, 239 companies from the Beijing-Tianjin-Hebei region have been listed in the two stock exchanges, excluding Trash Stocks and those lack of data (it means that no data has appeared on the regular reports or prospectuses by 2003), 138 of which are qualified and are analyzed. The statistics used in the paper are all from *http://www.cninfo.com.cn/* and *http://www.cnlist.com/*. The descriptive statistics of latent variable index employ SPSS software; confirmatory factor analysis and data processing of Structural Equation Modeling are conducted by using AMOS software; parameters are estimated by Maximum Likelihood Method.

2.4 Variable Selection

The paper selects the financial index to evaluate a company's social responsibility for shareholders, creditors and government in the evaluation system of a company's social responsibility. The commonplace financial index appraising a company's financial and operating performance is shown in the Table 1.

Table 1. Variable Selection

Measure Objects	Variable Name	Variable Calculation
CSR for Stakeholders	Return on Stockholders' Equity	After-tax Profits/Shareholder's Equity
	Addition of the value of Assets	Ending Ownership Interest/Beginning Ownership Interest
	Net Return on Assets	Net Return/Net Assets
CSR for Creditors	Quick Ratio	(Liquid Assets-Inventory)/Current Liabilities
	Assets-liability Ratio	General Assets/Total Liabilities
CSR for Government	Net Amount of Taxation Expenditure	Total Expenses of Taxation –Return of Expenses of Taxation
	Staff Number	Staff number
	Total Donation Expenditure	Non-business Expenditure
Financial Performance	Rate of Return on Total Assets	Total Amount of Earnings before Interests and Taxes/Average Total Assets
	net Profit Rate	Total Amount of Profits×(1- Income Tax Rate)
Operating Performance	Total Asset Turnover Ratio	Core Business net Income/Average Total Assets
	Inventory Turnover Rate	Core Business net Income/Average Inventory Balance

3 Analysis of SEM

3.1 SEM

Structural Equation Modeling, SEM is composed of such statistical methods as multiple regression, factor analysis, path analysis and simultaneous equations in econometrics. It is used to analyze the inner relationship between variables and variable groups which exist broadly in the fields of sociology, psychology and business management. In SME, those variables which can be directly measured are called Observed Variables, and those which can't be measured directly but can be shown by observed variable linear are called Latent Variables. In the model of Amos,

ξ means exogenous latent variables and η represents endogenous latent variables. X indicates external observed variables and Y internal observed variables.

Amos model includes two parts:

(1) Measurement Model: reflects the relationship between observed variables and latent variables. The formula is as below:

$$y = \Lambda_y + \varepsilon \quad (1)$$

$$x = \Lambda_x \xi + \delta \quad (2)$$

In the formula, Λ_x and Λ_y represent the coefficient matrix which reflects the intensity degree of the relationship between x to ξ and y to η. It can also be understood as the factor loading in factor analysis. ε and δ represent the measurement error between y and x.

(2) SEM: reflects the relationship between latent variables. The formula is as below:

$$\eta = B\eta + \Gamma\xi + \zeta \quad (3)$$

In the formula, B presents the interact between latent variables. Γ represents the influence of outside latent variables on inside latent variables. ζ is the error term of SE. The relationship between outside and inside latent variables is established through B and Γ coefficient matrix and ζ (error vector). The detail is shown in Figure 2.

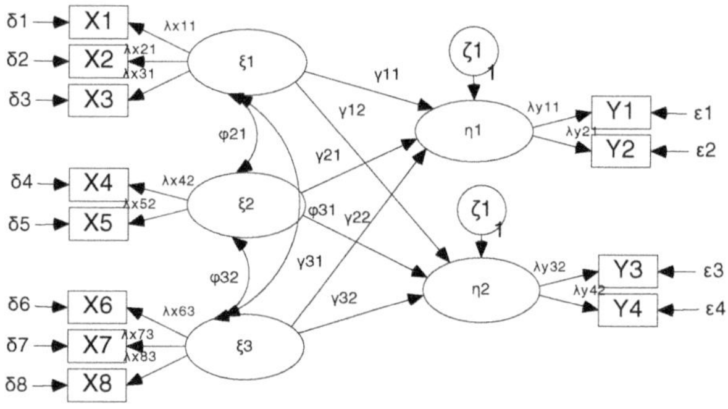

Fig. 2. Schematic diagram of structural

3.2 Initial Model Building

According to the above research hypothesis and the conceptual model, the initial model of the relationship between CSR and performance is set up, which is shown in Figure 3.

3.3 Estimation, Evaluation and Modification of Model Parameter

Applying the maximum likelihood estimate program of Amos 7.0, the research conducted the parameter estimate on the initial model. Figure 4 explains the standardized path coefficient.

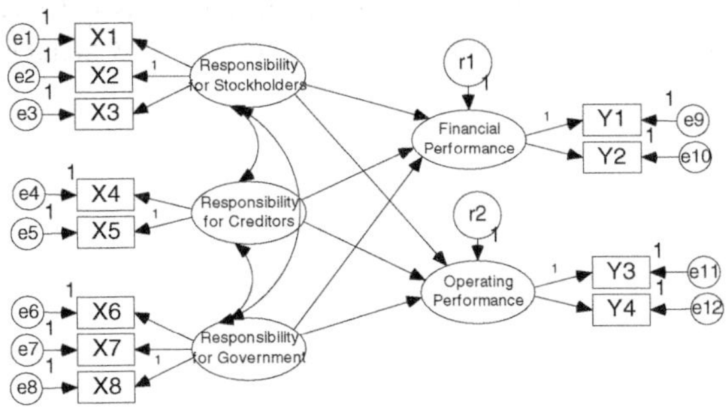

Fig. 3. Path of SEM Indicating the Relationship between CSR and Performance

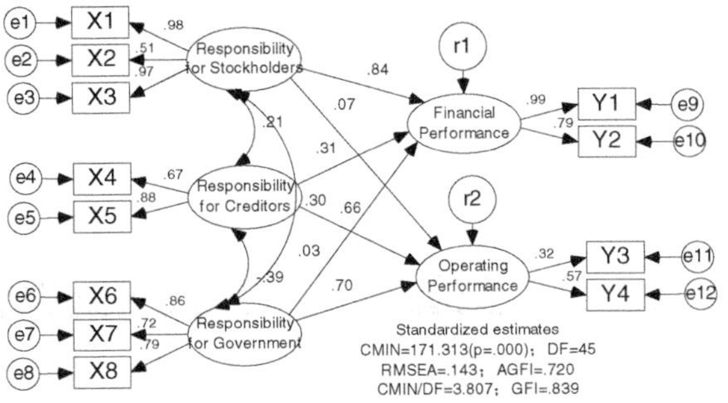

Fig. 4. Path of SEM Indicating the Relationship between CSR and Performance

The degree of freedom is 45. The chi-square of the fit of the whole model is 171.313. The significant probability value is p=0.000<0.05, which reaches the conspicuous level of 0.05. The null hypothesis being rejected means hypothesis model and sample data don't agree with each other. These values, including RMSEA value (0.143>0.08), the chi-square DOF ratio (3.807>3.000), AGFI value (0.720<0.900) and GFI value (0.839<0.900), shows that the fit of the whole model is not good enough.

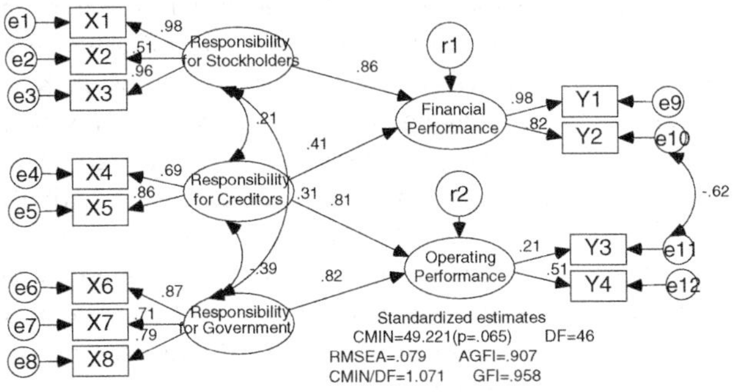

Fig. 5. Diagram of Modification Model Path Coefficient

Table 2. Modification Model Fitting Index

	$\chi2/df$	RMSEA	GFI	AGFI	NFI	RFI	CFI	PGFI	PNFI
Fitting Index	1.07	0.079	0.958	0.907	0.963	0.901	0.968	0.653	0.701

Figure 5 shows the result after modifying the initial model according to the modification value provided by Amos.

In the diagram of modification model, if we suppose that the error terms are not independent, according to the modification value, attention should be paid to the covariant relationship. Finally, no modification values higher than 4 are presented in the model and all the absolute residual values in the standardized covariance matrix are lower than 1.96. The result of the model testing indicates that the C.R. values of all the twelve λ are higher than 1.96, which means all the measurement index parameters reach the conspicuous level of 0.05. The DOF of the model equals to 45. The chi-square of the fit of the whole model is 49.221. The significant probability value is $p=0.065>0.05$, which doesn't reach the conspicuous level of 0.05. The null hypothesis being accepted means that hypothesis model and sample data agree with each other. It is found that the chi-square DOF ratio equals to 1.071 (lower than 3) and the values of AGFI, GFI, NFI, RFI and CFI are all higher than 0.9 and the value of PNFI is higher than 0.5. As a result, all the values reach the model fitting standard, which means the diagram of modification casual model can be accepted.

3.4 Hypothesis Testing and Path Analysis

As already discussed, the modification model displays a great fitting effect. The goodness-of-fit indices all reach the reference value: RMSEA equals to 0.079 lower than 0.8, which indicates the fitting degree between every latent variable and actual data.

The path parameter of CSR for stockholders and the financial performance is 0.86 and the path parameter of CSR for creditors and the company's performance is 0.41. This shows that CSR for stockholders and creditors can increase financial performance, provided that hypotheses 1a and 2a were verified. The path parameter of CSR for creditors and the operating performance is 0.85 and the path parameter of CSR for government and the operating performance is 0.65. This shows that CSR for creditors and government can effectively increase operating performance, provided that 2b and 3b are verified. Besides, the basic hypothesis—the effect of CSR for stockholders on operating performance and the effect of CSR for government on financial performance—is not verified, that is to say the model does not fully verify hypothesis 1, 2 and 3. However, generally speaking, CSR has a positive effect on performance, which is in accordance with the previous hypothesis.

4 Conclusion

The conclusion is reached from the empirical study on the relationship between CSR and a company's performance that the former is positively correlative with the latter and there is a conspicuous relationship of cause-and-effect between CSR and a company's performance within the companies in the Beijing-Tianjin-Hebei region. In a word, the fulfillment of the social responsibility of the companies in that region is able to enhance greatly a company's performance, instead of causing negatives. The reason for it is that the fulfillment brings a different and better competitive advantage to the company, despite the increase of cost. Stakeholders, shareholders, creditors and government are affected a lot by a company's performance, so, if their benefits are well protected via a company's fulfillment of responsibility, then a win-to-win situation is coming both for the company and stakeholders.

Name of Project. Humanities and social science research project of Department of education in Hebei Province. Project No: SZ2010225.

References

1. Bramrner, S., Williams, G., Zinkin, J.: Religion and Attitudes to Corporate Social Responsibility in a Large Cross-Country Sample. Journal of Business Ethics 71, 229–243 (2007)
2. Palmer: Multinational corporations and the social contract. Journal of Business Ethics 31, 245–258 (2001)
3. Cohen: Socially Responsible Business Goes Global. Business 23, 22 (2000)
4. Adams, Zutshi, A.: Corporate Social Responsibility: Why Business Should Act Responsibly and Be Accountable. Australian Accounting Review 14, 31–39 (2004)
5. Coldwell, D.A.L: Perceptions and Expectations of Corporate Social Responsibility: Theoretical Issues and Empirical Findings. South African Journal of Business Management 32, 49–55 (2001)
6. Carlisle, Y.M., Faulkner, D.O.: Corporate Social Responsibility: A Stages Framework. European Business Journal 16, 143–152 (2004)
7. Moore: Corporate social and financial Performance: An investigation in the U.K. supermarket industry. Journal of Business Ethics 34, 299–311 (2001)

Migration of Physicians: Causes and Effects in CEE Countries*

Cristina Boboc[1], Valentina Vasile[2], and Simona Ghiță[1]

[1] Bucharest Academy of Economic Studies, Department of Statistics and Econometrics, 15-17 Calea Dorobantilor, 010552, Bucharest, Romania
cristina.boboc@csie.ase.ro, simo_ghita@yahoo.com
[2] Institute of National Economy, Casa Academiei, 13 Calea 13 Septembrie, Sector 5, 761172, Bucharest, Romania
valentinavasile2009@gmail.com

Abstract. Physicians' migration revolves around the reasons of better structure of medical education, desire for better income, general security and improved prospects for family. Moreover, many Central and East European Countries are characterized by severe shortages, inappropriate skill mixes and gaps in health service coverage. This paper starts with a literature review about the determinants of migration. Most of the post-enlargement East-West migration flows have been pushed by the dissatisfaction with economic opportunities in new member states compared to the older ones. Is this the main reason as well for migration of physicians? And which are the effects of this migration in source countries? In order to answer to these questions, we have analyzed the health sector in CEE countries: health trends and patterns, education, employment, wages, physicians' migration by using descriptive statistics, factorial and regression analysis.

Keywords: physician's migration, health sector, CEE countries, statistical analysis.

1 Introduction

In Central and East European (CEE) countries, workers in health systems are facing increasing pressure and insecurity as long as they have to respond to a complex range of health threats. Financing policies, technological advances and consumer expectations have changed the workforce demand in health systems. In many CEE countries, health sector reform has captured the entire attention and financial resources, and the investments in human capital (education and employment) have been forgotten. Skill mix, distributional imbalances and inequalities compound today's problems. Many workers face discouraging working environments, poverty-level wages, unsupportive management, insufficient social recognition, and weak career development. Moreover, the skills of some professionals in health system are not well matched to the local profile of health needs. These two reasons accelerated international migration from the Eastern to the Western Europe and also to significant gaps in health service coverage.

* This paper is supported by the Sectorial Operational Program Human Resources Development (SOP HRD), financed from the European Social Fund and by the Romanian Government under the contract number SOP HRD/89/1.5/S/62988.

M. Zhou (Ed.): ISAEBD 2011, Part III, CCIS 210, pp. 514–520, 2011.

This paper starts with a literature review about the causes and effect of physician's migration. Afterward, we analyze the interdependencies on health sector in CEE countries by using descriptive statistics, factorial and regression analysis.

2 Literature Review

Despite the increasing pressure of globalization and of the knowledge economy which promote labour migration, Fouarge and Ester [8] find out that Europeans are not that willing to move to another country. Based on Eurobarometer Mobility Survey data (2005), only 5.4 per cent of the working-age population intends to move to another country within the next five years. Anyway, there are great disparities between countries, mostly between Eastern and Western countries. While family and other social relationships, as well as housing and local environment conditions, are important, Fouarge and Ester [7] and Bonin et al. [3] show that employment-related factors, such as higher income, better working conditions, and opportunities of finding a suitable job are key migration motivators in Europe, and in the new members states in particular. Furthermore, Bonin et al. [3] show that language and cultural barriers also play an important role. In the new member states of EU, Blanchflower et al. [2] show that the propensity to migrate is correlated with income per capita, unemployment rates, and life satisfaction. Unhappiness with their lives, dissatisfaction with their salaries and working conditions, small number of good jobs and employment insecurity are the key reasons for Eastern Europeans to migrate in the Western European countries [1].

Migration of physicians is not necessarily beneficial from a social point of view. The decision to migrate takes into account the private costs and benefits. In assessing the impact of physician migration it is important to distinguish between permanent and temporary migration. While temporary migration of physicians is generally beneficial through an upgrading of skills, technological and financial transfers, permanent migration represents a net transfer/export of human capital from the home to the host country. Permanent migration might improve the prospects of individual physicians, but substantial emigration flows which happened during the last years in CEE countries may weaken the capacity and efficiency of the home country's health care system. Temporary migration may be inspired by the desire to acquire higher professional qualifications or to gain experience with new techniques not available in the home country, but also to career development. However, if the skills that migrants have acquired during their stay abroad are too specialized, the home country may not be in a position to take advantage of them [6] on the short and medium term.

According to Buchan [4] the reasons of physicians' migration are often characterized as "push and pull" factors. To some extent, they are a mirror image on issues of relative pay, career prospects, working conditions and environment available in the source and destinations countries. When the gap or the perceived gap is significant the migration appears. Improvements in travel and communication, the availability of employment and the free circulations of persons and capitals between EU countries encouraged the temporary migration in health care sector. The similar educational curricula, the similar languages, the traditional links between countries may be also considered as important factors in choosing the destination countries for health professionals.

3 Empirical Analyses

3.1 Which Is the Main Road to Follow in the Near Future to Improve Health Outcomes in CEE Countries?

In order to identify which are the main determinants of health outcomes, we have used some factorial analyzes on all EU countries for which we had available data. The variables included in our analysis are divided in two categories: health outcomes and health determinants. To characterize the health outcomes we have chosen : life expectancy - LExp, infant mortality rate - IMR and the first two causes of death in Europe: Malignant neoplasm (C00-C97) - DMN and Diseases of the circulatory system (I00-I99) - DCS (source: Eurostat, year 2008 or the latest year available since 2006). As health determinants we have chosen on one hand: Relative wage in health system calculated as Wage in health system divided by average wage – RW; General practitioners: number on 100000 inhabitants – GP; Health expenditure: as % in GDP – HE, School life expectancy - SLE (source: Eurostat, year 2008 or the latest year available since 2006) and on the other hand: Improve sanitation facilities: % of population with access on sanitation facilities – ISF (source: World Bank, year 2008).

By applying Principal Components Analysis we have constructed two principal factors: the first one explains 50% of the total variation and the second one 17% of the total variation. The first principal component is determined by the variables: life expectancy, infant mortality rate, causes of death: diseases of circulatory system and malignant neoplasm, health expenditure and improved sanitation facilities. Western EU countries: Belgium, France, Germany, Austria, Sweden are characterized by high levels of both health outcomes and health determinants. On the other hand are Romania, Latvia, Lithuania, Poland and Slovakia with low levels of both health outcomes and health determinants. The inverse correlation between relative wage in health and the school expectancy is the main characteristic of the second principal component. This one puts in opposition countries like Bulgaria where the school life expectancy is very low and the relative wage in health is very high (high recognition of health professionals) and countries like Finland and Portugal where the school life expectancy is very high and the relative wage in health is low. The reasons for which the relative wage is low in Finland and Portugal are different. While in Finland the mean wage is high and therefore even if the wage in health is high compared with other EU countries, their ratio is lower than in other countries, in Portugal, the wage in health is very low compared with other Western EU countries. Another interesting fact is that almost all EEC do not have many general practitioners. These physicians are those who deliver the preventive services in health and who could identify what are the measures to be taken by their patients in order to prevent the death because of diseases of circulatory system or because of malignant neoplasm (by specific physical activities, alimentation, etc.). These preventive measures could improve health outcomes and should also reduce the health expenditure in time.

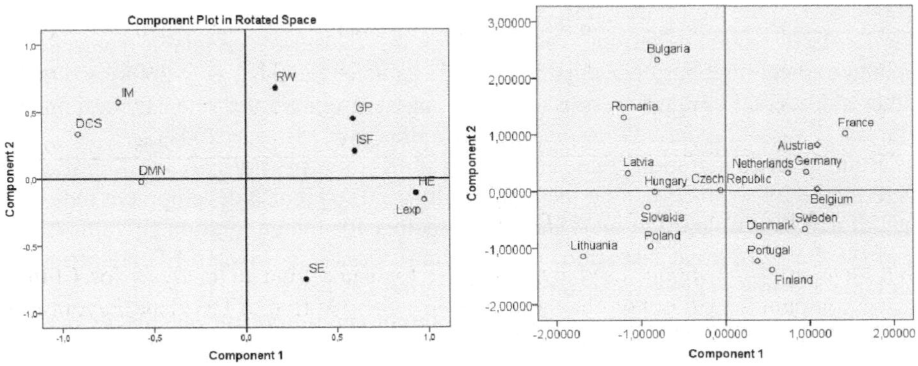

Fig. 1. Variables and countries representations on the two first principal components

In order to see which are the correlations between the two sets of variables, health outcomes and health determinants we have used a canonical analysis (Appendix 1). Life expectancy, infant mortality and Diseases of circulatory system are explained by health determinants with a level of significance of 0.01 as follows:

- Life expectancy is mainly explained by health expenditure (p-value<0.001) and improved sanitation facilities (p-value<0.05);
- Infant mortality rate is mainly explained by health expenditure (p-value<0.01) and school expectancy (p-value<0.1);
- Diseases of circulatory system are mainly explained by health expenditure (p-value<0.001) and school expectancy (p-value<0.05)

Therefore high levels of education and wealth (which means high levels of health expenditure) imply high levels of health outcomes. Improving education and wealth need a time lag. Anyway, substantial improvements in health should be obtained by some simple and not very expensive instruments. The first one should be the supervision of health workers which will improve the individual performance and the competition between them. Another very important issue is the reasonable compensation of work, wage package. Financial and non-financial supports will have effects on productivity and quality of care services. No matter how motivated and skilled health workers are, they cannot do their jobs properly if they do not have clean water, adequate lighting, heating, vehicles, drugs, working equipment and other supplies. Therefore, the authorities should offer all their assistance in assuring these basic support systems. Moreover lifelong learning should be encouraged in the workplace by organizing short term trainings, knowledge sharing, teamwork fostering etc.

3.2 Which Is the Main Road to Follow in the Near Future to Reduce the Brain Drain of Physicians?

So as to identify which are the main directions for reducing brain drain and increasing eventually the brain gain, we have used a canonical analysis on all EU countries with available data. The variables included in our analysis are on one side the: Human Development Index (source: UN database, year 2008), Improve sanitation facilities: % of population with access on sanitation facilities – ISF (source: World Bank, year

2008), School life expectancy - SLE (source: Eurostat, year 2008), Wage of physicians in Euro – Earn (source: Eurostat, year 2008 or the latest year available since 2006); Health expenditure, euro per inhabitant – HE (source: Eurostat, year 2008) and on the other side: Total emigration rate of physicians and emigration rate of physicians in Europe (Source: Frédéric Docquier and Alok Bhargava [5], year 2004).

Both total emigration rate and emigration rate in Europe are significantly determined by socio-economic factors (p-value<0.01). Human development index and health expenditure are the most important factors for the emigration (p-value<0.01). Even if there are great disparities in physician's earnings between EU countries, the variable Earning is not significant for emigration (Appendix 2). In addition, we have estimated two regression functions one for the emigration of physicians all over the world and one for the emigration of physicians in Europe. While Human Development Index is based on education, health and wealth indicators, we have used life expectancy and school life expectancy instead of HDI, the wealth factor being expressed by health expenditure. The results in Table 1 show that school expectancy and life expectancy are significant factors for emigration. Life expectancy is more important for emigration in Europe and school expectancy is more important for total emigration. Also, as a complementary push factor, healthcare services are closely related to economic development level and social insurance profile of the national social model. In this context, local demand of physicians and the quality of healthcare services increase depending to the level and dynamics of GDP/capita in a direct but not proportional correlation. So, in this context, the propensity for labour migration of the physicians is higher if the economic gap increase and the educational profile differences decreasing.

In EU developed countries, known as host countries for physicians' migration from the CEE countries, the healthcare services demand is more diversified, is related to the special services for elder persons, the quality and performances in preventing services, the public health expenditures and the quality and development level of private healthcare system. Diploma recognition and specialization abroad also during initial education provide for EU labor market competitive labor force supply of physicians from New Member States.

Table 1. Linear Regression – SAS results

Coefficients	**Physicians emigration – total**	**Physicians emigration – Europe**
Intercept	**0.61** (p-value < 0.03)	**0.577** (p-value < 0.01)
Health Expenditure	**0.000030** (p-value <0.001)	**0.000027** (p-value <0.001)
School Expectancy	**-0.01646** (p-value <0.01)	**-0.01138** (p-value <0.02)
Life Expectancy	**-0.00435** (p-value <0.2)	**-0.00505** (p-value <0.1)
R^2	**0.65**	**0.64**
Statistic F	**11.42** (p-value < 0.001)	**10.56** (p-value < 0.001)

4 Conclusions

A key factor in providing medical care is the availability of qualified and motivated health care professionals. The emigration of physicians is an important constraint that limits the satisfaction of the local needs in health care in the origin countries, with poorer performance healthcare system. The empirical evidence suggests that medical doctor's emigration in European Union appear because of poor distribution of physicians, low internal mobility and inappropriate skill mix. In case of migration from CEE countries to Western EU countries the main reasons are differences in working conditions, remuneration level and career opportunities. Substantial improvements in health and the conversion of the brain drain in brain gain in CEE countries should be obtained by some not very expensive measures. The first one is the motivation of doctors by offering system support and attractive working environment. The motivation goes to efficiency, quality and responsiveness. The second one is the increase of competence through short term trainings, knowledge sharing, transfer of knowledge from return physicians, teamwork fostering, and innovation. The third one is the coverage by appropriate skill mix and geographic distribution, numeric adequacy. Other more expensive measures which could sustain the health system and reduce migration flows of physicians are the increasing health expenditure and investments in medical research. Particularly for Romania, for example, there are also other types of motivation factors as unfinished reform of the healthcare system, under developed private healthcare system and low rate of wage payments at similar professional qualification and performances. The high quality of educational system in health associated to significant research results and practice performances is closely related to the level of RDI outcomes absorption in the system at national level and international research networks including Romanian teams of physicians. Some studies proved for Romania a relatively strong negative correlation between the returned migration ratio and the education index [9]. Nowadays, brain circulation has shown to be more efficient and attractive both for original and host countries, and also host/post workers can contribute in a large scale not only to increase the professional outcomes of mix team (from origin and host countries) but also to the quality of the healthcare services demand. For the CEE countries the future main challenge is to improve the national healthcare system and provide stimulative policies in order to reduce the physicians' emigration. Through proper policies to specialized high performing education, a real and an adequate institutional system reform and a stimulative work payment could generate lower or even inverse flows of migration and increased demand for quality of healthcare services, as base ground for better services in origin countries, reducing mortality, increasing life expectancy and quality of life.

References

1. Blanchflower, D.G., Lawton, H.: The Impact of the EU on the UK Labour Market. IZA Discussion Paper No. 3695 (2008)
2. Blanchflower, D.G., Saleheen, J., Shadforth, C.: The Impact of the Recent Migration from Eastern Europe on the UK Economy. IZA Discussion Paper No. 2615 (2007)
3. Bonin, H., Eichhorst, W., Florman, C., Hansen, M.O., Skiöld, L., Stuhler, J., Tatsiramos, K., Thomasen, J.H., Zimmermann, K.F.: Geographic Mobility in the European Union: Optimising its Economic and Social Benefits. IZA Research Report No. 19 (2008)
4. Buchan, J., Perfilieva, G.: Health Worker Migration in the European Region: Country Case Studies and Policy Implications. Division of Country Support WHO Regional Office for Europe, Copenhagen (2006)

5. Docquier, F., Bhargava, A.: The Medical Brain Drain: A New Panel Data Set on Physicians' Emigration Rates (1991–2004) (2007), http://www.ires.ucl.ac.be/csssp/home_pa_pers/docquier/filepdf/mbd1_description.pdf
6. Forcier, M.B., Simoens, S., Giuffrida, A.: Impact, regulation and health policy implications of physician migration in OECD countries. Human Resources for Health 2, 12 (2004)
7. Fouarge, D., Ester, P.: Factors Determining International and Regional Migration in Europe. In: European Foundation for the Improvement of Living and Working Conditions, Dublin (2007)
8. Fouarge, D., Ester, P.: How willing are Europeans to migrate? A comparison of migration intentions in Western and Eastern Europe. Open Access publications from Maastricht University, Maastricht University (2008)
9. Țițan, E., Todose, D.: A territorial approach of highly educated labor force migration in Romania, in the context of European integration process. Gospodarka Regionalna i Turystyka, Zeszyt 5/2008, Tom II. Wyższa Szkoła Ekonomii (2008) ISSN 1733-4314

Appendix 1 - Health Outcomes, Canonical Analysis – SAS Results

Squared Multiple Correlations and F Tests						
Numerator DF=5 Denominator DF=11						
	R-Square	Adjusted R-Square	Approx 95% CL for RSq		F Value	Pr>F
			Lower CL	Upper CL		
Lexp	0.925	0.891	0.672	0.962	27.12	<0.0001
IM	0.711	0.580	0.098	0.839	5.42	0.0093
DMN	0.216	-0.140	0.000	0.390	0.61	0.6968
DCS	0.938	0.910	0.723	0.969	33.29	<0.0001

	Raw Regression Coefficients			
	Lexp	IM	DMN	DCS
RW	2.497	0.472	-62.172	143.310
GP	-0.005	0.013	-0.076	0.354
ISF	0.029	0.005	0.001	-0.816
SE	0.396	-0.619	-5.077	-26.079
HE	1.787	-1.111	-3.801	-88.187
	Prob>|t| for the Regression Coefficients			
	Lexp	IM	DMN	DCS
RW	0.5338	0.9281	0.5330	0.4095
GP	0.5211	0.2628	0.7192	0.3437
ISF	0.0463	0.7845	0.9978	0.1724
SE	0.1397	0.0851	0.4291	0.0330
HE	<0.0001	0.0097	0.5832	<0.0001

Appendix 2 - Emigration, Canonical Analysis – SAS Results

Squared Multiple Correlations and F Tests						
Numerator DF=4 Denominator DF=13						
	R-Square	Adjusted R-Square	Approx 95% CL for RSq		F Value	Pr>F
			Lower CL	Upper CL		
Emigration Rate	0.644	0.535	0.106	0.809	5.89	0.0063
Emigration rate Europe	0.684	0.587	0.163	0.833	7.04	0.0030

	Raw Regression Coefficients				Prob>|t| for the Regression Coefficients	
	Lexp	IM			Lexp	IM
HE	0.000048782	0.000040962		HExp	0.0005	0.0002
HDI	-1.160814190	-0.929380565		HDI	0.0406	0.0083
ISF	0.000008507	-0.000051154		ISF	0.9844	0.878
Earn	0.000001036	0.000000493		Earn	0.2395	0.4587

The Research on Stock Market Volatility in China Based on the Model of ARIMA-EARCH-M (1, 1) and ARIMA-TARCH-M (1, 1)

Jingli Xing

Chengdu University of Information Technology, Chengdu, China, 610103
xjlxingjingli@126.com

Abstract. In order to reflect the volatility of financial time series with the character of clustering, asymmetry, peak and fat tail. Using the mode of ARIMA-EARCH-M(1,1) and ARIMA-TARCH-M(1,1) which is rarely used in the literature, choosing the Shanghai Composite Index and Shenzhen Stock Index of July 30, 2003 - July 30,2010 as the sample, we obtained the best appropriate model by empirically analysis of the Chinese stock market behavior. The results show that the stock market price has the character of clustering, asymmetry, peak and fat tail.

Keywords: ARIMA model, TARCH-M (1, 1) model, EGARCH-M (1, 1) model.

1 Introduction

China's stock market has been built for ten years. which has played an increasingly important part in the financial sector. The establishment and development of Stock markets, has played an important role in promoting China's economic reforms and economic development. Analysising and studying the trends of changes in the prices of stock market, summarizing the current characteristics of stock market price volatility, has not only some theoretical value for China financial markets , but it also has important reference value in the actual investment decisions. Compared with the international developed stock markets, China's stock market is still immature in many ways, showing the differences with each other. The Chinese stock market which is under the influence of the financial crisis, is not only of great significance for the research of China's stock market Volatility characteristics and the actual investment of our country decisions, but it is also of great in economic development and financial construction of China.

2 A Literature Review and Research Hypotheses

Many scholars had an empirical study about the relationship between the Shanghai and Shenzhen stock. Many financial economists, sociologists of financial markets began to try different models and methods to solve this problem. Engle [1] (1982) had proposed ARCH models and GARCH models one after another, ARCH models and GARCH

M. Zhou (Ed.): ISAEBD 2011, Part III, CCIS 210, pp. 521–527, 2011.

models was more successful for the prediction variance of the rate of return on financial assets under certain conditions, Bollerslev [2] (1986) had the conclusion of the stock returns distribution characteristics using the EGARCH model, which has a bias and a fat tail characteristics. Nelson [3] (1992) had proposed TARCH model which is based on the ARCH model, and used this model to study the leverage effect of stock market volatility. Han Gui [4] (2008), using EGARCH (1, 1) model to estimate the test results of the Shanghai Composite Index on December 19, 1990 to March 19, 2008 closing market volatility index based on five stages cycle, showed the conclusions there is a big volatility in the Chinese stock market, and there has alternating positive and negative leverage the phenomenon, and the impact of information asymmetry, which was significantly reduced in the Shanghai Composite Index.

A large number of empirical studies have shown that fluctuations in stock returns showing the character of clustering, asymmetry, peak and fat tail. However, there is rarely used empirical approach to forecast and study with the suitable models. In the paper, selecting recent data of Shanghai and Shenzhen Stock Market, choosing the model of ARIMA-EGARCH-M(1,1) and ARIMA-TARCH-M(1,1), which is different from the previous scholars .This is one of the innovation in this paper. Firstly, we establish the composite model of ARIMA-EPARCH-M(1,1) and ARIMA-TARCH-M(1,1).Secondly, we empirically analysis China's Shanghai and Shenzhen Stock Market, Finally, we draw the appropriate conclusions.

3 Model

ARIMA model estimation process, are usually assumed Conditional variance of the error term is constant, which, however, cannot effectively explain the often observed the volatility clustering phenomenon in financial time series , so we further introduced in the model of GARCH effects.

ARIMA-GARCH family model has two conditions: 1) conditional mean equation is the ARIMA model; 2) the conditional variance equation is the GARCH family model. The paper will choose models of non-symmetrical ARCH family——EGARCH and TARCH models. To describe the risk of changes in the stock market rate of return, it is necessary to introduce the conditional variance as a variable to the conditional mean equation.

Mean equation is:

$$\nabla^{\delta}\psi_{\tau} = \omega + \sum_{\iota=1}^{\pi}\varphi_{\iota}\nabla^{\delta}\psi_{\tau-\iota} + \upsilon_{\tau} + \sum_{\iota=1}^{\pi}\beta_{j}\upsilon_{\tau-j}$$

EGARCH (p, q)-M and TARCH (p, q)-M conditional variance equations are:

$$\lambda\nu(\sigma_{\tau}^{2}) = \omega + \sum_{\iota=1}^{\pi}\alpha_{\iota}\left|\frac{\upsilon_{\tau-\iota}}{\sigma_{\tau-\iota}} - E(\frac{\upsilon_{\tau-\iota}}{\sigma_{\tau-\iota}})\right| + \sum_{\kappa=1}^{\rho}\gamma_{\kappa}\frac{\upsilon_{\tau-\kappa}}{\sigma_{\tau-\kappa}} + \sum_{j=1}^{\theta}\beta_{j}\lambda\nu(\sigma_{\tau-j}^{2})$$

$$\sigma_{t}^{2} = \omega + \sum_{i=1}^{p}\alpha_{i}u_{t-i}^{2} + \sum_{k=1}^{r}\gamma_{k}u_{t-k}^{2}I_{t-k}^{-} + \sum_{i=1}^{q}\beta_{j}\sigma_{t-j}^{2}$$

$\sum_{k=1}^{r}\gamma_k u_{t-k}^2 I_{t-k}^-$ is Asymmetric effect terms, If $\gamma > 0$, it indicates leverage effect, the; if $\gamma < 0$, the main effect of non-symmetrical effect is to increase volatility.

4 Empirical Analysis

4.1 Data Preparation and Descriptive Statistics

This paper selects the number of the Shanghai Index and Shenzhen Component Index daily closing price, the sample data range from July 30, 2003 to July 30, 2010. The data has a total sample period of 1704 from Sohu Finance channel, including consecutive trading days. We note the closing price of the Shanghai and Shenzhen respectively, of P1, P2. To eliminate the base of the inconsistent influence on the natural logarithm of two indices, we recorded them as LNP1, LNP2. R1, R2 respectively, is the number of returns of the Shanghai Index and Shenzhen Component Index. R1 = LNP1 (t) - LNP1 (t-1), R2 = LNP2 (t) - LNP2 (t-1). Part of the sample period, includes a traditional Chinese festival, so it will not match the phenomenon of displacement between sample period of the trading day and Eveiws. In order to avoid the default date, we will establish the working paper file structure type (workfilestructure type), which is set to irregular data (unstructured / undated), so that it does not affect the regression results of the model.

Table 1. Descriptive statistics of data

	Mean	Median	Skewness	kurtosis	JB	S.E	LB(15)	LB^2(15)
R1	0.003	0.001	-0.286	5.842	596.479	0.019	36.365	460.29
R2	0.007	0.002	-0.314	5.302	403.901	0.02	40.81	414.76

Note: 1. JB Statistics is Jarque-Bera Normal test statistics. 2. LB (15) and LB ^ 2 (15) were tested and the Autocorrelation sequence and Autocorrelation corresponding to the square of the Ljung-Box statistics.

From Table 1, we show the conclusions as follows :(1) The Shenzhen Component Index on the Shanghai index R1 and R2, whose number of the kurtosis values are greater than the normal distribution the kurtosis value of 3, indicating that the return series are "peak" phenomenon. (2) The skewness number of R1 and R2 is negative shows that income distribution is not symmetric. There is a serious starboard. (3) JB result of the normal distribution of test statistics rejected the null hypothesis of normal distribution.

In order to study whether there exists a relationship in long-term equilibrium between Shanghai and Shenzhen stock index or not, we can use cointegration methods. If there is the relationship of Cointegration between the two variables, there is a long-term equilibrium relationship. After Cointegration test, if there exists Cointegration about the changes in Shanghai and Shenzhen stock index, we will use Granger causality test which can be further used to test whether there exists the short-term causal relationship between them and to what extent. Prerequisite for Cointegration analysis is the variables in the model are the entire sequence of I (1) sequence, Therefore, we had better take cointegration of the variables before the unit root test. Firstly, stability test. Secondly,Cointegration test. Finally, Granger causality test steps and we will empirical analysis in the paper.

4.2 Stationary Test and Cointegration Test

We will test Whether Day return series is or not subject to unit root process. In this paper, we will choose the ADF unit root test that is a commonly used method.

As can be seen from Table 2, we could know the Shenzhen Component Index R1and the Shanghai index R2 are stationary series.

Table 2. The unit root test of return series

Return series	ADF statistic	1% critical value	Conclusion
R1	-40.9479	-3.9634	stationary
R2	-39.4158	-3.9634	stationary

For Johansen cointegration test, there are two implementation ways: eigenvalue trace test and maximum eigenvalue test, the paper also examined the data by two methods. According to the characteristics of the sample interval time series, we would choose the Cointegration model which is a linear trend series, Cointegration equations have intercepts but no trend. The optimal number of Lag value is determined by the minimum of AIC and SC, the largest Log-likelihood values. As can be seen from Table 3, the results of cointegration test do not reject the null hypothesis at 1% significance level. We can determine, the Shenzhen Component Index R1and the Shanghai index R2 exists a stable cointegration relationship.

Table 3. Johanson Cointegration test results

H0: the number of cointegration equation	Trace statistic	5% critical value	P-value	The largest eigenvalue	5% critical value	P-value
None	622.144	15.495	0.000	347.094	14.265	0.000
At most one	275.050	3.842	0.000	275.050	3.842	0.000

4.3 ARCH-LM Test and Granger Test

There is a "volatility clusters “phenomenon by observing the residual plots of regression equation. We could initially determine the Errors may exist heteroskedasticity.

Therefore, we will test the regression equation on the Shanghai and Shenzhen Stock market about conditional heteroskedasticity of the ARCH effect test.

We have the conclusion there exists residuals of the ARCH effect from Table 4.

Table 4. Daily return of the Shanghai and Shenzhen ARCH test effect

Lag order	F-statistic		Probability		Obs*R-squared		Probability	
	The Shanghai Composite Index	The Shenzhen Component Index	The Shanghai Composite Index	The Shenzhen Component Index	The Shanghai Composite Index	The Shenzhen Component Index	The Shanghai Composite Index	The Shenzhen Component Index
1	31.8591	27.1237	0.0000	0.0000	31.3095	21.0224	0.0000	0.0000
5	17.9359	26.7282	0.0000	0.0000	85.4651	41.0992	0.0000	0.0000

The Granger causality test is very sensitive to the lag order, to ensure the robustness of the results, In the paper, we selected lag order of 5, to make Granger test for Shanghai Stock Index Returns R1 and Shenzhen Component Index Returns R2.The results are as follows,

Table 5. Granger Causality Test Results

Original hypothesis	Lag order	1	2	3	4	5
R2 is not R1 Granger cause	F-value	0.864	0.532	1.020	0.752	1.262
	P-value	0.353	0.587	0.383	0.557	0.278
R1 is not R2 Granger cause	F-value	5.625	4.349	2.890	2.679	3.265
	P-value	0.018	0.013	0.034	0.030	0.006

Table 5 shows that, in the Lag order delay within 5, the Shanghai Stock Index Returns R1 is the Granger causes of Shenzhen Component Index Returns R2. There exists a one-way Granger causality relationship between two variables.

4.4 The Estimation Results of Model

In this paper,we use EARCH-M (1,1) and TARCH-M (1,1) model. The results using Eviews 7.0 is as follows,

Table 6. ARIMA-GARCH estimation results under the assumption of normal distribution model

	ARMA(1,1)-EARCH-M(1,1)		ARMA(1,1)-TARCH-M(1,1)	
	The Shanghai Composite Index	The Shenzhen Component Index	The Shanghai Composite Index	The Shenzhen Component Index
ω	-0.25	-0.24	0.00	0.00
	(-6.47)	(-6.37)	(-4.12)	(-4.13)
α_1	0.16	0.16	0.06	0.06
	(-9.77)	(-8.76)	(-5.29)	(-5.36)
β_1	0.98	0.99	0.92	0.92
	(-245.18)	(-255.62)	(-104.39)	(-95.01)
γ	-0.02	-0.02	0.03	0.03
	(-2.50)	(-1.72)	(-2.36)	(-1.99)
φ	-0.73	1.69	-0.82	0.87
	(-0.35)	(-0.86)	(-0.38)	(-0.42)
AIC	-5.32	-5.14	-5.31	-5.13
SC	-5.29	-5.11	-5.29	-5.11
DW	2.04	2.01	2.05	2.01

From Table 6, we have the conclusion as follows, (1) ω、α1、 β can pass the significance test (t values in brackets), a good explanation. Four equations of the two markets in the 95% level are significantly greater than 0, which shows the positive impact of good news above the average (absolute value) of value will increase the price volatility effect. (2)Leverage items γ are non-0, showing a degree of leverage, but not very significant, indicating the presence of weak leverage. This phenomenon indicates that the current market of the degree of stock market which still has some characteristics of government-led or influence is low and lack of openness compared with international stock market. (3) TARCH model $\gamma > 0$, which means more bad news than good news causes market volatility, and there has $\gamma > 0$ in EGARCH model, which means more good news than bad news caused the market fluctuations. From Table 6, Shanghai and Shenzhen Stock market are good news than bad news is more sensitive to good news than bad news, more possibility to arouse fluctuations in the stock market, which is consistent with the reaction people's real life. bad news in the Chinese stock market is greater than the impact caused by the same size of good news. (4) β_1 ,which is used to measure the impact of persistent parameters is higher, but still less than 1.It indicates that both the response function in the stock market the impact of price fluctuations is at a relatively slow rate.

5 Conclusions

Through empirically analysising Shanghai Composite Index and Shenzhen Component Index of Stock Market in China, we have the following conclusions,

(1) The results show that Shanghai and Shenzhen stock index return have the character of clustering, asymmetry, peak and fat tail.

(2) There exsits a one-way Granger causality relationship between R1 and R2 in the5% significance level, rather than the two-way.

(3) Shanghai and Shenzhen Component Index Returns have leverage effect returns, but the Shanghai stock market is stronger than the Shenzhen stock market.

Compared with ARIMA-EGARCH-M(1,1) and ARIMA-TGARCH-M(1,1) model,we could capture the conclusion that EGARCH(1,1) is one of the best ways to describe asymmetrical influence of the recent news to the returns volatility in the stock market.what is not same as the Engleand Ng(1993) analysis's result is as follows, we believe that ARMA-EGARCH-M(1,1), but not TGARCH-M(1,1) is the best model, which fits the Shanghai Composite Index returns ratio sequence, reflecting the fluctuation asymmetry, the income - risk forward relations .

References

1. Engle, R.F.: Autoregressive conditional heteroscedasticity with estimates of the variance of UK inflation. Econo-metrica 50, 987–1007 (1982)
2. Bollerslev, T.: Generalized auto regression heteroscedasticity. Journal of Econometrica 31, 307–327 (1986)
3. Nelson, D.B., Cao, C.Q.: Inequality constraints in the univari-ate GARCH model. Journal of Business and Economic Statistics 10, 229–235 (1992)
4. Eric, Z., Wang, J-h.: ModelingFinancialTimeSeries. S-PlusSpringer-Verlag (2003)
5. Han, G., Wang, J.: EGARCH model based on the symmetry of stock market information in China. Southwest Jiao tong University (8) (2008)
6. Huang, D., Wang, H.: GARCH model to estimate the choice of methods and applications in the Shanghai index. Statistics and Management (5) (2010)
7. Gaotiemei: Econometric analysisand modeling-Eviewsapplications and examples. Tsinghua University, the Society (2006)
8. Yi, d.: Data Analysis and Eviews application. China Statistics Press, Beijing (2002)
9. Heyiqing, Caohuihong, Hou, J.: China's Shanghai and Shenzhen stock index returns of the EGARCH effect analysis. Statistical Observations (8) (2005)

Industry Development, Space Limitation, and Industry Transformation: Evidence from Wenzhou

Jie Zeng[1], Longbao Wei[1], and Changluan Fu[2]

[1] College of Management Zhejiang University, Yuhangtang Road, Hangzhou, 310058 P.R.C.
[2] School of International Business Administration, Zhejiang International Studies University

Abstract. This study explored the reason why the development of the Wenzhou economy, which is known as the "Wenzhou Model", has slowed down. Traditional research emphasized the effects of limitations from soft and hard environments, such as environment, resources, and capital. Built on acknowledging the factors mentioned above, the current study especially proved that there was limited development space for certain early-entered industries, that is, it became unrealistic for accelerating the development of certain industries after the industrial clusters in this area have occupied the most market share in China, even the whole world, which becomes the crux point to lead to the lag of the development of Wenzhou economy. The study first established a theoretical model for illustrating ideas delivered here and then proved the basic ideas in the model through analyzing materials and data collected through survey among Wenzhou industrial clusters. The conclusion subsequently followed.

Keywords: Wenzhou model, industrial clusters, industry space limitation

1 Introduction

Since 1980, China has been a real economic miracle (Zhang, 2009). In Wenzhou, Zhejiang, where the economic miracle was created by the private economy representatively, the rapid development of the regional economy created the impressive "Wenzhou model" (Shi, 2002). However, since 1998, Wenzhou economic growth began to lag behind other areas in Zhejiang Province. From the second half of 2003, same as the country, Zhejiang entered a new round of economic growth in the rapid expansion of the long-term period. In the new growth phase, the total amount of economic prosperity of the province significantly expanded and significant changes in industrial structure occurred. Unfortunately, in this round of the rapid expansion period, the economic growth of Wenzhou declined and the share of total provincial GDP was decreased from original 14% to 13.2%.

The "Wenzhou model" seems break out of the association between the model and the continual positive development of the Wenzhou economy. The issue that raises concerns both nationally and internationally is the lack of developmental stamina for the Wenzhou economy. The existing research emphasized effects of platform, space, environment, and other factors have been widely considered the main constraints for Wenzhou regional competitiveness and sustainable development.

M. Zhou (Ed.): ISAEBD 2011, Part III, CCIS 210, pp. 528–533, 2011.

Without denying the importance of these factors, the current paper answered the question from a different angle. We believe that limited space for the development of partial industries entered early is the crux reason which led to the lag of Wenzhou's economic development, because it has become unrealistic to increase the development after the industry cluster has accounted for most of the national and even global share.

To be specific, in the beginning of the reform, these complicated industrial technologies chosen by the entrepreneurs were easy to be divided into components. In fact, not all the industries fit for the cooperation based on the labor division, such as the steel industry.

Wenzhou's economy focused on light industries such as shoes, clothes, electronic machines, metals, and smoking instruments. These industries were easily divided into different components according to the producing process. Therefore, the cooperation system garnered great success in the beginning of the reform. However, some of these light industries have limited development potential. Once the industry developed to a certain point, it was hard for it to maintain the rapid development speed. The examples of such industries are lighter, button, and zip.

This article firstly builds an econometrical model to illustrate the above ideas. Then the data and case studies from Wenzhou industries are used to prove the econometrical model.

2 Theoretical Model

Development is constrained by the market (Liang, 2009). Based on the existent research, the authors firstly build a conceptual model. Then the authors construct an econometrical model to prove the core idea. At last, based on the analysis of the case study, the authors concluded that the overall small size of the industry is the reason why it is hard to maintain sustainable development for partial industries.

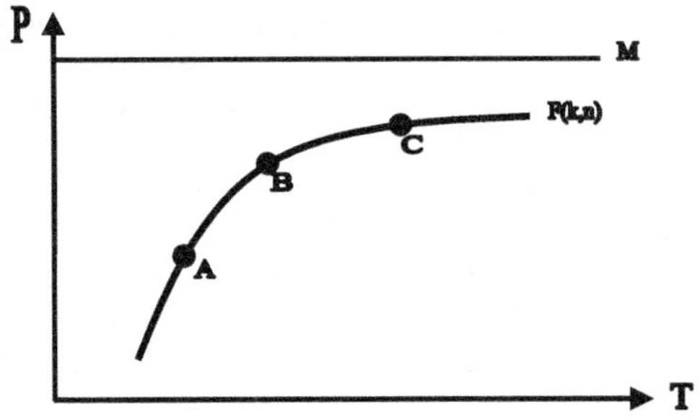

Fig. 1. Letting the horizontal axis represent time (T) and the vertical axis represent productivity (T). As indicated in Fig 1, the current market share is small, then it is far away from the horizontal line M, which means it will progress from point A to point B. On the other hand, if the total market is so small that the market share held by the regional area is relatively large, then it is close to the horizontal line M, such as in point B. If this occurs, then it is relatively difficult to develop to the point C compared to that of moving from A to B.

2.1 Conceptual Model

In the beginning of the reform, only limited local areas or companies owned enough capital to enter integrated production such as the steel industry. Most of the self-employed, private businesses or SME (small or median enterprises) entered cooperation system industries such as textile and hardware. During the period when the demand was greater than the supply, these light industries gained great success. The success made the foundation for the development of industrial clusters. However, when the industry shared most of the international and domestic market, the space for sustainable development was limited with the expansion of the industrial size. This is the reason why the Wenzhou economic model stagnated during recent years.

2.2 Mathematical Model

We establish a mathematical model to show the fundamental insight therein. Inspired by Liang's (2003) use of the Industrial Gini coefficient as an indicator of concentration to analyze the concentration of related industries, this paper used a location quotient to evaluate it, which is defined as:

$$\beta = \frac{q_{ij}/q_i}{q_{ji}/q_j} \quad (1)$$

Where q_{ij} is the total GDP of industry i in area j; q_i is the total market scale of industry i, and q_j is the total GDP of area j. Therefore, the numerator in the equation indicates the fraction of the industry i in the total GDP of the area j, and the denominator indicates the fraction of the industry i in area j in the total GDP of the national or global industry i. As a result, β stands for the difference of the industry share between the specific area and the nation/worldwide, and could be used as the criteria for the future potential of the industry section in the specific area.

This model shows that, if the numerator is large while the denominator is small, then the industry has comparative advantage and has potential for growth; otherwise the industry has no comparative advantage and has limited potential. Therefore, β indicates the potential for future development and contribution to the local economy.

The early entered industries in Wenzhou are primarily technically independent industries such as clothes and shoes. Zhang and Li (1990) studied the badge-making industry at Cangnan. A typical badge is made using 13 procedures, and each is done by specialized factories. To illustrate the core ideas of the theoretical model, the following sections analyzed some feature industries in Wenzhou in depth.

3 Case Study

The city of Wenzhou is located in the southern province of Zhejiang, facing the East Sea, and neighboring Fujian. Wenzhou was historically famous for its artifact industries. In the early stage of the reform and opening-up, Wenzhou is famous for the highly prospered private businesses, which was developing rapidly in that period. "Wenzhou Model" (Shi, 2002) attracted more attention nationally to Wenzhou.

There are 17 feature industries in Wenzhou, including shoe leather, clothes, plastic products, eye glasses, lighters, shavers, and so on. Four of them have more than 50 billion in annual production value, and five of them have between 10 billion and 50 billion. We put the 17 feature industries into the math model, and get the β.

Table 1. Betas of different industries (unit:0.1 billion)

Industry	Whole production value 2008(b)	Ratio of regional industries	Share in the country/world	β
Shoe leather	652	0.178	>40% (w)	>0.3
Appliances	610	0.167	< 50% (w)	>0.3
Clothes	520	0.142	<40% (w)	> 0.355
Plastic products	503	0.137	<40% (w)	>0.3
automobiles Accessories	380	0.104	< 40% (w)	>0.3
Pump valves	370	0.101	< 40% (w)	>0.3
Printing	190	0.052	< 5% (c)	>0.1
Synthetic leather	120	0.033	38.8% (c)	>0.1
Locks	102	0.028	5.7% (c)	< 0.1
Eyeglasses	45	0.012	25% (c)	< 0.1
Boats and ships	40	0.011	< 5% (c)	< 0.1
Zipper	31	0.008	<40% (w)	0.041
Pens	30	0.008	< 40% (w)	0.047
Shaver	20	0.005	60% (w)	0.009
Buttons	20	0.005	60% (w)	0.009
Lighters	15	0.004	80% (w)	0.005
Finance devices	14	0.004	#VALUE	#VALUE

Note: due to the lack of data of some industries' global market development space, we substitute the data of the national market, production volume and proportion, and divided it by 30067 billion (GDP in 2008).

The table above indicated that the global shares of buttons, shavers, and lighters are big, but it only takes a small portion in regional manufacturing. There are no relative advantages, and industry potential space is limited, which is indicated by the small β value. Therefore, future fast development is difficult. On the other hand, shoe leather, appliances, and clothing have bigger β value, which means they have bigger development space. This present argument confirms the math model.

From the table 2, the data indicate that the proportion of shoe leather, appliances, clothing, and plastic products in the Wenzhou economy is decreasing gradually. The plastic products are becoming less and less important, though it lead the fast growth of regional economy. Now the industry of plastic products is slowing down, especially industries like fasteners and lighters, which take 70%-80% of global market share, they can no longer lead Wenzhou economy to fast development. In the meantime, accessories on automobiles and pump valves are growing rapidly, which increased their economic proportions. Heavy industries, such as boats and ships, are entering the list of Wenzhou feature industries because of their increasing economic proportions. This proportion also confirms with the conclusion of the math model.

Table 2. The proportion of these feature industries in Wenzhou from 2005-2008 (units:%)

Industry\proportion	2005(%)	2006(%)	2007(%)	2008(%)
Shoe leather	20.58	18.92	18.36	17.80
Appliances	15.75	15.48	16.7	16.6
Clothes	15.17	13.58	14.2	14.2
Plastic products	14.93	14.19	14.6	13.7
Accessories to automobiles	6.19	10.80	10.3	10.3
Pump valves	8.25	8.79	9.48	10.1
Printing	6.19	5.68	5.33	5.19
Synthesized leather	3.69	3.41	3.42	3.28
Locks	3.09	2.87	2.81	2.79
Eyeglasses	2.39	2.43	2.22	1.23
Boats and ships	#VALUE!	#VALUE!	#VALUE!	1.09
Zippers	1.25	1.18	#VALUE!	0.86
Pens	1.24	1.05	0.89	0.82
Shavers	0.00	0.53	0.53	0.55
Buttons	0.78	0.64	0.57	0.55
Lighters	0.00	0.00	0.00	0.41
Finance devices	0.52	0.44	0.41	0.38

To sum up, as the regional industries take a large share of a limited market as a whole, if the growing pace of the whole market is not fast enough to catch up the regional growing pace, then the boundary of the whole market would limit the regional economic development. In the early stages of the economic reform in Wenzhou, some industries have had this exact same problems, therefore, their rapid development is now restricted.

This conclusion is consistent with the expectation of the total factor productivity theory (Yotopoulos, 1971; Barro, 1999)(Cai, 2009).

4 Conclusion

Based on the statement of the thoughts above, the construction of a theoretical model, and the practical evidence of the Wenzhou industry, it came to a conclusion: some industries confirmed the early development trend, but the total market is small, and the industry in Wenzhou has already occupied the majority of the share, the potential space for development is limited, therefore it is difficult to develop quickly again. In addition, the existing industrial structure and cost adjustment problem limited the economy development to a certain technical level. These factors constrained the speed of Wenzhou economy in the current stage.

References

1. Michael, E.P.: From competitive advantage to corporate strategy. BusinessAdministration Miscellaneous Papers Harvard Business Review 45 (1987)
2. Zhang, W.C.: The Economic System of China, vol. 118 China City Press (2009)
3. Michael, E.P.: The competitive advantage of nations (1998)
4. Ma, J.L.: The Return and Transcendence of Wenzhou Development. Zhejiang Social Science (2), 26–29 (2004)
5. Cai, F.: Flying Geese within Borders: How China Sustains Its Labor-intensive Industries? Economic Research Journal (2009)
6. Liang, Q.: Labor Division, Agglomeration and Growth, vol. 209. The Commercial Press (2009)
7. Zhang, R.S.: Re-innovation of Wenzhou Model. Decision Making Consultant, 14–15 (2002)

A Game Analysis on Salary Allocation of Corporate Executives and General Staff

Yuxia Zhao

Department of Business Administration, Henan University of Urban Construction, Ping Dingshan City, Henan Province, China, 467000
Zhaoyuxia@hncj.edu.cn

Abstract. The game theory has been widely applied in China's human resource management, but most of the researches focus on the static state of the game involving two persons. By adopting the multistage dynamic game model of incomplete information, this paper analyzes the game of inner interests allocation of the corporate staff ,finds out other conditions satisfying the demands for the fair salary allocation. The purpose of this paper is to provide new thoughts for the research on China's salary allocation management.

Keywords: Executive, General staff, Board of directors, Government regulators, salary allocation.

1 Introduction

Influenced by human resource scarcity in the knowledge economy age, the human capital value will rise rapidly. Nevertheless, owning to the lack of the advanced assessment skills and methods on human capital value and the sound matched professional manager market, the formulation of the executives' salary in state-owned enterprises or non-state-owned enterprises will inevitably be with blindness; meanwhile, owning to the imperfection of China's enterprise governance mechanism, the self-dealing salary of executives is quite popular. In recent years, despite the salary restriction system in China, the increasing salary disparity between corporate executives and general staff and the intensified unfair salary allocation have been a social phenomenon, which hasn't been effectively contained.

Currently, the entrustment relationship of China's state-owned enterprise is indistinct, which caused that the modern corporate governance becomes formalistic and doesn't work, severely affecting the fair and scientific income allocation of the cooperate stakeholders. Specifically, the problem in executives' salary in the state-owned enterprises is that the board of directors doesn't work normally (Jing Guo , The Soft Science of China, 2010). As for the state-owned enterprise, as one party of the salary contract, the enterprise or its shareholders have diversified goals. However, the goal of the other party — the manager, is not naturally consistent with the diversified goals of the society (Yuanxin Cheng and Donghua Chen, etc., Management World, 2009). The given salary contract includes various incentives, and the management level will maximize its own interests (Baiman, 1990). This indicates that the immediate

M. Zhou (Ed.): ISAEBD 2011, Part III, CCIS 210, pp. 534–540, 2011.

cause of triggering the salary unfairness is people's pursuit to maximum interests of their own.

Through the current documents on salary allocation, it is hard to see the game analysis on salary allocation stakeholders. This paper analyzes the stakeholders' game in corporate salary allocation cases and finds out other conditions satisfying the demands for the fair salary allocation. The purpose of this paper is to provide new thoughts for the research on China's salary allocation management.

2 The Game Model Hypothesis and the Players' Strategies

2.1 The Game Model Hypothesis

All the players are rational 'economic man', subjectively chasing the maximum interests of their own.

The information asymmetry exists between general staff and executives. Before the executives allocate the compensation, the general staff are not clear about the executives' decisions and the ideas of the board of directors.

The government regulators should randomly check the salary allocation plan.

The executives can gain excess earnings from the unfair salary allocation.

The general staff adopt negative slowdown, from which their earnings are less than those form positive working. Because of the hypothesis of 'economic man', under the conditions of fair interests allocation, the general staff must work hard.

It is of great possibility that the board of directors know about what are the salary allocation plan made by executives.

Assuming that in the salary allocation cases, the enterprise owners only pay the basic salary, the bonus is sheer an inner matter of the employees.

2.2 The Players and their Strategies

The corporate executives and their strategies. The rationality and fairness in the executives' salary allocation plan immediately affect the general staff's working results. The executives are an important variable of the general staff's working results. There are two strategies in the corporate management authorities when making decisions, namely, fairness or unfairness. And the executives have two strategies in the negotiation joined by the board of directors: adopting or abandoning the suggestions proposed by the board of directors. And there are also two strategies in treating the general staff: terminating or renewing the contract.

The general staff and their strategies. Since the decisions made by the executives are unknown to the general staff before they are announced, the general staff's strategies can only be made in line with the executives' decisions. There are two strategies of the general staff: acceptance or rejection; and there are two strategies in acceptance: positive working and negative slowdown.

The government regulator and its strategy. The probability of the government regulator's spot checking on corporate salary allocation plan is p_1, the probability of the unfairness found by the regulator in the executives' salary allocation plan is p_2. Because the government regulator focuses on social benefits instead of its own interests, its own strategy won't be affected by payoff function.

The board of directors and its strategies. In China's joint-equity-enterprise, the board of directors is entitled to joining the salary allocation process. However, as the components, functions and procedures of China's board of directors are under the control the supervisors of upper levels, it is hard to undertake the performance examination on executives and general staff independently and fairly. Therefore, for their own interests, the board of directors will compromise to the executives. There are two strategies in the board of directors: approval and objection.

From the hypothesis and statement above, we can take the players as executives, the board of directors, general staff and government regulator. Assuming that the players in the game are I= {1, 2, 3, 4}, in which 1 is an executive, 2 is the board of directors, 3 is the general staff, and 4 is the government regulator. The strategies and game process of all the players are described as a strategy set marked by S. S_{ixy} shows that the player i's y strategy in the x game stage, so $S = \{S_{11}, S_{22}, S_{13}, S_{34}, S_{35}, S_{16}, S_{47}\}$,

$S_{111} = Fairness$, $S_{112} = Unfairness$; $S_{221} = Agreement$,

$S_{222} = Disagreement$; $S_{131} = AdjustmentPlan$,

$S_{132} = UnadjustmentPlan$; $S_{341} = Acceptance$, $S_{342} = Rejection$,

$S_{351} = PositiveWorking$, $S_{352} = NegativeSlowdown$;

$S_{161} = Renewal$, $S_{162} = Dismission$; $S_{47} = RadomSpotChecking$。

3 The Payoff Function of the Game Model

3.1 The Game Payoff Function of the Board of Directors

Assuming that the annual average income of a member of the board of directors is a, if the board of directors knows the executives' salary allocation plan is unfair, but still agrees with the plan, the unfairness is verified by government regulator, who considers the board of directors negligent in its duty. The board of directors will be punished, and assuming that the punishment number is h_1, and the probability of agreement of the board of directors is p_5; if the board of directors makes objections to the executives, through negotiation, the executives adjust their plan until gaining the agreement of the board of directors. Certainly, the agreement doesn't mean the complete fairness of the plan, but just the bilateral acceptance of the plan. Once this agreement is verified by the regulator, the punishment is still inevitable but reduced. Assuming the punishment number is h_2, the payoff function of the board of directors is:

$$U_2(S_{111}, S_{22}, S_{34}, S_{35}, S_{16}, S_{47}) = a$$

$$U_2(S_{112}, S_{221}, S_{35}, S_{36}, S_{16}, S_{47}) = P_5 a - P_5[h_1 P_1 P_2 - h_1(1-P_1) - h_1 P_1(1-P_2)]$$

$$U_2(S_{112}, S_{222}, S_{35}, S_{36}, S_{16}, S_{47}) = (1-P_5)a - (1-P_5)[h_2P_1P_2 - h_2(1-P_1) - h_2P_1(1-P_2)]$$
$$U_3(S_{111}, S_{341}, S_{351}, S_{161}, S_{47}) = d_0 + b_1 + d_0'$$
$$U_3(S_{112}, S_{341}, S_{352}, S_{161}, S_{47}) = d_0 + b_2 - eP_3P_4 + e(1-P_3) + eP_3(1-P_4)$$

$$U_3(S_{112}, S_{342}, S_{35}, S_{16}, S_{47}) = b_4 - b_3$$

3.2 The Game Payoff Function of the General Staff

Assuming that the basic salary of the general staff is d_0 , and per capita bonus of the general staff fairly decided by the executives is b_1; and the per capita bonus of the general staff unfairly decided is b_2; the unfairness causes the rejection, the reassignment compensation is b_3, and the job-hopping earnings is b_4; the incentive award given by the executives for proactive working is d'_0, the punishment for negative slowdown is e, the probability of spot checking on the general staff is p_3 and the probability of the checked slowdown is p_4, so the game payoff function of the general staff is :

$$U_3(S_{111}, S_{341}, S_{351}, S_{161}, S_{47}) = d_0 + b_1 + d_0'$$
$$U_3(S_{112}, S_{341}, S_{352}, S_{161}, S_{47}) = d_0 + b_2 - eP_3P_4 + e(1-P_3) + eP_3(1-P_4)$$
$$U_3(S_{112}, S_{342}, S_{35}, S_{16}, S_{47}) = b_4 - b_3$$

3.3 The Game Payoff Function of the Executives

Assuming the per capita basic salary of the executives is d, when the executives' decision on salary allocation plan is fair, the bonus they get is d_1, when unfair, the bonus is d_2, obviously, d_2 is much more than d_1. If the board of directors collaborates with the executives, it agrees with the plan with the awareness of unfairness. If the unfairness is checked by the government regulator and the punishment to the executives is f_1; the board of directors makes objections and the unfairness remains through negotiation, the punishment to the executives is f_2, the executives follows the advice of the board of directors and adjust the plan with negligible cost, the bonus after adjustment is d_3; the influencing factor of the general staff's slowdown for their dissatisfaction for salary on the executives' benefits is f_3; the general staff are dismissed for their dissatisfaction for salary, and the lost amount of the executives for the enterprise's compensation is f_4; the general staff holds a positive attitude to the fairness , and the improved benefits of the executives is f_5. So the executives' payoff function is:

$$U_1(S_{111}, S_{22}, S_{34}, S_{35}, S_{16}, S_{47}) = d + d_1 + f_5$$
$$U_1(S_{112}, S_{221}, S_{341}, S_{352}, S_{161}, S_{47}) = P_5(d + d_2) - P_5[f_1P_1P_2 - f_1(1-P_1) - f_1P_1(1-P_2)] - P_5f_3$$
$$U_1(S_{112}, S_{221}, S_{342}, S_{162}, S_{47}) = P_5(d + d_2) - P_5[f_1P_1P_2 - f_1(1-P_1) - f_1P_1(1-P_2)] - P_5f_4$$

$$U_1(S_{112}, S_{222}, S_{131}, S_{341}, S_{352}, S_{161}, S_{47}) = (1-P_5)(d+d_3) - (1-P_5)[f_2P_1P_2 - f_2(1-P_1) - f_2P_1(1-P_2)] - (1-P_5)f_3$$
$$U_1(S_{112}, S_{222}, S_{132}, S_{342}, S_{162}, S_{47}) = (1-P_5)d + d_2 - P_5f_2[P_1P_2 - (1-P_1) - P_1(1-P_2)] - P_5f_4$$

4 The Nash Equilibrium Results Analysis on the Interests Allocation of the Executives and General Staff

4.1 The Active Working Conditions of the General Staff

The expected income of the slowdown:

$$E(U_3(S_{352}, S_{-1}) = d_0 + b_2 + e(1 - 2P_3P_4) \tag{1}$$

The expected income of the active working:

$$E(U_3(S_{351}, S_{-1}) = d_0 + b_1 + d_0' \tag{2}$$

The active working conditions:

$$b_1 + d_0' \geq b_2 + e(1 - 2P_3P_4) \tag{3}$$

The results analysis. Because all the letters in formula (3) are positive numbers it can be concluded that:

When $2p_1p_2 \geqq 1$, the bigger e is, the bigger p_3 and p_4 are, and the positive working conditions are easier to be satisfied; on the contrary, the slowdown is easier to be made.

When $2p_1p_2 \leqq 1$, the smaller e is, the bigger p_3 and p_4 are, and the positive working conditions are easier to be satisfied; on the contrary, the bugger e is, p_3 and p_4 are smaller, and the slowdown is easier to be made.

Besides, if b_4 is big enough, it is of great possibility that the general staff won't accept the salary allocation plan and resign for other jobs, which is also a direct reason for the great labor mobility nowadays.

4.2 The Conditions for Executives to Make Fair Salary Allocation Plan

When the allocation is unfair, the expected income of the executives with the general staff's slowdown:

$$E(S_{112}, S_{352}, S_{-1}) = P_5[d + d_2 + f_1(1 - 2P_1P_2) - f_3] + (1 - P_5)[d + d_3 + f_2(1 - 2P_1P_2) - f_3] \tag{4}$$

When the allocation is fair, the executives' income: In the fair salary allocation plan, the executives' income is:$d+d_1+f_5$. Meanwhile, the executives make the fair allocation conditions:

$$d + d_1 + f_5 \geq P_5(d + d_2) + (1 - P_5)(d + d_3) + P_5[f_1(1 - 2P_1P_2) - f_3] + (1 - P_5)[f_2(1 - 2P_1P_2) - f_3] \tag{5}$$

Namely,

$$d + d_1 + f_5 \geq P_5(d_2 - d_3) + d + d_3 + P_5(1 - 2P_1P_2)(f_1 - f_2) + f_2(1 - 2P_1P_2) - f_3 \tag{6}$$

Because the letters in (6) are positive numbers, and $d_2 > d_3$, $f_1 > f_2$, it can be concluded: The bigger a,f_3,f_4,f_5 and f_1- f_2 are, the more willingly he executives formulate the fair allocation plan, on the contrary, the less willingly they formulate it.

When $2p_1p_2 \geqq 1$, because the special position of the board of directors,p_5 is in inferior position, meanwhile, the major deciding factors are p_1 and p_2.When the smaller $p_1$and

p_2 are, the less easily the conditions are satisfied for executives to make fair plan; on the contrary, the more easily the conditions are satisfied for executives to make fair plan

When $2p_1p_2 \leqq 1$, p_1, p_2 and p_5 are the factors for executives to formulate the plan, meanwhile, the bigger p_5 is, and the smaller p_1 and p_2 are, the less easily the conditions for executives to make fair plan; on the contrary, the more easily the conditions for executives to make fair plan

4.3 The Conditions for the Board of Directors to Give Play to Its Functions

When the plan is unfair, the expected income of the board:

$$E(S_{112}\text{ , }S_{221}\text{ , }S_{-1}) = P_5 a - P_5[h_1 P_1 P_2 - h_1(1-P_1) - h_1 P_1(1-P_2)] \quad (7)$$

Namely,

$$E(S_{112}\text{ , }S_{221}\text{ , }S_{-1}) = P_5 a - P_5 h_1(2P_1P_2 - 1) \quad (8)$$

When the plan is unfair, the dissenting expected income of the board:

$$E(S_{112}\text{ , }S_{222}\text{ , }S_{-1}) = (1-P_5)a - (1-P_5)[h_2 P_1 P_2 - h_2(1-P_1) - h_2 P_1(1-P_2)] \quad (9)$$

Namely,

$$E(S_{112}\text{ , }S_{222}\text{ , }S_{-1}) = (1-P_5)a - (1-P_5)h_2(2P_1P_2 - 1) \quad (10)$$

The dissenting conditions of the board:

$$(1-P_5)a - (1-P_5)h_2(2P_1P_2 - 1) \geq P_5 a - P_5 h_1(2P_1P_2 - 1) \quad (11)$$

Namely,

$$(1-2P_5)a \geq 2P_1P_2(h_2 - P_5h_1) + P_5h_1 + h_2 \quad (12)$$

The constraint conditions should be proposed to this issue: p_5 cannot be too big, $h_1$and h_2 have the same range ability, otherwise it is meaningless to discuss it. Because all the letters in (12) are positive numbers, it can be concluded:

When $h_2 \geqq h_1p_5$, the smaller h_2, p_1 and p_2 are, the bigger h_1 is, the more easily the conditions are satisfied to make objections to the unfair plan; on the contrary, the less easily the conditions are satisfied to make objections to the unfair plan.

When $h_2 \leqq h_1p_5$, the bigger h_1 , p_1 and p_2 are, the smaller h_2 is, the more easily the conditions are satisfied to make objections to the unfair plan; on the contrary, the less easily the conditions are satisfied to make objections to the unfair plan.

5 Conclusions

The utility will be maximized when the government regulates corporate salary allocation without any personal interests. Meanwhile, the dependence of the executives or the general workers on the government regulation will both be maximized. When the bigger the probability of the government's spot checking on the allocation plan is, the more efficient the spot checking is, and the severer the punishment to the executives is, the more willingly the executives formulate the fair allocation plan; if the conditions above are satisfied, the bigger the probability of the executives' spot checking on the working of the general staff, the more efficient the spot checking is, and the more actively the general staff are willing to work; meanwhile, the board will be more willing to supervise and make objections to the salary allocation process and results. Otherwise, the executives won't stop the trend to their own interests, and maximize their own interests at last. The general workers' strategies are more likely to be: ① if there are better opportunities, they will resign. ② If there are not any opportunities, they will slow down their work, unless the non-enterprise management level punishes slightly the negative slowdown, satisfying some of their mental need, which will still make the workers work actively.

References

1. Wang, Z.: A Course in Game Theory, pp. 148–182. China Renmin University Press, Beijing (November 2004)
2. Zhang, W.: Accounting Study on Human Resources, pp. 131–148. China Finance and Economy Press (2002)
3. Zhao, B.: A Game Analysis on Audit Quality Control of Certified Public Accountant. Accounting Research, 58–62 (April 2009)
4. Bu, D.: A Research on the Fairness of Executives' Compensation. Accounting Research, 39-48 (May 2009)
5. Wang, F.: Methods and Enlightenment from Executives' Salary Reform of Some Countries in International Financial Crisis. Economic Review, 102–105 (February 2002)
6. Gou, J.: Some Thoughts on Regulating Executives Salary in China's State-Owned Enterprise. China Soft Science, 189–192 (January 2010)

The Co-integration and Causality Relationship Research of Stock Index Futures IF1006 and HS300 Stock Index

Yuanzheng Wang[1,*], Yajing Xu[1], and Peng Liu[2]

[1] Dept. of Math. And Infor. Sci., Zhengzhou Univ. of Light Ind., P.R. China, 450002
[2] Hongta futures, Zhengzhou 450002, China
wang_yz00@sina.com

Abstract. To explore the intrinsic relationship between the China stock index futures and Stock Index, in this paper, we study the China stock index futures IF1006 which recently come into market and HS300 Stock Index with co-integration theory. Furthermore, the unilateral causality relationship between stock index futures IF1006 and HS300 Stock Index is also found by Engle-Granger causality test. Last, we analyze the affect of stock index futures impacts on stock index by co-integration model and error correction model.

Keywords: stock index futures IF1006, HS300 Stock Index, Co-integration, causation test.

1 Introduction

The smooth coming-into market of HS300 stock index futures on Apr. 16th, 2010, indicates the time of stock index futures comes, which implies the big change of Chinese finance market.

From the quotation opening on Apr. 16th to the delivery on Jun.18th, stock index futures IF1006 dropped on the whole. Within this period, it dropped to 2684 on May. 21st and rebounded a little then. Finally, it dropped to 2716.8 from the quotation opening index 3482. During 60 days, it dropped more than 700. Meanwhile, HS300 stock index also dropped during Apr. 16th to Jun. 18th, and finally dropped to 2696.9.

The stock market dramatically dropped after the stock index futures came-into market. Meanwhile, the research on relation between stock index and stock index futures became hot topics among experts. There were three major opinions as follows. The first opinion is that the mechanism of bi-directional transaction and the interference from foreign investment for stock index futures are major reasons to cause the drop of stock index. The second opinion is that the relation between stock index and stock index futures are concomitant but not causal. This opinion is majorly based on the experience of mature stock index futures markets. The third opinion is that stock index drives stock index futures. The reason is that the stock index market is relatively mature and invested more while the stock index futures market is invested less since it came into market just a few days ago.

* Corresponding author.

M. Zhou (Ed.): ISAEBD 2011, Part III, CCIS 210, pp. 541–545, 2011.

We can obtain the macro and micro features of the stock index and stock index futures markets though the research on co-relations between them and provides the results for reference by market managers, agents and investors. In this paper, we take advantage of co-integration theory in econometrics to analyze the delivery data of stock index futures IF1006 and HS300 from Apr. 16th to Jun. 18th according to the trends of stock index and stock index futures in the perspective of technical analysis, for exploring the inner relationship between them and discovering whether there exists dynamic balanced relationship and causality between them.

2 Causality Test

2.1 Scatter Graph

Fig. 1 shows the trends of IF1006 and HS300 from Apr. 16th to Jun. 18th with the sampling rate 30 minutes. The data of stock index futures and stock index are represented by time series $IF1006_t$ and $HS300_t$.

The red curve is the trend of HS300 and the black one is the trend of IF1006. From the figure we can see that the two time series have similar trends. Primarily, they may have co-integration relation. We further make co-integration test for them.

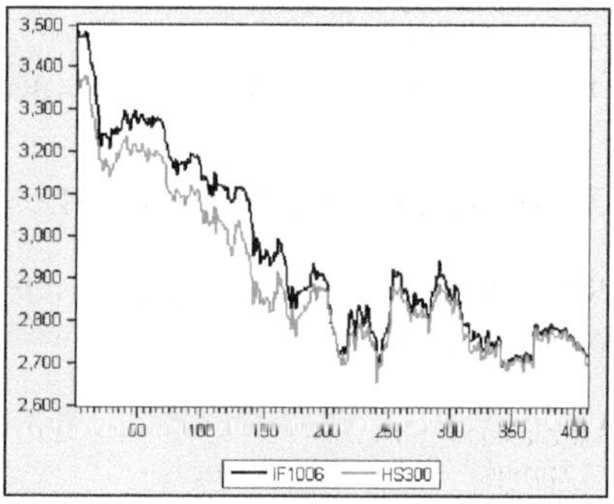

Fig. 1. The trends of IF1006 and HS3000 from Apr. 16th to Jun. 18th

2.2 Co-integration Test

According to the EG two step method of co-integration test[1], we further make co-integration test for $HS300_t$ and $IF1006_t$ by Eviews software[2].

Dependent Variable: HS300
Method: Least Squares
Date: 07/17/10 Time: 10:56
Sample: 1 410
Included observations: 410

Variable	Coefficient	Std. Error	t-Statistic	Prob.
C	332.3680	15.37125	21.62271	0.0000
IF1006	0.870804	0.005191	167.7589	0.0000

R-squared	0.985710	Mean dependent var	2904.498
Adjusted R-squared	0.985675	S.D. dependent var	185.0384
S.E. of regression	22.14687	Akaike info criterion	9.038136
Sum squared resid	200117.5	Schwarz criterion	9.057727
Log likelihood	-1850.818	Hannan-Quinn criter.	9.045887
F-statistic	28143.05	Durbin-Watson stat	0.201045
Prob(F-statistic)	0.000000		

Fig. 2. Regression model test

First, we build the regression model between the response series $HS300_t$ and the input series of $IF1006_t$ and show the result in Fig. 2. From the figure we can see that the F-test is significant and the coefficients of constant term and first order term derived from least square are also significant. The regression model is as follows.

$$HS300_t = 332.3680 + 0.870804\ IF1006_t + e_t \tag{1}$$

Second, we make the smoothness test for the residual error series $\{e_t\}$. Fig. 3 shows the ADF unit root test and PP unit root test for e_t

The first sub-figure of Fig. 3 shows the ADF unit root test without considering the heteroscedasticity of residual errors. The p value of t statistic $0.0063 < 0.01$, thus the zero assumption that e_t has unit root is denied. The second sub-figure shows the PP unit root test which considers the heteroscedasticity of residual errors. The p value of Adj-t statistic $0.0001 < 0.01$, thus the zero assumption that e_t has unit root is denied. Therefore, we can confirm e_t is smooth. In other words, the series $HS300_t$ and $IF1006_t$ have co-integration relation.

Augmented Dickey-Fuller Unit Root Test on E

Null Hypothesis: E has a unit root
Exogenous: None
Lag Length: 2 (Automatic based on SIC, MAXLAG=17)

		t-Statistic	Prob.*
Augmented Dickey-Fuller test statistic		-2.731008	0.0063
Test critical values:	1% level	-2.570656	
	5% level	-1.941604	
	10% level	-1.616177	

*MacKinnon (1996) one-sided p-values.

Phillips-Perron Unit Root Test on E

Null Hypothesis: E has a unit root
Exogenous: None
Bandwidth: 7 (Newey-West using Bartlett kernel)

		Adj. t-Stat	Prob.*
Phillips-Perron test statistic		-4.091933	0.0001
Test critical values:	1% level	-2.570628	
	5% level	-1.941600	
	10% level	-1.616180	

*MacKinnon (1996) one-sided p-values.

Fig. 3. Unit root test for e_t

3 Causality Test

Fig. 4 shows the result of causality test for $HS300_t$ and $IF1006_t$ by Eviews software.

Pairwise Granger Causality Tests
Date: 07/17/10 Time: 10:59
Sample: 1 410
Lags: 2

Null Hypothesis:	Obs	F-Statistic	Prob.
HS300 does not Granger Cause IF1006	408	0.73619	0.4796
IF1006 does not Granger Cause HS300		8.61620	0.0002

Pairwise Granger Causality Tests
Date: 07/17/10 Time: 11:01
Sample: 1 410
Lags: 3

Null Hypothesis:	Obs	F-Statistic	Prob.
HS300 does not Granger Cause IF1006	407	1.94932	0.1211
IF1006 does not Granger Cause HS300		6.44036	0.0003

Pairwise Granger Causality Tests
Date: 07/17/10 Time: 11:02
Sample: 1 410
Lags: 4

Null Hypothesis:	Obs	F-Statistic	Prob.
HS300 does not Granger Cause IF1006	406	1.72544	0.1435
IF1006 does not Granger Cause HS300		5.08129	0.0005

Fig. 4. Causality test result of Eviews

From the figure we can see that the test results with delay time with 2, 3, 4 periods indicate $HS300_t$ is not the reason of $IF1006_t$, but the vice versa situation exists.

4 Error Correctness Model

The co-integration regression model (1) reflects the long term and balanced relation between $IF1006_t$ and $HS300_t$.To study the short term and unstable feature, we take advantage of difference series $\nabla IF1006_t$, $\nabla HS300_t$ and early error series e_{t-1} to build ECM model.

$$\nabla HS300_t = \beta_0 \nabla IF1006_t + \beta_1 e_{t-1} + \varepsilon_t$$

Fig. 5 shows the least square model and the test result.

According to Fig. 5, the ECM model is as follows.

$$\nabla HS300_t = 0.781296 \nabla IF1006_t - 0.100431 e_{t-1} + \varepsilon_t \tag{2}$$

Dependent Variable: D(HS300)
Method: Least Squares
Date: 07/17/10 Time: 11:04
Sample (adjusted): 2 410
Included observations: 409 after adjustments

Variable	Coefficient	Std. Error	t-Statistic	Prob.
D(IF1006)	0.781296	0.026162	29.86336	0.0000
E(-1)	-0.100431	0.021340	-4.706176	0.0000

R-squared	0.686871	Mean dependent var	-1.705868
Adjusted R-squared	0.686101	S.D. dependent var	17.03020
S.E. of regression	9.541455	Akaike info criterion	7.354047
Sum squared resid	37053.02	Schwarz criterion	7.373674
Log likelihood	-1501.903	Hannan-Quinn criter.	7.361813
Durbin-Watson stat	2.382956		

Fig. 5. ECM model test

The result of model test and parameter test indicate that the model is significant, and the change of $IF1006_t$ impacts the change of $HS300_t$ significantly in the same period (the term of $\nabla IF1006_t$ β_0 is not zero significantly). Moreover, the early error of the co-integration model e_{t-1} impacts the change of $HS300_t$ significantly in the same period (β_1 is not zero significantly)

5 Conclusion

The co-integration test for $HS300_t$ and $IF1006_t$ shows that they have co-integration relationship. In other words, stock index futures and stock index have long term and balanced relationship; Granger causality test further shows that they have one-side causality, stock index futures IF1006 is the reason of stock index HS300, but not the vice versa. From the co-integration model (1) we can see that stock index will increase 0.870804 if stock index futures increases 1 point.

The error corrected model (2) shows that the change of stock index futures IF1006 impacts the change of stock index HS300 significantly in the same period (the term of

$\nabla IF1006_t$, β_0 is not zero significantly). In the view of its value 0.781296, the short term change of stock index futures IF1006 has relatively big impact on stock index HS300; The early error of co-integration model e_{t-1} impacts the change of stock index HS300 significantly in the same period (β_1 is not zero significantly), but the impact is not big. The unit adjusted ratio is – 0.100431.

The co-integration model and error corrected model make the long term balanced and short term relations between stock index futures IF1006 and stock index HS300 clear.

From the result of Granger causality test we can see that stock index futures drives the drop of stock index. The corresponding departments of the government should dampen the abnormal speculation by enhancing the monitoring to the cash flow of big or foreign investment organizations and properly adjusting the rule of stock index futures, for promoting the health development of stock market.

References

1. Wang, Y.: Applied Time Series Analysis, vol. 7. Renmin University of China Press, Beijing (2005)
2. Sun, J.: Ecnomitrics, vol. 9. Tsinghua University Press, Beijing (2004)
3. Box, G.E.P., Jenkins, G.M., Reinsel, G.C.: Time Series Analysis, Prediction and Control, vol. 9. China Statistics Press, Beijing (1997)
4. Pang, H.: Ecnomitrics, vol. 9. Science Press, Beijing (2004)

The Research on the Relationship between the Industrial Structure and Economic Growth in Henan Province — Positive Analysis Based on VAR Model

Yajing Xu* and Yuanzheng Wang

Dept. of Math. And Infor. Sci., Zhengzhou Univ. of Light Ind., P.R. China, 450002
xuyajing11@163.com

Abstract. To study the industrial structure of Henan province and reveal the inner rule of economy growth, in this paper, we take advantage of stable VAR model based pulse-response function and variance decomposition to analyze the relation between the tertiary industries of Henan and its economy growth. The data comes from the statistics of the GDP and ratios of tertiary industries in Henan from 1978 to 2009. The result shows that the primary and tertiary industries have no significant positive impact on the economy growth of Henan, while the latter is majorly influenced by the secondary industry. On the basis of these results, we give several suggestions to optimize the industrial structure of Henan.

Keywords: VAR model, pulse-response function, variance decomposition.

1 The Current Situation of Henan's Economy Growth and Industrial Structure

The classical theory of industrial economics shows that the change of a country's industrial structure is tightly related to its economy growth and the optimization and adjustment of the industrial structure inerrably reflect the well development of economy [1]. Therefore, we cannot avoid studying the evolution of industrial structure when studying economy growth. To study the industrial structure of Henan province and reveal the inner rule of economy growth, in this paper, we take advantage of stable VAR model based pulse-response function and variance decomposition to analyze the relation between the tertiary industries of Henan and its economy growth. The data comes from the statistics of the GDP and ratios of tertiary industries in Henan from 1978 to 2009.

Henan province is a big agricultural province and the agriculture of Henan plays an important role in China. To be specific, the plant area of wheat in Henan covers 21% of the total wheat plant area in China, and the output of wheat covers 27% of the total wheat output in China. Therefore, agriculture is the foundation for the development of

* Corresponding author.

M. Zhou (Ed.): ISAEBD 2011, Part III, CCIS 210, pp. 546–554, 2011.

Henan and may have strong impact on its economy growth. Moreover, Henan has a well developed transportation system, rich natural resource, and a relatively strong industrial foundation. In the end of 11th Five-Year, the increase of secondary industry, especially the increase of industrial output, covers almost half of Henan's GDP. Thus, we can conclude that the secondary industry plays an important role in Henan's economy and has significant positive impact on its economy growth. However, the irrational industrial structure of Henan has not been changed dramatically with economy growth ever since a long time ago: high energy consuming and high pollution resource industry is still the mainstay industry of Henan province. In 2009, the ratios of primary industry, secondary industry and tertiary industry in Henan are 14.2%、56.5% and 29.3%, respectively, where the ratio of the tertiary industry is still low and increases too slowly. With the enhancement of the environmental protection consciousness, such an irrational industry structure will be more and more improper for the rapid economy growth. Thus, there is a need to study the relationship between industrial structure and economy growth for Henan and find approaches for prompting the fast transformation of Henan's industrial structure.

2 Model Building and Data Analysis

2.1 Data and Variables

The representative indexes of industrial structure usually include the value structure, the labor structure, the capital structure, and technical structure of the primary, secondary, and tertiary industries, which describe the industrial structure from different perspectives[2]. In this paper, we use the macro economy index GDP to represent economy growth and use the ratios of tertiary industries' values in GDP (denoted as W1, W2, W3). The data are referred from 2010 Henan Annual Statistic (1978-2009). To remove the heteroscedasticity which is caused by introducing these variables into one model, we apply natural logarithm transformation to GDP, W1, W2 and W3, which are denoted as lnGDP、lnW1、lnW2, lnW3 respectively. In this way, we do not change the property and co-integration of the data and can obtain stable series easily[3]. The quantitative analysis tool used in this paper is EView 6.

2.2 Build VAR Model

2.2.1 Select Delay Order

The delay order should be selected before building the VAR model of lnGDP、lnW1, lnW2, lnW3. The delay order is usually expected to be big enough for reflecting the dynamic features of the model. Otherwise, the lag correlation of errors may be serious and cause the inconsistency of the estimated parameters. However, if a too big delay order is selected, the parameters to estimate will be too many to impact the effectiveness of estimated parameters. There are several metrics for selecting delay orders including LR statistics, AIC and SC[4]. Since the size of the data used in this paper is very limited, we just select a delay order from 1 to 3.

Fig. 1 shows the AIC, SC and LR statistics of different delay orders, respectively. According to the minimum AIC strategy and the stability of the models, and considering R^2, we select 2 as the delay order.

VAR Lag Order Selection Criteria
Endogenous variables: LNGDP LNW1 LNW2 LNW3
Exogenous variables: C
Date: 02/06/11 Time: 22:46
Sample: 1978 2009
Included observations: 29

Lag	LogL	LR	FPE	AIC	SC	HQ
0	133.4164	NA	1.56e-09	-8.925269	-8.736677	-8.866204
1	236.5283	170.6680*	3.90e-12	-14.93299	-13.99002*	-14.63766*
2	253.6112	23.56265	3.88e-12*	-15.00767*	-13.31034	-14.47609
3	265.5301	13.15182	6.22e-12	-14.72621	-12.27451	-13.95837

* indicates lag order selected by the criterion
LR: sequential modified LR test statistic (each test at 5% level)
FPE: Final prediction error
AIC: Akaike information criterion
SC: Schwarz information criterion
HQ: Hannan-Quinn information criterion

Fig. 1. Select delay order

2.2.2 Parameter Estimation

Fig. 2 shows the estimated parameters of the VAR model when the delay order is set to be 2.

Vector Autoregression Estimates

Vector Autoregression Estimates
Date: 02/13/11 Time: 06:18
Sample (adjusted): 1980 2009
Included observations: 30 after adjustments
Standard errors in ( ) & t-statistics in [ ]

	LNGDP	LNW1	LNW2	LNW3
LNGDP(-1)	-0.098140	-0.305046	0.514761	-0.292747
	(0.16023)	(0.36747)	(0.22688)	(0.19240)
	[-0.61874]	[-0.83013]	[2.26884]	[-1.52158]
LNGDP(-2)	-0.273514	0.201521	-0.163635	0.328057
	(0.17594)	(0.40351)	(0.24914)	(0.21127)
	[-1.55456]	[0.49942]	[-0.65681]	[1.55281]
LNW1(-1)	-0.125900	0.745184	-0.080270	0.117800
	(0.21122)	(0.48441)	(0.29909)	(0.25362)
	[-0.59607]	[1.53833]	[-0.26839]	[0.46447]
LNW1(-2)	0.131361	0.624897	-0.279964	9.76E-05
	(0.22922)	(0.52571)	(0.32458)	(0.27524)
	[0.57307]	[1.18868]	[-0.86254]	[0.00035]
LNW2(-1)	0.229637	-0.008757	0.698297	-0.067616
	(0.33622)	(0.77109)	(0.47609)	(0.40372)
	[0.68300]	[-0.01136]	[1.46674]	[-0.16748]
LNW2(-2)	-0.191738	0.874248	-0.537919	0.207255
	(0.32720)	(0.75040)	(0.46331)	(0.39289)
	[-0.58600]	[1.16505]	[-1.16103]	[0.52752]
LNW3(-1)	-0.549592	0.001183	-0.055215	0.969455
	(0.26403)	(0.60552)	(0.37386)	(0.31704)
	[-2.08157]	[0.00195]	[-0.14769]	[3.05787]
LNW3(-2)	0.470619	0.105223	-0.045332	0.030632
	(0.27169)	(0.62311)	(0.38472)	(0.32624)
	[1.73216]	[0.16887]	[-0.11783]	[0.09389]
C	6.568062	-4.396776	3.048181	-1.062555
	(1.77777)	(4.07716)	(2.51733)	(2.13469)
	[3.69455]	[-1.07839]	[1.21088]	[-0.49776]

Vector Autoregression Estimates

R-squared	0.534728	0.972117	0.835732	0.967579
Adj. R-squared	0.357482	0.961496	0.911249	0.955228
Sum sq. resids	0.018551	0.097571	0.037195	0.026747
S.E. equation	0.029721	0.068163	0.042086	0.035688
F-statistic	3.016866	91.51980	38.21955	78.34142
Log likelihood	68.25861	43.35740	57.82349	62.76981
Akaike AIC	-3.950574	-2.290494	-3.254899	-3.584654
Schwarz SC	-3.530215	-1.870134	-2.834540	-3.164295
Mean dependent	4.712041	3.272123	3.781556	3.311909
S.D. dependent	0.037079	0.347373	0.141269	0.168865

Determinant resid covariance (dof adj.)	1.32E-12
Determinant resid covariance	3.18E-13
Log likelihood	261.3877
Akaike information criterion	-15.02585
Schwarz criterion	-13.34441

Fig. 2. Parameter estimation of VAR model

The estimated VAR(2) model can be represented as follows:

$$\begin{bmatrix} \ln gdp \\ \ln w1 \\ \ln w2 \\ \ln w3 \end{bmatrix}_t = \begin{bmatrix} 6.568 \\ -4.397 \\ 3.048 \\ -1.063 \end{bmatrix} + \begin{bmatrix} -0.099 & -0.126 & 0.230 & -0.550 \\ -0.305 & 0.745 & -0.009 & 0.001 \\ 0.515 & -0.080 & 0.698 & -0.055 \\ -0.293 & 0.118 & -0.068 & 0.969 \end{bmatrix} \begin{bmatrix} \ln gdp \\ \ln w1 \\ \ln w2 \\ \ln w3 \end{bmatrix}_{t-1}$$

$$+ \begin{bmatrix} -0.274 & 0.131 & -0.192 & 0.471 \\ 0.202 & 0.625 & 0.874 & 0.105 \\ -0.164 & -0.280 & -0.538 & -0.045 \\ 0.328 & 0.001 & 0.207 & 0.031 \end{bmatrix} \begin{bmatrix} \ln gdp \\ \ln w1 \\ \ln w2 \\ \ln w3 \end{bmatrix}_{t-2} + \begin{bmatrix} \varepsilon_0 \\ \varepsilon_1 \\ \varepsilon_2 \\ \varepsilon_3 \end{bmatrix}_t$$

where the coefficients of determination for three regression functions are 0.419002, 0.966044 and 0.968977, respectively, which denotes that the explained information of lnGDP by the first and second delay orders of lnGDP、lnW3、lnE3 are not too much, while the other two ones have more explanatory information. It shows that the condition of the tertiary industry cannot significantly reflect the economy growth of Henan and thus cannot explain the latter well. In contrast, the economy growth can explain the development of the tertiary industry well in Henan.

2.3 Test VAR Model

2.3.1 The Stability of VAR Model

If the reciprocals of all solutions for the AR feature equations of a VAR are in the circle whose radius is equal to one, we can regard the model as stable[4]. Fig. 3 shows that all solutions are indeed in the circle whose radius is equal to one. Thus, the VAR(2) model is stable and the following analysis is effective.

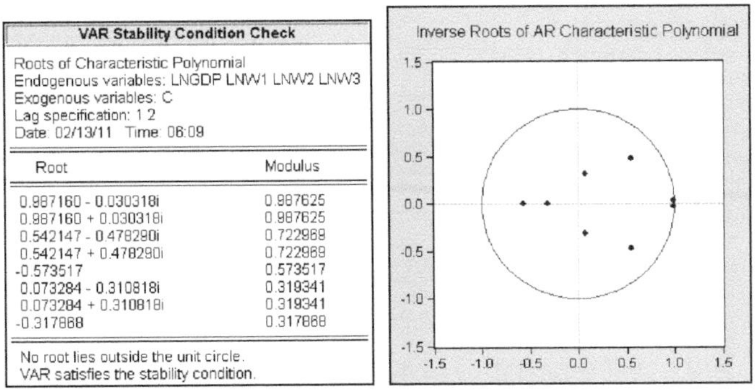

VAR Stability Condition Check

Roots of Characteristic Polynomial
Endogenous variables: LNGDP LNW1 LNW2 LNW3
Exogenous variables: C
Lag specification: 1 2
Date: 02/13/11 Time: 06:09

Root	Modulus
0.987160 - 0.030318i	0.987625
0.987160 + 0.030318i	0.987625
0.542147 - 0.478290i	0.722969
0.542147 + 0.478290i	0.722969
-0.573517	0.573517
0.073284 - 0.310818i	0.319341
0.073284 + 0.310818i	0.319341
-0.317868	0.317868

No root lies outside the unit circle.
VAR satisfies the stability condition.

Fig. 3. VAR stability Condition Check

2.3.2 The Normality Test of Residual Errors

The test of normality for the residual errors of a VAR model is the extension of J-B test of normality for residual errors in the case of multiple variables. It compares the third and fourth order residual error squares with the square from standard normal distribution[5]. Fig. 4 shows that the hypothesis that the residual errors follow a multiple variable normal distribution cannot be denied with the significance level 5%.

Component	Jarque-Bera	df	Prob.
1	2.287563	2	0.3186
2	2.907035	2	0.2337
3	4.620255	2	0.0992
4	4.535941	2	0.1035
Joint	14.35079	8	0.0731

Fig. 4. The normality test of residual errors

2.3.3 The Lag Correlation Test of Residual Errors

The original assumption of LM lag correlation test is that the series to test does not have at most m-th lag correlation. Fig. 5 shows that the hypothesis that the series of residual errors does not have lag correlation cannot be denied with the significance level 5%.

2.3.4 The Heteroscedasticity Test of Residual Errors

Heteroscedasticity test is done by using the series of residual errors to regress each explanatory variable and the time of their cross terms. Fig. 6 shows that the hypothesis that the series of residual errors does not have heteroscedasticity cannot be denied with the significance level 5%.

From the test we find that the statistic property of the VAR(2) model is good and it can be used for analyzing the relationship between the tertiary industry and the economy growth in Henan through pulse-response function and variance decomposition.

VAR Residual Serial Correlation LM T...
Null Hypothesis: no serial correlation ...
Date: 02/06/11 Time: 23:01
Sample: 1978 2009
Included observations: 30

Lags	LM-Stat	Prob
1	14.45497	0.5649
2	25.71014	0.0582
3	14.60297	0.5539
4	5.676507	0.9912
5	11.70509	0.7640
6	21.96196	0.1444
7	13.44728	0.6398
8	12.38342	0.7172
9	18.51770	0.2945
10	8.537889	0.9312
11	19.77313	0.2306
12	12.59333	0.7022

Probs from chi-square with 16 df.

Fig. 5. The lag correlation test of residual errors

VAR Residual Heteroskedasticity Tests: No Cross Terms (only levels and squares)
Date: 02/13/11 Time: 06:15
Sample: 1978 2009
Included observations: 30

Joint test:

Chi-sq	df	Prob.
167.9293	160	0.3180

Individual components:

Dependent	R-squared	F(16,13)	Prob.	Chi-sq(16)	Prob.
res1*res1	0.542770	0.964505	0.5341	16.28310	0.4334
res2*res2	0.406281	0.555993	0.8674	12.18844	0.7309
res3*res3	0.538223	0.947008	0.5477	16.14669	0.4428
res4*res4	0.532155	0.924186	0.5656	15.96465	0.4554
res2*res1	0.671149	1.658225	0.1814	20.13447	0.2142
res3*res1	0.704752	1.939427	0.1169	21.14257	0.1731
res3*res2	0.401789	0.545717	0.8747	12.05367	0.7403
res4*res1	0.700737	1.902505	0.1238	21.02212	0.1777
res4*res2	0.598683	1.212085	0.3676	17.96050	0.3262
res4*res3	0.579535	1.119883	0.4239	17.38604	0.3611

Fig. 6. The heteroscedasticity test of residual errors

2.4 VAR(2) Based Pulse-Response Function and Variance Decomposition Analysis

2.4.1 Pulse-Response Function Analysis

In a VAR system, the attack of an endogenous variable's stochastic disturbance will directly influence itself and propagate the influence to other endogenous variables by the dynamic structure of the model. Pulse-response function is used for measuring the impact of a standard deviation attack (pulse) from the disturbance term of an endogenous variable to the variable itself and other endogenous variables' current and future values.

Fig. 7 shows the response of lnGDP to the pulses of lnGDP, lnW1, lnW2, and lnW3, where the real lines denote pulse-response functions and dashed lines denote the differences between the plus and minus two times of standard deviation.

1) The first sub-figure shows the response of lnGDP to the pulse of itself. From the figure we can see that lnGDP responds to the pulse instantly and the response is 0.03 in the first year. After the first year, the impact from the pulse decreases fast and becomes zero after three years. In the fourth year the impact reoccurs but the value is minus. From then on, the impact gradually becomes zero.

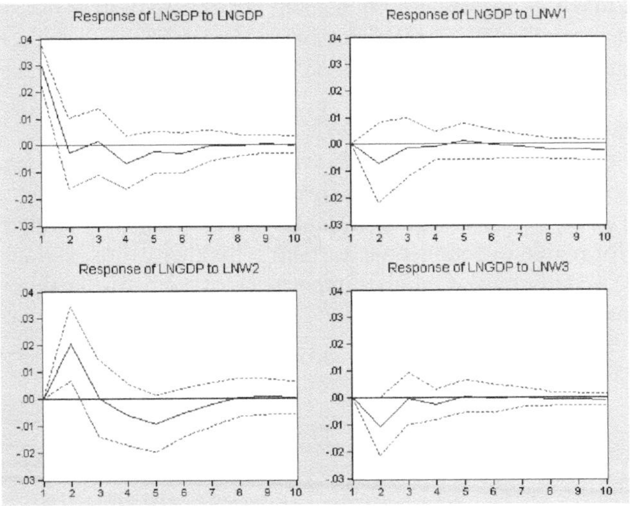

Fig. 7. Pulse-response function

2) The second sub-figure shows the response of lnGDP to the pulse of lnW1. From the figure we can see that lnGDP does not responds to the pulse instantly and the response is zero in the first year. In the second year, the response of lnGDP is biggest but negative. After the third year, the impact from the pulse gradually decreases to be zero. It implies that the economy growth of Henan does not respond to the change of the primary industry's ratio instantly. In the short term, the increase of the primary industry's ratio has no positive impact on the economy growth of Henan. In the long term, the positive impact exists but it is not significant.

3) The third sub-figure shows the response of lnGDP to the pulse of lnW2. From the figure we can see that lnGDP does not responds to the pulse instantly too and the response is zero in the first year. In the second year, the response of lnGDP is biggest and positive (0.02). From then on, the impact from the pulse gradually decreases. In the third year, the impact almost becomes zero and becomes negative in the following years. Finaly, it becomes zero again. It implies that the economy growth of Henan does not respond to the change of the secondary industry's ratio instantly. In the second year, the increase of the secondary industry's ratio has relatively big positive impact on the economy growth of Henan.

4) The fourth sub-figure shows the response of lnGDP to the pulse of lnW3. From the figure we can see that lnGDP does not respond to the pulse instantly and the response is zero in the first period. In the second period, the response of lnGDP is biggest but negative (-0.01). After the third period, the impact from the pulse gradually decreases to be zero. It implies that the economy growth of Henan does not respond to the change of the tertiary industry's ratio instantly. In the short term, the increase of the tertiary industry's ratio has no positive impact on the economy growth of Henan. In the long term, the positive impact exists but it is not significant.

Comprehensively, neither the response of lnGDP to the pulses of lnW1 nor that for the pulse of lnW3 is big while both of them are negative. In contrast, the response of lnGDP to the pulse of lnW2 is relatively big, which implies that the economy growth of Henan is majorly influenced by the secondary industry's development.

2.4.2 Variance Decomposition

Another method of analyzing the dynamic property of VAR models is variance decomposition. Its main idea is to analyze the contribution of each new information attack to the change of endogenous variables and thus knows the relative importance of each new information to endogenous variables. In other words, variance decomposition is a method of studying the relative importance of each stochastic disturbance which has impact on endogenous variables[5].

We analyze the contributions of lnGDP, lnW1, lnW2 and lnW3 to the change of lnGDP by variance decomposition.

Variance Decomposition of LNGDP

Period	S.E.	LNGDP	LNW1	LNW2	LNW3
1	0.029721	100.0000	0.000000	0.000000	0.000000
2	0.038481	60.19485	3.237558	28.77542	7.792175
3	0.038537	60.15880	3.369095	28.69179	7.780313
4	0.039685	59.59384	3.221642	29.40063	7.783887
5	0.040885	56.52920	3.100419	33.02172	7.348658
6	0.041338	55.81836	3.038802	33.93728	7.205558
7	0.041415	55.61524	3.073912	34.13194	7.178911
8	0.041468	55.47303	3.284770	34.04953	7.192672
9	0.041540	55.28573	3.554543	33.95773	7.201999
10	0.041621	55.07655	3.862060	33.82858	7.232809

Cholesky Ordering: LNGDP LNW1 LNW2 LNW3

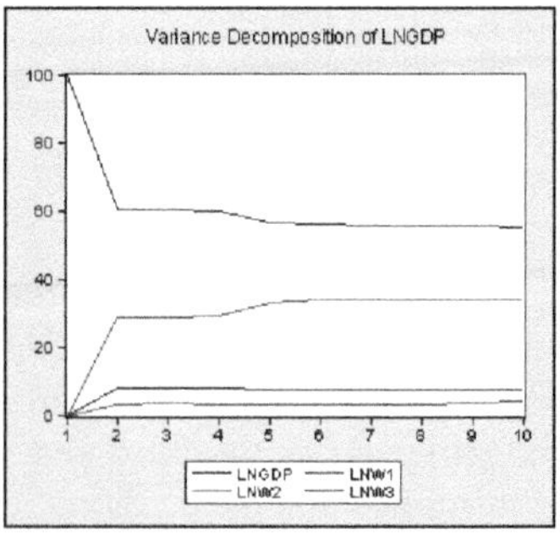

Fig. 8. Variance decomposition

The left sub-Fig. of Fig. 8 shows that in the first period, the variance of lnGDP's predictions is totally caused by the disturbance of lnGDP. In the second period, 60.19% of the variance of lnGDP's predictions is caused by the disturbance of lnGDP, while 3.24% of it is caused by the disturbance of lnW1, 28.78% of it is caused by the disturbance of lnW2and the remaining 7.79% is caused by the disturbance of lnW3. Then the decomposition of lnGDP is almost stable in the following periods, where 55.08% of the variance of lnGDP's predictions is caused by the disturbance of lnGDP, 3.86% of it is caused by the disturbance of lnW1, 33.83% of it is caused by the disturbance of lnW2 and the remaining 7.23% is caused by the disturbance of lnW3.

The right sub-figure of Fig. 8 shows the similar result, that is, the ratios of the variance of lnGDP's predictions caused by each disturbance term become stable after the first two periods.

The result of variance decomposition shows that the ratios of the variance of lnGDP's predictions caused by different disturbance terms become stable as time goes by. On the whole, the variance of lnGDP's predictions is majorly caused by the disturbance of lnW2 and minorly caused by those of lnW1 and lnW3, which is in line with the result of pulse-response function analysis.

3 Conclusion and Suggestion

In this paper, we took advantage of the VAR based dynamic economy quantitative analysis approach to perform positive analysis for the relationship between the tertiary industries of Henan and its economy growth. The result shows that the mainstay industry to push the development of Henan's economy is its secondary industry, while the contributions of the primary and tertiary industry are relatively low and have no significant positive impact on economy growth. It implies that the development of Henan's economy still suffers imbalance, inharmony and insustainability. The foundation of agriculture is still weak and the development of the tertiary industry is slow. According to the situation of Henan, we think that Henan province should follow the following action points for speeding up the economy growth:

1) Develop agriculture rapidly and push the modernization of agriculture positively

Henan is a big agricultural province and a major commodity grain production base of China. Agriculture should be a growth pole of economy development. In the recently released The outline of constructing Zhongyuan economic area, the Provincial Party committee and government of Henan have pointed out that we have to follow the theme of scientific thought of development and the masterstroke of changing the way of developing economy, for exploring a basic way of harmonic and scientific development which avoids sacrificing agriculture, grain, ecosystem and environment. The outline pinpoints the future direction of Henan's industrial adjustment. Henan should gasp the opportunity to speed up the construction of agricultural bases, enhance the adjustment of agricultural structure, optimize the types of plants, and push the transformations a) from plants to gardening; b) from agriculture to animal husbandry; c) from agricultural economy to agro-product processing, on the basis of enhancing the grain production. Moreover, Henan should help farmers to improve their skill of production and management, push the modernization of agriculture positively, change the way of running agriculture, widely take advantage of modern science and technology, improve the efficiency and benefit of agricultural production, and gradually realize the transformation from a big agricultural province to a strong agricultural province.

2) Enhance the competitive industries and adjust the industrial structure positively

Henan has rich natural resources such as minerals, power source, and has the foundation of manufacturing and mining industry. Henan has to take the way of New industrialization and informatization to change and improve the traditional competitive industries such as chemical engineering, nonferrous metal, food and spinning, start up new industries such as energy-saving, environment protection and new materials positively, develop the industries with high growthiness such as new power vesicles and electronic information rapidly, speed up the development of agro-product processing to promote the harmonic and good development of agriculture and industry, for enhance the pulling function of the development of industry to economy growth.

3) Optimize the structure of tertiary industry and develop modern service industry rapidly

In future, Henan should try hard to increase the ratio of service industry's value in GDP and the ratio of service industry's labor in the total labor, and invest more in modern service industry, especially the financial industry which can enhance the economy strongly and have good growthiness, and the cultural industry and the travel industry which already have dramatic advantages compared with other regions of China, for enhancing their industrialization. Meanwhile, Henan should enhance the industrialization of education by encouraging the diversity of school-running subjects and school-running mechanisms and make culture, education, fiancé and science directly enhance economy growth and thus enhance the GDP growth.

References

1. Ji, Y., Wu, Y.: The foundation and Realization of Relationship Co-integration Model of Industrial Structure and Economic Growth. Modern Economic Research (6) (2006)
2. Liu, W., Li, S.: Industrial Structure and Economic Growth. Chinese Industrial Economic (5) (2002)
3. Gao, T.: Econometrics Analysis Methods and Modeling. Tsinghua University Press, Beijing (2009)
4. Pan, S.: Econometrics Junior Tutorials, vol. 8. Tsinghua University Press, Beijing (2009)
5. Yin, X.: The Principle and Operation of Econometrics, vol. 8. ChongQing University Press (2009)

Analysis on Disclosure and Transparency in Published Accounting Information of Pakistani Listed Companies

Gohar Ali, Zhiwei Ni, and Chen Zhang

School of Management, Hefei University of Technology
Hefei, Anhui, China 230009
agafridipk@gmail.com, {nzwgd,zhangchen}@hfut.edu.cn

Abstract. This paper aims to analyze the published information by companies listed on Karachi Stock Exchange (KSE), Pakistan, for transparency & disclosure in order to check for the prevailing practices of corporate governances in the market. The published information from annual reports of 83 firms listed on KSE has been analyzed, using different performance measures in the form financial ratios. The ratios have regresses against market value for determination of any material relationship between these indicators and market valuation of these firms. We have found no significant link between these indicators and market valuation of stocks in our sample and concluded that thorough disclosure & transparency does not exist in these reports, which indicates poor corporate governance regime in the market. The market prices are mostly affected by speculations along with other macroeconomic and political factors.

Keywords: corporate governance, financial accounting information, disclosure & transparency, Pakistani capital market.

1 Introduction

Accounting information about the performance and financial position of every firm is declared by the management in the form of annual reports or interim reports, which provides the sole source of information for the shareholders to base their economic decisions of further investment or disinvestment in the firm's equity shares. These reports are compiled usually according to the local and international legal requirements. In a well organized and developed market, investors refer to these reports before making any investment decision with the premise of understandability, relevance, consistency, comparability, reliability and objectivity as the incorporated principles in compilation and content of these reports.

The information presented in any such reports has a very solid position in terms of the economic and efficient decision making process of all relevant stakeholders. It helps understand the existing situation of the firm and facilitates the forecasting efforts about the performance of the firms. It also gives an insight in the financial position and future profitability of the firm by providing the details of the available funds to the management for further investment thus ensuring future earnings and

M. Zhou (Ed.): ISAEBD 2011, Part III, CCIS 210, pp. 555–563, 2011.

growth. These reports also carry details about the level of education, skills, experience and overall ability of the management to handle the shareholders' wealth. There is an integral problem associated with the reports that these do not give any details about the intangible factors inside and outside of the firm affecting its operations, profitability and status.

Corporate governance cannot be imagined without the basic principles of transparency and disclosure. These are the essence of an efficient risk assessment process carried out by different stakeholders of the firms before taking any economic decision. Thorough disclosure and transparency should be incorporated in all disclosed information relating to financial & non-financial aspects of the firm in order to ensure safeguard of shareholders' interests, which is the prime motive of corporate governance.

Research has shown that high degree of disclosure and transparency can result in lower cost of capital for the firms. Chen et al. (2009) confirmed a strong negative relationship between corporate governance and cost of equity capital for firms in emerging markets, where investors are ready to pay high premium for shares of firm those have better governance practices and more open disclosure policy[1]. It not only enables the management to better exploit opportunities for further growth and profitability but also enable the outside stakeholders in their risk assessment process. Enough disclosure and transparency is also essential for judging the compliance level of the corporation to legal, social and environmental safety requirements thus ensuring high confidence of stakeholders, thus greatly reduce the stock market liquidity problems for firms.

There could be as many aspects as possible for judging the disclosure and transparency in the published reports of corporation. It must give details about the ownership pattern and voting rights of the shareholders along with complete details about the Board of Directors (BOD) and top management of the firm. There should be elaborate explanation about the distribution of authorities and responsibilities of shareholders, Board and management. The financial performance in the form of different statements presented must be duly audited by an independent auditor to show the reliability of the data disclosed. These reports must also contain information about existing material transactions concerning staff, stakeholders, managerial compensation, projects under progress and expected projects with relevant risk and return.

2 Literature Review

Corporate governance is a multifaceted phenomenon, where the governance carries aspects to be monitored and ensured in order to ensure high degree of regulatory and governance regime. A huge amount of literature is available on studies related to these different aspects. Financial accounting information is the data released by corporations in compliance with local and international accounting standards in the form of different reports for the purpose of understanding and analysis of all stakeholders. Research has proved the existence of a positive relationship between the accounting information and economic performance of firm in specific and overall economy in journal. It has been proved that financial accounting information plays a significant role of governance, which ultimately lead to high economic performance[2]. In contrast, there is evidence that poor governed firms at times have performed better than good governed firms but the associated risk with poor governed firms still remains the highest, thus resulting in low market efficiency and poor stock price performance for these poorly governed firms[3]. Brown et al. (2006) confirmed no significant relationship between market valuation and governance measure relevant to accounting and public policy including stock option expensing and other audit-related provisions[4]. Ammann et al. (2011) found a very strong link between firm valuation and firm-level corporate governance. They have analyzed the effects of corporate governance practices at both individual and aggregated form as indices and have observed the same strong relationship between corporate governance and market valuation.[5, 6]

The accounting system applicable in a country is affected by different factors including social, political, legal and economic. Any such difference has been confirmed by many studies. The existence of different accounting environments between different countries like China and France has been confirmed by Ding, Yuan. It has also been empirically proved that local circumstances positively affect the level of disclosure adequacy[7]. Country-specific factors affecting disclosure have been studied by numerous researchers e.g. the level of disclosure has been affected by sector of firms and no significant effects were observed for profitability, size and debt-equity ratio for different firms in United Arab Emirates (UAE)[8].

Disclosure and transparency are pre-requisites of good corporate governance. Firms with high degree of transparency and disclosure in accounting information and lower asymmetric information always enjoy placement of premium on their stock in market. Empirical studies have proved a positive relationship between float and degree of disclosure & transparency in the emerging markets especially Asian economies[9]. Transparency & disclosure have proved to be a set of strong corporate governance measures and resulting in high performance in firms possessing it in higher degrees in Taiwanese stock market[10].

Disclosure and transparency not only ensure economic performance but also safeguard against sharp decline and losses in case of financial crisis. Baek et al. (2004) studied the effects of financial crisis on different firm in 1997 Korean financial crisis and found a functional relationship between changes in market value and corporate governance measures adopted at firm-level. They found that firm with high degree of disclosure and accessibility to external finances also suffered less of the effects of the crisis[11]. Similar results were achieved by Barton, et al. (2004), where they observed lower decline in market prices, during New York Stock Exchange market crash in October 1929, of firms possessing high quality in their financial reporting. There was direct relation between managers' incentive and quality of information provided to the investors[12]. Tadessee (2005) suggested a strong relation between mandatory disclosure and banking industry stability in a study conducted over 49 different countries for 1990's[13]. Disclosure and transparency improve the investment efficiency of the firm also and results in less deviation from expected investment level or over sensitivity to other macroeconomic factors[14].

The availability of inside information might result in entrepreneurs' inclination for extracting private benefits instead of exploiting profitable investment opportunities. Increased disclosure limit any such possibility for entrepreneurs and can ensure high efficiency of investment. Along with efficient investment improved disclosure can also guarantee better legal shareholder protection[15].

The concept of corporate governance is relatively new in emerging markets and provides a vast area of research in this stage of development. Research needs to be done to explore further in this area in order to ensure stability of the development process. Countries like India also have evidence of positive relationship between firm market value and an overall governance index[16].

3 Pakistani Market

Pakistani stock market started developing in the early 90's when the government adopted the process of privatization and putting back the policy of nationalizing all financial and non-financial entities including banks and developing corporations in different sectors. Since then the Securities & Exchange Commission of Pakistan (SECP) has put forward different regulations and measures to ensure the development of market and investors' protection, including the enforcement of Code of Corporate Governance in 2002. There are three stock exchanges now operating in the country titled as Karachi Stock Exchange, Lahore Stock Exchange (LSE) and Islamabad Stock Exchange (ISE).

KSE is the biggest stock exchange and located in the financial and business hub of Pakistan i.e. Karachi, a city which is home to most of the head offices of different firms listed on KSE. Till 2011, there have been a net total of 827 listed companies listed on KSE while the total number of listed companies in the country tops 1000. At KSE different indexes are used name KSE 100 Index, KSE 50 Index, KSE 30 Index, which comprises of top 100, 50 and 30 companies of the market respectively. KSE 100 companies cover almost more than 90% of the total market capitalization. This index was launched in 1991 with a base of 1000 points.

There has been very limited research done so far on Pakistani market in the area under consideration and it can provide huge opportunities for the researchers to explore more into this emerging market. The accounting practices in Pakistan are quite well developed and based on its legal properties it can be assigned as a code law country. The country has adopted all accounting principles of IAS. There are certain limitations which affect the level of investors' protection including inefficient judicial system and law enforcement[17].

4 Research Scope

4.1 Sample and Selection Criteria

Initially all KSE 100 index companies were selected for analysis, but due to non-availability of annual reports for some of the companies for the period under study, i.e. 2005-2009, the sample was reduced to 83 companies which still consists of all companies included in KSE 30 Index and KSE 50 Index, comprising more than 90% of the total market capitalization. In order to analyze the exact role of data provided in the annual reports, all ratios have been calculated using the data provided in these reports instead of using the ratios published already there.

4.2 Tools for Analysis

This study has focused on assessing the extent of disclosure and transparency in published accounting information and its role in market valuation of stock on capital markets in two steps. Initially, with the assumption of being proper disclosure and transparency in the published annual reports, we have calculated different financial ratios using the published data instead of using the published ratios given in the annual reports of 83 firms in the sample. In the next stage, an econometric model has been used consisting market value of these firm, measured in terms of Tobin Q's ratio, being the dependent variable and the different financial ratios, being different performance indicators, as independent variables. A regression analysis has been conducted by Random-Effects GLS regression method using the STATA version 9. The purpose of the model is to look for any material relationship between market value of the firm, as perceived by the investors, and relevant performance results published by the management regarding these companies. A correlation matrix for all different indicators has also been calculated using the same software. The correlation analysis looks into any significant correlation existing between all these indicators. Any significant findings of relationship between these performance indicators and market valuation will highlight the existence of thorough disclosure and transparency in these reports else any such deviation will indicate the lack of thorough disclosure and transparency and it can be concluded that the market is operating mostly under forces of speculations.

In order to assess the performance of management in term of managing shareholders' wealth, different financial ratios have been utilized here so that the published results can be better explained and interpreted. These ratios have covered the areas of performances concerning activity, liquidity, and profitability, earning & return and capital structure of the firms. The ratios used here are given below.

$$\text{Activity Ratio}\ (\text{Assets Turnover Ratio}) = \frac{\text{Net Sales}}{\text{Total Assets}}. \tag{1}$$

$$\text{Debt Ratio} = \text{Total debt} \ / \ \text{Total Assets}. \tag{2}$$

$$\text{Earnings Per Share}\ (\text{EPS})\ (\text{Earning Ratio}) = \frac{\text{Operating Profit}}{\text{No. of Outstanding Shares}}. \tag{3}$$

$$\text{Price Earnings}\ (\text{P/E})\ \text{Ratio}\ (\text{Earning Ratio}) = \frac{\text{Market Value Per Share}}{\text{EPS}}. \tag{4}$$

$$\text{Return on Assets}\ (\text{Earning Ratio}) = \frac{\text{Net Profit}}{\text{Total Assets}}. \tag{5}$$

$$\text{Liquidity Ratio}\ (\text{Current Ratio}) = \frac{\text{Total Current Assets}}{\text{Total Current Liabilities}}. \tag{6}$$

$$\text{Market Value(TobinQ's Raio)} = \frac{\text{MVOS} + \text{BVLTD} + \text{BVCL} - \text{BVCA}}{\mathit{BookValueofTotalAssets}}. \tag{7}$$

MVOS = Market Value of Ordinary Shares; BVLTD = Book Value of Long Term Debt; BVCL = Book Value of Current Liabilities; BVCA = Book Value of Current Assets.

5 Data Analysis

Before embarking the data analysis stage, certain facts about the Pakistani stock market especially Karachi Stock exchange need to be added here to facilitate the understanding of movements of these performance indicators for all the firms in our sample. Pakistani economy is under constant pressure due to many social, political and infrastructural hurdles in the form of law & order, instable and poor political system, acute shortage of energy to run the economic infrastructure of the country. Although the stock market performed quite well till 2008 when KSE 100 index was declared as the best performer among major emerging markets with an increase of 7.4%. A sequence of event in the year 2008 resulted in a huge declined in the index and also affected the performance of the stock market very negatively and resulted in a net outflow of $36.9 billion in only 08 months period. Apart from the global financial crisis of 2008, the domestic factors that contributed to this decline were increasing level of inflation, rise in interest rate by the State Bank of Pakistan, weak coalition government at federal and provincial levels and setting of price floors for stock prices for stopping the plunge in share prices[18].

5.1 Ratio Analysis

We have given the summarized results of means of the above mentioned ratios, calculated from the annual reports of 83 firms in our sample for the period 2005 to 2009, in Table 1.

Table 1. Mean financial ratios calculated for the sample for the period 2005-2009

Year	Mean Tobin's Q Ratio	Mean Payout Ratio (After Tax)	Mean Return on Assets	Mean Price Earning Ratio	Mean EPS (After Tax)	Mean Current Ratio	Mean Asset Turnover Ratio	Mean Debt Ratio
2005	1.36	47.03	0.11	12.35	18.93	1.59	1.06	0.60
2006	1.37	49.34	0.12	9.03	25.60	1.66	1.07	0.59
2007	1.56	54.14	0.11	13.8	25.72	1.89	1.02	0.58
2008	1.55	40.77	0.05	4.24	19.66	1.73	0.97	0.63
2009	0.99	45.45	0.05	10.7	15.27	1.61	0.98	0.62

5.2 Transparency and Disclosure Check

We have used the model used by Fong[19] for same kind of analysis for Chinese listed companies with minor changes, including the addition of Dividend Payout ratio and two error terms. The model is given below.

$$Market\ Value_{it} = \beta_0 + \beta_1\ EPS_{it} + \beta_2\ Div\_Payout_{it} + \beta_3\ Liquidity_{it} + \beta_4\ Debt_{it} + \beta_5\ Activity_{it} + \beta_6\ ROA_{it} + \mu_i + e_{it} \quad (8)$$

Market $Value_{it}$ = Market value measured in terms of Tobin's Q ratio; EPS_{it} = Earning per Share ratio; Div_Payout_{it} = Dividend Payout ratio; $Liquidity_{it}$ = Measured in terms of Current ratio; $Debt_{it}$ = Debt to Total Assets ratio; $Activity_{it}$ = Measured in Term of Asset Turnover ratio; ROA_{it} = Return on Assets ratio; μ_i = Error term common to each of the i units, but differs between units; e_{it} = Error term unique to each of the i,t observations.

The data reveal that there is no fundamental relationship between the performance fundamentals and the respective market valuation of these firms. Individual measures like profitability, return, financing portfolio and liquidity all have no prominent effect on the market valuation of these firms measured in term of Tobin Q's ratio and the movement of these ratios over the period under consideration has negligible similarity in some cases while mostly defying expectations. By critically analyzing the different financial ratios we can deduce the poor corporate governance practices adopted by these firms. Different ratios like EPS, Liquidity, Debt, Asset Turnover and Return on Assets are showing an overall decline in the performance of the firms thus suggesting weak corporate governance practices.

Table 2. Regression results for market value of sample data

marketvalue	Coef.	Std. Err.	z	P > | z |	[99% Conf. Interval]	
eps	-0.0034274	0.0016988	-2.02	0.044	-0.0078033	0.0009484
div_payout	0.0015254	0.001089	1.40	0.161	-0.0012796	0.0043304
liquidity	0.195506	0.0496456	3.94	0.000	0.0676274	0.3233847
debt	1.036051	0.3246981	3.19	0.001	0.1996837	1.8724170
activity	0.2638612	0.0776773	3.40	0.001	0.0637778	0.4639446
roa	0.8403845	0.4400043	1.91	0.056	-0.2929915	1.9737610
_cons	0.0650928	0.28843	0.23	0.821	-0.6778537	0.8080393
sigma_u	0.79096936			R-sq:	within =	0.0633
sigma_e	0.79089667				between=	0.1179
rho	0.50004595	(fraction of variance due to u_i)			overall =	0.0974
No. of Obs.	415	Random effects u i ~		Guassian	Wald Chi^2 (6) =	33.15
No. of groups	83	Corr. (u_i, X) =		0 (Assumed)	Prob. > Chi^2 =	0.0000

As mentioned above the regression analysis has been done by using the statistical software STATA Version 9. The panel data was analyzed by the STATA using Random-effects GLS regression method. As evident in the regression results given above it can be observed that there is a negative relationship between dependent variable MARKETVALUE and EPS, which is against the available literature and also the market norm that market value should be positively affected by changes in EPS. We can also note the fact from the results that there is very weak relationship between other profitability and return indicators like DIV_PAYOUT (dividend payout) and

ROA (return on investment) and market value. The management efficiency indicators like LIQUIDITY and ACTIVITY also show quite weak effects on market value. The only factor which is showing a strong positive relationship is DEBT, which also is working quite the opposite way because the relationship here need to be negatively related with each other as the increased in debt mean lessen claim of shareholders in case of firm's liquidation.

Table 3. Correlation results for market value of sample data

	marketvalue	eps	div_payout	liquidity	debt	activity	roa
marketvalue	1.0000						
eps	0.0495	1.0000					
div_payout	0.2249	0.0318	1.0000				
liquidity	0.1573	0.1554	0.0382	1.0000			
debt	0.0201	-0.2289	-0.0354	-0.5380	1.0000		
activity	0.1711	0.2896	0.1494	0.0351	-0.1210	1.0000	
roa	0.1077	0.4858	0.2069	0.3189	-0.6452	0.2204	1.0000

As evident in the correlation results acquired from the data, there is a negligible correlation between the market value and different performance indicators including, EPS & Dividend Payout Ratio for profitability, Current Ratio for liquidity, Debt Ratio for financing portfolio, Asset Turnover Ratio for operating efficiency and Return on Assets Ration for measuring return on investments made in these firms by shareholders.

6 Conclusion

Our study has found that a strong corporate governance system is missing in the sample under consideration for the period 2005 to 2009. Regression results suggest the lack of thorough disclosure & transparency in the published reports of 83 firms in the sample for the five years period. These reports are the sole low-cost source of information available to investors, which can ensure high degree of corporate governance if the facts and figures disclosed in it carry though disclosure and transparency.

Factors affecting corporate governance might include weaknesses in local laws and its implementation, organizational structures and speculations in the market. The basic requirement for development of entrepreneurship and economy, industry needs access to low-cost funds with ease of access for financing purposes. Ensuring high standards of corporate governance can boost the efficiency of market and increased access to low-cost liquidity for firms.

Better regulatory regime is needed to ensure thorough disclosure & transparency in the published data by firms listed on stock market in order to strengthen the effectiveness and efficiency of stock market and ensure safeguarding of all stakeholders' interests. Further research is needed to explore the weaknesses in the legal and accounting system applicable in the country and corrective measures are suggested in order to strengthen protection of investors' interest and better regulate the market.

References

1. Chen, K.C.W., Chen, Z., Wei, K.C.J.: Legal protection of investors, corporate governance, and the cost of equity capital. Journal of Corporate Finance 15(3), 273–289 (2009)
2. Bushman, R.M., Smith, A.J.: Financial accounting information and corporate governance. Journal of Accounting and Economics 32(1-3), 237–333 (2001)
3. Aman, H., Nguyen, P.: Do stock prices reflect the corporate governance quality of Japanese firms? Journal of the Japanese and International Economies 22(4), 647–662 (2008)
4. Brown, L.D., Caylor, M.L.: Corporate governance and firm valuation. Journal of Accounting and Public Policy 25(4), 409–434 (2006)
5. Ammann, M., Oesch, D., Schmid, M.M.: Corporate governance and firm value: International evidence. Journal of Empirical Finance 18(1), 36–55 (2011)
6. Bai, C.E., Liu, Q., Lu, J., Song, F.M., Zhang, J.X.: Corporate governance and market valuation in China. Journal of Comparative Economics 32(4), 599–616 (2004)
7. Ding, Y.: International differences in disclosure adequacy: Empirical evidence from annual reports of French and Chinese listed firms. Advances in International Accounting 15, 155–179 (2002)
8. Aljifri, K.: Annual report disclosure in a developing country: The case of the UAE. Advances in Accounting 24(1), 93–100 (2008)
9. Patel, S.A., Balic, A., Bwakira, L.: Measuring transparency and disclosure at firm-level in emerging markets. Emerging Markets Review 3(4), 325–337 (2002)
10. Chi, L.C.: Do transparency and disclosure predict firm performance? Evidence from the Taiwan market. Expert Systems with Applications 36(8), 11198–11203 (2009)
11. Baek, J.S., Kang, J.K., Park, K.S.: Corporate governance and firm value: evidence from the Korean financial crisis. Journal of Financial Economics 71(2), 265–313 (2004)
12. Barton, J., Waymire, G.: Investor protection under unregulated financial reporting. Journal of Accounting and Economics 38, 65–116 (2004)
13. Tadesse, S.: The economic value of regulated disclosure: Evidence from the banking sector. Journal of Accounting and Public Policy 25(1), 32–70 (2006)
14. Biddle, G.C., Hilary, G., Verdi, R.S.: How does financial reporting quality relate to investment efficiency? Journal of Accounting and Economics 48(2-3), 112–131 (2009)
15. Östberg, P.: Disclosure, investment and regulation. Journal of Financial Intermediation 15(3), 285–306 (2006)
16. Balasubramanian, N., Black, B.S., Khanna, V.: The relation between firm-level corporate governance and market value: A case study of India. Emerging Markets Review 11(4), 319–340 (2010)
17. Ashraf, J., Ghani, W.I.: Accounting development in Pakistan. The International Journal of Accounting 40(2), 175–201 (2005)
18. KSE100Index, http://en.wikipedia.org/wiki/KSE_100_Index
19. Fong, M.W.L.: Financial Accounting Information and Corporate Governance: Chinese Listed Companies, in Corporate Governance: Challenges for China, pp. 200–222. Law Press, Beijing (2003)

Legal Issues on Copyright and Internet

Nor Sa'adah Abd Rahman

Faculty of Management and Human Resource Development
Universiti Teknologi Malaysia
Skudai, Johor Bahru
Malaysia

Abstract. The internet creates many legal questions and the legal challenges arise out of the internet had caused concern among on-line copyright owners on how their works are being used. Some internet activities have affected the concept of copyright law. The legal issue on accessing website involve the making of transient copies that clearly affect the reproduction rights of copyright owners. The paper concerns the legal issues of accessing website and storage in RAM. It is divided into three parts which will discuss the legal issue on copyright and internet and the law at international level in the first part followed by the laws at the regional level and lastly national level in order to establish whether any of those legal provisions are appropriate to address the issue. A summary of these relevant laws will be given, stressing those provisions which may be useful in formulating laws to regulate Internet activity.

Keywords: Copyright, Internet, Copyright infringement, Accessing website.

1 Introduction

With the creation of links or hyperlinks, appearing in the form of highlighted symbols or icons that appear on the computer screen, the user is able to hop from one web page to another. The act of going to and from whatever websites you want, whenever you want, is called 'browsing'. It is also known as 'surfing the net', and is always referred to accessing websites, and this issue has caused the most heated debate in the copyright and cyber world. This is due to the fact that whenever the website is accessed, something in the form of text, pictures, sounds or animation is copied. The software in the browser's computer, that is a 'web browser,' interprets the data and presents them to the user in the format intended.[1]

Nowadays, it appears that browsing is the most common activity of users on the internet. The complex problems raised by the internet mainly stem from the fact that it departs from traditional methods of using a copyrighted work. The internet, on the other hand, generally requires making a 'copy' of the work, and may also require distribution, transmission and access to the work as well.[2]

---

[1] See Johnston, David, Handa, Sunny, Morgan, Charles, Cyber Law, (Selangor: Pelanduk Publications Sdn. Bhd., 1998), p.153.

[2] See Hayes, David L, 'Advanced Copyright Issues on The Internet', 1998, Findlaw.Library, pp.48-49.

M. Zhou (Ed.): ISAEBD 2011, Part III, CCIS 210, pp. 564–571, 2011.

The problem of browsing which relates to copyright and the internet starts when someone puts up her work on a website, which is also a publicly accessible site where any user may access the material, and the material is housed in such a manner as to encourage its downloading.[3] It is the copyright holder's exclusive right to copy, distribute, and transmit the copyrighted work. However, the latter acts are essential and incidental to browsing a work on the internet. Hence it would appear that browsing might technically infringe multiple rights of the copyright holder. Moreover, browsing might also impeach the right of public display and/or public performance.[4]

The question of whether digital browsing can be considered as fair use was discussed in the case of *Religious Technology Centre v Netcom On-line Communication Services, Inc.*[5] Browsing raises important copyright problems that cannot be dismissed simply on the notion that doctrines such as fair use, implied licence or innocent infringement will remove the problems entirely.

In digital world copyrighted works have been converted into binary form which allows authors to make printed publications available for temporary use on-line. However, at present the copyright system has had to come to terms with 'dematerialised' works in digital form, where the supporting media are irrelevant or non-existent. For instance, a book can now be copied and used on a computer disk, on a CD-ROM (CD read-only memory) disk, or from an on-line service via the temporary random-access memory (RAM) of a computer. There are an increasing number of works that are only published in dematerialised form on such vehicles as the internet, for instance, newsletters and original databases.[6]

There is also an allegation that browsing technically causes an infringing copy of the digital information to be made in the screen memory. In *MAI Systems Corporation v Peak Computer Inc*[7], the court held that such a copy is fixed, even when information is temporarily placed in the RAM, such as the screen's RAM. The temporary copying involved in browsing is only necessary because humans cannot otherwise perceive digital information. It is the functional equivalent of reading, which does not implicate the copyright laws and may be done by anyone in a library without the permission of the copyright owner. However, it can be argued that the effects of digital browsing are different because millions can browse a single copy of a work in cyberspace, while only one can read a library's copy at a time.

In the absence of a commercial or profit-depriving usage, digital browsing is probably a fair use: there could hardly be a market for licensing the temporary copying of digital works onto computer screens to allow browsing. Unless such a use is commercial, such as where someone reads a copyrighted work online and therefore decides not to purchase a copy from the copyright owner, fair use is likely. Until reading a work online becomes as easy and convenient as reading paperback, copyright owners do not have much to fear from digital browsing and there is not likely to be much market effect. Through technology, the website can be protected by

---

[3] See Johnston, *op. cit.*, p. 153-154.

[4] *Ibid.*

[5] 907 F. Supp. 1361 (N.D.Cal. 1995).

[6] See Dixon, Allen N, Hansen, Martin F, 'The Berne Convention Enters The Digital Age', 1996, 11 European Intellectual Property Review, p. 605.

[7] 991 F.2d 511, 518 (9th Cir. 1993).

using a password to stop the public from having access to it. However the number of website that are password protected is limited mainly because of the reason behind putting any information on the internet itself, that is for the public to have access to those materials. Another problem is that the Act provides that any assignment or licence of copyright must be in writing and signed by the owner but in browsing cases there is no such agreement. The copyright owners also have the right to authorise the copying of work in material form and this shows that even without owning or licensing the copyright, material can be used that is reproduced.[8]

The Copyright Design Patent Act[9] (CDPA) states that: "copyright in a literary work, other than a computer program or a database, or in a dramatic, musical or artistic work, the typographical arrangement of a published edition, a sound recording or a film, is not infringed by the making of a temporary copy which is transient or incidental, which is an integral and essential part of a technological process and the sole purpose of which is to enable:

(a) transmission of the work in a network between third parties by an intermediary; or
(b) a lawful use of the work and which has no independent economic significance."

It can be argued that browsing fall under this section, because the temporary copying involved in browsing can be said to be a lawful use of work, because without that the user cannot browse.

A computer's permanent hard disk and RAM are totally different and under copyright law should be treated differently. The Copyright Act regarded the copies of a digital work on a semi-permanent or permanent computer memory device, such as a computer's hard drive or Read Only Memory (ROM) as fixed under that Act. This is because until they are actively deleted, they will remain in storage for more than a transitory duration. However, the digital data embodied in RAM is very transient and is not permanent. Due to the transient nature of RAM, which therefore distinguishes it from fixed storage, it needs special analysis under the reproduction provisions.[10]

The RAM embodiment once made cannot be easily transported and cannot survive without a constant supply of electricity and also has no market value. Even though one could technically load a copyrighted piece of software into the RAM of a portable, battery operated machine and be able to distribute it to others, the software would be lost forever as soon as the battery runs out or is taken out of the machine to be replaced. The redistribution would only be feasible if the RAM embodiment were copied into a permanent form, which in itself would be a copyright infringement. In short, RAM embodiment has only one use, as the only way that a digital file can be used or read. This kind of use of a RAM embodiment is harmless, and actually helps the copyright holder. Nobody would be able to use the copyrighted work if it were not for RAM, and thus no one would purchase it.[11]

---

[8] See Johnston, *op. cit.*, p.154-155.

[9] See Section 28A of The Copyright Design Patent Act 1988.

[10] See Matthews, Kristen J, 'Misundertanding RAM: Digital Embodiments and Copyright', 1977, pp.2-3.

[11] *Ibid.*, p.8.

2 International Level

At the international level, the World Intellectual Property Organization (WIPO) has provided the basis for the digital protection for the countries throughout the world through its convention and treaties. Therefore an analysis on the provisions of law provided by the Convention as well as the Treaties under WIPO as regards these legal issues will be made.

The Berne Convention covered the legal issues discussed in this paper that is the issue on accessing web pages and storage in RAM. The Berne Convention[12] has a provision dealing with the reproduction right, where it does not only provide protection but also the exclusive right to authors of literary and artistic works to authorize the reproduction of their works in any manner or form. Although the wording of the Article does not expressly stated that it applies to digitized works but the word 'in any manner and form' must be interpreted as wide as possible. Since we are in the digital age where works can be stored in digitized form therefore it is submitted that Article 9 (1) of Berne Convention applies to storage of works in electronic medium. If the Article only applies to the permanent copies, what will happen to the digitized work used by the online users without permission from the author? This includes uploading and downloading a work into or from a computer's memory. Clearly the Berne Convention covers the issues on accessing web pages and storage in RAM where it involve temporary copying.

The WIPO Treaties such as the WIPO Copyright Treaty (WCT) has also addressed the technological development. The preamble of the WCT states the desire to develop and maintain the protection of the rights of authors in their literary and artistic works in a manner as effective and uniform as possible. The Treaty also acknowledged the impact of the technological development on the creation and use of literary and artistic works and the need for new international rules. These new international rules are important in order to solve the problems raised by new economic, social, cultural and technological developments. All the member countries have to adhere to the requirement of the WCT and bring the copyright up to date to reflect technological change in particular, though not limited to the use of the internet as a means of disseminating and exploiting copyright works.

Since this paper is about the legal issues on the internet therefore the provisions on WCT were examined to see if it has provisions that relates to those issues. Due to the fact that one of the aim of the WCT is to address the question raised by the technological development therefore under the WCT[13] there is a provision specifically applies to the internet which states that "the authors of the literary and artistic works shall enjoy the exclusive right of authorizing any communication to the public of their works, by wire or wireless means including the making available to the public of their works in such a way that members of the public may access these works from a place and at a time individually chosen by them."

In general the WCT does not cover the legal issue discussed in this paper that is accessing web pages. It only covers the internet in general under Article 8. The WCT is too brief and does not provide relevant provisions as to the issues raised by the internet. It is submitted that the laws at the international level does not address all the

[12] See Article 9 (1) of The Berne Convention.

[13] See Article 8 of the WIPO Copyright Treaty.

digital issues. However, as regards the legal issue discussed in the paper, it is found that only Article 9 (1) of the Berne Convention covers the issue on accessing web pages and storage in RAM where it involves temporary copying. The law at international level however, only provides the basic framework for the protection of the internet for the Members States to come up with their own national laws.

3 Regional Level

At the regional level, the Directive on the Harmonisation of certain aspects of copyright and related rights in the Information Society (The Information Society Directive) was examined in order to find out whether there are provisions that will address the legal issues discussed in this paper. The aim of the Directive is to bring the copyright law up to date with the technological challenges as a response to the WIPO Copyright and Performances and Phonograms Treaties.

The Information society Directive[14] provides for the exclusive right to authorize or prohibit direct or indirect, temporary or permanent reproduction by any means and in any form. However Article 5 (1) of the Directive provides the only mandatory exception under the Directive on temporary acts of reproduction.

As regard the legal issue on accessing web pages which were discussed in the paper, there is a provision that covers the issue under the Directive that is under the Recital (33) of the Directive. This Recital states that the exclusive right of reproduction should be subject to an exception to allow acts of temporary reproduction which form an integral and essential part of technological process and it covers acts that will allow browsing to operate and this is expressly stated in Article 5 (1) of the Directive. Article 5 (1) provides the mandatory exception where it covers "temporary acts of reproduction, which are transient or incidental and an integral and essential part of a technological process, and whose purpose is to enable: (a) a transmission in a network between third parties by an intermediary, or (b) a lawful use of a work or other subject matter to be made, and which have no independent economic significance".

Clearly Recital (33) and Article 5 (1) of the Information Society Directive covers the legal issue discussed in the paper that are browsing. This legal issue involves the reproduction of works through the making of transient copies. If the acts are done with the permission of the right holder and not against the law then these acts is lawful. In general the Information Society Directive did not cover all the issues on the internet. The Information directive only addressed the issues on browsing which is under temporary reproduction that is transient or incidental forming an integral and essential part of technological process.

4 National Level

At the national levels the copyright law of the United Kingdom, Malaysia and USA will be examined in relation to the legal issue that is accessing website and storage of RAM.

---

[14] See Article 2 of the the Directive on the Harmonisation of certain aspects of copyright and related rights in the Information Society (The Information Society Directive).

4.1 United Kingdom

The Information Society Directive was implemented in the UK in 2003 by way of Statutory Instrument. The Copyright, design, patent Act (CDPA) Amendment Act will be examined to see whether the legal issues discussed in this paper are covered. As regards the legal issues discussed in this paper that is on accessing webpage and storage of RAM which is transient, the The Copyright, design, patent Act (CDPA) as amended had adopted and incorporated in the CDPA, Article 5 (1) of the Directive which provides for exemption for temporary acts of reproduction which are transient or incidental and essential part of a technological process. New section 28A[15] was added which covers the making of temporary copies. The issues on accessing webpages and storage of RAM involves the making of transient copies therefore are relevant to section 28A.

4.2 The United States

The analysis will be made to the US Copyright law in respect of the legal issues in this paper. Since US has the most advanced legislation on the internet therefore countries all over the world would observe the development of US law in that respect. The focus of the paper is on the legal issues on accessing web pages and therefore the US copyright law will be examined in this respect. It was found that the issue on accessing webpages was covered by safe harbour under DMCA[16]. Under this section the service provider are protected from action of infringement when they transmit, route or provide connections for materials through a system or a network controlled or operated by the service provider by intermediate and transient storage of that material in the course of such transmitting, routing or providing connections if they fulfill certain conditions.

From the above, it can be seen the difference between the protection of copyright offered by the WIPO, the Information Society Directive and the DMCA. In response to the WCT, The Information Society Directive provides far more provision on the digital issues as compared to the WIPO itself. At the international level only Berne Convention addressed the issue on accessing web pages, under Article 9. However the Information Society Directive addressed the issues discussed in this paper that relates to browsing as provided under Article 5(1) and Recital (33).

Although it cannot be denied that The US under the DMCA had addressed the legal issues in this paper. The safe harbour under the DMCA covers the issue on accessing webpages. The DMCA provide more solution to the existing digital problem compared to the EU Directive.

---

[15] Section 28A states that copyright in a literary works, other than a computer program or database, or in a dramatic, musical or artistic work, the typographical arrangement of a published edition, a sound recording or a film, is not infringed by the making of a temporary copy which is transient or incidental which is an integral and essential part of technologies process and the sole purpose of which is to enable.

(a) a transmission of the work in a network between third parties by the intermediary or
(b) a lawful use of the work

and which has no independent economic significance.

[16] See section 512 (a) Digital Millennium Copyright Act.

Both the DMCA and Information Society Directive tried to fulfill the needs to introduce new rules in order to provide solutions to the problems raised by the technological development which is the aim of the WCT. As for the Information Society Directive, the EU have to consider the views from its members states before passing the Directive and the member states have to adopt and implement the Directive under their own national law. However the US position is different where it can come up with its own law without having to consult other countries although it has to consider the WIPO treaties. Hence the US law regarding the internet is more advanced as compared to the EU. Another point is that since the internet itself originated from the US therefore it is not surprising that the law on internet in US is far more advanced than the EU and other countries for that matter.

4.3 Malaysia

The effort carried out by Malaysia in tackling the technological challenges will be examined. As regards the legal issue on accessing webpages there is no express provision on this under the Malaysian Copyright Act 1987. On the other hand, the definition of reproduction allows copies to be made in any form or version and this is provided under the Copyright Act[17]. Whereas the word 'material form' covers any form either visible or not. It is submitted therefore that the issue on accessing webpages falls under this section. Obviously there are gaps in the Malaysian Copyright law where there is no specific provision on the making of temporary copies. The Malaysian law is inadequate in handling the digital issues on internet and need to be improved.

In conclusion the law at the international level only provide the general framework of the law in handling the issues raised by the technological development. The treaties did not address all the digital issues and it is too brief. Therefore it is difficult for the member countries to come up with their set of laws in tackling the digital issues without precise guidelines. At the regional level, the EU through its Information Directive laid down rules on digital issues based on WIPO guidelines. As regards the legal issues discussed in this paper, the Information Society Directive covers the issue on browsing which is expressly stated in the Directive. At the national level the UK had implemented the EU Information Society Directive. The issue on accessing webpages were covered under section 28A of CDPA. The US position, the safe harbour under the DMCA provides for the legal issues in this paper that are accessing web pages and storage of RAM.

5 Conclusion

Therefore it can be said that the US offered better protection as regards the legal issues concerning copyright and internet. This is because the US not only the leader in internet law but also it can make law without having to consult other countries like the EU has to take into account the views from its member states. The US only has to follow the WIPO guidelines. As for Malaysia, the improvement has to be made to the existing Act in order to handle the internet issues more effectively.

---

[17] See Section 3 of the Copyright Act 1987.

Reference

1. Dixon, A.N., Hansen, M.F.: The Berne Convention Enters The Digital Age. European Intellectual Property Review 11 (1996)
2. Hayes, D.L.: Advanced Copyright Issues on The Internet. Findlaw, Library, 48–49 (1998)
3. Johnston, D., Handa, S., Morgan, C.: Cyber Law, p. 153. Pelanduk Publications Sdn. Bhd., Selangor (1998)
4. MAI Systems Corporation v. Peak Computer Inc. 991 F.2d 511, 518 (9th Cir. 1993)
5. Matthews, K.J.: Misundertanding RAM: Digital Embodiments and Copyright, pp. 2–3 (1977)
6. Religious Technology Centre v. Netcom On-line Communication Services, Inc. 907 F. Supp. 1361 (N.D.Cal. 1995)
7. The Berne Convention Berne Convention for the Protection of Literary and Artistic Works
8. The Copyright Act (1987)
9. The Copyright, Designs and Patents Act (1988)
10. The Digital Millennium Copyright Act
11. The Directive on the Harmonisation of certain aspects of copyright and related rights in the Information Society. The WIPO Copyright Treaty (1996)

Interest Groups and Sino-US Conflicts over Intellectual Property Protection

Li-Hong Yu[1,2]

[1] School of Economics, Huazhong University of Science and Technology, Luoyu Road 1037, Hongshan District, 430074 Wuhan, China
[2] Economy College of South-Central University for Nationalities, Minyuan Road 708, Hongshan District, Wuhan, China
yulihong0521@sina.com

Abstract. Interest groups have played an important role in Sino-US conflicts over Intellectual Property(IP) protection such as "Special 301", "337" investigations and dispute under TRIPS. This paper reviewed the evolvement of these conflicts and then analyzed the role of U.S. interest groups and U.S. government and Chinese government. An adjusted two-level game was put forward to illustrate the essential of Sino-US IP protection conflicts which is the U.S. government, standing for IP interest groups, demanded higher protection while Chinese government, trading off the interests of different groups, partly resisted and partly given up. The IP protection in China thus has been increasing by and by but the conflicts will not cease as long as there's still IP protection gap. Finally it concludes that IP conflicts have not materially hampered the trade relations between U.S. and China and the IP protection pressure is also a motive for China to promote indigenous innovation.

Keywords: Intellectual Property Protection, Interest Groups, Two-level Game, "Special 301".

1 Introduction

With the rapid development of trade and investment between US and China, many trade related disputes have aroused and the recurring conflicts over Chinese protection of foreign intellectual property (IP) have been hot since 1990s. IP protection conflicts take different forms, mainly "Special 301" investigation, "337" investigation and complaint about China's failure to enforce TRIPS to WTO. Behind these conflicts, the role of interest groups can not be ignored.

The role of interest groups in the Sino-US conflicts over IP protection has been discussed by some literature. Wu and Liu (2009) analyzed the inducing-mechanism of IP conflict between developed countries and developing countries. By assuming the goal of interest groups in both countries to be maximizing their profit and both governments to be maximizing the weighted political contribution and social welfare, different level of IP protection is demanded and supplied and conflict over IP protection induced. Croix and Konan (2001) focused on the economic and political foundations of the ongoing IP disputes between U.S. and China in 1990s as well as

M. Zhou (Ed.): ISAEBD 2011, Part III, CCIS 210, pp. 572–578, 2011.

the rapid convergence of Chinese IP law and enforcement to OECD standards. They argued economic considerations have played a fundamental role in these disputes. HE (2008) conducted an in-depth analysis of the causes of the intensification of dispute over IP between China and the United States after China's entry into WTO and pointed out that interest groups have directly promoted the disputes.

By emphasizing the specific role of interest groups, especially IIPA, this paper will help to deepen the understanding of the persistent IP protection conflicts and its future trends and effects to Sino-U.S. trade relations. After reviewing the evolvement of IP protection conflict between U.S. and China, this paper illuminates the role of interest groups and decision mechanism of US and Chinese government in these conflicts. An adjusted two-level game model is then constructed to illustrate the formation and solution of IP protection conflicts. And finally it concludes.

2 The Evolvement of Sino-US Conflicts over IP Protection

From 1980s the United States has threatened countries with weak IP laws and institutions through its "Special 301" provisions of U.S. trade law (Konan, et al 1995). Special 301 allows the U.S. Trade Representative to investigate foreign protection of U.S. intellectual property, to negotiate for higher standards of protection, and to retaliate with trade sanctions if negotiations fail.

In 1990s, three conflicts over IP protection which happed in 1991, 1994 and 1996 have almost led to trade wars. Each conflict happened with USTR's putting China in the "Priority country list" of its yearly "301 special report" and a trade sanction list announced by U.S. after six months' investigation which was responded by Chinese government's anti-sanction list. And each time at the last minute the sanction would have come into force, an agreement was concluded and trade wars avoided. The three agreements have greatly promoted the legislation of relevant Intellectual property laws and their enforcement in China and thus conflicts over IP protection between US and China have calmed down since then until 2004, three years after China's WTO accession.

After China's WTO accession, U.S. has turned its focus to supervise China's fulfillment of WTO obligation. With much of dissatisfaction with China's enforcement of TRIPS from commerce and industries since 2004, USTR has put China into the "priority watch list" in its 2005 "special 301 report" which was the first time to put China in this list since 1996. Though no investigation and trade sanctions against China, U.S. government has expressed its great dissatisfaction over China's enforcement of TRIPS and other bilateral agreement of IP and the first dispute about China's failure to enforce TRIPS was put forward to WTO on April 10th, 2007, complaining about four matters. The Panel report concluded that the Copyright Law and the Customs measures as US complained is inconsistent with the TRIPS Agreement and the report was adopted by the DSB. China has implemented the DSB recommendations and rulings in 2010.

"337" investigations which targets the imported goods infringed IP in USA have grown dramatically after China's WTO accession. From 2002 to 2010, China has suffered 110 of the total 286 "337" investigations this period, being No.1 object each year. "337" investigations have been one of the most tough barriers for many Chinese exporting enterprises, especially Medium-and-Small firms.

3 The Role of IP Interest Groups in Promoting IP Conflicts

With protection of IP, American IP owners can enjoy monopoly power and make more profit. Thus those IP-related interest groups have great incentives to lobby U.S. government to press China to enforce strict protection of foreign IP in China. Actually, U.S. IP-intensive industries became increasingly active players in the U.S. political arena as they became more export-oriented in the 1970s and 1980s. In the 1980s, numerous new industry trade associations were formed in the entertainment and computer industries, many with the narrow purpose of lobbying the federal government to obtain better enforcement of foreign copyrights on entertainment products and computer software. Among the hundreds of interests groups related to IP protection, International Intelligence Property Association (IIPA) has been very active in promoting international protection of IP owners in U.S.

3.1 IIPA Works for Stricter IP Protection

IIPA is a private sector coalition, formed in 1984, of trade associations representing U.S. copyright-based industries. IIPA's seven member associations represent over 1,900 U.S. companies producing and distributing materials protected by copyright laws throughout the world.

At the instance of IIPA and the copyright industries, Congress passed amendments to Section 301 in 1988, making the status of global Intellectual Property protection an annual exercise in "Special 301." Every year since 1989, IIPA has been filing its Special 301 submission with USTR. Its suggestion of putting China in the "Priority country list" of "Special 301" report in 1991, 1994 and 1996 was taken by the USTR and thus led three most prominent IP conflicts in 1990s.

After China became WTO member in December 11, 2001, IIPA's focus is to bring China fully into compliance with its obligation, especially to ensure TRIPS-compliant enforcement systems in place "in practice." In particular, it has been working to promote criminal laws are being used aggressively to fight against the criminal syndicates that are thought to be at the center of the "pirate trade."

Every few years, IIPA has issued economic reports since 1990 emphasizing the importance of copyright industries in U.S. Economy, employment and export. IIPA has also been reporting the trade loss owing to pirate. Such information has been widely accepted by USTR and other administration and affects their attitude and decisions in IP conflict with China. The reported loss from pirate by China was summarized in table 1.

Table 1. The trade loss from Chinese pirate estimated by IIPA: 1999~2008 (in million dollars)

Copyright loss	1999	2000	2001	2002	2003	2004	2005	2006	2007	2008
Cartoons	120	120	160	168	178	280	244	NA	NA	NA
CD & Music	70	70	47	48	286	202.9	204	206	451	564
Business software	437	765	1140	1637	1787	1488	1554	1949	2999	3005
Entertainment software	1383	455	455	568	568	510	590	NA	NA	NA
Books	128	130	130	40	40	50	52	52	NA	NA
Sum.	2138	1540	1932	2462	2859	2531	2644	2207	3502	3569

Source: http://www.iipa.com/statistics.html

Other interest groups which are active in promoting IP protection in China include The U.S. Chamber of Commerce, the Pharmaceutical Research and Manufacturers of America, International Trademark Association, Intellectual Property Owners Association, International Anti-counterfeiting Coalition, and so on.

3.2 U.S. Government's Decision in IP Conflicts with China

As an innovation country and net exporter of IP intensive goods, U.S. government and relevant interest groups share interests in strengthening IP protection in China, a growing and gigantic market. To spent more time and political resources on pressing China means the better chance of more export, rapid economic growth, more employment, and thus more political support in reelection. The main resources owned by U.S. government to press China are the retaliation under "Special 301", the veto to deter China's accession into WTO in 1990s, the DSU in WTO since 2002, and basically is the dependence of Chinese economy on U.S and world economy. For China, U.S. is the most important export destination and U.S. government has a lot of political power in international arena which will affect China's participation in global economy era.

When U.S. government faced with serious economic and political situations, like the 2008 international financial crisis and a recorded high rate of unemployment since WWII and a deteriorating trade deficit, there's even greater incentive for U.S. government to target China which has been the No.1 source of U.S. trade deficit. Selling more IPR-intensive goods will be both good to decrease trade deficit and to increase U.S. employment. That's why U.S. government and interest groups have been working to improve China's IP protection though which has been increasing rapidly and converged to that in most OECD countries by Ginarte-Park measurement.

Table 2. Measuring China's Intellectual Property Protection: 1984~2007

	1984	1985	1986	1987	1988	1989	1990	1991	1992	1993	1994	1995
GP	1.18	1.51	1.51	1.51	1.51	1.51	1.51	1.51	2.86	3.19	3.19	3.19
	1996	1997	1998	1999	2000	2001	2002	2003	2004	2005	2006	2007
GP	3.19	3.19	3.19	3.52	3.52	4.19	4.19	4.53	4.53	4.53	4.53	4.53

Source: Data of 1984 through 2002 is from HAN Yu-xiong and LI Huai-zu(2005); data of 2003 through 2007 is from Shen Guo-bing and Liu Jia(2009)

The degree of Chinese IP protection since 1984 is listed in table 2. The G-P value is calculated using Ginarte-Park (1997) method. Ginarte and Park (1997) also calculated the IP protection level in U.S. which is 3.86 in 1960 through 1975, 4.19 in 1980, 4.52 in 1985 and 1990. This means China's nominal IP protection in 2001 is the same as that of 1980 in US. From 2003 China has approached U.S. of 1990.

4 China's Decision of IP Protection: A Trade Off

Improving protection of U.S. intellectual property has different effects for different groups within China. For those industries imitating innovative products, stricter protection means high licensed fees or even means no chance to stay in market at all. For those innovation industries, stronger IP protection means better market chance and thus strong motive to innovate. Consumers may gain by more guarantee of commodity quality warranted by strong IP protection, or may lose by having to pay higher prices. Thus, a tradeoff exists. Too weak IPR protection discourages creative activity while too strong protection presses weak native industry. With the development of economy and technology, Chinese government has more incentives to strengthen IP protection with a view to inspiring indigenous innovation.

Foreign pressure has also affect the decision of Chinese government. Insufficient protection of IP has been a perennial source of contention in Sino-US relations as well as a stumbling block in China's bid for WTO membership. In most cases, foreign countries, especially U.S., have put the IP protection a clause into agreements which may expand bilateral or multilateral, regional cooperation. To be integrated into the more and more open world, China has to pay a cost by enforcing higher degree of IP protection to gain the benefits from opening economy than it would have enforced when without foreign pressure.

5 Sino-US Conflict over IP Protection: A Two-Level Game Model

Here I use the two-level game which originally put forward by Putnam (1988) to illustrate the mechanism of Sino-US conflict over IP protection. Two-level game theory is a political model of international conflict resolution between liberal democracies derived from game theory. The model views international negotiations between liberal democracies as consisting of simultaneous negotiations at both the intra-national (domestic) level and the international level. Over domestic negotiations, the executive absorbs the concern of societal actors and builds coalitions with them; at the international level, the executive tries to implement these concerns without committing to anything that will have deleterious effects at home. Win-sets occur when the concerns of actors at both levels overlap, a condition under which an international agreement is likely.

Considering Chinese government is of democratic centralism instead of liberal democratic government, here I slightly adjust the original model. My setting of the model is as follows: U.S. government absorbs the concern of IP-related interest groups and press Chinese government to improve IP protection by trade sanction promised under the "Special 301" clause or by an agreement in which U.S. promises no trade sanction but China has to be committed to higher standard of IP protection; Chinese government, trading off the interests of different groups within China of higher IP protection, responds by anti-sanction or an agreement which will promise higher IP protection but not as much as demanded by U.S. government. The payoff under different choices is as follows:

		U.S.	
		Trade sanction	Agreement
	Anti-sanction	$(-c1, -u1)$	$(0, -u1)$
China	Agreement	$(-c1-c2, u2)$	$(-c2, u2)$

The realistic choice combinations are (U.S. sanction and China Anti-sanction) and (U.S. and China enter into an agreement). $-u1$ stands for the loss of U.S. incurred by China's anti-sanction, $u2$ is the U.S. gains from exporting more IP or IP-intensive goods to China under higher IP protection and the gains are bigger the higher IP protection in China. $u2 > u1$ because U.S. is a net exporter of IP intensive goods and the net balance is quite bigger than the trade under retaliation. Thus the agreement-agreement combination is very beneficial for U.S. $-c1$ is China's loss caused by U.S. trade sanction, $-c2$ is the possible net loss China may suffer under higher protection level and $c2$ is positively related the actual protection level. So, China would try to make least concession in the agreement to minimize $c2$, while U.S. will ask the highest IP protection in China as long as possible to maximize $u2$. The win-set in their agreement negotiation is the overlap of the lowest IP protection level which can be accepted by U.S. and the highest IP protection level which can be accepted by China. Chinese interest groups play a minor role in affecting Chinese government's standing, and the agreement concluded by Chinese government is final and will not be denied by domestic interest groups. While the U.S. interest groups will lobby the Congress to deny the agreement which is not up to the demanded standard of IP interest groups. Thus the final results are usually an agreement which is more to the taste of U.S.

As long as China's actual protection of foreign IP can't reach the demanding of U.S. IP owners and U.S. government, "Special 301" can readily be applied and China will repeatedly be involved in a new negotiation or trade sanction. Thus the IP conflicts will not cease as long as there is IP protection gap between these two countries though three bilateral agreements about IP protection have been concluded in 1990s and China has been under the supervision of TRIPS since 2001.

6 Conclusion

The IP protection conflicts will not materially hamper the trade relations owing to the high degree of interdependency and complementation of U.S. and China. According to China's statistics, in 2010 China is the second biggest trade partner of U.S. with bilateral trade value reached 385 billion dollars and China's import from U.S reached 102 billion dollars. According to the WTO statistics, in 2009, U.S is China's biggest export destination and the fifth source of imports and China is the biggest source of U.S. imports and No. 3 destination of U.S. exports. Each country has the ability to retaliate and none can benefit from trade wars and thus each will not act too aggressively.

For China, the pressure is also a motive. The National Intellectual Property Strategy Outline started in 2008 aiming to improve China's ability to create, utilize, protect and manage intellectual property and thus to achieve the goal of innovative country by 2020. Higher IP protection may induce more indigenous innovation. With more IP owned by Chinese, China will gain more to enforce stronger IP protection. Though China has been increasing IP protection by foreign pressure, China has now taken an initiative step to meet the challenge of a more competitive world. Of course, to resists the persistent and too-demanding IP protection pressure from U.S. and other developed countries, China should be more active and professional in bilateral, multilateral negotiations and combine with other developing countries to fight for more fair obligations in international IP protection.

References

1. Ferrantino, M.J.: The Effect of Intellectual Property Rights on International Trade and Investment. Weltwirtschatliches Archiv 129(2), 300–331 (1993)
2. Ginarte, J.C., Park, W.G.: Determinants of Patent Rights: A Cross-National Study. Research Policy 26(3), 283–301 (1997)
3. Han, Y.X., Li, H.Z.: Quantitative Analysis for Intellectual Property Protection Level of China. Studies in Science of Science (6), 377–382 (2005)
4. He, X.Q.: The Dispute over Intellectual Property Rights between China and the U.S. since China's Entry into the WTO. Study of the United States (2), 49–62 (2008)
5. Maskus, K.E.: The International Regulation of Intellectual Property. Weltwirtschaftliches Archiv 134(2), 186–208 (1998)
6. Maskus, K.E.: Intellectual Property Rights in the Global Economy. Institute for International Economics, Washington, DC (2000)
7. Putnam, R.: Diplomacy and Domestic Politics: The Logic of Two-level Games. International Organization 42(3), 427–460 (1988)
8. Shen, G.B., Liu, J.: Nominal Level and Actual Strength of China's Intellectual Property Protection under the TRIPS Agreement. Finance & Trade Economics (11), 66–71 (2009)
9. Summer, La Croix, J., Konan, D.E.: Intellectual Property Rights in China: The Changing Political Economy of Chinese-American Interests. The World Economy (25), 759–788 (2002)
10. Wu, Y.Q., Liu, H.Y.: The Difference of Intellectual Property Right Protection Level and the Induced Mechanism of Trade Friction: Analysis from Interest Groups' Perspective. International Trade Problems (5), 105–112 (2009)

Marx and Engels' Harmonious Leisure Consumption Concepts

Zheng Lu

School of Art in Ludong University, Yantai, Shandong, China
happyluzheng@sina.com

Abstract. Marx and Engels insist on the harmonious leisure consumption concept, they think that leisure is the basic human need for human, leisure consumption is a kind of consuming behavior to meet the needs of individual development for all social members, leisure consumption can not go uncontrolled, it must be constrained by various external factors. Human can neither destroy ecological environment for the purpose of leisure, nor lead to the tense relationship between human and society because of leisure consumption. They advocate building a kind of leisure pattern that is appropriate for the overall development of human on the basis of the harmonious unity between natures and society. Marx and Engels' harmonious leisure consumption concept have an important practical significance in constructing a leisure consuming economic theory with Chinese characteristics, and also in creating a harmonious consuming environment, increasing consuming levels and consuming quality.

Keywords: Marx, Engels, leisure consumption, harmony, freedom.

1 Introduction

As the great thinkers in the 19th century, Marx and Engels have thought profoundly on the aspect of leisure time, leisure activities, leisure needs of human, leisure consumption and other issues. Leisure theory is an important part of the whole ideological theory. They insist on the harmonious leisure consumption concept, advocate building a kind of leisure pattern which is appropriate for the overall development of human on the basis of the harmonious unity between natures and society.

2 Main Body

2.1 Leisure Consumption Is the Basic Need for Human

Marx and Engels are both the great thinkers who thought the issue of leisure activities and leisure consumption at an early time. In *Das Kapital*, Marx divided the activities of workers into two major categories, the productive activity and the consumption activity. Correspondingly, time is also divided into working hours and free hours. Marx thought that, on one hand, the profit of the capitalism is created by surplus

M. Zhou (Ed.): ISAEBD 2011, Part III, CCIS 210, pp. 579–585, 2011.

laboring time; and on the other hand, the wealth of the capitalism liberates people from the manual laboring, and increases the free hours for people. The free hours, Marx said, is in fact the leisure time as we called today. In *The German Ideology*, Marx revealed three basic human living conditions, that is, the labor living conditions, physical living conditions and free living conditions. He called the free living conditions as the pursuit of "new needs."This new needs is actually human's leisure needs.

Marx and Engels thought the issue of leisure more from the angle of production and consumption, in their view, "leisure" is "the time that can be freely dominated" by human, it "will not be absorbed directly by productive labor, but used in the entertainment and rest, so as to open up a vast world for free activity and development."[1]The leisure"to make time available and create means for everyone"[2], so in free time, people can fully display their own preferences and expertise, develop their own intelligence, better meet their recreational and development needs and enjoy the beauty in spirit through civilized and scientific leisure consumption, so as to"make all social members can fully and freely develop and display their entire power and talent."[3]

Marx and Engels also analyze the important significance of the leisure consumption to the mass working class under the capitalism in detail, the importance of the vast working class, they point out: the leisure time at workers command is"not only necessary for the restoration of health and strength of the working class who constitute the backbone of every nation, but also necessary for ensuring workers have the opportunity to develop their intelligence, to conduct social interactions, social activities and political activities"[4].

So it can be seen in Marx and Engels' thought that leisure is a basic human right, leisure consumption is a kind of consuming behavior for all social members to meet their own development.

2.2 Leisure Consumption Influenced and Constrained by External Environment

One of the prominent features for Marx and Engels' research on the leisure consumption lies in that they did not study consumption only, but also to put leisure consumption into a larger economic system, to inspect from the whole social-ecological system.

Marx and Engels argued that all consumptions, including the leisure consumption, are an important part of the process of the overall social reproduction, and is closely related to the various aspects of the reproduction process, and influenced and constrained by the factors of other parts. Marx said: "The production displayed as starting point, the consumption displayed just as the ending point, distribution and exchange displayed as the intermediate linking parts, which is duplicate, because distribution is defined as an element from the prospect of society, exchange is defined as an element from the prospect of individual. In production, human objectification, in consumption, the object subjectification; in distribution, the society served as an intermediary between production and consumption in general, dominating and prescribed form; in exchange, production and consumption is intermediated by the requirements of the individuals accidentally. "[5] He further pointed out: "production and consumption unified directly, both served as each other's media, and create each other. If there is no consumption, there is no production; the entire production process is simultaneously the dual consuming process of both subject and object. The production behavior itself is the direct consuming behavior of all its elements. If there is no production, consumption lost its objects, thus there would be no consumption. Leisure consumption is the same ","just like the consumption of the elements and chemical substances in nature is the production of plants, "[6], this kind of consumption also produce the human body, enables human's physical and mental power to restore, maintain and develop.

Which is more valuable is that Marx and Engels also put the leisure consumption into the entire social-ecological systems to inspect. Marx thought that: "Human directly is a natural existence, as a natural existence, and is the natural existence with life." On the one hand, human has the initiative, on the other hand, as a natural object, human must rely on nature to exist, and is constrained by the external environment he existed, human is a "restricted existence."[7] Engels pointed out more clearly: "We must always remember: We rule in the natural world, not as conquerors rule the exotic nations, not as people who stand outside the nature, ...contrary, we, together with our flesh, blood and brain are all belong to the nature, and is existed in the nature. "[8] It can be seen in Marx and Engels's view that, all human consuming behaviors, including the leisure consumption can not be carried out uncontrolled; they are influenced and constrained by the various external factors.

2.3 The Alienated Leisure Consumption under Capitalism System

The consuming history of human being is a history of constantly pursue and realize self-interest of their own. Since the industrial civilization, when human beings are enjoying the tremendous material wealth brought by historical progress, meet the growing demand of consumption, they also should pay for a heavy price. As regard to this, Marx and Engels had a very deep understanding. Marx believed: The development of capitalist private ownership damaged the natural environment severely, the contaminated river water is no longer the essence of the existence of the fish, but become its opposite object, of course, it also goes to a state that is alienated and opposite to human beings . He said: "The essence of fish is its 'existence', that is water. The'essence' of river fish is river water. However, once the river is dominated by industries, once it is dyed and contaminated by other wastes, and there are ships travel in the river, once the river water is introduced into canals which can make the fish lose their living environment as long as discharging the water, then the river water is no longer the 'essence' of fish, it has become an environment not fit for fish to survive. "[9]Originally, the social labor is the objectification of human's essential power, people should feel happy and pleasure in labor, but the alienated labor under the capitalist system has become a kind of forcing labor, it is the loss of human nature, a torture of physical body and a destruction of the spirit. People's feelings and emotions to the natural are alienated, "the anxious poor people even have no feeling to the most beautiful scenery"[10]. In such cases, leisure, freedom, aesthetics, and etc are all meaningless to the workers, the leisure consumption under the capitalist system has undergone serious alienation. This kind of alienated leisure consumption is what Marx and Engels strongly opposed to.

2.4 The Essence of the Leisure Consumption is a Harmonious Unity between Human, Nature and Society

To Marx and Engels, the ideal leisure should be in a harmonious and united state between man and the nature, and the ideal leisure consumption should be harmonious consumption, without damaging the ecological environment for the aim of pursuing leisure, and without the tense relationship between human and social just because of the leisure consumption. Marx thought that, in harmonious leisure consumption, people can freely enjoy life and fully display their potential, "knowing how to produce according to the scale of any kind, and knowing how to apply the internal scale into the object everywhere,"" to build in accordance with the laws of beauty"[11].The so-called "law of beauty" is the harmonious unity of the law of nature and the law of human being, as well as the harmonious unity of the human and nature. Engels also pointed out: "We dominated the whole nature is that we are stronger than all any other animals, we can recognize and correctly apply the laws of nature."[12]

In their books, Marx and Engels have repeatedly talked about the issue of the harmony between human and nature, as well as human and society in leisure consumption activities. They believe that beautiful natural environment can not only enables people enjoy the rich gift given by nature, but also can develop human's mind, cultivate people's sentiments, enlighten people's mind, develop people's thinking and strengthen the body, which is favorable for the physical and mental health, as well as the overall development. Marx clearly saw that at the same time of human fully enjoy the tremendous civil achievements resulted by the constant transformation and conquering of nature, maintaining the harmony between man and nature is very important. Engels had warned people: "Do not over-intoxicated with the victory of human to nature. For such kind of victory each time, the nature has revenged on us. Every victory at the first step we have indeed achieved the expected results, but at the second and the third step, it turns out a completely different and unexpected results, which often has canceled the first result. "[13]

Marx and Engels thought further on the issue of the harmonious problems between human and society in the leisure consumption activities. "The essence of human is not single individual abstract existence. In its reality, it is the total sum of all social relations."[14] In all consuming activities, human must have some connections and relationships with the other people and the society. Marx consistently adhered to that the production and practice of any person is inseparable from the society, and is inseparable from the harmony between people. Human being's "activities and enjoyment, regardless of its content or its existence manner, are all social, they are social activities and social enjoyment. The essence of human in nature only exists when as regard to the society."[15]That is to say, the existence and development of any consumer are inseparable from various kinds of social relations, and social relations affect consumer's consuming preferences, consuming choices, consuming habits and consuming patterns at any time. Therefore, whether the relationship between human and society is harmonious or not is directly related to satisfaction degree of consumer, and is also related to the effects of leisure consumption.

2.5 Building a Leisure Consumption Pattern That Fit for the Comprehensive Development of Human

Marx and Engels opposed to in the narrow concept of individualism in the leisure consumption, they thought that on the basis of the harmonious unity of the human being, nature and society, and to increase the free hours through the development of productive forces, by abandon the private ownership to build a harmonious leisure pattern that fit for the needs of the comprehensive development of human.

Marx and Engels pointed out: "we should avoid reusing the 'society'as something abstract to against with individual. The individual is a social existence. Therefore, the manifestation of his life, even if it is not taking the direct form of the life manifestation that is common and being completed with the others, it is also the manifestation and confirmation of social life. "[16] To Marx and Engels, the demand for various consuming needs of human not only depends on people's consuming capacity, but also depends on the free hours which the workers possess. Only with more free time can human open up a vast world for their own free activities and development, so that can gradually from necessity to freedom.

Then how do we increase people's free time? Marx and Engels said: "The real economy –saving – is the saving of labor time ... ... and this saving is equivalent to the development of productive forces", to develop the productive forces, not only means to develop the consuming capacity, but also to develop the consuming material. " the saving of labor time is equal to an increase of free time, namely, increasing the time that enables the individual to develop themselves fully."[17] Marx further pointed out: only when productive forces is very developed can human beings be able to take a considerable amount of remaining hour from the socially necessary labor time, to constitute social free time. On the one hand, due to high development of productive forces, the working hours are shorter, free time is increased; on the other hand, the changing of the nature of labor itself provided a a broad space for the full development of individuals. To this, Marx put forward suggestions: "limit the working hours to 8 hours through legislation procedures"[18]. He also added that: "limiting the working hours is a prerequisite, and without this condition, all attempts on the pursuit of further improve the situation of workers and the liberation of workers would fail."[19]

In view of the alienation of the leisure consumption under capitalism system, the unprecedented confrontation between human and nature, and the deteriorating of the human living environment, Marx explicitly put forward that the ideal of abandoning the capitalist private ownership and rebuilding the harmonious relationship between human and nature, the beautiful ideal, he said: "the abandon of private property is the complete emancipation of all of the feelings and characteristics of human; but the reason why such abandon is such kind of liberation is that these feelings and characteristics are turning into people's whether subjectively or objectively Therefore, the needs and enjoyment lost their essence of individualism, and the nature lost its own pure usefulness, because the effectiveness of nature belongs to the effectiveness of human. "[20] By abandoning the private ownership, the leisure consumption of human abandoned the nature of individualism, pure utilitarian is removed from the relationship between human and the natural world, and thus to cultivate human's feeling of the essence of human is in accordance with the essence of the natural world, enables human to live in a real happiness and pleasure in the process of labour, and to enjoy the leisure life really.

To Marx, the fundamental criterion for measuring the progress of human, all to all, is the free and comprehensive development of human. Only Communism can provide healthy and useful work for all people, and provide adequate material life and leisure time for all the people, and provide true freedom to all people. Marx vividly described the leisure consumption in the communist society which is established on the basis of highly developed material production : "No one has a specific scope of activities, everyone can develop in any department, the society conditioned the entire production, so I might do this thing today and do that thing tomorrow at my wish, I can hunt in the morning, fish in the afternoon, and do farming at nightfall, and do criticism after dinner, but it does not therefore makes me become a hunter, a fisherman, a shepherd or a critics. "[21] It can be shown that Marx and Engels's harmonious leisure consumption concept is essentially an ecological consumption idea, it is not only beneficial for the environmental protection and the rational use of resources, but also reflects the scientific ethics, values and life outlook, and showed spiritual culture connotation at high levels.

3 Conclusion

Nowadays, we have stepped into the era of leisure, leisure has gradually become an important lifestyle for the people today, and leisure consumption has gradually become an important growth point in promoting national economic development. Therefore, the harmonious leisure consumption concept of Marx and Engels have an important practical significance in constructing a leisure consumption economic theory with Chinese characteristics, in creating a harmonious consuming environment, in increasing consumption levels and consumption quality, in establishing ecological civilization, as well as in realizing economic and social sustainable development.

References

[1] Marx, Engels: The Complete Works of Marx and Engels, vol. 26(III), p. 281. People's Publishing House, Beijing (1974)
[2] Marx, Engels: The Complete Works of Marx and Engels, Part 2, vol. 46, p. 219. People's Publishing House, Beijing (1980)
[3] Marx, Engels: The Selected Works of Marx and Engels, vol. 1, p. 217. People's Publishing House, Beijing (1972)
[4] Marx, Engels: The Complete Works of Marx and Engels, vol. 16, p. 216. People's Publishing House, Beijing (1964)
[5] Marx, Engels: The Selected Works of Marx and Engels, vol. 2, pp. 91–92. People's Publishing House, Beijing (1972)
[6] Marx, Engels: The Selected Works of Marx and Engels, vol. 2, p. 93. People's Publishing House, Beijing (1972)
[7] Marx, Engels: The Complete Works of Marx and Engels, vol. 42, p. 167. People's Publishing House, Beijing (1979)

[8] Marx, Engels: The Selected Works of Marx and Engels, vol. 3, p. 518. People's Publishing House, Beijing (1972)
[9] Marx, Engels: The Complete Works of Marx and Engels, vol. 42, p. 369. People's Publishing House, Beijing (1979)
[10] Marx, Engels: The Complete Works of Marx and Engels, vol. 42, p. 126. People's Publishing House, Beijing (1979)
[11] Marx, Engels: The Complete Works of Marx and Engels, vol. 42, pp. 96–97. People's Publishing House, Beijing (1979)
[12] Marx, Engels: The Selected Works of Marx and Engels, vol. 3, p. 518. People's Publishing House, Beijing (1972)
[13] Marx, Engels: The Selected Works of Marx and Engels, vol. 3, p. 517. People's Publishing House, Beijing (1972)
[14] Marx, Engels: The Selected Works of Marx and Engels, vol. 1, p. 18. People's Publishing House, Beijing (1972)
[15] Marx, Engels: The Complete Works of Marx and Engels, vol. 42, pp. 121–122. People's Publishing House, Beijing (1979)
[16] Marx, Engels: The Complete Works of Marx and Engels, vol. 42, pp. 122–123. People's Publishing House, Beijing (1979)
[17] Marx, Engels: The Complete Works of Marx and Engels, Part 2, vol. 46, p. 225. People's Publishing House, Beijing (1980)
[18] Marx, Engels: The Complete Works of Marx and Engels, vol. 16, p. 216. People's Publishing House, Beijing (1964)
[19] Marx, Engels: The Complete Works of Marx and Engels, vol. 16, p. 215. People's Publishing House, Beijing (1964)
[20] Marx, Engels: The Complete Works of Marx and Engels, vol. 42, pp. 124–125. People's Publishing House, Beijing (1979)
[21] Marx, Engels: The Selected Works of Marx and Engels, vol. 1, pp. 37–38. People's Publishing House, Beijing (1972)

The Analysis on the Factors of Developing Zhengzhou City into a Regional Center of International Logistics

Xia Li

School of Economics and Trade
Henan University of Technology
Zhengzhou, Henan, 450001, P.R. China
brief_mail@yahoo.com.cn

Abstract. International logistics centre, being an indispensable node in the process of international logistics, plays an important role in the development of international logistics. The creation of international logistics center involves multiple factors including traffic and geographic factor, infrastructure factor, function factor and environmental factor, etc. Through a thorough analysis, we conclude that the City of Zhengzhou possesses the prime factors of being a center of international logistics. In 2008, the State Council redefined the 10 rejuvenation industries in China. Among them, the logistics industry is the only one of the tertiary industry. Zhengzhou City boasts of the requisite resources to become the international logistics center in central and western parts of China by taking advantage of the preferential external conditions and policies.

Keywords: International logistics center Geographic location Infrastructure factor Function factor.

1 Introduction

International trade is one of the dynamic for national economic development in China. The gross value of cargo imports and exports amounts to US$ 2972.76 billion in 2010, compared with US$ 20.64 billion in 1978.It ranked the second place since 2009. International logistics underlies the cross-border transactions. International logistics center refers to large-scale collecting and distribution station featured by open operation, which deals in the storage, delivery, packing, loading and unloading, processing and logistics information processing and other business of commodities supported by international transport hub. It falls into 2 types, which are international logistics center with port and international logistics center without port respectively.

The westward movement of economic highlight hot spots is gradually becoming a reality along with the economic restructuring and the designed advancement of regional economy. The prospective international logistics centers will be allocated in central and western parts of China. The City of Zhengzhou, capital of Henan Province, is famous for being a transportation hub with wide range of radius to other areas of China. Zhengzhou could develop into an international logistics center in terms of connectivity and logistics capacity. In the wake of the integration of global economies, the implementation of the strategies of the rising of Central, western

M. Zhou (Ed.): ISAEBD 2011, Part III, CCIS 210, pp.586–591, 2011.

China, it is imperative that Zhengzhou reinforce its position as a logistics center. Hence it is urgent to have a general survey of the various factors that can help develop Zhengzhou into an international logistics center.

2 The Primary Factors on Building an International Logistics Center

An international logistics center is an integration of cargo delivery, information flow and capital flow which consists of buildings, premises, facilities, infrastructure as well as talents, management mechanism, etc.

2.1 Transport Geography Factor

The factor of geographic location and convenient traffic network tops other factors provided a city is to be built as an international logistics center since a international logistics center is supported by a transportation hub. A well-developed international logistics center must guarantee efficient functioning of every node to each economic sector. Every economic sector connects with each other and each node has its separate domain of service with no overlapping. The information exchange among all the nodes is easy and smooth and the logistics activities are of high efficiency.

2.2 Infrastructure Factor

In a logistics center, the transportation network of railway, highway, civil aviation, water carriage is available for use. The demand and the supply from each sector of the economy had been sufficiently exploited. The transport and storage service providers, wholesale and retailing companies and markets are well developed.

2.3 Information Network Factor

An international logistics center possesses a robust computer-based information management and electronic data interchange system. The logistics information network is an important constituent part of a logistics system which serves as the nerve center of logistics operation.

2.4 Function Factor

An international logistics center can provide the services of storage, packing, transport, distribution and value-added product processing. Other business includes exhibition, exposition and agency. In order to fulfill the above functions, it is necessary to equip the center with multi-functional, advanced storehouses which are suitable for entrepot trade and transit trade, standard workshops for product processing and large-area, multi-functional sites for exhibition.

2.5 Human Resources Factor

International logistics belongs to the tertiary industry which is featured by labor – intensive and talents-centered. Attracting more competitive personnel is one of the top priorities for the logistics businesses.

2.6 External Environmental Factor

Preferential government policies and a sound judicial system can support the development of an international logistics center.

3 The Corresponding Analysis on Matching the Essentials of Zhengzhou with the Factors on Building an International Logistics Center

3.1 Predominant Geographic Location and Convenient Transportation Network

The city of Zhengzhou is located in the central part of China, an intersection place of a couple of trunk lines including Beijing-Guangzhou Railway, Jiaozuo-Liuzhou Railway and Lianyungang-Lanzhou Railway. The talent, capital, technology-intensive, developed Pearl River Delta and Yangtze River Delta is to its south and east, the comparatively backward, resource-abundant, and vast-area western part of China is to its west. Zhengzhou is an important node along the Asia-Europe Continental Bridge from Lianyungang port to Rotterdam port. Zhengzhou acts as a forefront to link the Shanxin energy base, Tarim Oil and Gas Field with the provinces in East China.

In recent 10 years, Zhengzhou has been developed into a commercial center by taking advantage of its geographic location in Central China. Some of Fortune 500 multinational companies have their operations in Zhengzhou, such as Wal-mart, Carrefour and Metro, etc. There are a few leading spot-trading and futures-trading platforms headquartered in Zhengzhou including Zhengzhou Commodity Exchange, Zhengzhou Grain Wholesale Market and Huazhong Cotton Exchange. Large-sized, high-grade commercial outfits with national reputation can be found in Zhengzhou.

3.2 Well-Developed Infrastructure Facilities

The diversified modes of international logistics development justify the proposition of building Zhengzhou into an international logistics center although natural harbour is not available in the city. The traffic network of Zhengzhou is a combination of railways, civil aviation and highways.

Zhengzhou North Railway Station is the largest marshalling station in Asia; Zhengzhou East Railway Station is the largest piece goods station and one of the largest container transshipment stations in China. There are 5 international container transport routes linking Zhengzhou with Shanghai port, Kowloon, Lianyungang port, Tianjin port and Qingdao port.

The operation of Zhengzhou Xinzheng International Airport kicked off in August, 1997. It is approved by the State Council of China as the 21st national-level airport with 4E standard. It is one of the 5 civil aviation portals in China with access to urban area of Zhengzhou by expressway. 23 airlines have offered 67 domestic routes and 8 international routes as well as nonscheduled routes to Japan, Russia, Singapore, and Malaysia, etc.

Zhengzhou is located in the center of the traffic network in mid China and one of the 7 road transportation hubs in China. The Beijing-Zhuhai Expressway, Lianyungang-Horgas Freeway, national highways of G107, G310 and 18 trunk roads pass through Zhengzhou. The freeway access to large eastern ports is smooth.

3.3 Inefficient Information Network

The level of information development is slightly lower than it of other big cities. The wide application of Internet-based, EDI-aided logistics information system hasn't been achieved. The public logistics information platform is not available. The real-time data on cargo delivery cannot be provided. The separated information platforms hampered the efficiency of physical delivery and storage.

3.4 Availability of Comprehensive Logistics Service

There are 7 large logistics complex in the southeastern area of Zhengzhou by effectively integrating railroads, highways, airport and logistics ports. They are Zhengzhou National Trunk roads Logistics Port, Zhengzhou International Air Freight Center, Zhengzhou Railway Container Transport Center, Zhengzhou Piece Goods Railway Freight Center, Central China Postal Logistics Collecting and Delivering Center, Henan Import Bonded Zone and Zhengzhou Export Processing Zone. It is estimated that the logistics cost will decrease by 10%-20% at least. Quite a few industrial logistics centers have been set up, such as Yuantong Textiles Complex, Zhengzhou Airport Zone and Tianrong Construction Material Plaza, etc..

3.5 Shortage of Competent Work Force

The logistics industry is featured by talent-intensive. A constant supply of qualified personnel can warrant a healthy development of an international logistics center. It is reported that the number of individuals with national logistics certification is 200 or so. Many students of logistics choose to work outside Zhengzhou. The logistics companies in Zhengzhou can recruit over 150000 employees and a vacancy of about 50000 shall be filled in the coming years.

3.6 Strong Support from the Government Agencies

In 2005, the municipal government of Zhengzhou published the Compendium on Developing Zhengzhou into a Contemporary Logistics Center (2006-2010). Based on the bidding reports of A.T.Kearney and Roland Berger Consultancies, the local government unveiled the Compendium on Strategies and Layout of Building Zhengzhou into an International Logistics Center in March, 2010. Zhengzhou Customs Administration and Henan Entry-exit Inspection and Quarantine Bureau enter into cooperation agreement with local government of Zhengzhou to expedite the customs clearance and upgrade the level of exports in Zhengzhou to accelerate Zhengzhou's transition into an important inland entry-exit port and logistics center. The 11th Five-Year Plan of Henan Province highlights the logistics industry. National-level Henan Urban Agglomeration Development Program put for forward a proposition of building 3 Zhengzhou-centered platforms of logistics infrastructure, logistics information network and policy, law supporting system.

4 Proposals on Developing Zhengzhou into an International Logistics Center in Central China

4.1 Utilizing the Expedite Traffic Network and Encouraging Import and Export Trade

Zhengzhou commits itself to building into "a dry port" through its collaboration with Tianjin, Qingdao, Lianyungang and Shanghai and other sea ports. This arrangement can guarantee speedy inter-regional customs clearance; Zhengzhou strives to open more international container transport routes to become a "Oriental Land Port " with destinations to Central Asia, Russia and Europe by virtue of Eurasian Land Bridge, Zhengzhou Railway Container Central Station and Zhengzhou Railway Entry-exit Port(grade A). Furthermore, Zhengzhou plans to become regional distribution center of iron and steel, automobiles, textiles, garments, food, household appliances and machinery, etc.

The logistics network in Zhengzhou International Airport Zone is an important part of the logistics industry in Zhengzhou. 52 domestic flight courses and 20 overseas flight routes are available for service. Companies in the industries of electronics, information, clothing, food and cultured flower make their investment there. Foxconn is one of the big investors.

4.2 Playing a Supporting Role by the Zhengzhou Municipal Government to Ensure the Development of the Logistics Industry

The area expansion project of Zhengzhou Export Processing Zone is under way. The approval of Zhengzhou Bonded Zone is a potent impetus to the construction of a comprehensive customs clearance platform.

Trade fairs and expositions of automobiles, machinery, light industrial products, foodstuff, agricultural products, textiles, tourism and culture shall be sponsored in Zhengzhou to enhance the competitiveness of the local MICE industry. The city of Zhengzhou can make full use of the agglomeration effect of people flow, cargo movement, capital flow and information flow to accelerate the development of modern logistics industry.

The competent logistics companies shall be encouraged to tap logistics finance business. The banking firms are encouraged to tap logistics financial instruments to ease the dilemma of financing for small and medium-sized firms to keep the financial risks away, reinforce the competency in self-innovation and survive the fierce competition. Preferential policies on land, tax, price, financial support shall be made to boost the development of logistics industry based on a thorough investigation of the relevant policies in other peer cities.

4.3 Attaching Importance to Logistics Education

Firstly, since the science of logistics is an interdisciplinary subject of technology, economics and management which requires both theoretic education and practical training, the institutes of higher education shall collaborate with logistics companies to provide internship to both the students and teachers. Secondly, the logistics firms shall formulate talent incentive mechanism to attract more competent employees.

4.4 Establishing an Advanced Logistics Management Information System

An internet-based open platform shall be set up which integrates corporate MIS with EDI to realize share of data and logistics function between the logistics companies and clients.

4.5 Incubating the Backbone Logistics Companies to Survive the International Competition

More and more giant companies with overseas reputation have their business presence in the hinterland of China. It is imperative that the local large-scale logistics companies of Zhengzhou upgrade their management and sharpen their competitive edge to withstand the fierce competition. Zhengzhou-headquartered Yuxin Logistics Company and Changtong Logistics Company are encouraged to become competent players in domestic and international market. The manufacturers in the secondary industry and some renowned trading companies shall focus their efforts on their core business and outsource their logistics business to the third-party logistics(TPL) providers. The TPL providers will dominate a majority of the market share in the city of Zhengzhou.

References

1. Zhang, S., Du, H.: On the Construction of Logistics Center in China. Transport Standardization 11, 36–38 (2004) (in Chinese)
2. Gao, J., Xu, L., Pan, P.: Study on Setting up Regional Logistics Center. Urban Development Strategy 07, 37–40 (2009) (in Chinese)
3. Dobie, K., Rakowski, J.P.: Railroad and Motor Carrier Alliance: America's Global Logistics Competitive Advantage. International Advances in Economic Research 3, 4–6 (1997)
4. Hesse, M., Rodrigueb, J.-P.: The Transport Geography of Logistics and Freight Distribution. Journal of Transport Geography 5, 63–66 (2004)

The Financial Investment Projection Pursuit Model

Yan Chen

Business school of Ningbo University, Ningbo, China, 315211
chenyan999999@yahoo.com.cn

Abstract. In this paper, begin using projection pursuit approach in a new area - financial investment, trying to use projection pursuit analysis the financial investment process. Here the financial investment include the stock/option/etc investment. Assume the investment as a process from multi-dimensional variables to a one dimensional variable and establish the financial investment projection pursuit model. Finally point out the future research direction.

Keywords: new area, financial investment, projection pursuit, solution, model.

1 The New Area of the Projection Pursuit Application: Financial Investment

The projection pursuit is to locate the projection or projections from high dimensional space to low dimensional space that reveal the most details about the structure of the data set. It can overcome the "curse of dimensionality" and solve the problem of identification and extraction of higher dimensional characteristic variables for nonlinear system. The projection pursuit regressions is pioneered by Friedman and Stuetzle (1981) .The projection pursuit has been used in the flight/water/weather/etc engineering areas analysis. Like use the projection pursuit model of rotational speed of lower pressure turbine rotor of aircraft engine reveals the relation between rotational speed of lower pressure turbine rotor and other characteristic variables. In this paper, I begin use projection pursuit approach in a new area -financial investment ,trying to use it to analysis the financial investment process.here the financial investment include the stock/option/etc investment.

2 The Exploratory of the Financial Investment Projection Pursuit Model

Assume the (x,y) as a stomic variables, x is p dimensional financial investment like a stock characteristic variables, let us think that when we investment in financial market,the choice usually can be designed as from a p dimensional variables to a one dimensional variable. We assume the investment as a process from a p dimensional variables to a one dimensional variable. Here y is a one dimensional variable, and f(x)=E(y/x). f(x)is the Projection Pursuit regression function.In the Projection Pursuit Regression, we use a PPRA way which use a series functions gj(aj',x) pluses to nearly get the solution, this is as following

M. Zhou (Ed.): ISAEBD 2011, Part III, CCIS 210, pp. 592–594, 2011.

$$f(x) \sim \sum_{j=1}^{m} g_j(a_j'x) \tag{1}$$

Here we can find that when m=1last equation is as a liner regression equation. As the m become larger the .PP will be realized. We can prove that is right. We choose the aj, gj, j<m, find gm, etc, so that

$$r_m(x) = f(x) - \sum_{j=1}^{m} g_j(a_j'x) \tag{2}$$

's mode

$$\int r^2{}_m(x)dp$$

From m to m+1, reduce maxim, so that

$$g_m(a_m'x) = E[r_m(x)|a_m'x] \tag{3}$$

And we need prove only exist am, so that

$$Eg^2{}_m(a_m'x) \geq \rho \max_{|b=1|} Eg^2{}_m(b_m'x) \tag{4}$$

Here 0 <ρ<1, is a constant. so when m→∞,

$$\int \left[f(x) - \sum_{i=1}^{m} g_j(a_j'x)^2 dp \to 0 \right] \tag{5}$$

Here p is properblity. When m>1 constand, so that

$$f_m(x) = \sum_{j=1}^{m} g_j(a_j'x) \tag{6}$$

We should know that it is important to find g1. Generally when a' is contain, exist follow

$$g_1(a'x) = E(y|a'x)$$

T o find g1 is to minimum

$$Q = \sum r_j^2 = \sum [y_i - g_1(a'x)]^2 \tag{7}$$

If every a' exist g1, the Q is function of a', so we can use general optium way to solve the problem. This means the multi-dimensional investment financial stock characteristic variables problem transfer to one dimensional financial investment like stock characteristic variables problem.

3 The Future Research Direction

Exploratory financial investment projection pursuit model is a set of data analytic techniques for finding interesting low-dimensional projections of multivariate financial investment data. Application of the algorithms to real financial investment data sets reveals that these methods are very promising. In spite of the financial investment projection pursuit models is a great step forward in the problem of high-dimensional financial investment data analysis, although it has some limitations. We should design more projection pursuit software and do more financial investment analysis to abundant the financial investment projection pursuit models.

References

1. Friedman, J.H., Stuetzle, W.: Projection Pursuit Regression. J. Amer. Statist. Assoc. 76, 817–823 (1981)
2. Hall, P.: On Projection Pursuit Regression. Ann. Statist. 17, 573–588 (1989)
3. Domoho, D.L., JOhostone, I.: Projection-Based ApproximatiOn and a Duality with Kernal Methods. Ann. Statist. 17, 58–106 (1989)
4. Huber, P.J.: Projection Prsuit(with Piseussion). Ann. Statist. 13(2), 435–525 (1985)
5. Jones, L.K.: On A Conjecture of Huber Concerning the Convergence of Projection Pursuit Regression. Ann. Statist. 15, 880–882 (1987)

The Theory of the Labor Division

Yan Chen

Business School of Ningbo University, Ningbo, China, 315211
chenyan999999@yahoo.com.cn

Abstract. This paper analysis the labor division, proposes ten Chen theorems on the labor division. Ten theorems are that the division of labor in the firm is limited by the level of the firm management or the level of the resources possessed or the resources obtained ability, the division of labor is limited by the market capacity or the market volume(extent)or the market density, the division of labor in a nation is limited by the level of the government management or the level of government intervention or the level of the national institution ,the division of labor in the world is limited by the level of the world management or the level of international coordination or the level of the world institution. It has also discussed the application of these theorems.

Keywords: theorems, the labor division, application.

1 Introduction

The role of the labor division, in the general business of society, is the most important. The greater part of the skill, dexterity, and judgment with which it is anywhere directed, or applied in the market society, seem to have been the effects of the division of labor (smith,1776). The division of labor determines the improvement of social productive powers of labor and the economy growth. But what determine the division of labor?

2 The Theorems of the Labor Division

On the determination about the division of labor, there is Smith theorem in the economics. The content of the Smith theorem is that the division must always be limited by the extent of the market (smith, 1776). I affirm the partly importance and partly correctness of smith theorem, but I must also indicate its partly defects which at least consist of two aspects. One of the aspect is that its only emphasize the division of labor in the firm, but ignoring the industry and region division of labor in national scope or in world scope on the view of conception. Another is that its only emphasize the division of labor limited on the extent of the market, but ignoring others important factors or variables which limit the division of labor.

Regarding division of labor, I can analysis it on gradations as the division of labor in the firm and in the nation and in the world. On the division of labor in the nation, I also can make a distinction between macroscopic level and midroscopic level.

M. Zhou (Ed.): ISAEBD 2011, Part III, CCIS 210, pp. 595–598, 2011.

I consider the division of labor in the firm at first. The division of labor in the firm is mainly resources allocation .The resources be controlled by the firm, which includes human resources, material resources, social resources, etc. The resources allocation here is mainly realized by the firm management in fact. Generally speaking, the difference levels of the division of labor in the firm are determined by the difference levels of the firm management, therefore I give the first Chen theorem on the division of labor, which is that the division of labor in the firm is limited by the level of the firm management. Compared with different firms, we can discover that they have different resources possessed besides the management level. From the firm practice, it is quite good understanding that the difference levels of the division of labor in the firm are caused by the difference of the resources possessed or the resources obtained ability under the assumption that the firms management level are same, hence I give the second Chen theorem on the division of labor, which is that the division of labor is limited by the level of the resources possessed or the resources obtained ability. Because the status of different resources can change in different economic society, therefore I can give the first ratiocination that the division of labor is limited by the level of the land resources possessed or the land resources obtained ability in the agricultural society, the second ratiocination that the division of labor is limited by the level of the money capital possessed or the money capital obtained ability in the industrial society, the third ratiocination that the division of labor is limited by the level of the knowledge (information or human)capital possessed or the knowledge (information or human) resources obtained ability in the knowledge (information or human)society, the fourth ratiocination that the division of labor is limited by the level of the biological capital possessed or the biological capital obtained ability in the biological society, the fifth ratiocination that the division of labor is limited by the level of the ecological capital possessed or the ecological capital obtained ability in the ecological society, the sixth ratiocination that the division of labor is limited by the level of the social capital or authority capital possessed or the social capital or authority capital obtained ability in the society transformation.

Then I consider the industrial and regional division. I (1996, 2001) based on the economic analysis on the development fact of the region industry cluster, put forward the theory of productivity efficiency determined by the division—external economy. Comparatively the proposition that productivity efficiency determined by the division which was proposed by Smith, I proposed that the rising of productivity efficiency was affected together by the division and regional --industrial external economy. I extended the Smith theorem in advance, defined market volume and market density and market capacity, in which the market capacity is the first two products, pointed that the division of labor is limited by the market capacity and that the division of labor is limited by the market volume(extent) when the market density constants and that the division of labor is limited by the market density when the market volume constants .I call that the division of labor is limited by the market capacity and that the division of labor is limited by the market volume(extent) and that the division of labor is limited by the market density as the third, fourth and fifth Chen theorem on the division of labor. We can find that the fourth Chen theorem on the division of labor is similar to the Smith theorem on the division of labor.

Finally we consider the national level and the world level division of labor. Regarding national level division of labor, I base on the fact of government management and intervention, especially compare the planned economy government with the market economy government, find that the difference levels of division of labor in a nation are determined by the difference levels of the government management or the intervention level or the difference of the national institution, therefore I give the sixth Chen theorem on the division of labor which is that the division of labor in a nation is limited by the level of the government management, the seventh Chen theorem on the division of labor in a nation which is that the division of labor in a nation is limited by the level of the government intervention, the eighth Chen theorem on the division of labor in a nation which is that the division of labor in a nation is limited by the level of the national institution. Corresponds on the world level, I give the ninth Chen theorem on the division of labor in the world which is that the division of labor in the world is limited by the level of the world management or international coordination, the tenth Chen theorem on the division of labor in the world which is that the division of labor in the world is limited by the level of the world institution.

3 Application

About Chen theorems of division application, the first theorem which the division of labor in the firm is limited by the level of the firm management and the second theorem which the division of labor is limited by the level of the resources possessed or the resources obtained ability may use in for enhances the firm growth. The first, second, third, fourth, fifth, sixth ratiocination of the second theorem have the explanative and instructive functions for the different historical period firms. The third, fourth and the fifth theorem are helpful in to the cluster, the urbanization and the market development expansion, they have certain instruction functions. The sixth, seventh, eighth theorem may use in enhancing the government manage level or intervention level and promoting the national institution optimization choice. The ninth, tenth theorem may use in raising the world management level and promoting the international coordination and the optimized world institution. We also can use the Chen theorems in development growth theory.

4 Conclusions and Direction for Further Research

In this paper, I propose ten Chen theorems on the division of labor and give six ratiocinations of the second theorem. The Smith theorem is similar to the fourth Chen theorem on the division of labor. These theorems respectively in the firm, national and in the world three levels have the quite important theory and the practice significance.

This paper is adopted the similar method which proposed in the Smith theorem. Due to the limit, I mainly basis on the economical facts propose the division of labor Chen theorem. To its consummation, the application further discussion will be a direction which further research.

References

1. Gary, B., Kevin, M., Robert, T.: Human capital, Fertility, and Economy Growth. Journal of Political Economy 98(5), 12–37 (1990)
2. Gary, B., Kevin, M.: The Division of Labor, Coordination Costs, and Knowledge. The Quarterly Journal of Economics 107(4), 1137–1159 (1992)
3. Chen, Y.: The International Theory of Regional and Industrial External Economy—A Development in 'Smith Theorem' and 'Coase Theorem'. Nankai Economic Studies 5, 37–42 (1996)
4. Chen, Y.: The Economics of International Integration, pp. 59–71. China Commercial Press (2001)
5. Kim, S.: Labor specialization and the extent of the market. Journal of Political Economy 97(3), 692–705 (1989)
6. Paul, R.: Increasing Returns and Long- Run Growth. Journal of Political Economy 94(5), 1002–1037 (1986)
7. Smith, A.: An Inquiry into the Nature and Causes of the Wealth of Nations, pp. 1–30. China Commercial Press (1776) (1981)
8. Stigler, G.: The Division of Labor is limited by the extent of the market. Journal of Political Economy 59, 185–193 (1951)
9. Young, A.: Increasing Returns and Economic Progress. Economic Journal 38, 527–542 (1928)

Optimal Pricing and Replenishment for Deteriorating Items in B2B Electronic Markets

Liang-Tu Chen* and Chun-Yi Yeh

Graduate Institute of E-Business National Pingtung Institute of Commerce
51, Minsheng E. Rd, Pingtung 900, Taiwan
ltchen@npic.edu.tw

Abstract. The study proposes the inter-enterprise optimal dynamic decisions: retail price and replenishment scheduling/quantity under the retailer-managed inventory with price-only contract and the vendor-managed inventory (VMI) with consignment contract in electronic markets (EMs) respectively for deteriorating items. The numerical analysis shows that the proposed policy under the VMI with consignment can significantly increase the system efficiency and simultaneously achieve the Pareto improvements using slotting allowances for the decentralized channel in the EMs.

Keywords: Inter-enterprise, Electronic markets, Deteriorating item.

1 Introduction

In recent years, electronically-enabled supply chains have offered the potential for improving supply chain performance, including increasing coordination effectiveness and transaction efficiency, by changing the quantity and the velocity of information flow among channel partners [1]. Heinrich and Simchi-Levi [2] mentioned that there is a substantial link between information technology (IT) strategy, business processes, and supply chain performance according to a study by MIT, PERM and SAP. Numerous evidences show that enterprises applying business processes and IT systems outperform their competitors [3]. In practice, electronic markets (EMs) are an increasingly important research topic on the IT domain [4]. As advances in technology, internet-based EMs through low transaction cost and easy searching for buyers and sellers change the trade way in a channel from traditional markets into the EMs. In addition to increasing operational efficiency, the highly integrated system can strengthen strategic advantages and generate related benefits that have been well documented in the literature [4, 5]. An important building block in effective supply chain strategies is strategic partnerships between suppliers and buyers. The benefits of inter-organizational cooperation between upstream and downstream entities in a supply chain include cutting costs, enhancing profits, and other tangible and intangible rewards [6].

* Corresponding author.

M. Zhou (Ed.): ISAEBD 2011, Part III, CCIS 210, pp. 599–604, 2011.

One of the primary coordinating mechanisms is to streamline the business flows of goods and information and the decision-making processes among channel partners using vendor-managed inventory (VMI) for a vertically decentralized channel. The strategic partnerships change the ways to share information and manage inventory in a supply chain, possibly eliminating the impact of bullwhip effect [3]. Numerous channel partners engaging in collaboration and information sharing in supply chain management (SCM) via the VMI system allow vendors to harness latest retailer sales data to better forecast demand, reduce inventory and increase profit. For example, Buzzell and Ortmeyer [7] reported that these VMI projects at Dillard Department Stores, J.C. Penney and Wal-Mart have achieved sales increases of 20 to 25% and improvements in inventory turnover of 30%. However, the lately evolved enterprise resource planning systems can optimize the lot-size scheduling problem with time-varying demand over finite planning horizon, yet the dynamic aspects of pricing and other marketing related variables tend to be ignored in the highly computerized control systems. As a result, the system generates suboptimal solutions to the lot-size scheduling problem. This study uses calculus-based formulation coupled with DP techniques to solve optimal joint retail price and replenishment quantity/scheduling decision problem taking into account the dynamic nature of customer demand which is partially controllable through pricing scheme in a single-retailer and single-manufacturer channel over a multi-period planning horizon. Furthermore, the study proposes the two policies: the retailer-managed inventory with price-only (RMI with PO) and the VMI with consignment (VMI with consignment) in EMs respectively, while the channel sells a perishable product with multivariate demand function.

2 Problem Description

This study considers a single perishable item whose retail price and replenishment scheduling/quantity are reviewed periodically at time t, $t = 0, 1, 2,\ldots, H$, where H is the planning horizon. Each period begins with a joint decision regarding the scheduling of a new replenishment and its associated retail price. The problem is equivalent to determining the optimal sequence of issuance times for new replenishment z_{i-1}, $i = 1, 2,\ldots, n$, with the retail price being reset, and the lot-size simultaneously specified so as to maximize the profit stream over $[0, H]$. In the profit maximization problem, all the future revenue and costs are subject to the effects of inflation and time discounting. The net discount rate of inflation is assumed to be constant over time: $R = r - i$, where i is the inflation rate and r is the discount rate representing the time value of money.

3 The Model

Traditionally, a usual behavior for vertically decentralized channel coordination is the RMI system with PO contract, where the retailer is entirely responsible for replenishment scheduling/quantity and retail price decisions. Recently, the other substitute for channel coordination is the VMI system with consignment contract, where the manufacturer is fully responsible for the replenishment scheduling/quantity and retail price decisions. Hence, this study develops the mathematical models and solution procedures for decentralized channels under the RMI with PO and VMI with consignment settings in the EMs, respectively.

3.1 RMI with PO Setting

The base model considers a RMI with PO contract in EMs for a vertically decentralized two-echelon supply chain with one manufacturer and one retailer. The retailer has the right to decide the replenishment scheduling/quantity besides the retail price, and focuses only on her own profit maximization over the multi-period planning horizon, without considering her counterpart's reaction and channel-wide profit. The retailer owns the goods ownership and holds inventory of the goods which is subject to a constant deteriorating rate, and replenishes inventory from the supplier, which incurs a replenishment operations cost in order to meet a deterministic price-dependent and time-varying demand. The study in the section first derives a generic model for determining the optimal joint decisions: retail price and lot-size over an arbitrary selling period [z_{i-1}, z_i]. The model is further extended into a multi-period formulation where the optimal sequence of replenishments z_{i-1}, and associated retail price and lot-size for i = 1, 2,..., n, are determined using a DP approach.

In this study, a firm operating an EM is referred to as an independent third party, which advances the ability of marketing to optimally assign resources. The manufacturer and retailer have to pay the owner of the EM a transaction fee per unit when they join the EM. The transaction fee per unit in the EM may be a transaction-based commission fee charged by the owner of the EM which is usually a percentage of the transaction value, denoted ρ_R and ρ_M for the retailer and manufacturer respectively. According to the above definition, the retailer discount profit over the selling period [z_{i-1}, z_i] is the retailer discount revenue minus the relevant discount costs due to the purchase cost, holding cost, deteriorating cost, retailer transaction fee, and replenishment operations cost:

$$\pi_{RMIPO,R}(p) = \int_{z_{i-1}}^{z_i} pe^{-Rt}(a-bp)e^{\lambda t}dt - \int_{z_{i-1}}^{z_i} we^{-Rz_{i-1}}(a-bp)e^{\lambda t+\theta(t-z_{i-1})}dt - \int_{z_{i-1}}^{z_i} he^{-Rt}\int_t^{z_i}(a-bp)e^{\lambda t+\theta(u-t)}du\,dt$$

$$-\int_{z_{i-1}}^{z_i}\rho_R pe^{-Rt}(a-bp)e^{\lambda t}dt - S_R e^{-Rz_{i-1}}, \tag{1}$$

in which $D(p,t)=(a-bp)e^{\lambda t}$ which is the multivariate demand function with price-dependent (p) and time-varying (t), w is the purchase cost per unit, θ is the constant deteriorating rate, h is the holding cost per unit of time, and S_R is the replenishment operations cost per lot. The optimal retail price, denoted by p^*_{RMIPO}, under the RMI with PO contract in the EM that maximizes the retailer discount profit over period [z_{i-1}, z_i] can be obtained by taking the first-order derivative of Eqn. (1) with respect to p and setting the result equal to zero. The corresponding manufacturer discount profit generated from the selling period [z_{i-1}, z_i] is the discount wholesale revenue minus the discount variable production cost, manufacturer transaction fee and production setup cost:

$$\pi_{RMIPO,M} = \int_{z_{i-1}}^{z_i} we^{-Rz_{i-1}}(a-bp)e^{\lambda t+\theta(t-z_{i-1})}dt - \int_{z_{i-1}}^{z_i} ce^{-Rz_{i-1}}(a-bp)e^{\lambda t+\theta(t-z_{i-1})}dt - \int_{z_{i-1}}^{z_i} \rho_M we^{-Rz_{i-1}}(a-bp)e^{\lambda t+\theta(t-z_{i-1})}dt - S_M e^{-Rz_{i-1}}, \tag{2}$$

in which c is the production cost per unit and S_M is the production setup cost per run. Substituting p with p^*_{RMIPO} into Eqns. (1) and (2), the study yields the maximal retailer discount profit $\pi^*_{RMIPO,R}$ and manufacturer discount profit $\pi^*_{RMIPO,M}$, and associate maximal channel-wide discount profit, denoted by $\pi^*_{RMIPO,C}$, over an arbitrary period [z_{i-1}, z_i]. In the decentralized channel coordination under the RMI with PO contract in the EM, the retailer determines the sequence of replenishment besides the retail price. For further extending into a multi-period planning horizon formulation, the study applies the DP approach to determine the optimal replenishment scheduling, and the associated retail price, replenishment quantity, and discount profits of the retailer, manufacturer and channel-wide as follows

$$\Pi^{**}_{RMIPO,R,z_i} = Max\{\Pi^*_{RMIPO,R,z_{i-1}} + \pi^*_{RMIPO,R} : 0 \le z_{i-1} < z_i \le H\}, \tag{3}$$

with boundary condition $\Pi_{RMIPO,R,0} = 0$. The recursive procedure works in a forward fashion to determine the maximal total retailer discount profit over the time horizon. On the last stage of the procedure, $\Pi^{**}_{RMIPO,R,H}$ is found that is the maximal total retailer discount profit over the planning horizon. The optimal replenishment scheduling and retail price over the time horizon, denoted by $(z^{**}_{i-1,RMIPO}, p^{**}_{RMIPO,z^{**}_{i-1}})$, can be obtained by tracking backward from time H to time 0.

3.2 VMI with Consignment Setting

In the decentralized channel coordination with the VMI and consignment contract under the EM, the manufacturer owns the goods title and decides the sequence of replenishment besides the retail price over the multi-period planning horizon. Let r denote the fraction of channel revenue that the retailer keeps, so $(1-r)$ is the fraction that the manufacturer earns. According to the above definitions, the manufacturer discount profit during an arbitrary selling period [z_{i-1}, z_i] is the channel discount revenue that the manufacturer earns minus the associated discount costs, including the manufacturer transaction fee, variable production cost, holding cost, deteriorating cost, production setup cost, and replenishment operations cost:

$$\pi_{VMICS,M}(p) = \int_{z_{i-1}}^{z_i} (1-r)pe^{-Rt}(a-bp)e^{\lambda t}dt - \int_{z_{i-1}}^{z_i} ce^{-Rz_{i-1}}(a-bp)e^{\lambda t+\theta(t-z_{i-1})}dt - \int_{z_{i-1}}^{z_i} he^{-Rt}\int_t^{z_i}(a-bp)e^{\lambda u+\theta(u-t)}du\,dt$$
$$- \int_{z_{i-1}}^{z_i} \rho_M(1-r)pe^{-Rt}(a-bp)e^{\lambda t}dt - S_M e^{-Rz_{i-1}} - S_R e^{-Rz_{i-1}}. \tag{4}$$

The optimal retail price that maximizes the manufacturer discount profit over period [z_{i-1} , z_i] under the VMI with consignment contract can be obtained by taking the first-order derivative of Eqn. (4) with respect to *p*, and setting the result equal to zero. The corresponding discount profit of the retailer over the selling period [z_{i-1} , z_i] is the retail discount revenue minus the retailer discount transaction fee:

$$\pi_{VMICS,R} = \int_{z_{i-1}}^{z_i} (1-\rho_R) rpe^{-Rt}(a-bp)e^{\lambda t}dt \ . \tag{5}$$

Following a similar procedure developed for the RMI with PO contract, the optimal sequence of replenishment and the associated retail price for a multi-period planning horizon formulation under the VMI with consignment contract, denoted by $(z^{**}_{i-1,VMICS}, p^{**}_{VMICS,z^{**}_{i-1}})$, can be obtained by the DP approach:

$$\Pi^{**}_{VMICS,M,z_i} = Max\{\Pi^{*}_{VMICS,M,z_{i-1}} + \pi^{*}_{,VMICS,M} : 0 \le z_{i-1} < z_i \le H\}. \tag{6}$$

4 Numerical Analysis

The two policies in the study incorporating the proposed solution procedures were implemented on a personal computer with a Pentium CPU at 2.13 GHz under a Windows XP operating system running Mathematica. The numerical analysis reveals that the VMI with consignment contract outperforms the RMI with PO contract in EMs with slotting allowances $F \in (\min F, \max F)$, $\min F = Max((\Pi^{**}_{RMIPO,R,H} - \Pi^{**}_{VMICS,R,H}), 0)$ and $\max F = Max((\Pi^{**}_{VMICS,M,H} - \Pi^{**}_{RMIPO,M,H}), 0)$, in terms of channel system efficiency and Pareto improvements for the vertically decentralized channel.

5 Conclusion

This investigation summarizes the emerging research on managing a vertically decentralized single-retailer and single-manufacturer multi-period channel which produces and sells deteriorating goods in B2B e-markets. This study formulated two decision models for the decentralized channel coordination under retailer-managed inventory with price-only contract and vendor-managed inventory with consignment contract. The numerical results have shown that the proposed policy under the VMI with consignment contract can significantly increase the system efficiency and simultaneously achieve Pareto improvements using slotting allowances for the vertically decentralized channel. A natural extension of this investigation is to develop a prototype of a decision support system.

Acknowledgments. The author would like to thank the National Science Council (Taiwan) for financially supporting this research under Contract No. NSC97-2410-H-251-010.

References

1. Yao, Y., Palmer, J., Dresner, M.: An Interorganizational Perspective on the Use of Electronically-Enabled Supply Chains. Decision Support Systems 43, 884–896 (2007)
2. Heinrich, C., Simchi-Levi, D.: Do It Investments Really Change Financial Performance? Supply Chain Management Review, 22–28 (May 2005)
3. Simchi-Levi, D., Kaminsky, P., Simchi-Levi, E.: Designing and Managing the Supply Chain: Concepts, Strategies, and Case Studies. McGraw-Hill, Taiwan (2008)
4. Standing, S., Standing, C., Love, P.E.D.: A Review of Research on E-Marketplaces 1997-2008. Decision Support Systems 49, 41–51 (2010)
5. Power, D.J., Sharda, R.: Model-Driven Decision Support Systems: Concepts and Research Directions. Decision Support Systems 43, 1044–1061 (2007)
6. Lee, H.L.: The Triple-A Supply Chain. Harvard Business Review 82, 102–112 (2004)
7. Buzzell, R.D., Ortmeyer, G.: Channel Partnerships Streamline Distribution. Sloan Management Review 36, 85–96 (1995)

An Exploratory Study on the Internet Enabled Economic Patterns

Shiyang Wei

Institute of Policy & Management, Chinese Academy of Sciences,
No. 15, Zhong-Guancun Bei-Yitiao, Haidian District, Beijing, 100191, P.R. China
sywei@casipm.ac.cn

Abstract: In order to get an overview of the studies that have followed the positivistic research paradigm of the information society pioneered by Manuel Castells[1], this study has reviewed relevant theories and brought forward several new analyzing perspectives. Moreover, based on the general research methodology of social science, this study had designed a 4-dimension theory evaluation model to form a systematic perception of the relevant theories. Finally, this study makes an anticipation of the theoretical development in the internet enabled economy study area.

Keywords: internet, economics, review, anticipation, literature survey.

1 Introduction

Although scholars from various backgrounds are interested in the "Information Society" issue, no authorized definition of it has been reached up till now. What has been consented is that the human society began entering the information era in 1970s.

Besides "information society" [1], scholars have created many other terms to conclude the most distinct attribute of the influence that the technology development has done towards the modern society, e.g. knowledge economy [2], post-industrial society [3], post-modern society [4], digital capitalism [5], and virtual capitalism [6] etc.

In recent years, the term network society [7] has come into the vision of academics. Different from former scholars who have analyzed the problem from a rough integral perspective and pursued logical format, Manuel Castells (2000) [7] has done positivistic researches and founded the network society conjecture. He argued the network logic as one of the core attributes of the information technology paradigm (the others are information, pervasiveness, flexibility and convergence).

Following the positive network logic perspective of the information society, this study has made a literature survey about positive theories done on the internet economic patterns. Because internet poses as a dominate convergence of the information technology, the economic patterns those theories have studied are called

[1] (Spanish name: Manuel Castells Oliván, born in Hellín, Albacete,Spain, in 1942) is a sociologist especially associated with information society and communications research.

M. Zhou (Ed.): ISAEBD 2011, Part III, CCIS 210, pp. 605–616, 2011.

internet enabled[2] economic patterns. A systemic evaluation of those theories has been made afterwards. Problems that have occurred during theory construction have been analyzed and the trends of these theories' development have been anticipated.

2 Evaluation Model of the Positive Theory Construction

The evaluation model is consisted of 4 dimensions: 1) the theory construction process dimension which positions a theory's construction stage based on the general process of a scientific survey; 2) the research methodology dimension, in which the tactics of how to guarantee the scientificity of social science theory are discussed, and mistakes that are likely to make are concluded; 3) the social science theory classification dimension, in which social science theories are classified according to their research methods, research scales and research levels; 4) the more mature theory influence dimension, in which theories that are more capable of explaining the phenomena are introduced.

2.1 Theory Construction Process Dimension

Founded on positivism which emphasizes perceptions formed through experiences, modern scientific method is a bunch of techniques that are utilized to survey observations, correct and integrate knowledge. In order to guarantee its scientificity, a survey must base on observable, measurable, empirical evidence, moreover, accord with the basic principles of reasoning. A scientific research is mainly consisted of 4 steps below: 1) Use your experience: Consider the problem and try to make sense of it. Look for previous explanations. If this is a new problem to you, then move to step2. 2) Form a conjecture: When nothing else is yet known, try to state an explanation, to someone else, or to your notebook. 3) Deduce a prediction from that explanation: If you assume 2 is true, what consequences follow? 4) Test: Look for the opposite of each consequence in order to disprove 2 [8]. Generally speaking, theories that are at the 1st and 2nd step are called empirical theories, theories that are at the 3rd and 4th step are called normative theories. The two distinct attributes of a scientific survey are: 1) repeatable; 2) falsifiable.

2.2 Research Methodology Dimension

Social science, together with natural science, is a subtype of science. However, because social phenomena are only observable but not controllable or duplicable, a social science theory is further improved or disrupted only when supportive or opposite phenomenon takes place.

Based on the general research methodology of social science and research experiences, this study concluded 5 kinds of mistakes that are easy to make during theory construction: 1) explaining new phenomena through an old theoretic perspective. When an anomaly occurs, the incumbent theory usually neglects its

---

[2] Enable is a technological term in E&E, meaning to change the logic status of an electronic element. This study borrowed the term to hint the influence the information technology has done on society.

existence. If both the amount and influence of the anomaly are significant, the incumbent theory has the inertia of tailoring the phenomena according to its logic (happens at the 4th step of the theory construction process); 2) the causal analysis is done without approving that the observed phenomena are statistically significant (1st step); 3) enlarging a theory's applying scope by covering phenomena that do not have direct relationship with the theory (1st step); 4) simply considering correlation as causal relationship when forming a conjecture. This mistake is a common one when cluster and correlation analysis are well applied by means of the powerful statistical software (2nd step); 5) improperly introducing other theories to further develop the conjecture. Since there are differences between the contexts, introducing other theory as a way of deducing the conjecture may cause the validity of such reasoning be questioned (3rd step).

2.3 Social Science Theory Classification Dimension

There are generally two types of theories according to the positive theory construction stage: the empirical stage theory (1st and 2nd step) and the normative stage theory (3rd and 4th step).

According to the problem scale, social science theory could be divided into small scale theory, medium scale theory and large scale theory [9]. Because it is induced from phenomena which span limited time and space, small scale theory has exact causal relationship statements. Along with the expansion of the research scope, the possibility of stating exact causal relationship has gradually reduced. That is why a large scale theory is usually not falsifiable [9]. The majority of social science theories are small scale ones, the emergence of large scale theory always accompanies social revolution, e.g., the wealth of nation accompanied the industrial revolution, and the Das Capital accompanied the political revolutions of many countries.

According to the research level, theories could be divided into the individual level, the organizational level, the value network level, the industry/sector level and the national economic & political institution level [10].

2.4 Other Theory Influence Dimension

During the process of literature survey, it is found that there are other theories which have given more profound explanations of the relevant phenomena. Their perspectives facilitate to position the incumbent theory. A detailed explanation is going to be given in the later part.

3 Literature Survey Strategy

Because the internet enabled economic patterns study is a brand new area, relevant researches are dispersed in various fields without obvious searching key words. As a result, it is not feasible to grasp the research advancement by simply putting key words into the searching engine. It is necessary to design a literature survey strategy.

This study develops the literature survey along two directions: the research level direction and the disciplinary direction which involves futurology, economics, sociology and principles of management. There are two stages of the literature survey:

the initial stage aims at finding all relevant researches, and the second stage involves the researches that are cited or mentioned in the first stage surveyed theories. The literatures mainly come from CNKI (China National Knowledge Infrastructure), Jistor, National (Digital) Library of China, National (Digital) Science Library, Chinese Academy of Sciences.

Confined by time, energy, and literature sources, there is possibility that important researches are not included in the survey.

4 Theory Review and Evaluation

4.1 Marginal Utility Increase Theory

Marginal Utility Theory is the core theory of the Marginal Revolution which is claimed to be the starting point of economics entering the static general equilibrium research paradigm [11]. The Marginal Utility Theory is created by William S. Jevons[3] from studying the bilateral exchange process. He pointed out that unless the marginal importance of the acquiring commodity exceeded that of the abandoned one, the exchange process never happened.

$$\frac{\phi_1(a-x)}{\varphi_1(y)} = \frac{y}{x} = \frac{\phi_2(x)}{\varphi_2(b-y)} \quad (1)$$

The above formula indicates that the ratio of the marginal utility of abandoning x unites of A commodity to that of acquiring y unites of B commodity is inversely correlated with the ratio of y to x. In other words, the more commodity A one possesses, the less utility the last one unit will bring to him/her. As a conclusion, the marginal utility of a commodity decreases.

Marginal Utility Increase Theory is widely mentioned in books talking about the Network Economy. E.g., Network Economics [12], states that the consumption in network economy (mainly refers to the consumption of the information products) is highly related with technology, such attribute requires consumers must have computer and network knowledge, the more knowledge the consumers have, the more utility they will get while consuming. Moreover, strengthened by lock-in effect and network externality, marginal-utility-increase phenomena have become prevalent in the network economy.

However, this study argues that the consumption utility of the information products is not always dependent on the computer and network knowledge of the consumers. Such dependence exists on two occasions: 1) the consumers utilize the products as a tool to develop new products; 2) the interface of such products is not user-friendly enough. As technology develops, the second occasion will disappear in the future.

Moreover, the foundation of the marginal-utility-decrease conclusion is the exchange of a certain tangible commodity which might be owned in numbers. However, people do not need to buy the same information product for a second time. As a result, the information products do not suite the marginal utility logic at all.

[3] (1 September 1835 – 13 August 1882), is considered as the first one to use mathematics to analyze economy.

Since information products are duplicated with little costs, it is possible that their diffusions are not through exchange, but free broadcast. It is for protecting the interests of the producers has the exchange process of information products been manipulated by the tactics of intellectual property rights protection, fast technological upgrade behavior, and the not backwards compatible product policy.

The diffusion of information products will not deprive the ownership of initial producers or owners, but redistribute the control power which decides how relevant situations would develop, since un-anticipated participants join the situation by acquiring the information. Because the cost of blockading information is much higher than duplicating it, such attribute of information products is un-negligible.

As a conclusion, the marginal-utility-increase theory is not derived from facts, but deduced from the classical analyzing framework. It has made the 1st type mistake: explaining new phenomena through an old theoretic perspective. This theory is at the empirical stage since it has built up the conjecture, but has not further deduced a normative forecast, e.g. what products fit the conjecture, what adjustment should the competitive strategy complement. Because it studies exchange processes on the individual level, it belongs to small scale theory. This study argues that this analyzing perspective does not suite the attribute of information products, further studies might develop along the control power redistribution direction.

4.2 Competition Theory

Michael Porter (2009) [13], in his competition theory, queried the advantages the internet had done towards the economy. He argued that the market signal made by any emerging technology is un-dependable. The false impressions of the internet reflect in the following 3 aspects: 1) many internet firms set policies to transfer their profits to consumers in order to gain more share of the internet market; 2) many dealers make deals on the internet not because they need internet, but their curiosity; 3) the internet firms' survival depends largely on venture capital but not their profits.

This study argues that the competition theory generates in the 20th century, and serves the firms of the industrial age. The foundation of this theory is the existence of firms as the main organizational forms in economy, the products are tangible and the resources are scarce. Holding this perspective, it is not possible for Porter to see that internet has reshaped many industries' value chain system, e.g. the music industry, the retail industry, etc. The figure of the Amazon's profit change (as is shown in fig.1.) has also demonstrated that its dependence on VC is only temporary.

The competition theory is one of the most influential management theories in the 20th century. As the theory builder, Michael Porter is inclined to explain any phenomenon from his analyzing framework. That is why the vigor of the internet cannot be seen by him. The theory has made the 1st type mistake, namely explaining new phenomena through an old theoretic perspective. The competition theory is a theory that has finished both empirical and normative stages. It is a small scale theory which focuses on problems of the value network level and the organizational level.

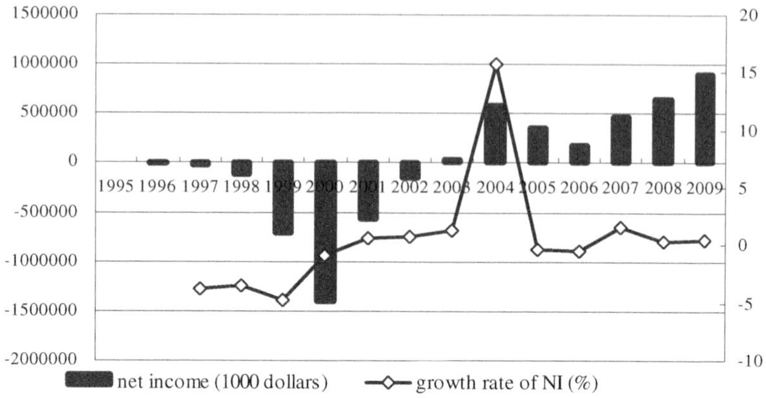

Data Source: annual reports of Amazon Inc. [14]

Fig. 1. Amazon's Annual Profit Changing Situation

4.3 Network Effect Theory

The term network effect (network externality) originated from the practice of the Bell company, and became well-known by means of the Metcalf's law. The research system of network effect consists of 3 parts: 1) the concept system, 2) the network effect classification, and 3) influences and solutions to diminish network effects. The delegate scholars are Katz, Shapiro, Farrell, Saloner, Liebowitz and Margolis, et al. [15].

The influences that the network externality does towards market are reflected in two aspects: 1) causing the actual production lower than the efficient social production; 2) causing the suboptimum technology gaining the market [16]. The new institutional economy has claimed that the externality could be absorbed through defining property rights. Many scholars then follow such route to solve the influence of the network externality.

However, this study argues that the defining property right method does not suit the network externality. According to the definition of network externality, it poses as a core function of a certain product. In other words, the reason why the product is worth buying is because its network externality.

As a result, although network externality causes less efficient production and the suboptimum technology gaining the market, there lacks institutional method to solve it. However, it does not mean that once formed, the network externality can not be removed. The incumbent network would collapse when opportunity windows emerge: the infrastructural technologies evolve into a new age; the product/service upgrades its user experience; accidental events cause the incumbent network paralyzed.

As a conclusion, because it has adapted the Coase's way of solving the negative influences of externality, the network externality theory has made the 5th mistake: improperly introducing other theories to further develop the conjecture. It belongs to small scale theory which develops on the individual level, and has accomplished the empirical stage, being at the normative stage.

4.4 Business Model Theory

Until now, the business model study can be divided into 2 stages. The first stage is the business model research aiming at the ICT industry since 1999; the 2nd stage is the business model research on various kinds of industries from 2005.

The delegate studies of the 1st stage are Timmers (1998), Afuah and Tucci (2001), Rappa (2000), Osterwalder (2002), Mahadevan (2000), Amit & Zott (2001), Gordijn & Akkermans (2001).

In this stage, scholars have done researches on business model concept, classification, analyzing framework and evaluation.

The common points of this stage's business model analyzing frameworks are 1) considering the relationship between enterprises and customers, and what value the enterprises provide as the most significant parts of the business model; 2) interested in the sustainability of the enterprises' profit gaining mode. It is easy to understand why the sustainability of profits is widely concerned, since it decides the enterprises' survival. The attention towards the firm & customer relationship is a consequence of the network technology which has reshaped such relationship and made the power of customers stronger than ever before.

As for the business model evaluation research of this stage, only one rough evaluation framework has been brought forward by Allan Afuah and Christopher L. Tucci (2001) [18].

The business model research of this stage is caused by people's curiosity towards the internet. Such curiosity vanished along with the 2000-2002 internet bubble, making people consider the internet more rational. Because the business model has not confined itself to a certain industry/sector, more scholars are joining in making various industries/sectors to be their research objects and contexts.

The main researchers of the 2nd stage are Osterwalder (2005), Morris (2002), Koo (2004), Jansen (2007) based on western contexts, and Yuan (2007), Qiao (2009), Wei et al. (2009) based on Chinese local contexts.

At the 2nd stage, the business model has evolved as a perspective. It is not feasible to make a classification of business models at this stage since numerous industries/sectors are getting involved. As a result, researches mainly focus on the analyzing framework and the evaluation of business model. Because most firms getting involved are not internet firms, their researches are not further discussed in this study.

In conclusion, the business model theory has provided an analyzing framework. Firms' complex operating activities are greatly simplified through it, this makes concluding the common places of the firms and inducing the rules behind become possible. However, because the empirical phenomena are changing fast, there are still further space for business model's definition and analyzing framework. It is possible that the emergence of the new phenomena will disrupt the original systems.

Business model research is developed on the individual and organizational level. Although many industries/sectors are involved in the 2nd stage, they are discussed separately, so the business model theory belongs to the small scale theory. The business model has undergone the evaluation process which has normative meanings, as a result, this theory is at the normative stage.

4.5 Review on the Observations of the Internet Enabled Economic Patterns

The observers who are interested in the internet enabled economic patterns are coming from various fields. E.g. technology professionals, like Hou Ziqiang[4], Wu Hequan[5], the futurologist Negroponte (1997), Kevin Kelly (1994), Alvin Toffler (1980), historians like Alfred Chandler (2008), Lin Jun (2009), and journalists and editors from the pioneering magazines who have the first hand information of the frontier, e.g. Duan Yongchao (2009), Hu Yong (2008), Fang Xingdong (2009), Li Li(2009), Nicolas Carl (2008), Chris Anderson (2009), Lawrence Lessig (2005) etc. Duo to lack of academic trainings and without clear research purposes, most of these works always span many facts and concepts, and did not logically converge. However, some of the works have indeed put forward new ideas. They are the long tail theory [17], the crowdsourcing theory [18], the wikinomics theory [19], and the post-modern economics theory [20].

4.5.1 Long Tail Theory

After observations, Anderson [17] has brought forward a conclusion which contradicts the classical economic theory: through internet retail platform, a variety economy is achieved, meaning that all kinds of products will sell out without considering the demand-supply relationship of the market.

This study argues that the long tail theory has made 2nd and 3rd type of mistakes which mean that the long tail statement was drawn without relevant phenomena showing statistical significance in a certain industry/sector (2nd mistake), moreover, the theory has enlarged its applying scope by covering phenomena that do not have direct relationship with the theory (3rd mistake). This theory belongs to small scale theory that does research on individual level. Since the long tail theory has formed its conjecture, but not made any further deduction, it is at the empirical stage.

4.5.2 Crowdsourcing Theory

After having observed the operational modes of many internet firms, Jeff Howe [18] considered that the term crowdsourcing could well summarize the common places of these operational modes. He argued that in the internet era, the performance of the crowd is always better than that of the same number employees in a company.

He had further concluded the necessary conditions for the emergence of the crowd sourcing, however, did not further research under what coordination mechanism the community could organize the people who are involved.

In conclusion, the theory is a small scale theory, done on the individual level. It has analyzed quite an amount of firms, and formed the initial conjecture. As a result, it is at the empirical stage.

4.5.3 Wikinomics Theory

Don Tapscott and Anthony D. Williams [19] have concluded the characteristics of the internet economy as Openness, Peering, Sharing and Global Operation.

---

[4] (born in 1937, Shanghai, China), An expert on signal & system from Chinese Academy of Sciences, being the chairman of the board of the China Kejian Inc. from 1992 to 2005.

[5] (born in 1941, Guangzhou, China), an expert on optical fiber transmission and broad band information network from Chinese Academy of Engieering.

The wikinomics stated the four characteristics of the new economy, however, did not dissertate the relationship between them. The information products' low cost duplicating attribute makes openness become a necessity of this economy. The direct outcome of openness is sharing, so it seems not necessary to make sharing as another characteristic. The characteristic Peering means that in the new context, the work relationship between people is not hierarchical but peering. This characteristic indicates the change of the organizational coordination mechanism. However, the cases that the consumers take part in the new product R&D process, and the cases that scientists build information platform for sharing their researches with colleagues are discussed in this part but cannot be explained by this characteristic. This study considers the word "collaborative" to be better. The cases used to induce the global operations characteristic are actually the cases of firms in traditional industries seeking rent during the economic globalization process. These cases happen because of the regional economic differences, not directly related with the IT technology, especially the internet. Thus, such characteristic could be called a characteristic of the globalization, but not that of the wikinomics.

As a conclusion, the four characteristics advanced by the author do not summarize the wikinomics' specialties properly, it seems more likely that they are coming from serendipitous ideas rather than rational cluster analysis. However, the phenomena that have been depicted while dissertating each characteristic are typical and should be paid attention to. As a theory, it has completed the 1st, 2nd step of the research process, so it is at the empirical stage. The mistake it has made does not belong to the theory construction mistakes which have been concluded in part 2, but basic logical mistake of not categorizing the phenomena properly.

4.5.4 Post-Modern Economy Theory

The post-modern economy theory [20] tries to discuss the post-modern economy from 7 aspects: value, exchange, organization, capital, institution and welfare.

The core part of this theory is the advancement of the information value. Jiang argued that the common value space is two-dimensional, containing the value in use (value of the product on its function) and the value (exchange value). The internet has enabled a third dimension: the information value or significance value (the psychological value of a product to its buyer/seller).

The information value has made the exchange process from homogeneous to heterogeneous. The individualized exchange requires the transition of the intermediary from pecuniary exchange to semantic exchange. Through semantic exchange, the heterogeneity like individuality and emotion can be better embodied. The pecuniary exchange happens when the values of the exchanging things are equal, however, the semantic exchange takes place when both of the exchanging sides consider it as proper.

In fact, the idea that the information value needs semantic exchange to fully realize is a way of articulating and exchanging the experienced utility[6] [21]. However, the post-modern theory does not give the attributes of such utility, or the rules of how to

---

[6] Refers to a person's psychological feelings towards gain or loss, was advanced by Daniel Kahneman (1997) [21]. It is measurable and can be divided into instant utility and remembered utility.

articulate and exchange it. This question has been answering by the behavioral economists. The main attributes of the experienced utility are expressed in Fig.2.

There are four attributes of the experienced utility: 1st, Loss Aversion [22]; 2nd, the endowment effect [23], 3rd, the sensitivity degression [24], and 4th, transaction utility [25].

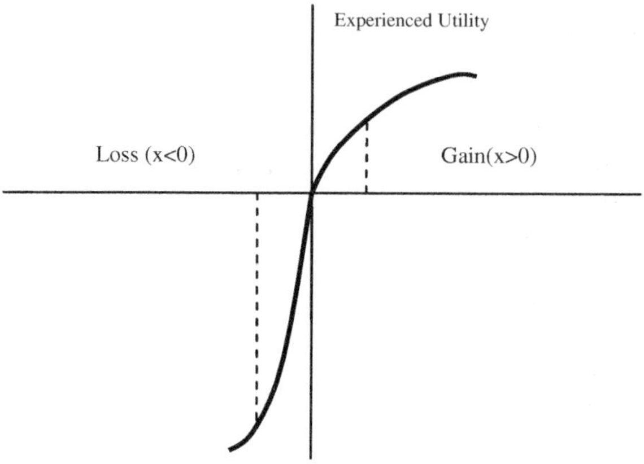

Fig. 2. the Attribute Function of Experienced Utility

In conclusion, the post-modern economy theory has put forward the information value through observing the internet cases. Such conclusion process belongs to the 2nd stage of the research process. The theory has tried to advance further deduction solving how the information value is exchanged, however, the solution is lack of feasibility. Another theory behavioral economics has been introduced because it explains such phenomena more deeply. As a result, the post-modern economy theory is beginning its normative stage, but needs to absorb the research conclusions of the behavioral economics to adjust itself. The post-modern economy theory belongs to small scale theory which develops on the individual research level.

5 Conclusions and Future Prospects

The critics of the theories are not repeated in this part. We could see from table 2 that most of the theories are small scale ones done on the individual, organizational level. This situation indicates that the researches on the internet enabled economic patterns are only at the initial stage. The 1st, 2nd and 3rd theories have places to adjust, while the theories from 4th to 8th need further improvements to complete their theory construction processes. Because the internet has not fully shown its influences towards the society, there is high possibility that un-anticipated phenomena will take place and disrupt original theories. As a result, the next stage research on such issue is supposed to focus on the field study continuously.

Table 1. The Overview of Theories on Internet Enabled Economic Patterns

stage	mistake	Scale
1-4	1-5	s,m,b

		Research Level														
#	Theory Name	Individual Level			Organizational Level			Value Network Level			Industry/Sector Level			National Political/Economic Level		
1	Marginal Utility Increase Theory	2	5	s												
2	Competition Theory				4	1	m	4	1	m						
3	Network Effect Theory	3	5	s												
4	Business Model Theory	3		s	3		s									
5	Long Tail Theory	2	2,3	s												
6	Crowdsourcing Theory	2		s												
7	Wikinomics Theory				2	B	m									
8	Post-Modern Economy Theory	3		s												
9	Network Society theory	4		b	4		b	4		b	4		b	4		b

References

1. Machlup, F.: The Production and Distribution of Knowledge in the United States. Princeton University Press, New Jersey (1962)
2. Stehr, N.: Knowledge Societies. Sage, London (1994)
3. Touraine, A.: The Post-Industrial Society. In: Tomorrow's Social History: Classes, Conflicts and Culture in the Programmed Society. Random House, New York (1971)
4. Lyotard, J.: The Postmodern Condition. Manchester University Press, Manchester (1984)
5. Schiller, D.: Digital Capitalism. MIT Press, Cambridge (2000)
6. Dawson, M., Foster, J.B.: Virtual Capitalism. Robert W. (1998)
7. Castells, C.: The Rise of the Network Society. Blackwell Pulishers, Oxford (2000)
8. Scientific Method, `http://en.wikipedia.org/wiki/Scientific_method`
9. Luo, J.: Social Network Analysis. Social Sciences Academic Press (China), Beijing (2010) (in Chinese)
10. Chesbrough, H., Vanhaverbeke, W.: Open Innovation: Researching a New Paradigm. Oxford University Press, Oxford (2006)
11. Blaug, M.: Economic Theory in Retrospect. R.D.Irwin, Homewood (1968)
12. Sheng, X.: Network Economy. Publishing House of Electronics Industry, Beijing (2009) (in Chinese)
13. Porter, M.: On Competition. Harvard Business School Pub., Boston (2008)
14. Annual reports of Amazon from 1995 to 2009, `http://phx.corporate-ir.net/phoenix.zhtml?c=97664&p=irol-reportsannual`
15. Blind, K.: The Economics of Standards: Theory, Evidence, Policy. Edward Elgar Publishing, Northampton (2004)
16. Nie, Q.: Study on Forming Mechanism and its efficiency of technical standards in network economy. Renmin University of China, Beijing (2007) (in Chinese)
17. Anderson, C.: The Long Tail: Why the Future of Business is Selling Less of More. Hyperion Books, New York (2008)
18. Howe, J.: Crowdsoucing: Why the Power of the Crowd is Driving the Future of Business. Three Rivers Press, New York (2008)
19. Tapscott, D., Williams, A.D.: Wikinomics: How Mass Collaboration Changes Everything. Penguin Group, New York (2006)

20. Jiang, Q.: The Post-Modern Economy: the Individualization and Diversification of the Network Era. CITIC Publishing Group, Beijing (2009) (in Chinese)
21. Kahneman, D., Wakker, P.P., Sarin, R.: Back to Bentham? Explorations of Experienced Utility. Quarterly Journal of Economics 112, 375–405 (1997)
22. Tversky, A., Kahneman, D.: Loss Aversion in Riskless Choice: A Reference-Dependent Model. Quarterly Journal of Economics 106, 1039–1061 (1991)
23. Thaler, R.: Toward a Positive Theory of Consumer Choice. Journal of Economic Behavior and Organization 1, 39–60 (1980)
24. Tversky, A., Slovic, P., Kahneman, D.: The Causes of Preference Reversal. American Economic Review 80(1), 204–217 (1990)
25. Camerer, C.F., Loewenstein, G., Rabin, M.: Advances in Behavioral Economics. Princeton University Press, Princeton (2004)

A Pilot Study on the Chinese Internet Environment

Shiyang Wei

Institute of Policy & Management, Chinese Academy of Sciences, No. 15, Zhong-Guancun Bei-Yitiao, Haidian District, Beijing, 100191, P.R. China
sywei@casipm.ac.cn

Abstract. After comparing the competitive conducts of the Chinese internet firms with their foreign counterparts, this study has put forward the characteristics of the Chinese internet environment. These characteristics pose as the influencing factors which shape the competitive behaviors of the Chinese internet firms on the environmental level. The aspects to which these characteristics belong respectively are the network trust, the intellectual property right appropriability, the consumer behaviors and the cultural tradition. Finally, this study has made a future research prospect.

Keywords: internet, environment, characteristics, comparison, firms.

1 Introduction

China has been undergoing the Reform and Opening Up policy for over 30 years. Foreign invested companies, especially U.S. companies, have entered into various kinds of Chinese industries, and most of them have achieved not only market share but also high profit margins. However, as far as the internet industry is concerned, all giants coming from the U.S. have failed and even withdrawn from the Chinese market. The state owned companies did not get a share either. Only the local private companies survived and have grown big. The well-known firm case and business history researcher Mr. Wu Xiaobo[1] has then made an optimistic estimation that the local internet industry would create a new mode of endogenous innovation[2], and may pose as the opportunity for China to become a leader in the 21st century. After systematically arranging and analyzing the 15 years history of the Chinese internet, Lin Jun (2009) [1] has concluded the reasons for the failures of the U.S. companies. The first one is that the temporal gap between China and U.S. applying the internet technology is no more than 3 years. This makes the Chinese internet industry need not to learn much from their U.S. counterparts. The second reason is that the foreign companies can not make contingent change according to the fast changing environment of this emerging industry, since their headquarters are not located in

[1] (Born in 1968) graduated from Fudan University majoring in journalism and is a visiting scholar of the Harvard University. He is well-known for business history writing.

[2] Refers to a kind of innovation that is different from technology absorption and simulation. Such innovation should realize new product/service innovation through owning intellectual property rights, and developing unique core technologies.

M. Zhou (Ed.): ISAEBD 2011, Part III, CCIS 210, pp. 617–621, 2011.

China; the third reason is that the professional managers of the U.S. firms are performance motivated, this makes them interested in profits only and neglect strategic advantages. Lin has also concluded the reasons for the absence of the state owned companies. The first reason is that the government will not permit such companies to do business in industries that are fast growing with un-imaginably high risk. The second reason is that the state owned companies are deeply embedded in the power infrastructure which makes them unable to adapt to the fast changing environment. However, do the advantages of the local private firms ever lasting? Are the Chinese winning the game or is there another possibility that they will suffer a decline in the future if nothing is done? After comparing Chinese internet firms with their counterparts in the U.S., the characteristics of the Chinese internet environment are concluded. These characteristics will tell another side of the story, and are expected to inform the relevant agencies to deploy certain arrangements.

2 Research Methodology

This study belongs to the pilot study (Yin, 2003) [2] which is not quite reputable in research methodologies since its conjecture is formed simply by observing the phenomena but not systematically measuring them. Such somehow intuitional survey is criticized as undependable, however, it always brings forward new perspectives and is considered as the overture of the rational academic research [3] [4].

3 Environmental Factors of the Chinese Internet

3.1 Network Trust

The e-commerce giant eBay entered the Chinese market in 2002, but exited 4 years later. The most important reason for such failure is that eBay did not adapt to the trust situation of China [5]. The U.S. has experienced the social trust forming process after entering into the industrial age for more than 200 years. However, trust has not yet come back to its original status in China, since the society had been fragmented and has been recovering for only 30 years[3]. In China, eBay simply duplicated the transaction process from its U.S. experiences. This process provided only the platform without regulating the buyer/seller's behavior. Since the transaction is depending on the trust between each side, it had caused many deceptions, and ruined eBay's reputation in China.

The problem was solved by eBay's Chinese counterpart, an internet company who is providing the transaction platform for small and medium enterprises in China, Alibaba. Two arrangements were executed. The first one is redesigning the transaction process by adding an intermediary between the buyers and sellers in form of temporarily storing the buyer's money before he/she receive the commodity. The second one is storing every transaction records to form a reputation archive of the seller.

---

[3] This study considers the rehabilitation of the Chinese society began after the setting out of the Reform and Open Up policy in 1978. The first 30 years after the establishment of P.R.China have been wasted in some way, since frequent political movements and events have done severe harm to the society.

However, this trust regulatory system has often been challenged. The buyers modify their reputation archives by hacking into the database or forming an alliance to beautify each other's reputation archives. Recently, an event happened that the staff inside the company facilitated the sellers to deceive buyers' from the other country. This is a managerial accident which is going to influence the reputation of Alibaba. Moreover, it disclosed how severe the trust crisis had been in China.

3.2 Intellectual Property Right (IPR) Appropriability

Digital music platform Napster provided free music download. However, it had been sued by many record companies for violating the intellectual property rights of their music works. As a result, it had stopped this free mode, however, could never regain its original status in the digital music area, because Apple had been providing the online music retailing store iTunes shortly after the accusation of Napster. iTunes designed a software process through which music is not sold by discs but by single piece. This way of selling music has preserved the record companies' rights & interests on the one hand, and enabled the consumers to listen to more favorable music with spending less money. Electronic books are also under the cover of this process.

Unlike their counterparts from U.S., the digital music platforms in China, e.g. Kuwo, Xiami, provide free music without being punished by law, moreover, they have been cooperating with the record companies as their new albums' first release platform. The reason for this phenomenon is that the appropriability of IPR is weak in China. By the time when information products like software, digital music, websites etc. were imported from U.S. to China, China was undergoing the industrial stage, and at the initial stage of informationalization. It was not feasible to protect IRP at that time, since the society as a whole had not realized the significance of IPR. Moreover, if IRP was protected properly at that time, information products would become too costly to be bought, as a result, China's entry into the information age would be delayed for many years. Although piracy at that time had positive meanings, it is not to say that IPR should not be protected. China's current situation of IPR appropriability has already caused problems. The free mode of online music download has not only decreased the profit margins of the record industries, but more severely, formed the consumers' psychological tendency that music creation is penniless. It could be deduced from this that the record industry in China would collapse because it could not interest talented individuals to live a life as a musician any more. The similar situation has happened on the network video websites. Until now, the network video websites have not yet found efficient profiting model, still relied on the subscription model and the advertizing model [6] to sustain their enterprises.

Another case is about the online publishing. The website named Qi Dian Zhong Wen which has been purchased by the famous online game operator SNDA is a pioneer of electronic publishing. Without the appropriability of IPR, the first dozens of chapters of novels published through Qi Dian Zhong Wen can be read online free. The authors are paid by the time length & ranks of their works getting on the rank list and the money that the consumers pay to read the final chapters of their works.

Such rank and the final-chapter-earning are highly correlated with the amount of people who have read the novel. As a result, in order to get more support of the consumers, novelists try to analyze what the consumers would like to read. Thus, a literature creation process becomes a transaction. However, in traditional publishing process, there exists an intermediary between the readers and the authors, the publishing press. The editors of the publishing press will use a professional standard to evaluate the books, because after publishing, the feedbacks from the minor readers who are usually highly educated and pose as the opinion leaders of the nearby people will greatly influence the commentary and sale of the books, those feedbacks always accord with the professional standard. Being an online selling mode, the iTunes mode does not destroy the completeness of the book by means of protecting its IPR, moreover, the vigor for such mode lies in the fact that it provides another way of getting feedbacks: the social community way. Through typing their comments below the introduction of the book on the website, readers and potential readers exchange their views towards a book. Suggestions at this time are not made by an acquaintance, but unidentified web surfers who are willing to share their own talents with the others.

3.3 Consumer Behavior

As the world's biggest online book retailer, Amazon is able to provide almost all the books that have been published in the recent 50 years. However, its counterparts in China like 8848 and joyo cannot simply duplicate its model. China's economy is at a different stage compared with U.S.'. The consumers from U.S. would like to seek individualized consumptions while in China, they ask for the same. Such characteristic could be seen from Bertelsmann's selling policy for China. Although having 1.5 million members in China, it only provides 120 kinds of books.

3.4 The Cultural Tradition

The social network platform named Facebook has started a new age of internet application. It originated from the campus of Harvard, and quickly expanded to the whole U.S. There are different versions of such websites in different countries, as for China, the counterpart is Renren. However, Renren in China is not so charming compared with Facebook in U.S. It is more like an upgraded BBS.

The reason why Facebook is popular in U.S. is that it provides opportunities for the youths to get to know the people who do not live around but share the same interests, moreover, it provides platforms to show individuality that can possibly bring a vocation. However, in China, people do not show much curiosity towards the others, because they live in a culture that values the entirety much higher than individualism. Moreover, the Chinese culture regards privacy so important and the Chinese express their feelings so wild and tactful that people are inclined to surf on the internet rather than expressing themselves on the web. In the contemporary society where social trust has not yet been built, people are more unwilling to let strangers know their personal information. As a result, the social network platform in China is more like a BBS system on which public information is shared, however, the core function of the social network has only partially implemented.

4 Conclusions

The environmental factors of the Chinese internet have shaped the behaviors of the Chinese internet firms. It is only through adapting these factors could the internet enterprises survive. However, we should not consider such factors as competitive advantages because the lack of trust will cause the deterioration of the business environment, the lack of IPR appropriability will cause the collapse of the industrial value chain. As a result, institutions and regulations should be designed to preventing such trends from happening.

Moreover, the consumer behaviors of Chinese people are developing towards those of U.S. The local internet companies should analyze the consumers from developed countries to get strategic advantages.

As for the cultural tradition aspect, until now, there are no products that are created based on the culture of the Chinese society. It is believed by this study that the emergence of the internet applications that are deeply rooted in Chinese culture poses as a milestone for the real boom of the Chinese internet industry.

5 Limitations and Future Prospects

Confined by the information channel, factors like the regulatory institutions and the informational extent have not been discussed. As for future study, first, systematic case survey and measurement should be done to verify the independence of these environmental factors, and explore whether other factors could be further induced. Second, a model depicting the causal relationship between the environmental factors and the competitive behaviors of the internet companies should be induced. Based on such model, policy intervention should be designed in order to find a method of ameliorating the internet environment. If this study sustains, an evaluation of the internet environment could be made periodically to be a reference of the relevant agencies and provide suggestions towards the internet companies.

References

1. Lin, J.: The Boiling 15 Years: Chinese Internet 1995-2009. CITIC Publishing Group, Beijing (2009) (in Chinese)
2. Yin, R.K.: Applications of Case Study Research. Sage Publications, Thousands Oaks (2003)
3. Ogawa, R.T., Malen, B.: Towards Rigor in Reviews of Multivocal Literatures: Applying the Exploratory Case Study Method. J. Review of Educational Research 61, 265–286 (1991)
4. Yin, R.K.: Advancing Rigorous Methodologies: a Review of "Towards Rigor in Reviews of Multivocal Literatures". J. Review of Educational Research 61, 299–305 (1991)
5. Hu, A.: The Enlightenment of eBay China. Publishing House of Electronics Industry, Beijing (2009) (in Chinese)
6. Rappa, M.: Managing the Digital Enterprise: Business Models, `http://ecommerce.ncsu.edu/topic/models/models.html`

Variance Analysis on Aesthetic Evaluation of Women's Collarless T-Shirt

Shan-Shan Wang[1,2], Xiao-Xia Zhang[1,2], Fang Qin[1,2,3], and Guo-Lian Liu[1,2]

[1] National Engineering Laboratory for Modern Silk
[2] College of Textile and Clothing Engineering, Soochow University Suzhou, China
[3] College of Arts, Jinling Institute of Technology, Nanjing, 211169, China
liuguolian@suda.edu.cn

Abstract. In this paper, women's collarless T-shirts with three necklines (round neckline, square neckline and V neckline) were selected as objects, and 72 young people were selected as target group. For the three collarless T-shirts, the influences of different neck drop and width on the aesthetic perception were studied based on visual cognition. Results in the paper can be a quantitative guide for the design of T shirts and will provide scientific references for the design of women's T-shirt to meet customers' requirements.

Keywords: T-shirt, aesthetic evaluation, vision cognition.

1 Introduction

With the coming era of emotional consumption, when consumers buy a T-shirt, they are not only pay attention to its comfortable and facilitate, but the feeling that the T-shirts give. The T-shirt which they bought is not just a piece of clothing, the more important is that it is a kind of self-satisfaction, and a high degree between the concept of life and the consumer's self-concept. In the face of the change of this consumer demand, we should grasp and understand the consumer psychology of T-shirts emotional needs, and design the T-shirt that can adapt to different consumers [1-2].

2 Experiment

2.1 Participants

72 undergraduate students from Soochow University (36 men, 36 women, 36 apparel, 36 non apparel) were selected as subjects who were volunteers to participate in this experiment without being forced or any boredom. All subjects had normal or correct vision and were unaware of the purpose of the experiment [3].

2.2 Stimulate Samples

In this paper, three popular neckline of women's collarless T shirt were selected. And the neck drop was divided into 11 equal levels between the collar dens and bust line,

M. Zhou (Ed.): ISAEBD 2011, Part III, CCIS 210, pp. 622–627, 2011.

and the neck width was divided into 9 equal levels between the shoulder point and lateral neck point. There are 242 women's collarless T shirt samples. The equal subintervals of neck drop and neck width can be seen in figue1 and figue2.

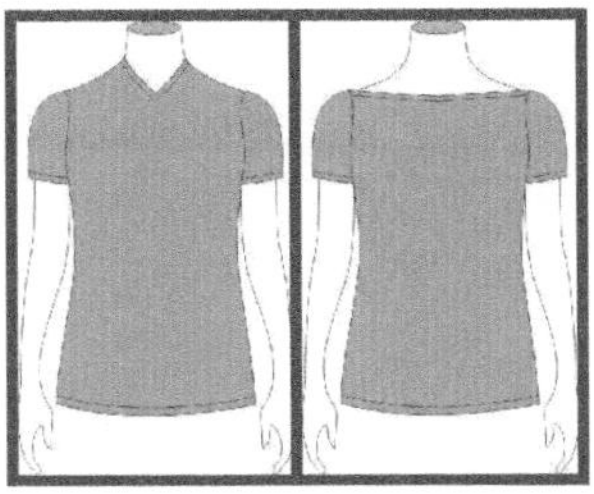

Fig. 1. The equal subintervals of neck drop

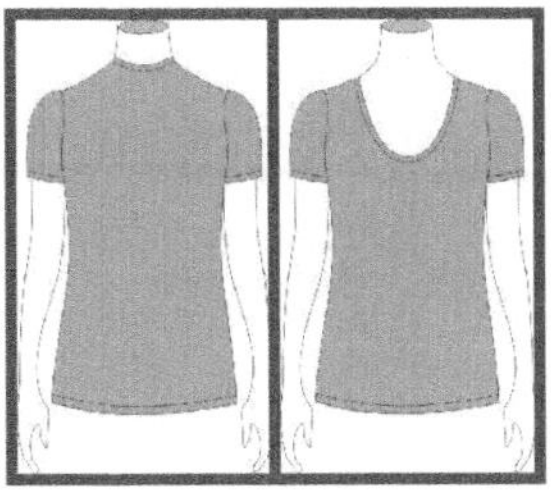

Fig. 2. The equal subintervals of neck width

2.3 Procedure Design

2.3.1 Experimental Apparatus

The stimuli were presented on a Pentium desktop computer with a 17-in monitor set at a refresh rate of 75HZ in a dimmed room, the distance between participant and monitor is about 60cm, and the visual angle was 12.3°×4.9°. Using E-Prime 2.0 (Psychology Software Tools, Inc.).

2.3.2 Experimental Procedures

Before the beginning of this experiment, the Participants were asked to know the procedure and operation. The procedure can be seen in figure 3. When the experiment

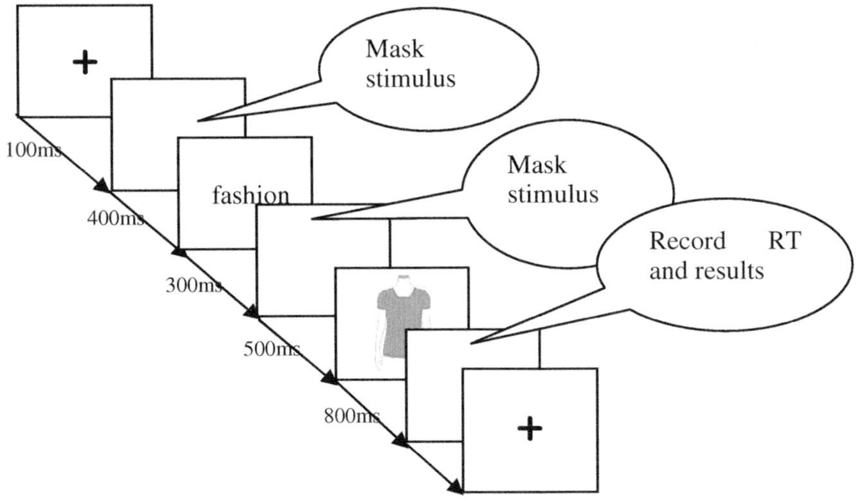

Fig. 3. Procedure of the experiment

began, at fist, a sign of "+" will be appeared on the centre of the screen to remind the beginning of the experiment for 100ms, followed with 400ms blank waiting; and then, the word "fashion" will be appeared on the same position for 300ms followed with 500ms bland waiting, at last, one women's collarless T shirt with different neck drop and neck width will be on this position randomly for 800ms [4-5].

3 Data Analysis and Discussion

3.1 Differences of Gender

3.1.1 The Aesthetic Differences of Neck Drop

The figure 4 and figure 5 shows that the fashion deferens of neck drop between men and women is significant, M=0.04935, P=0.006 < 0.05 and so is the prefer deferens, M=0.06481, P=0.000< 0.001. It can be seen from the figure that:

(1). with the neck drop increased, the aesthetics show first up and then decline both for men and women.
(2). When the neck drop is on the 8 level, the fashion reached the maximum both for men and women. While on the 9 level, the prefer reached the maximum.
(3). For the fashion sense, man believe the T-shirt to be more fashion when the neck drop is lower than 8, ; when higher, women to be more fashion. For the prefer sense, woman are more like the T-shirt with the neck drop of 7, 8,9.

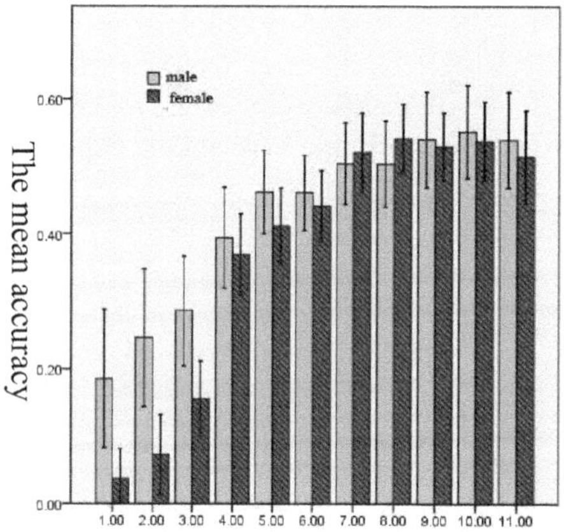

Fig. 4. The fashion sense difference of neck drop between young men and women

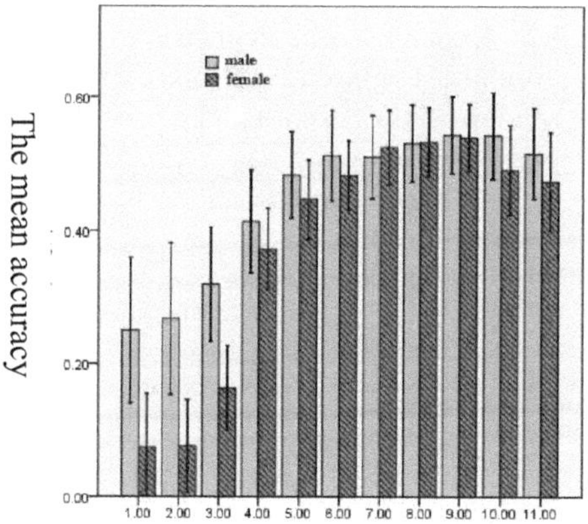

Fig. 5. The prefer sense difference of neck drop between young men and women

3.2 Differences of Professional

3.2.1 The Prefer Differences of Neck Width

The figure 6 shows that the prefer differences of neck width between apparel and non apparel is significant. M=0.05485, P=0.024< 0.05.

The curve of neck width's preference between apparel and non apparel are all show an overall upward trend. And subjects of apparel show more like the T-shirts. When the neck width increases gradually, this difference of preference will become less and less. When the neck width is on 1-7 level, the preference evaluation on T-shirts is higher. When on 8, 9, the results are on the contrary.

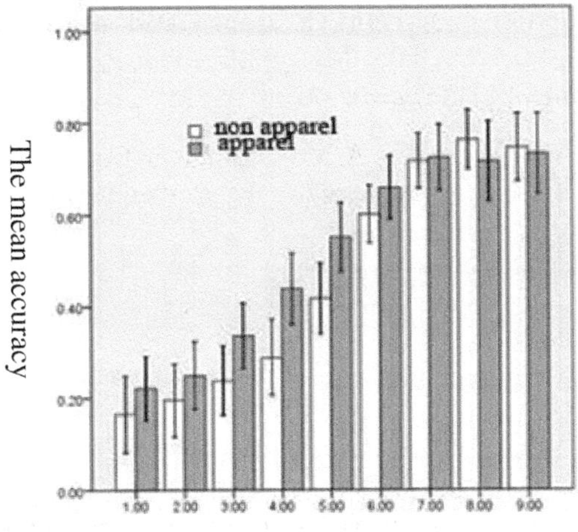

Fig. 6. The prefer sense difference of neck width between apparel and non apparel

3.2.2 The Prefer Differences of Neck Drop

Figure 7 shows that the prefer differences of neck drop between apparel and non apparel is significant. M=0.05098, P=0.005< 0.05.

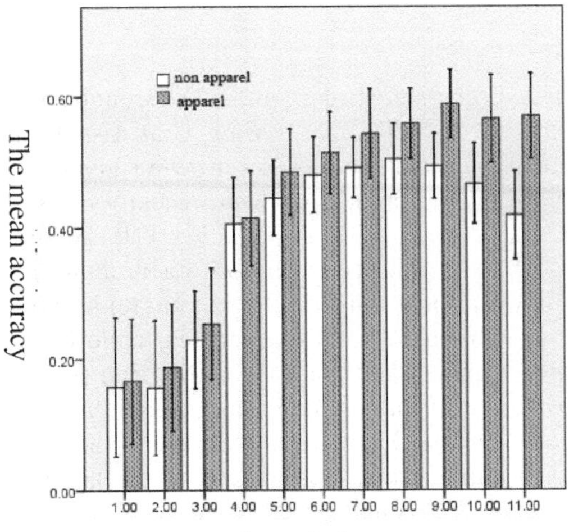

Fig. 7. The prefer sense difference of neck drop between apparel and non apparel

The differences in figure 7 show an overall upward trend. And subjects of apparel show more like the T-shirts. When the neck drop increases gradually, this difference of preference will become more and more. For subjects of apparel, who have deeply consciousness on clothing, the increase of neck drop can cause deep prefer for them.

3.2.3 The Differences of RT

The average prefer differences between apparel and non apparel is significant. M_{width}=-126.154, P_{width}=0.000< 0.05; M_{drop}=-127.4343, P_{drop}=0.000< 0.05. and so is the fashion. M_{width}=-143.1903,P_{width}=0.000< 0.05; M_{drop}=-129.174,P_{drop}=0.000< 0.05. It can be seen in figure 8 and figure 9.

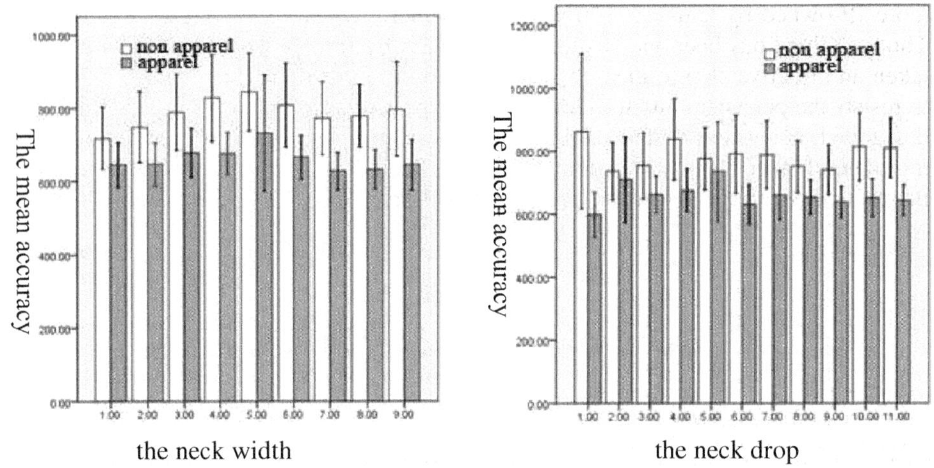

Fig. 8. The prefer sense difference of neck width between apparel and non apparel

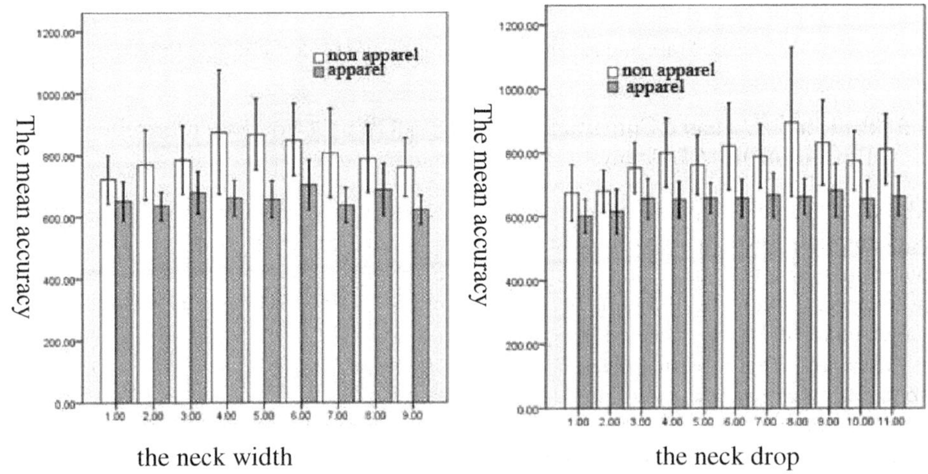

Fig. 9. The fashion sense difference of neck width between apparel and non apparel

It can be seen from the results of two groups; the prefer RT of T-shirts both have significant differences. The RT of apparel participants is rapid. The results demonstrate that the cognitive system of apparel is more mature and response is more sensitive.

4 Conclusion

1 The aesthetic evaluation on T-shirts is influenced by traditional and conservative attitudes for both men and women. For men, the traditional one is believed to be more fashion. While for women, their fashion sense of T-shirts is based on escape from the shackles of traditional ideas, they think that collarless T-shirts which deviate from traditional values is more fashionable.

2 Evaluation of differences between men and women still has the relationship of wear and appreciate. When women evaluate T-shirt, although their fashion evaluation is higher in non-traditional T-shirts, their prefer evaluation is very lower. Because their wearing habits are based on their knowledge and experience, and their wearing is conceited of the traditional values. So, for the non-traditional T-shirts, people usually would like to appreciate, but to acceptance or buy.

3 After systematic learning, the subjects of apparel have deeper understanding and knowledge, their understanding of clothing is wider than the other professional, the increase of neck drop can cause their overall prefer straightly.

4 The subjects of apparel have mature cognitive system and rich experience on clothing, and their reaction in clothing distinguish is faster than the other professional.

Funded by the First Phase of Jiangsu Universities' Distinctive Discipline Development Program for Textile Science and Engineering of Soochow University.

References

1. Zhang, L.: Illustrated Introduction to Fashion, vol. 77. China Textile and Apparel Press, Beijing (2005)
2. Yuan, T.Z.: Kansei Engineering research strategy. Arts and Sciences Research Center of Tsinghua University for: Expert Essays In Tsinghua International Design Management Forum 2, 186–187 (2002)
3. Jiang, X.F., Liu, G.L.: The Influence of Color Brightness on the Perception of Clothes Gorgeousness. In: Proceeding 2009 IEEE 10th International Conference, vol. 2, pp. 1273–1276 (2009)
4. Johnson, A., Jepma, M., Jong, R.: The Experimental Psychology Society 1406 (2007)
5. Qin, F., Liu, G.L: Study on Influences of Collar Types towards Women's T-shirt Fashionable Design Based on Visual Cognition. In: Proceeding 2009 IEEE 10th International Conference, vol. 2, pp. 1579–1583 (2009)
6. Huang, Q., Sun, S.Q.: State-of-the-art of Research on Product Style Computation. Jounal of Computer-Aided Design & Computer Graphics 18, 1629–1635 (2006)

Aesthetic Evaluation of Women's Collarless T-Shirt's Collar Style

Shan-Shan Wang[1,2], Xiao-Xia Zhang[1,2], Fang Qin[1,2,3], and Guo-Lian Liu[1,2]

[1] National Engineering Laboratory for Modern Silk
[2] College of Textile and Clothing Engineering, Soochow University Suzhou, China
[3] College of Arts, Jinling Institute of Technology, Nanjing, 211169, China
liuguolian@suda.edu.cn

Abstract. Collar-type is the main elements for the style of T-shirts. In this article, Aesthetic evaluation of women's T-shirts's collar style is researched from the view of visual perception targeting the young men and women consumers. It relies on the software E-prime, which is commonly used in psychological and behavioral experiments.

In this paper, women's collarless T-shirts with three necklines (round neckline, square neckline and V neckline) were selected as objects. The influences of different neck drop and width on the aesthetic sense were studied which can be a quantitative guide for the design of T shirts and will provides scientific references for the aesthetic design of women's T-shirt to meet customers' requirements.

Keywords: T-shirts aesthetic E-prime, visual perception.

1 Introduction

T shirt has been playing a very special role in the developing history of human clothing, which breaks through the gender, age, race, rich and poor countries, and is enduring worldwide popularity. With the growing of young people, their enthusiasm on T-shirts has never disappeared. And now, it has become a wardrobe essential for young people as casual wear. Although the T shirt has been loved by the majority of young people, the aesthetic elements which they loved has changed with the changing times and culture, and the classic T-shirts are no longer their love. They all rely on the ever changing aesthetic sensibility of young people.

Overall, the structures of T shirt are simple and its changes usually are shown in the neck, lap, cuffs, colors, patterns, fabrics and shapes. The neckline of T-shirt is the most important elements, which will directly affect the overall style of T-shirt and also can give the changes of personality, temperament and experience for wearers. Therefore, the collar of T-shirt as the key of overall shape cannot be ignored to observe the fashion trends. In this paper, the software E-prime was used which can accurately measure the determine time and it can also record the judgment results of each sample. The integrity and empirical characteristics of visual perception is based on to evaluate the beauty (fashion and preference) of T-shirt in order to speculate the psychological and emotional processing process. The process can be seen in figure 1.

M. Zhou (Ed.): ISAEBD 2011, Part III, CCIS 210, pp. 628–634, 2011.

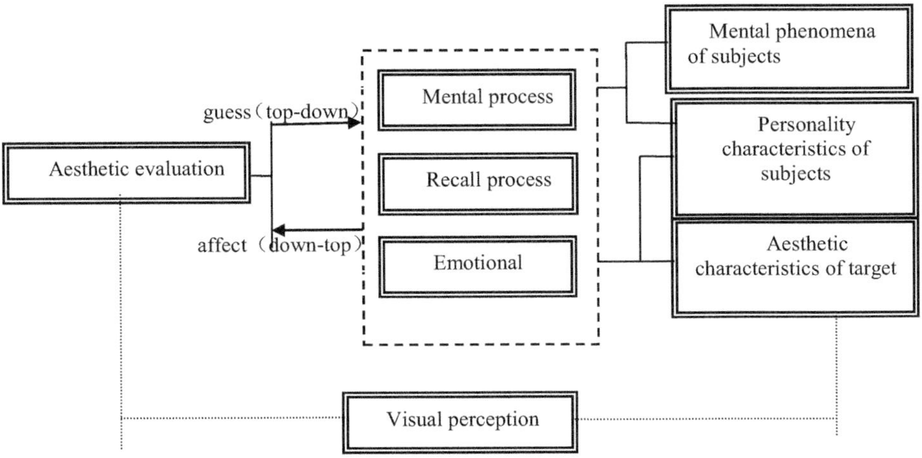

Fig. 1. Processing of visual perception T shirt

2 Experiment

2.1 Participants

A group of 72 undergraduate students from Soochow University were selected as subjects who were volunteers to participate in this experiment without being forced or any boredom. All subjects had normal or corrected vision and were unaware of the purpose of the experiment.

2.2 Stimulate Samples

The overall aesthetic of T-shirt is constituted by three elements, fabric, color and style. The T shirt in this paper is defined with the traditional sleeve, traditional length, mellow color of pink and it is right at the waist. The three neckline of T shirt can be seen in figure 3. CorelDraw graphics software is used to draw all the T shirts.

In this article, T shirts which were researched are symmetrical women's collarless T-shirts, whose neck drop is between the collar dens and bust line and neck width is between the shoulder point and lateral neck point.

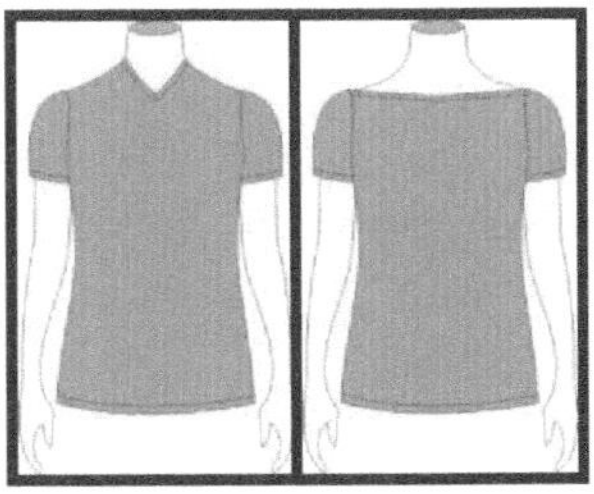

Fig. 2. The equal subintervals of neck drop

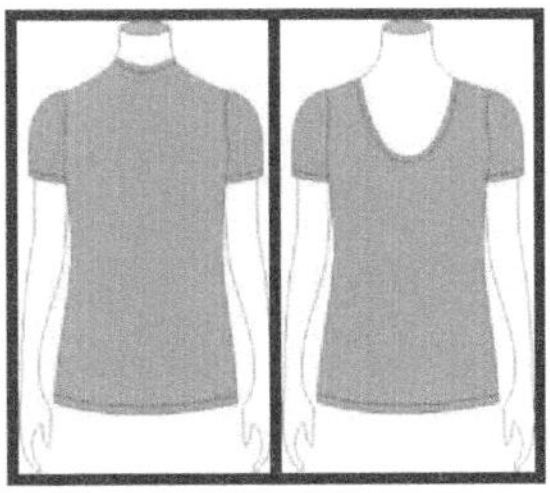

Fig. 3. The equal subintervals of neck width

In this article, the neck drop of T shirt was divided into 11 equal parts between the collar dens and bust line, and the neck width was divided into 9 equal parts between the shoulder point and lateral neck point. So there are 242 women's collarless T shirt samples in this article. The equal subintervals of neck drop and neck width can be seen in figue2 and figue3.

2.3 Procedure Design

2.3.1 Experimental Apparatus

The experimental computer must has been installed the software E-prime 2.0 , and the display is 17 inch , the resolution is 1024X768,color is 16 and the refresh rate is 75 HZ.

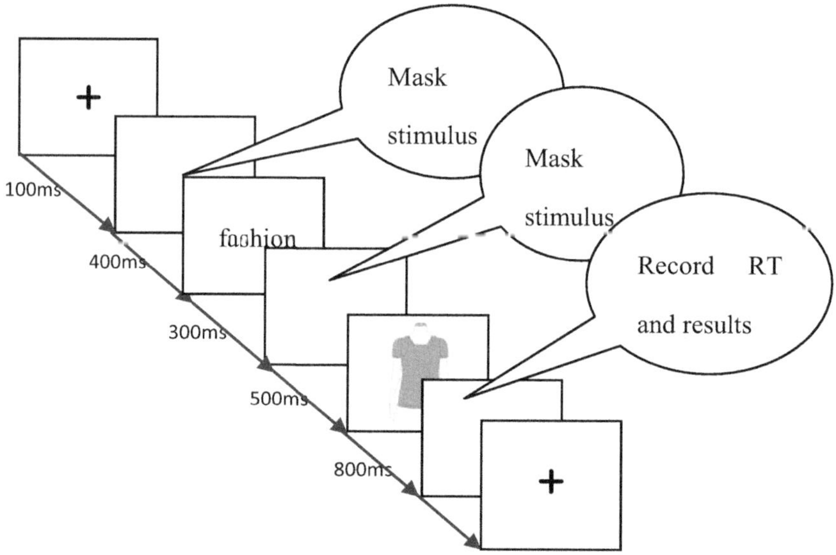

Fig. 4. Procedure of the experiment

2.3.2 Experimental Procedures

The subjects sat in front of the computer, the distance between subject and monitor is about 60cm, and the visual angle was 12.3°×4.9°.

Before the beginning of this experiment, the subjects were asked to know the procedure and operation. The procedure can be seen in figure 4. When the experiment began, at first, a sign of "+" will be appeared on the centre of the screen to remind the beginning of the experiment for 100ms followed with 400ms blank waiting; and then, the word "fashion" or "prefer" will be appeared on the same position for 300ms followed with 500ms bland waiting, at last, one women's collarless T shirt with different neck drop and neck width will be on this position randomly for 800ms.

3 Data Analysis and Discussion

3.1 Aesthetic Evaluation of Neck Width

The difference can be seen from the figure 5 and figure 6.

1. The difference among neck width has nothing to do with the collar necklines (F_{prefer}=0.58 P_{prefer}=0.618 > 0.05 $F_{fashion}$=1.398 $P_{fashion}$=0.276>0.05), but with the neck width size. (F_{prefer}=99.447;P_{prefer}=0.00 < 0.001 $F_{fashion}$=109.539, $P_{fashion}$=0.000<0.001).

2. And with the increasing of neck width, the mean accuracy of the aesthetic on T shirt shows an uptrend. When the neck width is near the shoulder point, the aesthetic value reached the maximum.

3. And when the neck width is in wider than the 6 part, the mean accuracy of the aesthetic accuracy stayed higher than 50%.

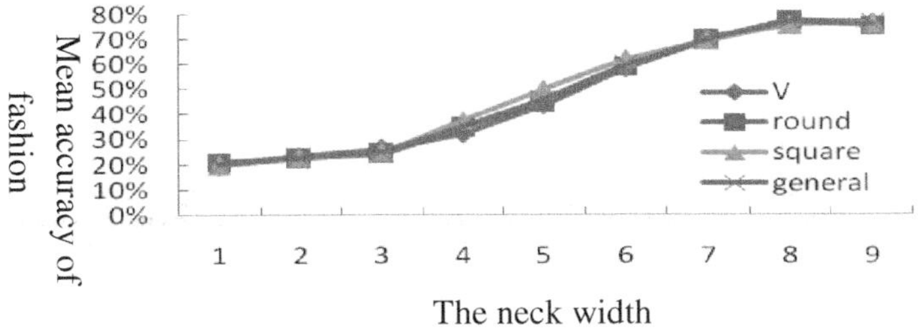

Fig. 5. The influence of neck width changes on the fashion sense

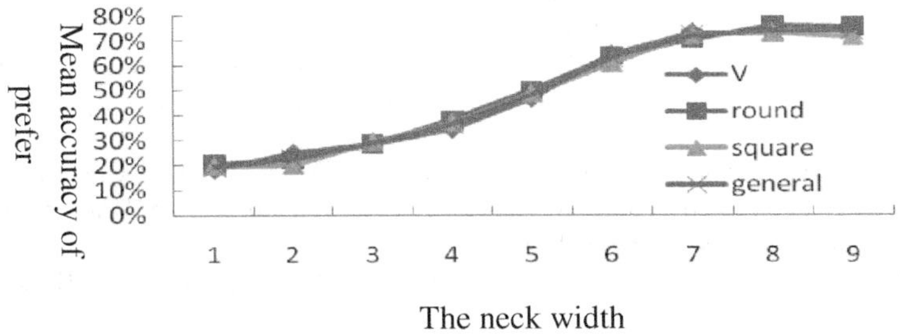

Fig. 6. The influence of neck width changes on the prefer sense

3.2 Aesthetic Evaluation of Neck Drop

The neck drop aesthetic can be seen from figure 7 and figure 8.

1. The difference among neck drop has nothing to do with the collar necklines (F_{prefer}=0.32 P_{prefer}=0.968>0.05 $F_{fashion}$=0.021 $P_{fashion}$=0.979>0.05), but with the neck drop size (F_{prefer}=540.44 P_{prefer}=0.00<0.001 $F_{fashion}$=71.8 $P_{fashion}$ =0.00<0.001).

2. With the increasing of neck drop, the mean accuracy of the aesthetic on T shirt shows an uptrend. And when the neck drops is on the level of 9 and 10, the fashion and prefers sense separately reached the maximum.

3. When the neck drop is on the level of 11, that is, the neck drop line is coincident with the bust line; its aesthetic value has declined.

With the progress and development of the times, for young people the classic T shirt is no longer their favorite, while T shirt with bigger neck width and drop was found to be more fashionable and easier to be loved and accepted by them. It also can be seen that the modern young people are more easily enjoy and accept fashionable T-shirts. But under the influence of traditional ideas, their acceptance of fashion elements stands on scruple. For example, when the neck width is on shoulder position, and when the neck deep is on the bust line, the aesthetic value has declined slightly.

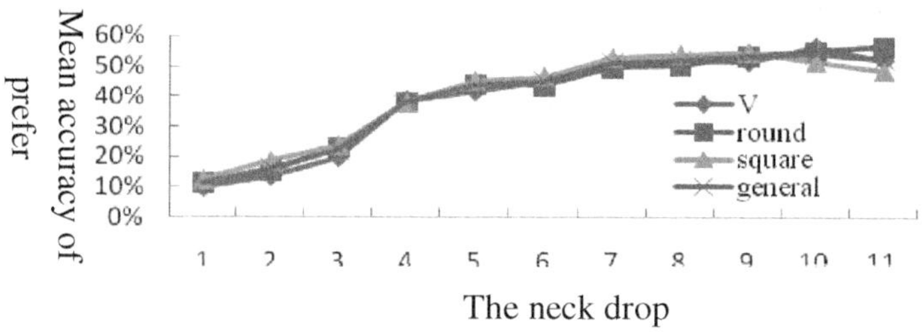

Fig. 7. The influence of neck drop changes on the fashion sense

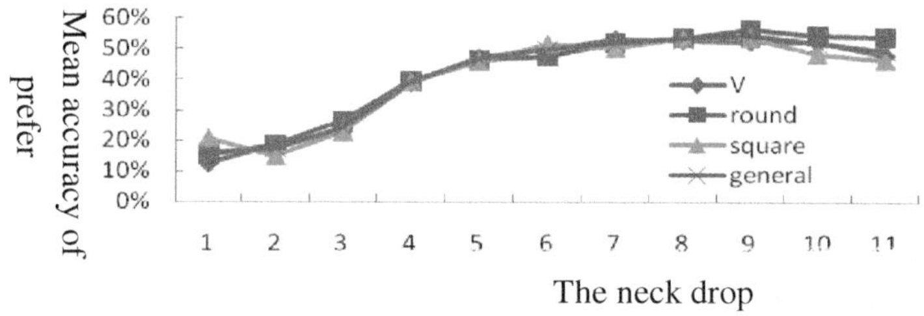

Fig. 8. The influence of neck drop changes on the prefer sense

3.3 RT of Neck Width

From the figure 9, we can see that among the 9 RT of neck width, there are significant differences for both the fashion and prefer sense. For the fashion, $F= 4.002$ $P=0.000 < 0.001$; and for the prefer sense, $F= 3.359$ $P=0.001 < 0.005$.

It can be seen from the figure 9 that with the increasing of neck width, the mean RT of the prefer sense on T shirt shows up and then trend. When the neck width is on 4 and 5 level, the RT reached the maximum; similarly, for the fashion sense, when on the level 4, 5 and 6, the RT is the longest. That is, when the neck width is in the middle of should, subjects showed a sense of hesitation and then longer the RT; while for the T shirt whose neck width is on the shoulder point (level 9), there is a tendency to increase reaction time. That is because for these T-shirts, which can give a good fashion sense for some ones, so in average extended RT.

For the two curves of fashion and prefer RT, the tendency are almost the same. When the T-shirts is higher fashionable, the RT was relatively longer, that is , when the T- shirt is in higher fashionable, the subjects must search memory to match the garments. so longer the RT ; while in lower fashionable, based on little experience, the subjects spend less RT to search memory.

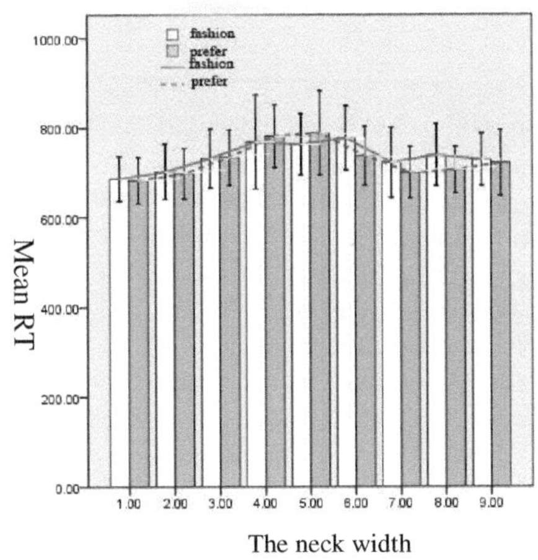

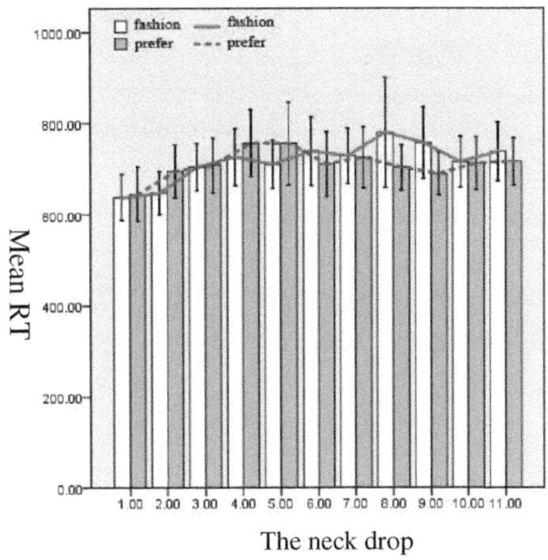

Fig. 9. The mean aesthetic RT of neck width **Fig. 10.** The mean aesthetic RT of neck drop

3.4 RT of Neck Drop

From the figure 10 we can see that among the 11 RT of neck width, there are significant differences for both the fashion sense. $F_{fashion}$= 5.687 $P_{fashion}$=0.000<0.05; for the prefer sense, there is no significant differences F_{prefer}= 0.633 P_{prefer}=0.786>0.05.

As the figure 10 shown, with the increasing of neck drop, the RT of fashion showed a rising trend. When the neck drop is on level 8, the RT reached maximum. For these T-shirts, when the subjects are judging the fashion sense, they have higher contradiction with the memory. Also we can see that these T- shirts the subject of fashion, while they are the potential fashion products.

4 Conclusions

1. The difference among subjects has nothing to do with the collar necklines but with the size of neck width and neck drop.

2. For the T-shirts, the neck width is on shoulder point or the neck drop is on bust line, whose aesthetic value is lower than the previous one. This kind T-shirt cannot meet aesthetic of the young generation.
3. When the neck width is in the middle of should, subjects showed a sense of hesitation and then longer the RT. For the aesthetic of this T-shirt, there is current controversy for young people.
4. For the T-shirt whose neck drop is on level 8, they are the potential fashion products for designers.

Funded by the First Phase of Jiangsu Universities' Distinctive Discipline Development Program for Textile Science and Engineering of Soochow University

References

1. Hong, d.: Present and Future of International T shirt. Screen Printing Industry 6, 76–79 (2001)
2. Lu, y.j.: T shirt of the aesthetic emotion and Cultural Studies. Enterprise Technology Development 8, 28 (2009)
3. Ge, y., Liu, g.: Perceptual image of male students characteristics of T-shirts. Silk 5, 10–14 (2007)
4. Hu, j.: Theoretical and applied cognitive psychology. Silk 8, 193–197 (2003)
5. Johnson, A., Jepma, M., de Jong, R.: The Experimental Psychology Society 60, 1406 (2007)
6. Vernon, D.: Cognitive vision:The case for embodied perception. Image and Vision Computing 26, 127–140 (2008)

A Positive Analysis of the Effect of Human Capital on Economic Growth: Evidence from Yunnan

Cunzhi Tian[1], Qiuping Guo[2], and Lijun Zhang[2]

[1] Economic Research Center, Kunming University of Science and Technology, Kunming, China, 650093
[2] Faculty of Management and Economics, Kunming University of Science and Technology, Kunming, China, 650093
tiancunzhi@sina.com, 154260472@163.com, kmlgzhanglijun@126.com.

Abstract. This article first reviews the history of human capital on the economic growth, then based on the data from 1978 to 2010 in Yunnan province, tests the impact of factors to the economic growth, the results show that Yunnan's economic growth show increasing returns to scale, during the economic growing, the human capital contributed the largest share. In order to keep the economic growing and developing, Yunnan province should change the economic increasing way, enlarge the investment in human capital.

Keywords: human capital, economic growth, positive analysis.

1 Introduction

The 'economic growth' is an ancient and also a new topic in the economic field. The policy makers can make better policies when they master the impact factors on economic growth, it is important to the developing country or regions especially. Human capital is regarded as a core factor on economic growth, this article mainly discuss the human capital on economic growth by positive analysis of Yunnan province and give some advice for Yunnan's economic growing and developing.

There are six parts of the article, the rest of the article is arranged as follow, part two is the literature review, part three is the model selection and the contribution rate's calculation, part four is the definition and description of the variables, part five is the description of data and the estimation of parameter, the last part is the conclusion and advice.

2 Literature Review

Adam Smith (1776) proposed the idea of human capital in "Wealth of Nations". Irving Fisher (1906) proposed the concept of human capital in the "nature of capital and income" firstly, and it was integrated into the framework of economic analysis, but the physical capital was the determinant of the production process at that time, the human capital was not due attention. R.Harrod and E.Domar created the modern

M. Zhou (Ed.): ISAEBD 2011, Part III, CCIS 210, pp. 635–640, 2011.

economic growth theory in the late 30 and early 40 in the 20th century, and it was called Harrod –Domar model, its important conclusion was that the fundamental driving force of economic growth was the accumulation of capital, the more capital accumulation, the faster economic growth. W.Schultz(1960) proposed the human capital theory, he elaborated the promotion of human capital on economic growth clearly in his speech "Human Capital Investment" ,he considered the human capital was the major driving force and the source of modern economic growth, but he put human capital as an exogenous variable, he did not establish a quantitative model to analyze either. Edward Denlson used quantitative methods tested the human capital on economic growth from 1927 to 1957 in America ,his research result showed that the education's contribution was 23% during the economic growing in America. Jacob Mincer(1957) proposed the revenue function in his doctor's thesis "Human Capital Investment and Personal Income", and used it to reveal the root causes of the income gap narrowing of worker were that people's level of education generally increasing and the results of human capital accumulation. Gary S.Becker's Book (1964) "Human Capital" was considered the beginning of human capital investment in economic thought, and it laid a good foundation for the human capital theory's developing. Lucas, R.E (1988) put the human capital into economic growth model as an independent element, created a core human capital endogenous growth model in his paper "The Mechanism of economic development". He believed that the source of a country's economic growth was the accumulation of human capital, he also believed that in an efficient economy, the higher accumulation of physical capital should match with the higher accumulation of human capital. In China, Jinying Wang(2001) used the data from 1978 to 1998 of China studied the relation between human capital and economic growth ,his study showed that the external model of human capital was more effective than the effective labor model. Yongyuan Hu(2003) Confirmed the truth that the Human capital contribution rate of economic growth was significantly positive .Many cross studies between nations have proved that the higher of a country or a region's human capital, the more of its output.

More than 30 years of reform and opening up in China, Yunnan province has made considerable economic development, its region's GDP to 6.905 billion yuan in 1978 rose to 142.4 billion yuan in 2010, its growth is 21 times at constant prices. Yunnan lies in the west of China, and the economic growth has its own characteristics, we try to analyze the impact of human capital of Yunnan's economic growth, and measure the human capital' contribution rate on economic growth in Yunnan.

3 The Model Selection and the Contribution Rate's Calculation

3.1 The Model Selection

Relation Xiangyin Kong's study (2000), we use the model as follow,

$$Y_t = AL_t^{\alpha} K_t^{\beta} H_t^{\gamma} e^{\varepsilon} \tag{1}$$

Y_t represent the real GDP, A represent technology, L_t represent labor stock, K_t represent physical capital stock, H_t represent human capital stock at t year respectively, we consider the technology as exogenous, α、β、γ represent labor's and physical capital's and human capital's output elasticity. ε represent random interference terms.

Take the natural logarithm on both sides of equation (1), we get,

$$LnY_t = LnA + \alpha LnL_t + \beta LnK_t + \gamma LnH_t + \varepsilon \quad (2)$$

We will estimate the coefficient of equation (2) by "Ordinary least squares"

3.2 The Contribution Rate's Calculation of Elements

Take the difference to time "t" on both sides of equation (2),we get,

$$\dot{Y}_t / Y_t = \alpha \dot{L}_t / L_t + \beta \dot{K}_t / K_t + \gamma \dot{H}_t / H_t \quad (3)$$

Chang equation (3) into differential equation, we get,

$$\Delta Y_t / Y_t = \alpha \Delta L_t / L_t + \beta \Delta K_t / K_t + \gamma \Delta H_t / H_t \quad (4)$$

$\Delta Y_t / Y_t$, $\Delta L_t / L_t$, $\Delta H_t / H_t$ $\Delta K_t / K_t$, represent economic growth, labor growth , physical capital growth, human capital growth respectively, $\alpha \Delta L_t / L_t$, $\beta \Delta K_t / K_t$, $\gamma \Delta H_t / H_t$ divide $\Delta Y_t / Y_t$ respectively will get their contribution rates in the economic growth.

4 The Definition and the Description of the Variables

The data of the article are from "Yunnan Statistical Yearbook 2010" and "60 years of New China, statistics compiled", the sample interval is from 1978 to 2010, and the variables are described as follow: (1)GDP, it is thought a standard of output ,we took 1978 as the base year, and then adjusted all the data of the years for the actual value. (2)Physical capital's stock, $K_t = (1-\delta_t)K_{t-1} + \Delta K_t$, K_t represents the current physical capital's stock, and K_{t-1} represents the last physical capital's stock, ΔK_t represents the current investment, and δ_t represents the discount rate of the year. We firstly took 1978 as the base year and added the data from 1952 to 1977 together as the stock of 1977, then calculated the physical capital stock by $K_t = (1-\delta_t)K_{t-1} + \Delta K_t$ (3)Labor stock: we took the total number of jobs in every years in Yunnan Province as the labor stock. (4)Human capital's stock: we took the expenditure on science, education, culture, health as the human capital's investment. The method is similar to deal with the physical capital. This is a try to use the expenditure of them to stand for the human capital. The education ages was regarded as the standard of the human capital stock in most of the articles before, we think the standard is partly. The standard we use is more completely than the past.

5 The Description of the Data and the Estimation of the Parameter

In table (1) L, H, P represent labor stock and human capital stock and physical capital stock respectively.

Before we estimated the coefficient, we tested the unit root to each variable and the cointegration among the variables, the results showed that we can do the regression analysis.

Table 1. The description of the data

variable	*mean*	*max*	*min*	*Std.D*
Y	439.17	1424.42	69.05	374.12
L	2051.87	2754.80	1313.40	409.64
H	712.73	3479.43	28.11	903.84
K	5129.50	29139.34	191.64	7337.57

Table 2. The estimation results of equation (2)

variable	*coefficient*	*Std.E*	*t-S*	*Prob*
C	-8.200	2.376	-3.451	0.002
LNL	1.484	0.328	4.523	0.000
LNH	0.171	0.151	1.133	0.266
LNK	0.222	0.102	2.179	0.038
R2=0.99, F=8970.37, D.W=0.814				

From table 2 we can see that the estimated model has a high goodness of fit, the natural logarithm of the labor stock is highly significant under 1% level ,the physical stock is significant under 5% level, the constant is significant under 1% level, but the human capital stock is not significant. according table2,we can get the production function as follow,

$$Y_t = e^{-8.200} L_t^{1.484} K_t^{0.222} H_t^{0.171} \tag{5}$$

From equation (5) we know that the economic growth is "Increasing returns to scale", and if the physical capital add one unit ,the output will add 22.2%, the human add one unit, the output will add 17.1%, the labor add one unit, the output will add 148.4%. From the data above we can also see that among the three elements, the labor stock has the most output elasticity, followed by physical capital, human capital minimum. If we simply consider the production function itself, higher labor input will make more output, because its output elasticity is most. If we compare human capital and physical capital investment, we will find the output elasticity of physical capital is greater than the output elasticity of human capital. Thus when the total input is fixed, rationalize investment between human capital and physical capital, the higher proportion of investment for physical capital, the higher output.

Now we come to analyze the input factors' contribution to economic growth, from 1978 to 2010, the labor's contribution rate to economic growth is 28.37%, and the human capital is 15.28%, the physical capital is 56.35%. From the data we know, although the elasticity of human capital is less than the elasticity of labor ,the growth rate of human capital is 122.77%, it is 111 times than the labor growth, this makes the human capital contribution rate of economic growth to 15.28, at the same time, we also notice that the labor's output elasticity is largest in the three elements, it reaches 148.4%, but its growth rate is not the largest, is for 28.37%, also we know that the contribution rate of physical to the economic growth is the largest.

6 Conclusion and Advice

We used the data from 1978 to 2010 of Yunnan province, tested the factors on economic growth, the results show that the economic growth of Yunnan province is "increasing return of scale", labor, physical capital, human capital, the output elasticity is less the same, but among the contribution rate to the economic growth, the physical capital's is largest, the human's is minimum. The fact also proved that more than 30 years of the reform and opening up, Yunnan provincial physical capital for economic growth is much higher than the contribution of human to economic growth, human capital contribution to economic growth is lower than physical capital contribute to economic growth. We know that the more human capital investment, the faster economic growth. This shows that the economic growth of Yunnan Province is drove mainly by investment in physical capital. Lisheng Shen (1999), had simulated and predicted the investment in human capital and physical capital on economic growth, the condition is that the total investment is fixed, with a certain percentage of human capital investment instead of physical capital, the result is the production of absolute value of the total increase. It can clearly be seen, compared to physical capital, the human capital is more important. At the same time more and more countries in the development of reality also tells us that investment in human capital play a very important role in increasing productivity, because through training more skilled workers can stimulate to innovate.

Human capital' and physical capital's productive property is that they can produce output. Physical capital's property is that it can produce itself, but human capital to be produced requires investment .Human capital investment is a major expenditure of an economy. Human capital is different from physical capital, human capital is added in the labor force, only when labor is working, and then the human capital to reflect the role. Human capital is fixed in the body of the labor, but the physical capital is independent of its owner, the presence of a person's physical capital is no limit on the amount, but there are limits to human capital, that is a person's health or education is limited, a person can accommodate the human capital stock is limited. But for Yunnan province, there are several places have no compulsory education, and health conditions are to be improved, there are great potential to transform human capital by increasing investment in human capital .Becker ever pointed out that in a new changing economy environment, only those countries and regions which used human capital effectively can sustain the economy to grow. Therefore, Yunnan province should increase investment in human capital to speed up economic development and growth. At the same time, Yunnan should also utilize the human capital effectively, make the human capital to play its potential, create conditions and atmosphere to stimulate the use of human capital, and put the existing human capital into productive forces. Finally, promote the rational flow of human capital in the province to improve the allocative efficiency and enhance the introduction of talent outside the province and prevent the outflow of talent.

In the article we used the expenditure on science, education, culture and health to stand for the investment on human capital, this is a new try to measure the human capital, whether it is fit for the human capital is still a topic to discuss in the future.

References

1. Schultz, W.: Human Capital Investment. Commercial Press, Beijing
2. Lucas, R.E.: On the mechanics of economic development. Journal of Monetary Economics (22) (1998)
3. Wang, J.: Human capital and economic growth: Theory and Evidence. China Financial and Economic Publishing House (2001)
4. Hu, Y.: Human capital and economic growth: An Empirical Analysis. Economic Science (01), 54–60 (2003)
5. Kong, X.: On Human Capital and Economic Growth. Economist (03) (2000)
6. Shen, L., Zhu, Y.: Human Capital and Economic Growth. Social Sciences Academic Press (1999)

Author Index

GPSR Compliance

The European Union's (EU) General Product Safety Regulation (GPSR) is a set of rules that requires consumer products to be safe and our obligations to ensure this.

If you have any concerns about our products, you can contact us on ProductSafety@springernature.com

In case Publisher is established outside the EU, the EU authorized representative is:

Springer Nature Customer Service Center GmbH
Europaplatz 3
69115 Heidelberg, Germany

Batch number: 10838023

Printed by Printforce, the Netherlands